I0824338
bark
tincture
goldenrod
sugar
300
200
100
ML

Essential Food Preserving

The Comprehensive Guide to Canning, Freezing, Drying, and Fermenting Vegetables, Fruits, Grains, Nuts, Beans, Meat, Dairy, and Eggs

JULIA SKINNER

The mission of Storey Publishing is to serve our customers by publishing practical information that encourages personal independence in harmony with the environment.

EDITED BY Carleen Madigan, Sarah Guare Slattery, and Nancy Ringer
ART DIRECTION AND BOOK DESIGN BY Ian O'Neill
TEXT PRODUCTION BY Jennifer Jepson Smith

COVER AND INTERIOR PHOTOGRAPHY BY © bagwellandprotasio
ADDITIONAL PHOTOGRAPHY BY aboodi vesakaran /Unsplash, 164; © Brian Brown/Alamy Stock Photo, 28 b.r.; Darío Méndez/Unsplash, 95; © Dayana Di /Shutterstock.com, 13; © Erin Kunkel, 48; © Joseph Keller, 372; Marek Studzinski/Unsplash, 324; Mars Vilaubi/© Storey Publishing, 19–20, 30–31, 140; Mockup Graphics/Unsplash, 105; Rodrigo dos Reis/Unsplash, 103; © Valentyn Volkov/Shutterstock .com, 89
PROP STYLING BY Kim Dergarabedian
FOOD STYLING BY Julia Skinner and Jessamine Starr

Be sure to read all of the instructions thoroughly before undertaking any of the techniques or recipes in this book and follow all of the recommended safety guidelines.

Storey Publishing
210 MASS MoCA Way
North Adams, MA 01247
storey.com

Storey Publishing is an imprint of Workman Publishing, a division of Hachette Book Group, Inc., 1290 Avenue of the Americas, New York, NY 10104. The Storey Publishing name and logo are registered trademarks of Hachette Book Group, Inc.

ISBNs: 978-1-63586-802-9 (hardcover); 978-1-63586-820-3 (ebook)

Printed in China by Toppan Leefung Printing Ltd. on paper from responsible sources
10 9 8 7 6 5 4 3 2 1

TLF

Library of Congress Cataloging-in-Publication Data on file

To the many hands, past and present, that shape the story of our food.

And to you, dear readers, who are adding your own hands and voices to our collective food story.

Contents

Preface 1

Introduction: Your Food Preservation Journey 2

Part 1: Food Preservation Techniques

Chapter 1: Pantries, Root Cellars, Refrigeration, Freezing 11

Chapter 2: Canning 25

Chapter 3: Fermentation and Pickling 43

Chapter 4: Syrup, Jam, Jelly, and Other Sweet Preserves 77

Chapter 5: Drying and Smoking 87

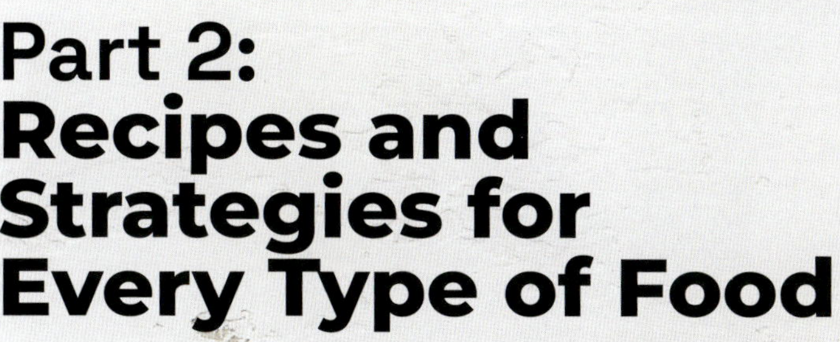

Part 2: Recipes and Strategies for Every Type of Food

Chapter 6: Vegetables 103

Chapter 7: Fruit 245

Chapter 8: Grains and Legumes 321

Chapter 9: Dairy, Meat, Seafood, and Eggs 341

Chapter 10: Other Preserving Experiments 395

Conclusion: Preserving in Community 404

Acknowledgments 408

Resources 410

Index 414

Preface

Food preserving is a practice rooted in possibility. And creativity. And love. Yes, preserving food is a practical act of making food last longer, but if we stop at this first junction in our preserving journeys, we miss out on what makes it really magical and special.

I first began preserving food more than two decades ago. As is the case for many people, I came to preservation from necessity, facing both an abundant garden and a less-than-abundant bank account. I grew food because I loved gardening, but also because I struggled to afford groceries, and when all the cabbages and peppers and tomatoes and everything else came in at once, preserving them gave me peace of mind and a bit of added security.

My first port of call was sauerkraut, then canned tomatoes, and from there my preservation practice has expanded in directions I never could have imagined. If you had told me 20 years ago that I'd be making my own miso paste or canning meat or stretching fish skin parchment or mixing up healing salves with leftover herb stems, I never would have believed you. But here I am, doing all of that, and it's because I took the time to develop a preserving practice that's all my own.

A lot of the preserved foods I make in my kitchen are ferments, which, if you've read my earlier book, *Our Fermented Lives*, probably won't surprise you. Fermentation has always had a special place in my heart because it's a collaboration with living beings who are so eager to work with us: Together, we're building a universe inside a jar. But fermenting isn't the only way I preserve food. My shelves are also groaning under the weight of dozens and dozens of canning jars; I have an entire mini-fridge dedicated to storing preserves (plus the dozens of preserves in my regular fridge) and a pantry full of vinegar infusions, tinctures, and any number of other edible and medicinal delights that I happily share with friends and family around the world.

Preserving started me down the path of a lifelong exploration, a journey that surprises and delights me and that teaches me something new every single day. I don't think I consciously realized it when I began, but I've always rooted my food preservation practice in excitement, curiosity, and an eagerness to learn. And whether you're well along your own path or just starting out, I hope your preserving journey is curious, expansive, creative, and, most of all, a lot of fun.

Introduction

Your Food Preservation Journey

Every person on earth plays a central role in the history of the world. And normally, he doesn't know it. —Paulo Coelho, *The Alchemist*

Most food preservation practices were and are rooted in the very practical need to make food last longer than it would fresh. We do that in all kinds of ways: fermenting, drying, canning, quick pickling, smoking, freezing, and beyond. Each offers its own benefits and its own best uses. Understanding how and what you eat can help you decide what to preserve and how.

For example, I eat a lot of vegetables, and I'm terrible at remembering to thaw things. So when I freeze food, it is typically vegetables that I can cook from frozen. I adore fermented foods and find that the practice of fermentation folds easily into my day. I dry food often, but I time it so I'm filling the dehydrator fully for each run, to conserve energy.

You get the idea.

You might want to embrace a preserving practice full of ready-made meals and ingredients that you can pop out of the freezer or a canning jar. You might want to put up a lot of the specific preserves that your family goes through quickly. You might just want to experiment and play and see what you like before you invest in equipment like a pressure canner. Whatever you do, you want a preserving practice that reflects the way *you* live.

Spending some time thinking about how you might easily weave preserving into your life will give you an entry point to the practice.

Some questions to consider:

- What kinds of foods do you like to eat?
- How much space do you have for preparing and storing food?
- What kinds of foods do you have access to in abundance? What are your favorite ways to prepare and enjoy them?
- What equipment do you have or want for preparing and storing food? Do you have a spare freezer? Canning jars? A dehydrator?
- Are there other specific considerations for your space? For example, limited access to electricity or water, or an HOA that forbids gardens?
- How many people do you want to feed with the food you preserve?
- If you live with others, how will your preserving practice fit into and around shared spaces?
- How does your preserving practice fit into other parts of your life? For example, how much time do you want to devote to preserving? What's your motivation behind preserving (e.g., sustainable eating, giving homemade gifts)?
- What kinds of preparations fit your lifestyle and habits? For example, if you can never remember to take food out of the freezer to thaw, maybe freezing isn't the best choice for you.

A Shared Tradition

When you embark on your preserving journey, you're traveling down a path walked by millions of people over thousands of years, adding yours to the countless hands that have shaped and created the food that sustains us.

This moment feels uncertain and sometimes scary, and we need practices to ground ourselves and find our feet. By tapping into these traditions and thinking of what I can grow, how I can preserve it, and who I can share it with, I find that I'm better able to navigate the uncertain parts of my (and our) path, when what's around the next bend is not clear. By joining my hands to those countless hands past and present, I'm able to shape my little corner of the world with greater intention. And, in doing so, I'm more resourced and hopeful as I help take on larger issues beyond my own little corner.

We often think of food preserving as something that happens at scale: big gatherings of people in a church basement canning hundreds of jars of tomato sauce, or kimjang (kimchi-making parties), for example. But traditions survive because we carry them forward to meet our lives where they are. And food preserving can happen in beautiful and sustaining ways that also fit into your life.

A sustainable practice looks different for everyone. Maybe it's tossing together a few jars of quick pickles after overbuying cucumbers at the store. Maybe it's canning a couple of batches of tomato sauce when your garden is really in full swing. Or maybe it's being in that church basement, spending hours over a hot canner. Every practice is different, but they're all important for preserving both our food and our traditions. Whatever and however you preserve, you're tapping into knowledge and intuition that has served our ancestors for millennia and continues to serve us today. If you and yours have special preserving traditions (say, a family pickle recipe), I encourage you to record it and pass it on so future generations can join their hands alongside yours in this work, too.

Quick-pickled peaches with herbs and edible flowers make a beautiful, delicious summer treat.

About This Book

This book is a treasure box of my most beloved recipes and foods—my staples, the ones you'll most often find in my kitchen. But it also includes some new favorite recipes that I discovered over the course of writing, which just goes to show that preserving really is a journey, and exploration is part of the process. Ultimately, this book is filled with food that makes me feel good and nourishes my body and soul. I hope it does the same for you.

The first part of the book is devoted to preservation techniques: freezing, canning, drying, and so on. Here you'll find step-by-step instructions, a guide to the equipment and tools, and tips and tricks I've learned along the way.

The second part of the book is organized by types of ingredients. I devote particular attention to fruits and vegetables, because that's what home cooks and restaurant kitchens are most likely to preserve, as well as use fresh. However, you'll also find chapters on animal proteins, grains and lentils, and "other experiments," a space where I offer an invitation to play and explore beyond those categories (think turning fish skin into parchment, making body care products, or baking with preserved leaves).

Common Themes

Food preserving is rooted in tradition and best practice, but the why behind my approach to preserving is also rooted in my personal experiences and my desire to connect others to these traditions.

Here are some themes that inform how and why I preserve food. Some of them might be (or become) guiding principles in your own practice, too!

GRATITUDE. Creating simply and fully with what we have reminds us of the abundance already in our gardens, pantries, and markets.

SUSTAINABILITY. I use the phrase "preserving abundance" to describe my practice because it reminds me of all the ways preserving supports abundance. It doesn't just make us more sustainable cooks (though it does that, too)—it helps us use what we have to the greatest effect.

COMMUNITY. Preserving offers a chance to create with and feed community. We're building community two times, sometimes three: in the growing, making, and sharing of food.

FOOD SECURITY. Throughout history, food preservation has allowed people to plan ahead and to be capable of nourishing ourselves through lean times. Food preservation is food security, but in a nourishing way that has our love in it, not in a "hiding in a bunker" kind of way. It helps us build the decentralized and localized food systems that make up a more resilient community and a healthier earth.

BEST PRACTICES. Food preserving is rooted in tradition and science, and by following both, you can make nourishing, delicious foods that are safe to eat.

FLEXIBILITY. Preserving is art and magic as well as science. There are some specific principles to observe so your preserved food doesn't spoil, but there's also flexibility. You might need to use specific ratios of salt or sugar for food safety (and rest assured, we'll cover food safety in detail), but you can easily alter flavoring factors (herbs and spices, for example) to suit your own tastes.

EXPLORATION. Preserving is an opportunity to explore new ingredients and techniques, and if you find one you love, I encourage you to keep exploring it beyond this book (see Resources, page 410, to guide you) so you can learn from multiple authors' experiences and perspectives and use each to strengthen your own. Each new rabbit hole you dive down is a great opportunity to really learn the why and how of that technique so you can customize it to meet your needs.

TRADITION. When we preserve food, we tap into the power of traditional methods and our ancestral connections to food making, whether it's the act itself or the foods we make or how we serve them.

SIMPLICITY AND PLEASURE. Preserving food can be about finding simple joy and pleasure. Most preserving techniques are low-tech and hands-on, manifestations of slow living and simple ways of creating.

Mindfulness and the Sensory Experience

Mindfulness, most easily defined as the cultivation of present-moment awareness, is often peddled to modern Westerners as a way to enhance productivity or to practice self-care as a product rather than a process.

Our culinary lives can teach us to return to mindfulness as a process: to give ourselves the messy, beautiful experience of being human by using the tools already around us, and the actions we're already engaged in, to live more fully.

Mindfulness allows us to connect more deeply with a daily practice we already have (cooking and eating), without a bunch of money for extra equipment or a perfect meditation room. All we have to do is show up, with our hands and our hearts, and create.

Preservation offers modern cooks an opportunity for mindful eating and mindful making, allowing us to build awareness and appreciation of the present moment into our everyday.

Cooking invites us to experience our food with every one of our senses. Especially with fermentation, I'm asked to engage my whole self in making, watching, and eating as the food transforms over a series of days.

Honoring our senses also means honoring our gut sense—our intuition. If you feel called to try a new flavor combination, or you have a gut sense that you need a little more of this or a bit less of that, why not follow those instincts and see where they lead you? Over the years, I've gotten to know my gut feelings for too much versus not enough seasoning, based on how I cook and how I like to eat (I prefer saltier condiments in smaller amounts, for example). That means I also recognize my gut feeling for what "just right" feels and tastes like, though sometimes the path to that feeling surprises me: adding lavender to soft caramels, for example, or pickling potatoes.

Preserving food is an opportunity to tap into deep wells of ancestral knowledge and into historic foods, and you never know what might come up. As my friend Doc used to say, "I add seasoning to my food until my ancestors tell me to stop."

Some Thoughts on Experimentation

Experimentation is one of the most enjoyable parts of building a preserving practice. Yet experimentation must exist within the boundaries of food safety. That necessitates finding the balance between adding your own touch and following proper technique. Some kinds of preserving offer more flexibility than others. Canning, for example, requires specific times, temperatures, processes, and measurements for safety. In this case, tested recipes are best, particularly when you're learning the process. I base the canning guidance in this book on recipes from the USDA, local Cooperative Extension Services, and other trustworthy sources that fastidiously test the best ways to can different types of foods.

Other processes, like lactofermentation, have some more wiggle room. You do have to keep your fermenting vegetables submerged in brine to prevent spoilage, but you can decide how long to ferment those vegetables, which ingredients to add, and how much salt to use (within the range at which fermentation happens).

Knowing the best practices for food preservation techniques, as outlined in this book, gives us clear boundaries to place around our experimentation. It might feel overwhelming at first, but I promise that it's easy to learn and implement a safe preserving practice. And when you do, you've got lots of room to play around within it.

Think of each recipe as a boundary line or fence, defining the area within which you can work. Within that boundary, you can play and explore freely. In a canning recipe, for example, you can exchange one set of spices and herbs for a different flavor combination. If you can make a basic pickling brine (which is so easy to do!), you can try pickling a new-to-you vegetable. If you know the basics of fermentation, you can play with savory, sweet, and funky flavors and with different types of foods. If you're experimenting with a new kind of preserve (like zucchini jam), you can make a small batch, maybe just a pint or so—I find that this makes me less inhibited in my experimentation because I'm not afraid of wasting (or being stuck eating) a batch I don't like the flavor of.

Preserving our food isn't just a tactic for making it last longer, it's a portal to new flavors and textures—perhaps ones you'd never considered before. This book is meant to be a playful exploration of possibilities, but it is only the beginning. Consider my suggestions a starting point, not an end point, in your own explorations. We'll use time-tested and science-backed methods for preserving, connect to culinary traditions from around the world, and learn the essentials of preserving. Whatever it is you're hoping to preserve, I hope you can find the information here.

You may just discover a newfound appreciation for a food or taste you'd overlooked or even disliked before. That's the magic of food preserving. It's a process of transformation and discovery that always offers us something new to learn.

Labeling and Storage Life

One important word of advice: After putting up food, be sure to label it! Include what it is, the date you processed it, and, if it's not something you can easily extrapolate from the processing date, the food's expiration date. You may think you'll remember what's in every jar and container, but trust me, once you really start to make a practice of preserving food, you absolutely will not.

A label with an expiration date is a useful benchmark, but it isn't always set in stone. Your senses, and your common sense, are important guides here. Sometimes foods don't last to the expiration date, depending on how they're stored, and they don't automatically go bad the hour after the expiration date passes, either.

It's important to work with fresh ingredients and check for signs of spoilage and infestation. Most spoilage is obvious. Jars with bowed or heavily rusted lids should be tossed immediately (not opened at all!), as should any vegetables that have become slimy. Some spoilage may not be as evident until closer examination: insects in grain, liquid in canned foods that's unusually cloudy, and, of course, changes in a food's smell and texture. The more you preserve food, the more comfortable you'll get making the call on what's safe to eat. I'm a devoted fermenter, and I often now eat fermented foods that the past me would have thrown out because I didn't know how to assess their safety.

Throughout this book, you'll find guidance on the proper storage and expected longevity of preserved foods. That said, use your best judgment and your senses. You can always turn to the advice echoed in many kitchens and cookbooks: "When in doubt, throw it out."

A UNIVERSE IN A JAR

Building a home food preserving practice gives us so much more than nice things to eat. When we preserve food, we are:

- Connecting to past traditions and carrying them forward into the future.
- Creating our own cupboard of magical culinary creations by choosing foods that best reflect our tastes.
- Devoting attention to nourishing ourselves and our loved ones.
- Living in closer relationship to the cycle of the seasons.
- Engaging in a fun and rewarding practice that's fulfilling and delicious.
- And, in the case of ferments, creating a whole community within a jar to nourish our bodies and our human communities.

It's a wonderful universe of creativity and possibility.

Why do you preserve?

Spring Greens Vinegar
(page 242)

PART 1

Food Preservation Techniques

We humans are resourceful, and we've found a way to preserve the abundance of just about everything. As a result of this millennia-deep, multicultural knowledge, modern cooks are blessed with an expansive, creative toolbox of techniques at our disposal. Our ancestors preserved food as a regular or even daily practice, and so can we.

The chapters in Part 1 offer an overview and step-by-step instructions for different preservation techniques. You'll find core recipes here, followed by lots of recipes and food-specific techniques in Part 2.

Today, many people preserve food as a hobby rather than a necessity. There are plenty of concerns about these traditions dying out as a result—and we stand to lose not just this critical ancestral knowledge but also the sensory experience of foods. As Southern folklorist April McGreger told me, "So many of these traditions are dying at the domestic level that people don't remember what the real versions tasted like."

Preserving food gives you the chance to taste food the way your ancestors tasted it, to find closeness to people you never knew but feel a bond with, to deepen your connection to place and time, and to experience the flavors of foods as they were traditionally made—often more nuanced, complex, and delicious than their mass-produced grocery-store counterparts. To me, it's an opportunity to experience and taste life more fully.

We are blessed to still have access to our preserving traditions, as well as to scientifically tested recipes that help us put up food safely. The combination may seem incongruent, but having a sense of how science undergirds our hands-on practices helps us use our preserving traditions safely while honoring their lineage and the many, many hands that shaped them for generations. And it deepens my sense of wonder: Because I preserve food and know the theory behind how to preserve it, the world feels just a little more magical.

Sometimes preserving can be challenging and stretch us to think in new ways, but it's also rewarding—a way to blend the science, art, and everyday magic of our culinary lives. Or as Terry Pratchett says in *Thief of Time*, "It doesn't stop being magic just because you know how it works."

It's up to us to choose what that everyday magic, and the adventure of making it, will look like.

CHAPTER 1

Pantries, Root Cellars, Refrigeration, Freezing

Properly storing ingredients is an important part of preserving. When choosing room-temperature storage spaces, you'll need to consider a few factors, especially temperature and humidity. For cool-to-cold storage, like freezing or refrigerating, match the scope of your preserving projects to the amount of freezer or fridge space you have.

Once you find preserved goods you like making, you'll be amazed how quickly the jars stack up and the freezer fills to bursting. You may have to come up with some creative storage solutions. (I write this while casting a sidelong glance at the bookshelf full of pickles and jam in my living room.)

Thinking ahead and giving yourself space to grow makes your future preserving life easier. It saves you the heartache of broken jars fallen from too-packed shelves, or of having to throw out ingredients because they were shoved in the back of the freezer and forgotten.

Pantry Storage

Shelf-stable preserved food keeps best when stored in a cool, dark place. So when you're choosing where to put your pantry (or which kitchen cabinets to delegate for food storage), look for a consistent, cool temperature and protection from light. The ideal temperature is 65 to 70°F/18 to 21°C. The more constant the temperature, the better.

Locating pantry storage out of direct sunlight and away from heat registers, radiators, and other heat sources (for example, your oven) goes a long way toward keeping the space consistently cool. So does choosing somewhere lower to the ground (a cabinet under your countertop rather than above it), since cool air falls and hot air rises. Some degree of airflow, and doors or other coverings that keep light out, will help, too.

Dried foods and canned foods can live in the pantry. Hardy produce, like apples, winter squash, onions, and root vegetables, will also store well in a consistently cool pantry. And, of course, many supplies you'll use for preserving foods—salt, sugar, vinegar, and so on—will last in a cool pantry for a good long while (some for years).

Rigid, durable containers made of food-safe materials are the best choice for storage. I like glass containers (like large mason jars) best, as the glass allows me to see and identify the contents without having to read the label, but ceramic, plastic, and metal also work. I don't generally recommend storing foods in plastic bags in the pantry; this can lead to disorganization and spills, and it's an open invitation to critters like roaches and rodents that can easily eat through the plastic to get dinner. Whatever containers you choose, clearly label them.

Storing Nuts

Nuts become rancid more quickly when stored at room temperature, so they are best stored in the fridge or freezer in an airtight container.

Storage times will depend on the food and the conditions of your pantry. Warm or fluctuating temperatures and humidity will shorten any pantry food's lifespan.

LIFESPAN OF PANTRY STAPLES

5 YEARS: salt, granulated sugar

2 TO 3 YEARS: whole spices, many store-bought canned goods, dried milk

18 MONTHS: dried legumes in airtight containers, freeze-dried foods, unopened nut butters

1 YEAR: home-canned foods, shortening, refined oils, flour, unopened cereals and whole grains, canned or packaged nuts, dried fruits, canned citrus fruits and juices

6 MONTHS: unrefined oils, ground spices

Root Cellaring

Prior to refrigeration, a root cellar was a common way to keep food at a relatively constant, cool temperature. Root cellars are typically dug into the ground or the side of a hill, taking advantage of the earth's cooling and humidifying properties. The cool temperature underground keeps food fresh for longer, much like a refrigerator. The natural humidity slows water loss from fruits and vegetables, so they don't shrivel up.

Root cellars can house many types of preserved foods, including shelf-stable items like canned goods and fermented foods like vinegar and wine, as well as fresh foods that have longer shelf lives, like root vegetables, winter squash, and apples. If you live off the grid or need to store more food than will fit in your fridge and pantry, a root cellar can expand your food storage possibilities.

Storing preserves in a cool, dark place helps extend their shelf life.

You can find plans for building your own cellar in many good homesteading books and online (see Resources, page 410, for some suggestions). But you may not have to dig a whole new root cellar, depending on your situation; I have used a dirt-floor crawl space as a root cellar, and some people use their basements. The key is to utilize a space that stays at a consistent cool temperature (33 to 40°F/0.5 to 4°C) and high humidity (90 to 95 percent).

If you want to see if a space is appropriate for root cellaring, put in a thermometer (for temperature) and a hygrometer (for humidity) and track the conditions in the space. A root cellar is a balancing act between temperature and humidity: If the humidity is too low, your veggies can shrivel. If it's too high, you can reach the dew point, resulting in condensation on produce, which can hasten spoilage. Over time, you'll learn exactly what your root cellar needs to stay within its ideal range, and you can add or remove water sources and increase or decrease airflow to help control conditions.

Some fruits and vegetables have different humidity requirements. Knowing the typical humidity levels in your root cellar will give you a sense of what produce will store best there. When storing produce in a root cellar, keep vegetables and fruit separate, as ripening fruit releases ethylene gas, which can hasten the ripening of nearby veggies and reduce their shelf life.

Follow best practices for keeping pests away from your stored food (for example, using chew-proof containers like metal, glass, or thick plastic). Avoid aerosolized bug sprays (commonly called bug bombs), which can settle on your food. And avoid using rat poison, which kills not just rats but any animals that come in contact with a poisoned rat, such as neighborhood cats and birds of prey.

Another note on storage: When I used to work in library special collections, we never stored materials on the bottom shelves. Why? To avoid damage in a catastrophic flooding event. I now apply this bit of library learning to my root cellaring life. Keep any food that would be damaged by water (e.g., fresh produce) off the bottom shelves.

Small-Space Storage

When I started preserving food, I lived in a 450-square-foot efficiency apartment, with maybe 2 feet of counter space, perpetually cold water, and constant freezing-but-also-humid conditions. There was a lot working against me and my budding love of preserving, but people have adapted preserving practices to their environments for millennia, and I did, too. Based on my experiences, and those of my friends, I've compiled this list of ideas to help you get creative in small spaces.

MAXIMIZE UNUSED SPACE. High, wall-mounted shelves running along the top of the wall, lined with jars, can make for visually striking and practical storage. Rolling bins under your bed might be another good option. Consider carts and custom-built shelves for small or irregularly sized spaces. If you have an attic or a crawl space, that might be a great place to store preserved goods, too.

UP, NOT OUT. This simply means maximizing vertical space. Instead of having shelves rising halfway up a wall, why not fill the whole wall instead?

TAKE IT DOWN AND OUTSIDE. Root cellaring can be a great way to store preserves if you're short on space in main living areas. If you store ferments in this space, make sure it's a comfortable temperature (the best rule of thumb is that if you're uncomfortable, your ferments are, too), and be sure to check them often for leaks and to release off-gassed pressure.

Refrigerator Storage

Refrigeration is a type of food preservation you probably use every day; it slows microbial and enzymatic action so food keeps longer. Prior to refrigeration, food preservation using cool temperatures looked a bit different—root cellars and ice boxes, for example—and often required ingenuity (like floating food in a bag in a cool stream). Your refrigerator is convenient, but to use it to its best effect, it's helpful to know where in the fridge to store different types of foods.

First, check your temperature: The fridge should be in the range of 35 to 40°F/2 to 4°C. Keep foods that need to stay extra cold (like meat) in the meat drawer, if your fridge has one, or toward the back of the bottom shelf, which tends to be the coolest part of the fridge (check this with a thermometer before reorganizing all your shelves!). The fridge doors are the warmest spots, as they're exposed to room-temperature air each time the fridge is opened.

Most produce does best stored in the crisper, which is cool and humid. Fruits that continue to ripen after harvest should be stored on the counter.

Dairy and eggs should be stored in cooler parts of the fridge (typically toward the back) and, importantly, away from strong-smelling foods that might infuse your butter or milk with unwanted flavors and smells.

An important note about egg storage: In some places, fresh eggs are not refrigerated (nor is butter), and if you raise your own birds or buy eggs from a local farmer, you might not refrigerate your eggs, either. If this applies to you, wipe fresh eggs with a cloth to remove any dirt, feathers, etc.—do not wash with soap!—and store them in a cool, dark place (like your pantry). Use unrefrigerated fresh eggs within one week or so. Once eggs have been refrigerated for any length of time, they cannot be left out on the counter. If you aren't sure whether your eggs have been refrigerated at any point in their journey to you, keep them in the fridge.

Whatever foods you're storing, don't overstuff every shelf, which prevents cold air from circulating. And follow the "first in, first out" rule: Keep the foods you need to use most quickly—those that are most perishable or are approaching their expiration date—visible and easy to grab so you use them first.

Freezing

One part of preserving abundance in our kitchens is preserving our time: putting that time to its best use when our storehouse is full, and drawing on what we've already put aside when fresh supplies are low. Though all food preserving helps us do just that, freezing can be a good solution for folks who don't have the time or inclination to can their food. As long as you have a freezer and some basic knowledge, you can freeze your food to preserve it.

Freezing is great for when you need to preserve something fast. When I have food to put up but little time to spare, sometimes dropping it into the freezer and walking away is perfect. Freezing is also a way to keep make-ahead meals and staples handy. If you love to cook but sometimes find preparation to be repetitive or a time suck, a freezer can help ensure you have ingredients prepped and ready to go (think: frozen chopped veggies, prepared sauces and herb blends, homemade stock, and so on). Then you can focus your efforts on joyful cooking when you're in the headspace to create.

BEST PRACTICES

Freezing helps slow the microbes that cause food to decay by turning water (which makes up the majority of produce and meats) into ice. Microbes simply cannot grow until the food is thawed.

As you might imagine, crystallization and thawing can alter a food's texture and flavor. Food tends to soften when frozen. Most fruits and vegetables freeze well, but once thawed, they can't be used exactly as they would be used raw because they lose some structural integrity. That said, freezing is a great, easy option for fruits and veggies that you'll be using in applications where texture matters less (like sauces, soups, and jams) and can be an absolute godsend for days when you need a meal fast (see, for example, Rainbow Roots Soup Starter, page 107).

For optimal results with freezing, observe the following three rules.

1. FREEZE FRESH

Freezers are a great tool for long-term food storage. However, they can't turn back the clock. Food that wasn't fresh going in won't be fresh coming out. For best results, freeze food at its freshest, which preserves nutrients, flavor, and texture and gives you a longer shelf life after you thaw it. For fresh fruits and vegetables, choose firm, fresh, young produce and freeze as soon after harvest as possible. Freeze meats while they're fresh, not after they've been sitting in your fridge for a few days. Freeze prepared foods as soon as possible after making them to maintain the quality of their taste and texture.

2. FREEZE FAST

Freezing is best done fast, which produces tinier ice crystals that result in less damage to the food. Cooling your food completely before freezing it helps it freeze more quickly, as does checking that your freezer isn't overstuffed and is circulating air properly.

3. AVOID FREEZER BURN

When frozen foods are directly exposed to cold, dry air, they "burn," meaning they lose moisture and oxidize, sometimes forming ice crystals on their exterior, with a negative impact on their texture and taste when thawed.

Freezer burn tends to happen when food is improperly packaged, kept in the freezer for too long, or exposed to temperature fluctuations. Remember that foods in the freezer don't keep well indefinitely, so try to use them within a year of freezing. Most importantly, package foods destined for the freezer carefully to minimize their contact with air. We'll look at the best preparation and packing methods for freezing below, and the profiles in Part 2 offer more detailed instructions for each type of food.

PREPARING FOOD FOR THE FREEZER

Most fruits and vegetables contain enzymes that can, over time, negatively impact their color, taste, and texture. Freezing slows but does not inactivate these enzymes, and fruits and vegetables stored for months in the freezer are likely to become mushy when thawed as a result. Briefly blanching fruits and vegetables (see page 17) deactivates those enzymes, allowing you to preserve your produce for the long term with minimal deterioration.

Meat and fish freeze beautifully, provided you create a barrier to protect them from the air. One way to do that is to wrap the meat or fish securely in butcher or freezer paper. Fish can also be ice glazed, which involves dipping it in water and then freezing it to create a thin ice barrier. (For instructions on wrapping and ice glazing, see page 376).

Blanching Fruits and Vegetables

To blanch fruits and vegetables, steam them over boiling water or boil them directly in the water and then "shock" them by submerging them in cold water to stop the cooking process. You'll find appropriate blanching times for specific fruits and vegetables in the profiles in Part 2.

1 Bring a pot of water to a boil. To steam blanch, suspend a steamer basket over the boiling water, making sure the basket does not touch the water.

2 Prepare an ice bath in your sink or in a large pot or bowl.

3 Chop, peel, or otherwise prepare your fruits or vegetables, as needed.

4 Drop your fruits or vegetables into the boiling water or place them in the steamer basket. If you are steaming them, don't overcrowd the basket, which will lead to inconsistent cooking.

5 Boil or steam the fruits or vegetables for the appropriate amount of time.

6 When the blanching time is up, immediately transfer the fruits or vegetables to the ice bath. If you are boiling them, a skimmer or spider is helpful for quickly removing the fruits or vegetables from the boiling water.

7 Chill the fruits or vegetables for 1 to 2 minutes. (You don't need to cool them to room temperature, just enough to get them down to 120°F/49°C.) Then drain and pat them dry.

NOTE: If you are planning to grate or grind fruit or vegetables that require blanching, like for the Rainbow Roots Soup Starter (page 107), blanch the vegetables first, then grate them.

STEP 5

STEP 6

Steamer Baskets

Steamer baskets are slotted baskets that hold your food above boiling water in a covered pan, allowing it to cook without touching the water itself. There are many different types of steamer baskets, and there isn't a definitive "best" version. Choose what fits your budget and your kitchen. Some options include expanding flower-style baskets that fit in any pan, double boilers, big bamboo steamers, flexible silicone baskets, and more. If you're working with food that might stick in a steamer basket, it can be helpful to lightly oil the basket or line it with clean banana leaves, corn husks, cabbage leaves, or some other food (lacking edible leaves, you can also use perforated parchment paper) to create a barrier between basket and food.

FREEZER-SAFE CONTAINERS

Many foods can be frozen in ziplock bags, whether plastic or (my preference) reusable silicone. Some foods might need to be first wrapped tightly in freezer wrap, waxed paper, or aluminum foil and then placed in a ziplock.

You might also use freezer-safe plastic containers or glass jars. If you opt for glass jars, note that not all jars are created equal! Make sure you use freezer-safe jars. This isn't the time to bust out those jars from the thrift shop, but rather the ones that you know will stand up to freezing without cracking (such as Ball, Kerr, and Kilner jars and those with a freezer safe symbol).

Some people use vacuum sealers, though these can produce a lot of plastic waste.

DRY PACKING

Most foods destined for the freezer are dry packed—that is, packed without any added liquid. If you're packing foods that are inherently moist, like chopped fruits and vegetables or raw meats, and you'd like to prevent them from becoming one giant, frozen, icy wad, a sheet pan that fits in your freezer is your new best friend. My go-to is a quarter sheet pan with a lip, and I use it for *everything*.

NEED TO FREEZE CHOPPED VEGETABLES OR FRUIT? Lay out the pieces in a single layer (not touching) on your sheet pan, freeze, then transfer to a ziplock bag or container. This helps prevent freezer burn and giant wads of frozen ingredients that you have to break apart.

NEED TO FREEZE BERRIES? Freeze them on a sheet pan until they rattle when shaken (a very fun test to perform!), then transfer to a ziplock bag or container.

NEED TO FREEZE MEAT? Cover a sheet pan with a silicone mat to prevent the meat from sticking, lay the pieces of meat on the mat, freeze, then transfer to a ziplock bag or container.

NEED TO FREEZE SAUCES, SOUPS, OR OTHER LIQUIDS? Place them in ziplock bags and freeze the bags on your sheet pan so they lie flat and stack neatly.

You'll also see my sheet pan at work when I'm freezing meal starters like the Rainbow Roots Soup Starter (page 107) and Frozen Mirepoix and Trinity (page 196), among many others.

SUGAR AND SYRUP PACKING

Fruits are sometimes packed in sugar or syrup in preparation for freezing. While this can help preserve texture and flavor, it isn't necessary for successfully freezing fruit. Syrup-packed fruit works well for uncooked desserts (it's perfect for the strawberries in syrup on strawberry shortcake), whereas sugar-packed or unsweetened dry-packed fruit is best for cooking because the final product contains less liquid.

Sugar-packed fruit works well for cooking.

Syrup-packed fruit is delicious in uncooked desserts.

TO PACK IN SYRUP: You'll need a syrup that is 40 to 50 percent sugar. To make it, combine 3 to 4 cups of sugar with 4 cups of water in a saucepan over medium heat (I always add a pinch of salt, too, for flavor, but that's optional). Stir until the sugar has dissolved, remove from the heat, and allow to cool completely. Pack your fruit into a ziplock bag or airtight container, pour the syrup over the fruit, seal, and freeze.

TO PACK IN SUGAR: Gently stir ¾ to 1 cup of sugar into 4 cups of fruit. Pack into a ziplock bag or airtight container, seal, and freeze.

NOTE: You can also pack fruit in water, juice, or pectin syrup, though I generally don't use these techniques because when the fruit is thawed it's not quite as plump or tasty.

HOW MUCH HEADSPACE?

Headspace is the space between the contents of a container and its lid. It's an especially important factor in freezing because food expands when it freezes. If you don't give it room, it can expand right out of its container, popping off the lid or even breaking the container. At the same time, you don't want to leave too much space in the container because contact with air is a prime cause of freezer burn.

If you're freezing food in ziplock bags, headspace is not a concern. Simply press as much air out as you can or use the air displacement method (see page 20). If you're freezing food in plastic containers or glass jars, the appropriate headspace depends on the food you're freezing and the container you're using.

DRY-PACKED FOOD

ALL CONTAINERS/JARS: ½ inch of headspace

LIQUIDS AND LIQUID-PACKED FOOD

WIDE-MOUTHED CONTAINERS/JARS:
½ inch of headspace per pint and 1 inch of headspace per quart

NARROW-MOUTHED CONTAINERS/JARS:
¾ inch of headspace per pint and 1½ inches of headspace per quart

Air Displacement Method

This is an easy way to remove air from ziplock bags packed with food. I like to fill all my bags at once, then do the air displacement method to minimize filling and emptying the sink. I use this technique with meat as well as fruits and vegetables; it's a great way to prevent freezer burn.

1. Fill a large bowl or your sink with enough water that you can submerge your zippered bags.
2. Fill the ziplock bags with whatever food you are freezing. Seal the zipper mostly closed, leaving the last inch or so open.
3. Submerge all but the open corner of each bag in the water. The water pressure will force out any remaining air.
4. While the bag is still underwater, press the zipper closed to seal the bag entirely.
5. Remove the bag from the water and pat dry.

STEP 2

FREEZER FAVORITE: SCRAPPY SOUP STOCK

Veggie scraps are great for making soup stock. Keep a container in your freezer for all the bits and bobs: carrot and celery greens, kale ribs, the remains of smashed garlic from your garlic press, onion ends, root veggie peels, herb stems, and whatever is in the crisper that you didn't get to in time and is starting to wilt. I keep a silicone zippered bag in my freezer and add my scraps to it each time I cook. I've even added fruit (like strawberry tops or apple peels) to the bag, though I'm mindful not to add too many bitter ingredients so I don't end up with a bitter final product.

When you're ready to make stock, toss the frozen scraps into a slow cooker with water to cover and cook on low for 6 to 12 hours.

You can do the same with meat bones and scraps, stockpiling them in the freezer until you're ready to make stock. When you do make meat stock, add a tiny splash of vinegar to the water. This helps break apart the connective tissue and makes for a richer stock.

You can make seafood stock by saving up shrimp shells and other leftover bits of seafood in the freezer. (Keep them in a separate container from your meat bones and scraps to prevent flavors from mingling.)

FREEZING IN CUBES

Freezing foods in ice cube trays gives you abundant grab-and-go add-ins for your cooking adventures. It's such a helpful convenience that you may want to have a few trays on hand. No need to be fancy—I use the plastic ice cube trays that were in my grandma's freezer. Most ice cube trays make 2-tablespoon frozen cubes. You can also find trays with larger compartments that will produce 2-cup frozen cubes, which are perfect for freezing broth and stock.

Consider making frozen cubes of the following.

- Fruit juices (lemon, lime, and so on)
- Fruit pulps and purées
- Smoothie Cubes (page 22)
- Mashed avocado (page 23)
- Blended or shredded vegetables
- Soup stock
- Beet Pasta-Sauce Cubes (page 122)
- Fresh herbs (float a tiny bit of olive oil on top to keep the herbs from discoloring)
- Herb pastes

Once the cubes are frozen, transfer them to a container or ziplock bag for long-term storage (and to free up your ice cube trays for making other frozen cubes!). I find it helpful to stack the fully frozen cubes intentionally rather than tossing them willy-nilly into a bag, which gives lots of surface area for freezer burn.

I like to combine different types of frozen vegetable cubes in one container, then grab a handful when I'm making soup or pasta sauce and toss them in to get some good variety of flavor and nutrition. If you want the easiest lunch ever, simmer a few cups of stock on the stove, add a handful of veggie cubes, and stir in a spoonful of miso paste as the soup comes off the stove.

Preparing for Power Outages

If you are concerned about power outages, you can do a few things to maximize the possibility of your frozen food staying safe.

If a power outage seems likely—for example, if a hurricane or blizzard is forecast—immediately turn your freezer down to its coldest setting. Fill your freezer (use containers of water, if necessary), because a full freezer stays cold longer. If the power goes out, do not open the freezer door. Don't open your fridge door, either.

If you *absolutely must* open your fridge or freezer, do so as briefly as possible. Think ahead to what you need and exactly where it is so you can reach in, remove the food, and close the door in a matter of seconds.

If the power will be out for more than 2 days, you can add dry ice, if you can source it, to the freezer to drop the temperature. Some people also wrap the freezer in blankets to help hold in the cold; if you do, tack the blanket away from the air vents, which will kick on again when the power does.

If you'll be away from home and worry about power outages while you're gone, follow an old trick from hurricane country. Freeze a container of water to completely frozen, then set a penny on top of the ice. When you get home after a power outage, check the penny. If it is still on top of the ice, the freezer maintained a cold enough temperature to keep food frozen the whole time, and the food in your freezer (and fridge) should still be safe to eat. If the penny is at the bottom of the container, the freezer was off for long enough to thaw your food, and, unfortunately, the food will have to be tossed.

Smoothie Cubes

Smoothie cubes are what you would imagine: cubes of ingredients you can put in smoothies. They offer a great way to use up fruits and veggies on the verge of being thrown out or to repurpose the leftover bits from other recipes. Consider not just the usual candidates—berries, stone fruits, bananas—but also spinach and other greens, carrots (or carrot peels), mashed avocado, and so on.

Smoothie cubes take mere minutes to make, allowing you to fold your preserving practice around the rest of your life on days when time is short. And they're great for busy mornings, too.

1. Put your fruits and/or veggies in a blender.
2. Add just enough liquid (juice, yogurt, or even whey from cheesemaking) that the mixture will blend, then process until it's a smooth, thick pulp.
3. Immediately pour the mixture into ice cube trays. Freeze for at least 6 hours, until the cubes are frozen through.
4. Once frozen, store your cubes in an airtight container or ziplock bag, leaving as little space for air as possible.
5. To use: Pop a couple of cubes in a blender with juice or yogurt, and blend for about 30 seconds.

Frozen Avocado Cubes

These cubes allow you to store avocado when it's ripe—an ever-so-brief window. The acidity helps keep the avocado from browning, but remember that you'll have to adjust the acidity when using these cubes in recipes, since they already contain acid.

1. Mash ripe, unblemished avocados.
2. Add ½ tablespoon fresh lemon juice or apple cider vinegar per avocado.
3. Scoop into ice cube trays, pressing to remove air. Freeze for 4 to 6 hours, until solid.
4. Once frozen, store your cubes in an airtight container or ziplock bag, leaving as little space for air as possible.
5. To use: 1 standard cube = about 2 tablespoons mashed avocado.

HOW LONG DOES FROZEN FOOD KEEP?

The exact length of time depends on your particular freezer and its temperature (and, importantly, the consistency of the temperature). Food kept at 0°F/–18°C or below will stay edible indefinitely. However, *edible* doesn't necessarily mean delicious or even palatable, so for best results, try to use foods within 1 year of freezing.

Foods with freezer burn should be composted or thrown out. A good way to avoid this, and avoid wasting food, is to rotate: When you add food to the freezer, put it in the back or bottom, and pull the food that was previously in the back or bottom to the front or top, so that you use it first. This means you use up everything that's in the freezer, rather than risking losing that pack of steaks or bag of veggies behind everything else for months (or years).

What Is Freeze-Drying?

Freeze-drying, or lyophilization, also uses low temperatures to preserve food but does so a bit differently than the freezer in your kitchen. Food is frozen at extremely cold temperatures, then dried under pressure to remove its water content. This is an effective form of preservation, but it's also an expensive and technical one that may not be ideal for the home preserver.

While you can buy freeze dryers for home use, they are expensive and bulky, so make sure it's something you know you'll use enough to justify the cost (or, if you have some preserve-making friends and neighbors, you could go in on a freeze dryer together).

CHAPTER 2

Canning

Canning is a relative newcomer to the world of food preservation. In 1795, the French army was desperate to find efficient ways to feed its troops. Yes, there were plenty of existing food preserving options available, but portable, shelf-stable (not dehydrated) food—something that could be opened and eaten without extensive cooking—was the dream. The army offered a 12,000-franc reward (equivalent to about $250,000 today) to whoever could find a way to safely store and transport food to the front lines without spoilage.

Many minds went to work on the problem, and in 1810, French chef Nicolas Appert devised a system of boiling food and sealing it in glass jars, winning him both the accolade of creating the first canned food and the prize money. Once he'd cracked the case, others soon followed. That same year, British shop owner Peter Durand began supplying the entire British navy with tinned foods, having received a patent for inventing the tin can several years prior. In 1812, the first American cannery opened, and canning operations branched out from there.

As commercial canning expanded in popularity, home canning grew as well. The mason jar was patented in 1885, followed by the two-piece metal lid we know today (invented by Alexander H. Kerr) in 1915. During World War I, home food preserving, including canning, was promoted in the United States as part of the home-front food security and rationing efforts. Home canning became even more popular during World War II: More than four billion cans and jars were processed in the United States in 1943 alone, according to the USDA. But canning began to decline just two years later, when home refrigeration started to become more common, lessening the need to put up vegetables and fruits to preserve them.

Since that time, the popularity of home canning has risen and fallen in response to larger shifts in technologies and the zeitgeist. With the increase in popularity of natural foods and DIY in the 1970s, home canning saw a resurgence, and the first USDA Complete Guide to Home Canning was published in 1988.

When I began canning and fermenting in the early 2000s, fellow preserving enthusiasts were harder to find, but today I regularly encounter more and more home canners. Perhaps we're in the middle of another resurgence?

Canning can feel intimidating to the uninitiated. But with some basic know-how, canning is a beautiful, fun practice that helps you preserve your favorite foods year-round, as home canners have done for generations.

Canning Basics

At its simplest, the canning process works like this:

1. Prepare food.
2. Prepare jars as necessary, heating or sterilizing according to your recipe.
3. Fill the jars with the food you've prepared. Remove air bubbles and wipe the rims. Put on the lids.
4. Heat the jars, either with boiling water or pressurized steam.
5. Let the jars cool.
6. Confirm that the jars have sealed properly, then store them.

Heating the food in the jars kills pathogens and deactivates the enzymes that lead to spoilage. Then, as the jars cool, a vacuum and airtight seal are formed, preventing air and microorganisms from entering and thus rendering the food safe for long-term storage.

There are two types of canning: hot water bath canning and pressure canning. For the hot water bath method, you submerge the jars in boiling water for the amount of time specified in your recipe. The temperature of the boiling water (212°F/100°C) renders foods safe for storage. Pressure canning uses a specialized stovetop canner with a locking lid; inside it, pressurized steam brings the jars to 240°F/115°C or higher.

The acidity of your food determines which process to use. Acidic foods (with a pH below 4.6), like pickles, can be safely canned in a hot water bath, but less acidic foods (with a pH above 4.6), like bean soup, need to be pressure canned.

Hot water bath canning is simpler and requires less of an up-front investment, but it is not as versatile as pressure canning, which involves specialty equipment but allows you to process meat and low-acid foods. If you haven't canned before, try hot water bath canning first to get comfortable with the process of filling and boiling jars. Then, if you want more canning options, extend your practice to pressure canning.

Understanding pH for Canning

The canning process you choose boils down to acidity and/or sugar content. The pH scale is how we determine a food's acidity or alkalinity. The scale goes from 0 to 14: 0 is the most acidic, 7 is neutral, and 14 is very alkaline.

Foods that fall toward the right of the pH scale (more alkaline, less acidic) need to be pressure canned, as they require the higher temperature in order to kill off any pathogens. More acidic foods and sugary foods (think quick pickles and jam) can safely be canned in a hot water bath canner.

Determining the pH of canned goods can be easily done with testing strips (there are many pH testing kits on the market today, in various price ranges). The pH of your food is determined by considering the acidity of all the ingredients. So, for example, not just the tomatoes in tomato sauce or the strawberries in jam, but also the onions and herbs you add to the tomatoes or the peaches you mix in with the strawberries. This means you need to consider the finished product's pH when canning.

For home canners, foods that are around a neutral pH (like tomatoes) can be hit or miss for hot water bath canning. In these cases, it's best to either pressure can or add some extra acidity (like citric acid).

Choosing Your Canner

Canning requires some up-front research and the right tools—specifically, a canner! Here's what you'll need to know as you consider which one is right for you.

HOT WATER BATH CANNERS

A hot water bath canner can be a purpose-built canning pot, but you can also use a stockpot or other large pot. The pot will need a lid, but more importantly, it will need a canning rack, which keeps jars off the bottom of the pot to prevent them from cracking and allows hot water to evenly circulate around them. You can purchase a canning rack to fit into most pots. Make sure your canner has enough room—you want space for the rack, for the jars themselves, and for water to boil 1 to 2 inches above the jars without bubbling over.

A canning rack transforms a large pot into a hot water bath canner.

PRESSURE CANNERS

First, make sure you're using a pressure canner, not a pressure cooker. A canner can cook, but a cooker can't can, according to my friend Christina Ward, a master food preserver and the author of *Preservation: The Art and Science of Canning, Fermentation and Dehydration*. Lovely though your Instant Pot is, it cannot reach the temperature and consistent pressure needed to can your food.

Dial gauge canners, like mine, show a pressure reading on the dial.

Weighted gauge pressure canners are another option for pressure canning.

For pressure canning, stovetop models are the only type tested and approved by the National Center for Home Food Preservation (NCHFP), a research center at the University of Georgia that is among the most authoritative sources of food preservation information in the United States. As of this writing, you can find electric pressure canners on the market; however, they have not yet passed the NCHFP's rigorous testing process (you can still use them for hot water bath canning, though, which is what I do with mine).

Pressure canners create a pressurized environment, hence the name, and there are two types: dial gauge and weighted gauge. The pressure required for a recipe will vary depending on which type of gauge your canner has. (Recipes throughout this book give you the pressure and processing time for both types.)

Entry-level models of pressure canners are relatively inexpensive; some are less than $100. If your canner is sealed by a rubber gasket, the gasket will eventually need to be replaced, but that's easily done. More expensive models are machined to seal without rubber gaskets. Replace gaskets and other components as recommended by the manufacturer.

When properly maintained, a good-quality pressure canner can last for lifetimes, which means that, yes, you can use a second-hand pressure canner—but make sure it's safe. Use only models manufactured after 1960, when safety-release valves became standard. If you've found a used post-1960 pressure canner but it's missing the rubber gasket and/or dial gauge, go ahead and get it, because both can be replaced. And, says Christina Ward, "in a rare gift to canners everywhere, replacement gauges are universal, so if, for example, you find a used Menomonie canner (an excellent canner but long out of business), a new Presto gauge will fit it." Of course, avoid any pressure canner with cracks in the vessel or lid, and make sure your canner has a safety-release valve and that the valve's opening is unobstructed. You can take your canner to your local Cooperative Extension office for inspection to have it checked for safety and accuracy.

The Jar Lifter

During the canning process, you'll need to get hot jars in and out of hot water. Some brave souls (my past self included) lift and place jars with an oven-mitt-clad hand. For safety and comfort, I recommend against that course of action. Instead, treat yourself to a jar lifter—a pair of funny-looking tongs shaped to fit canning jars. Your hands are worth it.

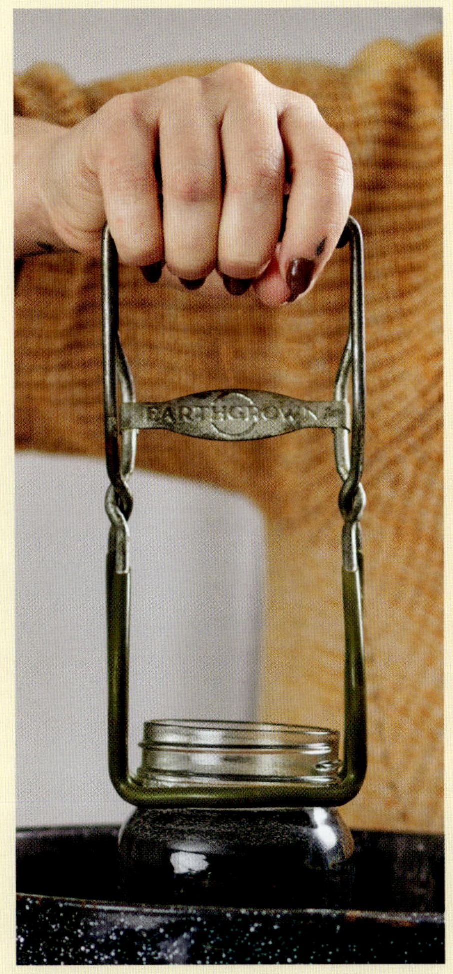

CANNER CAPACITY

Canners come in a variety of sizes. The bigger the canner, the heavier it is. The largest models require some arm strength to heft around (and a stove that can handle the weight—be very cautious if you want to use a large, heavy canner on a glass-top stove, and check your stove's specifications for use). In addition, some models won't work for certain things (e.g., not all sizes of pressure canners can safely can smoked fish). When deciding on a canner, decide what you want to use it for, how much food you plan to put up, and the size of jars you plan to use.

It is often best to start with a smaller canner, then buy a larger one later if you find you're consistently running multiple batches or otherwise not able to process as much as you'd like.

Choosing and Using Jars

It's important to use jars specifically made for canning, as they are sturdy enough to hold up to the heat and pressure of canning without cracking or exploding.

Ball and Kerr are two go-to choices for canning jars, and their names have become synonymous with home canning in the United States. You can find these canning jars at your local farm, hardware, or grocery stores and online.

In the United States, canning jars are either "regular-mouthed" (with a 2¾-inch opening) or "wide-mouthed" (with a 3⅜-inch opening). Both types come in a range of sizes, from tiny jam jars perfect for gifting to big half-gallon jars for large batches of pickles or meats, plus everything in between. For most home canning, half-pints, pints, and quarts will do the trick; pints are the size I reach for most often.

Before using your jars, make sure they have no hairline cracks or chips. To check, run a moistened finger gently along the rim of each one; you'll be able to feel any bumps or cracks your eyes might miss. Discard any damaged jars.

LIDS AND BANDS

Canning jars require canning lids, and for most modern canners, this means the two-piece lid and band invented by Kerr in 1915. The lid includes a rubberized coating on the outer edge of its underside, which forms a seal with the jar when processed.

Canning jars come in a range of sizes including half-pints, pints, and quarts.

Canning jars come with two sizes of openings: regular mouth (left) and wide mouth (right).

Until the 1990s, these lids needed to be boiled to soften their seal, and this is how I learned to can. Today's lids, though, have a more advanced seal that works without boiling, provided the jars are properly processed.

Standard canning lids cannot be reused; you can save them to use as lids for storage, but you can't reuse them for canning. You can reuse the bands again and again, though. Reusable lids and rubber rings exist, but there's a bit of a learning curve to using them, and they are more expensive.

GAUGING HEADSPACE

The space you leave unfilled, between the top of your food and the rim of the jar, is called headspace. Canning recipes will tell you how much headspace to leave in your jars, as determined by how much food expands during processing and the space needed to form a vacuum during cooling.

But there's no need to bust out your ruler to make sure you leave the correct headspace. Just look at your jar. Helpfully, mason jars with screw-top lids (like the usual two-piece lid plus band) have standard measurements built into the jar, as seen below.

WHEN TO STERILIZE JARS

According to the NCHFP:

- For foods that will be processed for less than 10 minutes in a hot water bath canner, the jars do need to be sterilized before you fill them with food.
- For foods that will be processed for 10 minutes or longer in a hot water bath canner, the jars do not need to be sterilized.
- For foods that will be pressure canned, the jars do not need to be sterilized.
- Jar lids and bands do not need to be sterilized for any type of canning.

To sterilize empty jars, simply boil them for 10 minutes. You can do this as part of the process of heating up the water for your canner. Place the empty jars on the canning rack in your hot water bath canner, fill the canner with water up to 1 inch above the tops of the empty jars, bring to a boil, and boil for at least 10 minutes.

Whether you are sterilizing your jars or not, preheat jars in your canner before filling them. This ensures that they won't crack once they are filled and then placed in the boiling water or hot steam.

Two-part canning lids include the lid with a seal and the band, which screws onto the jar.

Canning jar headspace can be measured by looking at the threading at the jar's top.

Raw Pack Versus Hot Pack

The terms *raw pack* and *hot pack* refer to whether fruits and vegetables are packed into jars raw or hot.

RAW PACK means packing raw food into jars before covering with boiling liquid (brine, water, juice, or syrup).

HOT PACK means heating food to boiling first, or cooking for a certain period, then packing with hot liquid into jars. These should be packed into jars fairly loosely.

In many cases, hot pack yields better color and flavor, but both work for most produce (be sure to follow recipe guidance, though, as not every fruit and vegetable can be packed both ways). Either way, make sure you add enough hot liquid to fill around and completely cover the food, and leave the required headspace.

Canning Recipes

When you preserve food by canning, always follow the recipe! Your recipe will tell you everything you need to know to can successfully and safely, including:

- How to prepare the food
- How much headspace to leave in the jars
- Which canning method to use: hot water bath or pressure
- How long to process jars in the hot water bath or pressure canner
- What pressure to use (if you are using a pressure canner)

LOOK FOR TRUSTED SOURCES

While you can freeze pretty much any recipe and feel confident that your frozen food will be safe to eat, you have to be more discerning when it comes to canning recipes. Done properly, home canning is absolutely safe—but you must use a recipe that follows the proper procedures for food safety.

So be sure that your recipe comes from a trusted source. Just because a canning recipe has been posted online or published in a community cookbook, for example, doesn't mean it's safe.

The NCHFP recommends using only recipes published after 1995 by reputable sources that follow best practices for canning. Master food preserver Christina Ward notes that 1995 is the year by which most reputable publishers had updated their cookbooks and guides to include the very important step of processing high-acid foods in a hot water bath. "Prior to that," she says, "canning instructions, especially for jams and jellies, might omit any type of processing or might not process for long enough to seal jars and prevent pathogen growth."

Modern recipes are tested and processed to follow the principles established by the NCHFP. Ward says, "A home canner can have confidence in the science that informs the recommended canning process as published by the National Center for Home Food Preservation. It's why canning recipes should be followed closely; it's the process of completely doing each step that assures your jarred creation is safe to store and safe to eat."

You can see more about evaluating the trustworthiness of sources, as well as lists of trustworthy preserving sources, in the Resources section (page 410).

All of the canning recipes in this book follow NCHFP safety principles.

CUSTOMIZING CANNING RECIPES

Let's say you've found a canning recipe you want to try, but you want to make some changes to it. Can you do that without compromising safety?

You can safely halve or double some canning recipes (do not triple or quadruple) if you keep the ratios of ingredients exactly the same. However, there are caveats. Doubling a recipe that is cooked before it is canned will increase the cook time, which, for some foods like jam and jelly, can change the flavor and texture. If you want to double these recipes, make two batches instead. In addition, Christina Ward cautions against increasing the volume of any canning recipe by more than 2 quarts (8 cups).

You can also switch up the herbs and spices. Note that the intensity of spices can increase over time in canned foods. If you want to subtly spice foods, put your herbs and spices in a tea ball or a bundle of cheesecloth, add to your food while cooking, then pull it out when it has a flavor you enjoy.

What about reducing salt or sugar? It depends. You can find recipes for reduced-sugar products, like jams, and some canned foods, like tomatoes, can be prepared with reduced or no salt, but these situations vary depending on the specific food and canning method. For guidance on canning for special diets, see the *USDA Complete Guide to Home Canning* and the University of Georgia Cooperative Extension's *So Easy to Preserve* (see Resources, page 410).

What Can't You Can?

People always want to can pumpkin butter, a delicious blend of puréed pumpkin with added sweeteners and spices. You can purchase canned pumpkin butter from commercial manufacturers, but there is no safe way to can it at home. Pumpkin purée, or any squash purée, is simply too dense for home canning; the interior does not always heat up sufficiently to ensure safety. (Christina Ward's workaround has become one of my favorites, too: Grind up dehydrated pumpkin into a powder, mix with spices, and add to applesauce before canning as a pumpkin butter substitute.)

Certain other foods, too, are not suitable for canning at home:

- Dense purées (banana, bean, potato, pumpkin, winter squash, and so on)
- High-fat red meats
- Dairy products (milk, butter, cheese, cream, and so on)
- Eggs
- Rice
- Pasta

Hot Water Bath Canning

If you are using the hot-pack method—that is, you are going to heat or cook the food, then pack it into jars—check the preparation time for your recipe. You'll want to have your canner and jars ready to go as soon as the food is ready to be packed.

1 Prepare your jars and canner: Run a moistened finger gently along the rims of the jars to feel for any microcracks or chips; discard any damaged jars. Fill your jars with warm water. Place a canning rack in your canner (or pot) and place the jars in it. Then fill the canner with enough warm water to cover the jars by a couple of inches and start heating it.

2 Sterilize the jars, if necessary: If you will be processing the food in the jars for less than 10 minutes, bring the water in the canner to a boil and boil the jars for at least 10 minutes to sterilize them.

STEP 2

3 Prepare the food as directed in your recipe.

4 Using jar-lifting tongs, carefully remove the jars from the canner, pouring the hot water inside the jars back into the canner, and set the jars on your countertop.

5 Fill the jars with the food you've prepared and any needed liquid, as directed in your recipe, leaving the appropriate amount of headspace.

STEP 4

STEP 5

6 Run a long, thin, nonmetal utensil—a plastic chopstick works well—around the inner edges of the jars to release any air bubbles trapped inside.

7 Seal the jars: Wipe the rim of each jar with a cloth to make sure it's clean and dry. Put a lid on each jar and secure it with a band. Tighten the bands only to fingertip tightness; they should be secure, but you really don't need to crank them down on the jars.

8 Using jar-lifting tongs, carefully transfer the filled jars to the rack inside the canner. Be sure to keep each jar upright as you move it; you don't want the contents of the jar sloshing up and getting under the lid, which will prevent it from sealing.

(continued on next page)

Hot Water Bath Canning *continued*

9 Make sure the water in the canner covers the jars by 1 to 2 inches. Put the lid on your canner and bring the water to a boil. Adjust the heat as needed to maintain a boil. Once the water has reached a boil, start your timer. Boil the jars for the amount of time specified by your recipe, adjusting for altitude (see page 39) if necessary.

NOTE: If you reduce the heat too much and the water stops boiling at any point during this process, bring the water back to a boil and restart your timer; the jars must be boiled without stopping for the complete length of time specified in your recipe.

10 When the processing time is up, turn off the heat and remove the canner lid. Let the jars sit in the hot water for a few minutes, if you like, until the canner water backs away from the boiling point. Then use your jar-lifting tongs to remove the jars from the canner, one by one, and place them on a towel, leaving a little space between them. As before, keep the jars upright as you're moving them.

11 Let the jars sit, undisturbed, for 12 to 24 hours. During this time, the food will cool and a vacuum will form inside the jars, creating a tight seal with the lids.

12 Test the seal on each jar: Remove the band and lift the jar by its lid (without pulling too hard on it). If the seal holds, success! If the seal doesn't hold, put the band back on (to secure the lid) and store the jar in your fridge, to be eaten first.

STEP 9

STEP 10

STEP 12

Pressure Canning

Pressure canning requires some technical know-how, but don't let that deter you. It is a rewarding and absolutely doable form of food preservation that opens up a world of canning beyond what's possible with a hot water bath canner. Whole meals, like soups, can be pressure canned, for example, along with most meats. Chicken soup, sans noodles, is a perfect pressure canner meal.

The first time you use a new pressure canner, start by canning some jars of water to become familiar with your new tool. Hands-on canning classes can benefit new canners. You can take a class or find an online tutorial from the NCHFP or a certified master food preserver.

1 Prepare your canner: Check to make sure the vent port is unobstructed, and if your canner has a gasket around the lid, make sure it is secure. Set your canner on your stove. Place a canning rack in it and then fill the canner with 2 to 3 inches of water (or however much water is called for in your recipe). Put the lid on the canner.

STEP 1

2 Prepare your jars: Run a moistened finger gently along the rims of the jars to feel for any micro-cracks or chips; discard any damaged jars. Warm the jars by placing them in a pot full of hot water or running them through a quick dishwasher cycle.

3 Prepare the food as directed in your recipe.

4 When you are almost ready to fill your jars, begin heating your canner. Make sure the vent port is open—you don't want to pressurize the canner yet.

(continued on next page)

STEP 3

STEP 4

STEP 5

STEP 7

Pressure Canning, *continued*

5 Fill the jars with the food you've prepared and any needed liquid, as directed in your recipe, leaving the appropriate amount of headspace.

6 Run a long, thin, nonmetal utensil—a plastic chopstick works well—around the inner edges of the jars to release any air bubbles trapped inside.

7 Seal the jars: Wipe the rim of each jar with a cloth to make sure it's clean and dry. Put a lid on each jar and secure it with a band. Tighten the bands only to fingertip tightness; they should be secure, but you really don't need to crank them down on the jars.

8 Using jar-lifting tongs, carefully transfer the filled jars to the rack inside the canner. Be sure to keep each jar upright as you move it; you don't want the contents of the jar sloshing up and getting under the lid, which will prevent it from sealing.

9 Vent the canner: Close the canner lid and secure it. Keep the vent port open. Increase the heat under the canner. When the water inside begins to boil, you'll see steam flowing from the port. Let the steam vent for about 10 minutes to drive air from the canner.

10 Pressurize: If you have a weighted-gauge canner, place the appropriate weight (as specified in your recipe) on the vent port. If you have a dial gauge canner, close the petcock (or close the vent port in whatever way is appropriate for your canner). The canner will now begin to pressurize.

STEP 8

STEP 9

STEP 10

STEP 12

11 Process: When the canner reaches your recipe's recommended pressure, the weight on a weighted-gauge canner will begin to rock or jiggle; check the manufacturer's instructions for guidance on monitoring the pressure. A dial gauge will simply give you a reading. Adjust the heat as necessary to keep your canner at the recommended pressure for the length of time specified by your recipe, adjusting for altitude if needed (see right).

NOTE: If the canner pressure falls below the level specified by your recipe at any point during this process, bring the pressure back to the specified level and restart your timer; the jars must be processed at that pressure or above for the complete length of time specified in your recipe.

12 Depressurize: When the processing time is up, turn off the heat under the canner. Let the canner depressurize, undisturbed, for the length of time recommended by the manufacturer. Do not open the vent port or the canner lid or attempt to cool the canner during this time. This can take hours, so just walk away and let it do its thing.

(continued on next page)

Altitude Adjustments

Water boils at lower temperatures as altitude increases. So whether you are canning in a hot water bath or pressure canner, if you are 1,000 feet or more above sea level, you'll have to make some adjustments.

- **For sterilizing jars:** Empty jars are typically boiled for 10 minutes to sterilize them. Add 1 minute of boiling time for each 1,000 feet of elevation above sea level.
- **For a hot water bath canner:** Add 5 minutes of processing time if you are at 1,000 to 3,000 feet of elevation, 10 minutes for 3,000 to 6,000 feet, 15 minutes for 6,000 to 8,000 feet, and 20 minutes for 8,000 to 10,000 feet.
- **For a pressure canner:** Pressure decreases at higher altitudes, so if you are 1,000 feet or more above sea level, increase the pressure by 5 pounds (which might be listed in your recipe as psi, or pounds per square inch). For example, if your recipe calls for 5 pounds of pressure, set your canner to operate at 10 pounds; if your recipe calls for 10 pounds, set your canner to 15 pounds.

Pressure Canning *continued*

13 Once the depressurization period is done, remove the weight from the vent port or open the petcock. Wait 10 minutes. Then open the lid (pointing it away from your face!).

14 Use your jar-lifting tongs to remove the jars from the canner, one by one, and place them on a towel, leaving a little space between them. As before, keep the jars upright as you're moving them.

15 Let the jars sit, undisturbed, for 12 to 24 hours. During this time, the food will cool and a vacuum will form inside the jars, creating a tight seal with the lids.

16 Test the seal on each jar: Remove the band and lift the jar by its lid (without pulling too hard on it; see step 12 photo on page 36). If the seal holds, success! If the seal doesn't hold, put the band back on (to secure the lid) and store the jar in your fridge, to be eaten first.

STEP 13

STEP 14

Storing Canned Food

Once your jars are securely sealed, you can and should remove the bands, because keeping them on the jars invites rust. Label your canned goods, including their contents and the date. Then store them at room temperature or cooler (but not freezing), and away from direct sunlight. Keep jars dry to avoid possible corrosion of the lids.

For best quality and flavor, eat canned foods within a year, though they generally can keep for 18 to 24 months.

Keep those bands handy! Once you open a jar, you'll need to keep it in the fridge, and you can use a band to secure the lid and prevent spills.

Connecting to Time and Place

Ashley English, author of *Canning and Preserving*, loves preserving food because it connects her to time and place. "Apples I picked up at the local orchard turned into apple butter become more than just a foodstuff; they become an edible memory. Or green beans I grew rendered into pickled dilly beans transport me to hot, humid, heady summertime in my garden, even in the icy depths of winter." Preserving allows us to capture our memories, then share them, too—perhaps even more evocatively and fully than we could through words alone.

Canning Safely: A Review of Best Practices

Canning doesn't need to be intimidating, and following basic safety practices ensures that it can be fun and safe.

CHECK YOUR JARS FOR HAIRLINE CRACKS AND CHIPS.

USE NEW CANNING LIDS ONLY.

RELY ON TESTED RECIPES FROM TRUSTED SOURCES (see page 411). The more you can, the more you'll notice commonalities among these sources (and this book), because canning safely relies on a certain set of best practices. Recipes from trusted sources incorporate those best practices.

FOLLOW RECIPE INSTRUCTIONS. Leave appropriate headspace. Process jars for the recommended time and (for pressure canning) at the recommended pressure.

ADJUST FOR ALTITUDE IF YOU ARE 1,000 FEET OR MORE ABOVE SEA LEVEL (see page 39).

CONSISTENCY IS KEY. Keep a hot water bath boiling or the pressure consistent throughout the canning process.

BE CAREFUL ABOUT WHAT YOU CAN. Do not can foods unless your recipe (from a trusted source!) says it is able to be canned.

LOOK FOR DAMAGED TOPS ON CANNED GOODS. If you find that one of your jars of canned goods has a bowed top, that's a sign of spoilage. Throw it away. Don't even open the jar and dump it out; just keep it closed and toss the whole thing.

CHAPTER 3

Fermentation and Pickling

Fermentation is a microbially driven, transformative process that gives us everything from cheese, wine, and bread to sauerkraut, kimchi, salami, yogurt, coffee, tea, chocolate, vanilla, and beyond. You probably eat something fermented every day, whether or not you realize it! This ancient food preservation method is found in every culture around the world, it encompasses a massive realm of culinary delights, and it is my greatest love in the preserving universe.

Vegetable lactofermentation is a form of pickling, where vegetables are fermented in brine over a period of days (or weeks) to produce a delicious, sour result. Many people are probably more familiar with "quick" pickling—preserving foods in a vinegar-based brine, rather than in a brine that's acidified by fermentation over a period of days (hence the "quick" part).

As a preservation technique, fermentation brings not just an extended lifespan for our foods but also, in various cases, improved digestibility, pre- and probiotics, enhanced nutrition, and incredible flavor profiles. Fermentation is magic, encompassing many different processes and foods, and it's woven throughout this book because it is so central to the human experience.

What Is Fermentation?

Technically speaking, *fermentation* refers to the breakdown of energy-rich compounds in organic matter by a range of bacteria, yeasts, and molds. There are, of course, multitudes of microbes devoted to breaking down organic matter and transforming it into the fermented foods we know and love. If conditions in our food favor the beneficial microbes—those that enhance our food as they break it down—they will outcompete the not-beneficial ones.

So when we practice fermentation as a food preservation technique, we set up conditions that favor those beneficial microorganisms. For example, when we make sauerkraut—fermented shredded cabbage—we keep the cabbage under a brine (water with salt) so that the fermentation is anaerobic (oxygen-free), and we add salt. Together, these two factors encourage the growth of beneficial microbes while inhibiting the growth of undesirable ones.

Some fermentation processes are wild, taking advantage of whatever microbial life is present in the immediate environment. Kimchi is an example of wild fermentation—we simply chop up the cabbage and seasonings, pack them into a container under a salty brine, and wait for beneficial microbes to kick-start the fermentation. Other forms use inoculation with a microbial culture (e.g., commercial bread yeast, brewing yeast, or koji). There are many, many fermented foods out there and many ways to go about fermenting, from cheesemaking (see page 345) to sourdough to pickles and beyond. In this book we just scratch the surface of possibilities, including:

LACTOFERMENTATION. This form of fermentation relies on bacteria that produce lactic acid as a result of fermenting carbohydrates. For this, we submerge our fermented foods in liquid and add salt, as described previously for sauerkraut and kimchi.

FERMENTATION WITH KOJI. For koji, we rely on a mold, typically *Aspergillus oryzae*, cultivated on a substrate like rice, barley, or soybeans. To encourage its growth, we steam the substrate, inoculate it with the mold, and then maintain heat and humidity.

ALCOHOL FERMENTATION. Alcohol production relies on yeast that converts sugars to alcohol, such as the *Saccharomyces cerevisiae* used to brew beer. To encourage the yeast, we feed it simple sugars at selective intervals and run it through a two-step aerobic-anaerobic process.

VINEGAR FERMENTATION. To make vinegar, we rely on acetobacter, or bacteria that convert alcohol to acetic acid. To encourage the bacteria, we make sure that the alcohol content is just

Using Ferments in Your Kitchen

People often ask me how to incorporate more fermented foods into their diets. Because so many things are fermented, there are endless possibilities. Here are a few ways I eat ferments every day:

CONDIMENTS. Thinking of ferments as condiments as well as side dishes can help you enjoy them in more ways. A couple of tablespoons of sauerkraut as a topping for a burger or sandwich is a great example.

SNACKS. Carrot sticks, for example, can be lightly fermented, then enjoyed as a snack. Or what about yogurt and fruit? Or, if you don't like yogurt, what about some lightly fermented berries in place of jam on your morning toast?

SAUCES, DIPS, AND BEYOND. Ferments can be folded into other dishes, too. Fermented bean pastes (like miso) can be whisked into sauces and dips, eaten as a soup, folded into baked goods, or added to marinades and dressings. Pickling brines can be used for flavoring and marinating.

Yogurt is my personal go-to for saucing and dipping. Whisk it with hot sauce for the easiest two-ingredient dip. Or blend it with handfuls of fresh dill weed, cloves of garlic, and whatever other herbs are fresh and ready (and maybe some spinach, too) to make ranch and green goddess–style dressings. I use it in place of buttermilk in baking and brining (just whisk in a bit of milk if you need it thinner), blend it into creamy beverages, and add it to sauces and chilled soups. Since I rarely have sour cream on hand, strained yogurt tends to make an appearance as a topping when I'm eating borscht or American-style tacos.

THE WONDERFUL WORLD OF BEVERAGES. Kombucha is forever a fermentation favorite, but other options include Beet Kvass (page 328) and herbal sodas (page 176). Shrubs made with homemade vinegar are a great add-in to cocktails and alcohol-free drinks.

LET YOUR CURIOSITY GUIDE YOU. Folding ferments into your meals is an opportunity to discover your own tastes and favorite flavors. If your gut is telling you to whisk some sauerkraut brine into a marinade for roasted vegetables, why not give it a try? You might discover a new favorite food.

right—not too high and not too low—and allow the fermentation to proceed aerobically, meaning in the presence of oxygen.

This is not an exhaustive list. Fermentation is so integral to the human diet that it intersects with almost every category of food preparation, and there are many ways to harness its power.

In many cases, there are higher-tech/more-equipment versions and lower-tech/less-equipment versions of ferments. To brew beer, for example, we can work with a whole cache of expensive homebrew equipment, or we can use simple vessels and take advantage of wild fermentation. It all depends on what we want to make and how we can set up the environment to support that outcome.

Ferments are living, active foods and will sometimes bubble or spill over when burped.

Lactofermentation

At its most basic level, lactofermentation needs only water, salt, and time. You tuck some vegetables or fruit into a salty brine and let them ferment until they are tangy and flavorful. This simple process is a form of lactofermentation, meaning fermentation that relies on bacteria that produce lactic acid as a result of fermenting carbohydrates.

Lactofermentation is one of the most common, and easiest, forms of fermentation. If you've never tried fermenting food before, I highly recommend starting with lactofermented veggies as your first experiment. You can try lactofermenting carrot sticks (page 144) or making Sauerkraut (page 135) or Beet Kvass (page 328).

A FEW BEST PRACTICES

While the specifics may vary between different ferments, there are some overarching best practices for lactofermentation.

KEEP FOODS SUBMERGED IN BRINE. Lactofermentation is an anaerobic (oxygen-free) process; keeping your fermenting fruits or vegetables submerged prevents contact with air and inhibits the growth of pathogens. There are a range of ways to hold your solids under the liquid, from specialty weights to a folded cabbage leaf.

USE RAW FOODS. Beneficial bacteria are naturally present on fresh, raw fruits and veggies. That's why we include raw fruits and vegetables in ferments. You can use cooked vegetables, as long as they're less than half the total amount of vegetables.

ACCOUNT FOR SPILLAGE. Fermentation is an active, living process (its name comes from the Latin *fervere*, "to boil"), and that activity can sometimes spill out of jars and onto your counter. Be sure to set fermenting foods in a tray or other container to catch overflow and prevent staining of your countertops.

BURP YOUR FERMENTS. Many fermented foods are made in a jar with a lid. "Burp" these ferments once a day while they're actively fermenting: Gently loosen the lid, allowing excess gas that has built up during the fermentation process to escape.

TOP OFF WITH BRINE WHEN NEEDED. If the brine bubbles out and your fruits or vegetables are no longer completely covered by liquid, top off with more brine (you can find brine ratios on page 49).

CONSIDER YOUR WATER SOURCE. Opinions vary about the type of water that is best for fermentation. Some people insist on distilled water, but I've had success with tap water. Ultimately, the best choice is to use the water that's most easily available to you; seek out another source of water if you aren't getting the results you'd like or have concerns about your local water source.

INTERACT WITH YOUR FERMENTS DAILY. Observe them, stir them, smell them, taste them. By doing so, you'll familiarize yourself with the ingredients and the fermentation process itself. There is no hard-and-fast rule for when ferments are done; they're finished fermenting when they taste the way you want them to, and by regularly tasting and smelling them, you're more likely to understand when that is.

REFRIGERATE WHEN DONE. Once your ferments have the desired flavor, put them in the fridge, which slows the fermentation process and allows you to enjoy them over time. When storing ferments with metal rings in the fridge, it can be helpful to put a piece of parchment or waxed paper between the top of the jar and the lid to prevent corrosion. Just make sure the paper doesn't come in contact with the ferment itself.

NOTE THE AMBIENT TEMPERATURE. It has a big impact on how quickly a ferment processes. When the temperature is hot, fermentation goes faster. In cooler temps, it takes longer.

Other Fermentation Equipment

Some people use specialty tools, like airlocks, for fermentation. These can be helpful for more consistent batches, and they can act like an insurance policy against air exposure. While airlocks are nice, they aren't necessary for wild lactofermentation: They just add another layer of protection from outside air. I prefer to ferment footloose and fancy-free most of the time, but if you want to explore the world of fermentation tools, by all means, use anything available to you. As you ferment more, you'll have a better sense of what tools you want (e.g., measurement equipment, airlocks, special stainless fermenting tanks). But when you're just starting out, learning the basics with simple tools will help point you in the direction you want to go. Fermentation is a practice that shapes itself to you, and shapes you in turn.

FERMENTATION CROCKS AND WEIGHTS

You can ferment in jars and other containers, but for larger batches or regular practice, you might consider obtaining a fermentation crock. These crocks are beautiful as well as functional. They can be purchased with or without lids or custom-fitted weights. You can find stoneware crocks commercially, and many artisans make them, too. You can also find Sichuan pickling crocks and onggi (Korean earthenware crocks) at some Asian markets and online.

If you're purchasing a secondhand crock, make sure it's watertight and free of cracks. Note that some antique ceramic glazes contain lead, so if you go that route, it's worth checking that the glaze on your crock is food-safe and lead-free.

To clean your crock, don't bust out the heavy-duty cleaners (and definitely not the bleach). When I asked master food preserver Christina Ward how she cleans her crock, she said, "Superstitiously!"

A water-filled ziplock bag acts as an improvised fermentation weight.

Airlock lids create an anaerobic environment for lactoferments.

Traditional onggi pots hold kimchi.

A smaller jar works as an improvised fermentation weight.

Over time and many ferments, your crock will come to host a community of all the beneficial fermentation microbes. These microbes will inoculate each new ferment you put in the crock, facilitating the fermentation. Scrubbing out the crock halfway to kingdom come defeats the purpose!

Instead, gently wash your crock in warm water by hand (not in the dishwasher), use a gentle soap if you really need to, and dry the crock before storing it.

You'll often need weights to keep your fermenting fruits and vegetables submerged in their brine, and, like fermentation crocks, these weights come in many different forms. Some crocks come with weights designed to fit in them, and you can purchase weights for different sizes and shapes of crocks or small weights made to fit inside jars.

But weights aren't limited to what you can buy at a store. For most of history, our ancestors employed materials from around them to successfully weight their ferments. You might use a plate, a bowl, a smaller jar, or some other item that fits inside your crock/jar/fermentation container. You might use a sealed plastic baggie of dried beans or a cabbage or banana leaf to hold food down. You can even use stones; just clean them very thoroughly before you do.

When choosing weights, look for something that will cover as much of the surface area of your ferment as possible without also being impossible to remove from the container. Of course, choose a material that's food-safe, too.

BRINE RATIOS

All lactofermented vegetables and fruits are made in a solution of salt and water—that is, brine. Lactofermentation can happen in brines that are anywhere between 1.5 and 5 percent salt, but 2 to 3 percent salt is best for flavor with most vegetables.

Some fermented foods require you to prepare a brine by dissolving salt in room-temperature water and then pouring the brine over the vegetables or fruits. To make pour-over brine, use the ratios in the table below.

For other fermentation processes, you'll massage salt into chopped vegetables, which releases their moisture and creates a brine. For krauts, kimchi, and other massaged cabbage ferments, you can assume that 1 head of cabbage will yield 3 to 4 cups of liquid (this can vary a bit, which is fine). So, using the measurements below, you would use roughly 1 tablespoon of salt to get at least a 2 percent brine. If your cabbage doesn't release as much liquid as you need, you can prepare a pour-over brine, again using the ratios below.

Brine Ratios

Desired Salt Percentage	Water/Liquid	Salt
2 percent	1 quart (4 cups)	20 grams, or about 1 tablespoon
3 percent	1 quart (4 cups)	35 grams, or about 2 tablespoons
5 percent	1 quart (4 cups)	50 grams, or about 3 tablespoons

Making Kraut

While *kraut* typically means sauerkraut, made with cabbage, the kraut-making technique offers lots of room for experimentation. If you can grate it or shred it, you can kraut it! For example, I love making kraut with grated root vegetables and their greens, plus fresh herbs. If you're adding softer ingredients (corn kernels or berries, for example), add them in after you massage your other veggies. You may have heard of this referred to as kraut-chi, which is *Wild Fermentation* author Sandor Katz's term for mixed vegetables (and sometimes even fruit) fermented in the sauerkraut style. It's a wonderful way to combine and enjoy local, seasonal vegetables!

1 Core (if relevant) and finely shred the vegetables. Transfer them to a large bowl.

2 Sprinkle the shredded vegetables with salt. Lightly massage the salt into the vegetables until they release enough liquid to form a brine. Stop while the vegetables still have some crunch. (Alternatively, chop or grate the vegetables in a food processor, pack them into a jar, and pour brine over them, using the brine ratios listed on page 49.)

Don't Toss the Brine!

Once you've eaten your fermented vegetables or fruits, don't toss your brine! It makes a great flavor addition to soups (be sure to adjust the salt in your recipe) and salad dressings/marinades, and you can use it as part of the liquid for boiling pasta, grains, and beans.

STEP 1

STEP 2

STEP 3

STEP 4

3 Give the brine a quick taste. It should taste salty like the sea. If it seems like the brine needs a bit more salt, add more and massage it in.

NOTE: If your vegetables are not releasing enough liquid for the brine, prepare a pour-over brine (see brine ratios, page 49), pour a few splashes over the vegetables, and massage again, or add brine to the jars to make up the difference.

4 Pack the vegetables into a jar or crock. Top them off with enough of the brine remaining in the bowl to completely cover the vegetables. If you don't have enough brine to cover the vegetables, prepare a batch of brine (page 49) and use it to top off the jar or crock here.

5 Press down on the vegetables to release any air bubbles. Top them with a weight to keep them submerged.

6 Let the mixture ferment at room temperature. Check it every day to be sure the vegetables stay submerged. Taste it every few days to monitor its progression.

7 When the ferment tastes the way you'd like it to, it's done (I usually do 2 to 3 weeks). Store it in the refrigerator; it will keep fermenting even in the cool fridge temperatures, but very slowly.

STEP 5

PERPETUAL BRINE FERMENTS

Perpetual brine ferments are, as you can probably guess, ferments where you keep the brine, adding new veggies to it and eating the old ones as they pickle. Paocai, a Sichuan pickle studded with spices, is one of my favorites. My adventure ferment, a perpetual pickle I bring with me on my travels, is another.

Perpetual brine can keep going for years, so long as you add new vegetables to it from time to time (I do every 2 weeks, usually) to give the microbes something to eat. Once your colony of bacterial friends is established, you'll notice that your pickles ferment pretty quickly, sometimes in a matter of days rather than weeks.

To make a perpetual brine ferment, start with a 3 to 4 percent brine (2 to 2½ tablespoons unrefined salt dissolved in 1 quart water), along with any spices you want, and ferment your vegetables as usual. When they're ready, keep the brine and add new veggies to the ferment, saving the brine and adding in vegetables each time you want a fresh batch, tasting to adjust for salt if needed. I store mine on the counter and just eat straight from the jar, which keeps the microbes active. (You can, if you need to, also store the ferment in the fridge if it'll take you a while to get through. Just take it back out before you add your new vegetables!)

I love the ease and simplicity of having pickles right when I need them, and of not having to make a new brine each time. The tart and sometimes slightly funky flavor is incredible, too.

Paocai

Paocai, a traditional Sichuan perpetual brine ferment, can be made with any vegetables, but cool-weather crops like carrots, onions, and cabbage are common. For spices, I love star anise, whole chile peppers, black peppercorns, and whole cloves; fermentation revivalist Sandor Katz adds pieces of licorice root. Paocai is traditionally made with malt sugar, but you can substitute light brown sugar or piloncillo if you need to.

— Makes about 1½ quarts

1–2 tablespoons malt sugar, light brown sugar, or piloncillo

1 cup hot water

2 tablespoons salt

6 cups room-temperature water

4–5 cups vegetables, prepared as desired (e.g., carrot sticks, onion wedges, and trimmed beans)

Spices, as desired (2 tablespoons is a good starting point)

1. To make the brine, dissolve the sugar in the hot water. In a separate bowl, whisk the salt into the room-temperature water until dissolved. Add the sugar solution to the salt solution and whisk again.

2. Pack the vegetables and spices into a nonreactive container. Pour enough brine over the vegetables to completely cover them.

3. Put the lid on the container. Set the container on a tray or plate (to catch any overflow) in a spot that is out of direct sunlight at room temperature.

4. Let the vegetables ferment for 1 to 2 weeks. Burp the container, if pressure has built up (burp every 1 or 2 days at first), by loosening the lid to release any built-up pressure, then tightening it again. Taste the ferment periodically. Once the pickles have a flavor you enjoy, they're ready to eat. Store the pickles in the fridge.

5. Once you've eaten all the pickles, add more vegetables to the brine and, again, set the container out of direct sunlight at room temperature. The new vegetables should need only a day or two to ferment in the mature brine.

6. Repeat forever! Over time, the salt, sugar, and spices in your brine will diminish; taste-test the brine occasionally and refresh these as needed.

Quick Pickles

Quick pickles can be canned or made in the refrigerator, and both have their benefits. Canned pickles are shelf-stable, though heat from the canning process can render them less crisp. Refrigerator pickles will keep for weeks or months before losing their texture; canned quick pickles are best used within 1 year.

Quick pickles are made simply by mixing up a brine and pouring it, hot or cold, over your prepared ingredients. See the table below for my core brine ratio.

You'll find specific guidance for pickling vegetables and fruits in Part 2. Most pickling recipes add seasonings, such as herbs and spices, to the brine. Some call for sugar, which yields a sweet-and-sour pickle, such as pickled strawberries (page 266). I encourage you to play around with the pickling technique. It's a simple, fast, and low-stakes way to preserve food.

CORE BRINE RATIO	LARGE BATCH	SMALL BATCH
8 parts vinegar	8 cups vinegar	1 cup vinegar
8 parts water	8 cups water	1 cup water
1 part salt	1 cup salt	2 tablespoons salt

Japanese Tsukemono

Tsukemono is a rich and diverse Japanese pickling tradition. Tsukemono (pronounced tsoo-key-MO-no) is a generic term for pickled foods: *tsuke* means "pickled/marinated/steeped," and *mono* means "things," so, pickled things. *Tsuke* becomes *zuke* when it is added to the end of another word, so, for example, vegetables preserved in salt are shiozuke, while those preserved in shoyu (soy sauce) are shoyuzuke. Tsukemono are served with every meal, and they provide balance and variety to whatever you eat.

As is the case for many other preserving traditions, these pickles are seasonal, made with whatever is fresh and abundant, to be enjoyed now and later. Some are quick pickles, preserved in a salty and acidic brine. Some are pressed to extract excess moisture. Others are nestled in a pickling bed of salt or miso. They include vegetables (just about any you can imagine) but also proteins like fish, tofu, and eggs, as well as fruits, seaweed, and flowers.

See the recipe for Shoyuzuke Eggs on page 390 to try making one of my favorite tsukemono at home.

Making Refrigerator Pickles

Refrigerator pickles offer a great opportunity for experimentation. Try cutting down on the salt and pulling back the vinegar to pickle fruits and veggies with delicate flavors and textures. Conversely, try ramping up the seasoning for more boldly flavored or tougher veggies. Or try adding sugar; a brine that is half salt and half sugar works well for fruit pickles.

While the acidity level in your vinegar is a crucial factor when you're canning pickles, it matters less for refrigerator pickles, which means this is a great place to use homemade vinegar (page 64).

1 Slice, chop, or otherwise prepare your vegetables and/or fruits, as desired. Smaller ones can be left whole.

2 Pack the prepared vegetables and/or fruits and any aromatics (herbs and/or spices) into glass jars, leaving ½ to 1 inch of headspace.

3 Make the brine: Combine 8 parts water, 8 parts vinegar, and 1 part salt (or whatever proportions your recipe calls for) in a nonreactive pot over medium heat. Stir until the salt is completely dissolved, then remove from the heat.

4 If the vegetables and/or fruits you are pickling are delicate, let the brine cool to room temperature. Otherwise, you can use it hot.

5 Pour the brine over the vegetables and/or fruits, making sure they are submerged, leaving ½ inch of headspace.

6 If you used hot brine, allow the jar to cool completely.

7 Put lids on the jars and then store them in the fridge. Most vegetables and fruits will be ready to eat after an 8- to 12-hour soak in the brine, but especially dense foods or large pieces will need longer. Refrigerator pickles will generally keep for at least a few weeks.

STEP 1

STEP 5

Making Canned Pickles

For canned pickles, be sure to use vinegar with at least 5 percent acidity. Some store-bought vinegars are diluted below 5 percent, so check the label of any vinegars you purchase.

1 Place canning jars in a hot water bath canner, fill it with enough water to cover the jars by a couple of inches, and begin heating it.

2 Slice, chop, or otherwise prepare your vegetables and/or fruits as desired (smaller ones can be left whole).

3 Make the brine: Combine 8 parts water, 8 parts vinegar, and 1 part salt (or whatever proportions your recipe calls for) in a nonreactive pot over medium heat. Stir until the salt is completely dissolved.

4 Using tongs, remove the jars from the canner. Pack the prepared vegetables and/or fruits and any aromatics (herbs and/or spices) into the jars, leaving ½ to 1 inch of headspace.

5 Pour enough hot brine over the vegetables and/or fruits to cover them, leaving ½ inch of headspace.

(continued on next page)

STEP 2

Making Canned Pickles *continued*

6 Run a chopstick or other thin, nonmetal utensil along the inner edges of the jars to release any air bubbles. Wipe the rims of the jars with a clean, damp cloth. Add the lids and bands on the jars, and screw down to hand tightness.

7 Process pint jars in a hot water bath for 10 minutes and quarts for 15 minutes, adjusting for altitude (see page 39), if needed.

8 Let the jars cool for 24 hours before testing the seals (see page 36), then store them out of direct sunlight at room temperature.

NOTE: Some people soak cucumbers in ice water for 4 to 5 hours before canning them; this can help preserve their crispness. You can also soak them in a food-grade lime solution (see the National Center for Home Food Preservation website for guidance) for 12 to 24 hours before canning them; however, you must then rinse them well, soak them in fresh water (without lime) for 1 hour, then drain, and repeat the process two more times before canning them. If you don't remove the excess lime, it increases the risk of botulism.

STEP 5

STEP 6

Alcohol and Soda

Alcohol is useful in food preservation in a couple of ways: It can be used to preserve food (think peaches packed in brandy or berries in vodka), or those foods can be used as a base for making alcohol (think dandelion or strawberry wine).

All alcohol is a product of yeast fermentation. Essentially, the yeasts convert sugar into ethanol (alcohol) and carbon dioxide (carbonation). The yeasts become inactive and die once the alcohol reaches about 14 to 15 percent, or 30 proof. So the first step in any alcohol-making process is to activate yeast fermentation of whatever it is you want to preserve. There is an incredibly vast array of possibilities here. Humans have a knack for turning things into alcohol, and as a result, we've turned just about anything you can imagine into a tipple over the years.

Strong spirits, like vodka and whiskey, are typically made from very starchy plants, like grains and potatoes, and all spirits require some form of distillation. Beer, wine, mead, and hard cider are more easily made at home.

If you ferment a beverage for less time and with less sugar, you end up with a naturally carbonated nonalcoholic "soft" drink—that is, soda. Sodas aren't typically classified as a preservation method, but they are a fun way to use up food scraps—which is itself a form of preservation.

You'll find recipes for various alcoholic fermented beverages throughout Part 2. Here I'll cover the basic process for the three forms that are easiest to experiment with as preservation techniques: soda (which, as noted, is fermented just like alcohol, but with less sugar and time), mead, and country wine.

In all these recipes, I opt for wild fermentation. The process is simple, and the flavors range from funky to sour to complex, depending on the microbes knocking around on your produce.

If you want less potential variability in your final ferment, you can instead pitch commercial yeast, which simply means boiling your substrate (the thing you're fermenting), then cooling it and adding a specific strain (or strains) of yeast. Since you'll have boiled (and thus killed) the existing wild yeasts, these added yeast strains can more easily establish a foothold in your ferment. I tend to prefer wild-fermented sodas, meads, and wines because I find the uncertainty exciting. If you don't, see Resources (page 410) for some excellent books on alcohol fermentation that include guidance for pitched yeast projects.

Ginger Bug

A "bug" is a wild-fermented starter culture for naturally carbonated sodas. It helps the soda ferment faster by introducing the microbes we need so they can start multiplying right away. You can use other starter cultures, like whey or kefir, but ginger bug is my personal favorite, and it has the most adorable name.

TO MAKE GINGER BUG: Grate some organic ginger and place it in a small jar. (It's critical to use organic ginger, as conventional ginger is often irradiated, which kills needed microbes.) Add enough water and sugar to give the grated ginger a thin porridge-y or slurry consistency: Start with a 1:1:1 ratio and adjust as needed. Cover the mixture with a cloth and rubber band and let it sit at room temperature. Add a bit more ginger and sugar each day for several days, until the ferment is bubbling vigorously. At this point, it's ready to use.

TO USE GINGER BUG: Add about ¼ cup of ginger bug to each quart of soda at the start of fermentation.

Refresh your bug with a bit more sugar and grated ginger whenever you use it. If you'll be using the bug infrequently, store it in the fridge between uses, and then feed it and let it sit out 8 to 12 hours before using. Your bug will be more active with regular feeding, so try to avoid storing it in the fridge too often if you can.

Making Naturally Carbonated Soda

Use the technique outlined here to make naturally carbonated beverages using whatever fruits, vegetables, or fruit-and-vegetable scraps you have. Be sure to include some exterior plant parts—peels, outer leaves, whole berries, tops, and so on. These will have the wild yeasts needed to start the fermentation process. Or use a ginger bug (page 57)—a starter culture that helps your soda ferment faster and sets you up for success—alongside your produce. A ginger bug can also be used with juices and syrups that don't contain their own microbes.

For the fermentation process, you'll need a glass or other nonreactive container. Once you're ready to carbonate the soda, transfer it to narrow-necked flip-top or capped bottles.

1. Add fruits and/or vegetables, chopped, or their scraps (peels, trimmings, etc.), totaling 1 to 2 cups per quart of water (the amount is very flexible) to a container. Add any flavorings and ginger bug (if using).

2. In a separate container, stir sugar into room-temperature water (1 to 1½ cups sugar per quart of water) until dissolved, then pour over the mixture. Add more water as needed to fill the container to its neck.

3. Top the container with an airlock, lid, or cloth.

4. Allow the soda to ferment for 2 to 4 days, or until you like the flavor. If you are not using an airlock on your container, stir or gently shake the mixture several times a day.

STEP 1

STEP 3

STEP 5

STEP 6

5 Strain the liquid.

6 Funnel or pour the liquid into narrow-necked bottles. Add about 2 tablespoons of sugar per bottle. This is called priming sugar, and it gives your yeasts a little extra boost so they're active enough to carbonate your soda for you. Gently shake to dissolve.

7 Allow the soda to ferment in the bottles for 2 to 3 days, depending on the temperature, until it is good and bubbly.

8 Once it's carbonated, store your soda in the fridge.

STEP 7

Making Mead/Melomel

Mead is a sometimes-sweet alcoholic beverage made by fermenting honey. Honey already contains all the yeasts it needs to ferment, as well as the sugars—mead really is a just-add-water ferment. Honey itself is shelf-stable, but mead is a wonderful way to bring in and preserve other ingredients that can flavor it.

Mead made with fruit is called a melomel, and most fruits, and even vegetables, work well for this. The fruits or vegetables not only impact the flavor but add their own microflora to the party, meaning your wild-fermented mead might be funky or sweet or complex—in other words, much more than the sum of its parts. I encourage you to take this basic recipe and run with it. Over time, you'll learn what works best for you, in your season and place, giving you a mead that's all your own.

1 Pour honey (1 cup honey per 4 cups water) into a fermentation vessel. I typically use a wide-mouthed crock, but a large glass jar or other food-safe container also works.

STEP 1

STEP 2

2 Pour room-temperature water into the fermentation vessel and stir until the honey is dissolved.

3 Add flavoring ingredients, such as fruits, vegetables, herbs, and or/spices (if using), and stir to distribute. Cover the fermentation vessel with a towel or cheesecloth (held in place with a rubber band, if needed) to keep insects out.

STEP 3

4 Let the mixture ferment at room temperature, stirring it several times a day. After 3 or 4 days, start tasting the mead once or twice a day. Continue this until the mead is good and bubbly and has the flavor you want, which should take 4 to 7 days.

5 When the mead has a flavor you enjoy, pull out any fruit, vegetables, herbs, or spices you may have added. (You can compost these, toss them into a dehydrator, or try topping your dinner or dessert with them—berries that have been used to make mead make a fantastic sauce for ice cream.)

The mead is now ready to drink. Store it in the fridge to slow further fermentation.

NOTE: If you would like to make a mead with a higher ABV or one that is carbonated, there are a lot of great resources out there with specifics on how to do so, including Jereme Zimmerman's *Make Mead Like a Viking*, Sandor Katz's *The Art of Fermentation*, and Christopher and Kirsten Shockey's *The Big Book of Cidermaking*.

STEP 4

The Myths of Mead

Mead lies at the core of many myths and legends. According to the Khoisan people of southern Africa, mead is a magical substance that was discovered fermenting in a tree stump, while according to Norse legend, mead was a gift passed from the gods to humans, giving us poetry, inspiration, and creativity.

Making Basic Country Wine

There's a special, meditative joy in wild winemaking. Daily stirring, watching bubbles gather and the ferment come alive, then watching the bubbles die back as this first stage of transformation draws to a close—it's a chance to watch the magic of fermentation in action.

This recipe is adapted from the grape wine recipe in the book *New Era Home Economics and Cookery*, published in 1903. Feel free to experiment with whatever ripe fruit, vegetables, and herbs you have on hand. Note that if you use low-sugar fruits, vegetables, or herbs (like dandelion flowers), you may need to increase the sugar.

1 Place 6 pounds of fruits, vegetables, and/or herbs (pitted, seeded, and chopped as needed) in a blender or food processor, and blend to a chunky pulp. Add liquid if needed. If you don't have a blender, you can use a potato masher.

STEP 1

2 Pour the pulp into a large jar or crock. Cover with a cloth and secure with a rubber band or twine.

3 Let the mixture sit at room temperature, stirring several times a day, for 7 to 10 days, until the mixture stops bubbling.

STEP 2

STEP 3

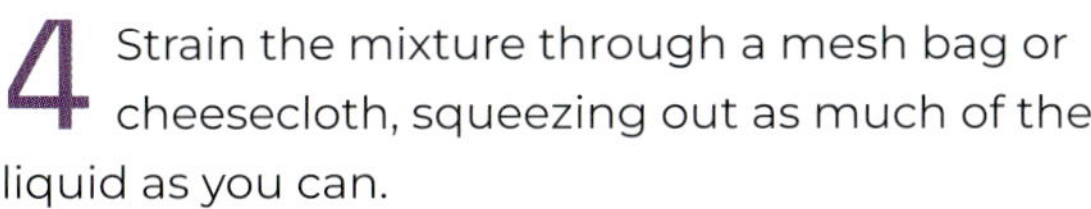

4 Strain the mixture through a mesh bag or cheesecloth, squeezing out as much of the liquid as you can.

5 Transfer the liquid back into your fermentation jar or crock. Add 5 cups of sugar and stir until it is dissolved. Cover the jar or crock with a cloth.

6 Let the liquid ferment again, stirring daily. It will bubble eagerly for the first few days, then start to slow down. Once the bubbling has mostly subsided and the brew tastes alcoholic, 7 to 10 days, it's ready to drink. (You can also test the alcohol level with a hydrometer, if you prefer to do so; I tend to let my taste buds guide me.)

7 Pour the wine into bottles. It will be quite sweet, as many country wines are. You can age it in the bottles in a cool place for 1 to 2 months to mellow out the sweetness a bit; just make sure your bottles are completely full and tightly capped to minimize the amount of oxygen coming into contact with the wine.

NOTE: If you like your wine carbonated, then before you pour it into bottles, add 2 tablespoons of sugar per gallon of wine (finely granulated sugar is easiest to work with here) and whisk to dissolve. Bottle the wine, tightly cap the bottles (swing-top bottles work great for this), and allow the wine to ferment at room temperature for several days until it's good and bubbly.

Vinegar

The word *vinegar* comes from the French *vin aigre*, or "sour wine," and it's likely that the invention of vinegar was a happy accident, resulting from a batch of wine left sitting out too long.

Vinegar is a boon to food preservation: It is itself a preserved food, made by fermenting wine, cider, juices, and other sweet liquids, and it can be used to preserve other foods, allowing us to flavor them quickly without waiting for them to ferment. It is a powerhouse for using up food waste. Scraps like strawberry and jalapeño tops can be added to sugar and water and fermented to make a flavorful vinegar. Even the waste from making alcohol (like pomace, the pulp left after pressing apples for cider) can be used for vinegar making.

I often wonder about the first batches of vinegar and the people who decided to eat them (or, perhaps, felt they had to in order to not waste food). How quickly did they figure out that vinegar might be useful for preserving? Or flavoring? We sometimes think our ancestors were pretty uninventive and narrow-minded with their cuisine, but the first people to use vinegar for flavor or pickling were at least as innovative as the most cutting-edge culinary minds today.

EXPERIMENTATION

Given the dizzying array of substrates you can use to make it—alcohol, cider, herbs, vegetables, fruits, food scraps—vinegar offers incredible space for exploration, and I strongly encourage you to play and experiment. How can you know if you've been successful? If it smells like vinegar and tastes like vinegar, congratulations, it's vinegar!

I also encourage you to experiment with using your vinegar. Try it in vinaigrettes, refrigerator pickles (see Chapter 3), and other preparations where the exact acidity level matters less. Vinegar's magic opens up such a wide expanse of flavor beyond what you can get from the store. I hope you'll experience some of that magic for yourself.

WHEN IS THE ACIDITY LEVEL IMPORTANT?

When you are using vinegar for canning and other preservation techniques (rather than for flavor), the level of acidity is important to food safety. In these cases, make sure your vinegar has 5 percent acidity (you can buy pH strips and meters to measure this at home, and most commercial vinegar lists the acidity on the label). For flavoring or for refrigerator pickles you'll eat relatively soon, your homemade vinegar with less acid is A-OK.

Making Vinegar

To make vinegar, you'll first need to make or obtain alcohol that is at least 4 percent alcohol by volume (ABV) but not higher than 14 to 15 percent. If your alcohol is too strong, your acetobacter (the bacteria that convert alcohol to acetic acid) won't be able to do their work (which is why distilled spirits do not turn into vinegar even when left out for years).

To this alcohol, you will add a vinegar "mother"—a gelatinous collection of acetobacteria, yeast, and cellulose—and let it sit until it's delightfully tart and sour. If you don't have a vinegar mother, don't despair. The microbes you need are everywhere, so a mother will grow on its own.

Step One (Optional): Making Alcohol

Alcohol is made using an anaerobic (without oxygen) yeast fermentation, a process that usually takes a week or two, sometimes more, depending on temperature and amount of sugar available. If you're new to making vinegar, apple cider is a great starter choice because it has the correct amount of sugar to give you the ABV you need to turn your alcohol into vinegar. Unpasteurized apple cider also contains the yeasts you need to ferment the juice into alcohol.

1 Pour 1 gallon of unpasteurized apple cider into a clean, dry container. You can use a carboy and an airlock, if you prefer, or put it in a crock or other food-safe container. If using a crock, place a cloth over the top and secure with twine or a rubber band. If using a jar, just twist the lid on tightly.

2 Allow the cider to ferment, stirring daily (unless you are using an airlock) for about 7 days, testing and tasting along the way. If your container has a tightly sealed lid, be sure to burp it (see page 46) at least once a day by loosening and retightening the lid to keep pressure from building up! As it ferments, the yeast will convert the sugars in your juice or honey mixture into alcohol, and you'll see bubbling.

3 The mixture will stop bubbling once the yeast activity has died down, which is your signal that alcohol fermentation is complete. You can buy equipment to measure the ABV, but I usually just go by taste. If it tastes like alcohol, it's ready.

Yeasts bubble and brew to turn cider to alcohol (left), then alcohol into apple cider vinegar (right).

Step Two: Vinegar Mother

This step involves bacterial, rather than yeast, fermentation. This process is aerobic (meaning it requires oxygen), so you'll want some exposure to air. Any liquid that is between about 4 and 15 percent alcohol by volume will naturally start to convert to vinegar after exposure to air. However, it can still be helpful to add a starter: A vinegar mother or a couple of healthy splashes of unpasteurized vinegar can speed things along.

1 Pour your alcohol into a nonreactive container with a wide mouth. Cover it with a cloth secured with twine or rubber bands to keep flies out.

2 Allow the alcohol to ferment for 2 weeks or more at room temperature, out of direct sunlight.

3 When it tastes like vinegar, it's vinegar! You can buy pH strips or meters to measure acidity if you want to get technical, but your taste buds really are a great guide here.

4 Transfer the vinegar to a storage container, seal it tightly, and store it in a cool, dark location. Be sure to limit your vinegar's exposure to air once it's done fermenting.

Infused Vinegars and Liquors

It's easy to infuse all sorts of vinegars and alcohols, store-bought or homemade, with herbs, spices, vegetables, and/or fruits, which impart their flavor. Wherever your vinegar comes from, the basic principle is the same: Pour your vinegar or liquor over whatever you're infusing into it, then let it steep. Once you like how it tastes, strain the liquid and store it in an airtight container.

Infusion offers a chance to get a lot of flavor payoff from a small amount of ingredients—a handful of herbs or other aromatics, for example. It's also a great way to use up food scraps (vinegar infused with strawberry and jalapeño tops is always a hit, as are spirits infused with herb stems). One of my personal favorites is vinegar infused with mirepoix scraps (onion, carrot, celery, and sometimes garlic; see recipe, page 196), which is aromatic, good for cooking, and good for reducing food waste.

You can layer the flavor of the vinegar or spirit with the flavors of what you infuse (think red wine vinegar with plums or cherries), or you can use a neutral base and just let the flavor of the infused ingredients shine through. You can infuse with just one ingredient (fresh summer peaches, for example), or you can layer ingredients (peaches and roses, or cherries and lavender). Sometimes I make infusions around a theme: flavors that remind me of a certain place or event, like peaches and mountain mint for Georgia in the summertime.

Making infused vinegars and liqueurs is a very easy, safe practice, but if you're infusing very juicy, watery ingredients, be mindful of not packing them too tightly in your jar. Why? Because the liquid in your substrate migrates into the alcohol or vinegar as it infuses, which can reduce your alcohol's ABV or vinegar's acidity. If the ABV/acidity gets too low, you risk the growth of pathogenic microbes. If you're worried about this, let your vinegar infuse in the fridge, and store it there, too.

Pasteurized Cider for Alcohol?

If all you have is pasteurized cider, you'll need to add an ingredient—like unpeeled raw fruit, fresh rose petals, or dates—that contains yeasts you need to make alcohol. The amount is flexible: I usually add a few cups of fruit per gallon or a couple of handfuls of petals.

Infusing Vinegar and Liquor

Since the processes of infusing vinegar and infusing alcohol are very similar, it can be fun to infuse the same ingredient in different vinegars and spirits and see how the flavor changes (or pair them in your food and drink across a single meal). These infusions make perfect gifts and great add-ins to your dinner or drinks.

For vinegar, I typically use apple cider vinegar, red wine vinegar, rice wine vinegar, and occasionally distilled white vinegar. For liquor, I generally use vodka or whiskey. You can use botanical spirits like gin, but note that they are already infused with other flavors, so you'll want to be intentional about what you pair them with. The more scraps you pack into your jar and the longer you let them infuse (up to a point, of course), the more flavorful your infusion will be.

1 Pack the aromatics (berries, vegetables, herbs, and/or spices) into a jar. The more you add, the stronger the flavor, but I usually do a 1:4 or 1:2 ratio of aromatics to vinegar or liquor. This means packing the jar one-quarter to one-half full.

2 Pour in enough vinegar or liquor to cover completely, leaving at least 1 inch of head-space. Secure the lid tightly.

3 Let steep until the vinegar or liquor reaches your desired flavor. I typically start taste-testing after 1 to 2 weeks.

4 When it's ready, strain out the aromatics, bottle and label the vinegar or liquor, and enjoy!

NOTE: Save the aromatics that you strain out! Eat them, use them as a garnish, dehydrate them . . . boozy fruit that's cooked down into a compote and served on top of ice cream is simply amazing.

Vanilla Extract

Vanilla comes from a flowering orchid whose pods are fermented to give them their characteristic aroma and flavor. Vanilla extract is basically an infused alcohol, and it is easy to make at home and better tasting than store-bought. And if you make your own vanilla extract, vanilla sugar (below) can be a happy by-product.

2 vanilla beans

8–9 ounces vodka or whiskey

Cut the vanilla beans lengthwise and place them in a half-pint jar. Add vodka to cover. Seal the jar and set in the pantry—the vanilla extract will be ready in 1 month. Remove the beans and store the liquid in an airtight container at room temperature. Use the beans for vanilla sugar or discard.

Vanilla Sugar

You can purchase vanilla beans for the purpose of making vanilla sugar, or you can use the leftover vanilla pods from other projects. For example, pods left over after scraping out the beans for ice cream still have tons of flavor and can be used to infuse your vanilla sugar. Even the pods you use for your extract probably have enough life left in them for vanilla sugar; just let them air-dry before packing them in.

2 vanilla beans

2 cups sugar

Cut the vanilla beans lengthwise and place them in a pint jar. Cover with the sugar and seal. Vanilla sugar will be ready in about 2 to 4 weeks. Whenever you have new or leftover pods, you can just toss them into the same jar and refill it with sugar for a continuous supply.

SHRUBS AND LIQUEURS

Sweetened infused vinegars are called shrubs, while sweetened infused liquors are liqueurs. Both are made in just the same way as unsweetened vinegars and liquors, but with the addition of a sweetener (sugar, honey, maple syrup, agave syrup, and so on).

We typically think of making shrubs and liqueurs with fruit, but vegetables and herbs are also great choices. Think sweeter root vegetables like carrots and beets or aromatic roots like turmeric and ginger. Or experiment with your favorites (I made a lovely shrub with sweet yellow cherry tomatoes and just a hint of basil several years ago). Fresh herbs, or herb stems if you have some left over from other dishes, are great for this, too.

To make:

1. Prepare an infused vinegar or liquor, following the instructions on page 66.
2. After straining the infused vinegar or liquor, stir in sweetener to taste. I typically use ⅛ to ¼ cup of sugar per 2 cups of vinegar or alcohol.
3. Store at room temperature, out of direct sunlight, or in the fridge.

To serve: Experiment with using shrubs and liqueurs in cocktails and mocktails. Or just mix them with a bit of soda water (I usually do 4 to 6 parts soda water to 1 part shrub). They're also great with other beverages, like Fermented Ginger Beer (page 110).

COCKTAILS AND MOCKTAILS

A mixology class is a bit beyond the scope of this book, but I use my preserves often in my drinks, and once you find some favorites, you very well might join me in that practice.

Drinks can be made with infused spirits and vinegars and with shrubs and liqueurs. But your preserving drinks cabinet doesn't have to stop there. Try stirring in bitters (see page 400), pickle brine (see page 69), jams, and syrups. Garnish your drinks with preserved lemons (see page 283) or dried fruit, or dust them with fruit or herb powders.

Many of the fruit and vegetable preserves in this book can, in whole or in part, be repurposed into cocktails, and scraps from your preserving projects can also be given new life through booze (or not-booze).

If you want mocktails that taste like cocktails, think about what the alcohol part of the cocktail brings to the table, flavor-wise: the "burn" from the distilled spirits, and a slight drying effect. The texture of alcohol can be mimicked by using tannic botanicals and tannic fruits, which help dry the mouth slightly (think tannins in a dry red wine). Hot peppers are often used to mimic the burn, but you can mimic it with other heat-giving foods, too, like black peppercorns or even horseradish. I also like to add tinctures and vinegar-based bitters (page 400) for flavor and medicinal purposes, and shrubs.

I often use apple cider vinegar as a base for my mocktail making, because it has a bold flavor and yet is not so sour as to overpower everything else. Infusing it with some tannic fruits and hot peppers is a good stand-in for whiskey in, say, a "whiskey" sour (adding a teeny tiny bit of charred fruit or other smoky flavor can be nice, too). I also like to make infused vinegars to mimic other spirits (think juniper berries in white wine vinegar if you're a gin fan). If you don't love your sour concoctions in drinks, don't despair: They're still great for eating, too.

Pickle Brine Martini

Just like pickles themselves, pickle brine martinis are all about experimentation. The flavors can be whatever you want them to be! If you like a dirtier martini, add more brine. The biggest concern is whether you like the flavor of the brine. Dip a spoon into your brine and give it a taste. These martinis may not be made "correctly," but they bring me joy, and at the end of the day, that's what it's all about.

— Makes 1 martini

Ice
2½ ounces gin or vodka (see note)
½–1 ounce pickle brine, strained
½ ounce dry vermouth
Pickle, for garnish (optional)

1. Fill a mixing glass or shaker with ice. Add the gin, pickle brine, and vermouth. Stir or shake for 20 to 30 seconds to combine.

2. Strain the mixture into a martini glass. Garnish with a pickle, if desired, and serve.

NOTE: Savory, spicy, garlicky brines stand up well to the botanicals in gin. If your brine has a gentler flavor, you might try it in a vodka martini.

Pickle Brine Martini

Koji Fermentation

Koji (*Aspergillus oryzae*) is a truly magical mold. The smell of it as it ferments is breathtakingly delicious and comforting, and it gives us many wonderful foods and drinks, including sake and amazake, miso, shoyu (soy sauce), tamari, and more.

Though koji is traditionally cultivated on beans and grains, it grows on just about any food you throw at it. Modern cooks are using it inventively, creating such delicacies as vegan charcuterie by growing koji on vegetables like butternut squash. Its superpower is the range of flavors it engenders as it ferments foods. It adds sweetness to sake and amazake and brings savory depth to dark miso pastes and shoyu. My friend Wade Fox, a fermentation enthusiast like myself, taught me to stir a spoonful of koji flour into alcoholic spirits a few hours before drinking them, which enhances the flavor. Try it!

Koji is deeply rooted in Japanese culinary and cultural traditions, as generations of shoyu, sake, and miso makers will attest. But it is also playful and experimental, as chefs and home cooks who experiment with it continue to show us. Koji asks us to learn about traditions and respect them, but also to be expansive as we carry those roots forward. Koji reminds us that we can preserve traditions, honoring them and the many hands and minds that went into crafting them through the centuries, while also creating new traditions informed by, but distinct from, what has come before.

CULTIVATING KOJI

I offer a few recipes for koji-based ferments in Chapter 8, including White Miso (page 339). You can purchase prepared koji for use in these recipes, but making koji from scratch using a starter culture (spores, or finished prepared koji, or even koji flour, which is just ground prepared koji) is relatively easy—and the results are worth the effort. When you pull back the covering of your koji bed, the sweet smell that hits you is intoxicating. It is, hands down, one of my favorite smells in the world, right up there with petrichor and sleepy kitten bellies. It's that good.

KOJIBAN

Many home fermenters cultivate koji using a variety of improvised incubators, but the traditional method is to use wooden trays, called kojiban, which help regulate temperature and humidity, resulting in a more consistent final product. A bamboo rice steamer lined with lint-free towels would also work. You want the koji to be able to breathe and regulate its temperature, so airtight containers won't work here. It also needs to be above room temperature—for example, kept in an oven turned off but with the pilot light on.

A kojiban is a traditional wooden box for fermenting koji.

DISPERSING SPORES

To cultivate koji on a substrate (whatever it is you're fermenting), you must use spores mixed with a dispersal medium so they will evenly coat the substrate. You can buy prepared koji starter, which is already dispersed and ready to use, but I usually prepare the spores myself, using rice flour and/or all-purpose wheat flour. Here's how to do it.

1. Turn off any fans or other air-circulating appliances (while koji is safe to eat, regular inhalation of aspergillus spores can cause issues, so try not to inhale it or make it airborne).
2. Mix the spores with your flour (the dispersal medium) at a 1:10 ratio: 1 gram of spores per 10 grams of flour. Measure out the appropriate amount of each.
3. Carefully open the packet of starter spores; you might just snip off a corner of the package. Empty the packet into the bottom of a jar, pouring slowly, keeping your hand still in the jar until the spores settle to prevent dispersing them.
4. Add the flour slowly, in several batches. Be very gentle to prevent spores from getting kicked up and becoming airborne.
5. Close the lid tightly, then shake to evenly distribute spores through the flour. Your starter is now ready to use.
6. Store the jar, tightly sealed, in a cool, dark place or the freezer. Spores can keep for up to 18 months if kept cool and dry, though I usually try to use mine within 6 to 12 months.

Once your starter is mixed up, the ratio of this starter to substrate is 1:1,000—that is, 1 gram of dispersed spores to 1,000 grams of cooked substrate (rice, soybeans, etc.).

Prepared koji can be made or purchased dried in blocks and crumbled to make a range of delicious products like shoyu, miso, and sake.

Growing Koji

Koji is traditionally made by steaming rice, barley, or soybeans, cooling to wrist temperature, then inoculating with koji spores. The substrate you choose depends on what you're making: soybeans for shoyu (soy sauce), for example. I most often use rice, which, once fermented by koji, gives you everything you need, enzymatically speaking, to make koji-fermented foods.

Once you learn the technique, you might experiment with growing koji on different substrates, like sourdough bread (see page 326) or other grains, and play with different koji strains.

1 Wash 4 cups of long-grain white rice until the water runs clear to remove excess starch.

2 Place the rice in a bowl, add water to cover, and soak the rice for 6 to 8 hours to partially hydrate it.

3 Line a steamer basket with a clean, lint-free cloth (like a linen dish towel) and place over a wide pot of boiling water. Add the rice to the steamer basket and spread into an even layer, then steam until just tender (like al dente pasta). This takes 45 to 70 minutes.

STEP 3

4 Remove the rice from the heat and spread out evenly on a large surface (like a baking pan), no more than 1½ inches deep. Let cool to wrist temperature.

5 Weigh the cooked rice to ensure you're using the proper amount of starter. For 2 grams of prepared koji starter, you'll want 2 kilograms of cooked rice.

6 Measure 2 grams of prepared koji starter into a spoon or small mesh strainer, then tap the edge of the spoon as you move it across the surface of your cooled rice.

7 Gently mix the rice and koji starter by hand to evenly distribute the starter throughout the rice, taking care to not crush or break the grains.

STEP 6

STEP 7

8 Transfer the inoculated substrate to an incubation container—a nonreactive pan (like a baking pan with 2-inch-tall sides or a hotel pan) lined with clean, lint-free cloths. Pile it up in the middle of the container to help the koji stay warm.

9 Set the incubation container in a spot that stays consistently warm. My go-to is an oven, turned off but with its pilot light on, provided it stays within the range of 86 to 95°F/30 to 35°C. You might also make a hot water bath (I use a sous vide machine in a large rolling cooler) as an incubator. There are many incubator options! Koji will begin to die off if the temperature goes above 115°F/46°C, so keep an eye on the temperature.

10 Check the substrate after 12 hours, mixing (gently!) by hand to aerate the rice and prevent the middle from getting too hot. Then spread the rice out in an even layer in your fermenting tray (like a kojiban; though many modern cooks also use nonreactive pans for this step, and they work well). Make ridges in the koji to increase surface area.

11 Continue this cycle of mixing and resting your koji, letting it rest for 8 to 12 hours after each time you mix it and spreading it in an even layer and then making ridges, until the mold covers the surface of each grain. Your koji is done when it's fragrant and covered in a fluffy, white mat of mycelia that binds the grains together. This usually takes about 2 days.

12 Use your koji right away, or store it in a ziplock bag, with air pressed out, in the fridge for about 2 weeks.

Shio Koji

USING KOJI FOR PRESERVATION

Koji is truly a magical mold, giving us foods and drinks we enjoy on their own, like sake, amazake, and miso, as well as seasoning like shoyu, which we can use to make a whole range of other dishes like Shoyuzuke Eggs (page 390). Traditional koji-based foods are a central part of the flavor profiles in Japanese cuisine. Today, many home cooks and chefs also experiment with koji in other ways.

Immersing food in shio koji—a magical mixture of koji, salt, and water—is a traditional seasoning and preserving technique. As a fermenting agent, shio koji is both delicious and versatile. Case in point: In *Preserving the Japanese Way*, Nancy Singleton Hachisu includes helpful graphs of various pickling methods and their effectiveness for a wide variety of fruit, vegetables, and seafood. In most cases, some methods work best for certain ingredients over others. But shio koji? It's the only method that works for every single ingredient on the list.

Shio Koji

In addition to its use in fermentation, shio koji can help tenderize ingredients when used as a marinade (thanks, enzymes!), and while traditional shio koji doesn't include extra flavors, it's a great canvas for flavor experiments. Think fresh rosemary and lemon peel, or orange and oregano, or baking spices—the sky's the limit! One of the best ones I ever made was a pine needle shio koji.

If you're using koji blocks, make sure to break them apart with your hands before using. Feel free to scale this recipe up or down as needed. The proportions noted here create a 10 to 12 percent salt solution.

— Makes about 3 cups

- **2 cups koji**
- **2 cups water**
- **4 tablespoons unrefined salt**
- **Flavorings, such as a couple of herb sprigs or 2 tablespoons whole spices (optional)**

Combine the koji, water, salt, and flavorings (if using) in a quart jar. Put on the lid and let ferment at room temperature for 1 to 2 weeks, stirring or shaking daily and burping the lid as needed. Store in the fridge, where it will keep for months.

Fermentation Guidance

The history of fermentation is fascinating in part because so many household-level fermentation practices were not recorded (and some, like brewing and breadmaking, are more commonly represented in historical records than, say, household-scale vegetable fermentation). This means that the written history of fermentation is incomplete, and some of it will unfortunately never be recovered. This is partially due to what we have historically chosen to record (both what processes and foods were considered important, and whose stories were considered worth telling), as well as what records survive.

Fermentation encompasses such a broad set of practices that we can't really paint its whole history with a single brush, but one thing that strikes me is that it's a hands-on, learned practice. Rather than gleaning information primarily from cookbooks, much of what we've learned historically about fermentation has happened in real time, from another cook, hands deep in bowls and jars and crocks.

So I hope you take the fermentation guidance in this book as the beginning of your own journey. While I may not be there teaching and learning alongside you in your kitchen (wouldn't it be great if that were the case?), we're still learning together from afar, and I encourage you to seek out the wisdom of knowledgeable fermentation teachers, including community elders, folks at your county Cooperative Extension offices, professional cooking instructors, or your best friend who's been making sauerkraut since they were five. Even with a familiar practice, there's always a chance to learn something new by watching someone else do it.

CHAPTER 4

Syrup, Jam, Jelly, and Other Sweet Preserves

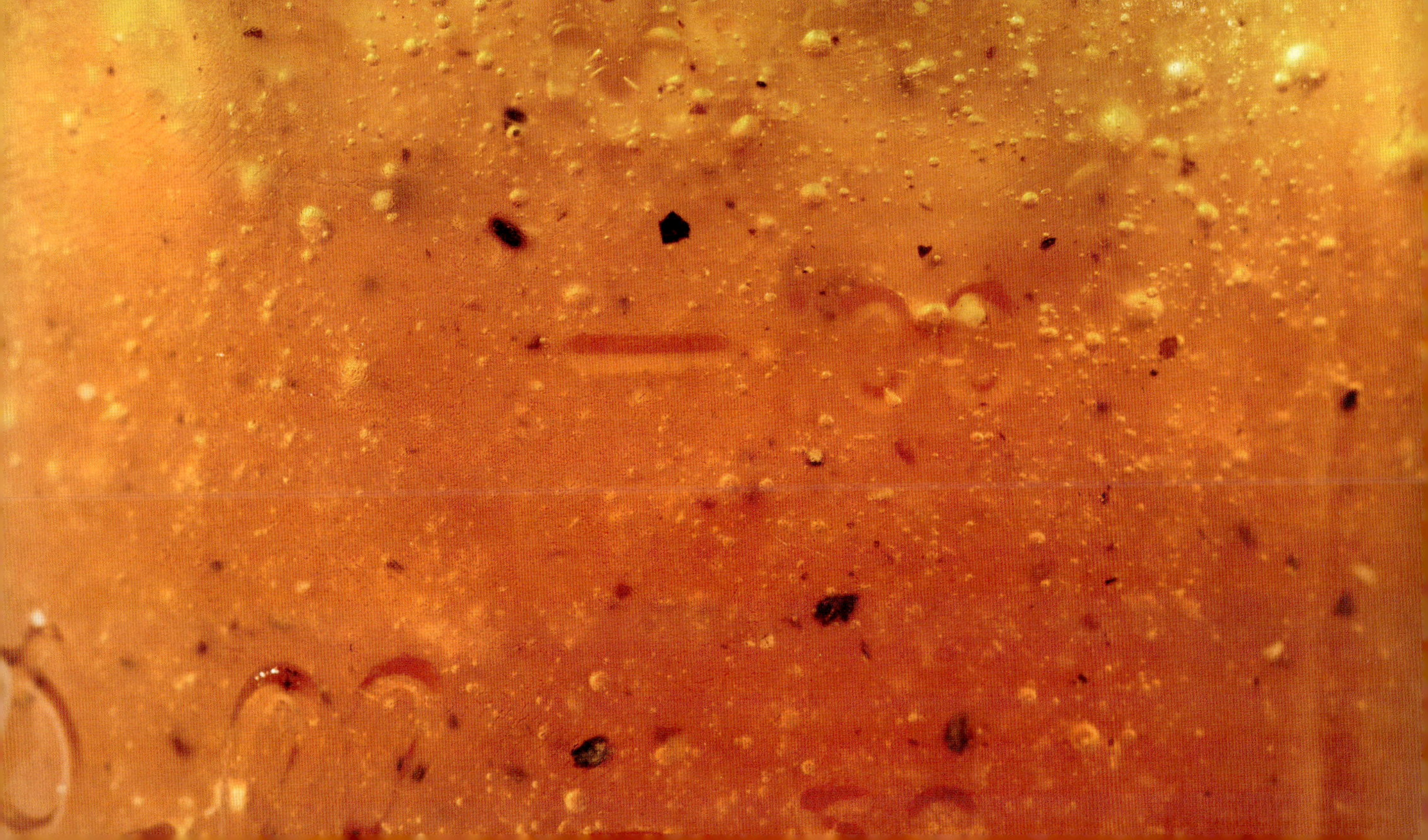

Preserving fruits (and vegetables) with sugar is a time-honored tradition and easy to do in a home kitchen. Jam and fruit preserved in syrup, in particular, are friendly entry points to preservation.

The difference between a jelly and a jam, broadly speaking, is that jelly is made from cooked, sweetened, strained juice, which is then thickened with gelatin or pectin. Jam is made from mashed-up fruits or vegetables; it may or may not have additional thickeners, and it tends to be (or at least can be) chunky. Syrups are made with fruit (and/or other flavors), sugar, and water, or from fruit juice, thickened by cooking but still pourable. They're like jellies without the added gelling ingredients. In fact, if you attempt a jelly and it doesn't set, don't fret. Instead of jelly, now you have some nice jars of syrup.

The history of jam goes back at least to ancient Persian sugar cultivation, and Greek and Roman traditions of preserving fruit in honey (though undoubtedly, fruit was being sweetened and eaten long before and in many places). Jam made with cane sugar, as we often think of it today, showed up in Europe with the import of sugar from the Americas. The process of cooking down fruit with sweetener is not, however, uniquely European. Around the world, jammy preserves are made with whatever sweetener is ready to hand. You can find fruit chutneys in India, grass jelly in China, marmalades in the UK, and more. Cheong, a Korean specialty, yields both a syrup and sugar-preserved fruit.

Syrups, jams, jellies, and other sweetened preserves are a great way to use up food waste, offering a simple option for processing fruits and vegetables while they're still fresh. I especially love them for produce that is slightly bruised, asymmetrical, or otherwise not grocery-store perfect. Just trim off any not-so-good bits and jam away!

Syrups

Syrups are sweetened, pourable liquids made from sugar, honey, agave syrup, or other sweeteners plus, in the case of this chapter, fruit. They can be thick or thin. They can have chunks of fruit or be strained. Syrups can be whatever your imagination asks of them—and they're flexible enough that your imagination really can ask a lot.

You can make syrup from all kinds of fruits: the blueberries in your fridge that are still edible but getting squishy, the peels (but not the bitter pith) from grapefruit paired with rosemary stems, and even some vegetables (try making a beet and raspberry syrup, preferably with a strip of lemon zest; see page 268).

Store syrups in the fridge, where they'll usually keep for at least 2 weeks, though that timing depends on the sugar versus water content. You can also freeze them. If you wish to can a syrup but are experimenting on your own rather than following a tested recipe, you must either pressure can it or make sure it is acidic enough (the pH must be less than 4.6) to be canned in a hot water bath. To do this, you can test it with pH strips and adjust the acidity as needed with bottled lemon juice or citric acid.

Making Syrup

Fruit syrup at its simplest is 1 part sugar, 1 part water, and 1 part fruit. I often add a pinch of salt or a small splash of vinegar or lemon juice just to make the flavors sing, but you can leave that out if you wish. From there, you can play with more fruit, more sugar, adding spices, or whatever else you desire.

1. Combine sugar, fruit, water, and any flavorings you're using in a saucepan over medium heat. Bring to a simmer, then reduce the heat to medium-low and cook, stirring often, until the fruit has softened and released its flavor into the syrup, and the syrup has thickened but is still pourable. It should have about the same thickness as maple syrup. This can take 10 to 20 minutes or more, depending on the fruit you're using.

STEP 1

2. Strain the syrup, then let it cool.

3. Store the syrup in an airtight container in the fridge.

STEP 2

Making Cheong

Cheong, from Korean cuisine, is a sweetened preserve made by layering raw fruit and sugar. It is basically a long-term maceration and fermentation process. The sugar pulls the liquid from the fruit, making a flavorful syrup as well as sugar-preserved fruit.

Cheong is a nice way to repurpose fruit scraps with minimal up-front effort. It can be made with whatever fruits you want, and you can also use edible flowers or fresh herbs (Italians make a similar sugar-packed ferment, called mugolio, from green pine cones; see page 242). Note that some fresh herbs, like thyme, will give you a delicious sugar but won't necessarily contain enough water to make a syrup.

The amount of sugar varies. A 1:1 ratio, or equal parts fresh fruit and sugar, is a standard starting place. Some people use less sugar (2 parts fruit to 1 part sugar), which can result in alcohol fermentation, giving you a boozy, delicious fruit-and-syrup treat. Others might use more sugar. And you can add other flavors, like a strip of citrus zest, if you wish.

1 Layer sugar and fruit/flowers/herbs in a clean jar, finishing with a layer of sugar on top to completely cover.

2 Seal the lid and let the mixture sit at room temperature until it has a flavor you like and the syrup is, well, syrupy. (Some people let it sit for a month, others for 100 days, others for a year—and anywhere in between.)

3 Enjoy the syrup as is, in drinks, or drizzled on food. The fruit makes a great topping for desserts or is delicious on its own. Or you can experiment: I've put preserved blueberries on salads, for example, and eaten preserved fruit with sticky rice.

STEP 1

Vegan Fruit Honey

Fruit honey, a vegan stand-in for regular honey, is basically a kind of syrup, and it offers a fun opportunity to play with the flavors of different fruits. Pear is a common version, but you can also make this with strawberry juice, peach juice, or whatever is your favorite, or even with fruit scraps (peels and pieces) from other projects, as the authors of *So Easy to Preserve* recommend.

1. Wash your fruit and add it to a large saucepan. Cover with water and simmer, covered, until the fruit is very soft, then strain it through cheesecloth or butter muslin, pressing to remove the liquid.
2. Measure the volume of liquid, then add it back to your saucepan and bring it to a rapid boil.
3. Add sugar at a ratio of ½ cup of sugar per cup of fruit liquid, then continue to vigorously boil, stirring frequently, until it has the consistency of honey.
4. If refrigerating, let the fruit honey cool, and store it in an airtight container in the fridge. It will last for at least 2 weeks.
5. If canning, sterilize jars (see page 31) by boiling for 10 minutes. Add ½ teaspoon citric acid or 2 tablespoons bottled lemon juice per quart of fruit honey, stirring to combine. Pour the mixture into hot jars, leaving ¼ inch of headspace.
6. Run a chopstick or other thin, nonmetal utensil along the inner edges of the jars to release any air bubbles. Wipe the rims of the jars with a clean, damp cloth. Add the lids and bands and screw down to hand tightness.
7. Process half-pints and pints for 5 minutes in a hot water bath, adjusting for altitude (see page 39) if needed.
8. Let the jars cool for 24 hours before testing the seals (see page 36), then store out of direct sunlight at room temperature.

Jams and Jellies

Some people classify jams, jellies, marmalades, fruit butters, and fruit curds as sweet spreads, a term I find very fun to say and an apt description. The preparation for your sweet (fruit) spreads varies depending on the type, but each is mostly preserved via the addition of sugar and thickened or jellied to greater or lesser extents.

THE SCIENCE OF JELLY AND JAM

There's a lot more going on in your jam pot than you might think. Each ingredient plays an important role in the texture and flavor of the final outcome.

ACID. Acidity reduces the likelihood of pathogenic growth and improves the flavor. Acids also interact with pectin to help jams and jellies set.

HEAT. Canning uses heat to destroy pathogens, then creates a vacuum inside the jar to prevent any new pathogens from forming. In jam and jelly, heating to 220°F/105°C activates the interaction between sugar and pectin, allowing your preserve to gel. Follow basic canning guidance (see page 27) and eat within a year. (If you don't can your jam or jelly, store it in the fridge and use within 1 month.)

PECTIN. Pectin is naturally found in fruit, especially underripe fruit, and aids in gelling when added to the right combination of sugar and acid.

SUGAR. Obviously sugar contributes to the sweet taste of jams and jellies, but it is a preservative, too, drawing out and binding to the water in your fruit and thus preventing microbial growth.

TO PECTIN OR NOT TO PECTIN

Some fruits are naturally high in pectin, like apples, crabapples, gooseberries, some plums and grapes, as well as quince, and thus don't need any added. But other fruits, like berries and cherries, are not. So if you want to make berry jellies, you'll need to use pectin. The correct combination of fruit, acid, pectin, and sugar is what makes the jellied texture we're used to.

Pectins are a type of fiber that will gel if combined with sugar and an acid. The amount of pectin in your fruit lessens as it ripens, which means fully ripe fruit has less pectin than underripe fruit. This is why it's recommended that one quarter of fruit used in making jellies without added pectin should be underripe.

Acidity matters, too. Without enough, the pectin won't set. But too much, and it will lose liquid. For low-acid fruits, add bottled lemon juice or other acids as listed in your recipe (bottled lemon juice, rather than fresh, is used for canning recipes because it has a consistent acidity). Commercial pectin powder or liquid contains acid to ensure proper gelling.

And finally, sugar preserves the fruit, adds flavor, and helps your fruit gel. Recipes typically use cane or beet sugar, and in some cases you can swap corn syrup or honey for part of the sugar, following tested recipes and guidelines as in the *USDA Guide to Home Canning*. Yes, jams and jellies have a lot of sugar in them. However, do not reduce the amount of sugar. An insufficient amount of sugar not only prevents gelling, but it also invites pathogen growth.

One note: If you're experimenting with jams or jellies rather than following tested recipes, refrigerate your products rather than canning them just in case they aren't quite acidic or sweet enough to safely can.

Making Jam

The specifics of jam making depend on what fruit you're using, but you can use this general process as a guide.

1 Prepare the fruit: Remove pits, and peel or dice if needed. Berries can be used whole.

2 Combine fruit and sugar (and any other ingredients your recipe calls for, like water or lemon juice) in a heavy-bottomed pot and slowly bring to a boil until the sugar is dissolved. Once it is, rapidly heat it to get the fruit to, or almost to, the jellying point (220°F/105°C), stirring frequently to prevent burning.

NOTE: When you are making jam with low-pectin fruits, recipes may call for adding pectin, dissolved in hot water, to the fruit as it cooks.

STEP 2

3 Once your jam is thickened, remove from the heat. You can test your jam by dipping a spoon into it and noticing if it coats the back of the spoon. If, when you run your finger over the spoon, it makes a space, you know it's ready. Alternatively, place a drop of jam on a cold plate and poke it with your finger to see if it's set.

4 If you're going to can the jam, immediately pour it into hot jars. (If the jars will be processed for less than 10 minutes, they'll need to be sterilized first.) Process according to your recipe, adding citric acid or bottled lemon juice if needed. Or you can pour the jam into a heatproof container (like a mason jar), let cool, and then store in the fridge for up to 1 month.

Freezer Jam

Freezer jam (a misnomer, because it can also be refrigerator jam) is a no-cook version of jam. Most jam recipes involve cooking the fruit with sugar until it reaches 220°F/105°C, when the sugar interacts with the pectin naturally found in the fruit and begins to gel. But with freezer jam, you mash fresh fruit, add sugar, and then stir in pectin dissolved in boiling water. Let sit for several minutes, then pack the jam into containers, leaving ½ to 1 inch of headspace. Freezer jams cannot be canned. Store them in the refrigerator, where they'll keep for several weeks, or in freezer-safe jars in the freezer for up to 1 year.

Making Jelly

Like jam, the specifics of jelly making depend on what jelly you're making. But, also like jam, there's an overarching common method. While jams may or may not have added pectin, many jellies will. Here's how to make them.

1 Prepare fruit juice: You can purchase prepared juice (without additives), or crush or cook fruit according to your recipe, then strain out the solids. Pour the juice into in a heavy-bottomed pot.

2 Measure and add pectin, according to your recipe and whether you're using powdered or liquid pectin. (Some recipes for high-pectin fruits omit this step.)

3 Add sugar according to your recipe, stir, and heat the mixture to a rolling boil, then boil for the length of time called for in your recipe.

4 Remove from the heat and skim off any foam or scum from the surface.

STEP 1

STEP 2

5 If you're going to can the jelly, immediately pour it into hot jars. (If the jars will be processed for less than 10 minutes, they'll need to be sterilized first.) Process according to your recipe, adding citric acid or bottled lemon juice if needed. Or you can pour the jelly into a heatproof container (like a mason jar), let cool, and then store in the fridge for up to 1 month.

STEP 4

Vegetable Jellies and Jams

We tend to think of jellies and jams as being made from fruit, but you can make them with vegetables, too. Pepper jelly is a classic example. Tomato jam, zucchini jam, onion jam—many vegetables can be cooked down to a sweetened pulpy mash. You can even combine fruits and veggies; consider Raspberry-Beet Jam (page 272) or Tomato-Peach Refrigerator Jam (page 312).

CHAPTER 5

Drying and Smoking

Drying food simply means removing moisture from it, which prevents mold and bacteria growth and thus makes it shelf-stable for a longer period. Drying uses a simple combination of time, heat, and air circulation to remove moisture from food. Smoking does the same, but with fire as a heat source, which produces smoke that flavors food as it dries. In this chapter, we'll look at all the different methods used for drying and smoking foods, from low-tech to high-tech.

Air-Drying

This is by far one of the easiest ways to put up food, and one seen around the world, from bunches of peppers seductively draped across doorways to herbs hanging from the rafters of a barn. I remember driving through North Carolina with my grandma one autumn in high school and seeing garlands of apple-squash rings drying on some of the covered porches—a beautiful, low-tech way to preserve.

Important factors for air-drying include good air circulation and low humidity. Sun-drying adds the warmth of the sun to the process of air-drying, and drying in the sun is faster than drying in the shade. (If you've ever hung clothes on a clothesline on a sunny day versus an overcast one, you've already experienced this in action.) Air-drying works best with fruit, whose higher acidity means a lower risk of pathogen growth, and some vegetables. Sun-drying is not recommended for animal proteins, because the low temperature and slow drying time can lead to spoilage. Sun-drying can be as simple as drying fruit on screens in a single layer laid out on a sunny patio, or as high-tech as a purpose-built solar dehydrator.

There are many techniques out there, and the one you choose should depend on your needs and where you live. The focused drying power of a solar dehydrator is useful in humid environments, whereas food dried in a desert may not need the extra oomph to dry quickly. If you're in a buggy, critter-heavy place, you may want to put screens or other critter prevention on your air-drying projects to keep from sharing the bounty.

Oven Drying

You can also simply use your oven to dry fruits and vegetables. Note, though, that this is a very energy-inefficient way to dry food (and quality can be inconsistent, compared to a purpose-built dehydrator), so if you plan to do it more than occasionally, investing in a dehydrator is the way to go. That said, if you just want to try dehydrating to see if it makes sense for your life, using your oven is a good starting point before investing in another appliance or building a solar dehydrator.

The trick with an oven is to get it to the right temperature: It should be under 200°F/93°C to avoid scorching your food. The ideal temperature

is around 140°F/60°C (if your oven has a "keep warm" function, it may work well for this).

Place your produce on racks and set them in the oven. For ovens without good airflow, crack the door at least once an hour to prevent moisture buildup. After a few hours, check your food to see if it's drying evenly. It's helpful to flip it at least once to prevent it from sticking to the racks. Oven drying can take more than 8 hours.

Dehydrating

Many people use electric dehydrators, and these are certainly helpful for keeping food at a low, steady temperature with airflow, which can help with more even, faster drying. A dehydrator can dry vegetables, fruits, herbs, grains, and nuts. You can make fruit leather, dried soup mix, powdered herb blends, and more; you can mix and match ingredients, repurpose leftovers, and experiment in the kitchen.

If you're shopping for an electric dehydrator, look for one with a fan at the back; when you load up the trays and set them inside the dehydrator, the fan will blow air evenly across all of them. Some models have a fan at the top, but this doesn't work as well for consistently moving air across your food—the food at the top tends to dry more quickly. If you use a model with a fan on top, make sure to check (and possibly rotate) your trays regularly to ensure even drying. Some dehydrators have a fan on the bottom of the unit, but I don't recommend this style; this setup not only dries unevenly but also risks shorting or failing as liquid from your drying food drips onto the electrical components below (and, as you'd imagine, these dehydrators are not terribly easy to clean).

Solar Dehydrators

If you live off-grid or just want to minimize your energy use, you might consider buying or building a solar dehydrator. If you're building your own, here are some key elements to include. First, make sure it is able to provide airflow while keeping pests away from your food. Second, make sure it has sufficient surface area to dry things in a single layer. And third, make sure it can dry food without scorching it or drying it so slowly that mold or bacteria growth becomes a problem.

PRETREATING FRUITS AND VEGETABLES

Fruits and vegetables usually need to be pretreated to stop their natural enzymatic activity, thereby preserving their color, texture, and nutrients during storage. There are several methods: blanching, an ascorbic acid dip, a fruit juice dip, or a honey/sugar syrup dip.

BLANCHING

I generally recommend steam or hot-water blanching as a pretreatment for vegetables, as it is simple and doesn't require additional supplies. See page 17 for instructions. Appropriate blanching times are noted for each type of vegetable in Part 2.

ASCORBIC ACID DIP

Ascorbic acid is just vitamin C, and using it in a solution as a dip is probably the easiest way to prevent fruit from browning as it dries. It is often available as a powder sold with canning supplies or in tablet form. You can even use the kind sold as a nutritional supplement.

To use ascorbic acid for drying, mix 1 teaspoon of powder (or 3,000 mg in tablet form, crushed) into 2 cups of water until dissolved. Add your fruit to the solution and let it sit for 3 to 5 minutes. Then remove the fruit and drain it well before drying.

You can use a batch of solution two times, then refresh the water with more ascorbic acid at the same ratio.

FRUIT JUICE DIP

If you want to experiment, it can be fun to use fruit juices that are high in vitamin C for drying fruit. This is more hit-or-miss than pure ascorbic acid because different juices have different acidity levels and amounts of vitamin C. But they can add some interesting flavors to the final product. Just make sure you're using 100 percent juice, not the artificial stuff.

Citrus, pineapple, or cranberry juice are all good choices, as is any juice with added vitamin C. Add enough juice to your container to cover the cut fruit, then soak for 3 to 5 minutes before draining the fruit well and drying.

You can reuse your juice two times, and then drink it or use it in other dishes, make homemade ice pops, or freeze it in ice cube trays.

HONEY/SUGAR SYRUP DIP

If you want things a bit sweeter, try dipping your fruit in a honey solution or sugar syrup before drying. To make a honey dip, dissolve 1 cup of sugar in 3 cups of hot water, cool to wrist temperature, and then whisk in 1 cup of honey until it is dissolved. For a vegan version, use 2 cups of sugar and no honey. Dip the fruit in the cooled syrup and allow it to sit for 3 to 5 minutes before draining the fruit well and drying.

Sulfuring or Sulfite Dip

Sulfur is the most effective pretreatment for long-term preservation, but unless you're a winemaker, you're unlikely to have sulfur lying around, and the methods for using it are less practical (and maybe more intimidating) than other options. Sulfuring is an old method of pretreating fruit, done by burning sulfur in a box or other container with the fruit. This has the longest-lasting effect against oxidation (browning) and is also supposed to guard against the loss of nutrients. If you decide to give this a try, make sure you do it outside in an area with good air circulation!

Sodium bisulfite is a liquid form of sulfur that serves as an antioxidant. Sulfite dips rely on dissolving ¾ to 1½ teaspoons of food-grade sodium bisulfite per quart of water, placing fruit in the mixture, and soaking for 5 minutes (for slices) or 15 minutes (for halved fruit). Then rinse the fruit lightly under cold water before drying. Make a fresh batch each time you dip.

To learn more about either method of using sulfur, contact your local Cooperative Extension office.

DRYING TEMPERATURES AND TIMES

Times for dehydrating can vary considerably based on the moisture content of the ingredients, the size of the pieces, and the humidity in the air. So use the times suggested for foods in Part 2 as a guide, and rely on your senses to test for dryness rather than just your clock. (Is your vegetable dry enough to snap? Does your fruit ooze any liquid when you cut it? Is it tacky?) As common sense would suggest, smaller pieces dry faster than larger ones, and whole fruits or vegetables take longer to dry than cut-up ones.

Check your food more frequently toward the end of the drying time, as you want to pull it when it is dried but before it cooks or loses flavor. If the food you are dehydrating is very wet or in large pieces, turn it over partway through the drying process so the pieces dry more evenly.

Follow your dehydrator's recommendations, but here are basic temperature guidelines for drying foods.

FRUIT AND VEGETABLES. Dry at 125 to 140°F/52 to 60°C, which dries them at an adequate speed without cooking them.

DELICATE HERBS AND SPICES. Dry at 95 to 115°F/35 to 46°C to prevent scorching.

MEAT AND FISH. Dry at a higher temperature (think 160 to 165°F/71 to 74°C), in part because of the density of the muscle tissue but also to limit the time for pathogens to grow.

NUTS. Dry raw nuts at 115 to 125°F/46° to 52°C; whole nuts will need 10 to 14 hours and nutmeats (shelled nuts) 8 to 12 hours.

RAW FOODS. For anyone on a living food diet (raw, uncooked, plant-based foods), dehydrating can help extend storage times while still leaving enzymes intact—useful for extending the shelf life of homegrown veggies. To keep enzymes intact, do not pretreat foods, and keep dehydrator temps below 140°F/60°C. These partly dried foods will keep for 1 to 2 months.

Using a Dehydrator

If you're new to using a dehydrator, start with sliced fruits and vegetables or fresh herbs. These are some of the easiest things to dry and offer an inexpensive introduction to the process.

1 Prepare the food you are going to dehydrate.

PRODUCE. Core, peel, or trim fruits, vegetables, or herbs, if necessary. Chop or slice as desired. If you are leaving fruits whole, check the skins (see Checking Whole Fruits and Vegetables, opposite).

GRAINS/LEGUMES. Remove any shells or husks as appropriate. Some recipes recommend blanching beans before drying. (Do not do this if you want to plant them later, and for shelled beans I've found this is not usually necessary.)

MEATS AND FISH. Slice, if necessary. Season or marinate in the fridge as desired.

2 Pretreat fruits or vegetables, if appropriate. Vegetables are generally blanched and shocked (see page 17). Fruits are often dipped in an acidic solution (see page 90).

3 Arrange the food in a single layer on dehydrator trays, without overcrowding. Put the trays in your dehydrator, set the dehydrator to your desired temperature, and let it run.

4 Check the progress of the dehydration every hour or so, especially toward the end, when foods can go from underdried to overdried pretty quickly. It's often helpful to turn the food halfway through for even drying.

5 When the food is fully dehydrated, remove it from the dehydrator and let it cool. Store it in an airtight container at room temperature, out of direct sunlight and away from temperature and humidity fluctuations.

NOTE: If you've dehydrated fruit, store it in an airtight container and shake the container daily for the first 7 to 10 days, making sure the shaking separates the individual pieces of fruit. This process is called conditioning, and it helps equalize the moisture content across all the pieces of fruit, which notoriously tend to dry unequally. While conditioning, check for moisture buildup (which means you need to dehydrate your fruit for longer). Once dehydrated fruit is conditioned, you can store it long-term in an airtight container out of direct sunlight.

STEP 3

STEP 5

Checking Whole Fruits and Vegetables

If you are drying whole fruit with skins intact (or vegetables that you want peeled, like bell peppers), you'll want to "check" (crack open) the skins. Do this by dipping the fruit in boiling water and then immediately submerging it in ice water. This will shock the fruit and introduce cracks in the skin, which allows the skins to slip off more easily, if you're removing them, or will allow air to penetrate your unpeeled fruit more deeply in the dehydrator.

Whole, unpeeled plums before being submerged in boiling water

Plums after checking to crack skins

Tips for Dehydrating Success

Here are a few practices that will help ensure consistently delicious dried fruits and vegetables.

USE EVENLY SIZED PIECES. That way, the pieces will dry at the same rate.

DEHYDRATE VEGETABLES FULLY. Unless your recipe says otherwise, dehydrate vegetables until they're completely dry to the touch and crisp.

DEHYDRATE FRUITS TO A PALATABLE TEXTURE. You can dry fruits until they are crisp if that is how you like to eat them, but most fruits need to be dried only to a texture that renders them palatable. In practical terms, this means the fruit can be still pliable (though not always), but it should not be sticky or tacky. When cut or squeezed, it shouldn't ooze any liquid. Note that the more moisture the fruit contains, the shorter the shelf life.

LET DRIED FOODS COOL COMPLETELY BEFORE STORING. Then store them in an airtight container. If the air is very humid, package your dried foods as soon as they cool, or they might absorb moisture from the air.

Making Fruit Leather

Fruit leather is a nice way to stretch out a few cups of fruit. A whole tray takes less fruit than you might think (about 2 cups of cubed fruit), because the fruit is spread so thinly. You can dry fruit leather in a dehydrator or by air-drying it in the sun. I've had minimal success drying fruit leather in the oven, as it tends to dry unevenly without regular turning, but if you want to give it a try (and remember to rotate it as it dries), by all means, do.

1 Combine the fruit, sugar (if using), and lemon juice in a blender and blend to a pulp. For every cup of cubed fruit, use ¼ cup sugar (if using), and 1 teaspoon of lemon juice.

2 Line a dehydrator tray or baking sheet with a silicone mat (preferred) or plastic wrap that's smoothed to press out wrinkles (don't use foil or waxed paper, which stick to your leather). Pour the fruit pulp onto the mat, spreading it evenly and avoiding the edges, to about ⅛-inch thickness.

3 Dry in a dehydrator at 140°F/60°C for 6 to 12 hours or in the sun for 1 to 2 days. Test for dryness by touching the center: It should feel tacky, not wet, and your finger should not leave an indent behind.

4 Peel the fruit leather up from the tray while it is still warm and roll it up. Let it cool.

5 Wrap the rolled-up fruit leather in plastic wrap or waxed paper. Store it in an airtight container at room temperature for 1 month, or freeze for up to 1 year.

STEP 1

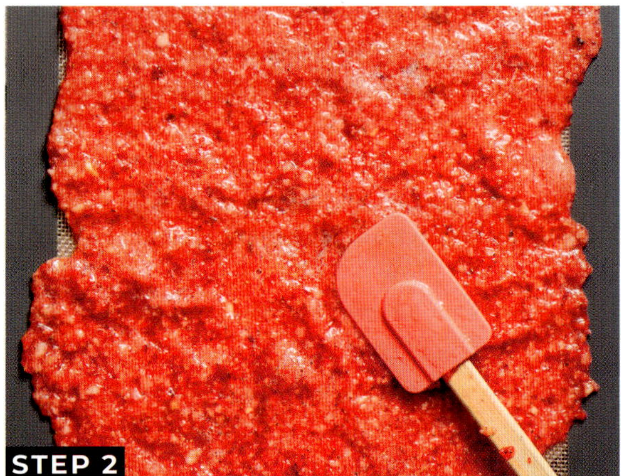

STEP 2

STEP 3

STEP 4

Pickle Powders and Seasoning Blends

Dried foods can also be powdered and added to other foods as seasoning blends to amp up the flavor and nutrition. Some of my favorite seasoning blends are what I call pickle powders, which are simply the leftovers from fermentation projects, dehydrated and powdered. Fermented or not, the process for drying and grinding is the same.

1. Dehydrate your fruits, vegetables, or scraps until they are bone-dry; any moisture could cause mold later on. If you are using an electric dehydrator, set it to 135°F/57°C. If you're drying in an oven, set it to its lowest heat.
2. Once the scraps are dry, use a mortar and pestle, coffee grinder, food processor, or blender to grind them to the desired consistency.
3. Store the powder in an airtight jar out of direct sunlight.

I make seasoning blends with just about anything I can get my hands on, including scraps from other preserving projects. Here are a few favorite leftovers I repurpose as dried seasoning blends.

FERMENTS AND PICKLES. Sometimes fermented and quick-pickled foods taste great but don't have the best texture. This is a good way to salvage a tasty pickling experiment turned to mush.

SOLIDS FROM MAKING BEVERAGES. Strained fruit from melomel (fruit mead), wine, soda, and homemade syrup can make nice seasoning powders. Vegetables left over from beverage making, like the beets from beet kvass, can also shine as a powder.

SCRAPS FROM INFUSING VINEGAR. You can dehydrate and powder any fruits, vegetables, herbs, or spices you've infused in vinegar. Fire cider seasoning, made from the scraps left over from making Fire Cider vinegar (page 399), is one of my go-to gifts; it's aromatic, a bit sour and funky, and absolutely divine on roasted veggies and grilled things.

FISH SAUCE SCRAPS. When I make fish sauce (see page 386), I save the salt and fish solids after I remove the liquid (I also remove any large bones), pulse in a food processor, then spread out the paste to let it dry. Then I powder it and use it as a seasoning.

Aromatic Herbal Salt

The magic of this salt lies in its versatility. You can make it from any of the things you would use to make a pickle powder (see page 95), or you can make it seasonally, harvesting and drying herbs, vegetables, and fruits that come into season together and then mixing them with salt for a year-round seasoning bursting with the flavors of that particular harvest window. As with all magic, what makes it powerful is when you make it your own.

— Makes about 2 cups

1 cup dried herbs, fruits, or vegetables

1 cup coarse grain sea salt

1 Using a mortar and pestle, coffee grinder, or burr grinder, grind the dried herbs until they are the same consistency as your salt grains, or finer. (If you're using a coffee grinder, use one dedicated for grinding herbs, not the same one you make your coffee with!)

2 Combine the ground herbs with the salt in a pint jar. Close the lid and shake until evenly combined. Use liberally.

Smoking

Smoking is a traditional method of preserving food, especially meats and seafood, in many regions where the climate is not conducive to air-drying. It is a form of drying that's done over smoldering (rather than flaming) wood chunks or chips, using the long, slow exposure to heat to remove moisture from the food, which takes on a smoky flavor as well. It can be done simply, in barrel smokers, for example, or in smokers with more bells and whistles, which may require additional investments like brand-name wood pellets. Some smokers are huge, while some are relatively small and easier to store. As with all cooking equipment, choose the smoker that works for your lifestyle and budget.

How you use your smoker depends almost entirely on the type you have. Always follow the manufacturer's instructions for use. In general, smokers fall into one of two categories: hot smoke and cold smoke.

HOT SMOKE. These are the most commonly available style of smoker, and they operate at a higher temperature, cooking food as well as flavoring it. Food is cooked over smoldering wood, typically 190 to 300°F/88 to 150°C. Hot smokers can be used at their lowest temperatures to dehydrate jerky and other foods, provided the temperature is consistent, or they can be used to add flavor at the end of the preserving process.

COLD SMOKE. Cold smoking takes place at a cooler temperature, closer to 90°F/32°C. For preservation, food is usually first cured, then cold smoked to impart flavor while also removing some additional moisture. (Without proper pre-smoke curing, like brining or salt curing, cold smoking can allow pathogen growth.) Smoked salmon is a well-known example of a cold-smoked food.

Smokers can get hotter than dehydrators, so keep an eye on the temperature gauge to ensure that your food doesn't overcook. To determine doneness, use the same touch and texture tests as for dehydrated foods (see page 93).

Storing Dried Foods

Store dried foods in airtight containers, like mason jars, plastic containers with tight-fitting lids, ziplock bags, or vacuum-sealed bags. Store in a cool, dark, dry place with minimal temperature fluctuations (so, not right next to your heating vent or above your stove).

The ideal temperature for long-term storage of dried foods is 50 to 60°F/10 to 16°C, but don't worry if your house doesn't exist in that 10-degree range: Just keep them in a cool, dark cupboard (or similar) away from pests and moisture, and try to keep the temperature as consistent as possible. The shelf life for dried foods depends on storage conditions (particularly humidity), but they typically keep for 4 to 12 months. Jerkies will last longer if frozen or refrigerated.

Reconstituting Dried Foods

Dried foods make great snacks, but you can also reconstitute them for use in cooking. You might, for example, want to rehydrate dried apple slices to make them into pie filling. You can reconstitute dried ingredients in any number of ways.

STEAMING. Simply place your dried food in a steamer basket over simmering water and steam until plumped.

SOAKING. Place your dried food in a shallow dish and add liquid to cover. You can use water or a flavorful liquid, like fruit juice or tea, that complements whatever you're cooking. Allow to rehydrate for 1 to 2 hours, or cover your dish and place in the fridge for 8 to 12 hours for larger or denser pieces.

SOAKING IN BOILING WATER. Reconstituting with hot water works best for more dense, hearty vegetables; it can be too much for delicate foods. Place dried vegetables (or dense dried fruits) in a heatproof dish. For every cup of vegetables, add 1 cup of just-boiled water, making sure your vegetables are evenly distributed and covered. Let soak for 15 to 20 minutes, then drain.

SIMMERING. You can also place equal parts water with dried vegetables or fruit in a saucepan and simmer just until tender. You might toss dehydrated vegetables directly into a soup or stew to reconstitute while it simmers. Delicate produce might break down when simmered, so only simmer if you *want* them broken down (as in a fruit sauce or syrup) rather than whole.

Reducing Food Waste

We can open to a more expansive and creative culinary practice by thinking about how to better use every part of our food. Using what we have to the fullest is a way to honor all of the hands that touched that food on its way to our plates, and a way to connect with the living tradition of food preservation.

Weaving waste reduction and repurposing into our kitchens doesn't need to be daunting. Here are a few places to start.

THINK IN TERMS OF THE WHOLE FOOD. With carrots, for example, most of us just eat the root, but the greens are also edible, nutritious, and delicious. How might you work them into a dish you're already cooking today or this week? Think about what familiar foods they remind you of and treat them in a similar manner. What about the peelings or the root ends you cut off before roasting carrots? Can they be repurposed, like in Beet Kvass (page 328) or Carrot Cake Jam (page 146), or added to your bag of scraps for making stock (see page 20)?

TURN SCRAPS INTO SEASONING BLENDS. You can make wonderful seasoning blends from the herbs, spices, and other ingredients that you use to infuse vinegars, spirits, and more. See page 95 for more information.

REUSE LEFTOVER BRINE. Lactofermentation and quick pickling give us flavor-rich, nutritious brine, but often in such abundance that it can be hard to know what to do with it! You can use it to add an extra punch (and extra nutrition) to soups, stews, and marinades. Use it to culture butter and buttermilk (see below). Cook rice and pasta in it, or even try it in cocktails!

USE FERMENTATION SCRAPS TO CULTURE BUTTER AND BUTTERMILK. The scraps from your liquid ferments, including the vinegar or brine from lactofermentation, make fantastic starters for culturing cream for butter and buttermilk. The scraps you use will, to varying extents, transfer their flavors to your butter and buttermilk, an excellent way to deepen and diversify the flavors in a dish.

Carrot Cake Jam (page 146) is a fun way to repurpose a bumper crop of carrots.

INFUSE, INFUSE, INFUSE. Using scraps to flavor vinegars and spirits is an easy way to repurpose creatively. You can expand your practice from there: Dehydrate citrus rounds that were once used to flavor other foods and garnish drinks with them; make syrups with stems from the herbs you used to make dinner; or make avocado pit liqueur.

COMPOST! Of course, a simple compost pile is a fantastic way to use up scraps you don't know what to do with, and some municipalities also have food scrap collection, which in turn results in affordable (or free) compost that you can go pick up and use in your garden. There are a million resources out there on building a simple compost heap as well as specialized compost tumblers and other containers you can build or purchase.

MAKE SACHETS. Sachets are a simple way to use herb stems or other aromatic scraps. Simply dry the scraps, if needed, and then place them in the center of a square of fabric. Lift up the corners and tie to secure—done! When the scent begins to fade, untie the sachets and replace the contents. As a no-waste bonus, you can use old T-shirts or other fabric scraps to make these sachets.

MAKE CLEANING SPRAY. You can infuse vinegars with scraps from foods or herbs whose scent you like (lavender or oregano stems, for example) and then dilute the vinegar to make a wonderful-smelling and effective cleaner. Vinegar is an especially potent cleaning agent; a vinegar solution as weak as 0.1 percent (that's 1 teaspoon of standard-strength vinegar in 1 cup of water) will inhibit the growth of many microorganisms. (Don't use vinegar on granite or marble, as it can etch the surface.)

USING A DEHYDRATOR TO REDUCE WASTE

Tossing food scraps in a dehydrator is a wonderful way to get creative in the kitchen and cut down on waste. I've been using my dehydrator for seasoning blends and more for years, but the possibilities are endless. Jeanette Hurt, a food writer and dehydrator expert, and master food preserver Christina Ward shared some of their favorite ideas with me.

POWDERS AND SEASONINGS. Dehydrating fruits and vegetables until they're crisp and then grinding them into powders makes great flavor boosters. Think of powdered tomato added to marinara or powdered apple added to pies. As I mentioned before, you can't can pumpkin purée (it's too dense to can safely), but Ward has a great work-around: Dehydrate pumpkin, grind to powder, add spices as you wish, then add it to applesauce and can it!

WILTED VEGGIES AND OVERRIPE FRUIT. Hurt says, "You know that celery that's going bad in your refrigerator? Chop it up and toss it in a dehydrator, then throw it into soups or sauces when you need it." The same is true for fruit that's going soft, bananas that are turning brown, or any other fruit or veggie that's approaching its end. Dry them all for later use.

FRUIT LEATHER. If you're chronically finding overripe berries stagnating in your fridge, Ward suggests turning them into a base for fruit leather. Her technique is to purée, mix with applesauce, then dehydrate. Hurt uses rhubarb—a prolific springtime producer—as a base for fruit leather; she also recommends chopping and dehydrating rhubarb to make summery pies in the middle of winter.

DOG TREATS. Hurt dries fish skins and sweet potato skins as dog treats. She does the same with chopped poultry gizzards. "I call those bits magic fairy dust for dogs," she says. "They go wild for them."

MYSTERY MIXES. Save all the little edible vegetable bits (peels, ends, and so on) left over from a cooking project, chop them into uniformly sized pieces, and dehydrate to make "mystery soup mix." Ward keeps a storage container of these dehydrated veggies that she adds to over time; she notes: "When you reach about 4 cups' worth, use them to make a slow-cooked vegetable stock." Ward does the same with fruits, though she separates them by family (stone fruits in one batch, berries in another, and so on), and grinds them into powder or uses them in chunks for winter fruit cakes and steamed puddings.

COCKTAIL GARNISHES. Dried citrus is perfect for garnishing cocktails and other beverages. If you've zested an orange, chop up the sections, dehydrate them, and then float them on a cocktail. As Hurt says, "They taste like sweet-and-sour candies." Before you juice a lemon, zest it, then dry that zest for use as a garnish. Ward stirs her mystery mix fruit powders into sugar to rim cocktail glasses.

CRACKERS. If you use a juicer, you likely have a lot of pulp left over. Ward mixes vegetable pulp with seasonings, soaked chia seeds, and even nuts, and then dehydrates the mixture like a fruit leather to make raw vegan crackers. You can do the same with fruit pulp, chia seeds, and maple syrup for sweet crackers.

PART 2

Recipes and Strategies for Every Type of Food

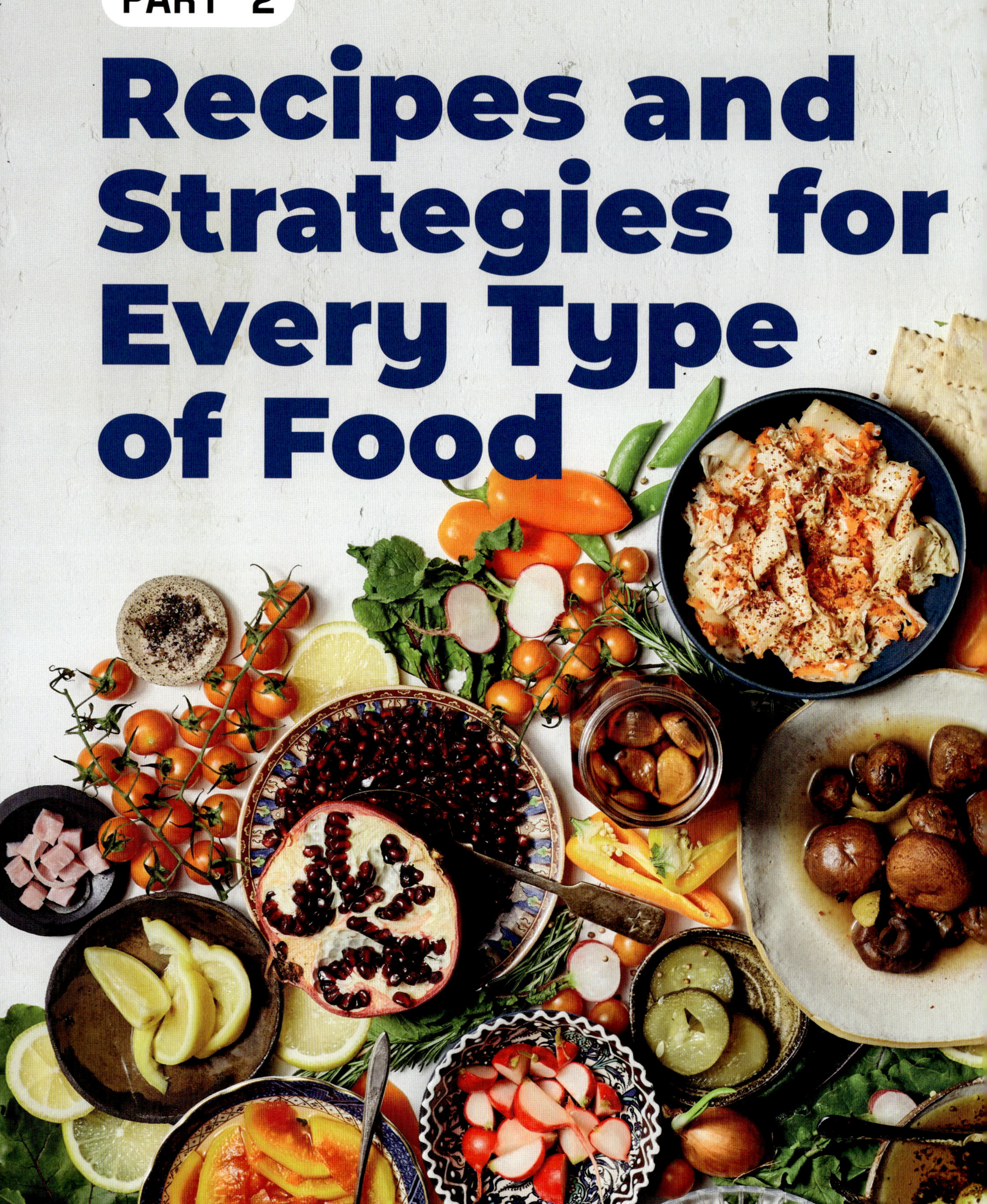

Busyness is glorified in this period in history, and whether or not you love that fact (I do not), it's true that many of us are, in fact, busy. So to keep food preserving as a *sustainable* habit that you love and that fits into your life, rather than a burnout- and panic-inducing chore, it's helpful to do a bit of planning ahead.

Consider the following:

What foods do you have access to in abundance?

What kinds of preserved foods do you like to eat?

What storage space do you have for preserved foods?

How much time do you have for preserving?

What preserving methods are you familiar with, and what methods would you like to learn?

Your answers will shape your approach to preserving food. The goal is to find preserving methods that enrich your life and your meals but don't stress you out.

Time and energy are two key factors here. I preserve food in the mornings because that's when I have energy and time (I'm privileged to work from home and write about this for a living). When do you have energy and free time? Also think about how you can preserve food when you *don't* have much energy or free time. Because if you're reading this book, you want to preserve more food, right? The best way I've found to do this is to work small tasks into daily life.

Maybe you keep a container in the freezer to fill with food scraps for stock, or plan a few minutes a day to harvest from the garden and then ferment or pickle whatever you pick. Maybe you have a couple of different kinds of preserving tasks you like: your luxurious, all-the-time-in-the-world preserving days (for canning jam, for example) and your "I have five minutes to throw these blueberries in the freezer before I leave for work" days.

The following chapters offer comprehensive coverage of preservation methods for every type of food, from vegetables and fruits to grains, nuts, legumes, dairy, meats, and eggs. Browse through them, pick some tasks you can easily do without tons of prep time (fermenting, freezing, or making things like infused vinegars, quick pickles, or simple syrups are all good choices here), and start working those into your life as your core preserving practices. When you have time, do more. When you feel overwhelmed by life, go back to basics. After all, the best preserving practice is the one that works for you.

Fermented Carrot Sticks (page 144)

CHAPTER 6

Vegetables

Aromatic Roots	104
Artichokes	115
Asparagus	117
Beets	121
Brassicas	128
Carrots	142
Celery	148
Corn (Fresh)	150
Cucumbers	155
Eggplant	161
Fennel	165
Green Beans	167
Greens (Dark and Leafy)	169
Herbs and Tender Greens	172
Leeks	178
Lettuce	180
Mushrooms	182
Okra	191
Onions and Shallots	195
Peppers	200
Potatoes	212
Radishes	214
Rhubarb	218
Scallions and Scapes	220
Summer Squash and Zucchini	222
Sweet Potatoes	225
Tomatoes and Tomatillos	227
Winter Squash	236
Wild Plants	241

The term *vegetable* here basically refers to any plant that isn't a fruit or a grain (it's botanically messy, but so is our language about plants in general). This means that I include herbs, for example, with the vegetables, along with everything from green peanuts to peppers to carrots.

Aromatic Roots

Garlic, Ginger, Horseradish, Turmeric

I group aromatic roots together because you can use many of them in the same way. Some recipes, like ginger beer, might not work quite as well with other roots (like garlic), but most, including aromatic pastes and infused vinegars, can be applied to any aromatic root you wish (or a combination of them). This offers a wonderful opportunity to experiment.

For garlic, choose bulbs with tight, closed heads with the paper intact. For roots like ginger and turmeric, choose firm, dense roots without any cuts, bruises, or peeling skin; they should snap easily when bent.

DRYING

Unlike many other vegetables, aromatic roots do not require blanching. Simply peel and grate or finely chop them, and dehydrate in a single layer. You can thinly shave or slice, too, for pieces to add to soups or other long-simmered dishes. Make sure the slices are thin, though, for more even, faster drying. It also makes them easier to grind, should you decide to do so.

Because these roots are aromatic, be mindful of what else you put in the dehydrator with them: The flavor will seep into everything else in that same batch.

To dry garlic, ginger, and turmeric, place prepared pieces in a single layer in the dehydrator. Dry them at 135°F/57°C for 6 to 8 hours or until dried through. Check halfway through and break them apart, if needed, to aid in drying.

You can also dry horseradish, which can be added to cooked dishes as is, or powdered in a coffee grinder (see pickle powders, page 95) and sprinkled on food. Dried horseradish is not as pungent as fresh, but it will work in a pinch. Dry grated horseradish in a single layer in the dehydrator at 125°F/52°C for 6 to 8 hours or until brittle enough to snap. Cool completely and store in an airtight container.

FREEZING

The best way I find to freeze aromatic roots is as ingredients for other things, like Rainbow Roots Soup Starter (page 107) or as prepared meals that are then frozen. However, you can freeze peeled, minced garlic in ice cube trays, then pack the frozen cubes into a freezer-safe container with no headspace. Note that garlic's smell will linger in the plastic of the ice cube tray, so don't use that one for your drinks. Other aromatics can be minced and frozen in a similar manner.

Ways to Preserve Aromatic Roots

	Shelf-stable	Fast	Low waste	Ready meals and ingredients	Big flavor
Rainbow Roots Soup Starter (page 107)				X	X
Fermented Horseradish Paste (page 107)		X		X	X
Three-Root Paste (page 108)		X		X	X
Garlic in Honey (page 109)				X	X
Fermented Ginger Beer (page 110)		X		X	X
Quick-Pickled Horseradish and Scallion Paste (page 111)		X		X	X
Prepared Horseradish (page 111)				X	X
Horseradish and Orange "Kosho" (page 113)				X	X
Citrus-Pickled Turmeric (page 113)				X	X
Kimchi-Inspired Pickle Brine (page 113)				X	X
Horseradish Vinegar (page 114)				X	X
Masala Syrup (page 115)		X			X
Fermented Beet-and-Carrot Sauce (page 127)				X	X
Fire Cider (page 399)			X	X	X

Rainbow Roots Soup Starter

Rainbow Roots Soup Starter

I love this soup base. I toss it in stock or water for a few minutes, then maybe stir in some miso paste. Something about it just smells like home to me! Use this recipe as a template for your own soup-starter explorations.

—— Makes about 1 gallon

- **2 or 3 large beets**
- **4 large carrots**
- **1 yellow onion**
- **4 cloves garlic, minced**
- **2 stalks celery, finely diced**
- **½–1 tablespoon red pepper flakes**
- **½–1 tablespoon cumin seeds**
- **½–1 tablespoon caraway seeds**

1 Grate the beets, carrots, and onion with a box grater or food processor. Add the garlic, celery, pepper flakes, cumin, and caraway, and toss until evenly mixed.

2 Transfer to a freezer bag or airtight container, filling completely or pressing the extra air out of the bag. Freeze and use within 6 months.

Using Your Greens

If you grow your own aromatic roots or purchase them with the greens attached, don't throw away the greens! I use these like fresh herbs (page 172), infusing them in vinegar, drying into seasonings, freezing, or adding to ferments and quick pickles.

FERMENTING

Fermenting brings shelf stability and packs a big punch of flavor. And it's an easy way to turn your aromatic roots into pantry staples for quick meals. I use Three-Root Paste (page 108) in place of minced garlic and toss fermented vegetables on top of salads or sandwiches for some extra zip. And have you ever tried garlic fermented in honey? It's a mellow, rich ingredient that's divine with roasted vegetables. It very well might become a new favorite!

Fermented Horseradish Paste

This is a tangy, funky stand-in for your standard prepared horseradish paste, but it can be used in all the same ways.

—— Makes 1 pint

- **4 teaspoons sea salt**
- **2 cups water**
- **1 (3- to 4-inch) horseradish root, sliced (1½–2 cups)**

1 Dissolve the salt in the water to make a brine. Add the horseradish root to your jar and cover with the brine to submerge completely.

2 Ferment for 7 to 10 days, until the root has softened slightly and has a flavor you enjoy.

3 Place the finished ferment in a blender or food processor and blend to your desired consistency. Store in an airtight container in the fridge, where it will keep for several weeks or more.

Three-Root Paste

This paste and the Rainbow Roots Soup Starter (page 107) are two of my favorite ways to fully honor the last bits of the root-vegetable harvest. And they are two of my tried-and-true standbys for quick, healthy meals. Toss them in the water you're boiling for pasta, add them to a miso soup, or use them in sauces. This is a great way to use up those last little knobs of aromatic roots you have lying around. This process works for other roots, too (like those last little nubs of carrots, beets, horseradish, or burdock), so you can make it your own.

— Makes 1 pint

- **1 bulb garlic**
- **3 (2- to 3-inch) pieces fresh organic turmeric, sliced**
- **1 large piece fresh organic ginger, sliced (see note)**
- **½ tablespoon sea salt or other unrefined salt**

NOTE: When using ginger as the basis for a wild-fermented food, always use organic ginger (and other organic roots, to the extent possible). Nonorganic ginger is often imported and irradiated, which kills the microbes that you want present to kick-start your ferment.

1. Fill a pint jar one-third full with a layer of unpeeled garlic cloves, followed by a layer of turmeric, and finally a layer of ginger. The skins will soften as they ferment, so there's no need to peel!

2. Add the salt and cover with water. Seal tightly and shake until the salt is dissolved. Make sure the brine is still completely covering the roots; if it isn't, push the roots back under the brine.

3. Ferment at room temperature for 7 to 10 days, until the mixture reaches a flavor you enjoy.

4. Pour the contents of the jar into a food processor or blender and blend to your desired consistency. For best flavor, store in the refrigerator, where it will keep for at least 1 month.

VARIATION: ADDING SPICES

You can make this paste with your favorite roots and customize it further with your favorite spices. For big flavor, add-ins might include black peppercorns, hot peppers, and woody stemmed herbs (or even your leftover herb stems).

Before blending

After blending

Garlic in Honey

This can ferment for as short as a month or as long as a year: The flavor mellows over time and is sweet and rich. It's perfect on toasted sourdough! You can also mix it up by adding hot peppers or spices.

—— Makes 1 pint

3 heads garlic

1–2 cups honey (raw and local if available)

1 Peel the garlic cloves and crack lightly (this helps the honey seep in).

2 Add the garlic to a pint jar and add honey to cover (you may have to add honey in several increments to let it seep to the bottom).

3 Cover the jar with a lid and place it out of direct sunlight to ferment. Start tasting the honey after 1 month, and continue fermenting until it reaches your desired flavor. Store the jar at room temperature out of direct sunlight, and make sure the cloves and any additional flavorings stay under the honey. It will keep for several months.

Garlic in Honey

Fermented Ginger Beer

Ginger beer is a delicious classic and a staple in my beverage rotation. Enjoy it on its own or mix it with a bit of rum or whiskey for an excellent cocktail.

Feel free to adjust the amount of ginger or the soak time to make the beer more or less spicy. Add in other aromatic roots like turmeric, burdock, and dandelion root (though maybe not garlic). Or adjust the amount of lime juice or sugar for a less sour or sweet drink. You can add herbs and spices to the ginger as it soaks if you want to experiment (I like brewing ginger beer with tulsi). Just be sure to use organic ginger, as conventional ginger is sometimes irradiated when imported, removing many of the beneficial microbes that you need to initiate fermentation.

—— Makes 1 gallon

1 pound fresh organic ginger
1 gallon water
Juice of 4–6 limes
1–2 cups turbinado sugar

1. Rinse and scrub the ginger to remove any dirt. Do not peel.

2. Grate the ginger by hand using a box grater, mince it in a food processor, or chop it roughly. Combine it with 1 to 2 cups of the water, enough to make it blend, then blend in a blender.

3. Combine the ginger and the remaining water in a large bowl and stir to distribute the ginger. Cover the bowl with cheesecloth or a tea towel to keep bugs and dust out. Let it sit at room temperature for 8 to 12 hours, or until it has the flavor you like.

4. When the ginger is done soaking, strain it through a fine-mesh strainer into a nonreactive bowl. Squeeze the ginger pulp to release all the remaining gingery goodness.

5. Add the lime juice and sugar to taste to the liquid, whisking until the sugar dissolves.

6. Transfer the ginger beer into glass bottles or other narrow-necked, food-safe containers. For a still, nonalcoholic beverage, refrigerate immediately. For a fizzy or slightly alcoholic drink, let the mixture bottle-condition for a couple of days by leaving it out at room temperature to ferment until carbonated. Store in a swing-top bottle in the fridge, where it will keep for 2 weeks or more.

Fermented Ginger Beer

PICKLING

Quick pickling is a fast, simple way to preserve your aromatic roots with flavor-packed effect. Plus, the aromatic roots impart their flavor to the vinegars used for pickling, which creates another delicious ingredient to play with later on.

Pickling is easy: Either toss your thinly sliced roots, like ginger, or your whole peeled cloves of garlic into a jar and cover them completely with vinegar, or make a brine using my core brine recipe (see page 53), adjusting salt up or down to your taste. Store your pickles in the fridge or in a cool, dark place, making sure your roots stay under the brine. You can also can these pickles in a hot water bath canner, if you wish. Can half-pints for 10 to 12 minutes and pints for 12 to 15 minutes, adjusting for altitude (see page 39) if needed.

Note that garlic sometimes turns blue when pickling due to an enzymatic reaction—this isn't harmful and doesn't impact the flavor.

As with any other quick pickle, add spices and herbs as desired.

FLAVOR VARIATIONS FOR PICKLED GARLIC: Try hot pepper–infused vinegar, dried dill weed, oregano, or strips of lemon zest. Garlic is delicious pickled in apple cider vinegar or in white or red wine vinegar.

FLAVOR VARIATIONS FOR PICKLED GINGER: Pickle thinly sliced ginger in rice wine vinegar, make red wine vinegar pickles, or pickle with strips of citrus zest and baking spices for a different twist.

Quick-Pickled Horseradish and Scallion Paste

Use this paste as you would prepared horseradish. It's great for when you want a little bit of an oniony bite; I love spreading a little on a toasted bagel along with Cream Cheese (page 351).

—— Makes 1 pint

- **1 (4- to 5-inch) horseradish root, grated (about 2 cups)**
- **3–5 scallions, finely diced**
- **2 teaspoons distilled white vinegar, plus more if needed**
- **1 teaspoon sea salt**

1. Add the horseradish and scallions to a bowl and stir in the vinegar and salt (adjust these to your taste—I usually add a little at a time), until the salt is dissolved.

2. Pack horseradish and scallions into a pint jar, add liquid from the bowl, and add additional vinegar if needed to cover.

3. Let sit overnight in the fridge. If you want a finer texture, run it through a food processor or blender. Store it in the refrigerator, where it will last for at least 2 weeks.

Prepared Horseradish

Use in place of jarred prepared horseradish from the store.

—— Makes about 1 pint

- **1 (4- to 5-inch) piece horseradish, grated (about 2 cups)**
- **⅔ cup apple cider vinegar or distilled white vinegar**
- **½ tablespoon salt**

1. Combine the horseradish, vinegar, and salt in a blender or food processor and blend until smooth.

2. Store the mixture in an airtight container in the fridge. For best results, use within 1 to 2 months, after which time horseradish's pungency fades.

Preserving Around the World

Eastern Europe, with Katsu Lask

Katsu Lask is the founder of Fermentation Love. She lives in northern Germany, and her eastern European roots stretch through northeast Germany, Poland, and Belarus. Her cooking is rooted in this part of the world. Food preservation and fermentation—in particular sour vegetables, including her childhood favorite, pickled beetroot—as well as curdled milk, fruit compotes, and juices, weave through her childhood memories: "A very familiar sight was seeing my grandmother in the kitchen cooking applesauce and juice, and I regularly found a carton of milk in the cupboard left there to turn thick and sour. When my father was young, he was set in the barrel to stomp sauerkraut with his feet. My grandmother also took me foraging. I had not known that buckwheat is something you can buy in a store before I was an adult; we always gathered it in the fall." People gather to harvest, then process, fruits and vegetables in community gatherings, while festivals, like sauerkraut festivals, celebrate the harvest and its delicious results.

Sauerkraut and quick pickling are common preserving methods where Lask lives. In addition to cabbage, people often pickle cucumbers, beets, and onions. Herbs and fruits are hung to dry or turned into pesto, milk is turned to yogurt or left to sour, and fruits are cooked into jams and compote as well as applesauce. In coastal areas, fish is smoked; in the countryside, pork is smoked or cooked in sour jelly or canned with spices. Preserves are eaten as sides or stirred into dishes, and pickles offer a contrast to fatty, rich foods.

Beet kvass, made with bread and water, is another staple: "I actually learned how to make kvass from my Latin teacher. He was from eastern Germany and taught me the traditional way, burying the vessel with the bread and water in the ground during fermentation. That was an awesome experience."

For Lask, who learned from her grandparents, passing on knowledge is an important part of keeping traditions alive.: "The knowledge of preserving techniques is passed down through generations, with children learning from their parents or grandparents. In my generation it was more learning from the grandparents; now I'm passing it on to my children so they learn from their parents. My parents were the silent generation; my mother did cook fresh daily, but she did not preserve. That was just not done by her generation; it belonged to the generation before."

Horseradish and Orange "Kosho"

Inspired by the citrusy, spicy kick of Yuzu Kosho (page 285), this sauce swaps out the original hot peppers for the zing of horseradish. It's best when mixed into vinaigrettes or marinades (such as for fish) rather than poured on as a sauce.

— Makes 1 half-pint

- **2 large oranges**
- **1 (4-inch) piece horseradish, grated (about 1 cup)**
- **¼ cup apple cider vinegar**
- **½ teaspoon salt**

1 Remove the orange peel in strips with a vegetable peeler, then roughly chop the peel. Juice the oranges.

2 Add the orange peel and juice, horseradish, vinegar, and salt to a blender or small food processor. Blend to a paste.

3 Store in an airtight container in the fridge, where it will keep for at least 1 month.

Citrus-Pickled Turmeric

I fell in love with using fresh turmeric when I moved to Tallahassee for my PhD. It was an ingredient I rarely encountered fresh living up north, but since it grew in the warm Florida climate, it became a staple. This recipe emerged from a bounty of fresh turmeric root and fresh citrus juice. Remember: Turmeric stains all things, so bear that in mind when using.

— Makes about 1 pint

- **½ pound fresh turmeric**
- **Juice of 3–4 oranges or lemons**
- **1½ tablespoons salt**

1 Wash and peel the turmeric (I peel it by scraping it with a spoon) and then slice it into ¼-inch pieces.

2 Place the turmeric in a pint jar. Add the juice and salt, put the lid on, and shake to combine.

3 Pop it in the fridge, shaking gently each day. It will be pickled through in 2 to 4 days and will keep in the fridge for 1 to 2 months.

Kimchi-Inspired Pickle Brine

This is a garlicky, peppery brine that you can whisk up and pour over whatever vegetables you want to ferment: beets, daikon, carrots, even corn on the cob. My favorite types of chile to use here are Urfa chiles, New Mexico Hatch chiles, and, of course, Korean chiles.

— Makes 1 quart

- **4 cups water**
- **1–2 tablespoons salt**
- **4 or more cloves garlic, peeled and sliced**
- **2–4 teaspoons of your favorite ground, dried chile**

1 Combine the water, salt, garlic, and chile powder in a bowl and whisk until the salt is dissolved.

2 To use: Add your vegetables to a food-safe, nonreactive container, pour the room-temperature brine over to completely cover them, and let them ferment at room temperature for 1 to 2 weeks, or until they have a flavor and texture you enjoy. For more on lactofermenting vegetables, see page 46.

VARIATION: REFRIGERATOR PICKLE BRINE

Replace half the water with vinegar and let your veggies pickle in the fridge for 1 to 2 days before eating.

VARIATION: FISH SAUCE–INSPIRED PICKLED BRINE

Replace the salt with fish sauce, add shredded and dried seaweed, or replace some/all of the pepper with gochujang (Korean fermented chile paste).

INFUSING

Aromatic roots infuse beautifully in vinegar. They give us part of the basis for Fire Cider (page 399) as well as flavorful infusions using only one root, like horseradish vinegar, which is great splashed in vinaigrettes to go with hearty vegetables.

Horseradish Vinegar

This is an easy way to use up those last bits of horseradish after grating for Fermented Horseradish Paste (page 107), Prepared Horseradish (page 111), or Horseradish and Orange "Kosho" (page 113).

— Makes 1 pint

1 cup thinly sliced horseradish (add more for a stronger flavor)

Apple cider vinegar or distilled white vinegar, to cover

Put the horseradish in a pint jar and pour vinegar over to cover. Let it steep for at least a week until it has a flavor you enjoy. Strain and store at room temperature, where it will keep for at least 1 month.

MAKING SYRUPS

You may not think of sweet syrups when you think of aromatic root vegetables, but roots that have sweet or savory applications, like fennel or ginger, make wonderful syrups, perfect for everything from pancakes to cocktails to your morning coffee.

Masala Syrup

I use this ready-to-go dirty chai syrup for my morning coffee. Just 1 to 2 tablespoons does the trick! If you want to mix things up, you can swap tea or coffee for the water in the syrup.

— Makes about 1 pint

12 green cardamom pods
1 tablespoon fennel seeds
1 teaspoon black peppercorns
½ teaspoon whole cloves
½ teaspoon coriander seeds
1 (4-inch) cinnamon stick
1 (3- to 4-inch) piece fresh ginger, sliced (about 3 tablespoons)
2 cups sugar
Pinch of salt
1 cup water

1. Split the cardamom pods with the tip of a knife.
2. Place the cardamom, fennel, peppercorns, cloves, coriander, and cinnamon in a cast-iron skillet and toast over medium-low heat for 5 minutes, or until they are very fragrant.
3. Add the toasted spices, ginger, sugar, salt, and water to a saucepan and bring to a boil over medium-high heat.
4. Reduce the heat to a simmer and cook for 5 to 10 minutes. The syrup will get stronger the longer you simmer it.
5. Strain the syrup through a fine-mesh sieve to remove the spices. Store in an airtight container in the fridge, where it will last for at least 2 weeks.

VARIATION: SPICED ROOT SYRUP

You can adapt the herbal syrup core recipe (see page 174) for aromatic roots like turmeric and ginger, with or without the spices listed above. I love having these spicy syrups around in winter for my cocktails and coffee. Use this as a template for other syrups, too. I make a variation with a cup or so of fresh turmeric, plus a tablespoon or more of rose petals and a strip of orange zest.

Artichokes

Artichokes are typically eaten fresh, but they also make for some tasty preserves. If you've ever had Cynar, a liqueur, you've already had a form of artichoke-based preserve. If you have an abundance of artichokes, try infusing or pickling them for a new twist on old favorites.

INFUSING

Artichokes, part of the thistle family, are delicious as is but also make great infusions. The flower bud itself (what we normally eat and call "artichoke leaves") can be infused in vinegar or alcohol for a mild-flavored artichoke-y ingredient for your salad or your drinks. You can also infuse the leaves or stems for a lower-waste version (homemade Cynar uses artichoke leaves).

Artichoke Vinegar or Liquor

Trying to get to that sweet, sweet artichoke heart? Don't throw out your leaves: Make artichoke vinegar instead! Artichoke vinegar is also good for pickling oysters and fish, if you're into that.

You can also use the artichoke leaves to make a bitter infused liquor, which you can sweeten (see liqueurs, see page 174) or leave as is. Simply swap out the vinegar for vodka.

Raw artichoke leaves

Distilled white vinegar or white wine vinegar (for artichoke vinegar) or vodka (for artichoke liquor), to cover

Pack the raw artichoke leaves into a jar and pour vinegar or vodka over them to completely cover. Let the mixture sit for about 1 month, then strain. Store out of direct sunlight or in the fridge, where it will last for 3 weeks or more.

Ways to Preserve Artichokes

Ways to Preserve Artichokes	Shelf-stable	Fast	Low waste	Ready meals and ingredients	Big flavor
Artichoke Vinegar or Liquor (page 115)	X	X		X	X
Feta and Herb Salad with Artichoke Vinaigrette (page 116)				X	X
Pickled Artichoke or Cardoon Stems (page 116)		X	X	X	X

Feta and Herb Salad with Artichoke Vinaigrette

Once you've made your artichoke vinegar (see page 115), try it out in this tasty feta salad. It's great with crusty bread, on top of fresh greens, or as an accompaniment to fish or white beans.

—— Makes 1½ cups

- ¼ cup artichoke vinegar
- ⅛ cup extra-virgin olive oil
- Salt and freshly ground black pepper
- 1 cup cubed feta
- 1–2 tablespoons chopped basil
- 1–2 tablespoons chopped mint
- 1 tablespoon finely diced shallot
- Red pepper flakes (optional)

In a medium bowl, whisk together the vinegar, oil, and salt and pepper to taste. Add the feta, basil, mint, shallot, and pepper flakes (if using) and toss until evenly coated. Let the salad marinate in the fridge for at least 2 hours.

PICKLING

Quick pickling is an easy way to preserve an abundance of artichokes or their cardoon relatives. I developed this recipe for pickling stems after a bumper crop of cardoons in my garden several years ago, and I like it enough that I continue to make it every spring when my cardoons burst to life.

Pickled Artichoke or Cardoon Stems

This is an amazing, bright topper for salad or a side for cheese plates and seafood. Artichoke and cardoon stems are tough and should be peeled and blanched before pickling. This also helps remove bitterness. You can reduce the cooking time by a few minutes for a firmer pickle, but still make sure they're tender enough to be edible.

—— Makes 1 pint

- 1 tablespoon distilled white vinegar
- 4½ cups water
- 12–16 artichoke or cardoon stems, peeled and sliced ¼ inch thick (about 1 cup)
- Juice of 2 lemons
- 3–4 (2-inch) strips lemon zest
- 1½ teaspoons salt
- 1 teaspoon herbes de Provence

1. Combine the vinegar and 4 cups of the water in a saucepan and bring to a boil.
2. Add the artichoke stems and blanch for 15 minutes, until tender. Drain the stems and let them cool before transferring them to a pint jar.
3. Make the brine: Combine the remaining ½ cup water, lemon juice, lemon zest, salt, and herbes de Provence in a small bowl and whisk until the salt dissolves.
4. Pour the brine over the artichoke stems. Let them pickle for 8 to 12 hours in the fridge. Eat within 3 weeks.

Asparagus

Asparagus is a harbinger of spring, its tender stalks emerging from the soil just as the weather begins to warm. This goofy, wonderful springtime friend, as I've often called it, looks like a child's drawing as it grows—single stalks poke upright out of the ground, like someone walked by and stuck them there.

Fresh asparagus snaps easily and has a satisfying crunch. Choose asparagus with tight, fresh heads and firm stalks. And preserve or use your asparagus relatively quickly. It tends to wilt and go off after just a handful of days in the fridge.

Many recipes for asparagus call for you to snap off the ends. Asparagus-End Relish (page 120) is a great way to use these up, or just pop the ends in the freezer with your other ingredients for Scrappy Soup Stock (page 20).

DRYING

Dried asparagus is best as an ingredient rehydrated in soups and stews rather than eaten as a snack. For the best texture, choose young, tender stalks or cut thicker asparagus stalks in half lengthwise. Blanch asparagus in boiling water for 3½ to 5 minutes, or in steam for 4 to 5 minutes. Shock to cool in an ice bath (see page 17), then drain well. Dry it at 140°F/60°C for 4 to 6 hours or until brittle.

FREEZING

Wash asparagus thoroughly, taking care to not damage it. Blanch your asparagus in boiling water for 2 minutes (small spears) to 4 minutes (large spears), then immediately shock in an ice bath to cool. Drain asparagus thoroughly and package, leaving no headspace. Seal and freeze. Or, after blanching, freeze in a single layer on a rimmed sheet pan, then transfer to airtight freezer-safe containers with no headspace once frozen through.

CANNING

Asparagus, unless it's pickled, needs to be pressure canned. Choose asparagus with tight, closed tips and fresh, crisp stalks. Asparagus works best in wide-mouthed jars, as packing it into regular-mouthed jars can snap the stalks and damage the delicate tips.

Ways to Preserve Asparagus	Shelf-stable	Fast	Low waste	Ready meals and ingredients	Big flavor
Herbes-de-Provence-Pickled Asparagus (page 118)	X				
Asparagus Refrigerator Pickles (page 119)		X			X
Asparagus-End Relish (page 120)	X		X		X

Pressure Canning Asparagus

1 Place jars in your pressure canner and heat it up. Then, using tongs, remove the hot jars from the canner.

2 Wash the asparagus thoroughly, but gently, so as not to damage the tips. Cut off any tough scales and snap the ends off of your asparagus. Leave the pieces whole (they should be 4- to 6-inch-long stalks) or cut them into 1-inch pieces so they fit in your jar with 1½ inches of headspace.

3 Hot pack or raw pack your jars.

- Hot pack: Cover the asparagus with boiling water, boil for 2 to 3 minutes, then drain. Pack the hot asparagus into hot jars, leaving 1 inch of headspace. Add salt, if desired—½ teaspoon per pint or 1 teaspoon per quart—and dried herbs and spices (if using). Fill the jar with boiling water, leaving 1 inch of headspace.
- Raw pack: Pack the asparagus tightly into hot jars, taking care to not damage it. Add salt, if desired—½ teaspoon per pint or 1 teaspoon per quart—and dried herbs and spices (if using). Fill the jar with boiling water, leaving 1 inch of headspace.

4 Run a chopstick or other thin, nonmetal utensil along the inner edges of the jars to release any air bubbles. Wipe the rims of the jars with a clean, damp cloth. Add the lids and bands and screw down to hand tightness.

5 Set your pressure canner to 11 pounds pressure (dial gauge) or 10 pounds pressure (weighted gauge), and process pints for 30 minutes and quarts for 40 minutes, adjusting for altitude (see page 39) if needed.

6 Allow your canner to depressurize completely. Let the jars cool for 24 hours before testing the seals (see page 40), then store out of direct sunlight at room temperature.

PICKLING

Pickled asparagus is quite a treat. The tartness of the vinegar and the zip of salt play beautifully with the bitter-but-sweet flavor of fresh asparagus stalks.

Herbes-de-Provence-Pickled Asparagus

Simple and delicious, this is the perfect accompaniment to fish or an entrée salad. I like these pickles with Niçoise salad, or anything else with a bit of heaviness from oily fish or eggs. They're also great on a springtime cheese platter, or as a garnish for chilled spring and summer soups (think cold pea soup or vichyssoise).

— Makes 1 pint

1 small bunch asparagus (about 12 ounces)
1 cup apple cider vinegar, white wine vinegar, or distilled white vinegar
¾ cup water
2 teaspoons salt
1½–2 teaspoons herbes de Provence

1 Snap off the asparagus ends so the stalks fit in a pint jar, leaving 1 inch of headspace.

2 Combine the vinegar, water, salt, and herbes de Provence in a small bowl and whisk until the salt is dissolved. Pour over the asparagus to cover, leaving ½ inch of headspace.

3 Screw the lid on the jar and allow the asparagus to pickle in the refrigerator for 1 to 2 days before using. It will last in the fridge for weeks.

VARIATION: CANNING ASPARAGUS PICKLES

Pack the raw asparagus into hot jars, leaving 1 inch of headspace. Pour in brine, leaving ½ inch of headspace, wipe rims and tighten lids, then process pints in a hot water bath for 15 minutes, adjusting for altitude (see page 39) if needed. Let the jars cool for 24 hours before testing the seals (see page 36), then store out of direct sunlight at room temperature.

Asparagus Refrigerator Pickles

Asparagus Refrigerator Pickles

While the Herbes-de-Provence-Pickled Asparagus (page 118) is wonderful with French food, this red wine vinegar–pickled asparagus is a nice side to go along with congee or miso soup. Use this as a base recipe for asparagus refrigerator pickles. Feel free to mix up the flavors to match your mood or whatever cuisine you plan to cook that week.

—— Makes 1 pint

- 1 bunch asparagus (about 12 ounces)
- 1 cup red wine vinegar
- 1 cup water
- 1 tablespoon salt
- ½–1 tablespoon five-spice powder
- 1 teaspoon red pepper flakes
- 1–2 cloves garlic, crushed
- Sprigs of your favorite fresh herbs (optional)

1 Trim the ends off the asparagus and place the stalks upright in a pint jar, leaving 1 inch of headspace.

2 Make the brine: In a medium bowl, combine the vinegar, water, salt, five-spice powder, pepper flakes, garlic, and herbs (if using) and whisk until the salt is dissolved.

3 Pour the brine over the asparagus until covered (you can mix up a little extra if needed).

4 Screw the lid on the jar and allow the asparagus to pickle in the refrigerator for at least 8 hours, or until pickled through. Store in an airtight container in the fridge, where it will last for at least 2 weeks.

VARIATION: HERB-FORWARD ASPARAGUS REFRIGERATOR PICKLES

This red wine vinegar and herb-forward version pairs nicely with Italian food. Simply replace the five-spice powder and red pepper flakes with 1 tablespoon herbes de Provence, 1 teaspoon black peppercorns, and 1 teaspoon dried rosemary. This recipe also works with apple cider vinegar instead of red wine vinegar, if you prefer.

Asparagus-End Relish

When it comes to woody asparagus ends, my favorite technique is to very finely slice them with a mandoline or by hand to make this relish. If you want a more traditional relish texture, you can try grating, though I prefer slicing, as it keeps a crisper texture. If the very ends are still so woody that they aren't usable, just add them to your Scrappy Soup Stock (page 20) container.

Unlike most relishes, this one is packed in brine, so you'll want to drain it before using it on burgers and sandwiches. Then use that beautiful brine to marinate meat or mushrooms, or in a vinaigrette.

—— Makes 2 half-pints

- **Asparagus ends from 2 asparagus bunches (the ends from one 1-pound bunch will give you roughly half a pint)**
- **3 teaspoons salt**
- **2 teaspoons sugar**
- **1 cup distilled white vinegar, apple cider vinegar, or white wine vinegar**
- **1 cup water**
- **1 teaspoon red pepper flakes or Turkish biber pepper**
- **½ teaspoon coriander seeds**
- **½ teaspoon yellow mustard seeds**

1 Slice the asparagus ends very thinly with a mandoline or by hand.

2 Make the brine: Add the salt, sugar, vinegar, and water to a saucepan and heat until boiling.

3 If canning, place two half-pint jars in your hot water bath canner and heat it up. Then, using tongs, remove the hot jars from the canner.

4 Divide the asparagus slices, pepper flakes, coriander, and mustard seeds evenly between the two jars. Pour hot brine over the slices to completely cover, leaving ½ inch of headspace.

5 If refrigerating, add the lids and let the asparagus pickle in the refrigerator for at least 2 days before using.

6 If canning, take a chopstick or other thin, nonmetal utensil and run it along the inner edges of the jars to release any air bubbles. Wipe the rims of the jars with a clean, damp cloth. Add the lids and bands and screw down to hand tightness.

7 Process half-pints for 12 minutes or pints for 15 minutes in a hot water bath canner, adjusting for altitude (see page 39) if needed.

8 Let the jars cool for 24 hours before testing the seals (see page 36), then store out of direct sunlight at room temperature.

Beets

Few things make me happier than beets. Yes, they can stain your countertop. And yes, to some palates they taste a lot like dirt, but their color and flavor give them bonus points in my book. Their rich color makes food beautiful and makes a fantastic ink and dye. And their earthy flavor is so comforting, particularly layered with beets' sweetness and satisfying crunch. If you come into my kitchen, it will be quickly apparent how much I love beets. I love to mix them in with my aromatic root seasoning pastes (see page 108), add them to ready-to-go recipe starters (like Rainbow Roots Soup Starter, page 107), use them as a meat substitute (page 124), and make them into their own recipes where their flavor shines through.

Choose beets that are firm and free of cuts, scrapes, or blemishes. If they have greens, these should be fresh, not limp. For longest storage life, trim greens to 2 inches above the beets, then store the beets in the crisper drawer of your refrigerator. You can repurpose the greens in all kinds of ways: Braise them, chop them up in salads, add them to smoothies, or use them in multi-greens pestos.

DRYING

Uncooked, dehydrated beets are incredibly tough, so for the best results, dry beets that have been cooked until tender. If you have leftover

Ways to Preserve Beets	Shelf-stable	Fast	Low waste	Ready meals and ingredients	Big flavor
Rainbow Roots Soup Starter (page 107)		X		X	X
Beet–Pasta Sauce Cubes (page 122)				X	X
Fermented Pastrami Beets (page 124)					X
Pickled Pastrami Beets (Refrigerated or Canned) (page 125)				X	X
Fermented Beet-and-Carrot Sauce (page 127)				X	X
Kimchi Beets (page 127)				X	X
Root Vegetable Jam (page 146)	X		X	X	X
Raspberry-Beet Syrup (page 268)				X	X
Raspberry-Beet Jam (page 272)					X
Beet Kvass (page 328)			X	X	X

roasted, steamed, or boiled beets, this is a good way to preserve them.

To prepare raw beets for drying, cook them whole and peel, or peel and cut them in ⅛-inch-thick slices (my preference, as they cook faster) and cook until tender, then let cool. Cut whole cooked beets into ⅛-inch-thick slices or shoestrings; cut your sliced beets into ⅛-inch-thick shoestrings. Lay them out in a single layer on a dehydrator tray and dry for 10 to 12 hours at 140°F/60°C, or until brittle.

Dried beets add color, flavor, and nutrition to soups, sauces, or even the boiling water for pasta (just add them in close to the beginning to give them time to soften). To make a beet powder that can be used to color your dishes and sometimes as a natural pigment (depending on the type of beet), grind your dried beets as you would for other seasoning blends and pickle powders (see page 95).

FREEZING

For best results, cook beets before freezing. Steam or simmer whole, unpeeled beets until the peels come off easily, then cool and peel and cut into cubes or slices. Pack into freezer bags, removing as much air as possible (see page 20), label, and freeze.

Beet–Pasta Sauce Cubes

Years ago, I watched an episode of Nadiya Hussain's *Time to Eat* where she made a quick, delicious, and beautiful beet pasta sauce using prepackaged beets, fresh dill weed, and a handful of other ingredients. Once I tried it, I was immediately hooked. So when I wrote this book, I decided to take a preserving spin on this beet pasta sauce that's become a staple in my kitchen.

You can, if you prefer, freeze this in freezer-safe containers with headspace (see page 19); however, I love the convenience of having smaller portions ready for single-serving meals.

— Makes about 16 cubes

- **2 large beets, unpeeled and washed, cut into 1-inch cubes**
- **¼ cup red wine**
- **Zest and juice of 1 lemon**
- **1 teaspoon honey or agave syrup**
- **2 red bird's-eye chiles, stems removed**
- **2 cloves peeled garlic**
- **Salt and freshly ground black pepper**
- **¼ cup packed fresh basil or dill weed**
- **¼ cup extra-virgin olive oil**
- **Pasta, for serving**
- **Crumbled feta cheese, for serving**

1. Steam the beets until fork-tender and drain, reserving the liquid. Let cool.
2. Add the beets, wine, lemon zest and juice, honey, chiles, garlic, and salt and pepper to taste to a blender. Add enough reserved cooking liquid to blend, and blend until smooth.
3. Add the basil and blend until chopped and evenly distributed.
4. Spoon into an ice cube tray, tapping the tray gently on the counter to remove any air bubbles.
5. Float a splash of the olive oil on top of each cube, just to cover the surface.
6. Freeze for 6 to 10 hours, or until frozen through, then pop out the cubes and store them in an airtight, freezer-safe container with no headspace, where they will last for at least 2 months.
7. To serve: Cook pasta and drain, reserving a couple of spoonfuls of cooking water. Add 1 or 2 beet–pasta sauce cubes per 1 cup of cooked pasta to the empty pot, along with the reserved cooking water, and cook until heated through. Toss with the pasta and top with crumbled feta cheese or your favorite toppings.

VARIATION: QUICK BEET SOUP

These cubes also make a nice soup starter. I add 3 or 4 cubes (or more, if I'm craving lots of flavor and color) to 1 quart of simmering stock, maybe with other ingredients like leftover roasted vegetables or shredded chicken. You might add other flavors, too (like a pinch of cumin seeds), and toppings like a dollop of sour cream, a drizzle of olive oil, or some fresh pesto.

VARIATION: EASY YOGURT SAUCE

This is my go-to for when I want a unique dipping sauce and am short on time. I defrost 1 beet–pasta sauce cube (on the stovetop over medium heat in a small pan or in the microwave in 30-second intervals). Once thawed, I whisk it into ¼ cup of plain yogurt along with some salt and freshly ground black pepper to taste.

INFUSING

Beet-infused vinegar can be enjoyed as a colorful, playful addition to meals or sweetened and made into a shrub (drinking vinegar). You can also infuse it with raspberries for a wonderful addition to your salads (it's like a fancy version of the raspberry vinaigrette we all enjoyed in the '90s), or add your favorite fruits and vegetables (peaches and carrots are two of mine). Follow the guidance for making infused vinegars on page 66.

CANNING

Beets, unless they are pickled, need to be pressure canned. For best results, stick to smaller beets (1 to 2 inches in diameter) if canning whole beets. Larger beets should be cut into pieces for canning.

Pressure Canning Beets

1 Cut off the greens 1 inch from the top of the beets, and wash and scrub the beets thoroughly.

2 Bring a pot of water to boil. Add the beets and boil for 18 to 25 minutes, or until the skins can slip off easily (check by pulling off a small piece of skin).

3 Meanwhile, place jars in your pressure canner and heat it up. Then, using tongs, remove the hot jars from the canner.

4 Cool the beets, remove the skins, and trim off the tops and tails. Leave little baby beets whole; cut larger beets in halves or quarters.

5 Pack your beets into hot jars, leaving 1 inch of headspace. If you wish, add ½ teaspoon of salt to pints and 1 teaspoon of salt to quarts. Fill the jars with boiling water, leaving 1 inch of headspace.

6 Run a chopstick or other thin, nonmetal utensil along the inner edges of the jars to release any air bubbles. Wipe the rims of the jars with a clean, damp cloth. Add the lids and bands and screw down to hand tightness.

7 Set your pressure canner to 11 pounds pressure (dial gauge) or 10 pounds pressure (weighted gauge), and process pints for 30 minutes or quarts for 35 minutes, adjusting for altitude (see page 39) if needed.

8 Allow the canner to depressurize completely. Let the jars cool for 24 hours before testing the seals (see page 40), then store out of direct sunlight at room temperature.

PICKLING AND FERMENTING

Pickled beets are truly one of nature's perfect foods. Tart, yet a bit sweet, they have a great texture and are substantial enough to sit at the center of the plate as well as complement other dishes as a side. There are plenty of options for playing with pickled beets.

PACK BEETS IN SAUERKRAUT, in kimchi, or in leftover pickle brine and let them steep in the fridge (or on the counter) for a few days or until pickled through.

NESTLE YOUR BEETS IN A PICKLING BED made with fermented rice bran to make nuka-zuke. Just bury sliced beets along with any other veggies you want. Check them every 1 to 2 days. Once they're pickled through and have a flavor you like, they are done! Pull them out and store in the fridge, reusing your pickling bed for other veggies. You can also make a nontraditional pickling bed from whatever you feel like pouring or pressing into a tray or box or other flat, food-safe container. You might use koji-based ferments (like miso) or lactoferments (like strained and blended pickled vegetables; this is a great way to repurpose those fermented pickles that got mushy but still have a nice flavor!).

MAKE BEET KVASS (page 328), which also works well with bits of other vegetables (like carrot ends). Or grate them and add to sauerkraut or kraut-chi—one of my favorite breakfast additions is made with grated beets, red cabbage, and pomegranate seeds!

Pastrami-Spiced Beets

I'm a big fan of vegetable-based meat substitutes that are, well, actual vegetables, and I love finding ways to use savory flavors we typically associate with meats on earthy, rich veggies.

Enter the pastrami-spiced, fermented beets. These are truly incredible on a sandwich with some slaw or on a bed of grains. I've also taken to eating them out of the jar, always intending to take just one but instead having to stop myself after half the container is gone.

They're an embodiment of the changing seasons: The warming spices feel so at home when the weather is cold but you can sense the possibility of warmer days on the horizon. The rich, sweet flavor is both familiar and rooted in fall and winter, but also liminal and flexible. To me, their flavor speaks to the pleasures of the moment and to my eagerness and excitement for the changes to come.

Fermented Pastrami Beets

You can make pastrami-cured beets by rubbing beets in spices and baking them, but I prefer this fermented version. For a thin-shaved "pastrami," ferment whole or quartered/halved beets and shave with a mandoline or food processor. If fermenting thicker slices (¼ to ½ inch), let sit for an extra couple of days until flavorful and softened.

— Makes 1 quart

- **3 large beets, cut in ¼-inch slices or thinly sliced using a mandoline or food processor**
- **2 cloves garlic, peeled and halved**
- **1 teaspoon coriander seeds**
- **1 teaspoon coarsely ground black pepper**
- **½ teaspoon red pepper flakes**
- **½ teaspoon yellow mustard seeds**
- **⅛ teaspoon celery seeds**
- **1 quart 2–3% brine (1–2 tablespoons unrefined salt dissolved in 1 quart water)**

1 Pack the beets, garlic, coriander, black pepper, pepper flakes, mustard seeds, and celery seeds into a quart jar.

2 Pour the brine over to cover completely, to the bottom of the band.

3 Ferment for 4 to 7 days or until flavorful and softened (but not mushy).

4 Store the beets in the fridge, where they will last for at least 1 month.

VARIATION: SMOKED PASTRAMI-FERMENTED BEETS

I don't smoke my beets before fermenting, since I don't want to risk killing off the microbes that are going to turn them into delicious pickles. But if you do decide to smoke your beets, just make sure to add another source of microbes before fermenting them—maybe some old lactofermented pickle brine from your last batch of beets, or some other raw veggies (carrots, perhaps). You could also swap smoked salt for the regular salt to build in a bit of that flavor, or add a dash of smoked paprika.

Pickled Pastrami Beets (Refrigerated or Canned)

These are delicious as is, and they also benefit from smoking. If you want to go that route, smoke your beets at 125 to 135°F/52 to 57°C for 15 minutes, or until fragrant and flavorful and ever so slightly softened. Note: You'll have some brine left over, perfect for quick pickling other veggies on the fly!

— Makes 2 pints

- **2 cloves garlic, minced**
- **1 teaspoon coriander seeds**
- **1 teaspoon coarsely ground black pepper**
- **½ teaspoon yellow mustard seeds**
- **½ teaspoon red pepper flakes**
- **⅛ teaspoon celery seeds**
- **3 large beets, thinly sliced using a mandoline or food processor**
- **4 cups apple cider vinegar**
- **4 cups water**
- **½ cup salt**

1 If canning, put two pint jars in your hot water bath canner and heat it up. Then, using tongs, remove the hot jars from the canner.

2 Divide the garlic, coriander, black pepper, mustard seeds, pepper flakes, and celery seeds between the two pint jars. Pack the two jars with the beets.

3 Make the brine: Combine the vinegar, water, and salt in a saucepan over medium heat. Once hot, pour the brine over the beets, leaving ½ inch of headspace.

4 If refrigerating, allow the beets to cool to room temperature, cover, and place in the fridge for 2 days or until pickled through. Store them completely submerged in brine in the refrigerator, where they will last for at least 3 weeks.

(continued on next page)

Pickled Pastrami Beets *continued*

5 If canning, run a chopstick or other thin, nonmetal utensil along the inner edges of the jars to release any air bubbles. Wipe the rims of the jars with a clean, damp cloth. Add the lids and bands and screw down to hand tightness.

6 Process pints in a hot water bath for 15 minutes, adjusting for altitude (see page 39) if needed.

7 Let the jars cool for 24 hours before testing the seals (see page 36), then store out of direct sunlight at room temperature.

Pickled Pastrami Beets

Fermented Beet-and-Carrot Sauce

This tangy, versatile sauce is perfect slathered onto roasted veggies or meat, mixed up with fresh pesto for a bright, summery sauce, or shaken with olive oil and a splash of vinegar for an easy salad dressing. My favorite way to use it is inspired by my beet pasta sauce (see page 122): I blend the sauce with a bit of garlic, hot pepper, lemon zest, and fresh dill, then serve it on pasta topped with feta.

—— Makes 1 pint

2–3 cloves garlic, unpeeled

1 beet, cubed or cut into chunks

1 carrot, cubed or cut into chunks

½ tablespoon sea salt

1. Place the garlic in the bottom of a pint jar and top with the beet and carrot.
2. Add the salt and fill the jar with enough water to cover the vegetables. Seal it tightly and shake until the salt is dissolved.
3. Ferment at room temperature for 5 to 7 days or until it reaches a flavor you enjoy.
4. Pour into a food processor or blender and blend to your desired consistency. Store the sauce in the fridge, where it will last for at least 2 weeks.

Kimchi Beets

Try a single layer of these beets in a grilled cheese sandwich and thank me later. This recipe also works with carrots, parsnips, daikon, and other root vegetables. Make sure to save your ends to make beet kvass or beet-infused vinegar. Mix up ingredients/flavoring to make it your own.

—— Makes 1 quart

2 large beets, shaved or thinly sliced

4 cloves garlic, halved

4 scallions or garlic scapes, sliced ¼-inch thick

1–2 tablespoons minced ginger

1–2 bird's-eye or other small red chiles, thinly sliced, or 2 teaspoons red pepper flakes or gochujang (Korean fermented chile paste)

1–2 teaspoons fish sauce, or seaweed for a vegan version (optional)

2 cups distilled white vinegar, apple cider vinegar, or rice wine vinegar

2 cups water

2 tablespoons salt

TO FERMENT:

1. Place the beets, garlic, scallions, ginger, chiles, and fish sauce (if using) in a quart jar.
2. Make the brine: Combine the vinegar, water, and salt in a medium saucepan. Bring the brine to a boil and then pour it over the beet mixture to completely cover, leaving ½ inch of headspace.
3. Put the lid on and place your ferment on a tray or plate to catch overflow. Place it out of direct sunlight at room temperature.
4. Ferment for at least 1 week, or until the beets have a flavor you enjoy. Burp your ferment, as needed, when the pressure builds up.
5. Store the fermented beets in an airtight container in the fridge, completely submerged in brine, where they will last for at least 2 weeks.

(continued on next page)

Kimchi Beets *continued*

TO CAN:

1. Place two pint jars in your hot water bath canner and heat it up. Then, using tongs, remove the hot jars from the canner.

2. Divide the beets, garlic, scallions, ginger, chiles, and fish sauce (if using) evenly between the hot jars, leaving ½ inch of headspace.

3. Make the brine: Combine the vinegar, water, and salt in a medium saucepan. Bring the brine to a boil and then pour over the vegetables to completely cover, leaving ½ inch of headspace.

4. Run a chopstick or other thin, nonmetal utensil along the inner edges of the jars to release any air bubbles. Wipe the rims of the jars with a clean, damp cloth. Add the lids and bands and screw down to hand tightness.

5. Process pints in a hot water bath canner for 15 minutes, adjusting for altitude (see page 39) if needed.

6. Let the jars cool for 24 hours before testing the seals (see page 36), then store out of direct sunlight at room temperature.

Brassicas

Bok Choy, Broccoli, Brussels Sprouts, Cabbage, Cauliflower, Kohlrabi

Brassicas are a family of vegetables that includes bok choy, broccoli, Brussels sprouts, cabbage, cauliflower, and kohlrabi, among others. Kale, mustard greens, and some other dark leafy greens are also brassicas, but they are preserved in the same way as other non-brassica dark leafy greens, like spinach and beet greens; we discuss all these hearty greens on page 169.

In many cases, you can swap one brassica for another in a recipe, though smaller or more tender brassicas will take less time to pickle or ferment than larger, denser ones.

DRYING

Drying brassicas is a great way to have shelf-stable ingredients on hand that can be easily tossed into a stew or rehydrated and added to other dishes like casseroles, mac and cheese, pasta salad, or grain dishes. Broccoli and cauliflower dry well, but kohlrabi can dry out; I find the results with kohlrabi to be more hit or miss than with some other brassicas. If you do decide to dry kohlrabi, peel it first and slice it thin (some people eat it as kohlrabi chips). Leafy brassicas, like cabbage, can be dried, too, though other preservation methods (like fermentation) will tend to yield a better end result. Bok choy can be treated like cabbage.

If you wish, toss brassicas in a solution of 1 teaspoon citric acid per gallon of water before drying. This pretreatment can help them keep color and flavor longer after they've been dried.

BROCCOLI

Cut broccoli into pieces as if you were serving it fresh, and wash it thoroughly. If the stalks are big and thick, quarter them lengthwise. Blanch the pieces for 3 to 4 minutes in steam or 2 minutes in boiling water, then shock them in an ice bath to cool (see page 17). Dry at 140°F/60°C for 12 to 15 hours, or until brittle and crisp.

BRUSSELS SPROUTS

Because of their layered leaves, Brussels sprouts don't always have great texture when dried (and can dry inconsistently), and they tend to retain a strong flavor. If you decide to dry yours, don't add other ingredients alongside them in the dehydrator.

Cut each sprout in half. Blanch for 6 to 7 minutes in steam or 4 to 5½ minutes in boiling water, then shock in an ice bath to cool. Dry at 140°F/60°C for 12 to 18 hours, or until the leaves are brittle.

CABBAGE

Remove the outer leaves from the cabbage, then quarter and core the head. Grate the core into kraut-chi (see page 50), or add it to your freezer for Scrappy Soup Stock (page 20). Cut the quartered cabbage into ⅛-inch-thick strips. Blanch until wilted—for 2 to 3 minutes in steam or 1½ to 2½ minutes in boiling water—then shock in an ice bath to cool. Dehydrate at 140°F/60°C for 10 to 12 hours, or until brittle.

Ways to Preserve Brassicas

	Shelf-stable	Fast	Low waste	Ready meals and ingredients	Big flavor
Quick-Pickled Cauliflower (page 131)		X			X
Kimchi (page 132)				X	X
Canned Cauliflower Pickles (page 134)		X			X
Kimchi-Lemongrass Infused Vinegar (page 134)		X			X
Sauerkraut (page 135)				X	X
Curtido (page 138)				X	X
Coriander-and-Mustard Canned Sauerkraut (page 138)				X	X
Fermented Chowchow (page 139)	X				X
Quick-Pickled Chowchow (page 140)	X				X
Broccoli-Stem Refrigerator Relish (page 141)			X		X
Fermented Stems and Ends (page 141)			X		

CAULIFLOWER

Cut the cauliflower into pieces as if you were serving it fresh, and wash thoroughly. Blanch for 4 to 5 minutes in steam or 3 to 4 minutes in boiling water, then shock in an ice bath to cool. Dry at 140°F/60°C for 12 to 15 hours, or until brittle and crisp.

FREEZING

Choose firm, fresh vegetables for freezing. The process is largely the same (blanch, shock, freeze) for all brassicas, but the specifics vary.

BOK CHOY

The base of bok choy should be firm and the leaves not wilted. Bok choy can be cut into 1-inch pieces and prepared the same way as cabbage.

BROCCOLI

Broccoli should have tight, compact heads and tender rather than tough or woody stalks. Remove any leaves and woody parts of the stem and split it lengthwise. Cut broccoli into florets—whatever size is ready-to-eat for you. For home-harvested broccoli, immerse in a brine of 1 tablespoon salt per gallon of water for 30 to 45 minutes to remove any insects.

Blanch the broccoli for 5 minutes in steam or 3 minutes in boiling water, then shock in an ice bath to cool (see page 17). Pat dry, transfer to a ziplock bag or airtight container (or sheet pan, if you want to freeze it in individual pieces before packing it up), and freeze.

BRUSSELS SPROUTS

Brussels sprouts should be tight and firm. Remove any tough outer leaves and sort the sprouts by size: small, medium, and large. Blanch in boiling water for 3 minutes (small), 4 to 4½ minutes (medium), or 4½ to 5 minutes (large). Shock in an ice bath to cool. Pat dry, transfer to a ziplock bag or airtight container (or sheet pan, if you want to freeze it in individual pieces before packing it up), and freeze.

CABBAGE

Cabbage that has been frozen should be reserved for use in dishes that are cooked; the texture doesn't lend itself well to fresh eating once frozen cabbage is thawed. Remove any tough outer leaves and cut the head into shreds or thin wedges (less than 1 inch wide), or just separate all the leaves to freeze whole. Blanch in boiling water for 1½ to 2 minutes, then shock in an ice bath to cool. Pat dry, transfer to a ziplock bag or airtight container (or sheet pan, if you want to freeze it in individual pieces before packing it up), and freeze.

CAULIFLOWER

Cauliflower is processed in the same manner as broccoli.

KOHLRABI

Trim off the tops and roots of the kohlrabi and then peel the bulb. Leave small bulbs whole or cut into ½-inch cubes. Blanch in boiling water: whole bulbs for 3 to 3½ minutes and cubes for 1½ minutes. Shock in an ice bath to cool. Pat dry, transfer to a ziplock bag or airtight container (or sheet pan, if you want to freeze it in individual pieces before packing it up), and freeze.

PARSNIPS

Parsnips are prepared in the same manner as kohlrabi.

RUTABAGA

Rutabaga is prepared in the same manner as kohlrabi when chopped into cubes. Or you can boil rutabaga until tender, drain, season if desired, mash until smooth, and pack into containers, leaving the appropriate headspace (see page 19).

TURNIPS

Turnips are prepared in the same manner as kohlrabi.

PICKLING AND FERMENTING

I revel in the delights of fermented and pickled brassicas on a daily basis, adding a scoop of sauerkraut or kimchi as a side dish to pretty much every meal I make. There are colors, textures, and flavors in abundance to explore. If you're new to the magical world of pickling and fermenting, then welcome: You're in for a delicious journey.

Quick-Pickled Cauliflower

This is a favorite ingredient for cheese boards (which make a frequent appearance in my home), and it's also great on tempeh sandwiches.

— Makes about 1 quart

- **4 cups cauliflower florets**
- **1 bay leaf**
- **1 teaspoon black peppercorns**
- **½ teaspoon coriander seeds**
- **Parsley stems or leaves (optional)**
- **Red pepper flakes (optional)**
- **2 cups white wine vinegar or apple cider vinegar**
- **2 cups water**
- **2 tablespoons salt**

1. Place the cauliflower in a quart jar. Add the bay leaf, peppercorns, coriander, and parsley and pepper flakes (if using).
2. Make the brine: Combine the vinegar, water, and salt in a saucepan over medium-high heat and whisk until the salt is dissolved.
3. Pour the hot brine over the cauliflower to cover completely.
4. Let cool, then cover the jar and transfer it to the fridge to pickle for 1 to 2 days.
5. Store the pickles in the fridge, where they will keep for at least several weeks.

Quick-Pickled Cauliflower

Kimchi

Kimchi dates back to at least the third or fourth century in Korea, beginning as simple pickled vegetables and, over time, evolving to encompass greater variety in both ingredients and techniques. This is my small-batch recipe, which I use when I have a head of cabbage and just a few things to mix in. You can also make kimchi the more traditional way with whole heads of cabbage, rubbed and filled with salt, spices, and other ingredients, then packed into a crock or other large container.

Use this recipe as a template and a jumping-off point to your own kimchi traditions. As with sauerkraut, you can add other ingredients (like grated apples) or adjust the spice level to suit your fancy. For a vegan version, replace the fish sauce with some shredded seaweed.

Note: You may want a pair of latex gloves for massaging the ingredients to protect your hands from stains, stings, and smells.

—— Makes 2–3 quarts (depending on cabbage size)

- **1 large head napa cabbage**
- **2 quarts 2–3% brine (2–4 tablespoons unrefined salt dissolved in 2 quarts water)**
- **1 carrot, grated**
- **1 daikon radish, grated**
- **1 bunch garlic scapes, finely chopped**
- **1 (4-inch) piece fresh ginger, grated**
- **½–1 cup gochujang (Korean fermented chile paste), dried pepper flakes, or ground chiles**
- **3–4 tablespoons Korean fish sauce**

1 Remove 6 to 8 outer leaves from the cabbage and set aside. Quarter and core the cabbage, then chop it into bite-size pieces. Place the chopped cabbage in a large nonreactive bowl. Pour the brine over the cabbage and let it soak for 8 to 12 hours.

2 Drain the liquid from the bowl, reserving it to use later.

3 Add the carrot, daikon, garlic scapes, ginger, and gochujang to the bowl of cabbage. Put on a pair of latex gloves. Massage the pepper paste into the mixture to evenly coat the vegetables.

4 Add the fish sauce to taste and toss until evenly distributed. Massage the mixture to begin breaking down the cell walls of the cabbage leaves, allowing them to soften somewhat.

5 You have a couple of options for fermenting. Like with sauerkraut, you can pack the kimchi into individual jars, filling them about three-quarters full and topping each with a folded cabbage leaf to hold the mixture under the brine. Alternatively, you can pack the mixture into one large container and place the leaves on top, topped with a weight and a tea towel or other cloth secured with twine, or topped with a lid.

6 Pour the reserved brine into each jar or container, as needed, until the vegetable mixture is covered, then put on the lids loosely. Set the kimchi aside to ferment at room temperature, away from direct sunlight or heat. The speed of fermentation varies dramatically depending on environmental factors, so check the kimchi every day—open the jars or containers, smell the kimchi, and pluck a piece out to taste. If it's not done, you'll know (it will taste like fresh cabbage rather than pickled).

7 Once it gets to a level of softness and flavor that you like, move the kimchi to the fridge, where it will keep for weeks or even months. Just be sure the vegetables stay under the brine.

Kimchi

Kimchi-Lemongrass Infused Vinegar

This vinegar infused with kimchi and lemongrass is perfect for a quick salad dressing, or for dressing banchan (small side dishes served alongside meals).

—— Makes about 1 quart

- **1 stalk lemongrass, chopped into ½- to 1-inch pieces**
- **2 cups kimchi**
- **Rice wine vinegar or apple cider vinegar, to cover**

1. Combine the lemongrass and kimchi in a quart jar and add enough vinegar to cover.
2. Place the lid on the jar and let steep at room temperature, shaking the jar every few days, until it has a flavor you enjoy (I steep it for 2 to 4 weeks). Then strain out the solids.
3. Store the infused vinegar at room temperature or in the fridge, where it will last for months.

Flavorful Brines

The classic brine for quick pickles is just vinegar, water, and salt. For fermentation, it's even simpler: just water and salt. But for either, you could use an herbal infusion or tea in place of water, cooled to room temperature (for fermentation). You can, of course, add spices or herbs, or play around with color (like I do in flowerkraut; see page 136). You might try a brine that includes sourdough starter in addition to the water and salt. So long as you maintain the basic ratios, brine offers endless possibilities for experimentation.

Canned Cauliflower Pickles

Pickled cauliflower is crunchy, bright, and delicious. It is always welcome as a side to my sandwiches or as a zingy addition to pasta salad.

—— Makes 2 pints

- **4 cups cauliflower florets**
- **1 bay leaf**
- **1 teaspoon black peppercorns**
- **½ teaspoon coriander seeds**
- **2–4 parsley stems or leaves (optional)**
- **⅛–¼ teaspoon red pepper flakes (optional)**
- **2½ cups white wine vinegar or apple cider vinegar**
- **1 cup water**
- **2 tablespoons salt**

1. Place two pint jars in your hot water bath canner and heat it up. Then, using tongs, remove the hot jars from the canner.
2. Distribute the cauliflower, bay leaf, peppercorns, coriander, and parsley and pepper flakes (if using) evenly between the hot jars.
3. Make the brine: Combine the vinegar, water, and salt in a saucepan over medium-high heat and whisk until the salt is dissolved.
4. Pour the hot brine over the cauliflower, leaving ½ inch of headspace in each jar.
5. Run a chopstick or other thin, nonmetal utensil along the inner edges of the jars to release any air bubbles. Wipe the rims of the jars with a clean, damp cloth. Add the lids and bands and screw down to hand tightness.
6. Process in a hot water bath canner, half pints for 12 minutes and pints for 15 minutes, adjusting for altitude (see page 39) if needed.
7. Let the jars cool for 24 hours before testing the seals (see page 36), then store out of direct sunlight at room temperature.

Sauerkraut

This is the way I learned to make sauerkraut almost two decades ago. I was taught to make it in jars rather than in a big crock, which was better suited to my small apartment and limited equipment. You can also ferment in a crock, of course, or another food-safe, nonreactive container. To ferment in a crock, pack your cabbage in and weight it down with fermentation weights, a plate, a bowl, or other food-safe, nonreactive weights. Make sure your sauerkraut is completely covered in brine. Cover and allow to ferment as you would in jars.

— Makes 2 pints

1 head cabbage

Sea salt

Spices, such as caraway, fennel, or juniper berries (optional)

1 Remove the outer two layers of leaves from your cabbage and set them aside. Quarter and core the cabbage, then thinly shred it.

2 Add the shredded cabbage to a bowl and sprinkle liberally with salt (I use about 1 teaspoon). Toss and allow to sit for 10 minutes.

3 Massage the salt into the cabbage until it releases enough liquid to form a brine (you'll know it's ready when it releases a thin stream of liquid when squeezed). If it doesn't seem like the cabbage is releasing liquid, add a bit more salt and keep massaging.

4 Give the brine a quick taste: It should taste salty like the sea. If it seems like the brine needs a bit more salt, you can always add more and massage it in.

5 Pack the cabbage and brine tightly into two glass pint jars. Using your hand—either flat or balled into a fist—or the back of a ladle or a wooden sauerkraut pounder, press your cabbage down firmly to release any air bubbles and ensure that the brine will cover it. If your cabbage is not completely covered, add more brine. If you find there are still air bubbles, gently slide a chopstick or knife down the edge of your jar to release them.

6 Fold over one of the reserved outer cabbage leaves and place it on top of the shredded cabbage in the jar. This top leaf keeps the shredded cabbage in the brine. Make sure the leaf itself is also submerged in the brine.

7 Place a lid on each jar and set the jars on a baking sheet or plate. Allow them to ferment out of direct sunlight for 2 to 3 weeks (or longer, if desired, which will soften the cabbage and make it more sour). Loosen each lid and check your ferment at least every couple of days, making sure all the cabbage stays submerged in the brine. If you need to add more brine, use a solution of 1 teaspoon salt dissolved in 2 cups water.

8 Once your kraut is as sour as you'd like, store it in the fridge in an airtight container (like the jars you fermented it in). It can keep for several months if it stays submerged in brine.

Sauerkraut

Playing with Kraut

Sauerkraut is a delicious template for your wildest flavor imaginings. It's a flexible, forgiving, and fun ferment that offers endless possibilities. Add grated carrot, pomegranate seeds, lemon zest, or those caraway and fennel seeds you've been itching to use. Challenge yourself to make new flavor combinations just with what's available on a given day in your garden, at the farmers' market, or on your foraging adventures. Sauerkraut sparks a sense of wonder and excitement in me—and I hope it does the same for you, too.

PLAYING WITH FLAVORS

You can put just about anything in sauerkraut. Some vegetables work better than others (a primarily kale-based kraut, for example, can get sulfuric quickly), but just about any flavor combination you can imagine is worth trying.

Try dried herbs and spices: These may include classic pickling spices like dill and black peppercorn, classic sauerkraut spicing like caraway and fennel seeds, or any other favorites. Or try a warming kraut made with baking spices.

Try aromatics: Classic pickling aromatics like garlic work great, but try other aromatic roots like ginger or turmeric, or expand your scope to include other concentrated flavors, like citrus zest.

Try other vegetables: Carrots, celery, and onion make a wonderful mirepoix sauerkraut. Beets add color and flavor.

Try fruit: Yes, fruit works well in sauerkraut. Add it after massaging if you don't want it to get mushed up (though a sauerkraut with mashed fruit can be fun, too). Apples are classic, but berries and pomegranate seeds are nice as well. With fruits that might go soft, add them to your kraut toward the end of the fermentation period if you want to preserve their texture.

PLAYING WITH FLOWERS

We often put herbs in our sauerkraut, but why not flowers? I started making flowerkrauts years ago, and now they're a popular staple in my kitchen and in my classes. Flowers are beautiful in kraut, whether as whole heads or just as petals, or cut into a chiffonade and distributed throughout. Fresh flowers tend to have a brighter flavor than dried flowers.

Some of my favorite flowers to use in kraut include:

- **Fresh flowers:** calendula, goldenrod, lavender, nasturtium, rose, violet
- **Fresh flowering tops:** agastache, basil, mint
- **Dried flowers with mild flavor:** blue butterfly pea, linden, violet
- **Dried flowers with more flavor:** calendula, hops, lavender, marigold, rose petals

I tend to go light on the salt in flowerkrauts and to ferment them for only 2 to 3 weeks. But there's lots of room to experiment!

You can also use flowers to make quick pickles by infusing vinegar with flowers (see page 173), then using that vinegar in your brine.

PLAYING WITH COLOR

If you love a good home science experiment, this is the sauerkraut for you. Blue butterfly peas change color when exposed to acid; adding them to your brine gives you a real-time visual measure of the brine's acidity. (Violets have a similar effect.)

To try it, make sauerkraut (page 135), but before packing into jars, add 2 to 3 tablespoons of dried blue butterfly pea flowers and mix to distribute evenly. For this experiment, pack the kraut into a quart jar rather than two pint jars.

As the kraut acidifies, the brine will go from a deep indigo blue to a vibrant purple. You'll probably notice a color change within a day or so. Interestingly, the cabbage itself doesn't turn that deep color, but it is still dyed a bit (and, of course, because it's kraut, it's still delicious).

Tip: You can reuse the colorful brine in other recipes later, which is a fun experiment and can turn your food . . . creative colors. If you're curious to try tofu the color of blue jeans, marinate it overnight in this leftover brine.

Flowerkraut before color change

Flowerkraut after color change

Coriander-and-Mustard Canned Sauerkraut

I vastly prefer fermenting sauerkraut rather than canning it (a ferment will retain its probiotic value, unlike a canned version), but canned sauerkraut can have its place, and if you use a purple cabbage, you'll get a nice red color at the end. If you do can your kraut, I encourage you to try the fermented version, too, noticing the differences in flavor and texture that come from different methods. With canned sauerkraut, the flavor remains stable over time. With fermented sauerkraut, the flavor changes as the fermentation process goes on.

— Makes 2 pints

- **2 teaspoons coriander seeds**
- **1 teaspoon yellow mustard seeds**
- **2 cups apple cider vinegar**
- **½ cup water**
- **1 medium head cabbage, shredded (4–5 cups)**
- **1 clove garlic, minced**
- **1 tablespoon salt**

1. Heat a heavy, high-sided pan over medium-high heat. Add the coriander and mustard seeds and toast them, shaking or stirring regularly, until fragrant but not burnt, 1 to 2 minutes.

2. Add the vinegar, water, cabbage, garlic, and salt. Reduce the heat to medium-low and simmer until the cabbage is softened (but al dente), 20 to 25 minutes.

3. Meanwhile, place two pint jars in your hot water bath canner and heat it up.

4. When the cabbage is softened, remove the pan from the heat. Using tongs, remove the jars from the canner. Scoop the cabbage out of the brine and pack it into the hot jars, pressing down to remove air bubbles and leaving ½ inch of headspace.

5. Pour in enough brine to cover the cabbage, again leaving ½ inch of headspace. If you run out of brine, top off the jars with a splash of vinegar.

6. Run a chopstick or other thin, nonmetal utensil along the inner edges of the jars to release any air bubbles. Wipe the rims of the jars with a clean, damp cloth. Add the lids and bands and screw down to hand tightness.

7. Process pint jars in a hot water bath canner for 15 minutes, adjusting for altitude (see page 39) if needed.

8. Let the jars cool for 24 hours before testing the seals (see page 36), then store out of direct sunlight at room temperature.

VARIATION: CARAWAY AND JUNIPER SAUERKRAUT

Replace the coriander and mustard seeds with caraway seeds and juniper berries, using 1 to 1½ tablespoons in total.

Curtido

Curtido is a tangy cabbage slaw from El Salvador that's the perfect complement to pupusas (or just about anything else). This quick-pickled version reminds me of ones I've enjoyed in food stalls and restaurants over the years. Oregano and carrots are key ingredients; some recipes use scallions or thinly sliced red onions. I've seen other add-ins, too, like sliced zucchini and fresh peppers.

As with any quick pickle, you can adjust these flavors up or down to suit your tastes. Curtido is most delicious when bright and crisp, so it works best as a refrigerator pickle, but if you must can it, do so following the instructions for canned sauerkraut.

— Makes about 2 quarts

- **1 medium head cabbage, outer leaves removed**
- **3 large carrots**
- **1½ tablespoons dried oregano**
- **¼ cup salt**
- **1 tablespoon plus 2 teaspoons sugar**
- **2 cups distilled white vinegar**
- **2 cups water**

1 Finely shred the cabbage, place it in a large bowl, and separate the pieces with your fingers.

2 Finely slice or grate the carrots. Add the carrots and oregano to the bowl with the cabbage and toss to combine.

3 Pack the mixture into two quart jars.

4 Make the brine: Combine the salt, sugar, vinegar, and water in a medium saucepan over medium-high heat. Whisk until the salt and sugar are dissolved.

5 Pour enough of the hot brine over the cabbage mixture in the jars to cover it completely.

6 Let the jars cool, then cover and transfer them to the fridge to pickle for 1 to 2 days.

7 Store the curtido in the fridge, where it will keep for at least 2 weeks.

VARIATION: FERMENTED CURTIDO

To make a fermented version, massage the cabbage and carrots together like you're making sauerkraut (page 135), then add the remaining ingredients and ferment like sauerkraut for about 2 weeks, or until it's as sour as you'd like.

Fermented Chowchow

Chowchow is a pickled relish that is popular in many parts of the southern Appalachians. Like kimchi in Korea or sauerkraut in eastern Europe, it's a pickle with many variations. You can find chowchow made with onion, garlic, corn, and more, but this simple version is how I've had it most often. The key to achieving optimal relish-y consistency is finely shredding your cabbage and finely dicing your pepper and tomatoes.

Chowchow can also be made as a sweet-and-sour quick-pickled relish, which is how you'll find it served most often (see page 140).

— Makes about 3 pints

- **½ head green cabbage**
- **½ tablespoon finely ground sea salt**
- **1 banana pepper or other pepper of your choice, diced**
- **2 large, firm green or red tomatoes, diced**

1 Core and finely shred the cabbage.

2 Transfer the cabbage to a large bowl and sprinkle it with the salt. Lightly massage the salt into the cabbage until it releases enough liquid to form a brine. Stop while the cabbage still has some crunch to it.

3 Give the brine a quick taste: It should taste salty like the sea. If it seems like the brine needs a bit more salt, add more and massage it in.

4 Pack the cabbage into jars or a crock. Top off with the brine, completely covering the cabbage. Press down on the cabbage to release any air bubbles. Then weight the cabbage to keep it submerged.

(continued on next page)

Fermented Chowchow *continued*

5 Let the mixture ferment at room temperature, checking it every day; mine usually takes about 1 week. Once it has the desired taste (chowchow is usually sour but not as lip-smackingly sour as, say, a long-aged kraut), add the pepper and tomatoes and allow the chowchow to ferment for 1 or 2 days longer.

6 Store your finished chowchow in the fridge, where it will keep for at least 3 weeks.

NOTE: You can experiment with adding the peppers and tomatoes at the beginning of the fermentation or at the very end if you want them to be extra firm (just let the chowchow sit in the fridge for 1 or 2 days before serving to let the flavors blend). As always, use your intuition and let your taste buds guide you!

Quick-Pickled Chowchow

Quick-Pickled Chowchow

As a fermentation lover, I usually gravitate toward fermented chowchow, but a lot of the chowchow I enjoy from other folks is quick pickled. It's a great, quick way to make a versatile side and condiment when your garden is in full swing.

— Makes about 2 pints

- **4 large, firm green or red tomatoes, diced**
- **1 banana pepper or other pepper of your choice, diced**
- **¾ cup apple cider vinegar or distilled white vinegar**
- **Pinch of salt**
- **½ head green cabbage, finely shredded**

1 Combine the tomatoes and pepper in a large saucepan over medium heat and bring them to a simmer.

2 Stir in the vinegar and salt. Add the cabbage and cook for 10 to 20 minutes, or until the desired texture is reached.

3 Let the chowchow cool, then transfer it to an airtight container and store in the refrigerator, where it will keep for several days.

Broccoli-Stem Refrigerator Relish

This is an easy way to use up broccoli stems. I like this as a stand-in for traditional cucumber relish on burgers and sandwiches and in potato salad. Feel free to experiment with the spices—you might try your favorite bread-and-butter pickle combo, or hot peppers and turmeric.

—— Makes about 1 pint

Stems from 2 heads broccoli, diced (1–1½ cups)

2 large cloves garlic, peeled and halved

¾–1 teaspoon dried dill weed

¼–½ teaspoon red pepper flakes

½ tablespoon salt

½ teaspoon sugar

½ cup apple cider vinegar

½ cup water

1. Combine the broccoli stems, garlic, dill, and pepper flakes in a pint jar.

2. Make the brine: Combine the salt, sugar, vinegar, and water in a saucepan over medium-high heat. Whisk until the sugar and salt are dissolved.

3. Pour enough of the hot brine over the broccoli stems to cover them completely.

4. Let the jars cool, then cover them and transfer to the fridge to pickle for 12 to 24 hours.

5. Store in the fridge, where the relish will keep for about 1 month.

Fermented Stems and Ends

This is another way to ferment and preserve foods in brine, and an easy way to use up things like kale and collard ribs or broccoli and chard stems. I tend to find that brassicas develop a sulfurous flavor if fermented for too long, so I'll let them go just long enough to soften slightly but not long enough to get pungent (maybe a couple of days). However, I know others who love a longer-fermented flavor, so experiment and find what you like it to taste like.

Brassica stems and ends (like broccoli stems)

2–3% brine (1–2 tablespoons unrefined salt dissolved in each quart of water)

Any desired flavorings (herbs, spices, aromatics)

Pack the brassica stems and ends into a jar. Pour the brine over the veggies. Secure the lid and let ferment, remembering to burp the jar at least once a day, until the vegetables have a flavor you enjoy. Store the finished fermented pickles in the fridge, where they'll last for 2 weeks or more if stored completely submerged in brine.

Carrots

Choose firm, crisp carrots that snap easily. If they have greens still attached, the greens should be fresh and bright. Store carrots in the refrigerator crisper in a ziplock bag; they'll stay fresh and crisp for 2 to 3 weeks. Some people wrap them in a damp paper towel before storing.

Carrot greens hasten the wilting of carrots, so take them off as soon as you get your carrots into the kitchen. But don't toss them! Store carrot greens as you would fresh herbs, wrapped in a damp paper towel or kitchen towel in an airtight container. You can use them to make pesto, as a stand-in for parsley, or in any dish that would benefit from the addition of fresh greens.

DRYING

It's important to use fresh, crisp, tender carrots for drying if you want them to have good texture when you rehydrate them in dishes later. While you don't have to peel them, the final texture can be improved by doing so (save your peels for making jam; see page 146).

Thoroughly wash the carrots to remove any dirt, then cut off the tops and root tips. Cut into ½-inch-thick rounds or strips. Blanch for 3 to 3½ minutes in steam or boiling water, then shock in an ice bath to cool (see page 17). Dehydrate at 140°F/60°C for 10 to 12 hours, or until brittle and crisp.

FREEZING

Trim off any greens and the ends, and peel. Small carrots can be left whole; cut larger carrots into strips, cubes, or slices. Blanch in boiling water for 5 minutes (for small whole carrots) or 2 minutes (for pieces). Drain and pat dry. Lay the carrots in a single layer on a rimmed sheet pan, freeze, then transfer to containers and store in the freezer.

Ways to Preserve Carrots	Shelf-stable	Fast	Low waste	Ready meals and ingredients	Big flavor
Rainbow Roots Soup Starter (page 107)				X	X
Fermented Beet-and-Carrot Sauce (page 127)				X	X
Carrot "Lox" (page 143)				X	X
Fermented Carrot Sticks (page 144)		X		X	X
Quick-Pickled Carrots (page 144)		X		X	X
Bread-and-Butter Carrots (page 145)	X				X
Root Vegetable Jam (page 146)	X		X		X
Frozen Mirepoix and Trinity (page 196)		X		X	

You can also freeze carrots as a purée: Cook until tender, drain, and mash. Allow to cool completely, then pack into containers, leaving the appropriate headspace (see page 17), and freeze.

PICKLING AND FERMENTING

Quick-pickled carrots and fermented carrots are staples in my house: Carrot sticks make a quick, healthy addition that rounds out my lunch, even when I'm just reheating leftovers; and because carrots' hearty and floral flavor can go in so many directions, I never run out of ways to experiment and create. Here are a few of my favorites.

Carrot "Lox"

While I find most vegetable-based meat replacements hit-or-miss, carrot "lox" is delicious in its own right. Miso is an important ingredient here: Red or barley miso is best, but you can use other types of miso if needed.

This vegan topping is great on sandwiches, bagels, and salads. I use just enough liquid smoke to give that traditional lox-like smoky flavor; feel free to skip the liquid smoke if you don't like the taste—or add an extra splash if you love it!

—— Makes about 1 pint

- **1 pound carrots**
- **½ cup water**
- **1½ tablespoons mugi (barley) miso or red miso**
- **1 tablespoon drained capers**
- **¾ tablespoon dark soy sauce**
- **½ tablespoon rice wine vinegar**
- **⅛ teaspoon liquid smoke (optional)**
- **1 sheet nori or 1 tablespoon fish sauce**
- **Juice of 1 lemon**
- **3 (2-inch) strips lemon peel (optional)**

1. Shave the carrots into long, thin strips with a vegetable peeler. Set aside.
2. Place a large saucepan of water over high heat.
3. While the water heats up, make your marinade: Add the water, miso, capers, soy sauce, vinegar, liquid smoke (if using), nori, and lemon juice to a blender, and blend until combined. (If you don't have a blender, finely chop the capers and whisk them together with the remaining ingredients.)
4. Place the lemon peel (if using) in the bottom of a pint jar or other container.
5. When the water in the pot comes to a boil, add the carrot strips and blanch for 2 to 3 minutes, until just tender, then drain.
6. Transfer the hot carrots to a mixing bowl and pour the marinade over them. Toss until evenly coated.
7. Place the carrots in the jar and let them cool. Press the carrots down gently to make sure the marinade covers them, then cover the jar and transfer it to the fridge.
8. Your lox is already delicious, but for best flavor, let it sit in the fridge for 1 to 2 days. It will keep in the fridge for at least 1 month.

Fermented Carrot Sticks

I don't mean to be dramatic here, but I eat fermented carrot sticks *every day*. They are easy to make, and you can offer them with dip for a snack, cut them up on salads, serve them as a dinner side, or do whatever else strikes your fancy. Ferment these carrot sticks for just a few days for a mild flavor or longer for a stronger, more sour bite. I never peel mine (I do scrub them thoroughly, though). I suggest a few spice ideas in the recipe, but feel free to use any spices you desire.

— Makes 1 pint

2 carrots, halved or quartered and cut into 2-inch sticks

Herbs and spices, like peppercorns, crushed red pepper, or dill seeds (combined as desired; optional)

2 cups water

½ tablespoon salt

1 Pack the carrots and spices (if using) into a pint jar, leaving 1 inch of headspace.

2 Make the brine: Combine the water and salt in a small saucepan over medium heat. Whisk until the salt is dissolved.

3 Pour enough hot brine into the jar to cover the carrots completely. Lightly screw on the lid.

4 Set the jar on a tray or plate out of direct sunlight. Let the carrots ferment for 4 to 7 days, or until they have a flavor you enjoy. Store the fermented carrots in the fridge, where they will keep for at least 2 weeks.

Quick-Pickled Carrots

I find pickled carrots to be a gift that everyone is happy to receive. I usually use distilled white vinegar or apple cider vinegar for a light flavor, and I keep the seasoning simple. I love using multicolored carrots here. Preserving them as refrigerator pickles rather than pouring hot brine over them helps maintain their color. Serve these pickled carrots alongside appetizers and snacks, or finely dice them and toss with yogurt or oil and vinegar for a simple salad dressing.

— Makes about 1½ quarts

⅓ cup salt

4 cups distilled white vinegar or apple cider vinegar

4 cups water

8 medium carrots, thinly sliced (4 cups)

A few parsley or dill stems for flavoring (optional)

1–2 teaspoons dill seeds

1 Make the brine: Combine the salt, vinegar, and water in a saucepan over medium heat, whisking until the salt is dissolved. Cool to room temperature.

2 Add the carrots, parsley (if using), and dill to a jar or other food-safe container.

3 Pour the brine over the carrots, making sure they are completely covered. Seal tightly and transfer to the fridge. Allow to pickle for 1 to 2 days.

4 Store the carrots in the fridge, where they will keep for at least 1 month (just be sure they stay under the brine).

Bread-and-Butter Carrots

I'm rarely a bread-and-butter pickle fan, but I make an exception for these carrots. Their minimal sweetness is layered with plenty of spices to make them more complex than your standard store-bought versions.

They're great as a garnish and topping, of course, but they're also really good alongside sweet and savory snacks and as an end-of-meal treat. I enjoy them as a palate cleanser between dinner and dessert. This recipe makes a lot, so they're great as gifts, too.

—— Makes about 2 quarts

- ⅛ cup salt
- ⅛ cup sugar
- 4 cups distilled white vinegar
- 4 cups water
- 16 medium carrots, sliced (8 cups)
- 1 bay leaf
- 2 teaspoons black peppercorns
- 1 teaspoon coriander seeds
- ¼ teaspoon celery seeds
- ¼ teaspoon brown mustard seeds
- ¼ teaspoon yellow mustard seeds
- ⅛ teaspoon whole cloves

1. Make the brine: Combine the salt, sugar, vinegar, and water in a saucepan over medium heat and whisk until the salt and sugar are dissolved. Cool to room temperature.

2. Divide the carrots, bay leaf, peppercorns, coriander, celery seeds, brown mustard seeds, yellow mustard seeds, and cloves between two quart jars or other food-safe containers.

3. Pour the brine over the carrot mixture, making sure everything is completely covered.

4. Seal tightly and transfer to the fridge. Allow to pickle for 1 to 2 days. The carrots will keep in the fridge for at least 1 month (just keep them under the brine).

Carrot-Top Pesto Is Magic

If you've never had carrot greens, you're in for a treat (and if you have, you know what I'm talking about!). Carrot greens are my go-to stand-in for parsley; they have a similar but milder flavor. I recommend chopping them fine, as their texture is coarser and denser than parsley, before sprinkling on your dishes.

You can also blend carrot greens for pesto, add them to your favorite green herbaceous sauces (I particularly like them in chimichurri), blend them into soups, infuse them in vinegar, or use them to flavor sauerkraut. To make carrot-top pesto, simply swap carrot tops for basil in your favorite pesto recipe.

MAKING JAM

"Vegetable jam? Really?!" I hear you ask. Trust me, vegetables have as much a place in your jam pot as your favorite fruit. Some vegetables, like carrots, are naturally sweet, lending themselves to jammy applications. The texture of these jams tends to be a bit different than fruits high in pectin, but they're just as delicious.

Root Vegetable Jam

If you've got a bumper crop of carrots and beets, this sweet-yet-savory jam is a wonderful and unexpected way to use them up. It maintains a bit of texture from the dense roots. The color is amazing, too!

— Makes 4 half-pints

- **6 cups grated carrots and/or beets (from 6–8 large carrots, 4–6 large beets, or a combination)**
- **3 cups sugar**
- **2 cups water**
- **½ cup dried raisins, golden raisins, or dried cranberries**
- **¼ cup honey**
- **Zest of 1 lemon**
- **2 tablespoons bottled lemon juice**
- **1 teaspoon ground cinnamon**
- **¼–½ teaspoon fine sea salt**
- **Freshly ground black pepper**

1 Combine the grated root vegetables, sugar, water, raisins, honey, lemon zest and juice, cinnamon, salt, and pepper to taste in a large saucepan over medium-high heat. Bring the mixture to a boil, then reduce the heat and let it simmer uncovered, stirring occasionally, for 45 to 50 minutes, until the root vegetables are soft and the liquid is reduced by about half, creating a syrup.

2 Meanwhile, place four half-pint jars in your hot water bath canner and heat it up.

3 Once the shredded veggies are toothsome but tender, remove the saucepan from the heat. Using tongs, remove the jars from the canner. Scoop the veggies out of the syrup and into the hot jars, leaving 1 inch of headspace.

4 Pour enough of the hot syrup into the jars to cover the vegetables, leaving ½ inch of headspace. (Note: If you have extra syrup left over, it is great in cocktails or drizzled over desserts.)

5 Press the vegetables down gently with the back of a spoon to remove any air bubbles. Wipe the rims of the jars with a clean, damp cloth. Place the lids and bands on the jars and screw down to hand tightness.

6 Process half-pints in a hot water bath canner for 15 minutes, adjusting for altitude (see page 39) if needed.

7 Let the jars cool for 24 hours before testing the seals (see page 36), then store out of direct sunlight at room temperature.

VARIATION: CARROT/BEET PEEL JAM

If you have carrot and/or beet peels left over from another cooking project, roughly chop them and use them in place of some or all of the grated vegetables in this recipe.

VARIATION: CARROT CAKE JAM

Carrot cake with cream cheese icing was my mom's favorite. She often put raisins in it, though that wasn't traditional to our official family recipe, handed down from my great-grandma and grandma. So I sometimes skip the beets and make root vegetable jam entirely with carrots, a version inspired by my family's traditional carrot cake recipe but made in honor of my mom.

Carrot Cake Jam

Celery

Choose crisp, fresh celery in compact bunches that are heavy for their size, with firm rather than wilted leaves (if there are leaves) and without pink discoloration on the cut ends. You can cut celery into pieces for a ready-to-add ingredient for stir-fries and other dishes, or keep heads whole. Wrap in foil, then store in the crisper drawer.

Celeriac (celery root) is a celery variety grown for its root rather than stems. Select firm, young roots that are dense and heavy for their size (older roots can become tough and woody). Scrub the root thoroughly with a brush to remove dirt, be sure to *very* thoroughly pat dry, keep any stalks in place, and store in a zippered bag in the fridge. It will keep for a very long time—even months, in some cases. Trim off any remaining roots from the outside and peel before using.

DRYING

While I often have carrots and onions, I don't always have celery, so dried celery (or frozen; see opposite) is a great option to have on hand when I want to make a soup and don't want to head to the store to round out my mirepoix.

Trim the celery stalks and wash thoroughly. Slice them ¼ inch thick, then blanch (in steam or boiling water) for 2 minutes. Shock in an ice bath to cool (see page 17). Drain and pat dry. Arrange your pieces in a single layer on a dehydrator tray at 140°F/60°C, then dry for 10 to 16 hours, or until brittle. (If you prefer, you can slice your stalks ¼ inch thick lengthwise rather than in small pieces; still blanch for 2 minutes, but note the drying time may be shorter.)

Ways to Preserve Celery

	Shelf-stable	Fast	Low waste	Ready meals and ingredients	Big flavor
Rainbow Roots Soup Starter (page 107)				X	X
Celery Vinegar and Celery Vodka (page 149)		X			X
Celery Salt and Celery-Leaf Seasoning (page 149)	X		X	X	X
Pickled Celeriac (page 150)					X
Frozen Mirepoix and Trinity (page 196)		X		X	

CELERY SALT AND CELERY-LEAF SEASONING

Celery salt can be made by mixing ground dried celery or celery seeds with salt.

Or you can dry celery leaves in a 200°F/93°C oven for 20 to 25 minutes or a dehydrator at 135°F/57°C for 40 to 60 minutes, or until they are crisp, brittle, and crumble easily. Allow them to cool completely. Mix them with salt (start at a 1:1 ratio), or use ground leaves as is for a salt-free seasoning. Store in an airtight container at room temperature and use within several months.

FREEZING

Frozen celery becomes soft when thawed, but it is still a wonderful ingredient for cooked dishes like soups and stews. Remove any thick strings from the celery stalks, then wash and cut them into 1-inch-long pieces. Blanch them in boiling water for 3 minutes, then shock in an ice bath to cool (see page 17). Package with no headspace and freeze, or freeze in a single layer on a rimmed sheet pan and then transfer to freezer-safe containers with no headspace.

You can also freeze celery in ready-made mixes for soups—check out Rainbow Roots Soup Starter (page 107) or Frozen Mirepoix and Trinity (page 196).

Celeriac also freezes well. Wash it, trim off any remaining roots from the outside, peel, and cut into ½- to 1-inch cubes. Blanch in boiling water for 4 minutes. Shock in an ice bath to cool, then freeze in a single layer on a rimmed sheet pan and transfer to freezer-safe containers with no headspace.

INFUSING

Celery can be infused in vinegar, which is a nice way to add celery flavor to your meals if you find you ran out of the fresh stuff (using dried celery seeds is, of course, another great option). It also infuses well in clear spirits; try infusing vodka with celery to bring some extra flavor to Bloody Marys.

Celery Vinegar and Celery Vodka

This is perfect for Bloody Marys! You can make these infusions using full stalks of celery, as described here, or use celery leftovers from other projects—the trimmings, leafy bits, or scraps of the root. If using vinegar, use white wine vinegar, distilled white vinegar, or apple cider vinegar. Also note that the same method can be used with chopped celeriac.

Celery, cut into 1-inch-long batons

Vodka or vinegar, to cover

1. Fill a jar about one-third to half full of loosely packed celery. Because celery is watery, you don't want it too full, or it will dilute your alcohol or vinegar, introducing the possibility of pathogen growth.

2. Add vodka or vinegar to cover completely, making sure the celery stays submerged.

3. Let steep for 2 to 4 weeks. Strain and store out of direct sunlight.

PICKLING

Celery's savory flavor naturally lends itself to pickling. You might already be aware of its pickle magic if you use celery seeds as a seasoning for pickles (try it with Fermented Carrot Sticks, page 144). Thinly sliced pickled celery makes a fantastic topper for sandwiches or addition to chicken or egg salad, and the spears (and pickling brine) are great additions to a Bloody Mary. I also love the brine for a Pickle Brine Martini (page 69).

Pickled Celeriac

Celeriac, or celery root, is delicious roasted, but I also love it pickled. Cut into thin slices to top sandwiches, or in matchsticks to serve as a side. This same method also works with other dense root vegetables, like turnips. You could also substitute 1½ teaspoons five-spice powder and ½ teaspoon red pepper flakes for the spices, if you like.

—— Makes about 1 quart

- **1 (1–2-pound) celery root**
- **1⅓ cup water**
- **¾ cup distilled white vinegar, apple cider vinegar, or white wine vinegar**
- **½ tablespoon salt**
- **1 teaspoon pink peppercorns**
- **¼–½ teaspoon green or black peppercorns**
- **1 strip lemon zest**

1. Scrub the celeriac with a brush under water to remove dirt, then peel. Cut in half, then cut into thin slices or into thick or thin matchsticks.

2. Add the celeriac to a jar or other food-safe, nonreactive container.

3. Make the brine: Add the water, vinegar, salt, peppercorns, and lemon zest to a saucepan over medium-high heat and heat just until boiling and fragrant.

4. Pour the hot brine over the celeriac, then allow to cool. Seal and transfer to the fridge. Let pickle for 24 to 48 hours, or until pickled through (the thicker the pieces, the longer it takes). It will last for a month or more in the refrigerator.

Corn (Fresh)

Choose corn with tender, plump kernels. If harvesting corn fresh, harvest it at the milk stage, and choose ears with a tight husk that peels back in single pieces rather than breaking apart. For preserving dried corn, see Chapter 8.

DRYING

Use only tender, fresh sweet corn with plump, mature kernels. Blanch the whole, husked cobs for 3 to 4 minutes (boiling water) or 4 to 5 minutes (steam). Shock in an ice bath to cool (see page 17), then cut the kernels from the cobs. (To remove the kernels, place each corncob upright in a bowl and carefully run a knife from top to bottom to cut the kernels from the cob. The bowl will catch the kernels, and you can set the cob aside for other uses.) Lay the kernels in a single layer on dehydrator trays and dry at 140°F/60°C for 6 to 8 hours or until brittle. Allow the kernels to cool completely, then label and store in an airtight container out of direct sunlight.

You can also dry corn silk for tea, which is a traditional remedy for some gastrointestinal complaints. Dry it in a thin layer at 135 to 140°F/57 to 60°C for several hours or until crisp and brittle. Allow it to cool completely, then label and store in an airtight container out of direct sunlight.

FREEZING

Blanch kernels in boiling water for 3½ to 4 minutes, shock in an ice bath to cool (see page 17), and drain well. Package leaving ½ inch of headspace, or freeze in a single layer on a rimmed sheet pan, then place in an airtight container with no headspace.

Corn on the cob can be frozen: Blanch small ears (1¼ inches or less in diameter) in boiling water for 7 to 7½ minutes, medium-size ears (1¼ to 1½ inches in diameter) for 8½ to 9 minutes, and large ears (over 1½ inches in diameter) for 10½ to 11 minutes. Shock in ice water immediately after blanching to prevent them from tasting like their cobs. Drain well. Freeze in a single layer on a rimmed sheet pan, then place in an airtight container with no headspace.

Ways to Preserve Corn

	Shelf-stable	Fast	Low waste	Ready meals and ingredients	Big flavor
Corncob Stock (below)			X		
Sour Corn (page 152)		X			X
Sunny Blueberry-Corn Jam (page 273)	X				X

Corncob Stock

Fresh corncobs can also be frozen after the kernels have been removed and saved to make corncob stock. Use the stock in place of water in recipes where you want a bit of extra corn flavor.

Fresh corncobs, kernels removed

1 Freeze corncobs in a single layer on a rimmed sheet pan, then store in an airtight container with no headspace.

2 When ready to use, either add other aromatics to make a stock, or make corncob stock. Place the corncobs in a large pot and add just enough water to cover. Simmer over low heat until fragrant and flavorful, roughly 20 to 30 minutes, depending on the number of cobs and the amount of water. The goal is to pull the last bits of corn flavor from your cobs but not to cook them so much that the stock just tastes like the cobs themselves.

3 Cool completely and store in the fridge.

PICKLING AND FERMENTING

Sweet corn is a treat fresh, but it's perfect as a pickle, too. The plump, sweet kernels stay firm with shorter fermenting times and with quick pickling. And the burst of sweet-and-sour flavor you get when you bite into sour corn is absolutely divine.

QUICK-PICKLED CORN

I especially love making quick-pickled corn with finely diced fresh jalapeño and shredded carrot. Add corn kernels, and whatever other vegetables you want, to a pint jar with my basic pickling brine (see page 53) and 1 to 2 teaspoons of your favorite spices. Let sit in the fridge overnight before serving.

Sour Corn

Sour Corn

Sour corn is a food I associate with the southern Appalachians and is a dish that, according to regional oral traditions, has been prepared by the Eastern Band of Cherokee Indians since precolonial times. You can ferment the whole corn on the cob, you can cut the corncobs into a few pieces, or you can strip the kernels from the cobs and ferment them. (You can then save the cobs to simmer for corn stock or slice them, dry them, and grind them to make flour.) Sour corn ferments relatively quickly, so it's a great choice if you're looking for a ferment with a minimal time investment.

I sometimes throw in some grated or diced vegetables, particularly grated carrot, but sour corn is already amazing all on its own.

—— Makes about 2 quarts

- **6–8 whole ears of corn**
- **4–5% brine (2½–3 tablespoons unrefined salt dissolved in 1 quart water)**
- **Handful of shredded carrot (optional)**
- **Handful of diced green bell pepper (optional)**

1. If you have a large crock or barrel to play with, it can be fun to ferment whole corn on the cob. Shuck your corn (remove the husks and silk) and pack it into a large crock. Alternatively, cut each corncob into rounds and stack them in a container, or remove the kernels and just ferment those.

2. Pour the brine over the corn, completely covering it; use additional brine if needed. Add the carrot and diced pepper (if using).

3. Put a weight on your corn, or be ready to give it a stir a couple of times a day to keep yeast from growing on top of the brine.

4. Cover the corn with a cloth or lid and let it ferment at room temperature, checking daily. Once the corn tastes as sour as you'd like (usually a few days in warm weather and 5 to 7 days in winter), store it in the fridge, where it will last for at least 2 weeks.

Preserving Around the World

The Chinese Diaspora, with Su-Jit Lin

For food writer Su-Jit Lin, preserved foods are a thread that ties the cuisine of her family to their ancestral home in China and their adopted home in the United States. Lin's parents were born in Fuzhou: Her mom moved to Hong Kong and then the States at 12, her dad at 18.

"In my family and experience, which is Fuzhounese with strong Cantonese influences and American Chinese, fermentation is a core part of creating deep, intense flavors," Lin says. This includes black bean paste in sauces, pickled and fermented foods in stir-fries, fish sauce, and a mix of sweet-and-sour pickled items alongside jook (plain congee/rice porridge), which is eaten for breakfast.

Lin's family relies on dried foods like salted and dried seafood to season soups and vegetables, but they aren't eaten dried. "The key is rehydration of the dried things. We subscribe to hot and cold foods (*yeet hay* in Cantonese), which really, now that I think about it, translates to 'water content.' For example, lettuce is a cooling food and so would steamed broccoli be; roasted Brussels sprouts or dry-fry green beans are not. Because Chinese food is all about blended balance in most regions, we do a lot of reconstitution to bring the energy levels to an equilibrium."

For many immigrants, being in a new place means finding new ways to cook familiar dishes, but for Lin's family, restaurateurs with access to Manhattan's Chinatown plus Flushing's Chinatown in Queens, finding what they need is easier than for many. Or they make it themselves, as in the case of Fuzhou hong zhao, red rice wine, which her dad ferments: "He keeps a jar of the starter in the fridge like a prized sourdough!"

Movement between places, and sharing information between generations, also means a risk of loss, whether of a long-standing preserving tradition or a beloved family recipe: "It makes the food my family serves at get-togethers more precious—I'm more conscious that it could disappear. And in the United States, especially now that we're even entering the era of second-generation immigrants and many first-genners are creating their own food brands in preservation of their own cultural food histories, [I'm conscious] that individual families are losing some of our own personal recipes as well, since we look to convenience and packaged solutions—quick ways to recapture a taste memory, where close enough is good enough."

Lin's cooking has veered more American over time, though not entirely. She mixes American vegetables with Chinese flavors and techniques, or she adds Chinese ingredients to Japanese, Korean, and Mexican dishes because she knows how the flavors will build on each other.

And preserving cultural traditions also becomes harder when your traditions are devalued in Western culture at large: "Slow cooking is a luxury white cuisines have—they're the fine dining pinnacle and can advertise the painstakingness and charge accordingly for the time. Asian cuisine, outside of Japanese, is still largely expected to be fast and cheap, with little to no education about how long prep takes to create fast and cheap on the spot. My dad's brown sauce concentrate took hours to make and days to steep . . . and in this way, he was able to throw together entrées in 10 minutes."

Fermented Cucumbers: Adapting Preserves to Place

Cucumbers can be a challenge to ferment because they have a high water content, and they also contain an enzyme that hastens their decline from delicious to mush. This is particularly true in hot weather: Cucumber pickles were traditionally made in cooler climates, so folks in hot places might find their cucumbers get squishy quickly.

Pickled cucumbers are a reminder of how important it is to think about the food you're preserving within the context of its historical space. Many recipes for and traditions of fermented cucumbers come from eastern Europe, where temperatures are quite different from a summer day in, for example, Georgia, where I live.

That's not to say it's impossible to make full sour cucumber pickles in Georgia; we just have to adjust the original technique. After all, our preservation practices change depending on where we are. It's a reminder that many of our beloved foods come from different places, and they've been adapted to root into each place as we and our recipes move around the world.

Preservation is not only about the preservation of food but also the adaptation to a new culture and a new geographic environment, because food preservation of all kinds is deeply intertwined with geographic space: What seasons are things prevalent (or not prevalent), and how long are those seasons? How hot and cold does it get, and for how long? All these factors influence what can grow, along with what, when, and how much we will be able to preserve. When we learn more about the history of the foods we preserve, our knowledge of them deepens.

PREVENTING MUSHY FERMENTED PICKLES

There are a few ways you can prevent mushy pickles, for cucumbers or other similar watery vegetables like zucchini.

ADD TANNINS. A must-do when making fermented cucumber pickles is to add something that will put tannins into your brine. Grape leaves are traditional; you can also use tea leaves, oak leaves, or other edible tannic leaves. You can also add brewed tea into your brine rather than whole leaves.

SHORTEN YOUR FERMENTATION TIME. Especially in warm weather, this can help reduce the risk of mush. Instead of setting your sights on making monthlong fermented full sours, if you live in Georgia and it's August, focus your attention on making a much shorter fermented half sour. The best way to do this is to ferment your cucumbers until the color *just* starts to change. It should be a little brighter and lighter than it was when your cucumbers were raw (this just takes a matter of days!).

INCREASE YOUR SALT. Adding more salt can help slow the rate of fermentation slightly, which can keep your pickles from zipping past perfectly tart to mush before you can blink.

REMOVE THE BLOSSOM END. This is where those squish-making enzymes are concentrated. Just cut off the last ¼ inch to help keep pickles crisp.

Cucumbers

In addition to having my favorite botanical family name, cucurbits include some of my favorite veggies—such as cucumbers, summer squash, and winter squash. In this section we're focusing on cucumbers, which, if you grow them yourself, ripen in droves when in season, making preservation a must.

DRYING

Dried cucumbers lose most of their volume, stick to the trays, and do not maintain much flavor. That said, you *can* dry your Canned Dill Pickle Chips (page 159) into, well, dried pickle chips, because the pickling brine removes some of their water and imparts flavor that holds up to the drying process. Dry at 140°F/60°C for 4 to 10 hours (no need to blanch beforehand); just be sure to pat dry very thoroughly before drying to keep them from sticking to the trays.

PICKLING AND FERMENTING

When most people think "pickles," they're thinking of pickled cucumbers, so much so that the word *pickles* is interchangeable with *cucumber pickles* in the English language. Pickled cucumbers have a long, long history, particularly in more temperate climates where they can be fermented easily, and you'll find thousands of variations to the theme in cookbooks and online. Here are the ways pickled and fermented cucumbers show up in my kitchen.

Ways to Preserve Cucumbers	Shelf-stable	Fast	Low waste	Ready meals and ingredients	Big flavor
Half Sours and Full Sours (page 156)		X			
Dill Refrigerator Pickles (page 156)		X			
Garlic Refrigerator Pickles (page 157)				X	X
Cornichons (page 157)	X				X
Sweet-and-Sour Cucumber Salad (page 158)				X	X
Summery Cucumber Salad (page 158)				X	X
Canned Dill Pickle Chips (page 159)	X				
Mountain Cabin Cucumber Salad (page 160)				X	X

Half Sours and Full Sours

Making half-sour and full-sour pickles follows the same process: The difference is the amount of time you let the pickles ferment. Half sours are only fermented for a short time; they have a brighter green flavor and a crisp, crunchy texture. Full sours are fermented longer; they have more of a deep, dull, or olive green color and more of a sour bite. As always, play with the spices to adjust to your taste.

Here's a tip: You can use the leftover brine like you would the brine from quick-pickled cucumbers—in marinades and brines for meat and vegetables, in sauces and dips, or as a chaser for a whiskey pickleback shot (the only shot you can convince me to take).

—— Makes 1 quart

4–8 whole cucumbers, depending on size
1–2 cloves garlic
1–2 teaspoons dill seeds
½–1 teaspoon red pepper flakes
½ teaspoon coriander seeds
½ teaspoon black peppercorns
1 quart 3% brine (2 tablespoons unrefined salt dissolved in 1 quart water)

1 Place the cucumbers, garlic, dill, pepper flakes, coriander, and peppercorns in a quart jar or other food-safe, nonreactive container.

2 Pour room-temperature brine over the cucumbers to completely cover them, ensuring that they stay submerged.

3 Cover the jar, place it on a tray or plate in case the ferment bubbles over, and allow the pickles to ferment out of direct sunlight. Fermentation time can vary depending on temperature and your final goal. Half sours may take several days, and full sours usually take at least 1 week, often longer. Store finished pickles in the fridge, where they will last for at least a few weeks.

Dill Refrigerator Pickles

Quick-pickled cucumbers are what most modern folks are familiar with from the grocery store—all the shelf-stable major brands are pickled in vinegar rather than fermented.

Most store-bought varieties leave me wanting, but not these homemade dill pickles. I cut them into spears after pickling and before serving, leaving the pickles whole in the brine until I'm ready for them, but you can cut them up (or not) however you want. Note that you can adapt this recipe to summer squash (particularly zucchini) if you have those rather than cucumbers.

—— Makes about 4 quarts

1 head garlic, cloves removed and peeled (about 12 cloves)
1 bunch fresh dill weed
4 sprigs thyme
About 5 pounds pickling cucumbers, 3–4 inches in length
3 tablespoons coriander seeds
4 bay leaves
¼ cup black peppercorns
2–3 teaspoons red pepper flakes
½–¾ cup salt
8 cups water
6 cups apple cider vinegar
2 cups distilled white vinegar

1 Add half of the garlic, plus all of the dill and thyme, to a 1-gallon food-safe container, or divide between four quart jars.

2 Add the whole cucumbers, leaving 1 inch of headspace.

3 Make the brine: Combine the remaining garlic, coriander, bay leaves, peppercorns, pepper flakes, salt, water, and vinegars in a large pot. Heat until simmering. Remove from the heat and let cool slightly before pouring over the

cucumbers to cover. If using separate jars, evenly divide the spices between jars (using 1 bay leaf per jar). Leave ½ inch of headspace.

4 Allow the pickles to cool completely, then cover and place in the refrigerator. Let sit for 24 hours, or until pickled through, before eating. Store pickles in the refrigerator, where they will last for 3 weeks or more.

Garlic Refrigerator Pickles

I love garlic, and these pickles are a versatile ingredient to have in your fridge; you'll be ready to add a garlicky, sour-and-salty bite to whatever it is you're cooking. I use them to jazz up sandwiches and burgers or dice them to add to potato salad.

— Makes about 4 quarts

- **About 5 pounds pickling cucumbers, 3–4 inches in length**
- **¾ cup salt**
- **8–10 cloves garlic, peeled**
- **2–4 bay leaves**
- **2–3 tablespoons black peppercorns**
- **2–3 tablespoons dill seeds**
- **1 tablespoon brown mustard seeds**
- **½ tablespoon coriander seeds**
- **½ tablespoon fennel seeds**
- **½ tablespoon yellow mustard seeds**
- **½ teaspoon celery seeds**
- **⅛ teaspoon whole cloves**
- **2 quarts water**
- **1½ quarts distilled white vinegar**
- **½ quart apple cider vinegar**

1 Add the whole cucumbers to a 1-gallon food-safe container or divide between four quart jars, leaving 1 inch of headspace.

2 Make the brine: Combine the salt, garlic, bay leaves, peppercorns, dill seeds, brown mustard seeds, coriander, fennel seeds, yellow mustard seeds, celery seeds, cloves, water, and vinegars in a large pot. Heat until simmering. Take off the heat and let cool slightly before pouring over the cucumbers to cover. If using separate jars, evenly divide the spices between jars (using 1 bay leaf per jar). Leave ½ inch of headspace.

3 Allow the pickles to cool completely, then cover and place in the refrigerator. Let sit for 24 hours, or until pickled through, before eating. Store pickles in the refrigerator, where they will last for 3 weeks or more.

Cornichons

Cornichons are adorable, tiny baby pickled cucumbers—a must-have in my kitchen and on the plates of cheese and crackers I eat for quick lunches. I've seen versions with apple cider vinegar instead of white wine vinegar, with peeled pearl onions instead of sliced shallot, and with all kinds of spices (but always mustard seeds). If you have a bumper crop of cucumbers and have some small ones on the vine, this is a nice way to enjoy them.

— Makes about 1 quart

- **3½–4 cups baby cucumbers, 2–3 inches in length**
- **½ small shallot, sliced**
- **2 sprigs tarragon**
- **1 bay leaf**
- **2 teaspoons yellow mustard seeds**
- **1½ teaspoons brown mustard seeds**
- **1 teaspoon black peppercorns**
- **¼ teaspoon whole allspice berries**
- **Freshly grated nutmeg**
- **¼ cup salt**
- **2 cups white wine vinegar**
- **2 cups water**

(continued on next page)

Cornichons *continued*

1 Put the cucumbers, shallot, tarragon, bay leaf, mustard seeds, peppercorns, allspice, and nutmeg to taste into a quart jar or other food-safe container, leaving 1 inch of headspace.

2 Make the brine: Combine the salt, vinegar, and water in a pot over medium heat, just until simmering. Take off the heat and let cool slightly.

3 Pour the brine over the cucumbers to cover, leaving ½ inch of headspace.

4 Allow the jars to cool completely, then cover and place in the refrigerator. Let sit for 24 hours, or until pickled through, before eating. Store in the refrigerator, where they will last for 1 month or more.

Sweet-and-Sour Cucumber Salad

This recipe is straight from my mom's recipe box. If you grew up going to lots of potlucks in the US Midwest or South, you have probably had some variation of this sweet-and-sour cucumber salad. I've encountered many iterations across many cultures, and it's a great template for whatever spicing you want to try.

What differentiates a cucumber salad from a bowl of cucumber pickles? To me, it's a slightly less acidic, slightly sweeter brine, relatively clean flavors, and thin slices of cucumber rather than thick coins or spears.

— Makes about 1 pint

1 large cucumber
½ cup sugar
1 teaspoon salt
½ teaspoon dried dill weed
½ cup distilled white vinegar
¼ cup water

1 Score the cucumber lengthwise with a fork, thinly slice, and place it in a mixing bowl.

2 Make the brine: Add the sugar, salt, dill, vinegar, and water to a saucepan and heat, stirring constantly, to just boiling.

3 Pour the brine over the cucumber slices, cover, and let cool. Chill for at least 1 hour before serving. This salad will last for 2 to 3 weeks in the fridge.

Summery Cucumber Salad

I developed this version of a sweet-and-sour cucumber salad using thinly sliced onions and cucumbers (use a mandoline and mind your fingers!) and fresh dill for a bright, summery flavor.

— Makes about 1 quart

1 large or 2 medium cucumbers, thinly sliced
1 small yellow onion, thinly sliced
1 small bunch fresh dill weed, chopped
¼ cup sugar
2 tablespoons salt
1–2 teaspoons black peppercorns
2 cups distilled white vinegar
2 cups water

1 Put the cucumbers, onion, and dill in a quart jar.

2 Make the brine: Combine the sugar, salt, peppercorns, vinegar, and water in a saucepan and heat, stirring constantly, to just boiling.

3 Pour the brine over the cucumbers and onions, cover, and let cool. Chill for at least 1 hour before serving. Lasts for 2 to 3 weeks in the fridge.

Canned Dill Pickle Chips

These dill pickle chips are perfect for topping sandwiches. They are also an excellent way to use those cucumbers that are still firm but a bit too large to pickle whole. Cucumber pickles lend themselves well to canning. Just note that the texture won't be as crisp as refrigerator pickles since they're heat processed. As with refrigerator pickles, you can season these with any spices you want; I love adding turmeric and hot peppers to make my own achar.

— Makes about 7 pints

CUCUMBER/ONION MIXTURE

- **3½–4 pounds cucumbers, cut into ¼-inch-thick rounds (discard ⅟₁₆ inch of each cucumber's blossom end)**
- **1 large yellow onion, halved and cut into ¼-inch-thick slices**
- **½ cup salt**
- **8 cups cold water**

SPICE BLEND

- **1½ tablespoons dill seeds**
- **1 tablespoon yellow mustard seeds**
- **½ tablespoon brown mustard seeds**
- **2 teaspoons black peppercorns**
- **1–2 teaspoons red pepper flakes**
- **1 teaspoon white peppercorns (optional)**
- **1 teaspoon coriander seeds**
- **1 teaspoon dried dill weed**
- **4 cloves garlic, peeled and halved**

BRINE

- **½ cup salt**
- **2 tablespoons sugar**
- **4 cups distilled white vinegar or apple cider vinegar (5% acidity)**
- **4 cups water**

1. Prepare the cucumber/onion mixture: Place the cucumbers and onions in a large bowl. In a separate bowl, combine the salt and water, whisking to dissolve the salt, then pour over the cucumber mixture. Let sit in the refrigerator for 2 to 3 hours, stirring halfway through. Drain thoroughly.

2. Make the spice blend: Mix the dill seeds, mustard seeds, black peppercorns, pepper flakes, white peppercorns (if using), coriander, and dill weed in a small bowl. Set aside.

3. Make the brine: Heat the salt, sugar, vinegar, and water in a large pot over medium heat, whisking to dissolve the sugar and salt. When the brine is at a simmer, add the cucumber mixture to the pot and bring it just to a boil.

4. Meanwhile, place seven pint jars in your hot water bath canner and heat it up. Then, using tongs, remove the hot jars from the canner, and divide the spice blend and garlic evenly among the jars.

5. As soon as the cucumbers and onions boil, divide them among the jars, leaving ½ inch of headspace.

6. Run a chopstick or other thin, nonmetal utensil along the inner edges of the jars to release any air bubbles. Wipe the rims of the jars with a clean, damp cloth. Add the lids and bands and screw down to hand tightness.

7. Process pints in a hot water bath canner for 10 minutes, adjusting for altitude (see page 39) if needed.

8. Let the jars cool for 24 hours before testing the seals (see page 36), then store out of direct sunlight at room temperature. Let the pickles sit for 4 to 5 weeks before eating to let the flavors fully develop.

Mountain Cabin Cucumber Salad

Mountain Cabin Cucumber Salad

During my artist's residency at Wildacres Retreat while writing this book, this salad accompanied many of my meals out on the porch. Dill is a classic choice—and the perfect way to use up your dill stems from other dishes—but you can substitute any herbs you wish.

—— Makes about 1 pint

- 2 tablespoons finely chopped fresh dill leaves or stems
- 1 clove garlic, minced
- 1 teaspoon salt
- ½ teaspoon freshly ground black pepper
- 1 cup apple cider vinegar
- ½ cup water
- 1 medium English cucumber, sliced ¼ inch thick

1. Make the brine: Combine the dill, garlic, salt, pepper, vinegar, and water, and whisk until the salt is dissolved.

2. Place the cucumber slices in a nonreactive bowl. Pour the brine over the cucumber and allow it to sit, covered, in the refrigerator for 2 to 8 hours.

3. Store the salad in the refrigerator, where it will last for at least 1 week.

Eggplant

Small, compact eggplants are lovely for roasting and pickling, while larger, more watery eggplants are typically sliced for eggplant parmesan and the like. I prefer preserving the smaller eggplants whole, but big eggplants are absolutely perfect for caponata.

Choose eggplants that are heavy for their size with firm skin. Store whole eggplants in a paper bag with the top slightly open so they can breathe, in a cool, dark place. Or wrap in a paper towel in the fridge crisper. Do not peel or cut until you're ready to use. Eggplants can decline in quality quickly, so eat them or preserve them as soon as you can.

DRYING

Dried eggplant can be rehydrated in stews where you'd like a bit more body and texture. Wash your eggplant, trim the ends, and cut into ¼-inch slices (you may wish to halve or quarter larger eggplants before slicing). Steam blanch for 3 to 3½ minutes or boiling-water blanch for 3 minutes. Shock in an ice bath to cool (see page 17), drain and pat dry, then arrange the slices in a single layer on a dehydrator tray. Dry at 140°F/60°C for 12 to 14 minutes, or until pliable but dry. Store in an airtight container out of direct sunlight.

FREEZING

Peel your eggplant and slice it ½ inch thick. Eggplant oxidizes quickly, so only slice enough for one blanching session at a time. Blanch for 4 minutes in a gallon of boiling water with ½ cup of lemon juice added to prevent oxidation. Shock in an ice bath to cool. Package leaving ½ inch of headspace, or freeze in a single layer on a rimmed sheet pan until frozen through, then place in an airtight container with no headspace. You can interweave freezer paper between slices before freezing, too, for single-serve slices for frying.

PICKLING AND FERMENTING

Pickling eggplant is a balancing act: The spongy texture means eggplant soaks up whatever brine you make, so if your brine is super vinegary or salty, your eggplant will be, too. I usually stick to eggplant as a refrigerator pickle or cooked down into a relish or caponata, which allows me to play around with acid levels with abandon. I've included a few of my favorite pickled eggplant recipes here. To dive deeper into the world of eggplant pickling, look to achar: a diverse world of pickles from India that includes some of my favorite pickles (eggplant and beyond).

Ways to Preserve Eggplant	Shelf-stable	Fast	Low waste	Ready meals and ingredients	Big flavor
Caponata (page 162)	X			X	X
Pickled Mini Eggplant (page 164)				X	X

Caponata

I tend to pickle small eggplants to add a spongy, sour bite to my salads and charcuterie boards. For the bigger ones, I make caponata. I love the texture, flavor, and convenience—with the addition of some cheese and some crackers or bread, I have a meal fit for a queen even on days when cooking feels hard. You can even use it with pasta, hot, or as a pasta salad.

This is best made in the summer, when everything is at its peak, but if your eggplants and tomatoes don't all come in at the same time, you can substitute one (14.5-ounce) can of diced tomatoes for the fresh tomatoes.

—— Makes about 2 pints

- **1 large eggplant, peeled and cut into ¼-inch cubes**
- **1 tablespoon salt**
- **2 tablespoons extra-virgin olive oil**
- **1 large red bell pepper, seeded and cut into ½-inch dice**
- **1 small to medium yellow onion, cut into ½-inch dice**
- **2 large stalks celery, cut into ½-inch slices**
- **2 cloves garlic, minced**
- **3–4 large tomatoes, cut into 1-inch dice, juice reserved**
- **1 tablespoon lemon juice**
- **Whole nutmeg**
- **¼ cup drained capers**
- **¼ cup chopped, pitted kalamata olives**
- **1 tablespoon good-quality honey**
- **1 teaspoon red pepper flakes**
- **Freshly ground black pepper**
- **½ cup white wine vinegar, red wine vinegar, or sherry vinegar**
- **¼ cup dry white wine**
- **1 small bunch fresh parsley, chopped**

1 Toss the eggplant with the salt, then let it sit for 20 minutes to remove liquid and some bitterness. Drain and pat dry.

2 Meanwhile, heat the oil in a large high-sided skillet or saucepan over medium heat. Add the bell pepper, onion, and celery. Cook, stirring occasionally, until the vegetables start to soften, about 8 minutes.

3 After patting the eggplant dry, add it to the vegetable mixture. Cover and cook for 10 minutes, stirring occasionally. Add the garlic and sauté until fragrant, 2 to 3 minutes.

4 Reduce the heat to medium-low and add the tomatoes, with their juices, and the lemon juice. Grate in nutmeg to taste and stir to combine. Stir in the capers, olives, honey, pepper flakes, and black pepper to taste. Add the vinegar and wine. Cook until very soft, about 10 minutes.

5 Remove from the heat, add the parsley, and stir to combine. Allow the caponata to cool completely. Store it in the fridge, where it will keep for at least 1 week.

VARIATION: CANNED CAPONATA

For canned caponata, make sure you're using a vinegar with 5 percent acidity, and use 3 tablespoons bottled lemon juice.

Instead of sautéing the eggplant and peppers with oil, cut them into 1-inch cubes and roast at 350°F/180°C for 15 to 20 minutes, until tender.

Sauté the onions, garlic, and celery with ¼ cup of water until translucent, then add the remaining ingredients following the directions above. Add the eggplant and peppers during the last 5 minutes of cooking.

Place four half-pint jars in your hot water bath canner and heat it up. Then, using tongs, remove the hot jars from the canner.

Add the hot caponata to the hot jars, leaving ½ inch of headspace. Remove air bubbles, wipe the rims, add the lids and bands, and screw down to hand tightness. Process the jars in a hot water bath for 35 minutes, then allow them to cool for 12 to 24 hours before checking the seals (see page 36). Store out of direct sunlight.

Caponata

Pickled Mini Eggplant

Pickling fairytale eggplant, or another small eggplant, is a nice and relatively easy way to preserve it. It makes a delicious sour side with heavy stews or other hearty dishes to help cut their richness. You can cut the eggplants into quarters when serving or leave them whole.

—— Makes 1 quart

- **2–3** cloves garlic, peeled
- **4–5** stems fresh parsley
- **½–1** teaspoon red pepper flakes
- **⅛** teaspoon cumin seeds
- About 1 pound small eggplant, like fairytale eggplant
- **1–1½** tablespoons salt
- **2** cups red wine vinegar
- **2** cups water

1. Add the garlic, parsley, pepper flakes, and cumin to the bottom of a heatproof quart jar.
2. Cut a small X at the base of each eggplant to help the pickling liquid soak in. Loosely pack the eggplants into your jar, leaving 1 inch of headspace.
3. Make the brine: Combine the salt, vinegar, and water in a saucepan and heat until just boiling, then pour over the eggplant.
4. Allow to cool, add the lid, and place in the refrigerator. Let sit for 24 hours, or until pickled through, before eating. Store pickled eggplant in the refrigerator, where it will last for 2 to 3 weeks or more.

Fennel

Fennel is fragrant and delicious. My go-to preserving techniques for it are pickling and infusing, which uphold its bright flavor. Choose firm, tight, bruise-free heads with fresh, plump fronds (if present).

FREEZING

Cut the fennel into 1-inch slices and blanch them in boiling water for 3 to 4 minutes. Shock in an ice bath to cool (see page 17). Package and freeze, leaving ½ inch of headspace, or freeze the slices in a single layer on a rimmed sheet pan overnight or until frozen through, then place them in an airtight container with no headspace.

INFUSING

Fennel makes wonderful, anise-scented vinegars and infused spirits for drinking as shrubs (sweetened vinegars) or as sweetened liqueurs, or for using in cooking. This is a great place to use up stalks and cores that otherwise might get tossed.

Fennel-Strawberry Vinegar

This is a delightful infused vinegar that can be made with the scraps from other cooking projects. If using strawberry tops rather than whole strawberries, use 1½ cups.

— Makes 1 quart

¾–1 cup strawberries, halved
1–2 fennel cores, sliced (about 1 cup)
1 teaspoon black peppercorns
White wine vinegar or apple cider vinegar, to cover

1. Add the strawberries, fennel, and peppercorns to a quart jar or other food-safe, nonreactive container.

2. Add vinegar to cover, leaving ½ inch of headspace.

3. Let steep for 2 to 4 weeks, until the vinegar has a flavor you enjoy. Strain and store at room temperature or in the fridge. It will last for 1 month or more.

Ways to Preserve Fennel	Shelf-stable	Fast	Low waste	Ready meals and ingredients	Big flavor
Fennel-Strawberry Vinegar (above)			X		X
Quick-Pickled Fennel (page 166)	X			X	X

Quick-Pickled Fennel

PICKLING AND FERMENTING

Fennel's heady fragrance and anise flavor make it perfect for pickling, as its natural sweetness rounds out the sharp acid tang of vinegar. I love fennel in ferments, too. You can add some to your soda (page 58) or mead (page 60); or for a quick pickle, try the following recipe.

Quick-Pickled Fennel

Quick pickling is one of the easiest and most delicious ways to preserve fennel. Here's my base recipe, with a few herbal flavoring suggestions—mix up the seasonings as you see fit. I make this as a refrigerator pickle to keep fennel crisp; the thin slices of fennel can become soft when exposed to heat during canning.

— Makes about 1 quart

- **1 large or 2 medium fennel bulbs, fronds removed, cored and thinly sliced**
- **1 sprig rosemary, 1 bay leaf, or several sprigs thyme (or a combination)**
- **½ tablespoon green, white, or pink peppercorns**
- **1 teaspoon black peppercorns**
- **2 tablespoons salt**
- **2 cups white wine vinegar, apple cider vinegar, or white balsamic vinegar**
- **1½ cups water**

1. Add the fennel, rosemary or other spices, and peppercorns to a quart jar or other food-safe, heatproof container.
2. Make the brine: Bring the salt, vinegar, and water to a simmer in a medium saucepan and heat until the salt is dissolved.
3. Pour the hot brine over the fennel and allow to cool.
4. Store in an airtight container in the refrigerator and let pickle for 18 to 24 hours, or until pickled through. Pickled fennel will keep in the refrigerator for at least 2 weeks.

Green Beans

Green beans (and their close cousin, wax beans) are technically legumes, but I discuss them here with the other vegetables because they are prepared and eaten similarly. (I explore other legumes, like shell beans, peas, and peanuts, in Chapter 8.)

Fresh green beans should have crisp pods that snap, and the beans themselves should be firm, not mushy or squishy. As with all fresh vegetables, you'll want to preserve your green beans as quickly as you can after harvesting them or bringing them home.

DRYING

Wash your beans, trim the ends, and cut them into ½- to 1-inch-long pieces. Blanch them in boiling water for 2 minutes, then shock in an ice bath to cool (see page 17). Drain well. Dehydrate at 140°F/60°C for 8 to 10 hours or until brittle (in a humid climate or with larger pieces, this may take longer). Store in an airtight container at room temperature, out of direct sunlight and away from high humidity and temperature fluctuations (not, for example, next to or above the stove).

Tip: Freezing blanched, shocked green and wax beans for 30 to 40 minutes before drying them helps improve the texture of the final product.

FREEZING

Frozen green beans are a staple, perfect for tossing into a curry or soup or enjoying as a side dish. If you've ever grown your own, you know that these verdant legumes tend to come in by the bushel, and freezing is a simple way to preserve their fresh flavor year-round.

Wash beans and trim off the ends, then cut them into 2- to 4-inch-long pieces. Blanch them in boiling water for 3 minutes, then shock in an ice bath to cool. Drain thoroughly to remove water, and package leaving ½ inch of headspace. Or freeze in a single layer on a rimmed sheet pan until frozen through, then package leaving no headspace.

PICKLING AND FERMENTING

Dilly beans taste like summer to me, but these magical legumes are just the tip of the iceberg when it comes to pickled-bean possibilities. You can quick pickle dilly beans (and other fresh beans, too), but I especially love them fermented, which gives that nice depth of flavor that only fermentation can provide.

Quick-Pickled Dilly Beans

I developed this recipe when I was working in a restaurant kitchen and ran out of apple cider vinegar halfway through making dilly beans. To improvise, I substituted distilled white vinegar for the remaining cider vinegar, and I still make them that way to this day. You can use all of one vinegar or the other (or your own favorite vinegar) instead.

(continued on next page)

Ways to Preserve Green Beans

	Shelf-stable	Fast	Low waste	Ready meals and ingredients	Big flavor
Quick-Pickled Dilly Beans (above)				X	X
Fermented Green Beans (page 168)				X	X

Quick-Pickled Dilly Beans *continued*

Any leftover brine is perfect for pickling some other last-minute veggies on the fly. I use cooled brine to keep the beans as crisp as possible.

—— Makes about 2 quarts

- **¼ cup salt**
- **4 cups water**
- **2 cups apple cider vinegar**
- **2 cups distilled white vinegar**
- **1½–2 pounds fresh green beans, trimmed (6 cups)**
- **1 large bunch fresh dill weed**
- **6 cloves garlic, peeled and sliced**
- **4–6 stems parsley (optional)**
- **2 tablespoons black peppercorns**
- **2 teaspoons red pepper flakes**

1. Make the brine: Combine the salt, water, and vinegars in a saucepan. Heat just enough to dissolve the salt, then remove from the heat and allow the brine to cool.

2. Meanwhile, divide the beans, dill, garlic, parsley (if using), peppercorns, and pepper flakes between two quart jars or four pint jars, leaving 1 inch of headspace.

3. Pour the brine over the beans to cover completely, leaving ½ inch of headspace.

4. Seal the jar lids and refrigerate the beans overnight before enjoying. These will last in the fridge for weeks.

VARIATION: CANNING QUICK-PICKLED DILLY BEANS

To can your beans, which gives a softer texture but a longer shelf life, heat the brine to boiling. Swap the fresh dill weed for 1 to 2 teaspoons dried dill weed per pint, and increase the salt to ½ cup. Pack beans in hot pint jars, leaving 1 inch of headspace, and pour brine over to cover completely, leaving ½ inch of headspace.

Process pints for 10 minutes in a hot water bath, adjusting for altitude (see page 39) if needed. Allow them to cool for 12 to 24 hours before checking the seals (see page 36). For best results, let your dilly beans sit for at least 2 weeks before opening and eating, which allows the flavor to fully develop.

Fermented Green Beans

Beans are a very common ferment in many places around the world. And they are as simple as other lactofermented vegetables: Just add brine to the beans and let them sit. Fermented green beans are so delicious that I actually dream about them if I haven't had some in a couple of weeks.

—— Makes about 2 quarts

- **1 pound fresh green beans**
- **2 quarts 3% brine (¼ cup unrefined salt dissolved in 2 quarts water)**

1. Snap the beans in half and place them in a crock or two quart jars, pressing them down slightly. Pour the brine over the beans.

2. Place a weight on the beans to hold them under the brine. Cover the crock or jars with cheesecloth or a dish towel.

3. Allow to ferment at room temperature, checking the beans each day. When they have developed a level of sourness that you like, put them in the refrigerator. I usually ferment these for 4 to 7 days, but the time varies based on temperature and personal preference. They will last in the fridge for at least 3 weeks if kept under the brine.

VARIATION: FERMENTED DILLY BEANS

Add 1 to 2 tablespoons dried dill weed, a few whole peeled cloves of garlic, and 1 to 2 teaspoons of red pepper flakes to your brine before fermenting.

Greens (Dark and Leafy)

Beet Greens, Chard, Collards, Kale, Mustard Greens, Spinach

"Dark leafy greens" refers to hardy greens like kale and spinach, as well as the tops and tips of certain vegetables, like beet greens, which we tend to overlook but have a ton of nutritional and flavor potential. Use the tops and tips in pestos, freeze them for future use like you would other greens (see page 172), or use them fresh or in any of the other ways you would use more dense greens.

DRYING

To dry dark leafy greens, trim away any thick stalks (like those on kale) and cut larger greens (again, like kale) into 1-inch-wide pieces. Wash very thoroughly. Blanch in steam or boiling water (see page 17) for 1½ to 2½ minutes, until they're just about to wilt and the color has brightened. Shock in an ice bath to cool. Drain well. Dry at 120°F/49°C for 4 to 10 hours (depending on how thick they are) or until brittle. Allow dried greens to cool completely before storing in an airtight container out of direct sunlight, where they will keep for months.

FREEZING

Freezing hardy greens is best done if you plan to use them from frozen (as in smoothies) or in cooked applications (like tossing a handful into soup toward the end of cooking).

To freeze hardy greens like collards, chard, kale, mature spinach, and mustard greens, start by removing any tough midribs (save these scraps for stock, if you want, or compost them). Tender midribs can stay put. More tender young greens should be blanched in boiling water for 2 minutes; blanch tougher, thicker greens for 3 minutes. If you prefer, you can also stir-fry them for several minutes until wilted. Let your greens cool completely, then pack into containers and freeze.

Green Smoothie Cubes

Hardy greens add a vitamin-rich punch to morning smoothies. For a ready-to-go option, try freezing greens into smoothie cubes (for more smoothie-cube ideas, see page 22).

Hearty greens

Liquid to blend (juice, yogurt, kefir, etc.)

(continued on next page)

Ways to Preserve Dark Leafy Greens

	Shelf-stable	Fast	Low waste	Ready meals and ingredients	Big flavor
Green Smoothie Cubes (above)		X		X	
Fermented Rainbow Roots and Spinach Salad (page 170)				X	X

Green Smoothie Cubes *continued*

1 Clean the greens. Keep greens like spinach whole; for big greens like kale, remove ribs and cut into ribbons. If you plan to use these up within a month or so, no need to blanch. If not, blanch whole greens in boiling water for 2 minutes, then shock to cool before preparing (see page 17).

2 Add greens to a blender or food processor with enough liquid to make it blend down. Blend until smooth, then pour into ice cube trays and freeze.

3 Once frozen, pop the cubes out and store in the freezer in an airtight zippered bag or airtight container with no headspace, where they'll last for several months or more.

INFUSING

Tough greens, like tender greens, can be infused in vinegar. But note that the vinegar will taste like those greens, so for ones that are particularly strong or bitter, your vinegar will be, too. Mustard greens do, in fact, make a somewhat mustardy-flavored vinegar with a verdant kick (it is strong, though).

Infusing greens in vinegar is simple. Just pack your greens into a jar (the fresher and more local your greens, the better!), pour your favorite vinegar (I love apple cider vinegar) over the top until completely covered, and let the mixture sit out of direct sunlight for 2 to 4 weeks to infuse.

FERMENTING

Tough, flavorful greens can be fermented, as any vegetable can, but they can pose issues if fermented for too long because their strong flavor tends toward the sulfuric after a bit of time in the brine. To avoid this, I let them *just* start to ferment and soften using the same method I use for pickled lettuce (see page 180), then pull them and refrigerate them, to either enjoy as a slaw or topping, or blend up as a slightly funky pesto to dress my salads and noodles.

Fermented Rainbow Roots and Spinach Salad

This recipe was inspired by Kirsten Shockey's fermented spinach recipe in *Fermented Vegetables*, which opened my eyes to the delicious possibilities of fermenting spinach. Play around with using other favorite root vegetables. It's the perfect ready-made spinach salad!

— Makes 1 quart

- **2 carrots, grated (about ½ cup)**
- **1 medium shallot, grated or minced**
- **¼ medium beet, grated (about ¼ cup)**
- **Zest of 1 lemon**
- **1½ teaspoons salt**
- **5 ounces spinach**
- **1 cup 2% brine (¼ tablespoon unrefined salt dissolved in 1 cup water; optional)**

1 Combine the carrots, shallot, beet, lemon zest, and salt in a bowl. Massage together until brine pours out when squeezed.

2 Pack the spinach in a quart jar and pack the grated root mixture on top. If needed, pour 2 percent brine on top until the vegetables are completely covered.

3 Place your ferment on a tray or plate to catch overflow and place out of direct sunlight at room temperature. Burp your ferment, as needed, when pressure builds up.

4 Ferment for 3 to 7 days, until the spinach has softened but before it gets mushy. Then store in the fridge, where it will last for 2 weeks or more.

VARIATION: ADDING SPICES

For a twist, add about 1 teaspoon total of cumin seeds, caraway seeds, and red pepper flakes. Or use 1 to 2 teaspoons of rosemary (dried or fresh) or another favorite herb.

Preserving Seaweed

Seaweed is wonderfully nutritious, contributing depth, umami, and a taste of the ocean to whatever it's added to. Different types of seaweed have different uses and flavor profiles, and it has long been eaten and preserved by coastal communities around the world. I asked chef Melanie McIntosh, from Speck restaurant in London, about her favorite ways to preserve seaweed. She says, "I love the texture and the nutritive qualities of sea vegetables—a little goes a long way. They are so easy to keep at home dried and have a relatively long shelf life. The umami flavors you get from seaweeds are massive but less punchy than something like, say, parmesan. You can layer sea vegetables with many other ingredients, and it doesn't have to dominate the dish. There is a whole flavor scale from sea-salty to nutty."

If you're foraging your own, learn to identify seaweed before harvesting. McIntosh notes that the biggest problem from beached seaweed is rot or pathogens. "Cutting fresh is usually best, and if possible, cut while leaving the holdfast (like a root), as some species can continue to grow new blades (leaves)." Or source from your favorite supplier (see Resources, page 410).

Seaweed can be dried in a dehydrator or in the sun, preserved in vinegar, or made into tsukudani. If you have access to seaweed, you have a wonderful chance to explore a versatile ingredient.

TSUKUDANI

Tsukudani, a method of preserving by simmering in shoyu and mirin or sugar, is used for everything from mushrooms to seafood to grasshoppers. And, of course, seaweed. "I love preserving seaweeds in this style, especially British and Irish seaweeds," McIntosh says. She also uses this method on Irish or Scottish sugar kelp, sea spaghetti, channel wrack, and nori or laver, which results in a flavorful paste. She steers clear of high-alginate seaweeds like Irish sea moss or dulse, which create a mucilaginous gel and/or break down.

Here McIntosh shares her recipe for breathing new life into kombu that has been used for making dashi (Japanese soup stock). Rather than tossing it out, she puts the used kombu in the freezer, and when she has about 10 ounces she follows this method:

1. Cut the kombu into strips or squares (it doesn't shrink, so cut it to the size you want it to be as a finished product).
2. Add it to a pot with a mixture of equal parts water and shoyu, enough to cover your kombu, and bring to a boil.
3. Turn the heat down to a simmer and cook, stirring often, until the liquid has reduced to about half or a bit more, 45 to 60 minutes.
4. Add sugar (the amount is flexible—I do ½ to 1 cup of sugar per cup of reduced cooking liquid) and continue heating until it thickens to a syrup. It's important to add the sugar at the end to prevent drying out the seaweed. Remove the pot from the heat and let it cool.

McIntosh says, "Making tsukudani is a low-risk, high-reward project. If something goes wrong, you can likely try again. It's also no waste if you are using up pieces of kombu, which might be expensive and imported. It's not salty or high sugar enough to be shelf stable but can last in the fridge for months or years." It goes remarkably well with a variety of Japanese meals as well as other cuisines. Try it with rice or pasta, with cream cheese on a bagel or crumpet, in stew for extra umami, or as a topping for savory porridge or congee. You can even dehydrate it and sprinkle it on ice cream!

While the tradition is less common in Japan today, McIntosh hopes it will revive and spread. "Food moves around the world in different ways, and it would be lovely to see people embrace it and make it their own wherever they might be making it."

Herbs and Tender Greens

I divide my herbs into two broad categories based on how I tend to approach preserving them: soft-stemmed herbs, like basil and cilantro, and woody-stemmed herbs, like thyme and rosemary. Soft-stemmed herbs lend themselves well to herbal pastes (like pesto), while woody-stemmed herbs are perfect for other applications like infused vinegar. Tender greens, like arugula and baby spinach, are often preserved in the same way as herbs, so I've included them here. Lettuce is its own beast and handled differently. For more on that, see page 180.

DRYING

Aromatic herbs are one of my favorite things to dry. You can also dry tender young greens, but the resulting texture is not—by and large—terribly appealing, so if you try it, I recommend grinding your dried greens into powder and using it as a nutritional add-in for smoothies and soups.

There's no need to blanch herbs before you dry them. When drying fresh herbs, I often tie them into small bundles and hang them upside down out of direct sunlight (and away from steamy places like next to the stove) until brittle. Another option: Lay the herbs on a dehydrator tray and dry at a very low temperature (90 to 100°F/32 to 38°C) for 1 to 3 hours or until brittle. If you're out foraging and find some herbs you want to dry, you can also lay them flat on the

Ways to Preserve Herbs and Tender Greens	Shelf-stable	Fast	Low waste	Ready meals and ingredients	Big flavor
Herb-Infused Vinegar (page 173)	X	X	X		X
Herbal Liqueurs (page 174)	X	X	X	X	X
Rosemary and Thyme Syrup (page 174)				X	X
Basil Burst Syrup (page 175)				X	X
Herb Bud Salt (page 175)	X	X	X	X	X
Pickled Herb Buds (page 176)	X		X	X	X
Choose-Your-Own-Adventure Herbal Soda (page 176)					X
Herbal Sauce (page 177)				X	X
Savory Sage Refrigerator Paste (page 178)				X	X

dashboard of your car for an hour or two until dry (just keep an eye on them and pull them when they're brittle but before they bake).

To dehydrate tender greens, wash them very thoroughly, and blanch for 1½ to 2½ minutes (in steam or boiling water; see page 17) until they're just about to wilt and the color has brightened. Shock in an ice bath to cool, drain, and pat dry. Dry at 120°F/49°C for 2 to 6 hours (depending on thickness) or until brittle. Allow to cool completely before storing. You can also grind them into a powder. Store dried herbs and greens in airtight containers out of direct sunlight, where they will last for months.

FREEZING

Freezing herbs in ice cube trays lets me enjoy a burst of fresh herbaceous flavor even in the middle of winter—just toss a cube or two in your soup or sauce. To make these cubes, chop herbs (by hand or in a food processor) finely enough that they can fit neatly inside your ice cube tray compartments with a bit of room at the top. Then pour olive oil over them to cover, and freeze. (The olive oil serves as a barrier to keep your herbs from getting discolored and freezer burned.) Once the cubes are frozen through (4 to 6 hours), transfer them to an airtight container with no headspace. These will keep for at least 2 to 3 months.

INFUSING

Herbs lend themselves beautifully to being infused in vinegar, and the resulting vinegars offer an instant flavor burst to anything you add them to. Herbal-infused vinegars can last for years, too: I have a tulsi-infused vinegar that's 4 or 5 years old, and it has aged like fine wine.

Herb-Infused Vinegar

You can infuse your herbs in any vinegar you wish. I prefer apple cider vinegar, red wine vinegar, or white wine vinegar. If I'm making a vinegar to clean with or just want the flavor of the herbs without anything else, I use distilled white vinegar. I don't use balsamic because the intense flavor tends to overwhelm the herbs, but if you love balsamic, give it a try.

Fresh or dried herbs of your choice

Vinegar of your choice, to cover

1. Pack your jar about half full of fresh or dried herbs.

2. Add vinegar to cover completely.

3. Let the jar sit out of direct sunlight, checking to ensure all the ingredients remain under the vinegar and that no mold has grown on the surface (which is unlikely).

4. Check the flavor after about 2 weeks. Once you enjoy the flavor, strain out the herbs and store the vinegar in an airtight container, like a narrow-necked swing-top bottle or a repurposed screw-top wine bottle, out of direct sunlight. Stored properly, it will keep for months.

VARIATION: FLORAL VINEGAR

Flowers make a great addition to your vinegar: Spicy nasturtium adds a nice kick, roses are divine in mocktails, and goldenrod flowers offer a piney and bright addition (goldenrod is also nice for making an herbal-infused salt; see page 96).

For a beautiful jar of vinegar with a floral, herbaceous punch, use the flowering tops from herbs like basil, agastache, and mint.

Colorful flower vinegars are a delight to the eyes and tastebuds, too: I like to use my favorite colorful flowers (like roses or marigolds) to add visual interest to my pantry and my vinaigrette

(continued on next page)

Herb Infused Vinegar *continued*

(try them in drinks, too!). Some flowers, like violets and blue butterfly pea flower, even change color: The acidity of the vinegar turns their pigments from blue to a beautiful purple as they infuse.

VARIATION: HERB-STEM VINEGAR

You can infuse vinegar with the leftover woody stems from herbs like rosemary and thyme that are too tough to chop and add to recipes but still have plenty of flavor. Herb-stem vinegar is about the easiest low-waste food you can make, and it makes a wonderful gift (no one needs to know you made it from herb scraps!).

Another option? Save those stems and add them to soups, stocks, and sauces, or just to your Scrappy Soup Stock container (page 20) for an extra punch of flavor.

HERBAL LIQUEURS

Herbs are prime candidates for making some delicious drinks. They pair well with fruit: I especially love blueberry and basil, blackberry and lavender, rosemary and citrus, thyme and apple, and sage and apple. This is also a great place to use up your herb stems from other projects!

If you're making a liqueur to drink on its own or in cocktails, fill a jar about halfway full of herbs, then add your desired spirit to cover. You can add more herbs if you want it to be very flavorful. Let steep for at least 2 weeks, or until you like the flavor (I let most of my infused liqueurs go for about 1 month). Strain; then, if you wish, sweeten with simple syrup (1 part sugar to 1 part water). Store liqueurs at room temperature out of heat and direct sunlight.

MAKING SYRUPS

Syrups are an easy, accessible way to play with preserving herbs. They are a reminder of the beauty and simplicity of preserving, and they can be customized to your heart's desire.

Rosemary and Thyme Syrup

This recipe makes a concentrated, flavorful syrup, perfect for working with those last stragglers in your autumn garden. It's delicious when added to drinks and desserts (try it on poached pears). For me, pungent, punchy herbs really shine when added to a cocktail. They're also great in a shrub mocktail because they can stand up to the sour punch of vinegar. Feel free to substitute other herbs, depending on what's growing in your garden.

Think of making herbal syrups like making an herbal tea: Steep your herbs in the liquid until it's flavorful and fragrant by gently simmering rather than boiling, which can damage delicate aromatics. If you want a mild flavor, just use half the amount of herbs. Since this makes such a small amount, it's best to can it only if you already have the canner going for other projects.

— Makes about 1 pint

About 1 cup thyme, stems and all
3 sprigs rosemary
2½ cups sugar
Pinch of salt
1 cup water

1. Combine the thyme, rosemary, sugar, salt, and water in a medium saucepan. Simmer over medium-low heat until the water is very fragrant and flavorful and thickened, 15 to 20 minutes.

2. If canning, place jars in your hot water bath canner and heat it up. Then, using tongs, remove the hot jars from the canner.

3. Strain out the herbs with a fine-mesh strainer, pressing with the back of a spoon to release any remaining liquid. Pour the hot syrup into the jars, leaving ½ inch of headspace.

4. If refrigerating, add the lids and store in the refrigerator, where the syrup will keep for at least 2 weeks.

5 If canning, run a chopstick or other thin, nonmetal utensil along the inner edges of the jars to release any air bubbles. Wipe the rims of the jars with a clean, damp cloth. Add the lids and bands and screw down to hand tightness.

6 Process in a hot water bath for 15 minutes for pints or 12 minutes for half-pints, adjusting for altitude (see page 39) if needed.

7 Let the jars cool for 24 hours before testing the seals (see page 36), then store out of direct sunlight at room temperature.

Basil Burst Syrup

This syrup calls for a lot of basil, but thankfully it's a great use for the flowers on your basil plant that starts to bolt, or the basil that's starting to wilt in your fridge, as well as fresh, perky basil leaves. You can also use the stems, roughly chopped, in addition to the leaves.

If you don't have a ton of basil, try swapping out other herbs and playing with combinations. I also use this same approach with edible, flavorful flowers like roses, and the flowering tops and tender stems of herbs when my garden is in full swing. When you have a lot of herbs in your garden in summer, this is a good way to preserve their flavor for a bit longer.

—— Makes about 2½ pints

- **4½ cups granulated sugar**
- **4 cups water**
- **Pinch of salt**
- **4 cups basil (packed)**

1 Combine the sugar, water, and salt in a saucepan and bring to a simmer over medium-low heat, stirring to dissolve the sugar.

2 Add the basil and gently simmer until fragrant and flavorful and reduced slightly, 15 to 20 minutes.

3 Pour the finished syrup through a fine-mesh strainer, pressing with the back of a spoon to release any remaining liquid.

4 Store the syrup in the refrigerator, where it will keep for at least 2 weeks.

VARIATION: CANNED BASIL BURST SYRUP

To can, increase the sugar by 1 cup and add 2 tablespoons of commercially bottled lemon juice or 1 teaspoon citric acid. Pour it into canning jars, leaving ½ inch of headspace, and process in a hot water bath for 15 minutes for pints or 12 minutes for half-pints (see page 34 for complete canning instructions).

PICKLING, SALTING AND FERMENTING

I first started preserving herb buds with the ample invasive shiso in my yard. Pickling and salting the buds gave me a new way to explore how shiso's flavor expresses itself in different formats (it's less minty and more earthy when preserved in salt), and I've found this to be true of other herbs as well. Pickled herb buds are an interesting substitute for capers and can add fun new dimensions to dishes where you want that pop of briny flavor. But the magic of herbal fermentation doesn't end there. Herbal sodas, for example, are a simple way to play with flavors and make a delicious beverage that's healthier (and cheaper) than something store-bought.

HERB BUD SALT

Unlike herbal salt (see page 96) where dried herbs are blended with salt, here we're keeping the buds whole. Herb bud salt is simple to make: Put a layer of salt, about ¼ inch thick, in the bottom of a jar, then add a single layer of herb buds, removed from their stems, followed by another layer of salt. Repeat layers as desired, ending with a layer of salt on top. Let it sit for at least a couple of weeks. You can use the herb buds as tiny, flavorful, salty garnishes in dishes—I use them as a sort of stand-in for capers—and the salt, which takes on the herbal flavor, as an aromatic seasoning or finishing salt.

Another option? Nestle your herb stems into a bed of salt for a low-waste flavored salt option.

PICKLED HERB BUDS

Pickled herb buds are made in brine, and flavor-wise, they are closer kin to those vinegary jars of capers at the supermarket. When you want a juicier version of herb bud capers rather than the dry salted ones, this is a nice approach.

To make pickled herb buds, mix up a pickling brine of 1 part salt, 8 parts water, and 8 parts vinegar. Use your favorite 5 percent acidity vinegar (red or white wine vinegar, apple cider vinegar, and rice wine vinegar all work well here). Fill your jar(s) with herb buds, removed from their stems, leaving 1½ inches of headspace, then pour the brine over them, leaving ½ inch of headspace. Let pickle for at least a week, giving the jar a very gentle shake every 1 to 2 days to redistribute any buds that have floated to the top. Store in the fridge or at room temperature.

Herb Bud Salt

HERBAL SODA

Herbal sodas, which are ready to drink in just a handful of days, rely on a two-step process: first, fermenting herbs with sugar and water, then straining and pouring the liquid into a bottle for a second fermentation, which carbonates it. The key to soda-making success is to use narrow-necked bottles with a tight-sealing lid, such as screw-top wine bottles or flip-top bottles.

Choose-Your-Own-Adventure Herbal Soda

The flavor possibilities of this soda are endless. You can use just herbs (as called for in this recipe) or a blend of herbs and spices or flower petals. You can also add fruit, though the extra sugar in the fruit may make your soda ferment more quickly and/or result in a sweeter final product, so bear this in mind. Some of my favorite combinations are lavender and rosemary, rose petal and violet, and blueberry and lavender. This soda works best with fresh herbs or fresh flower petals, but dried herbs can be substituted as long as they are used in tandem with fresh ingredients (e.g., fresh fruit), which provide the yeasts needed for fermentation.

— Makes 1 gallon

1½ cups sugar
1 cup fresh herbs of your choice
1 gallon water

1. In a 1-gallon crock or glass jar, combine the sugar, herbs, and water, and stir to dissolve the sugar.

2. Cover the container with a tea towel or clean cloth, stirring twice a day for 3 days, or until fragrant and bubbly.

3 Strain your soda and taste. If needed, add extra herbs or other flavorings during bottling.

4 Pour your soda into capped bottles, filling just up to the neck.

5 Seal tightly and allow to sit at room temperature for 2 to 3 days until bubbles are visible. Store in the fridge, where the soda will last for at least 1 week.

CANNING

Canned herbal sauces are a great option for when you're traveling and want to bring a flavorful herbal ingredient to mix into meals. Think of this as the base of a vinaigrette or marinade that's ready to go rather than traditional pesto, which uses oil (and thus can't be canned).

Note that this isn't a thick paste, but more of a pourable, vinegary sauce, and the addition of salt and acid renders it safe for canning. It can also be stored in the fridge to use less energy than canning.

To make a dressing, take a scoop of paste and whisk it with olive oil (or your favorite oil) to the desired consistency. Give it a try on white bean salad! Rub it on vegetables and proteins as a marinade before roasting. I've even rubbed it on a halved cauliflower before baking for a dramatic center-of-the-plate dish.

Herbal Sauce

This is an adaptable base recipe that works with whatever combination of herbs you want. However, limit intensely flavored, woody-stemmed, or bitter herbs to about one third or less of the total amount of herbs. You can add other things, too, like minced garlic, cracked black pepper, or other leafy or floral ingredients (think carrot greens or beet greens—just note that these won't have as strong an herbal flavor as culinary herbs).

— Makes 1 pint

1 cup herbs, loosely packed

¾ cup apple cider vinegar or your favorite 5% acidity vinegar, plus more if needed

1 teaspoon salt

1 If canning, place jars in your canner and heat it up. Then, using tongs, remove the hot jars from the canner.

2 Remove the stems from woody-stemmed herbs (soft-stemmed herbs can stay on the stem).

3 Add the herbs, vinegar, and salt to a blender or food processor and blend them into a sauce consistency, adding more vinegar if needed. This should be more liquid than standard pesto; if the paste is thick, it can't be safely canned.

4 Loosely fill your jars, leaving ½ inch of headspace.

5 If refrigerating, use within 2 weeks.

6 If canning, run a chopstick or other thin, nonmetal utensil along the inner edges of the jars to release any air bubbles. Wipe the rims of the jars with a clean, damp cloth. Add the lids and bands and screw down to hand tightness.

7 Process half-pints for 12 minutes or a pint for 16 minutes in a hot water bath canner, adjusting for altitude (see page 39) if needed.

8 Let the jars cool for 24 hours before testing the seals (see page 36), then store out of direct sunlight at room temperature.

NOTE: Herbal sauces tend to separate when canned: This is natural! Just give the jar a shake when you're ready to serve.

Savory Sage Refrigerator Paste

This tastes like the holidays to me. When I want to eat cozy food in cool weather, I brush this on squash before baking or stir into marinades or soups.

—— Makes 1 pint

- **1 cup sage leaves, loosely packed**
- **Leaves from 1 large sprig fresh rosemary**
- **2 cloves garlic, peeled**
- **1½ teaspoons salt**
- **½ teaspoon red pepper flakes (optional)**
- **¼–½ teaspoon lemon zest**
- **¼ teaspoon freshly ground black pepper**
- **¾ cup apple cider vinegar, plus more if needed**

1. Add the sage, rosemary, garlic, salt, pepper flakes, lemon zest, black pepper, and vinegar to a blender or food processor and blend them into a sauce consistency, adding more vinegar if needed.
2. Loosely fill your jars, leaving ½ inch of headspace.
3. Store in the fridge and use within 2 weeks.

Leeks

Leeks are notoriously sandy and hard to clean, but they're worth the effort. And preserving your leeks all at once means you have clean, ready-to-use leeks later: a gift to your future self.

CLEANING

To clean leeks, cut them into pieces ¼ to ½ inch thick. Place them in a large bowl of water, separating gently with your fingers while shaking and stirring the leeks to remove grit. Carefully scoop into a strainer to drain, taking care to not disturb the dirt that's settled to the bottom of the bowl.

DRYING

Cut leeks into ¼- to ½-inch-thick pieces (both green and white parts) and clean. Drain well. Spread them in a single layer on dehydrator trays. Dehydrate at 125°F/52°C for 4 to 6 hours, until brittle. Store in an airtight container out of direct sunlight.

FREEZING

Cut and clean leeks as directed above and pat dry. Lay out the pieces in a single layer on a baking sheet lined with parchment paper or a silicone mat. Freeze for 4 to 6 hours, or until frozen through. Store in an airtight container with no headspace. Toss into soups and sauces frozen, or thaw in the fridge for 8 to 12 hours, then use.

INFUSING

Leeks can be infused in vinegar for a ready-to-go flavor enhancer (I splash a bit into stock when I make it). The greens, when blended in a vinaigrette or into yogurt, make fantastic sauces and dressings.

LEEK-INFUSED VINEGAR

This is a perfect use for all parts of the leek, tops or bottoms. Clean your leeks and pat them dry. Fill a pint jar halfway with leek pieces (2- to 3-inch-long tops, or slices of bottoms), then add your favorite vinegar to cover. Let steep for at least 2 to 3 weeks, giving it a gentle shake every few days. Enjoy the vinegar when it has a flavor you like. The pickled leeks are a great garnish on salads, fried tofu, seafood, and beans.

Leek-Top Dressing

This is a great way to quickly jazz up a meal. It makes a very thin sauce, which easily coats bowls of beans, grains, or greens.

— Makes 1 cup

- **1 cup leek tops, cut into 1-inch-long pieces**
- **½ teaspoon salt**
- **1 fresh chile, 1 clove garlic, or other desired flavors (optional)**
- **½ cup apple cider vinegar or lemon juice**
- **¼ cup extra-virgin olive oil**

Add the leeks, salt, chile (if using), vinegar, and oil to a blender and blend until smooth. Store in the fridge, where the dressing will last for about 1 month.

Yogurt Leek Sauce

This is a nice dip or topping for kebabs, grilled vegetables, savory sourdough pancakes, salads, or anything else that calls out for a creamy, tangy, cold condiment.

— Makes about 3 cups

- **Tops of 1 large leek, finely sliced (about 2 cups; see note)**
- **2 cloves garlic, peeled**
- **1 small chile (optional)**
- **1½ cups plain yogurt**
- **1 teaspoon salt**

NOTE: The green leek tops are thick, so be sure to slice them very finely.

Add the leek, garlic, chile (if using), yogurt, and salt to a blender or food processor. Blend until smooth. Store the sauce in the refrigerator, where it will keep for about 2 weeks.

VARIATION: SPICIER YOGURT LEEK SAUCE

For a spicier version, add 1 to 2 green bird's-eye chiles or 1 green jalapeño, seeded, plus 1 (2-inch) knob ginger, peeled and finely diced, to the base recipe.

Ways to Preserve Leeks

	Shelf-stable	Fast	Low waste	Ready meals and ingredients	Big flavor
Leek-Infused Vinegar (page 178)	X	X		X	X
Leek-Top Dressing (above)				X	X
Yogurt Leek Sauce (above)				X	X

Lettuce

I'm often asked the best way to preserve lettuce. Sadly, there aren't many options, as this watery, tender vegetable turns to mush in the freezer and dust in the dehydrator. That said, if you're eager to experiment with lettuce preserving, you'll have the best luck with sturdier, thicker-stemmed types (like romaine) rather than delicate spring greens or butter lettuce, which are best eaten fresh.

FREEZING

One option for preserving lettuce—especially smaller leaves of some of the colorful delicate varieties you find in a spring mix—is to blend it with *just enough* water, juice, or other preferred liquid to make it blend smoothly, then freezing it like herb cubes (see page 20) or turning it into Smoothie Cubes (page 22). Just make sure the lettuce is packed under your liquid or oil completely when freezing to prevent discoloration (and when you use the cubes, stick to dishes where their thawed lack of structure won't matter, like smoothies and soups).

You probably haven't ever considered putting lettuce in your smoothies, but a single cube, in tandem with other more flavorful ingredients, tends to blend into the background and provide some extra nutrition. A single cube in soup or stew also adds a little nutrition and helps you work through your bounty of lettuce.

For science, I've made a smoothie entirely out of lettuce before, and while I do not recommend this course of action, I don't want to deny you the full, richly textured experience of your own life, so please make a lettuce-only smoothie if you so desire.

You can also try infusing lettuce in vinegar by filling a jar about half full with loosely packed leaves, then adding vinegar to cover them completely (packing it too tightly can cause the watery lettuce to dilute the vinegar). It won't be particularly flavorful, but the lettuce will add some minerals, and you will, technically, be repurposing them (and it's certainly better than just waiting until they go bad and tossing them).

FERMENTING

Finding a viable lettuce-preserving technique involved turning to the past and to a seemingly once-common (now more rare) fermentation practice from Ukrainian Jewish traditions. I first learned about this in Sandor Katz's *Art of Fermentation*, where he mentions lettuce kvass. This method produces a refreshing, drinkable brine as well as the lightly pickled lettuce itself.

This fermentation is best done in cooler weather, and you must keep an eye on it: Be ready to pull it, pack it in jars, and bundle it off to the fridge when it's just lightly fermented and before it gets mushy. The addition of sugar is optional, and while it is slightly sweeter, of course,

Ways to Preserve Lettuce	Shelf-stable	Fast	Low waste	Ready meals and ingredients	Big flavor
Lettuce Kvass (page 181)		X		X	X
Soy Sauce–Pickled Romaine Lettuce (page 181)		X		X	X

it is not terribly sweet. I offer the dill profile that Katz mentions, but you can make pickled lettuce (and drink pickled lettuce kvass) using whatever flavors you wish.

All lettuce pickling works best with lettuce that has some good crunch and body to it already: Iceberg works some of the time, and romaine works best. You may have luck with other greens like endive if they're especially toothsome.

Lettuce Kvass

Lettuce kvass makes for a light, refreshing beverage, and the lightly pickled lettuce is nice as a side dish, on sandwiches, or mixed into salads with other greens. Kvass is traditionally made with stale bread. By using a heel from yesterday's loaf, for example, you add more food for lactic acid bacteria and some additional depth of flavor.

—— Makes 1 gallon

- **2 heads romaine lettuce**
- **2 cloves garlic, peeled and halved**
- **½ tablespoon dried dill weed (or 1–2 large sprigs fresh)**
- **2 tablespoons salt**
- **1½ tablespoons sugar (optional)**
- **8 cups water**

1 Cut the lettuce into 1-inch-wide pieces (you should end up with about 8 cups), reserving the two outer leaves to weigh down the lettuce during fermentation.

2 Add the chopped lettuce, garlic, and dill to a 1-gallon or 2-liter food-safe container. Top with folded lettuce leaves.

3 Combine the salt, sugar (if using), and water in a large bowl and mix until dissolved. Pour over the lettuce to cover. Place the lid on the container.

4 Let the lettuce ferment until it is slightly bubbly and sour but still crisp (3 to 7 days, shorter in hot weather). Store the kvass in the fridge, where it will last for at least 1 week, often longer.

Soy Sauce–Pickled Romaine Lettuce

This variation is loosely based on Chinese pickled celtuce (stem lettuce) traditions. The firmer stems of celtuce help it hold up to pickling, but if you take care in preparing the lettuce, this recipe can work with romaine lettuce, too. Keeping the brine cool is critical for a crisp texture. Eat as a pickle or add to a stir-fry. You can substitute other vegetables for the lettuce, like celtuce or celery.

—— Makes about 1 quart

- **1 head romaine lettuce**
- **2 tablespoons sugar**
- **1–2 teaspoons red pepper flakes**
- **1 small whole star anise, or ½ to 1 teaspoon five-spice powder (optional)**
- **½ cup dark soy sauce**
- **½ cup brown rice vinegar or rice wine vinegar**
- **1 tablespoon toasted sesame oil**

1 Cut the lettuce into 1-inch-wide pieces and place it in one quart jar or divide between two pint jars, with 1 inch of headspace.

2 Make the brine: Add the sugar, pepper flakes, star anise (if using), soy sauce, vinegar, and oil to a small bowl and whisk until the sugar is dissolved.

3 Pour the brine over the lettuce until covered, add the jar lids, and set the jars in the fridge, where the pickled lettuce will last for about 2 weeks.

Mushrooms

There are many varieties of mushrooms that offer culinary, medicinal, and in some cases mind-altering benefits. You're probably familiar with some popular cultivated varieties (such as portobello and button) and maybe some wild varieties (morels, chanterelles, etc.). Mushrooms range from decadent truffles to daily drivers like cremini and everything in between, encompassing a range of flavors and culinary possibilities.

It goes without saying, or it should, but *if you decide to forage for mushrooms, please, oh please, make sure to identify them correctly and harvest them sustainably.*

Whether they're store-bought or freshly foraged, clean your mushrooms as soon as you get home: Wipe off any dirt with a damp cloth and cut away any areas that have started to decay. If the mushrooms are especially dirty (or, like every batch of morels I've ever brought home, full of ants), you may want to submerge them in water, though some people think this cleaning method makes your mushrooms waterlogged and alters the texture.

There's a lot of conflicting advice out there about how to store mushrooms, but you want cool, dark storage and some amount of airflow. If you smash your fresh mushrooms together in an airtight container, they'll go bad much

Ways to Preserve Mushrooms	Shelf-stable	Fast	Low waste	Ready meals and ingredients	Big flavor
Dried Mushroom Tea (page 184)	X			X	
Mushroom Jerky (page 184)	X	X		X	X
Freezer-Safe Lion's Mane Mushroom Cutlets (page 185)		X		X	X
Frozen Mushroom "Scallops" (page 186)				X	X
Mushroom Broth (page 186)				X	X
Tea-Pickled Mushrooms (page 187)					X
Quick-Pickled Mushrooms (page 188)		X		X	X
Mushroom Ketchup (page 188)				X	X
Marinated Mushrooms (page 189)				X	X

more quickly than if you give them some breathing room. Avoid storing mushrooms in plastic bags and containers, which causes them to become soft and decay rapidly. Paper bags keep mushrooms contained but allow for air circulation. Storing your mushies in the main part of the fridge in a closed paper bag helps ensure they'll stay fresh longer (but still aim to use them quickly, as some mushrooms have a very short shelf life even when stored properly).

Working with Mushrooms: An Invitation to Intuitive Cooking

Many of these recipes work with a variety of mushrooms, and I encourage you to play around with different mushrooms and different flavors, as the nuances of each will become apparent as you do.

Different mushrooms also require different preparation times: Delicate and moist oyster mushrooms, for example, don't need quite as long as denser cremini mushrooms to give up their liquid in Mushroom Ketchup (page 188), but they may take a bit longer to dry than thin slices of reishi mushrooms because of their higher moisture content.

It's best, then, to use these recipes as guidelines but to trust your senses to tell when your preserve is done. Here are some sensory ways to engage with mushroom preserves.

DRIED: Are your mushrooms dried all the way through and dry to the touch? Do they snap, rather than fold, when you bend them?

PICKLED AND FERMENTED: Are your mushrooms evenly pickled through to the center? Do they have a consistent texture and flavor?

MUSHROOM KETCHUP: Has all the liquid been extracted from your mushrooms? In other words, has the amount of liquid in the bowl remained the same for an hour or more?

FROZEN: Are your mushrooms frozen all the way through? Or does the middle feel squishy when pierced with the tine of a fork or a skewer? Depending on how they're cut, your mushrooms might also break apart when bent once frozen through.

Just as different mushrooms require slightly different processing, different mushrooms also have different uses. Reishi really shine when they're dried, then simmered and used for flavorful teas and stocks. Lion's mane can also be dried, but it works great as a main dish, whether fresh or frozen (page 185). Many grocery-store mushrooms like button, cremini, and portabello (which are all actually the same species at different levels of maturity) are incredibly versatile kitchen workhorses—probably the reason why they are so widely available and beloved. Shiitakes are versatile, too, as are oysters and trumpet mushrooms.

And finally, some people are more sensitive to raw mushrooms than others are. Cooking mushrooms is the safest way to ensure everyone can enjoy them.

DRYING

Dehydrating is a nice set-and-forget option that will leave you with mushrooms that can be rehydrated in soups, made into teas, or powdered and added to other dishes for an umami kick. Dried mushrooms can last for months (sometimes many months) when made and stored properly.

Mushrooms are best dried in a dehydrator. I find that an oven, even at its lowest heat, is a little intense for them.

To dehydrate mushrooms, start by cleaning them and patting them dry. Cut off and discard parts that are starting to go bad, as well as any tough, woody stalks. Mushrooms do not require blanching prior to drying. Slice the mushrooms and arrange the pieces on dehydrator trays in a single layer without touching. Set the dehydrator at 120 to 125°F/49 to 52°C (for very delicate mushrooms) and up to 140°F/60°C (for sturdier, more dense mushrooms), and dehydrate until completely dried through. The time required varies depending on the mushrooms' size and water content, but it usually takes 4 to 6 hours for thinly sliced mushrooms (less for very thinly sliced mushrooms) and 8 to 10 hours for big pieces, whole mushrooms, or ones with a high water content.

Make sure your mushrooms are completely cooled and dehydrated before storing. I prefer to use a mason jar or similar; I label the jar with the date and mushroom variety and store it out of direct sunlight.

DRIED MUSHROOM TEA

To make a tea from dried mushrooms, prepare a decoction: This means simmering plant matter for a long time rather than pouring boiling water over plant matter to steep. Simmer dried mushrooms (1 to 2 tablespoons per 10 ounces of water) over low heat, covered, for 20 to 40 minutes, until the mushrooms are soft and the liquid is flavorful. Sweeten or otherwise flavor to taste.

Mushroom Jerky

Mushroom jerky is one of my favorite road-trip snacks. It can be made with just the marinade, or the marinated mushrooms can be tossed in your favorite seasonings before drying. Mix and match marinades and coatings to suit your taste. You'll want about ½ cup marinade per 8 ounces of fresh mushrooms. This works well with all but the most delicate mushrooms.

This marinade is bright, lightly flavored, and slightly spicy. Seasoning options include salt and maple sugar; red pepper flakes and fresh herbs like oregano and dill; black pepper, salt, and sugar; berbere, sesame seeds, garam masala, or your favorite spice blend.

— Makes about 2 cups

- **1 pound fresh, firm mushrooms, such as shiitake or porcini**
- **2 cloves garlic, peeled**
- **½ tablespoon salt**
- **½ teaspoon red pepper flakes**
- **¼–½ teaspoon freshly ground black pepper**
- **½ cup dry white wine, dry light-bodied rosé, or orange wine**
- **¼ cup water**
- **½ teaspoon honey**
- **Juice and zest of 1 lemon**
- **Seasoning of your choice (see headnote for ideas; optional)**

1 Clean the mushrooms, cut off any brown or soft spots, and slice them ¼ inch thick.

2 Make the marinade: Put the garlic, salt, pepper flakes, black pepper, wine, water, honey, and lemon juice and zest in a blender. Blend until well combined and the garlic is minced.

3 Place the mushrooms in a nonreactive container with an airtight lid. Add the marinade and toss to coat.

4 Refrigerate for 1 to 3 days, depending on how flavorful you like your jerky, tossing or stirring several times a day to evenly season the mushrooms. I usually just give them a quick stir every time I open the fridge.

5 Drain the mushrooms in a mesh colander. (Note: You can save your marinade to use for another batch; store it in the fridge and use within 2 weeks.) Blot the mushrooms lightly with paper towels and then toss them with seasoning (if using).

6 Dehydrate the mushrooms at 100°F/38°C for 5 to 7 hours: They should be pliable but not so dry that they snap. Store the jerky in an airtight container in a cool, dark place, where it will last for 3 weeks or more.

VARIATION: MUSHROOM JERKY MARINADE #2

This marinade has more of a traditional jerky flavor profile. It's great tossed with seasonings such as oregano and thyme or hot pepper, or with maple sugar. Combine in a blender: 3 cloves garlic, 1 teaspoon red pepper flakes, ¼ cup dark soy sauce, ¼ cup apple cider vinegar, 1 tablespoon maple syrup, and 1 tablespoon Worcestershire sauce.

FREEZING

Frozen mushrooms are great for weeknight meals. I cut them small enough to be tossed into sauces and soups (or the boiling water for pasta or other starches) while still frozen. You need to cook mushrooms before freezing to maintain their texture and flavor when thawed.

To prepare mushrooms for freezing, cut your mushrooms into similar-size pieces—quartered, sliced, etc. (For best texture, don't slice them less than ¼ inch or so.) Then sauté or steam the mushrooms until soft and cooked through. Allow to cool, then drain off any liquid and press gently with a paper towel or tea towel to remove any excess moisture.

Place them in a single layer on a baking sheet lined with parchment paper or a silicone mat and freeze for 3 to 5 hours or until frozen through. Store in an airtight, freezer-safe bag or container with no headspace.

Freezer-Safe Lion's Mane Mushroom Cutlets

These cutlets will last for several months in the freezer, though they're so delicious that they tend to disappear very quickly in my house. Lion's mane mushrooms are famed for supporting memory and brain function. This recipe is a godsend for ready-made weeknight meals: Enjoy the mushrooms as cutlets, or shred them with BBQ sauce or another favorite sauce. The size of mushrooms varies a lot: I find I can get anywhere from 3 to 7 cutlets from a single mushroom, depending on how big it is!

Large lion's mane mushroom(s)

Salt and freshly ground black pepper

Oil

1 Cut the mushroom(s) into 1-inch-thick slabs widthwise. Season with salt and pepper to taste.

2 Lightly oil a large skillet and set it over medium heat. Sauté the mushroom pieces until just golden, for several minutes, then flip. Press down with your spoon or spatula to remove as much water as possible. Continue cooking, flipping, and pressing every few minutes until the mushrooms are cooked through and golden brown, 15 to 20 minutes.

3 Remove the mushroom slices from the heat and let them cool completely. Place them in a single layer on a baking sheet lined with parchment paper or a silicone mat and freeze for 8 to 12 hours or until completely frozen through. Store in a single layer in a silicone freezer bag, taking care to press out as much air as you can (see page 20).

(continued on next page)

Freezer-Safe Lion's Mane Mushroom Cutlets *continued*

4 To use: Thaw in the fridge for 8 to 12 hours or until thawed through, then bake in a 350°F/180°C oven for 15 minutes, or sauté over medium heat, turning once, until heated through.

Frozen Mushroom "Scallops"

Like lion's mane cutlets, this is a nice main-course vegan option to have ready to go. It's perfect with black trumpet and king oyster mushrooms, which have big, hearty stems! (You can save the rest of the mushrooms to dry, freeze, or use fresh.)

Keep these in the freezer, then take out the number of scallops you need, place on a rimmed plate or in a container with sides in the fridge, and thaw overnight. You can sauté them until golden on both sides and cooked through, or you can broil them. I love using these as a stand-in for shrimp in a scampi.

— Makes about 2 cups

- **2 cups water**
- **¼ cup seaweed flakes, or 2–3 large strips seaweed**
- **3 large mushroom stems (1–2 inches in diameter), cut into 1-inch-thick slices**
- **2 cloves garlic, minced**
- **4 (2-inch) strips lemon peel**
- **¼–½ teaspoon black peppercorns**
- **½ teaspoon red pepper flakes (optional)**
- **Juice of ½ lemon**
- **1 tablespoon dark soy sauce**

1 Make a seaweed tea brine: Combine the water and seaweed in a saucepan and bring to a boil over medium-high heat. Reduce the heat to medium and simmer, covered, for 12 to 15 minutes.

2 Meanwhile, add the mushrooms, garlic, lemon peel, peppercorns, pepper flakes (if using), lemon juice, and soy sauce to a heatproof quart jar.

3 Allow the unstrained seaweed brine to cool just slightly, then pour while still hot into the jar to cover the mushroom stems.

4 Let the jar cool, screw on the lid, and place it in the refrigerator to marinate for about 2 days.

5 Remove the "scallops" from their marinade and press them between paper towels to remove extra moisture. Freeze them on a baking sheet lined with parchment paper or a silicone mat for 6 hours or until frozen through, then store in a container with no headspace. These will last in the freezer for at least 1 month. In the fridge, in the seaweed tea brine, they'll last for 1 to 2 weeks, depending on freshness and size.

Mushroom Broth

An umami-rich vegan alternative to meat stocks or to cooking water for grains and beans, mushroom broth is also a fantastic way to use up leftover mushroom stems and other bits. You can add mushroom stems to a Scrappy Soup Stock container (page 20) in the freezer, but sometimes it can be nice to separate out mushroom bits and reserve them, along with some other favorite mushroom-friendly flavors (like celery and thyme), for a fragrant, delicious mushroom stock. If you're cooking directly from frozen mushrooms, add another 15 to 20 minutes of simmer time. This is a flexible technique that works with what is available; use the scraps and veggies you have around.

— Makes about 1 quart

- **2 pounds mushroom stems and trimmings (or whole or sliced mushrooms) and mushroom-friendly veggies (think celery and carrots)**
- **1 onion, peeled and halved**
- **4 cloves garlic, peeled**
- **1 bay leaf**
- **Dark soy sauce**

1. Combine the mushrooms, vegetables, onion, garlic, bay, and soy sauce to taste in a pot. Add enough water to cover (there should be about twice as much water as other ingredients) and bring to a boil. Cover, reduce the heat, and simmer for about 30 minutes, then remove the lid and continue simmering for 15 to 25 more minutes uncovered.

2. Let cool, then strain, pressing the mushrooms with the back of a spoon or squeezing with clean hands to remove excess liquid.

3. Refrigerate in an airtight container and use within a week, or freeze (see freezing instructions for liquids on page 18).

PICKLING AND FERMENTING

Pickled mushrooms are both nostalgic and innovative in my world, reminding me of the salad-bar restaurants of my 1990s childhood on the one hand while giving me new horizons to grow into and explore as a cook on the other. Mushrooms are exciting and playful additions to my fermentation and pickling practices, and I hope these recipes will help you feel the same.

Tea-Pickled Mushrooms

I like fermented mushrooms: There's something about fermenting the fruiting body of mycelia that really appeals to me on an existential level as well as a culinary one.

Mushrooms are typically cooked before being fermented, which means your brine needs raw ingredients or a starter culture to get your bacteria to grow. Here I add raw garlic and ginger—I love how both intersect with the flavor of the tea and the mushrooms. Sometimes I use a starter culture from an established ferment, like sauerkraut brine.

— Makes about 2 quarts

- **11 cups water**
- **1½ tablespoons tamari**
- **1½ pounds whole cremini or other firm mushrooms, cleaned**
- **4 (2-inch) strips lemon peel**
- **2 tablespoons salt**
- **1½ tablespoons sugar**
- **1 tablespoon loose black tea leaves**
- **1 teaspoon black peppercorns**
- **1 teaspoon red pepper flakes**
- **½ teaspoon whole coriander seeds**
- **½ teaspoon dried mint**
- **2 (2-inch) unpeeled knobs of ginger, cut in half**
- **2 cloves garlic, peeled**

1. Combine 5 cups of the water and the tamari in a large saucepan and bring to a boil.

2. Add the mushrooms and boil, covered, until just softened, about 5 minutes. Drain them and cool to room temperature on a tray lined with tea towels or paper towels to absorb excess liquid.

3. Meanwhile, make your tea brine: Combine the lemon peel, salt, sugar, tea leaves, peppercorns, pepper flakes, coriander, and mint. Bring the remaining 6 cups of water just to a boil. Pour the hot water over the tea brine mixture and stir to dissolve the salt and sugar. Let this steep for 12 to 15 minutes, then strain and cool. (You'll have enough brine left over for another jar of mushroom pickles, or another project.)

4. Place one knob of ginger and one clove of garlic in each quart jar or similar food-safe container. Divide the cooled mushrooms between the jars and put a weight on top. Ladle the tea brine and seasonings equally between the two jars. Screw on the lids.

5. Ferment the mushrooms for 3 to 10 days, until they have a flavor you enjoy, burping the lid once daily. Store them in the fridge, where they will last for 1 month or more.

Quick-Pickled Mushrooms

Easy to make, quick-pickled mushrooms are nice to have in the fridge. This works best with mushrooms that are somewhat dense and firm, so they hold up to steaming and pickling—think shiitakes, chanterelles, cremini, or button mushrooms. I recommend steaming the mushrooms beforehand if you're concerned about the possible GI distress some mushrooms can cause.

— Makes about 1 quart

- About 1 pound firm, fresh mushrooms
- 1–1½ tablespoons salt
- ½ tablespoon sugar
- Spices (see below for ideas)
- 2 cups apple cider vinegar, rice wine vinegar, or white wine vinegar
- ½ cup water
- ½ cup dry red or white wine or ¼ cup sake

1. Clean your mushrooms and steam them for 10 to 15 minutes until slightly softened.
2. Meanwhile, make the brine: Combine the salt, sugar, spices, vinegar, and water in a saucepan and bring to a boil. Remove from the heat and stir in the wine.
3. Gently strain your mushrooms and drain them for a few minutes on clean kitchen towels to let excess water drip off.
4. Loosely pack the mushrooms into a quart jar. Pour brine over to cover, leaving ½ inch of headspace. Cool, refrigerate, and let steep 2 to 3 days before eating. The pickled mushrooms will last for at least 2 weeks.

VARIATION: SPICE IDEAS (PER QUART)

- 1–2 tablespoons five-spice powder and 1 fresh chile
- Zest and juice of 1 lemon, 2 cloves garlic, 2 teaspoons black peppercorns, and 1 teaspoon whole coriander seeds
- 3–4 sprigs (or more) of dill weed, 1–2 large cloves garlic, 1–2 teaspoons black peppercorns, 1 teaspoon dill seeds, red pepper flakes to taste, and 1 bay leaf

Mushroom Ketchup

Mushroom ketchup is a delicious throwback to ketchup's early days before it became all tomatoes, all the time. Like other seventeenth-century ketchups made from fish, walnuts, and more, it is thin like fish sauce. Thick tomato ketchup didn't come on the scene until the nineteenth century. This recipe is from *Our Fermented Lives*, where I talk about the history of ketchup in more depth. You can try different types of mushrooms, play with spices, swap shallot for onion—all for the pure pleasure of experimentation and to match your tastes.

I've been asked if you can adjust the salt, and the answer is yes: Just note that less salt results in a less shelf-stable product. Like fish sauce or soy sauce, this is meant to be a condiment, so don't worry if it's too salty to eat alone. Think of it as an ingredient to use in place of other salts, and taste test as you add it to keep your dish balanced.

— Makes 1–2 cups

- 1 pound mushrooms, rinsed and finely diced
- ¼ cup fine sea salt, plus more if needed
- 1 small yellow onion, chopped
- 1 tablespoon prepared, grated horseradish (see note)
- ½ teaspoon whole allspice berries
- ¼ teaspoon whole cloves
- 1 bay leaf
- Pinch of ground cayenne or a splash of fermented cayenne hot sauce
- ¼ cup good-quality apple cider vinegar

NOTE: Be sure to use grated, not creamy, horseradish for this recipe. I often use homemade pickled horseradish, which I make by fermenting sliced horseradish root in brine until soft, then chopping in a food processor until smooth. See page 107.

1 Combine the mushrooms and salt in a nonreactive bowl. Using your hands, toss the mushrooms until they're evenly coated and then massage the salt into them slightly. You'll be able to feel them start to release liquid.

2 Cover the bowl and let sit at room temperature. Check the mushrooms after 20 minutes or so to make sure that they are releasing liquid. If they aren't, add 1 more teaspoon salt and massage again. Allow them to sit at room temperature for around 24 hours.

3 Pour the mushrooms and their liquid into a saucepan. Add the onion, horseradish, allspice, cloves, bay leaf, cayenne, and vinegar. Simmer for 15 to 20 minutes, then remove from the heat and let cool.

4 Line a strainer with muslin or cheesecloth and set it in a mixing bowl. Pour the mushroom ketchup into the strainer. Wrap the cloth up around the mushroom mixture and squeeze it to release the rest of its juice. (When you're done, don't throw out those spent mushrooms! They're infused with a lot of tasty spices and can be dried and ground into a fantastic umami-rich seasoning blend.)

5 Transfer the mushroom ketchup to a jar or bottle and store in the fridge, where it will last for several months.

Marinated Mushrooms

As a child in the 1990s, I *loved* salad-bar restaurants—and one thing that was always on those salad bars was marinated mushrooms. Today I still love marinated mushrooms, particularly as one of the few people who secretly revels in the nostalgic, though admittedly rubbery, texture of canned mushrooms. This is my take on those salad-bar mushrooms from my childhood. I recommend serving them alongside a salad, of course—preferably one with lots of tasty toppings—though they go beautifully with most meals.

For the most authentic salad-bar mushrooms, I use distilled white vinegar, but feel free to substitute another vinegar with 5 percent acidity like apple cider vinegar, red wine vinegar, or white wine vinegar. I recommend plain old olive oil or salad oil for this recipe; extra-virgin olive oil also works but can make it bitter, so use with care.

—— Makes about 8 half-pint jars

MUSHROOMS

- 3 pounds small fresh mushrooms (button or cremini) with tight, unopened caps
- ½ cup lemon juice or vinegar (5% acidity)

BRINE

- ½ small yellow onion, finely diced (about ⅓ cup)
- 2 tablespoons salt
- 1½ tablespoons dried oregano
- 1 tablespoon dried basil or tarragon
- ½–1 tablespoon red pepper flakes
- 2½ cups distilled white vinegar or other favorite vinegar
- 2 cups olive oil

SEASONING

- Peel of 1 lemon, cut into 8 (1-inch) strips with a vegetable peeler
- 8 cloves garlic, peeled and halved
- 2 tablespoons black peppercorns

(continued on next page)

Marinated Mushrooms *continued*

1 Wash the mushrooms and trim their stems to ¼ inch. Add them to a pot with water to cover and the lemon juice.

2 Bring to a boil, stirring frequently to make sure all mushrooms are submerged most of the time, then drain. Or steam for 5 minutes.

3 Make the brine: Combine the onion, salt, oregano, basil, pepper flakes, vinegar, and olive oil in a saucepan and bring to a boil. Reduce to a simmer and cook until fragrant, 5 to 8 minutes.

4 Divide the lemon peel, garlic, and peppercorns equally between the jars.

5 Pack the mushrooms into the jars and pour the hot brine over them, leaving ½ inch of headspace.

6 Cool and refrigerate for 4 to 5 days or until pickled through (see note). The mushrooms will last in the fridge for at least 2 weeks.

NOTE: The oil will solidify in the fridge but will reliquefy at room temperature, so bring the jar out of the fridge about 30 minutes before serving.

Marinated Mushrooms

Okra

Choose firm pods without cracks or bruises. Store okra unwashed and wash it just before using, which keeps away excess moisture; storing wet okra can quickly turn it to mush. Store okra in the vegetable crisper in perforated bags or a paper bag. Airflow is important to preserve freshness.

DRYING

Thoroughly wash whole pods, trim, then slice into ¼- to ½-inch-thick discs. Okra does not require blanching prior to drying, so arrange your raw slices in a single layer on a dehydrator tray. Dry at 140°F/60°C for 8 to 10 hours or until brittle. Store in an airtight container out of direct sunlight and away from high humidity, where it will last for at least 4 months.

TIP: Dried okra, along with dried aromatics like onion and garlic, makes a great ready-to-go soup base.

FREEZING

Select tender, fresh young pods and separate your pods by size—smaller pods (under 4 inches) and larger pods (over 4 inches). Wash the pods and trim off their stems without cutting down far enough to expose the inside of the pod.

To freeze, blanch in boiling water for 3 minutes (small pods) and for 4 minutes (large pods), then cool in ice water for the same period of time. After blanching, leave the pods whole or cut them in slices. Package, leaving about 1½ inches of headspace, label, and freeze.

Ways to Preserve Okra	Shelf-stable	Fast	Low waste	Ready meals and ingredients	Big flavor
Ready-to-Go Okra Soup Cubes (page 192)				X	X
Okra and Tomatoes: Small Batches (page 193)				X	X
Lauren's Pickled Okra (page 194)	X			X	X

Ready-to-Go Okra Soup Cubes

Okra and okra soup were brought from West Africa across the Middle Passage with enslaved Africans, and the traditions they preserved and shared made it part of US Southern cuisine. You can adapt this technique to your favorite okra soup. These cubes are single-serving additions to soup stock for a quick meal that can be eaten alone or with rice or your favorite starch, loosely based on Zoe Adjonyoh's Ghanaian version. For a thicker soup, chop okra more finely. For a less slimy texture, leave it in larger pieces, as here.

— Makes 12–16 cubes

- **1½ tablespoons tomato paste**
- **1 cup water**
- **1–2 tablespoons additional flavorings, such as your favorite spice blends, dried shrimp powder, fish sauce (adjust for salt), grated ginger, or Three-Root Paste (page 108) (optional)**
- **3 tablespoons sustainable palm oil or peanut oil**
- **1 medium carrot, thinly sliced**
- **1 medium yellow onion or red onion, cut into ¼-inch dice**
- **3 cloves garlic, minced**
- **1 small jalapeño, finely diced (for a mild soup, remove seeds)**
- **1 pound okra, trimmed and sliced ¼ to ½ inch thick**
- **2 large tomatoes, cut into ½-inch dice, juices reserved**
- **Salt and freshly ground black pepper**
- **2 green onions, thinly sliced**
- **Stock, for serving**
- **Rice (optional), for serving**

1 In a small bowl, whisk the tomato paste into the water along with any additional flavorings (if using). Set aside.

2 Heat the oil in a large pan over medium-high heat. Add the carrot and onion, and sweat until the onion is just translucent. Then add the garlic and jalapeño, and sauté until the garlic is a light golden brown color.

3 Reduce the heat to medium-low and add the okra, tomatoes, and tomato paste mixture. Add salt and pepper to taste. Cover and let simmer, stirring occasionally, until the okra is softened, about 15 minutes.

4 Uncover and continue cooking until thickened, about 10 minutes. If you want the okra to be more broken down, continue cooking until it is very soft.

5 Adjust seasoning as needed, add the green onions, and remove from the heat. Let cool; the consistency will be slightly thicker than stew. Ladle into two ice cube trays and freeze. Once frozen, remove the cubes from the tray and place in airtight containers. They will last for months in the freezer.

6 To serve: Add 2 or 3 cubes per 1 cup of stock to a pot and simmer until heated through. (If the stock is unsalted, add salt as needed.) Serve alone or with rice.

PRESSURE CANNING

Choose tender young pods, and wash and trim the ends. You can leave the okra whole or cut it into 1-inch-thick pieces. Add the okra to a saucepan, add hot water to cover, and boil for 2 minutes. Drain and pack the hot okra into heated jars, leaving 1 inch of headspace. Add salt, if you'd like: ½ teaspoon to pints and 1 teaspoon to quarts. Then add boiling water to the jars, leaving 1 inch of headspace. Remove air bubbles, wipe the rims, and tighten the lids. Set your pressure canner at 11 pounds pressure (dial gauge) or 10 pounds pressure (weighted gauge) and process pints for 25 minutes and quarts for 40 minutes, adjusting for altitude (see page 39) as needed.

Okra and Tomatoes: Small Batches

There are as many variations of okra and tomatoes as there are people who cook it. My version keeps spicing to a minimum to let the flavor of the vegetables shine through, but this dish is also a wonderful place to experiment with spices. Flavors from West Africa and the southern US both work well in this traditionally West African dish. I also add more acid for two reasons: because I love the flavor and because tomato acidity differs between varieties. Adding vinegar makes me more confident that this recipe's pH is safe to process in a hot water bath canner.

—— Makes about 3 pints

- **1 tablespoon peanut or sunflower oil**
- **1 onion, cut into ½-inch dice**
- **2–3 cloves garlic, minced**
- **½ cup apple cider vinegar (5% acidity) or bottled lemon juice**
- **5–6 large tomatoes, cut into 1-inch dice**
- **½ pound okra, cut into ½-inch slices**
- **Salt and freshly ground black pepper**
- **1 teaspoon citric acid**

1. Add the oil to a large, high-sided skillet over medium-high heat.

2. Once warm, add the onion and sauté until translucent and just starting to brown, 5 to 7 minutes.

3. Add the garlic and cook until it starts to turn golden, just about 1 minute.

4. Reduce the heat to medium-low and add the vinegar, tomatoes, okra, and salt and pepper to taste. Simmer until the okra is softened and the tomatoes have mostly broken down, 15 to 20 minutes. Adjust the seasoning if needed. Stir in the citric acid.

5. Meanwhile, place three pint jars in your hot water bath canner and heat it up. Using tongs, remove the hot jars from the canner, then fill them, leaving ½ inch of headspace. I find it helpful to press gently on the okra with the back of a spoon to remove any air bubbles.

6. Run a chopstick or other thin, nonmetal utensil along the inner edges of the jars to release any air bubbles. Wipe the rims of the jars with a clean, damp cloth. Add the lids and bands and screw down to hand tightness.

7. Process pints in a hot water bath for 15 minutes, adjusting for altitude (see page 39) as needed.

8. Let the jars cool for 24 hours before testing the seals (see page 36), then store out of direct sunlight at room temperature.

Okra and Tomatoes

PICKLING

I do a lot of bartering, and pickled okra is my number-one choice: It's paid for everything from haircuts to car repairs over the years. It's hands down one of the most popular pickles I make (along with Mimi's Pickled Watermelon Rind, page 298). I get such regular requests for it that I plan whole shopping trips and subsequent afternoons around procuring and pickling okra.

Lauren's Pickled Okra

Lauren's Pickled Okra

This recipe is over 100 years old and comes from the recipe box of my dear friend Lauren Harris, who has graciously given me permission to reprint it here. I typically can this okra, but you can make them as refrigerator pickles. In the original recipe, they are made by pouring hot brine over okra and letting it sit at room temperature for 3 weeks, then chilling before serving. If you make these as refrigerator pickles, let them sit in the fridge for at least a week (but really, longer is better) to pickle all the way through.

—— Makes 10 pints

1 cup salt

8 cups vinegar

8 cups water

About 3 pounds okra (see note)

2 small chiles, chopped, or ½ tablespoon red pepper flakes

2 cloves garlic, chopped

1 teaspoon dill seeds

NOTE: Choose smaller, firm pods that are very fresh for the best final texture. Larger, tougher pods work better when frozen for later use (see page 191) or in okra soup (page 192).

1. Make the brine: Combine the salt, vinegar, and water in a large pot and boil for about 10 minutes.

2. Meanwhile, if canning, place 10 pint jars in your hot water bath canner and heat it up. Using tongs, remove the hot jars from the canner, and pack the okra into them, leaving 1 inch of headspace.

3. Divide the chiles, garlic, and dill seeds evenly among the jars.

4. Pour the hot brine over the top, leaving ½ inch of headspace.

5 Run a chopstick or other thin, nonmetal utensil along the inner edges of the jars to release any air bubbles. Wipe the rims of the jars with a clean, damp cloth. Add the lids and bands and screw down to hand tightness.

6 If canning, process pints in a hot water bath for 15 minutes, adjusting for altitude (see page 39) if needed.

7 Let the jars cool for 24 hours before testing the seals (see page 36), then store out of direct sunlight at room temperature.

VARIATION: SMOKY OKRA

Using the same brine ratio and amount of okra, substitute the following spices per pint:

1 small clove garlic, crushed
2 whole cloves
½ teaspoon smoked paprika
½ teaspoon red pepper flakes
¼ teaspoon ground allspice

Onions and Shallots

Aromatic, versatile onions and shallots add a familiar depth and roundness to most any savory dish. Onions can be stored at room temperature for quite a while, but sometimes we have so many that it would take months to go through them all. So when you have an abundance of onions or shallots, how do you best preserve them for later? Thankfully you have a lot of options, which you can tailor to how you cook and eat—from frozen, diced onions as a ready ingredient to pickled onions as taco and sandwich toppings.

Choose firm onions and shallots without mold, blemishes, or soft spots, with paper that is dry underneath and peels away cleanly. Store at room temperature in an area with some air circulation, out of direct sunlight.

Ways to Preserve Onions and Shallots

	Shelf-stable	Fast	Low waste	Ready meals and ingredients	Big flavor
Rainbow Roots Soup Starter (page 107)				X	X
Frozen Mirepoix and Trinity (page 196)		X		X	X
Soup à l'Oignon Cubes (page 197)				X	X
Pickled Sweet Onions (page 198)				X	X
Pickled Red Onions with Mustard (page 199)				X	X
Rosemary Cocktail Onions (page 199)				X	X
Fire Cider (page 399)	X		X		X

DRYING

Drying is not usually my go-to with onions, but dried onions can be a nice, lightweight option to take traveling and camping and are good to have in the pantry in a pinch. Unlike many vegetables, onions do not require blanching prior to drying.

To dry onions (or shallots), remove the paper from outside the onion, then wash to remove any dirt. Cut off tops and root ends (save, if desired, for Scrappy Soup Stock, page 20), and cut into ⅛- to ¼-inch-thick slices. Arrange the slices in a single layer on dehydrator trays and dry them at 130 to 140°F/55 to 60°C for 3 to 8 hours (this varies widely depending on the onion variety and its water content; check them every couple of hours). Pull when they are crisp or brittle. Store in an airtight container out of direct sunlight and away from high humidity, where they will last for at least 4 months.

FREEZING

Freezing is, for the most part, not the most effective way to preserve onions and shallots, as they already keep well in a cool, dry place, and blanching and freezing them alters their texture. As a result, I rarely put onions in my freezer. The exception to this rule in my kitchen are the frozen soup starters like Frozen Mirepoix and Trinity on this page as well as the Rainbow Roots Soup Starter (page 107). You can also caramelize onions, cool completely, then freeze in containers with ½ inch of headspace.

Frozen Mirepoix and Trinity

Premade frozen batches of mirepoix and trinity make it easy to answer the siren song of soup whenever I want. And you can transfer the mixtures straight from freezer to pan. Do take care to not overcrowd your pan, though, if you plan to sauté your soup base before adding stock: A bigger pot works best here so that your aromatics brown rather than steam.

I use roughly equal parts of each aromatic, but the measurements here aren't an exact science. If you don't plan to use this within 1 or 2 months of making, be sure to blanch your vegetables for 1 to 2 minutes, then shock to cool before freezing (see page 17). This recipe makes relatively small batches, but you can increase it to your heart's content.

—— Makes about 1 quart

MIREPOIX

- 2 medium carrots, cut into ½-inch dice or ¼-inch slices
- 2 medium stalks celery, cut into ½-inch dice or slices
- 1 medium onion, cut into ½-inch dice

TRINITY

- 1 large carrot, cut into ¼- to ½-inch dice
- 1 medium onion, cut into ½- to 1-inch dice
- 1 large green bell pepper, cut into 1-inch dice

1 For mirepoix, toss the carrots, celery, and onion together to combine; for trinity, toss the carrot, onion, and pepper together to combine. Spread out in a single layer on a rimmed quarter sheet pan.

2 Freeze for 6 to 12 hours until frozen through, then seal in an airtight, freezer-proof container with no headspace. Both mixtures will keep in the freezer for about 6 months.

Frozen Mirepoix

Soup à l'Oignon Cubes

I love French onion soup for its richness and depth of flavor that comes from a long cook time and deep caramelization, and I especially love Julia Child's recipe. But the same things that make it delicious also make it inaccessible for daily cooking, and thus an unlikely member of my regular mealtime rotation as someone who lives alone half the year. I adapted Child's recipe from my battered old copy of *The French Chef* to make a version that can be frozen in cubes for quick, easy meals.

—— Makes 12–16 cubes

- 5 tablespoons butter
- 1 tablespoon olive oil
- 8 medium yellow onions, peeled, halved, and thinly sliced
- 1 teaspoon salt
- Freshly ground black pepper
- 1 teaspoon sugar
- 5 cups beef or vegetable stock, plus more for serving
- 3 cloves garlic, peeled and sliced
- 3 tablespoons flour
- ½ cup full-bodied red wine
- 1 bay leaf
- 1 sprig sage
- 1 sprig fresh thyme
- Toasted bread, for serving
- Gruyère cheese, for serving

1 Set a pan over medium-high heat. Once hot, add 4 tablespoons of the butter and the oil. After the butter has melted, add the onions, salt, and pepper to taste.

2 Cover and cook over medium-low until the onions are soft and translucent, 15 to 20 minutes.

(continued on next page)

Soup à l'Oignon Cubes *continued*

3 Uncover, increase the heat to medium, and stir in the sugar.

4 Cook until the onions are a deep caramel color, stirring occasionally, 25 to 30 minutes.

5 As needed while browning onions, deglaze the pan with 1 cup of the stock, 1 to 2 tablespoons at a time, scraping to remove bits. Continue browning, deglazing, and scraping as needed, until the onions are chocolaty brown and fragrant but not burnt.

6 Add the garlic and sauté for 2 to 3 minutes until the garlic is fragrant.

7 Add the remaining 1 tablespoon butter and let it melt, then sprinkle in the flour, stirring to mix. Let cook for several minutes to remove the raw flour taste.

8 Reduce the heat to low and whisk in the remaining 4 cups stock. Bring the mixture back to a simmer to allow it to thicken slightly.

9 Add the wine, bay leaf, sage, and thyme, and adjust the salt and pepper if needed. Simmer until reduced by about one third, about 30 minutes.

10 Remove from the heat, fish out your herbs, and let cool.

11 Scoop into ice cube trays and freeze for 8 to 12 hours. Transfer the cubes to an airtight, freezer-safe container with no headspace. It will keep for at least 2 months.

12 To serve: Add 1 cube per 1 cup stock and simmer until hot. Top with toasted bread and Gruyère cheese, then broil until the cheese is browned. For a more flavorful soup, add 2 cubes per 1 cup of stock.

PICKLING

Pickled onions are no one-trick pony: They can range from sweet to tart to pungent to spicy and beyond. Customize the spicing in these recipes to fit your palate and the dishes you like to cook. Use your pickled onions to top everything from salads to sandwiches to cooked fish to cheese trays to roasted vegetables. Or just enjoy them on their own.

Pickled Sweet Onions

When I was a kid, my mom used to make this delicious cucumber salad with dill, sugar, and vinegar (see page 158), and over the years I've adapted it to also include a version made with sweeter yellow and white onion varieties. These onions are super easy and packed with flavor: They taste wonderful on pitas and burgers but also as a tart, tangy side to heavy holiday meals!

— Makes 1 pint

- **1 medium yellow onion, thinly sliced**
- **2½ tablespoons sugar**
- **2 tablespoons dried dill weed**
- **1 teaspoon salt**
- **1½ cups white vinegar, plus more if needed**
- **½ cup water**

1 Place the onion in a pint jar.

2 Combine the sugar, dill, salt, vinegar, and water in a large glass or jar. Stir until the sugar and salt are completely dissolved.

3 Pour the mixture over the onion slices until they are completely covered (you can top it off with extra vinegar if needed).

4 Screw the lid tightly onto the jar and place it in the fridge.

5 Wait for 24 hours and enjoy! The onions will last for a couple of months in the refrigerator if submerged in their brine.

Pickled Red Onions with Mustard

Pickled red onions are the perfect accompaniment to sandwiches and salads: I love how they cut the richness of creamy dressings and crumbled cheeses. I make these with toasted mustard seeds, but the possibilities are endless.

—— Makes about 2 pints

2–3 red onions, thinly sliced
2 tablespoons salt
1 tablespoon yellow mustard seeds, toasted
2 cups red wine vinegar, plus more if needed
2 cups water

1 Divide the onions equally between two pint jars.

2 Add the salt, mustard seeds, vinegar, and water to a large glass or jar. Stir until the salt is completely dissolved.

3 Pour the mixture over the onions until they are completely covered (you can top it off with extra vinegar if needed).

4 Screw the lids tightly onto the jars and place them in the fridge.

5 Wait for 24 hours and enjoy! The onions will last for a couple of months in the refrigerator if submerged in their brine.

VARIATION: PICKLED SPICED RED ONION

Follow the same steps for pickling as above, but use 3 tablespoons of salt instead of 2, and instead of yellow mustard seeds, use ½ tablespoon black peppercorns and ½ tablespoon dried thyme.

Rosemary Cocktail Onions

I'm kind of addicted to tiny vegetables—baby carrots, mini eggplants, and, of course, tiny onions. Sadly, I've found many of the commercial cocktail onions I've tried over the years to be either bland or so vinegary it's almost a mind-altering experience to bite into one. This recipe is my version of cocktail onions: herbaceous and just the right amount of pickle-y. I can these in half-pint jars; you can also simply tuck them away in the fridge for later use.

—— Makes 2 half-pints

1 bay leaf
6 peppercorns
2 tablespoons salt
3 cups vinegar
1 cup water
2 cups white pearl onions
2 small sprigs rosemary

1 Make the brine: Combine the bay leaf, peppercorns, salt, vinegar, and water in a pan and simmer for 10 minutes.

2 Meanwhile, bring a pot of water to boil. Drop the onions (peels and all) into the boiling water and boil for 3 minutes. Remove the onions to a bowl of ice water. Cut off just the root end of each onion and gently squeeze the top to push the onion out of its skin.

3 If canning, place two half-pint jars in your hot water bath canner and heat them up. Then, using tongs, remove the hot jars from the canner. Add a rosemary sprig to the bottom of each jar.

4 Divide the onions between the hot jars and ladle hot brine over them to cover, leaving ½ inch of headspace.

(continued on next page)

Rosemary Cocktail Onions *continued*

5 If making refrigerator pickles, allow the jars to cool, top with lids, and let the onions pickle in the refrigerator for 2 to 3 days before enjoying.

6 If canning, run a chopstick or other thin, nonmetal utensil along the inner edges of your jars to release any air bubbles. Wipe the rims of the jars with a clean, damp cloth. Add the lids and bands and screw down to hand tightness.

7 Process half-pints in a hot water bath canner for 15 minutes, adjusting for altitude (see page 39) if needed.

8 Let the jars cool for 24 hours before testing the seals (see page 36), then store out of direct sunlight at room temperature.

Peppers

Hot peppers and sweet peppers are a delicious addition to your kitchen. In most cases, both can be used in these applications, depending on the final flavor profile you want. You can swap out hot peppers to showcase your favorite varieties, blend sweet and hot, or go all sweet. Here are some of my favorite ways to preserve the abundance of peppers in my kitchen.

DRYING

Dried peppers, hot or sweet, are a nice addition to the pantry, as they can be easily added to dishes or, if you wish, ground up and used alone as a seasoning or as part of a spice blend. Years ago, I worked with the folks at Burlap & Barrel to make a pickling spice blend: I lactofermented hot peppers for 2 to 3 weeks, then drained them from their brine, dried them, ground them up, and blended them with black peppercorns, fermented white peppercorns, coriander, and allspice. Crushed or ground peppers offer a wonderland of spice-blend possibilities, perhaps including a signature spice blend all your own!

To dry peppers, wash and stem your peppers, then remove cores and seeds. Cut out the white ribs from the peppers (note that for hot peppers, if you want to keep all the heat, keep the ribs intact, and the seeds, if you wish, but still stem them).

Small peppers, like bird's-eye chiles, can remain whole; cut larger peppers, like red bell peppers, into rounds about ⅓ inch wide.

Peppers do not require blanching. Arrange raw peppers in a single layer on dehydrator trays and dry at 135 to 140°F/57 to 60°C for 8 to 12 hours or until crisp and brittle. Store in an airtight container out of direct sunlight and away from high humidity, where they will last for at least 4 months.

FREEZING

Sweet peppers can be frozen for later use in dishes, as can hot peppers (though with those, I prefer to make hot sauce, like on page 207; Hot Pepper Vinegar, page 203; or other preserves). Sweet peppers should be washed and stemmed, then halved and seeded. You can freeze them in halves or cut into strips or rings, packing with no headspace. Hot peppers should be washed and stemmed, dried completely, then packaged leaving no headspace.

Freezing without blanching will give you a crisper texture (this is how I freeze peppers in Frozen Trinity, page 196). If you only plan to use them cooked and texture is less of an issue (say, in casseroles), boiling-water blanch halves for 3 minutes or strips or rings for 2 minutes. Shock in ice water, drain, and package with ½ inch of headspace.

Ways to Preserve Peppers	Shelf-stable	Fast	Low waste	Ready meals and ingredients	Big flavor
Roasted Pepper Cubes (page 202)		X		X	
Sofrito Cubes (page 202)		X		X	X
Hot Pepper Vinegar (page 203)	X			X	X
Hot Honey (page 203)				X	X
Aji Dulce Pepper Relish (page 205)				X	X
Jalapeño Relish (page 205)				X	X
Fermented Hot Sauce (page 207)				X	X
Red Chile Chocolate Hot Sauce (page 207)				X	X
Doc's Hot Sauce (page 209)				X	X
Hot-and-Sour Bird's-Eye Sauce (page 209)				X	X
Easy Candied Jalapeños (page 210)				X	X
Sweet-and-Sour Roasted Red Pepper Jam (page 211)				X	X

Roasted Pepper Cubes

Roasted pepper cubes are a nice ingredient to have in the freezer and can be made with sweet or hot peppers. To use: 1 cube equals about 2 tablespoons of roasted pepper sauce.

Fresh peppers, sweet or hot

1 Place the peppers on a baking sheet lined with parchment paper. If roasting sweet peppers, cut peppers in half, remove the seeds and veins, and place cut side down on the pan.

2 Blister the skins in a 450°F/230°C oven for 6 to 8 minutes (for hot peppers) or 30 to 40 minutes (for sweet peppers), or place the peppers on the flame of a gas burner, rotating regularly, until their skins are blistered all over.

3 Place the peppers in a paper bag and seal, or in a bowl covered with a tea towel, to hold in steam and make them easier to peel. Cool for 10 to 20 minutes, until the skins peel away easily, then peel your peppers and discard the skins (you can also save the skins and dry them, then crumble and try them out as a seasoning).

4 Put the peppers in a blender or food processor and blend to a smooth consistency. Cool, then pour them into ice cube trays and freeze for 6 to 12 hours. Pack frozen cubes in a freezer-safe container with no headspace.

Sofrito Cubes

Sofrito comes in many forms, depending on where you have it. This version is a bit of a mishmash, combining tomatoes with cilantro and using bell peppers instead of small sweet peppers since they are easier to find. I encourage you to dive down your own sofrito rabbit hole and find the version you like best. I freeze mine in ice cube trays for a ready-to-go seasoning to add to beans, soups, stews, and slow-simmered meat, fish, or vegetables.

— Makes about 24 cubes

1 bunch cilantro, cut into 2-inch-long pieces
1 medium yellow onion, peeled and quartered
1 green bell pepper, seeded and quartered
1 red bell pepper, seeded and quartered
1 large tomato, quartered, juice reserved
3–4 cloves garlic, peeled
½–1 red jalapeño, stem removed (optional: remove seeds and ribs for less heat)
2 tablespoons apple cider vinegar
Salt
Freshly ground black pepper

1 Add the cilantro, onion, green pepper, red pepper, tomato, garlic, jalapeño, and vinegar to a blender or food processor and blend until smooth, adding salt and black pepper to taste.

2 Divide the sofrito evenly between two ice cube trays and freeze for 6 hours or until frozen through. Store it in the freezer in an airtight container, where it will last for at least 2 months.

3 To use: Add frozen cubes directly to simmering beans, soups, and the like.

INFUSING

Hot peppers' strong, spicy flavor infuses wonderfully in vinegar. The same technique works for vodka or bourbon, making a spicy base for cocktails. Hot honey is another favorite: Sweet, yet balanced, it's perfect drizzled on proteins and roasted vegetables or served with soft, spreadable cheeses.

HOT PEPPER VINEGAR

In my experience, making pepper vinegar usually means combining whatever hot peppers are in one's garden with distilled white vinegar or maybe apple cider vinegar. Slice your peppers (or just halve them) and add them to a food-safe container. Add vinegar to completely cover and let them steep for several weeks. You can pack your peppers into narrow-necked bottles for gifting, or just use regular old jars (if you use jars and your pepper slices float to the surface, give them a gentle shake every few days). You can eat those peppers as pickles as you go through the vinegar, or add more vinegar to get a second (somewhat less potent) batch. See the core recipe for infusing vinegar (page 66) for more.

HOT HONEY

Hot honey has become popular in recent years as a condiment, and it's incredibly easy to make. If you add a lot of peppers, your honey will ferment slightly (never a bad thing), as the mixture will have a higher water content. If you don't want that, use fewer peppers and opt for lower-water varieties (like bird's-eye chiles rather than jalapeños).

Fill a half-pint jar about one-third to halfway with stemmed, halved hot peppers. Add honey to completely cover, leaving ½ inch of headspace. Let it steep out of direct sunlight, burping the jar occasionally if pressure builds up, for at least 2 weeks or until it has a flavor you enjoy.

PICKLING AND FERMENTING

Peppers are the perfect entry point to the world of pickling and fermenting, offering a primer in the versatility of both techniques. Peppers can be lactofermented and used whole or sliced, or allowed to go a bit longer until soft, then blended up into hot sauce. Quick-pickled peppers can be eaten as, well, pickles, or turned into relishes and hot sauces. Both techniques play well with just about any spice, herb, or other flavoring you can throw at them. The playground of possibilities is limited only by your imagination.

Quick-Pickling Peppers

Pickled peppers follow the same basic formula: Make a brine, prepare the peppers, and pack (along with other ingredients, like garlic and spices) in jars, pour the brine over, and then refrigerate or can. Refrigerator pickles have more of a crisp crunch and a fresh bite, whereas canned peppers are softer. This technique can be applied to whatever peppers you have, in whatever quantities.

Making the Brine

1 Use 5 parts vinegar (5 percent acidity) to 1 part water (so 5 cups vinegar to each 1 cup water), and ½ teaspoon salt per pint. For sweeter pickles, add 1 to 2 teaspoons of sugar per pint.

2 Simmer the brine for 5 to 10 minutes with any spices or aromatics desired (see flavoring ideas on page 204), and pour over peppers while hot.

Peeling and Preparing Your Peppers

3 Thicker-skinned peppers (like jalapeños) can best if peeled, as the peels can get tough. Follow the guidance under canning peppers (see page 210) or slit and blanch the peppers in boiling water for several minutes, allow them to cool

(continued on next page)

Quick-Pickling Peppers *continued*

enough to handle, then peel. However, when I make refrigerator pickles, I tend to just slice them, skins and all, in slices up to ½ inch thick, then let them pickle away.

4 Bell peppers should be seeded and quartered. Smaller peppers can be stemmed and left whole but should be flattened after peeling and before canning.

Packing Your Jars and Canning Your Peppers

5 Pickled peppers are acidic, so they can be canned in a hot water bath.

6 Pack peppers into clean hot jars with ½ inch of headspace. Add hot brine to cover, leaving ½ inch of headspace.

7 Run a chopstick or other thin, nonmetal utensil along the inner edges of the jars to release any air bubbles. Wipe the rims of the jars with a clean, damp cloth. Add the lids and bands and screw down to hand tightness.

8 Process pints in a hot water bath canner for 10 minutes, adjusting for altitude (see page 39) if needed.

9 Let the jars cool for 24 hours before testing the seals (see page 36), then store out of direct sunlight at room temperature.

VARIATION: REFRIGERATOR PICKLES

For refrigerator pickles, pour hot brine over peppers in a heatproof jar or other container, let cool, and add the lid. Place in the fridge. Let the peppers sit for 1 to 2 days or until completely pickled through.

Pickled Pepper Flavoring Ideas

CILANTRO AND JALAPEÑO: For each 10 cups sliced jalapeños, add 1 cup fresh cilantro leaves or stems (if canning, use ½ cup dried), 1 thinly sliced small yellow onion, the peel of 1 lemon cut into strips, 2 teaspoons black peppercorns, and the juice of 1 lemon. This tastes best with a brine using distilled white vinegar.

ONION AND CORIANDER: Combine 3 sliced poblano peppers with 1 sliced yellow onion, 2 tablespoons black peppercorns, and 1 tablespoon coriander seeds. This tastes best with distilled white vinegar as well.

STRAWBERRY OR BLACKBERRY: For each pint, add a spoonful of strawberry or blackberry jam to your pickling brine, stirring to dissolve completely. To each pint jar, add ¼ teaspoon coriander seeds and ¼ teaspoon black peppercorns. This works well with a brine of apple cider vinegar, distilled white vinegar, or white wine vinegar.

ROASTED PICKLED PEPPERS: Roast bell peppers as you would to remove the peels, but blacken the peels in some places (without annihilating the pepper underneath) to get a roasted flavor. Add ¼ to ½ teaspoon smoked paprika per pint of brine for an extra-smoky flavor, if desired. Add 1 clove garlic per pint, if desired. One to 2 peppers will typically fit in a pint jar.

Aji Dulce Pepper Relish

These sweet, bright peppers need very little to make them sing. Use this relish as is, whisk it with extra-virgin olive oil or sesame oil for a dressing, or blend it to make a tasty, tangy pepper sauce. Adjust flavorings as needed.

— Makes 1 quart

- **About ⅓ pound fresh aji dulce peppers**
- **Zest of ½ lime**
- **Juice of 1 lime**
- **1½ teaspoons salt**
- **1⅓ cups water**
- **⅔ cup apple cider vinegar**

1 Halve and stem the peppers, then cut them into ¼-inch slices (or thinner). Add the peppers to a quart jar along with the lime zest and juice.

2 In a small bowl, whisk together the salt, water, and vinegar until the salt is dissolved, then pour the brine over the peppers to cover completely.

3 Let the peppers pickle in the fridge for 4 to 12 hours before using. They will last for at least 2 weeks in the fridge.

VARIATION: AJI DULCE PEPPER SAUCE

If you just want to make pepper sauce, stem and halve the peppers, but don't bother slicing them. Follow the recipe above and let the peppers pickle in the fridge for 1 to 2 days, then blend until smooth. You can strain before using or use as is.

Jalapeño Relish

You can add or change amounts here (more onion or less jalapeño, for example) to suit your tastes. Since this is a refrigerator pickle, there's more flexibility with ingredient ratios than with canning. This relish is the perfect topping for tacos, rice and beans, or whatever else your imagination dreams up! It can also be used as a sauce or dressing—just whisk with a bit of olive oil, sour cream, or yogurt.

— Makes 1 pint

- **2 large jalapeños, finely diced**
- **½ small red onion, cut into ¼-inch dice**
- **1 small stalk celery, thinly sliced**
- **1 clove garlic, minced**
- **1 small bunch fresh cilantro leaves or stems, chopped**
- **½ teaspoon lime zest**
- **1 teaspoon salt**
- **⅔ cup apple cider vinegar**
- **⅔ cup water**

1 Combine the jalapeños, onion, celery, garlic, cilantro, and lime zest in a pint jar or bowl and gently shake or mix.

2 Make the brine: Add the salt, vinegar, and water to a saucepan set over medium heat and stir until the salt is dissolved.

3 Pour the brine over the relish until completely covered.

4 Cool the relish and store it in the fridge. For best results, let it pickle for at least several hours before serving. The relish keeps for 2 weeks or more in the fridge.

Fermented hot sauces, here made with seawater and regular old brine, can encompass a world of colors and flavors.

Fermented Hot Sauce

This recipe is a template you can use for whatever you like and have on hand. I've made wonderful hot sauces with hot peppers and everything from peaches to carrots to cocoa nibs and beyond. Let your imagination run wild!

—— Makes 1 pint

2–3 cloves garlic, unpeeled
1 pint whole hot peppers, hot pepper tops, and any other add-ins you want
½ tablespoon sea salt

1 Arrange the garlic cloves at the bottom of a pint jar. Tightly pack in the hot peppers and any other add-ins to fill the jar, leaving 1 inch of headspace.

2 Add the salt and fill the jar with enough water to cover, leaving ½ inch of headspace. Seal tightly and shake to dissolve the salt. Make sure the brine is still completely covering the botanicals (if it isn't, push them back under the brine).

3 Ferment at room temperature for about 3 weeks or until it has a flavor you enjoy.

4 Pour the contents of the jar into a food processor or blender and blend to your desired consistency. Store in the fridge, where it will keep for months.

VARIATION: BIRD'S-EYE AND SERRANO SAUCE

Use green bird's-eye chiles and/or serrano peppers (you can do half and half or all of one or the other) plus ¼ teaspoon black peppercorns for a tangy green pepper sauce. I typically double the garlic, too.

VARIATION: HABANERO SAUCES

VERSION 1: Use 2 cloves garlic and about 2 cups fresh habanero peppers.

VERSION 2: Use about 2 cups fresh habanero peppers and 2 cloves garlic with ¼ teaspoon black peppercorns and 1 to 2 sprigs thyme.

VERSION 3: Use about 1 cup fresh habanero peppers and 1 cup fresh strawberries or strawberry tops with 2 cloves garlic. Note that the sugar in the fruit can make it ferment vigorously, so check often.

Red Chile Chocolate Hot Sauce

Inspired by mole, this variation on basic hot sauce incorporates cocoa and cinnamon for depth and richness. Shaking the jar *at least* once a day, preferably more, is critical because the powdered ingredients will float to the top—disrupting the surface keeps them from inviting pathogen growth.

—— Makes 1 pint

1 pint whole hot peppers (I use red guajillo)
2 cloves garlic, peeled
1 (4-inch) strip orange peel
3 tablespoons unsweetened cocoa powder
1 teaspoon ground cinnamon
1½ teaspoons salt

1 Pack a pint jar with the peppers, garlic, orange peel, cocoa powder, and cinnamon.

2 Add the salt and fill with enough water to cover, leaving ½ inch of headspace. Seal tightly and shake to dissolve the salt.

3 Ferment at room temperature for 2 to 4 weeks (give it a smell test after 2 weeks), shaking the jar daily.

4 Pour the contents of the jar into a food processor or blender and blend to your desired consistency. Store in the fridge, where it will keep for months.

Preserving Around the World

Thailand, with Leela Punyaratabandhu

Leela Punyaratabandhu is a food writer, illustrator, and expert on Thai food, which she discusses in her books and on her blog, *SheSimmers*. She says that Thailand employs a wide variety of preservation methods influenced by the regional climate:

> The mountainous, landlocked north is typically cold and dry in the winter, while the sea-flanked south is warm and humid almost year-round. In the north, you'll find unique preservation methods like salted beef hung out to dry in the open air (nuea nam khang, literally "dew beef") or fermented soybeans (thua nao, literally "rotten beans"), which are more effective in cooler, less humid weather. In contrast, riverine regions feature various types of fermented freshwater fish, and the coastal areas in the east, west, and south are known for a wide range of fermented seafood products, such as shrimp paste and fish sauce.

Some preserved products, like fish sauce and dried chiles, are central to Thai cuisine and always in high demand, and preserves are staples across every region of Thailand. "If you were to remove even just a few basic staples, like shrimp paste, fish sauce (nam pla), fermented freshwater fish sauce (pla ra), or dried chiles, many Thai dishes that we know would no longer exist."

Freshwater fish sauce is made in the riverine upper central region during rainy season, when the freshwater fish known as pla soi (*Henicorhynchus siamensis*) is caught by the truckload, then fermented for a year. "By the time the rainy season returns the following year," Punyaratabandhu explains, "this year's catch will have transformed into fish sauce, while a new batch of fish is being salted and fermented in large clay jars, ready to be turned into fish sauce the following year." In the northeast, a similar ritual results in a fish sauce made by fermenting freshwater fish with pineapple—a uniquely microregional food not found anywhere else in Thailand.

Punyaratabandhu notes that the primary driver for food fermentation in Thailand is reducing waste, but flavor and health benefits are also important factors. Sticky rice is a prime example: Rice is shelf-stable for long periods, so it is not fermented for preservation. "People ferment cooked sticky rice because they enjoy its flavor, and it serves as both a tasty snack and a source of probiotics—long before the benefits of pre- and probiotics were widely understood. In a culture where dairy isn't traditionally consumed, this fermented rice acts as a nondairy equivalent to yogurt or kefir in Thailand," Punyaratabandhu says.

Doc's Hot Sauce

Danielle Holliday (Doc) was my best friend, my soulmate in all things culinary, and a big believer in and frequent consumer of my fermented hot sauces. This was one we made together along with our dear friend Jeremy Fisher. I still have a bottle of that original batch from 2018 in my fridge, and I cherish it like a prized family heirloom (though at this point it has lost nearly all its heat). Our hot sauce was a versatile and delicious concoction of bird's-eye chiles, garlic, and ginger. Here's how to make your own.

—— Makes 1 quart

3 cups green bird's-eye chiles

4–6 cloves garlic, peeled or unpeeled

1 (3-inch) knob ginger, unpeeled if organic

1½–2 tablespoons salt

1 Combine the chiles, garlic, and ginger in a quart jar, leaving 1 inch of headspace.

2 Add the salt and fill with enough water to cover, leaving ½ inch of headspace. Seal tightly and shake to dissolve the salt. Make sure the brine is still completely covering the botanicals (if it isn't, push them back under the brine).

3 Ferment at room temperature for about 3 weeks or until it has a flavor you enjoy.

4 Pour the contents of the jar into a food processor or blender and blend to your desired consistency. Store in the fridge, where it will keep for months. It will be hottest within a few months of making.

Hot-and-Sour Bird's-Eye Sauce

This is one of the hotter sauces I make—use sparingly when you need a front-of-the-palate kick of heat. After the peppers have sat and softened in their brine for just a couple of days, they're ready to be blended. You can swap the bird's-eye chiles for other peppers, like cayenne, to get different flavor profiles.

—— Makes about 1 pint

2 cups red bird's-eye chiles, stems removed

2 cloves garlic, peeled or unpeeled

2 cups apple cider vinegar or distilled white vinegar, plus more if needed

1–2 teaspoons salt

1 Add the chiles and garlic to a pint jar, leaving about 1 inch of headspace.

2 Pour in the vinegar, adding more if needed to cover the chiles completely.

3 Place the container in the fridge. Or weight your peppers and set the container out of direct sunlight. Let sit for 2 to 3 days to soften the peppers.

4 Place the entire contents of the jar in a blender and blend until smooth. Strain the solids out, if desired, or leave them in for a thicker sauce.

5 Store in an airtight container. You can keep this out of direct sunlight in a cool place for at least 2 to 3 weeks, or in the fridge for at least a couple of months. Shake before using if the sauce separates.

CANNING

Pickled peppers can be canned in a hot water bath, but peppers canned just in water or light brine need to be pressure canned.

Pressure Canning Peppers

1 For sweet peppers and thin-skinned peppers, remove the stems and (for large peppers like bell peppers) quarter and remove the seeds. Blanch them for 3 minutes in boiling water.

Thick-skinned chiles need some extra preparation: Blister the skins in a 400°F/200°C oven for 6 to 8 minutes, or place the peppers on the flame of a gas burner, rotating regularly, until their skins are blistered all over. Place the peppers in a paper bag and seal, or in a bowl covered with a tea towel, to hold in steam and make them easier to peel. Cool for 10 to 20 minutes, until the skins peel away easily, then peel your peppers and discard the skins (you can also save the skins and dry them, then crumble and try them out as a seasoning).

2 Place jars in your pressure canner and heat it up. Then, using tongs, remove the hot jars from the canner.

3 Pack the peppers loosely into hot jars with 1 inch of headspace, adding ½ teaspoon of salt per pint if you wish. Fill the jars with boiling water, leaving 1 inch of headspace.

4 Run a chopstick or other thin, nonmetal utensil along the inner edges of the jars to release any air bubbles. Wipe the rims of the jars with a clean, damp cloth. Add the lids and bands and screw down to hand tightness.

5 Process pints in a dial gauge pressure canner at 11 pounds or a weighted gauge pressure canner at 10 pounds for 35 minutes, adjusting for altitude (see page 39) if needed.

6 Allow the canner to depressurize completely. Let the jars cool for 24 hours before testing the seals (see page 40), then store out of direct sunlight at room temperature.

Easy Candied Jalapeños

I enjoy these candied jalapeños because they're not cloyingly sweet, and the spices add a bit of complexity. These are nice alongside eggs or other rich proteins, or even on top of a spinach salad with strawberries.

If you prefer, you can swap two or three poblano peppers for the jalapeños; just cut them in half before slicing. I tend to make these as refrigerator pickles, but I opt to can them when I've already got the canner running for other projects.

— Makes 1 pint

- **1⅛ cups sugar**
- **½ teaspoon coriander seeds**
- **½ teaspoon black peppercorns**
- **¼ teaspoon salt**
- **½ cup apple cider vinegar**
- **4–6 jalapeños, cut into ¼-inch slices**

1 Make the brine: Combine the sugar, coriander, peppercorns, salt, and vinegar in a saucepan and heat just until boiling, whisking to dissolve the sugar and salt.

2 If canning, place a pint jar in your hot water bath canner and heat it up. Then, using tongs, remove the hot jar from the canner.

3 Pack the jalapeños into a jar and pour the brine over them, leaving ½ inch of headspace. Top off with an extra splash of vinegar, if needed.

4 For refrigerator pickles, let them cool and refrigerate for 2 days or until pickled through. They will last in the fridge for at least 3 weeks if they stay under the brine.

5 If canning, run a chopstick or other thin, nonmetal utensil along the inner edges of the jars to release any air bubbles. Wipe the rims of the jars with a clean, damp cloth. Add the lids and bands and screw down to hand tightness.

6 Process the pints for 15 minutes in a hot water bath canner, adjusting for altitude (see page 39) if needed.

7 Let the jars cool for 24 hours before testing the seals (see page 36), then store out of direct sunlight at room temperature.

Sweet-and-Sour Roasted Red Pepper Jam

I love using this as a sauce more than as a jam—it's a sweet-and-sour dip for everything from fried snacks, like eggrolls, to vegetables and beyond. It's also a nice stand-in for pepper jelly on cream cheese to get that traditional potluck food without quite as much sweetness. If you want to get experimental, try swapping the apple cider vinegar for Herb-Infused Vinegar (page 173) to layer your flavors in fun ways; just make sure your vinegar has 5 percent acidity.

— Makes about 2 pints

- **5 red bell peppers**
- **2 cups apple cider vinegar**
- **2 cups sugar**
- **1 teaspoon salt**
- **Freshly grated nutmeg**

1 Halve and seed the peppers and lay them on a baking sheet skin side up.

2 Broil on high for several minutes until the skin is charred and blistered, or char them over an open flame (see page 202). The skin should be blackened in some places but not all over.

3 Place the hot, charred peppers in a paper bag or a bowl covered with a tea towel to hold in steam and make them easier to peel.

4 Allow the peppers to cool for 10 to 20 minutes, until the skins peel away easily, then peel your peppers.

5 Place half of your peppers in a blender with 1 cup of the apple cider vinegar and blend until smooth. Repeat with the remaining peppers and 1 cup vinegar.

6 Combine the pepper mixture, sugar, and salt in a large saucepan over medium heat. Cook, stirring occasionally (stir frequently toward the end of cooking), until it coats the back of a spoon: For a loose jam or sauce, cook for 20 to 35 minutes, and for a thicker jam texture, cook for an additional 5 to 10 minutes.

7 Remove the jam from the heat, add nutmeg to taste, and stir to combine.

8 If canning, place two pint jars in your hot water bath canner and heat it up. Then, using tongs, remove the hot jars from the canner. Pour the jam into the jars, leaving ½ inch of headspace.

9 If refrigerating, pour the jam into the jars, leaving no headspace. Allow the jam to cool completely before storing in the refrigerator. It will last for at least 2 weeks.

10 If canning, run a chopstick or other thin, nonmetal utensil along the inner edges of the jars to release any air bubbles. Wipe the rims of the jars with a clean, damp cloth. Add the lids and bands and screw down to hand tightness.

11 Process the pints in a hot water bath canner for 15 minutes, adjusting for altitude (see page 39) if needed.

12 Let the jars cool for 24 hours before testing the seals (see page 36), then store out of direct sunlight at room temperature.

Potatoes

Choose fresh, firm potatoes without scrapes or blemishes. Potatoes are best stored in a cool, dry place with some airflow and away from pests. Potatoes with thin skins do not last as long as thicker-skinned potatoes, and red potatoes don't last as long as white potatoes.

If you're harvesting your own potatoes, clean them before storing. Brush off potatoes grown in sandy soil, and wash those grown in clay that may stick to the potatoes, then allow them to dry completely before storing. Cure your newly dug potatoes for 7 to 10 days in a dark, well-ventilated area with a moderate temperature (like a very cool room temperature) and high humidity. This helps the potatoes last longer. After they've cured, store potatoes between 40 to 46°F/4 to 8°C for the best flavor and shelf life.

Keeping potatoes away from light helps prevent them from turning green. While eating a small amount of the green on potatoes is probably safe, eating a lot can cause illness. Be sure to peel or cut away any greening, and discard any bitter-tasting potatoes.

DRYING

Thoroughly wash potatoes and peel if desired. (I often leave them unpeeled, but the peels can add a bit more texture and a slightly more bitter flavor, so remove them if you don't enjoy them.) Cut into ¼-inch-thick shoestrings or ⅛-inch-thick slices. If you choose slices, you may want to halve or quarter very large potatoes so the final size of the slices is more manageable.

Steam blanch for 6 to 8 minutes, or hot-water blanch for 5 to 6½ minutes. Dehydrate at 135 to 140°F/57 to 60°C for 6 to 12 hours, or until crisp and brittle. Store in an airtight container out of direct sunlight and away from high humidity, where they will last for at least 4 months.

Dried potatoes can be rehydrated in soups, stews, and other dishes.

FREEZING

Baked and boiled potatoes do not freeze well, turning into a mealy, mushy mess upon thawing. Barely cooked new potatoes, though, freeze quite well for later use.

New potatoes should be washed and peeled or scraped. Blanch potatoes in boiling water for 3 minutes for small new potatoes and 5 minutes for larger new potatoes. Cool, drain, then package either whole or cut into halves or quarters, leaving ½ inch of headspace.

Ways to Preserve Potatoes	Shelf-stable	Fast	Low waste	Ready meals and ingredients	Big flavor
French Fries (page 213)		X		X	

French Fries

I've encountered many methods over the years for freezing fries, but my favorite remains the one from the University of Georgia Cooperative Extension's publication *So Easy to Preserve*, in part because the prep when you're ready to serve your fries is so easy. The potatoes are partially fried before freezing to maintain their texture. Use mature white potatoes that have been stored for 30 days.

Mature white potatoes

1 Wash and peel the potatoes. Cut first into ½-inch-thick slices and then into ⅓- to ½-inch-thick matchsticks. Rinse the matchsticks in cold water and dry thoroughly.

2 Deep-fry small batches of potatoes at a time in oil heated to 360°F/182°C until just tender but before they turn brown, about 5 minutes. Drain on a paper towel and cool.

3 Package with ½ inch of headspace, seal, and freeze, where they will last for at least a couple of months.

4 When it's time to serve, brown them in a 475°F/240°C oven for 10 to 15 minutes, or until golden brown.

CANNING

Potatoes can be canned for a convenient grab-and-go ingredient, particularly if you want to make soup or mashed potatoes but have very little energy for cooking. I typically freeze my potatoes or simply store them since they store well; however, a few jars of canned potatoes are welcome for days when I need a comforting starch and am running on empty.

Potatoes need to be pressure canned. And note that potatoes stored in especially cold places might discolor when canned.

Pressure Canning Potatoes

1 Prepare a solution of 1 teaspoon ascorbic acid to 1 gallon of water.

2 Wash and peel the potatoes. If you're canning whole potatoes, choose small (1- to 2-inch-diameter) potatoes. Or cut larger potatoes into ½-inch cubes.

3 Immediately after peeling and/or cutting, place the potatoes in the ascorbic acid solution, then drain.

4 Place the potatoes in a large pot of hot water. Boil whole potatoes for 10 minutes; boil cubed potatoes for 2 to 3 minutes.

5 Meanwhile, place jars in your pressure canner and heat it up. Then, using tongs, remove the hot jars from the canner.

6 Drain the potatoes and pack them into hot jars, leaving 1 inch of headspace. Add salt (½ teaspoon per pint, 1 teaspoon per quart) if you wish.

7 Fill the jars with fresh boiling water, leaving 1 inch of headspace.

8 Run a chopstick or other thin, nonmetal utensil along the inner edges of the jars to release any air bubbles. Wipe the rims of the jars with a clean, damp cloth. Add the lids and bands and screw down to hand tightness.

9 Set your pressure canner to 11 pounds pressure (dial gauge or weighted gauge) and process for 35 minutes for pints or 40 minutes for quarts, adjusting for altitude (see page 39) as needed.

10 Allow the canner to depressurize completely. Let the jars cool for 24 hours before testing the seals (see page 40), then store out of direct sunlight at room temperature.

PICKLING AND FERMENTING

You can quick pickle thinly sliced potatoes and add whatever flavoring you like. I use the same brine ratios as for making pickled okra (see page 194), then add 3 teaspoons to 1 tablespoon of seasoning per pint. (Since potatoes are mildly flavored, the pickles taste like very little without seasoning, so I tend to have a heavy hand.) Some of my favorite seasonings include a very light sprinkle of lavender with a heavier sprinkle of rosemary and a strip of lemon zest, or a few teaspoons of a masala spice pickling blend.

Potatoes can also be fermented in a 2 to 3 percent brine (see brine ratios, page 49) as either ½-inch cubes, ½-inch-thick slices, or ½-inch-thick matchsticks. I ferment them for several days, then store them in the fridge to make fries and other dishes. Note that for potatoes, fermenting isn't a preservation strategy so much as a flavor- and nutrition-enhancing one. But it's a delicious strategy nonetheless.

Radishes

One thing I love about radishes is that they have a lot of range: from sweet to spicy, sharp and biting to mellow—there really is a ton of radish possibilities to explore.

PICKLING AND FERMENTING

Not every preservation technique works well for radishes: Drying, for example, tends to alter their flavor and aroma in unpleasant ways, and the texture isn't great. They also don't freeze well, as their famously crisp texture is lost, and they become discolored and not-so-great tasting. But when it comes to preserving radishes, acidity is your friend: Pickling and fermenting keep textures palatable and flavors bright.

Ways to Preserve Radishes	Shelf-stable	Fast	Low waste	Ready meals and ingredients	Big flavor
Pickled Red Radishes (page 215)				X	X
Slightly Sweet-and-Sour Pickled Radishes (page 217)				X	X
Fermented Daikon (page 217)				X	X

Pickled Red Radishes

My grandpa loved radishes. Each place he would move as a kid, he would plant radish seeds. Even if the place was unfamiliar, once those radish seeds were in the ground, he told me, it felt like home. He mailed me his last packet of radish seeds, fished out of a drawer or cupboard in his overstuffed garage and dating back to probably the 1950s. He insisted I plant them and, while they unsurprisingly never sprouted, they did instill in me an association of this particular food with home, so much that I now have a radish tattooed on me as a reminder to find home wherever I am.

These pickled radishes are a good example of the way we can allow our recipes to be guides on a journey rather than a set-in-stone map. I use this recipe as a guide to making pickled radishes that remind me of my grandpa. Depending on the journey you're on, you might use it to make another kind of pickle or add different spices.

— Makes about 2 quarts

- **½ cup salt**
- **4 cups distilled white vinegar**
- **4 cups water**
- **2 pounds red radishes**
- **½ tablespoon dill seeds**
- **½ teaspoon celery seeds**

1. Make the brine: Combine the salt, vinegar, and water in a pot and heat, stirring until the salt is completely dissolved.

2. Thinly slice the radishes (or use a mandoline). Divide the radishes, dill seeds, and celery seeds between two quart jars.

3. Pour the brine over the radishes until they are completely covered.

4. Seal the lids tightly and let the radishes pickle in the fridge for at least 4 hours, or until they have a flavor you like. The sooner you eat them, the crisper they'll be: I tend to eat these within about a week, but they will last longer.

NOTE: This recipe makes more brine than you need, so it's the perfect excuse to pickle any extra veggies you happen to have knocking around in the crisper.

Preserving Around the World

Vietnam, with Nguyễn Thiên Ân

Nguyễn Thiên Ân is the founder of the Under the Squash Vines website and an avid gardener, cook, and collector of stories. She says:

> At its core, Vietnamese food is about family, community, and sharing. Vietnamese are very open-minded and love to explore new cuisines and incorporate them into our own melting pot of complex flavor profiles, as seen with the French-influenced bánh mì (Vietnamese sandwich) and cà phê sữa đá (Vietnamese iced coffee), just as long as we can share them with our family and friends. If you've ever been invited to dinner at a Vietnamese person's home, then you know that our meals are served family-style. The components of a Vietnamese meal are a stir-fry dish (đồ xào), a braised dish (đồ kho), and a soup dish (canh), all to be served with jasmine rice.

She says the art of food fermentation and pickling "is ingrained in our heritage, as deeply as the rich rivers that engrave the map of the country." She loves quick pickling, but nothing replaces the flavor of fermented vegetables, and fermented shrimp or fish or dưa món (a mixture of daikon radishes, chiles, garlic, and carrots fermented in fish sauce) are often served as side dishes to complement less flavorful foods, which is especially important "when the bulk a family can afford is rice." Pickles like dồ chua (pickled carrots and daikon radishes, always present on a banh mi sandwich, but also in fried spring rolls or vermicelli bowls) add flavor and texture. "Those dishes are already delicious in their own right, but when paired with tangy, crunchy carrots and daikon radish, they become magical."

Dưa món is made with vegetables that are dehydrated, then pickled, giving them their unique texture. During the month leading up to Tết (Vietnamese Lunar New Year celebration), vegetables for the pickles are sun dried: "Every year, about two weeks before Tết, every balcony and rooftop of everyone, young and old, rich and poor, would be decorated with the natural colors of Tết vegetables." She says, "Dưa món is the cultural emblem that brings us all together and lights the communal fire of anticipation and hopefulness for the new year."

She connects food preservation not only to skills passed between generations but to survival and ancient legends. In one legend, the Water God Thủy Tinh and the Mountain God Sơn Tinh were rivals for the love of Princess Mỵ Nương. Thủy Tinh lost, and in anger summoned monsoons and torrential rain to destroy Sơn Tinh. To defend his home, Sơn Tinh conjured the spirits of the mountains to ascend and assembled the mountain fortresses that still weave their way through the Vietnamese landscape. Thủy Tinh was forced to retreat but never forgot his old wound, so each year, Thủy Tinh batters the Earth with storms. Thiên Ân writes:

> So when the very rivers that nourish our livelihoods morph into cruel tidal floods that wash away our crops, we retreat to higher ground: often the cramped loft space under the roof, where we store rice and other provisions—the fermented/pickled foods we've been saving in anticipation of the gods' vindictive rage.
>
> And so as our parents instructed us as their parents instructed them: "When the water god is angry, climb as high as you can on the roof, and make sure you have plenty of preserved foods up there with you."

Slightly Sweet-and-Sour Pickled Radishes

This is a good base recipe for larger radishes like daikon and some of the big, round heirloom varieties (though small red radishes will work, too). I pour room-temperature brine over my radishes, then pickle them in the refrigerator, to preserve the texture.

—— Makes 1 quart

- **2 cups distilled white vinegar**
- **2 cups water**
- **1 tablespoon sugar**
- **1½–2 tablespoons salt**
- **2–3 pounds daikon or other large radishes, sliced ¼ inch thick**
- **2 teaspoons red pepper flakes**
- **1 (2- to 3-inch) strip lemon peel**

1. Make the brine: Whisk together the vinegar, water, sugar, and salt in a bowl until the sugar and salt dissolve.

2. Place the radishes, pepper flakes, and lemon peel in a quart jar. Add brine to cover. Let pickle for 1 to 2 days in the fridge, where the radishes will last for 1 month or more if kept under the pickling brine.

VARIATION: WARMING SPICE BLEND

For another flavor profile, use ½ teaspoon fennel seeds, ¼ teaspoon whole cloves, and ½ teaspoon red pepper flakes (optional).

FERMENTED DAIKON

One of my greatest fermentation memories is of sitting at Sandor Katz's kitchen island, tucking into daikon radishes that he fermented in the large stainless steel tank in his yard. The radishes, grown by a friend, were sour, still slightly crisp, and utterly delicious. Prior to this, I had only fermented daikon in kimchi. Having them as a standalone ferment was an epiphany.

Daikon radishes are naturally suited to fermentation and the perfect complement to so many spices. I've had wonderful ones made with turmeric and mustard, others with garlic and hot peppers, and plenty just fermented with nothing but water, salt, and time.

Scrub any dirt from your radish and gently rinse. Make a 2 to 3 percent brine (see brine ratios, page 49), cool to room temperature if heated, and pour over your sliced radish (and any flavorings, if using) to cover completely.

Seal the lid, place on a plate or tray to catch any drips, and allow to ferment, burping every day during the early stages when it's very actively fermenting.

You can let these go for as long as you want. I've pulled some just a few days in when they're still crisp and barely pickled, and let others go for months. If you have enough space, you can pickle whole radishes, then slice when you're ready to serve. Just make sure they're completely submerged in brine.

Rhubarb

Rhubarb, a member of the buckwheat family, is tart and bright and is most often used in desserts like rhubarb pie. I love it in relishes and syrups, which allow me to enjoy its tangy taste without having to bust out the pie tins.

Rhubarb gets its tart flavor from oxalic acid, which is fine in small doses but toxic in larger ones. (You know the old saying, "The dose makes the poison"? Oxalic acid is an example of that.) The stems have minimal oxalic acid and are safe for most people to consume, but the leaves contain a toxic amount of oxalic acid and should never be eaten.

Choose rhubarb with crisp, firm stems without blemishes. If you grow your own, preserve your rhubarb as soon as possible after harvest for the best flavor. Separate stems from leaves before cooking and add the leaves to your compost. Harvest rhubarb when the stalks are big enough to use (maybe about as big around as your thumb) but still snap easily; older rhubarb stalks can be tough and stringy, so continue harvesting as leaves mature for the best result.

FREEZING

Cut rhubarb stalks to the desired length and pack in 40 percent syrup (page 19) with headspace, then freeze. You can also freeze rhubarb in juice, if preferred.

PICKLING

Pickled rhubarb is a boon to my fellow sour food aficionados looking for a new direction to take their passion for pickling. Basic pickled rhubarb is a template for your mind's wildest imaginings in the realm of sour foods—crank the acid and salinity up or down, add seasonings (or don't), and use it as a relish or on cheese trays. Speaking of relish, rhubarb and black pepper relish is a springtime favorite. I hope you will enjoy it as much as I do as the days lengthen and the weather warms.

BASIC PICKLED RHUBARB

Slice the rhubarb into ¼-inch slices, then add them to a jar with ½ inch of headspace. Add any flavorings you want (a teaspoon or so of baking spices or a bit of five-spice powder are great, as are strips of citrus zest). Make a brine with the same ratio as pickled okra (see page 194), cool to room temperature, and pour over the rhubarb to completely cover. Add the lid, pop the jar in the fridge, and wait at least 24 hours until the rhubarb is pickled through. Since rhubarb floats to the top of the brine, I like to give the jar a little shake halfway through the pickling process to redistribute it. Store it in the fridge, where it will last for several weeks.

Since this is a refrigerator pickle, you can adjust the acid and/or salt a bit to suit your tastes. This does make a pretty sour and salty pickle, so think of it as more of a condiment than a pickle you eat by itself.

Ways to Preserve Rhubarb	Shelf-stable	Fast	Low waste	Ready meals and ingredients	Big flavor
Basic Pickled Rhubarb (above)				X	X
Rhubarb and Black Pepper Relish (page 219)				X	X

Rhubarb and Black Pepper Relish

Rhubarb tastes like springtime to me, and I can almost feel the sun on my skin when I take a bite. This recipe calls for macerating the rhubarb before cooking it quickly, which results in a loose jam consistency (plus the bits of rhubarb) that is perfect on things like Halloumi (page 349) or fried goat cheese, or as a dip or side for fruit and charcuterie plates. It is an easy, low-effort way to use just a little bit of rhubarb. Mix things up by swapping strips of citrus peel for the black pepper, or use both.

—— Makes about 1 half-pint

2 stalks rhubarb, cut into ¼-inch dice

¼ cup sugar

½ teaspoon freshly ground black pepper

1 Toss the rhubarb with the sugar and pepper and let it macerate for 3 to 4 hours until it is sitting in a pool of liquid.

2 Pour the mixture into a saucepan over medium-low heat. Simmer until thickened, 5 to 10 minutes, stirring at regular intervals and stirring constantly toward the end.

3 Cool the relish completely and store it in the fridge, where it will last for a couple of weeks.

Rhubarb and Black Pepper Relish

CANNING

Stewed rhubarb can be canned as a quick addition to desserts throughout the year. Remove and discard the rhubarb leaves. Cut the stalks into ½- to 1-inch-long pieces and place them in a large saucepan. Mix in ½ cup sugar per quart of sliced rhubarb, and let the mixture stand for 15 minutes or so until juice appears.

Heat the jars in your canner, then remove them with tongs. Bring the rhubarb mixture to a boil over medium-high heat. Once it's boiling, pour it immediately into hot jars, leaving ½ inch of headspace.

Using a plastic chopstick or other nonmetal utensil, remove any air bubbles, wipe the rims, add the lids and bands, and process, adjusting for altitude (see page 39) if needed. In a hot water bath, process pints and quarts for 15 minutes. In a dial gauge canner, process for 8 minutes at 6 pounds pressure; in a weighted gauge canner, process for 8 minutes at 5 pounds pressure.

MAKING SYRUPS

Rhubarb lends itself well to syrup making. Strawberry-rhubarb syrup is a sweet-and-sour favorite over ice cream or in summertime drinks (try it with soda water or in lemonade or limeade). To make it, follow the instructions for making fruit syrups (page 79), using a 3:1 ratio of strawberries to rhubarb (so 3 cups strawberries to 1 cup rhubarb). Adjust that ratio up or down based on your tastes and whatever fruit you have around. Feel free to swap in other berries, like blueberries. Store it in the fridge and use it liberally on just about everything.

Scallions and Scapes

Scallions (also called green onions) and garlic scapes (the edible, curly green shoots from hard-neck garlic) are a must-have topping for baked potatoes and hearty, creamy soups, but they're perfect in so many other dishes, too. I'll mix an herb cube (see page 21) into my pasta-cooking water, for example, or toss frozen scallions into a chowder at the end of cooking if fresh aren't available.

Look for scallions and scapes that are fresh (not wilted or slimy) with upright stalks and tight bulbs. Once you use the scallion greens, replant the bulbs in your garden or in a planter conveniently near (or in) your kitchen so you always have fresh scallions at hand.

FREEZING

Freezing offers an easy way to bring the flavor of scallions and scapes into your meals. Freezing them sliced means that, once thawed, they will maintain their flavor but will have an altered texture—not crisp, and perhaps a bit tough, but still usable. I use frozen scallions and scapes in soups, stews, and sauces when I don't have raw ones.

Scallions and scapes do not require blanching before freezing. To freeze, slice to desired thickness, then dry pack into freezer bags or freezer-safe containers, leaving ½ inch of headspace. Or (my preference): Freeze in a single layer on a baking sheet lined with parchment paper or a silicone mat for about 4 hours or until frozen through, then package leaving no headspace.

You can also blend up (or thinly slice) your scallions and scapes and add to ice cube trays to make herb cubes that you can add to sauces, soups, pasta, etc. See the directions for making herb cubes on page 20.

PICKLING

Pickled scallions and scapes are an easy staple to have in the fridge, great for adding lots of flavor to dishes quickly. Use these blended up as a quick, pickle-y sauce (or whisk the blend with oil for a quick vinaigrette) or finely slice them and add to dishes. You can can these, which results in a softer texture, or (my preference) make refrigerator pickles. When I make the refrigerator pickles, I like to pour the hot brine over the scallions, but for a firmer final product, cool the brine first.

Ways to Preserve Scallions and Scapes	Shelf-stable	Fast	Low waste	Ready meals and ingredients	Big flavor
Pickled Scapes and Scallions (page 221)		X		X	X

Pickled Scapes and Scallions

In *A Rising Tide*, DL Acken and Emily Lycopolus share their recipe for extending the garlic scape season though pickling. I like their simple approach and over the last couple of seasons have adapted it to my own kitchen. This is that adapted version. I've found this method works well for not just garlic scapes and scallions but any similar shoots, like onion greens (from your regular mature, full-size onions as they grow), ramps, and wild garlic.

Serve these pickles on salads, blended into sauces, as toppings on soups and pasta, or with meat and fish, and be sure to save your pickling liquid to whisk into vinaigrettes or use as you would any other extra brine (see page 50).

—— Makes 1 pint or 2 half-pints

- **1–2 tablespoons spices (see note; optional)**
- **1½ cups apple cider vinegar, distilled white vinegar, or white wine vinegar**
- **½ cup water**
- **2 tablespoons salt**
- **2 tablespoons sugar (optional)**
- **About ½ pound scapes or scallions, ends trimmed and reserved**

NOTE: Spices are optional, but these pickles do well with many pickling flavors like basic dill pickle brine (see page 159), or with mustard, black peppercorns, hot peppers, white pepper, thyme, and rosemary. Go easy on very floral or strong flavors (like fennel and coriander), which can overpower some other notes.

1. If canning, sterilize your jars by processing in a hot water bath for 10 minutes. Then, using tongs, remove the hot jars from the bath.
2. Add the spices (if using) to the bottom of the jar(s).
3. Make the brine: Place the vinegar, water, salt, and sugar (if using) in a medium saucepan and bring to a boil.
4. Coil your scapes tightly and pack them into the jar(s), continuing to pack your greens toward the center until the jar is full, leaving ½ inch of headspace. If space remains, add the ends trimmed from your scapes into the middle.
5. Pour the hot brine over the scapes, leaving ¼ inch of headspace. Ensure the scapes are entirely covered by the brine (if they start to pop up, press them down with a sterilized spoon or butter knife).
6. If making refrigerator pickles, cool to room temperature and refrigerate. Let them sit for a couple of weeks before using. They'll last for several weeks in the fridge.
7. If canning, run a chopstick or other thin, nonmetal utensil along the inner edges of the jars to release any air bubbles. Wipe the rims of the jars with a clean, damp cloth. Add the lids and bands and screw down to hand tightness.
8. Process for 7 minutes for half-pints and 10 minutes for pints in a hot water bath canner, adjusting for altitude (see page 39) if needed.
9. Let the jars cool for 24 hours before testing the seals (see page 36), then store out of direct sunlight at room temperature. Let them sit for a couple of weeks before opening.

Summer Squash and Zucchini

Summer squash is perhaps infamously abundant, as the zucchini left on unsuspecting friends' and neighbors' porches in summertime can attest. Choose firm summer squash with tender skin; they shouldn't have any soft spots or blemishes. If you won't be using them right away, store them whole in the refrigerator rather than sliced or cubed.

DRYING

To dry summer squash, wash your squash and trim the ends, then slice ¼ inch thick. Steam blanch for 2½ to 3 minutes or boiling-water blanch for ½ to 1 minute before shocking in an ice bath to cool (see page 17). Drain well. Dry in a dehydrator at 140°F/60°C for 10 to 12 hours or until pliable but dry.

FREEZING

Freezing works best with young, tender squash rather than big, watery ones.

Wash and slice squash ½ inch thick, boiling-water blanch for 2½ to 3 minutes, then shock to cool in an ice bath. Drain well. Freeze in a single layer on a rimmed sheet pan lined with parchment paper or a silicone mat for 8 to 12 hours or until frozen through. Place in an airtight container with no headspace, or, to freeze in a container, package leaving ½ inch of headspace.

For future baking projects, steam blanch grated zucchini for 1½ to 2 minutes, rinse with cold water, then drain very well, squeezing *gently* to remove water. Package into portions in freezer-safe containers, leaving ½ inch of headspace. Thaw before using, draining off any extra water. This process can work with large zucchinis, if needed, provided you use the firmer outer flesh rather than the watery, seedy center.

PICKLING

Like cucumbers, summer squash (which are in the same botanical family) lend themselves well to pickling. Zucchini, in particular, are a good substitute for cucumbers in quick pickles. For pickling, choose smaller, firm summer squash that aren't overly spongy or watery.

Ways to Preserve Summer Squash and Zucchini	Shelf-stable	Fast	Low waste	Ready meals and ingredients	Big flavor
Dill Squash Refrigerator Pickles (page 223)				X	X

Dill Squash Refrigerator Pickles

You can adapt any classic cucumber pickle recipes to summer squash, particularly zucchini. I usually make this recipe with spears, but you can also cut your squash into ¼- to ½-inch-thick rounds if you prefer pickle chips.

—— Makes about 1 gallon or 4 quarts

- 1 head garlic, cloves removed and peeled (about 12 cloves)
- 1 bunch fresh dill
- 4 sprigs thyme
- About 5 pounds summer squash, cut into 3- to 4-inch lengths
- ½–¾ cup salt
- ¼ cup black peppercorns
- 3 tablespoons coriander seeds
- 2–3 teaspoons red pepper flakes
- 4 bay leaves
- 8 cups water
- 6 cups apple cider vinegar
- 2 cups distilled white vinegar

1. Add half of the garlic, the dill, and the thyme to a 1-gallon food-safe container (or divide among four quart jars).
2. Add the summer squash, leaving 1 inch of headspace.
3. Make the brine: Add the remaining garlic along with the salt, peppercorns, coriander, pepper flakes, bay leaf, water, apple cider vinegar, and distilled white vinegar to a pot and heat until simmering.
4. Cool the brine slightly and pour it over the squash to cover, leaving ½ inch of headspace.
5. Allow the pickles to cool completely, then cover and store in the fridge, where they'll last for several weeks or more if kept submerged in brine.

Things to Do with a Large Zucchini

SEEDS

Giant zucchini seeds are usually soft, but they are occasionally firm enough to roast. Heat your oven to 325°F/160°C, toss your seeds in a bit of neutral oil and some seasonings (such as Lawry's seasoning salt, five-spice powder, or salt and dill weed), then toast in the oven until just golden. (If you are used to roasting pumpkin seeds, be aware that zucchini seeds toast up more quickly.) I start checking them after 5 to 7 minutes and usually pull them at 10 to 15.

Softer seeds can go in your freezer stock bag (page 20); just squeeze all the liquid out first.

FLESH AND SKIN

I dry my giant zucchini in rings or strips (see Five Spice Apple Rings, page 250, for the process). Then I rehydrate them in some stock that's simmering on the stove, maybe with some herb cubes (see page 21), Three-Root Paste (page 108), and Frozen Mirepoix and Trinity (page 196). Serve as is or toss in the blender to break up the squash.

Pickles are great, too: I *highly* recommend using the flesh closer to the stem end, as the base is full of seeds and water. Zucchini is best as refrigerator pickles (see page 54), not canned.

Or grate and freeze: Remove seeds before grating, then put the shredded squash in a bowl. For every 6 cups squash, mix in ½ to 1 tablespoon salt. Let sit for 10 to 20 minutes to pull out some moisture, then squeeze to remove liquid. Freeze in ice cube trays overnight, then store in ziplock bags.

Preserving Around the World

Ireland, with Dr. J. P. McMahon

Outside of Ireland, people often associate Irish food with stews, soda bread, and potatoes. But as chef and author J. P. McMahon says, it's a complex cuisine: "For me, what is most interesting about Irish food is the way in which people have been eating food in Ireland for about 10,000 years, and the different foodstuffs they've eaten along that time." Beginning with hunter-gathering and shifting to rural farming, Irish culinary traditions are unique to the island, even though, as McMahon notes, there are similarities with other European countries based on climate.

The introduction of the potato by the English in 1589, after its introduction in mainland Europe, altered the Irish culinary landscape considerably, gaining a foothold in the 1700s, despite Europeans' initial skepticism. While the two are heavily intertwined in our minds today, Ireland's dependence on the potato "wasn't unique in Europe. A lot of peasant communities in Europe were dependent on the potato." However, in Ireland, a lack of access to other food sources under colonization made the potato a main source of nutrition, and this meant people went hungry during An Gorta Mor (the Great Famine). Nowadays, we know it was a human-made famine caused by English colonizers' demands for food supplies to the detriment of local populations. McMahon notes that just "because the potato crop failed—it didn't mean there wasn't food in the country." The Irish just couldn't access that food.

Prior to the potato's introduction, much of the Irish diet was rooted in milk and oats. Meat was also eaten, but dairy and oats were the mainstays. Oats almost certainly would have been fermented as porridges or beers, and "there are all sorts of different sour milks and curds, many different processes [. . .] They would have gotten about 20 products from milk."

Wild vegetables were often preserved through drying, though they were dried indoors because of the rain. In summer, fish was dried, sometimes by laying it out on rocks in the sun:

> They would have dried it without salt; I suppose the sea is salty, so it's naturally salted [. . .] They used to catch the Ray Wing, and they used to skin it and the fisherman would drag it through the sea on the way back so it would be kind of brined, and they'd hang it on the washing line to dry it. I don't know how long they dried it for, but the guy who was talking said they would keep up to 6 months, so they must have been pretty dried. And I assume they would have rehydrated them in milk . . . presumably the whole street would do this, so you can only imagine the whole street drying fish on the washing line would be the most bizarre thing you'd encounter.

Today, the Irish food landscape includes more and more chefs, home cooks, and other food enthusiasts who are tapping into traditional methods, including foraging for seaweed, fermenting, and cheesemaking. You can see some of my favorites in Resources (page 410).

Sweet Potatoes

Sweet potatoes are utterly divine. They offer all the comfort of a potato, the sweetness and color of carrots (though with their own unique flavor), and the versatility of both. Choose firm sweet potatoes without soft spots or blemishes, and store them in a cool, dark place.

DRYING

Dehydrated sweet potato cubes are a simple, shelf-stable staple. Rehydrate them in soups, stews, and sauces until soft, or simmer in stock until soft, then blend.

To make them, wash and peel your potatoes, then cut them into ¼-inch slices. Steam blanch for 3 to 4 minutes, shock to cool in an ice bath (see page 17), and drain well. Dry at 125°F/52°C until brittle. Store in an airtight container in a cool, dark place.

FREEZING

Freezing is the only safe, tested method for preserving thick vegetable purées, like puréed sweet potatoes, but you can also freeze sweet potatoes in cubes. Allow your sweet potatoes to cure for at least 1 week (see page 212), then wash well after curing.

Cook your sweet potatoes before freezing:

- For purée, bake at 350°F/180°C, or peel and steam or simmer, until very tender. Cool and purée.
- For slices and cubes, peel and steam, simmer, or bake until tender.

Once they have cooled completely, place in freezer bags, or wrap in freezer wrap and place in an airtight container, leaving ½ inch of headspace. Alternatively, seal with a vacuum sealer. Label and freeze. Use within 1 year of freezing.

CANNING

Sweet potatoes grace my table in many forms, one favorite being sweet potato casserole: mashed sweet potato roasted with a sweet pecan topping and marshmallows. Normally I use freshly roasted sweet potatoes, but if you're in a bind, canned work wonderfully for this or other mashed–sweet potato applications.

Sweet potato can only be canned as chunks, never as a purée. So if you want puréed sweet potato, can the chunks, then purée when you're ready to serve.

To can sweet potatoes, boil or steam them until partially softened (15 to 20 minutes, depending on size). Remove the skins. Small potatoes can be kept whole, if desired, or cut into pieces; cut medium potatoes into uniformly sized pieces (do not mash them).

Ways to Preserve Sweet Potatoes	Shelf-stable	Fast	Low waste	Ready meals and ingredients	Big flavor
Sweet Potato Fly (page 226)			X		X

Fill jars, leaving 1 inch of headspace, and add 1 teaspoon of salt per quart, if desired. Cover with boiling water or with syrup (see page 79 for syrup-making instructions), remove air bubbles, wipe rims, and adjust lids. Set your pressure canner at 11 pounds pressure (dial gauge) or 10 pounds pressure (weighted gauge) and process pints for 65 minutes or quarts for 90 minutes, adjusting for altitude (see page 39) if needed.

FERMENTING

Sweet potatoes can be fermented before turning into delicious fries, just as you would do for potatoes (see page 214). But they can also be turned into one of my very favorite soft drinks: sweet potato fly.

Sweet Potato Fly

I learned how to make this fermented soda from Sandor Katz, and you'll notice our recipes are somewhat similar (you can see his in *The Art of Fermentation*). However, mine often varies in flavor from batch to batch, as I rely on building flavor with whatever bits I have lying around (an extra strip or two of citrus zest, or whatever spices I'm in the mood for). This means mine is not always traditional sweet potato fly, but it is still quite good.

Sweet potato fly is a wonderful beverage from Guyana and is traditionally made with sweet potatoes, sugar, water, eggshells (which are used to neutralize sourness), and flavorful add-ins like baking spices and lemon. This is a good way to use up the peels from sweet potatoes (or extra whole sweet potatoes, if you grow or buy too many). And while it doesn't last as long as some other preserves, it allows us to engage with another aspect of preserving: using all parts of our food with intention and care. If you use whole sweet potatoes, make sure to grate them and rinse them until the water runs clear to remove some of their starch.

— Makes about 1 gallon

1–2 cups sweet potato peels or grated, rinsed sweet potatoes

1 eggshell, crushed, with membrane removed

1 teaspoon ginger bug (see page 57)

1 eggshell, crushed, with membrane removed

Other flavors, as desired

2 cups sugar

1 gallon water, at room temperature

1. Place the sweet potato, eggshell, ginger bug, and other flavorings in a large container.
2. Add the sugar and water to a bowl and stir to dissolve the sugar. Pour over the sweet potato mixture.
3. Allow the mixture to sit at room temperature for 1 to 2 days, until it becomes good and bubbly.
4. Strain the mixture through cheesecloth or a fine-mesh sieve and funnel it into capped or flip-top bottles.
5. Allow the fly to sit at room temperature for another 1 to 2 days until pressurized (carbonated), and then place it in the fridge, where it will last for at least 1 week.

Tomatoes and Tomatillos

Tomatoes and tomatillos are the stars of many of my summer preserves, as I often have them in abundance in my garden (or from trading for them from friends' gardens). Blessedly, they offer many preserving options to enjoy a taste of summer year-round.

Look for firm, heavy fruit without soft spots or broken skin. If the skins are split, cut off the split portion and discard, and immediately process the tomatoes in purées or with other methods that do not require firm whole or sliced fruit.

DRYING

I like to dry my tomatoes in slices because they are easiest to store, I can add them to stews or other dishes, and they'll break down well. Slices are also nice because they don't require peeling and blanching. If you are preserving enough tomatoes in summer, any method that doesn't require peeling is welcome! I dry green tomatoes as well as red ones that are ripe but still firm, and tomatillos.

To dry tomato slices, wash your tomatoes, then trim out the core. Cut the tomatoes crosswise into ¼- to ⅓-inch-thick slices. Arrange the slices in a single layer in your dehydrator and dry at 135 to 140°F/57 to 60°C for 5 to 11 hours. Tip: You

Ways to Preserve Tomatoes and Tomatillos	Shelf-stable	Fast	Low waste	Ready meals and ingredients	Big flavor
Tomato-Skin Powder (page 228)			X	X	
Green Tomato Dill Chips (page 228)				X	X
Summer Harvest Tomato Sauce (page 231)	X			X	X
Tomato Refrigerator Pickles (page 232)				X	X
Bread-and-Butter Green Tomatoes (page 233)				X	X
Tomatillo Salad (page 233)				X	X
Fermented Salsa (page 234)				X	X
Tomato Cocktail Syrup (page 234)				X	X
Green Tomato Refrigerator Jam (page 235)				X	X
Tomato-Peach Refrigerator Jam (page 312)				X	X

can also enjoy these slices as a summer snack. I like to sprinkle them with dried herbs and spices before drying (I enjoy basil or oregano, or even cinnamon, plus a tiny bit of salt).

To dry tomato sections for stewing: Steam tomatoes for 3 minutes, or dip in boiling water for 1 minute to loosen the skins, then shock to cool in ice water. Slice or cut into ¾-inch-thick sections, or halve smaller tomatoes. Dehydrate for 10 to 18 hours at 135 to 140°F/57 to 60°C and allow to cool completely before storing.

TOMATO-SKIN POWDER

If you've peeled a lot of tomatoes for other projects (like tomato sauce, or drying tomatoes for stewing, above), the skins can be reserved and dried, then ground to make a powder to add to other dishes as a seasoning or garnish. If you're already using the dehydrator, pop them in for 1 to 2 hours until crisp, then allow to cool completely before grinding. Or dry in a single layer in direct sunlight until crisp.

Green Tomato Dill Chips

Dusting green tomatoes with spices and then drying them gives you a nice pickle-chip flavor and some very rewarding snacking. You can double or triple this recipe to fill your dehydrator as needed.

—— Makes about 1 quart

- **2 large green tomatoes, cut into ¼-inch-thick slices**
- **½ teaspoon cayenne pepper**
- **½ teaspoon dried dill weed**
- **¼ teaspoon dried parsley**
- **¼ teaspoon salt**

1. Sprinkle the tomatoes evenly with the cayenne, dill, parsley, and salt.

2. Arrange the slices in a single layer in your dehydrator and dry them at 135°F/57°C for about 6 hours or until crisp. Check the tomatoes after about 3 hours and peel them up from the tray to keep them from sticking when dry.

3. Let cool completely, and store in an airtight container.

CANNING

If you remember our canning pH scale (see page 27), you'll recall that the acidity of food is how we determine whether to pressure or hot water bath can. Tomatoes fall *riiiight* in the middle of that scale, meaning they might or might not be acidic enough to hot water bath can, depending on the variety and size. For this reason, you should either introduce extra acid or pressure can them. Tomatillos are, by and large, slightly more acidic than tomatoes, but for simplicity and safety's sake, I treat them as tomatoes when I am canning.

To acidify tomatoes (whole, crushed, or juiced), add 1 tablespoon of bottled lemon juice or ¼ teaspoon citric acid per each pint of tomatoes, or 2 tablespoons of bottled lemon juice or ½ teaspoon citric acid for quarts. You can also use 2 tablespoons of vinegar per pint or 4 tablespoons per quart, if you wish, but note that you'll be able to taste the vinegar in the finished product. Green tomatoes are more acidic than red tomatoes, but they should still be acidified as you would do with ripe tomatoes.

Canned whole tomatoes

Canning Tomatoes

Leave your tomatoes whole or cut them in half, and can them in tomato juice.

1 Cut a shallow X in the base of each tomato. Dip the tomatoes in boiling water for 1 to 2 minutes until the skins are loosened, shock them in cold water, then peel them and remove cores by cutting around the top of the tomato where the stem attaches.

2 Place jars in your canner and heat it up. Then, using tongs, remove the hot jars from the canner. If canning in a hot water bath, prepare hot jars by adding bottled lemon juice or citric acid (see page 228). For either canning method, add salt to the jars (½ teaspoon to pints and 1 teaspoon to quarts), if desired.

3 Hot pack or raw pack your jars:

TO HOT PACK, place the tomatoes in a saucepan with enough tomato juice to completely cover them, and boil gently for 5 minutes. Pack them into hot jars with enough juice to cover them, leaving ½ inch of headspace.

TO RAW PACK, heat the tomato juice in a saucepan. Pack the raw tomatoes into hot jars, then pour hot juice over them to cover, leaving ½ inch of headspace.

4 Run a chopstick or other thin, nonmetal utensil along the inner edges of the jars to release any air bubbles. Wipe the rims of the jars with a clean, damp cloth. Add the lids and bands and screw down to hand tightness.

5 To can in a hot water bath, process pints or quarts for 85 minutes. To pressure can, process pints or quarts at 11 pounds pressure (dial gauge) or 10 pounds pressure (weighted gauge) for 25 minutes. Adjust times for altitude (see page 39) if needed.

6 Allow the canner to depressurize completely, if pressure canning. Let the jars sit for 24 hours before testing the seals (see page 40), then store out of direct sunlight at room temperature.

Canning Tomatillos

To safely can tomatillos in a hot water bath, acidify them as you would tomatoes. Can tomatillos whole, without peeling or seeding, after removing their dry, papery husks and rinsing to remove sticky residue. Mixtures of tomatoes or tomatillos and other things (like okra and tomatoes) should be pressure canned unless you're using a tested recipe (like one from the USDA), which will ensure the correct acidity.

1 Add tomatillos to a saucepan with enough water to cover and boil them gently until tender, 5 to 10 minutes. Drain.

2 Meanwhile, place jars in your canner and heat it up. Then, using tongs, remove the hot jars from the canner. Prepare hot jars by adding bottled lemon juice or citric acid to acidify (see page 228).

3 Add the hot tomatillos to the jars, leaving ½ inch of headspace. Then fill the jars with boiling water to cover, leaving ½ inch of headspace.

4 Run a chopstick or other thin, nonmetal utensil along the inner edges of the jars to release any air bubbles. Wipe the rims of the jars with a clean, damp cloth. Add the lids and bands and screw down to hand tightness.

5 To can in a hot water bath, process pints for 40 minutes or quarts for 45 minutes. To pressure can, process pints or quarts at 11 pounds pressure (dial gauge) or 10 pounds pressure (weighted gauge) for 10 minutes. Adjust times for altitude (see page 39) if needed.

6 Allow the canner to depressurize completely, if pressure canning. Let the jars cool for 24 hours before testing the seals (see page 40), then store out of direct sunlight at room temperature.

Summer Harvest Tomato Sauce

This is my place-based adaptation of the marinara sauce recipes I made when I first started canning and gardening. I used to rely on traditional Italian flavors, but over time I began swapping in other herbs from my own garden or foraging walks, ingredients that maybe don't fit in a traditional marinara but taste like that place and time. Choose what you like (or have a lot of) and make the flavor of this sauce your own. This is, to me, preservation at its best. You get a delicious, easy pantry staple made by preserving things your garden is already producing.

As with other canned tomato recipes, this needs to be acidified (see page 228) to can it safely in a hot water bath.

— Makes about 3 pints

- **10 medium-large tomatoes, diced (about 10 cups)**
- **1 medium onion, diced large**
- **½ tablespoon olive oil**
- **3–5 cloves garlic, minced**
- **¼–½ cup red wine vinegar or apple cider vinegar (optional)**
- **1 teaspoon black pepper**
- **1 teaspoon salt**
- **1 teaspoon sugar**
- **½–1 teaspoon red pepper flakes**
- **1–1½ cups fresh herbs, packed**
- **3 tablespoons bottled lemon juice or 1 teaspoon citric acid**

1 To remove the tomato skins, cut a shallow X in the base of each tomato, drop the tomatoes in boiling water for 1 to 2 minutes, then shock in cold water. Peel off the skins and cut the tomatoes in ½- to 1-inch dice, preserving their juices.

(continued on next page)

Summer Harvest Tomato Sauce

Summer Harvest Tomato Sauce *continued*

2 In a large, high-sided skillet or Dutch oven, sweat the onion in the olive oil over low heat. Then add the garlic and sauté for 1 to 2 minutes. Increase the heat to medium and continue to sauté until golden. For a bit of extra flavor, deglaze the pan with the vinegar, or you can just use water if you prefer.

3 Reduce the heat to low, then add the tomatoes and their juices, black pepper, salt, sugar, and pepper flakes. Simmer over low heat, covered, until the tomatoes have broken down, 20 to 30 minutes.

4 Meanwhile, chop the herbs and add them to the sauce during the last 5 minutes of cooking. Place jars in your canner and heat it up.

5 Remove the sauce from the heat and blend it with a blender, an immersion blender, or by pressing it through a food mill.

6 Return the sauce to medium heat and cook until slightly thickened, stirring frequently, about 10 minutes. Add bottled lemon juice or citric acid to the sauce and stir to evenly distribute.

7 Using tongs, remove the hot jars from the canner. Pour the hot sauce into the jars, leaving ½ inch of headspace.

8 Run a chopstick or other thin, nonmetal utensil along the inner edges of your jars to release any air bubbles. Wipe the rims of the jars with a clean, damp cloth. Add the lids and bands and screw down to hand tightness.

9 To can in a hot water bath, process half-pints or pints for 35 minutes, adjusting for altitude (see page 39) if needed. To pressure can, process in a dial gauge pressure canner at 11 pounds pressure or a weighted gauge pressure canner at 10 pounds for 15 minutes, adjusting for altitude if needed. Allow the canner to depressurize completely.

10 Let the jars sit for 24 hours before testing the seals (see page 36), then store out of direct sunlight at room temperature.

PICKLING AND FERMENTING

Pickled, firm tomatoes are summer at its best. Tiny cherry tomatoes bursting with sour brine make a punchy, enlivening snack and can be mashed up with a fork for a quick dressing or topping. And pickled green tomatoes are the only bread-and-butter pickle I routinely eat.

Tomato Refrigerator Pickles

When I have a bounty of ripe, fresh cherry tomatoes, I make them into refrigerator pickles, which allows them to hold their shape and texture. I offer my go-to recipe here, but feel free to swap in your favorite vinegar, spices, or herbs.

You can eat these straight from the jar, use them to top sandwiches or burgers, or mash them up with olive oil for an instant vinaigrette. I've even mashed them, added a bit of sugar, and cooked them for a few minutes on the stove for a quick and easy relish to top foods or add to cheese boards.

— Makes about 1 quart

- **4 cups fresh, ripe cherry tomatoes**
- **2–3 cloves garlic, peeled and sliced**
- **2–3 sprigs thyme**
- **1 teaspoon black peppercorns**
- **¼–⅓ cup salt**
- **2 cups apple cider vinegar, white wine vinegar, red wine vinegar, or distilled white vinegar**
- **2 cups water**

1 Add the tomatoes, garlic, thyme, and peppercorns to a quart jar.

2 Make the brine: Combine the salt, vinegar, and water in a bowl and whisk until the salt is dissolved.

3 Pour the brine over the tomato mixture to cover, leaving ½ inch of headspace.

4 Let the tomatoes pickle in the fridge for 8 to 12 hours before eating, stirring the jar very gently after a few hours if tomatoes have floated to the top, to ensure they pickle evenly.

5 Store the pickles in the fridge, where they will last for at least 2 weeks.

Bread-and-Butter Green Tomatoes

I am not normally a bread-and-butter pickle person. But there's an exception to every rule, and these pickled green tomatoes are one of mine. Some recipes call for canning whole, small, pickled tomatoes, but I prefer them sliced, then pickled in the refrigerator when I have the space to do so, because they maintain a crisp texture I adore.

—— Makes about 4 quarts

- **8–10 pounds firm, green tomatoes**
- **1 large yellow onion**
- **⅛ cup whole peppercorns**
- **3 tablespoons celery seeds**
- **3 tablespoons coriander seeds**
- **3 tablespoons mustard seeds**
- **2 tablespoons whole cloves**
- **¾ cup sugar**
- **½ cup salt**
- **8 cups apple cider vinegar or distilled white vinegar**
- **8 cups water**

1 Slice the tomatoes and onion in ¼-inch-thick slices and pack them into quart or pint jars. Divide the peppercorns, celery seeds, coriander, mustard seeds, and cloves equally among the jars.

2 Make the brine: Combine the sugar, salt, vinegar, and water in a saucepan over medium heat. Heat until just simmering and the salt and sugar have dissolved.

3 Pour the brine over the tomatoes and spices, leaving ½ inch of headspace.

4 Allow to cool completely, then tighten the lids and store the jars in the fridge. Let pickle for 1 day before serving. The tomato pickles will last for at least 2 weeks in the refrigerator.

Tomatillo Salad

Like Bread-and-Butter Green Tomatoes, this pickle-y salad is best made in the fridge to keep textures crisp and flavors bright. I adore the slightly spicy, deep flavor of this particular salad on top of rich braised meats or with rice and beans. If you find yourself with a few quarts of tomatillos, this is the way to use them.

—— Makes 3–4 quarts

- **6 pounds tomatillos**
- **4 poblano peppers**
- **1 small red onion**
- **1 jalapeño (optional)**
- **¾ cup salt**
- **1–2 tablespoons oregano, preferably fresh**
- **12 cups water**
- **4 cups apple cider vinegar or distilled white vinegar**

1 Cut the tomatillos, poblanos, onion, and jalapeño (if using) into ¼-inch-thick slices (or slightly thinner). Divide the vegetables equally among the quart jars, leaving 1 inch of headspace.

2 Make the brine: Combine the salt, oregano, water, and vinegar in a large pot and heat until the salt is dissolved. Pour over the vegetables, leaving ½ inch of headspace.

3 Allow to the jars to cool, top with lids, and store them in the fridge. Let the salad pickle for 1 to 2 days before eating. It will last in the fridge for at least 2 weeks.

Fermented Salsa

This is a great way to easily preserve a few tomatoes at a time as they become ripe. My general formula is to fill the jar half to three-quarters full with tomatoes, then one-quarter to half full of "other stuff" (corn, onions, garlic, herbs, cilantro, etc.).

Fermented salsa is very flexible! As long as you've got some salt to make a brine and enough liquid to cover your vegetables completely, your salsa can look however you want it to.

—— Makes 1 quart

- **3 large or 4 medium ripe tomatoes, cut into ¼- to ½-inch dice, juices reserved**
- **½ yellow or white onion, cut into ¼-inch dice or smaller**
- **½ jalapeño, finely diced and deseeded (optional)**
- **3 tablespoons diced fresh cilantro or tarragon, or 1 tablespoon dried**
- **Freshly ground black pepper**
- **1 tablespoon salt**
- **1 cup water**

1. Put the tomatoes and their juices, onion, jalapeño (if using), cilantro, and pepper in a quart jar.

2. Combine the salt and the water in a small bowl and whisk until the salt is dissolved. Pour the brine into the jar, leaving ½ inch of headspace. Screw on the lid and shake gently to distribute the salt.

3. Let the salsa ferment for 3 to 7 days at room temperature, shaking and burping once a day. When it's bubbly and has a flavor you enjoy, place it in the fridge, where it will last for at least 2 weeks. (Note: The texture of the tomatoes gets softer the longer it sits.)

MAKING SYRUP AND JAM

We usually treat tomatoes as a vegetable, but whole worlds of culinary possibilities open up when we remember that they are actually fruit. These recipes will help you embrace the sweeter side of cooking with tomatoes.

Tomato Cocktail Syrup

Cocktails made with in-season summer tomatoes are a thing of beauty. You can juice tomatoes fresh, but a syrup is helpful if you want to be ready to make a cocktail on a whim, or to make batches for guests. I like this syrup with gin or the various nonalcoholic gin-style beverages out there, but it works with whiskey or vodka, too. Garnish with fresh basil, if you have it.

—— Makes about 1 pint

- **About 1 pound tomatoes, cut into 1-inch cubes, juices reserved**
- **⅓ cup sugar**
- **1 bay leaf**
- **Pinch of salt**
- **¼ cup water**
- **Juice from ½ lime**

1. Combine the tomatoes and their juices, sugar, bay leaf, salt, water, and lime juice in a large saucepan over medium-low heat.

2. Simmer until the tomatoes are soft and have expressed most of their juice, 13 to 18 minutes.

3. Let cool, then strain through a fine-mesh strainer. Store the syrup in the fridge, where it will keep for around 2 weeks.

Green Tomato Refrigerator Jam

Green Tomato Refrigerator Jam

This chunky, fresh, summery jam is perfect with goat cheese, crackers, or toast. It's also an easy and slightly unexpected way to use up a handful of plump, tart green tomatoes. I love having a jar in the fridge, ready to reach for whenever I have friends over or just want to liven up a quick lunch for myself.

—— Makes about 1½ pints

- **8 medium green tomatoes (about 4 pounds), cut into ¼-inch dice**
- **1 green apple, peeled, cored, and grated**
- **1 cup sugar**
- **⅛ teaspoon salt**
- **Juice of 1 lemon**

1. Combine the tomatoes, apple, sugar, salt, and lemon juice in a high-sided pan and bring to a boil over medium-high heat.

2. Reduce the heat to low and simmer, stirring occasionally, until the mixture has a thin jam consistency and coats the back of a spoon, 45 to 50 minutes.

3. Allow the jam to cool completely, then spoon it into a food-safe container, leaving ½ inch of headspace. Store it in the fridge, where it will last for at least several weeks.

Winter Squash

Winter squash is pretty magical. The variety of shapes and colors alone make me love it, as does the cozy flavor that reminds me of cool weather and warm blankets and sweaters. I also love that winter squash keeps for months when held in the correct conditions. There is a wide variety of winter squash available, from pumpkin to butternut to acorn to kabocha and more. North Georgia candy roaster, an heirloom from the southern edge of the Appalachian Mountains, is perhaps my all-time favorite.

Select firm, fresh squash that are heavy for their size and have no soft spots or bruises. If you're growing your own squash, stem "corking" (the stem's shift from bright green to dark green or brown, plus development of brown, woody strips where it meets the fruit) is a good sign that the squash is mature enough to harvest. Be sure to harvest before frost.

Squash are typically stored for at least a few weeks after harvesting and before eating, as they begin to convert their starches to sugars and become more palatable. Squash should be stored in a cool, dry area like a root cellar or basement. Depending on the variety, squash will last for 2 to 6 months in storage under the right conditions (50 to 60°F/10 to 16°C).

DRYING

To dry winter squash, begin by breaking it down into manageable pieces. You can do this either with a knife or by actually breaking it. (For especially tough squash, I've literally dropped them on the ground to break them apart more easily: Just put a clean tarp or other covering down first to keep dirt off them and make the pieces easier to collect.)

Squash rings, along with Five-Spice Apple Rings (page 250) are two of my favorite winter pantry staples, as both can be rehydrated in a variety of dishes.

Remove the seeds—which you can save for roasted spiced pumpkin seeds (see page 223) or for planting, if you wish—and the pulp. Next, cut your squash pieces into 1-inch-thick strips, or, for smaller squash, into rings. Remove the rind with a vegetable peeler. Finally, cut your peeled strips down again, crosswise (side to side) in ⅛-inch-thick pieces.

Blanch in steam for 2 to 3 minutes or in boiling water for 1 to 1½ minutes. Shock in an ice bath to cool (see page 17) and drain well. Then dehydrate at 135 to 140°F/57 to 60°C for 9 to 15 hours, or until dry but pliable.

Ways to Preserve Winter Squash

	Shelf-stable	Fast	Low waste	Ready meals and ingredients	Big flavor
Fermented Squash-and-Apple Relish (page 238)				X	X
Quick-Cooked Squash-and-Apple Relish (page 239)				X	X
Butternut Squash Peel Bitters (page 239)		X	X		X
Pumpkincello (page 240)				X	X

FREEZING

Squash freezes best as a purée. You can freeze cooked, cubed squash, but the texture tends to get mushy upon thawing, and it's more prone to freezer burn, so freezing purée is my preference. To prepare the purée, cook the squash (steam, boil, pressure cook, or roast) until it is very tender. Scoop the flesh from the peel and purée. Let it cool. (To speed up the cooling process, transfer the purée to a container and then place that container in a cold-water bath, stirring the squash to cool throughout.)

Once cool, pack the purée into rigid containers, leaving ½ inch of headspace, and freeze. Or scoop the purée into ziplock bags. To avoid freezer burn, press out all the air and smooth the bags flat; each one should have a layer of purée about ½ inch thick. Freeze flat. You can also freeze squash purée in an ice cube tray for single-serving cubes. Remove the frozen cubes and store in an airtight container or freezer bag.

If you want to try freezing cubed winter squash, make sure it's cooked to tender. Cool it completely, then freeze in a single layer on a baking sheet lined with parchment paper or a silicone mat until frozen through. Package it leaving ½ inch of headspace.

CANNING

Cubed squash can be pressure canned; however, squash butters and purées *cannot safely be canned using any method.* Why? Because they are so thick that they cannot be adequately heated all the way through, introducing the possibility of pathogen growth. Prior to the 1970s, the USDA offered recipes for canned squash purées, but these were withdrawn after studies at the University of Minnesota showed too much variation in density to offer safe, consistent guidelines. As a result, all guidelines were changed in 1994 to reflect current safe canning practices.

Cubed squash is perfect to mash for pies or cook up for quick soups and stews.

Pressure Canning Winter Squash

Canning renders the squash cubes quite soft, so when it's time to use them, drain and mash your cubes, then reheat. You can use them for savory dishes (like soups, sauces, and ravioli filling) or sweet ones (like pies).

1 Select firm, stringless squash (not spaghetti squash) free of rot and blemishes, and peel them.

2 Cut the peeled flesh into 1-inch cubes. Set a pot of water to boil over high heat; boil the cubes for 2 minutes, then drain.

3 Meanwhile, heat your jars in your pressure canner. Then, using tongs, remove the hot jars from the canner.

4 Fill the hot jars with the squash cubes, leaving 1 inch of headspace. Add salt (½ teaspoon per pint or 1 teaspoon per quart) if desired. Then add hot water to the jars, leaving 1 inch of headspace.

5 Run a chopstick or other thin, nonmetal utensil along the inner edges of the jars to release any air bubbles. Wipe the rims of the jars with a clean, damp cloth. Add the lids and bands and screw down to hand tightness.

6 Set your pressure canner to 11 pounds pressure (dial gauge) or 15 pounds pressure (weighted gauge) and process pints for 55 minutes and quarts for 90 minutes, adjusting for altitude (see page 39) if needed.

7 Allow the canner to depressurize completely. Let the jars cool for 24 hours before testing the seals (see page 40), then store out of direct sunlight at room temperature.

FERMENTING

Winter squash makes a nice pickle, like squash-and-apple relish, which can be either fermented or quick-cooked for a delicious holiday side.

Fermented Squash-and-Apple Relish

This is an unexpected way to combine squash and apple into a healthy treat to grace your holiday table. Crisp, tart, and savory, it helps cut the richness of festive foods. It will store in the fridge for several weeks—perfect for making ahead of time. Some of my favorite additions include nuts (walnuts and pistachios are good!), cubed beets, dried or fresh cranberries, and citrus peel.

— Makes about 2 quarts

- **1 medium butternut squash, peeled and cut into 1-inch cubes**
- **4 apples (any variety), peeled and cut into 1-inch cubes**
- **1 (2-inch) piece fresh organic ginger, sliced**
- **¾ cup toasted pecans**
- **2 cinnamon sticks**
- **1 star anise pod**
- **1 teaspoon black peppercorns**
- **½ teaspoon whole cloves**
- **Additional nuts or other add-ins (see headnote; optional)**
- **4 teaspoons sea salt**
- **4 cups water**

1 Place the squash and apples in your fermentation vessel. Add the ginger, pecans, cinnamon, star anise, peppercorns, cloves, and any add-ins (if using).

2 Make the brine: Combine the salt and water in a bowl and stir to dissolve the salt. Pour the brine over the squash-apple mixture, making sure it is completely submerged.

3 Place a weight on your ferment to keep everything under the brine. Ferment at room temperature, covered, out of direct sunlight, and check it every couple of days. I usually let this ferment for about a week. When it has developed a flavor you like, it's finished! If you want a sweeter flavor, add a bit of sugar or honey to taste after fermenting. It will last in the fridge for 2 weeks or more.

Quick-Cooked Squash-and-Apple Relish

This quick-cooked relish is a sweet-and-sour side that can be ready in a pinch. Add sugar if you want your relish on the sweeter side. Some of my favorite additions include nuts (walnuts and pistachios are good!), grated beets, dried or fresh cranberries, citrus peel, and other spices (like star anise).

—— Makes about 1 quart

½ tablespoon olive oil
1 medium butternut squash, peeled and diced
½ cup water
4 apples (any variety), peeled and diced
½ teaspoon grated ginger
¾ cup toasted pecans
1 teaspoon ground cinnamon
¼ teaspoon ground cloves
¼ teaspoon ground nutmeg
¼ teaspoon freshly ground black pepper
½–¾ cup apple cider vinegar
Sea salt
Sugar (optional)
Additional nuts or other add-ins (see headnote; optional)

1 Add the oil to a pan over medium heat. When the oil is hot, add the squash and sauté until it begins to brown, about 5 minutes. Add the water, cover, and simmer until the squash begins to soften.

2 Add the apples, ginger, pecans, cinnamon, cloves, nutmeg, pepper, and vinegar to the squash, stirring to combine. Add salt to taste, and sugar and add-ins (if using).

3 Cook for 5 to 10 minutes, adding a splash of water if needed, until the squash and apples are softened.

4 Cool the relish completely and store it in an airtight container in the refrigerator, where it will keep for 1 to 2 weeks.

INFUSING

When you think of infusing, winter squash might not come immediately to mind. But squash offers us the chance to play with beverages and vinegars, bringing new dimensions to your drinks and meals.

Butternut Squash Peel Bitters

We tend to think of winter squash as a fall or winter food, but when infused with citrus and spices in vodka, it creates a mildly bitter treat that can be enjoyed year-round. It's perfect for adding a little brightness to a gin and tonic or even a mocktail with soda water and a squeeze of lemon. The peels add some bitterness that the flesh does not, but you still get a bit of butternut flavor from those last bits of squash left clinging to the peels. Make it with vinegar for a nonalcoholic version: The presence of tannins in the peels mimics the drying effect you get from alcohol.

(continued on next page)

Butternut Squash Peel Bitters *continued*

— Makes about 1 cup

- Peel of 1 medium butternut squash
- Peel of ½ orange
- ½ teaspoon coriander seeds
- ½ teaspoon black peppercorns
- ¼ teaspoon white peppercorns
- Vodka, to cover

1 Add the squash and orange peels, coriander, and peppercorns to a pint jar with 1 inch of headspace. Pour in vodka to cover.

2 Steep the bitters for about 1 month or until they have a flavor you like, then strain and store in an airtight container at room temperature, where they will last for 1 month or more.

Pumpkincello

Back in the salad days of food blogging (circa 2010s), I had a small, not-at-all-widely-read blog called *A Bloggable Feast*. It was a graduate school hobby: Posts were infrequent, but all represented very fun experiments that turned out well, sometimes to my great surprise. Pumpkincello is one such example.

I make this with raw squash, but I know that isn't everyone's cup of tea. You can use cubes of roasted squash if you want a more traditional pumpkin spice profile.

— Makes about 1 liter

- 1 small (2- to 3-pound) pie pumpkin
- 1 liter vodka (depending on the size of your container and your pumpkin, you may have some left over)
- 12 whole allspice berries
- 1 green cardamom pod
- 1 cinnamon stick
- Grating of fresh nutmeg
- 1 cup sugar
- 2 cups whole milk or soymilk (can replace with water for noncreamy drinks)

1 Peel, seed, and cut the pumpkin flesh into ½-inch cubes. Roast until tender, if desired.

2 Put the pumpkin in a nonreactive container and pour vodka over it to cover.

3 Let it sit for 1 to 4 weeks in the refrigerator until it has a flavor you enjoy.

4 After your vodka is infused, pour it through a fine-mesh strainer to remove the pumpkin. You can strain it again through cheesecloth if tiny pumpkin bits in your drinks bother you.

5 Toast the allspice, cardamom, cinnamon, and nutmeg in a cast-iron skillet until fragrant.

6 Transfer the spices to a saucepan and add the sugar and milk. Heat over medium-low to medium heat, stirring occasionally, until the sugar is completely dissolved. Let the mixture cool to room temperature.

7 Strain the spices from the milk, then add the spiced milk to the vodka. Mix and store in an airtight container in the fridge. Drink within 1 to 2 weeks.

Wild Plants

DRYING

For drying guidance, check out the domesticated ingredients that are closest to what you've harvested. Wild blackberries, for example, will be the same as store-bought ones when it comes to drying. And tender wild greens can be air-dried using the guidance on page 88.

FERMENTING

Kraut (page 50) is a fun way to play with wild greens. Try violet dandykraut: Combine violet leaves cut into a chiffonade with chopped dandelion greens (go a bit light on violet leaves, as they're mucilaginous; I use them for about a quarter of my total greens), plus shredded carrots and anything else you'd like in there (shiso leaves are good). Because of the delicate texture of the violet leaves, I make a roughly 3 percent brine (see brine ratios, page 49) and pour it over the kraut rather than my usual approach of massaging salt in, and let it sit for just 1 week (or maybe less) to keep the texture more firm.

Sugar clings to pine cones in Mugolio (page 242), a green pine cone syrup.

Ways to Preserve Wild Plants

	Shelf-stable	Fast	Low waste	Ready meals and ingredients	Big flavor
Mugolio (Green Pine Cone Syrup) (page 242)	X			X	X
Spring Greens Vinegar (page 242)	X			X	X

Mugolio (Green Pine Cone Syrup)

This is one of my most frequently requested recipes and a good one to have handy in early spring for any green pine cones you might find on your local edible conifers. Mugolio is originally from the Italian Alps, relying on the immature pine cones from *Pinus mugo*, but it works with other immature edible cones, too. This is my personal favorite add-in to whiskey drinks and is also a nice syrup for desserts.

Green pine cones

Sugar

1 In spring, gather the green pine cones that fall from edible species of pine, or harvest a small number from the branches. This can be sticky work, but it's worth it.

2 Put your pine cones in a jar (or jars) large enough to hold them with a bit of extra room. (I do two to four pine cones per pint, depending on how large they are.)

3 Fill the rest of the jar with sugar. Make sure the pine cones are completely surrounded by sugar! It can help to shake or tap the jar a bit to get the sugar to settle.

4 Top with the lid and set the jar aside for about 1 month. You can leave it in the fridge or at room temperature. The sugar will draw the sap from the pine cones; you should end up with a jar that's half syrup and half pine-infused sugar, so you can scoop out one or both when you're ready to enjoy. Both are very fun to experiment with in the kitchen! Store in the fridge or at room temperature in an airtight container out of direct sunlight, where it will last for 1 month or more.

INFUSING

Infused vinegars are delicious and endlessly customizable, but each spring I eagerly await fresh, tender wild greens to make my favorite: greens-infused vinegar. It's packed with minerals (vinegar is a superstar at extracting minerals from plants), and its bright, verdant flavor is perfect in sauces, soups, and dressings.

Wildflowers make nice infused vinegars, too, like piney-fresh goldenrod vinegar. Or try pine-needle vinegar (tip: The pickled pine needles make a great snack).

Spring Greens Vinegar

My favorite green for this, hands down, is chickweed, but it works well with dandelion, nettle, cleavers, henbit, violet leaf, or deadnettle. If you prefer store-bought greens, give this a try with arugula or even spinach. Really any green or herb works here, as long as you like its flavor. Especially for more watery herbs, don't pack your jar too tightly, as the water from the leaves can dilute the vinegar and reduce the acidity.

Greens or herbs of your choice

Apple cider vinegar or your favorite 5% acidity vinegar

Pack your greens in a jar (I aim for about half to three-quarters full). Pour vinegar over the top until completely covered. Let the jar sit out of direct sunlight for 2 to 4 weeks, then strain and bottle. Store at room temperature or in the fridge, where it will last for months.

Infused greens vinegar (left) captures the garden bounty, and vinegar mothers (right) can be used to start other vinegar projects.

Working with Stinging Nettle

Nettle is a nourishing springtime treat but one that intimidates some cooks and gardeners because of its sharp, stinging hairs. I like to remember that nettle is both a fierce protector with strong boundaries and a deeply loving, nourishing caregiver for those willing to work with it respectfully. Here is how I do that.

SAFE HANDLING: Wear gloves when handling raw nettles and keep nettles away from uncovered skin (like on your forearms). Drying, blanching, or infusing in vinegar all deactivate the stinging hairs.

DRYING: Air-dry like other dried herbs (see page 88).

BLANCHING: Blanch for 2 to 3 minutes until softened and quite bright green. Strain and shock in an ice bath to preserve color, then store in the fridge and use whole, chopped, or blended for hot or chilled soups, smoothies, and more. Or blanch, chop, and store like herb cubes in the freezer (see page 21).

INFUSING IN VINEGAR: Use nettles to make Spring Greens Vinegar (page 242).

Pickled Papaya (page 316)

CHAPTER 7

Fruit

Apples, Pears, Quinces, and Crabapples	246
Bananas	259
Berries and Currants	263
Cherries	275
Citrus	279
Cranberries	287
Figs and Dates	289
Grapes	292
Melons	297
Pomegranates	302
Stone Fruits	305
Tropical Fruits	313

There's something about having a bounty of fruit that makes me feel like a goddess and makes my kitchen feel like a luscious, sensual playground. Fruit may not give you divine aspirations, but it can give you some great preserves. The exact preservation process depends on the fruit. While stone fruits and berries both make excellent jams, for example, you have to prepare them for cooking a bit differently (removing pits from your peaches, for instance). But while each fruit may have particularities, the overall process is often similar.

Apples, Pears, Quinces, and Crabapples

These fruits are all part of the rose family, and I group them together because their techniques are largely interchangeable. These are pome fruits, which means they have dense cores with seeds surrounded by edible flesh.

Firm, fresh pears can be substituted for apples in pickled apple recipes, for example, and crabapples can be swapped out in some recipes, too (just note that they are tart, so adjust your seasoning/sugar accordingly!). Quinces tend to be very firm-fleshed and tannic and are best when cooked, so while they may not make the best pickles, they'll make an absolutely divine jam.

DRYING

Apples and other rose family members are, by and large, delicious and versatile when dried. They can be added to oatmeal or other dishes, eaten as snacks, or rehydrated and used in desserts. These fruits also make excellent fruit leathers; follow the general guidance on page 94. (Note that crabapples should not make up the majority of a fruit leather because their flavor is tart and concentrated.)

APPLES

Apples dry incredibly well. Dried apples can be rehydrated and used in pies or other desserts or added to sauces for meat and roasted vegetables. I also enjoy dusting my apples with spices, like ground five-spice powder or citrus zest and sugar or cinnamon before drying, for a flavorful snack.

To dry your apples, core them and cut them into ⅛-inch-thick rings or slices. Steam blanch them for 6 to 7 minutes, blanch in syrup for 10 minutes, or dip in an ascorbic acid (vitamin C) solution for several minutes (see page 90 for more on each method). Apples are typically peeled first, but they don't have to be. Dehydrate at 125 to 135°F/52 to 57°C for 6 to 12 hours. Dried apples may be slightly pliable but should not be sticky or tacky at all.

PEARS

Pears are also lovely dried, to be used later as an ingredient or eaten on their own. Like apples, you can toss them in your favorite seasoning before drying.

To dry pears, peel, halve, and core your fruit (or cut into quarters or slices). Steam blanch them for 6 to 7 minutes, blanch in syrup for 10 minutes, or dip in an ascorbic acid (vitamin C) solution for several minutes (see page 90 for more on each method).

Dry your halved fruit for 24 to 36 hours at 125 to 135°F/52 to 57°C. For quarters, halves, and slices, the drying time is reduced, and the time is less the smaller your fruit pieces are. Remember to keep an eye on your fruit, especially toward the end. When dried, your pears may be slightly pliable, but they should not be sticky or tacky at all.

Ways to Preserve Apples, Pears, Quinces, and Crabapples

	Shelf-stable	Fast	Low waste	Ready meals and ingredients	Big flavor
Fermented Squash-and-Apple Relish (page 238)				X	X
Persimmon, Apple, and Cranberry Refrigerator Pickles (page 249)				X	X
Sweet-and-Sour Five-Spice Apples (page 249)				X	X
Five-Spice Apple Rings (page 250)	X				X
Apple Relish (page 251)				X	X
Pickled Apples with Sage (page 251)				X	X
Old Apple Vinegar (page 252)			X	X	
Mapple (Maple and Apple) Butter (page 253)		X		X	X
White Quince Marmalade (page 254)				X	X
Red Quince Marmalade (page 256)				X	X
Apple Cider Molasses (page 256)				X	X
Apple Pie Filling (page 257)		X		X	X
Basic Applesauce (page 258)				X	X

QUINCE AND CRABAPPLES

While pears and apples dry up nicely, quince does not, as it relies on cooking to make it palatable. When dried on its own, it is sharply acidic, and the texture is tough and almost grainy. Crabapples, while delicious in many other applications, are not terribly well suited to drying, either. Their small size and tart texture make for a punchy but unpalatable treat. They can, however, be combined with other fruit in fruit leather (see page 94), while quince is best left out of dehydrator-based preserves in general.

FREEZING

While you *can* freeze whole apples and pears, these can get mushy, so once thawed they are best used mashed up. The same is true of quince and crabapple; I typically reserve all fruits in this family for other preservation methods.

Dried Apples: An Ancient Tradition

Apples have been sun dried across Asia and Europe and North Africa for thousands of years: Dried apples were even found in an ancient Sumerian tomb of Queen Puabi, who was buried around 4,000 years ago. Apples were an important food in Sumeria, even mentioned in the *Hymn to Inanna*. For dried apples that will make you feel like royalty, brush them with a solution of honey, warm water, and rose water before drying.

Freezing Apples

Here's how I prepare, slice, and freeze apples to use later in things like pies and pancakes.

1. Peel your apples and cut them into ¼-inch-thick slices.
2. Steam blanch for 2 minutes, then immediately shock in ice water and thoroughly drain.
3. Sprinkle or brush with 1 teaspoon ascorbic acid mixed in a little water (or use lemon juice).
4. Freeze in a single layer on a baking sheet lined with parchment paper or a silicone mat.
5. Stack the frozen apples in an airtight container or freezer bag with no headspace. Apples will keep for at least 2 months if properly stored.

PICKLING

You may not think of pickling when you think of pome fruits, but they shine in relishes and pretty much any sweet-and-sour application. The recipes here are for apples, but you can substitute quince (in cooked recipes only; they may be too tart for refrigerator pickles) or firm, fresh pears. All these fruits oxidize quickly when cut, so having your pickling solution at the ready is a great way to keep their colors bright and their texture firm.

Spicing possibilities for this group of fruits are incredibly expansive. You can lean into citrus, play with floral flavors, add baking spices, or do whatever your heart desires.

Persimmon, Apple, and Cranberry Refrigerator Pickles

A really nice late-autumn snack, this is a colorful addition to meals or cheese boards. You can mix up the ratio of apple to persimmon. Note that apples are denser and take a little bit more time to pickle. Likewise, bigger chunks take longer to pickle than smaller ones, so I recommend dicing the fruit, though you can experiment with slices and rounds, too. To preserve texture, I prefer to use a cool brine instead of a hot one and refrigerate rather than can.

— Makes about 2 quarts

- **½ blood orange, cut into slices**
- **½ cup sugar**
- **2 tablespoons salt**
- **1 teaspoon fennel seeds**
- **½ teaspoon whole cloves**
- **4 cups distilled white vinegar or apple cider vinegar**
- **4 cups water**
- **3–4 pounds persimmons and apples, cut into ½- to 1-inch dice**
- **½ cup dried sweetened cranberries**

1. Make the brine: Combine the orange, sugar, salt, fennel, cloves, vinegar, and water in a large saucepan. Bring to a simmer and stir until the salt and sugar are dissolved. Remove from the heat and allow to cool.

2. Meanwhile, divide the persimmons, apples, and cranberries between two quart jars, leaving 1 inch of headspace. Pour the cooled brine over the fruit until completely covered, then allow it to steep in the fridge for at least 8 hours and up to 2 days until the fruit is pickled through.

3. Store the pickles in the refrigerator, where they will last up to 2 months, softening more the longer they sit.

Sweet-and-Sour Five-Spice Apples

This is a good side for pork and holiday meals. Sometimes I blend it into a sauce and toss it with stir-fried chicken, shrimp, and vegetables with a splash of soy sauce and a serving of apples on top or on the side. It also makes for a not-too-sweet dessert, and the syrup makes a nice drink with soda water or kombucha.

— Makes 2 pints

- **1½ cups sugar**
- **1–2 teaspoons red pepper flakes (optional)**
- **1 teaspoon five-spice powder**
- **⅛ teaspoon salt**
- **¾ cup apple cider vinegar**
- **3–4 medium apples, peeled, cored, and cut into ½-inch-thick slices**
- **½ teaspoon citric acid (if canning)**

(continued on next page)

Sweet-and-Sour Five-Spice Apples

Sweet-and-Sour Five-Spice Apples *continued*

1 Make the syrup: Combine the sugar, pepper flakes (if using), five-spice powder, salt, and vinegar in a pot. Bring to a simmer and heat until the salt and sugar are dissolved.

2 Divide the apples between two pint jars and pour the syrup over the top. Let them cool, then refrigerate for 2 to 3 days before enjoying. They will last a month or more in the fridge, softening more the longer they sit.

3 For a softer texture and longer shelf life, you can also can them. If canning, add ¼ teaspoon of the citric acid per pint. Place two pint jars in your hot water bath canner and heat it up. Then, using tongs, remove the hot jars and pack the apple slices into them, leaving 1 inch of headspace. Pour hot syrup over the top, leaving ½ inch of headspace.

4 Run a chopstick or other thin, nonmetal utensil along the inner edges of your jars to release any air bubbles. Wipe the rims of the jars with a clean, damp cloth. Add the lids and bands and screw down to hand tightness.

5 Process pints in a hot water bath canner for 15 minutes, adjusting for altitude (see page 39) if needed.

6 Let the jars cool for 24 hours before testing the seals (see page 36), then store out of direct sunlight at room temperature.

Five-Spice Apple Rings

Spiced apple rings are typically a holiday and wintertime treat, and the traditional flavor profile is heavy on the baking spices or just cloves. Some home preservers also add red or green food coloring. My version uses five-spice powder for the warmth of traditional apple rings with the roundness of star anise. I also like to add dried rose petals, as they pair nicely.

Makes about 5 pints

- **1 teaspoon ascorbic acid**
- **1 gallon plus 2½ cups water**
- **About 4 pounds apples**
- **5 cups sugar**
- **¼ cup apple cider vinegar**
- **2 teaspoons five-spice powder**
- **1 teaspoon salt (optional)**
- **Dried rose petals, about 1 teaspoon per jar (optional)**
- **1¼ teaspoons citric acid (if canning)**

1 Mix the ascorbic acid into 1 gallon of water. Peel, core, and cut the apples into ½-inch rings. Immediately submerge the apple rings in the ascorbic acid solution to prevent oxidation.

2 Make the syrup by bringing to a boil 2½ cups of water, the sugar, vinegar, five-spice powder, and salt (if using).

3 Meanwhile, if canning, place five pint jars in your hot water bath canner and heat it up. Then, using tongs, remove the hot jars.

4 Place rose petals (if using) in the bottom of each jar. Stack the apple rings in the jars, leaving 1½ inches of headspace. Pour the boiling syrup over the apples to cover.

5 If refrigerating, allow the apple rings to cool and refrigerate, where they will keep at least 2 weeks.

6 If canning, add ¼ teaspoon of the citric acid per pint. Run a chopstick or other thin, nonmetal utensil along the inner edges of the jars to release any air bubbles. Wipe the rims of the jars with a clean, damp cloth. Add the lids and bands and screw down to hand tightness.

7 Process pints in a hot water bath canner for 10 minutes, adjusting for altitude (see page 39) if needed.

8 Let the jars cool for 24 hours before testing the seals (see page 36), then store out of direct sunlight at room temperature.

Apple Relish

Loosely inspired by a traditional Italian condiment called mostarda di frutta, this relish is spicy and tart, perfect for pairing with rich meats and cheeses, vegan cheeses, or high-fat nuts. Play around with the spices here, if you wish.

— Makes about 4 pints

- **2½ tablespoons yellow mustard seeds**
- **7 apples, cored and diced (peel for a smoother final texture, if desired)**
- **5 dried figs, cut into ¼-inch dice**
- **1 shallot, finely diced**
- **¾ cup golden raisins**
- **½ cup packed light brown sugar**
- **⅓ cup dried cranberries**
- **½–1 tablespoon herbes de Provence**
- **¼ teaspoon salt**
- **Zest of ½ lemon**
- **Zest of ½ orange**
- **1 tablespoon Dijon mustard**
- **1½ cups apple cider vinegar**
- **1 cup ginger beer, homemade (page 110) or store-bought**
- **1 teaspoon citric acid (if canning)**

1. Toast the mustard seeds in a large saucepan until fragrant.

2. Add the apples, figs, shallot, raisins, sugar, cranberries, herbes de Provence, salt, lemon zest, orange zest, mustard, vinegar, and ginger beer to the saucepan. Simmer until the apples are tender and cooked through, about 30 minutes.

3. If refrigerating, allow the apple mixture to cool completely, pack it in airtight containers, and refrigerate. The relish will last for at least 3 weeks in the fridge.

4. If canning, stir in the citric acid. Place four pint jars in your hot water bath canner and heat it up. Then, using tongs, remove the jars from the canner and pack the apple mixture into the hot jars, leaving ½ inch of headspace. Divide the liquid between jars, leaving ½ inch of headspace.

5. Run a chopstick or other thin, nonmetal utensil along the inner edges of the jars to release any air bubbles. Wipe the rims of the jars with a clean, damp cloth. Add the lids and bands and screw down to hand tightness.

6. Process pints in a hot water bath canner for 15 minutes, adjusting for altitude (see page 39) if needed.

7. Let the jars cool for 24 hours before testing the seals (see page 36), then store them out of direct sunlight at room temperature.

Pickled Apples with Sage

This recipe relies on one of my favorite cool-weather combinations: apples and sage. I've been a longtime fan of this pairing, after making dozens and dozens of apple-and-sage waffles at a restaurant (RIP Fair Grounds) I worked at while living in Iowa. This recipe also works beautifully with thyme or rosemary, too. You can play with the amount of herbs to make it your own.

Choose sweeter apples (like Fuji) to balance the sweet-and-sour pickling brine. The black tea lends some tannins to help keep your apples crisp for longer. Enjoy on salads, as a side with grilled summer dishes, or on waffles or pancakes drizzled with a bit of honey.

— Makes about 1 pint

- **2 medium sweet-yet-firm apples, cored and sliced ¼ inch thick**
- **1 bunch sage**
- **3 teaspoons fine sea salt**
- **1 teaspoon black tea (or 1 tea bag)**
- **1¾ cups water**
- **1 cup apple cider vinegar**
- **1 tablespoon good-quality honey**

(continued on next page)

Pickled Apples with Sage *continued*

1 Add the apples and sage to a pint jar or another nonreactive container with an airtight lid.

2 Make the brine: Combine the salt, tea, water, vinegar, and honey in a separate container and stir until the salt and honey are dissolved.

3 Pour the brine over the apple mixture until completely covered (it may be helpful to use a fermentation weight to keep your apples under the brine).

4 Allow the apples to pickle for 8 to 12 hours. Store them in the fridge, where they will keep for 1 to 2 weeks, or longer, softening the longer they sit.

Working with Quince

Quince, a once-popular fruit from ancient times until a century or two ago, has a divine fragrance and an equally divine taste. The catch? It only tastes heavenly when cooked. This fruit is high in tannins, which means in most cases you get a mouth-puckeringly tart bite if you try to eat it raw. When cooked, however, it's soft, sweet, and fragrant. And its high pectin content makes it perfect for preserves and fruit pastes, like the quince paste that graces many cheese and charcuterie boards.

Try my recipes for quince marmalade (pages 254–56), which can also be run through a food mill to make quince butter. Or swap out quince in cooked apple recipes.

FERMENTING

APPLE SCRAP VINEGAR is, as you might have guessed, made from scraps from your other apple projects: cores, peels, and other bits and bobs. These are combined with sugar and water and fermented into vinegar. The more apple scraps you add, the more appley your final product tastes and the more nutrient-dense it is.

APPLE CIDER VINEGAR is, on the other hand, made from the pressed cider that is then fermented into vinegar. It has a deeper, richer flavor and darker color than apple scrap vinegar. You can make it by fermenting fresh cider into alcohol, then either letting it wild-ferment into vinegar or adding some raw apple cider vinegar or a vinegar mother to kick-start the process.

You can also make a mishmash between the two that I call Old Apple Vinegar.

Old Apple Vinegar

This is one of my favorite ways to use up apples that are old or a bit mushy. It works well with other pome fruits, too, so you could create old crabapple vinegar, old pear vinegar, or even old quince vinegar.

Old apples
½–1 cup sugar per quart

1 Start by puréeing your old apples and sugar in a blender. Add a splash of water and a bit of sugar if you need to, but you most likely won't. If you do, add water ¼ cup at a time.

2 Transfer the purée into a clean wide-mouthed jar. Cover your jar with cheesecloth, a clean piece of sheet, or other permeable covering secured with a rubber band or twine, and set it out at room temperature out of direct sunlight. Let it ferment into alcohol (1 to 2 weeks), stirring daily.

3 Strain the solids out after 7 to 10 days. Some people add a vinegar mother or a hefty splash of apple cider vinegar at this point to speed the fermentation process, while others wait until the mixture turns to vinegar naturally.

4 Keep fermenting your liquid for 1 to 2 months, tasting and testing once or twice a week, until it smells and tastes like vinegar.

5 Store the vinegar in the fridge or in a narrow-necked bottle out of direct sunlight.

MAKING BUTTERS, JAMS, SYRUPS, AND SAUCES

Apple butter and applesauce are two famous apple preserves, but they just scratch the surface of possibilities for sweetened (and often also canned) preserves from the rose family.

Mapple (Maple and Apple) Butter

Maple and apple butter is autumn in a jar. You can use maple syrup or maple sugar, whichever you have on hand. It's perfect over cinnamon apple pancakes, on biscuits or English muffins, or just spread on your weekday-morning toast.

Early apple butters were, so far as I can tell, made from apples boiled in cider, while the modern versions like mine are essentially a thick applesauce that's run through a food mill. These early apple butters were a shelf-stable way to preserve apples: cooked down to a thick mash, then stored in earthenware vessels. Today, apple butter is stored in the fridge or canned.

— Makes about 4 pints

5 pounds sweet apples (I use 3 pounds Gala and 2 pounds Fuji)

Juice of 2 lemons

3 whole cloves, crushed with a mortar and pestle

2 bay leaves

¼ cup sugar

½ teaspoon salt

1¼ cups real maple syrup or 1½ cups maple sugar

Apple cider (preferred) or water, as needed

1 teaspoon citric acid or 2 tablespoons bottled lemon juice (if canning)

1 Core and chop the apples and add them to a large, nonreactive pot, tossing with the fresh lemon juice as you go to prevent oxidation.

2 Put the cloves and bay leaves in a looseleaf tea bag or pouch so you can retrieve them later.

3 Add the seasoning pouch, sugar, salt, and maple syrup to a pot over medium-low heat.

4 Increase the heat to medium and cook, stirring frequently, until the apples are very soft, about 1 hour. You can add a little cider, 1 to 2 tablespoons at a time, if needed to keep the mixture from sticking and burning.

5 Remove the seasoning pouch. Use an immersion blender and/or a food mill to blend the apples until very smooth. The texture should be a little thicker than applesauce but still spreadable. If it's too thin, cook it a bit longer, stirring frequently, to reduce.

6 If refrigerating, allow the apple butter to cool and store it in an airtight container; it will keep for at least 2 weeks.

(continued on next page)

Mapple (Maple and Apple) Butter *continued*

7 If canning, stir in the citric acid. Place eight half-pint jars in your hot water bath canner and heat it up. Then, using tongs, remove the hot jars from the canner and fill them, leaving ½ inch of headspace.

8 Run a chopstick or other thin, nonmetal utensil along the inner edges of the jars to release any air bubbles. Wipe the rims of the jars with a clean, damp cloth. Add the lids and bands and screw down to hand tightness.

9 Process half-pints in a hot water bath canner for 15 minutes, adjusting for altitude (see page 39) if needed.

10 Let the jars cool for 24 hours before testing the seals (see page 36), then store out of direct sunlight at room temperature.

Repurposing Mushy, Bruised Apples

If your apples are starting to go soft, preserving them in rings (canned or dried) may not work, since you'd have to cut off spots, leaving you with lop-sided rings.

So what can you do? Basically, anything that involves turning the apples into mush, paste, or liquid: applesauce, vinegar, apple syrup, apple butter, or dicing and freezing the fruit for smoothies and pancakes. Just make sure to preserve them as soon as you're able. Once one apple goes bad, the whole bunch goes soon after. There's a whole saying about it, after all.

White Quince Marmalade

Quince makes for a deliciously flavorful and color-changing treat—as the fruit oxidizes, it goes from white to a rich red. Nearly every quince product you can buy is red, but if you want to experiment with this color-changing fruit, make white quince marmalade, which is cooked quickly enough to preserve its light color. This recipe is also made with less water than red marmalade, which allows it to heat more quickly, thus minimizing the possibility for oxidation.

These recipes for white and red quince marmalades are adapted from a 1615 cookbook, *The English Housewife* by Gervase Markham, and the flavor is almost like apples and honey (though they're completely vegan).

— Makes about 2 pints

2¼ cups sugar
2 cups water
1 pound quince
1 teaspoon citric acid or 2 tablespoons bottled lemon juice (if canning)

1 Add the sugar and water to a pot and bring to a simmer.

2 Right before cooking, peel, halve, and core the quince. Then cut into 1-inch cubes and add immediately to the pot.

3 Bring to a rapid boil and cook until a thick syrup develops and the fruit is softened, about 30 minutes. Remove from the heat and mash the fruit with a spoon or potato masher to your desired smoothness.

4 If refrigerating, allow the marmalade to cool and store it in an airtight container; it will keep for 1 month.

5 If canning, stir in the citric acid. Place four half-pint jars in your hot water bath canner and heat it up. Then use tongs to remove the hot jars; fill them, leaving ½ inch of headspace.

6 Run a chopstick or other thin, nonmetal utensil along the inner edges of the jars to release any air bubbles. Wipe the rims of the jars with a clean, damp cloth. Add the lids and bands and screw down to hand tightness.

7 Process half-pints in a hot water bath canner for 12 minutes, adjusting for altitude (see page 39) if needed.

8 Let the jars cool for 24 hours before testing the seals (see page 36), then store out of direct sunlight at room temperature.

White Quince Marmalade

Red Quince Marmalade

This recipe harnesses the color-changing magic of quince with a long, slow cook time that allows the beautiful red color to develop. Quince marmalade (red or white) is perfect on crackers, with cheese, or dolloped on overnight oats.

— Makes about 2 pints

- **1 pound quince**
- **2¼ cups sugar**
- **4 cups water**
- **1 teaspoon citric acid or 2 tablespoons bottled lemon juice (if canning)**

1. Peel, halve, and core the quince, then cut it into 1-inch cubes.
2. Add the quince, sugar, and water to a medium saucepan over low heat.
3. Simmer, loosely covered, for about 2 hours, stirring occasionally.
4. Once most of the water has evaporated and the fruit is in a thick syrup, use a spoon or potato masher to mash the fruit if needed.
5. If refrigerating, allow the marmalade to cool and store it in an airtight container; it will keep for 1 month.
6. If canning, add the citric acid. Place four half-pint jars in your hot water bath canner and heat it up. Then use tongs to remove the hot jars; fill them, leaving ½ inch of headspace.
7. Run a chopstick or other thin, nonmetal utensil along the inner edges of the jars to release any air bubbles. Wipe the rims of the jars with a clean, damp cloth. Add the lids and bands and screw down to hand tightness.
8. Process half-pints in a hot water bath canner for 12 minutes, adjusting for altitude (see page 39) if needed.
9. Let the jars cool for 24 hours before testing the seals (see page 36), then store out of direct sunlight at room temperature.

Apple Cider Molasses

Apple cider molasses, also called boiled cider, dates back to New England in the mid-seventeenth century. This sweet condiment was a practical way to lengthen the shelf life of apple cider. Apple cider molasses has a concentrated cider flavor and tastes warm and comforting. You can boil it down to the consistency of molasses or leave it thinner—whatever you prefer.

My version, inspired by James Beard Award–winning chef Alan Bergo, a.k.a. Forager Chef, is great as a pancake and dessert drizzle or in coffee, tea, or evening drinks. The spice sachet is optional, especially if you want to use this as a versatile vegan honey replacement.

— Makes about 1½ pints

- **1 gallon apple cider**
- **1 cinnamon stick (optional)**
- **7 whole allspice berries (optional)**
- **4 whole cloves (optional)**
- **½ teaspoon citric acid (if canning)**

1. In a large, high-sided pot, bring the cider to a boil over medium-high heat.
2. Make a sachet with the cinnamon, allspice, and cloves (if using) and add it to the pot.
3. Reduce the heat to a strong simmer and cook, stirring occasionally, for 45 minutes. Scrape off any scum from the surface as it rises and discard. Remove the sachet.
4. Continue cooking for 2 to 2½ hours, until the cider is reduced by about three-quarters and has a thin, syrupy consistency.

5 If refrigerating, pour the syrup into an airtight container. Note that refrigerated apple cider molasses may need to be warmed before using if it's very thick.

6 If canning, whisk in the citric acid. Place three half-pint jars in your hot water bath canner and heat it up. Using tongs, remove the hot jars; fill them, leaving ½ inch of headspace.

7 Run a chopstick or other thin, nonmetal utensil along the inner edges of the jars to release any air bubbles. Wipe the rims of the jars with a clean, damp cloth. Add the lids and bands and screw down to hand tightness.

8 Process half-pints for 12 minutes in a hot water bath canner, adjusting for altitude (see page 39) if needed.

9 Let the jars cool for 24 hours before testing the seals (see page 36), then store out of direct sunlight at room temperature.

Molasses Varieties

You can use the same molasses-making process with many different juices, like pomegranate, for example. I've even made it with beet juice and carrot juice, which are naturally sweet, alongside fruit juice. Just make sure you're using juice with enough sugar in it to become a sweet syrup. If you make beet molasses, try adding 1 teaspoon of ground sumac per pint of beet juice.

Apple Pie Filling

The flavor profile of this filling is inspired by a pippin pie recipe I've re-created many times from *The English Housewife* (1615). In that pie, whole small apples are filled with dates and whole spices and baked. In this version, apples are sliced and ground spices added. This works best with firm, fresh apples—as tart or sweet as you wish. As Luke Dilbeck from the Folk Collaborative in the North Georgia mountains once told me, the best pies and ciders are made with a mix of apples, and I've certainly found that to be the case.

— Makes about 3 quarts

- 11 apples, peeled, cored, and cut into ½-inch dice or slices (about 10 cups)
- 2 tablespoons lemon juice
- 1 cup chopped dates (optional)
- 4½ cups sugar
- ¾ cup cornstarch
- 3 teaspoons ground cinnamon
- 1 teaspoon salt
- ⅔ cup orange juice
- ½ teaspoon whole cloves
- 7 (4- to 5-inch) strips orange peel
- 4 cups water
- 1½ teaspoons citric acid or 6 tablespoons bottled lemon juice, if canning

1 Toss the sliced apples with the lemon juice immediately after cutting, to prevent browning.

2 Combine the apples, dates (if using), sugar, cornstarch, cinnamon, salt, and orange juice in a pot and bring them to a simmer. Put the cloves and orange peels in a sachet. Once the mixture is simmering, add the sachet and water.

3 Boil over high heat, stirring gently and constantly until thickened, 5 to 8 minutes.

(continued on next page)

Apple Pie Filling *continued*

4 Remove the pot from the heat and stir in the citric acid, if canning, and let the sachet steep while you pack the jars. Remove the sachet before canning or storing.

5 If refrigerating, allow the apples to cool, pack them into jars, and store them in the refrigerator for 2 to 3 weeks.

6 If canning, place three quart jars in your hot water bath canner and heat it up. Then, using tongs, remove the hot jars from the canner and pack them tightly with the apples, pressing down (it's okay to crush a few). Pack the jars to about ½ inch below the bottom thread of each jar. Add syrup if needed to completely cover, leaving 1 inch of headspace.

7 Run a chopstick or other thin, nonmetal utensil along the inner edges of the jars to release any air bubbles. Wipe the rims of the jars with a clean, damp cloth. Add the lids and bands and screw down to hand tightness.

8 Process quart jars in a hot water bath canner for 25 minutes, adjusting for altitude (see page 39) if needed.

9 Let the jars cool for 24 hours before testing the seal (see page 36), then store out of direct sunlight at room temperature.

VARIATION: FIVE-SPICE FILLING

Use 4 to 5 teaspoons five-spice powder in place of cinnamon and cloves.

Basic Applesauce

Applesauce is simply apples cooked down a bit until thickened, but not as thick as a spreadable preserve. Unlike apple butter, which is blended (or passed through a food mill) until very smooth, applesauce often has more texture. Applesauce is great plain or with your favorite flavors. Cinnamon is a classic addition, or try cinnamon and rose water for a Persian twist. Save the peels and cores for apple scrap vinegar (page 252)!

— Makes about 2 pints

- **8 medium apples, peeled, cored, and cut into ½-inch dice**
- **½ cup water or rose water**
- **1 tablespoon apple cider vinegar**
- **½–1 cup sugar**
- **½–1 tablespoon ground cinnamon or 1–2 teaspoons dried sage (optional)**
- **¼–½ teaspoon salt**

1 Add the apples, water, and vinegar to a pot over medium heat and cook until the apples are very tender, about 20 minutes.

2 Leave the applesauce chunky or, for a smoother texture, process it with a food mill, food processor, immersion blender, or just a potato masher.

3 Add the sugar and adjust the salt as needed.

4 If refrigerating, allow the applesauce to cool and store it in airtight containers for 2 to 3 weeks.

5 If canning, place two pint jars in your hot water bath canner and heat it up. Then use tongs to remove the hot jars; fill them with hot applesauce, leaving ½ inch of headspace.

6 Run a chopstick or other thin, nonmetal utensil along the inner edges of the jars to release any air bubbles. Wipe the rims of the jars with a clean, damp cloth. Add the lids and bands and screw down to hand tightness.

7 Process pints in a hot water bath canner for 20 minutes, adjusting for altitude (see page 39) if needed.

8 Let the jars cool for 24 hours before testing the seals (see page 36), then store out of direct sunlight at room temperature.

Bananas

Most people think of bananas as a fresh food, but there are many wonderful ways to preserve them, from banana chips to banana vinegar and beyond. Choose fresh, firm bananas without bruises or blemishes. Store at room temperature out of direct sunlight and away from heat.

DRYING

I have, historically, not been a fan of dried bananas. However, it turns out that if done correctly, drying is an easy and delicious way to preserve this fruit. Case in point? The banana chip recipe on page 260.

Ways to Preserve Bananas

	Shelf-stable	Fast	Low waste	Ready meals and ingredients	Big flavor
Banana Chips You'll Actually Want to Eat (page 260)	X			X	X
Banana "Ice Cream" (page 261)		X			
Banana Vinegar (page 261)				X	X
Banana Jam (page 262)				X	X

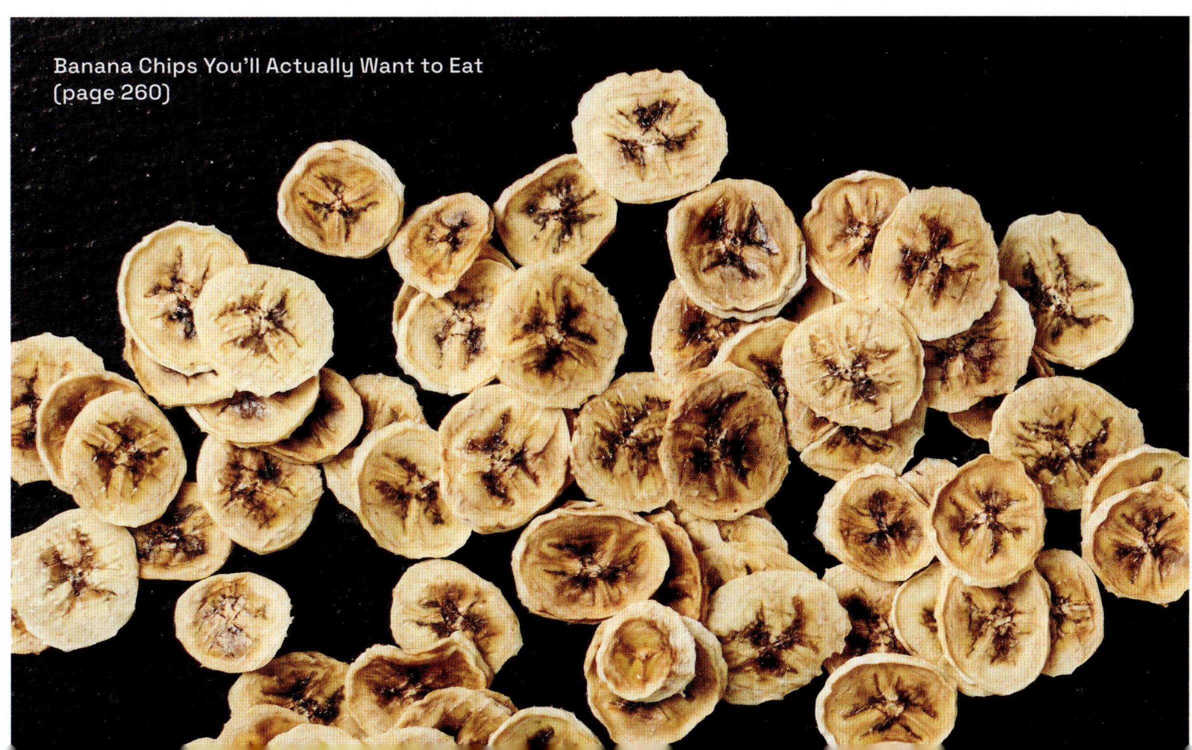
Banana Chips You'll Actually Want to Eat (page 260)

Banana Chips You'll Actually Want to Eat

I was once a strict avoider of banana chips. Most store-bought banana chips have a terrible texture and taste artificially banana-y or like nothing at all. They're about as exciting as munching on a chunk of drywall. If I saw them in my trail mix, I would eat everything else and save those chips for the compost. However, after many trials, I'm pleased to say that I have found a process for making crisp, flavorful banana chips that *I actually want to eat.*

—— Makes about 1 cup dried chips

- **2 ripe, peeled bananas, sliced ⅛–¼ inch thick**
- **1–2 tablespoons seasoning (see suggestions below; optional)**

Coat the banana pieces with your choice of seasoning, if desired. Arrange them in a single layer on dehydrator trays and dehydrate at 135°F/57°C for 6 to 10 hours, turning over once, halfway through. When they're done, the chips will easily snap in half. Allow them to cool completely, then store in airtight containers with no headspace. Properly dried banana chips will last for at least 2 months.

VARIATION: FLAVOR OPPORTUNITIES

When you make your own banana chips, the sky's the limit, so any flavors you like with bananas elsewhere can be brought to your banana-chip game.

Here are some of my favorites.

BLACK PEPPER. Just use plain old black pepper, or equal parts salt and sugar along with pepper, which makes for an almost kettle corn–esque banana chip.

CINNAMON. Try ground cinnamon with or without cocoa powder (and maybe a dash of hot pepper powder if you want a banana chip in the style of Mexican hot chocolate).

CITRUS ZEST AND HEAT. Some spice and brightness bring out the banana flavors. I like pairing warm or cool colors, like orange zest and red pepper flakes, or lime zest and green chiles.

COCOA POWDER. Chocolate and banana is a classic combination. Plain old unsweetened cocoa powder works perfectly. If you have vanilla powder or peanut butter powder, those might be fun to play with, too.

SPICE AND CITRUS ZEST. Warming spices and spice blends, especially when cut through with some citrus zest, really shine here. My favorite is garam masala and lime zest.

FREEZING

The typical guidance for bananas is to freeze them mashed. If you mash them, add ½ teaspoon ascorbic acid per cup of banana to prevent browning.

You can also freeze whole, peeled bananas—perhaps with a popsicle stick inserted lengthwise—and then dip them in chocolate as a dessert. Note that the texture of these frozen banana treats will vary based on your freezer temperature and how fast the bananas cool (and thus how big the ice crystals in them are).

Or slice your bananas in ½- to 1-inch-thick rounds and lay them out in a single layer with space between them on a baking sheet lined with parchment paper or a silicone mat. Freeze for 6 to 8 hours or until frozen through. Store in an airtight container with no headspace. Sliced frozen bananas can be added to smoothies and desserts with minimal fuss.

Banana "Ice Cream"

This is a simple way to make vegan ice cream using just bananas. You can add chopped nuts or chocolate after you stir the ice cream base, if you like (finely chopped or shaved chocolate, rather than whole chocolate chips, will have a better texture post-freezing).

— Makes about 2 cups

2 large overripe bananas, peeled

1 In a mixing bowl, mash the bananas with a potato masher until smooth.

2 Spread the mixture in a small baking pan and place it in the freezer.

3 Freeze until the top begins to harden, about 1 hour, then run a fork through the mixture to break up the ice crystals.

4 Repeat this process several times until the mixture is frozen and has the consistency of ice cream.

5 Pack the ice cream into an airtight container—all the way to the top to prevent freezer burn—and return it to the freezer. It will keep for at least 1 month if properly stored.

FERMENTING

Yes, you can ferment bananas! While I've experimented with adding banana to other ferments, banana vinegar is my favorite.

Banana Vinegar

This is an easy (mostly set-and-forget) way to use up your overripe bananas. Use banana vinegar to add some tang to banana bread and baked goods, to lend an unexpected sour note in dressings or fruit salad, or even to culture butter (page 358): Banana vinegar–cultured butter is great in desserts, too.

Very ripe bananas

Unpasteurized vinegar or a vinegar mother (optional)

1 Make the alcohol. Thoroughly mash a banana (or several) in a jar. Let the mash sit in the jar, covered with a lid or a tea towel secured with string or rubber band, stirring at least once a day, for 15 to 20 days, or until it becomes liquid, bubbly, and alcoholic. It may have small pieces of banana in it. That's okay! It will still be alcoholic enough to become vinegar.

2 Turn the alcohol into vinegar. Pour the banana alcohol into in a nonreactive bowl, crock, or other vessel with a large surface area, then cover it with a cloth to keep out bugs while allowing air to circulate. Whatever container you use, fill it no more than half full to maximize the surface area. (For a speedier fermentation, add about 2 tablespoons of unpasteurized vinegar or vinegar mother per 1 cup of banana alcohol.)

3 Let the liquid ferment at room temperature, out of direct sunlight, for 2 to 4 weeks, or until the alcohol has turned to acetic acid. After 2 weeks, begin testing your vinegar. You can buy chemical titration kits to test whether any alcohol is left, or you can test it the old-fashioned way: by smell and taste. If it smells and tastes like vinegar, it's vinegar; and if you like the taste, go ahead and pull it. If it's not very sour yet, try letting it go a little longer. And if it's too sour, you can dilute it a bit before use. Store the vinegar in an airtight container with no headspace in the fridge for at least 2 months, or at room temperature out of direct sunlight for up to 1 month.

Banana Jam

MAKING JAM

Jam is a great use for overripe bananas, which are very soft, break down easily, and have a strong banana flavor and scent.

Banana Jam

Recipes for mashed and sweetened bananas in various forms are often seen in Australia and in many other places where bananas grow. If you're using less-ripe bananas and they aren't breaking down as they simmer, just use a potato masher and mash them down a bit in the pan as you cook. Add the lemon and lime zest if you like things very citrusy!

—— Makes about 1½ pints

- **6 overripe bananas, peeled and cut into 1-inch rounds**
- **2¼ cups sugar**
- **Pinch of salt**
- **Juice of 1 lemon**
- **Juice of 1 lime**
- **Zest of 1 lemon and 1 lime (optional)**

1. Add the bananas, sugar, salt, lemon and lime juice, and lemon and lime zest (if using) to a large high-sided skillet or a small stockpot.

2. Bring to a simmer over medium-high heat, then reduce the heat to medium and cook, stirring frequently, until the liquid is reduced by a bit more than half and the jam coats the back of a spoon, about 15 minutes.

3. If you want a smoother jam, mash it with a potato masher or blend with an immersion blender.

4. Cool the jam completely and store it in an airtight container in the refrigerator, where it will last for 2 weeks or more.

Berries and Currants

This is a very broad, and very delicious, group of fruits that includes blackberries, blueberries, currants (red and white), dewberries, gooseberries, elderberries (see sidebar, page 267), ground cherries, huckleberries, lingonberries, mulberries, raspberries, and strawberries. The great thing about them is how interchangeable many of them are, so if you want to swap strawberries into your Raspberry-Beet Jam (page 272) or use blueberries rather than strawberries in Solstice Refrigerator Jam (page 274), the world is your oyster.

DRYING

Many berries lend themselves well to drying, with the exception of berries with lots of seeds like blackberries. You *can* dry them, but the texture of those seeds is really emphasized. (I recommend freezing or making other preserves instead.)

For berries *without* a ton of big seeds (blueberries, boysenberries, cranberries, currants, or strawberries, among others), drying is a fantastic way to preserve them. Berries are best dried whole, but you can also dry halved or sliced strawberries, cut ¼-inch thick, if desired (just adjust the time, as slices dry more quickly).

Thoroughly wash and drain your berries. Unlike most fruits, you don't need to pretreat these with a sulfur or acid dip. Instead, plunge your berries into boiling water for just 20 to 30 seconds, then immediately submerge in ice water, which will crack the skins and allow them to dry more evenly. Drain well on a clean tea towel or paper towels before drying.

Dry your whole fruits in a single layer on dehydrator trays at 135°F/57°C for 18 to 24 hours (depending on the size of berries/currants and water content) or until dry. I've had very large, watery berries take about 30 hours. Berries may still be somewhat pliable but should not be sticky or tacky, even when cut in half.

You can keep dried berries whole or grind them up into berry dust to sprinkle on drinks, ice cream, oatmeal, or anything else you want. Store in an airtight container out of direct sunlight and away from high humidity, where they will last for at least 4 months.

FRUIT LEATHER

Berries and currants are fantastic for fruit leathers: They're sweet, they mash up and dry well, and they play nicely with lots of other flavors. The main consideration with these is to think about the flavor profile of the final product. Lots of tart currants, for example, might be best balanced with sweeter fruits, like strawberries. To make fruit leather, see page 94.

FREEZING

Berries' structure does break down a bit in the freezer, so when thawed they won't be as firm as they were when fresh. They're still great for cooking, though, from tossing into cake batter or pancakes to making a quick batch of jam.

For the best texture, keep your freezer below 0°F/–18°C and don't freeze too much food at one time, which causes the temperature to fluctuate. If you're able to, freeze your fruit at –10°F/–23°C and serve just as it's almost thawed.

Berries can be dry packed, syrup packed, or sugar packed.

- **DRY PACKED:** Pack whole berries into containers, leaving ½ inch of headspace, seal, and freeze.
- **SYRUP PACKED:** Pack whole berries in a 40 to 50 percent syrup, leaving headspace (see page 19). To make your syrup, combine 3 to 4 cups of sugar with 4 cups of water in a saucepan over medium heat (I always add a pinch of salt, too). Stir until the sugar is dissolved, remove from heat, and allow the syrup to cool completely before pouring it over fruit, sealing, and freezing.
- **SUGAR PACKED:** Gently stir 1 quart of berries with ¾ cup of sugar, leaving headspace (see page 19), then pack and freeze.

Berries last for 8 to 12 months when properly stored in the freezer.

Ways to Preserve Berries and Currants

	Shelf-stable	Fast	Low waste	Ready meals and ingredients	Big flavor
Fennel-Strawberry Vinegar (page 165)			X		X
Chilled Blueberry Soup (page 265)		X		X	X
Strawberry-Top Shrub (page 265)			X		X
Strawberry-Jalapeño Shrub (page 266)			X		X
Refrigerator Pickled Blackberries (page 266)				X	X
Refrigerator Pickled Strawberries (page 266)				X	X
Elderberry Syrup (page 267)				X	X
Raspberry-Beet Syrup (page 268)				X	X
Sweet-and-Savory Macerated Strawberry Sauce (page 268)				X	X
Strawberry-Top Lime Syrup (page 269)				X	X
Ginger-Berry Syrup (page 269)				X	X
Strawberry Jam (page 270)				X	X
Strawberry-Wine Refrigerator Jam (page 271)				X	X
Blueberry-Lavender Refrigerator Jam (page 271)				X	X
Raspberry-Beet Jam (page 272)				X	X
Blue Strawberry Jam (page 273)				X	X
Sunny Blueberry-Corn Jam (page 273)				X	X
Solstice Refrigerator Jam (page 274)				X	X

Chilled Blueberry Soup

The height of summer is the perfect time to make chilled soup from berries frozen in spring.

Fresh blueberries

Yogurt or coconut milk

Fresh mint

Salt

Herbs, spices, or other fruits (optional)

1 Either freeze the blueberries whole (see page 263) or blend and pour the pulp into ice cube trays and freeze.

2 Combine equal parts frozen blueberries and yogurt in a blender. Add a sprig of fresh mint per about 2 cups of soup, and salt to taste. Add your favorite fruit-loving herbs and spices or other fruits like fresh peaches, if desired. Blend well. Use extra splashes of coconut milk as needed to thin out the soup. Serve chilled.

INFUSING

Those last, lingering fruits clinging to your berry bushes might not seem like enough to make much of anything. Thankfully, infusing fruit into vinegar or spirits helps stretch the flavor, giving you an abundance even with just a little fruit. Don't have berries? This will work well with sliced stone fruits, too, as well as other flavorful foods like fresh herbs.

Making berry vinegar couldn't be simpler: Fill a container about halfway with your favorite ripe berries, add vinegar to cover completely, top with a lid, and let sit out of direct sunlight until it has a flavor you enjoy. I let mine sit for at least 2 weeks, but you can do more or less as you wish. Check your vinegar each day, giving it a gentle stir or shake if berries have floated to the surface. Berry vinegar can be stored at room temperature or in the fridge in an airtight, narrow-necked bottle. Note that the water from the fruit can dilute the acidity of the vinegar, so if you're concerned about this, storing it in the fridge is the best choice.

Strawberry-Top Shrub

Strawberry-Top Shrub

A shrub is a sweetened vinegar for drinking. The strawberry flavor shines with this technique, and using the tops trimmed from the berries is one of my favorite ways to reduce food waste. I like to use red or white wine vinegar, apple cider vinegar, or sometimes even distilled white vinegar.

— Makes 1 pint

About 1 cup strawberry tops

¼ cup sugar

1 (3-inch) strip lemon peel

½ teaspoon lavender flowers (optional)

Vinegar, to cover

1 Add the strawberry tops, sugar, lemon peel, and lavender (if using) in a pint jar. Pour vinegar over to cover and fill the jar.

2 Steep the shrub for about 3 weeks, shaking occasionally, then strain. Store it in an airtight container in the fridge or at room temperature.

Strawberry-Jalapeño Shrub

This fruity, spicy shrub is my go-to for holiday mocktails with a bit of a flavor kick (just add soda water or ginger beer) or for cocktails with whiskey or tequila. For a low-waste version, swap out strawberry and jalapeño tops left over from cooking.

—— Makes 1 pint

- **¾–1 cup sliced strawberries**
- **¼ cup sliced jalapeños (or more if you like things really spicy!)**
- **Apple cider vinegar or distilled white vinegar, to cover**
- **⅛–¼ cup sugar**

1. Put the strawberries and jalapeños in a pint jar. Add vinegar to cover.
2. Let the mixture steep for 2 to 3 weeks, shaking or stirring every couple of days.
3. Strain the vinegar. Add sugar to taste, whisking to dissolve.
4. Decant the shrub into a pint jar, small gift jars, or small swing-top bottles. Store in the refrigerator, where it will last for 1 month or more.

PICKLING

Delicate fruits, like berries and currants, don't hold up well as canned pickles: The fruits dissolve into mush. These fruits work best when a cooled pickling brine is poured over the top, which helps them maintain their texture. Choose only very firm and fresh berries and currants for pickling. Here are two basic refrigerator pickle recipes to get you started on your pickled-berry journey, one sour and one sweet.

Refrigerator Pickled Blackberries

Tart pickled berries are wonderful on a salad, or as a garnish for summertime drinks.

—— Makes about 3 quarts

- **Scant ½ cup salt**
- **4 cups distilled white vinegar**
- **4 cups water**
- **4 pounds (6 pints) blackberries**
- **3 small sprigs sage**
- **½ teaspoon black peppercorns**

1. Make the brine: Combine the salt, vinegar, and water in a pot over medium heat. Heat just enough to dissolve the salt. Take off the heat and cool completely.
2. Meanwhile, divide the blackberries, sage, and peppercorns among the containers.
3. Pour the cooled brine over the berries to cover. Let them pickle for 8 to 12 hours in the fridge before eating. They'll last for at least 1 week.

Refrigerator Pickled Strawberries

This is the only pickle recipe I use balsamic vinegar in; I use white balsamic vinegar here, but swap out regular balsamic if you prefer.

—— Makes about 3 quarts

- **½ cup sugar**
- **¼ cup salt**
- **4 cups water**
- **4 cups distilled white vinegar**
- **1¼ cups white balsamic vinegar**
- **6 pounds strawberries, sliced or quartered**
- **1 tablespoon fresh rosemary**
- **1 tablespoon mace or ground nutmeg**

1 Make the brine: Combine the sugar, salt, water, distilled white vinegar, and balsamic vinegar in a pot over medium heat. Heat just enough to dissolve the salt and sugar. Remove from the heat and cool completely.

2 Meanwhile, divide the strawberries, rosemary, and mace among the containers.

3 Pour the cooled brine over the strawberries to cover. Let them pickle for 8 to 12 hours in the fridge before eating. They'll last for at least 1 week.

MAKING SYRUPS, SAUCES, AND JAMS

Syrups, sauces, and jams are the perfect way to use up a lot of berries at once. They're also a great way to preserve the taste of the season for yourself or for gifts to share with others.

Working with Elderberries

Elder trees are beloved by foragers, and for good reason. Elderflowers make a delicious cordial; the berries make a nice syrup to have on hand for winter colds (follow my fruit syrup guidance, page 79) or they can be dried for later use. Be sure to properly identify them before harvesting, and always harvest sustainably. Note that elderberry stems need to be completely removed and that elderberries need to be processed before consuming (not eaten raw).

Elderberry Syrup

I adore elderberries. The ravine next to my house is studded with them, and each summer I make this syrup that's equal parts medicinal and delicious.

— Makes about 2 pints

- **4 cups ripe elderberries**
- **4 cups sugar**
- **1–2 teaspoons spices of your choice, like baking spices, or 1 cinnamon stick (optional)**
- **½ teaspoon salt**
- **1 cup water**
- **3 tablespoons bottled lemon juice, if canning**

1 Combine the elderberries, sugar, spices (if using), salt, water, and lemon juice (if using) in a large saucepan and bring to a boil.

2 Reduce to a simmer and cook until the fruit starts to break down and the syrup is rich and dark, about 20 minutes.

3 Strain the syrup through a fine-mesh strainer to remove the pulp and seeds.

4 If refrigerating, allow the syrup to cool completely, pack it into an airtight container, and refrigerate or freeze. It will last in the fridge for at least a few weeks.

5 If canning, place four half-pint jars or two pint jars in your hot water bath canner and heat it up. Then, using tongs, remove the hot jars from the canner and pack the hot syrup into them, leaving ¼ inch of headspace.

6 Run a chopstick or other thin, nonmetal utensil along the inner edges of the jars to release any air bubbles. Wipe the rims of the jars with a clean, damp cloth. Add the lids and bands and screw down to hand tightness.

7 Process in a hot water bath canner for 10 minutes for half-pints or 12 minutes for pints, adjusting for altitude (see page 39) as needed.

(continued on next page)

Elderberry Syrup *continued*

8 Let the jars cool for 24 hours before testing the seals (see page 36), then store out of direct sunlight at room temperature.

Raspberry-Beet Syrup

This deep red syrup is an easy way to add a colorful pop to beverages, desserts, or your morning pancakes.

— Makes about 3 half-pints

- **4 cups sugar**
- **2 cups raspberries**
- **½ cup grated beets**
- **1 (3-inch) strip lemon zest**
- **1 cup water**
- **1½ tablespoons bottled lemon juice (if canning)**

1 Combine the sugar, raspberries, beets, lemon zest, and water in a large saucepan and bring to a boil over medium heat.

2 Reduce the heat and simmer until the fruit starts to break down and the syrup is rich and thick, 15 to 20 minutes.

3 Strain through a fine-mesh strainer to remove the pulp and seeds.

4 If refrigerating, pack the syrup into an airtight container and store in the fridge (or freezer). It lasts in the fridge for at least 2 weeks.

5 If canning, add the lemon juice. Place three half-pint jars in your hot water bath canner and heat it up. Then, using tongs, remove the hot jars and pack the hot syrup into them, leaving ¼ inch of headspace.

6 Run a chopstick or other thin, nonmetal utensil along the inner edges of the jars to release any air bubbles. Wipe the rims of the jars with a clean, damp cloth. Add the lids and bands and screw down to hand tightness.

7 Process in a hot water bath canner for 10 minutes for half-pints or 12 minutes for pints, adjusting for altitude (see page 39) as needed.

8 Let the jars cool for 24 hours before testing the seals (see page 36), then store out of direct sunlight at room temperature.

Sweet-and-Savory Macerated Strawberry Sauce

Maceration is simple. Just add sugar to fruit in a jar and *gently* shake (or to a bowl and gently stir), let it sit in the fridge, and voilà: The longer it sits, the more syrupy and less firm the fruit will become. Use it right away or keep it in the fridge as a soft fruit syrup. Slice the fruit for quicker maceration or leave berries (even strawberries) whole. This syrup is sweet enough for dessert, but the vinegar and soy sauce give the flavor more complexity than that of standard macerated strawberries.

— Makes about 1 pint

- **1 pound strawberries, sliced ¼ inch thick**
- **1 tablespoon sugar**
- **2 teaspoons apple cider vinegar**
- **1½ teaspoons dark soy sauce**

1 Combine the strawberries, sugar, vinegar, and soy sauce in a jar and gently shake. Let sit at least 1 hour in the fridge before using.

2 To store the sauce in the fridge, pack it into an airtight container with no headspace and use within 1 month. Or freeze in an airtight, freezer-safe container with headspace (see page 19), where it will last for 8 to 12 months.

Strawberry-Top Lime Syrup

This is the perfect addition to soda water in summertime and a great way to use up those strawberry tops from your other preserving projects!

— Makes 2 pints

- **2 cups sugar**
- **1 cup strawberry tops**
- **½ teaspoon salt**
- **2 cups water**
- **Juice and zest of 1 lime, zest cut into strips with a peeler**
- **1 teaspoon citric acid (if canning)**

1 Combine the sugar, strawberry tops, salt, water, and lime juice and zest in a pot. Cook over medium-high heat until flavorful and fragrant and reduced by half, 15 to 20 minutes.

2 Strain through a fine-mesh strainer, pressing on the strawberry tops to release the syrup.

3 If refrigerating, cool the syrup, pack it into an airtight container, and store in the fridge. It will last for at least 2 weeks.

4 If canning, add the citric acid. Place two pint jars in your hot water bath canner and heat it up. Then, using tongs, remove the hot jars from the canner and pack the hot syrup into them, leaving ½ inch of headspace.

5 Run a chopstick or other thin, nonmetal utensil along the inner edges of the jars to release any air bubbles. Wipe the rims of the jars with a clean, damp cloth. Add the lids and bands and screw down to hand tightness.

6 Process pints in a hot water bath canner for 12 minutes, adjusting for altitude (see page 39) as needed.

7 Let the jars cool for 24 hours before testing the seals (see page 36), then store out of direct sunlight at room temperature.

Homemade Berry Soda

Strawberry soda was a childhood classic, but I prefer the flavor of fresh, ripe fruit over the store-bought stuff. You can make berry sodas with a fruit syrup (see page 79), adding soda water to taste, or by wild-fermenting the fruit with water and sugar, then doing a second fermentation to carbonate it (see page 58).

Ginger-Berry Syrup

This process works with any berries, but blueberries and strawberries are my favorites. If you use strawberries, slice them before cooking. Use on desserts and in drinks. I offer a few non-ginger variations here.

— Makes about 1 pint

- **2 cups berries**
- **1 (2-inch) piece fresh ginger, cut into ⅛-inch pieces**
- **2 cups sugar**
- **¼ teaspoon salt**
- **1 cup water**
- **2 teaspoons apple cider vinegar, red wine vinegar, or white wine vinegar (5% acidity)**

1 Combine the berries, ginger, sugar, salt, water, and vinegar in a large saucepan over medium-high heat.

(continued on next page)

Ginger-Berry Syrup *continued*

2 Bring just to a boil, then reduce the heat and simmer, stirring occasionally, until the fruit is soft and the syrup is fragrant and flavorful, about 15 minutes. It can help to break up whole fruit with a potato masher 5 minutes into cooking.

3 Skim off any foam and strain the syrup through a fine-mesh strainer.

4 If refrigerating, cool the syrup completely and store it in an airtight container. It will last for 2 weeks or more.

5 If canning, place a pint jar in your hot water bath canner and heat it up, then remove the jar from the canner with tongs and pack the hot syrup into it, leaving ½ inch of headspace.

6 Run a chopstick or other thin, nonmetal utensil along the inner edge of the jar to release any air bubbles. Wipe the rim of the jar with a clean, damp cloth. Add the lid and band and screw down to hand tightness.

7 Process the pint in a hot water bath canner for 12 minutes, adjusting for altitude (see page 39) as needed.

8 Let the jar cool for 24 hours before testing the seal (see page 36), then store out of direct sunlight at room temperature.

VARIATIONS: BEYOND GINGER

Consider swapping out the ginger for one of these flavor profiles.

CITRUS. Use a 2- to 3-inch strip of your favorite citrus peel (also nice with 1 teaspoon of black peppercorns).

FIVE-SPICE POWDER. Use ½ to 1 teaspoon of five-spice powder.

STRAWBERRY ROSE. Use all strawberries for the berries in the recipe, and add ¼ cup of dried rose petals.

BLUEBERRY LAVENDER. Use all blueberries and 1 tablespoon of dried lavender flowers.

Strawberry Jam

A lot of sugar, maceration, and a high cook temperature mean that this jam takes less time on the stove than some of my other recipes. You can use other berries, along with or instead of strawberries, depending on what you have on hand.

— Makes about 4 pints

- **4 pounds strawberries, tops removed**
- **7 cups sugar**
- **1 teaspoon salt**
- **½ cup white or red wine vinegar (5% acidity) or bottled lemon juice**

1 Put the strawberries in a large pot and crush the fruit, one layer at a time. Stir in the sugar, salt, and vinegar. Let sit for 30 minutes to macerate.

2 Bring the fruit to a boil over high heat, stirring frequently, until it reaches the jelling point (220°F/105°C), about 15 minutes.

3 If refrigerating, allow the jam to cool completely and store it in airtight containers with ¼ to ½ inch of headspace. It will last for 2 weeks or more in the fridge.

4 If canning, place eight half-pint jars or four pint jars in your hot water bath canner and heat it up. Then, using tongs, remove the hot jars from the canner and add the jam, leaving ½ inch of headspace.

5 Run a chopstick or other thin, nonmetal utensil along the inner edges of the jars to release any air bubbles. Wipe the rims of the jars with a clean, damp cloth. Add the lids and bands and screw down to hand tightness.

6 Process half-pints or pints for 10 minutes in a hot water bath canner, adjusting for altitude (see page 39) as needed.

7 Let the jars cool for 24 hours before testing the seals (see page 36), then store out of direct sunlight at room temperature.

Strawberry-Wine Refrigerator Jam

I adapted this simple recipe from Gervase Markham's *The English Housewife* (1615) to my kitchen for small-batch jam making. I like the depth of flavor the wine adds. Feel free to use whatever wine (or even a dark stout or fruit juice) or fruit you'd like.

—— Makes about 1 pint

4 cups strawberries, sliced

¼ cup red wine (such as cabernet sauvignon)

¼ cup sugar

1 Place the strawberries in a medium saucepan and add enough water to cover. Bring to a boil and cook until very soft, about 20 minutes.

2 Using a fine-mesh strainer, strain the liquid from the strawberries. Combine the strawberry liquid and wine in a high-sided skillet and bring to a boil. Cook until the liquid is reduced by half, about 5 minutes.

3 Add the strained fruit back into the liquid and use a potato masher to mash the fruit into a pulp.

4 Turn off the heat and add the sugar, then stir until dissolved.

5 If jam is thinner than you'd like, using a fine-mesh strainer, strain excess liquid from the mixture and place the jam into a heatproof container. Store it in the refrigerator, where it will last for 2 weeks or more.

Blueberry-Lavender Refrigerator Jam

This is one of the first jam recipes I ever wrote. Nowadays I often make this with overripe berries and herb stems, simply pulling the stems out when I'm done cooking.

I like lavender in fruit jams, in moderation, because lavender complements the floral notes of the fruit. But if you overdo it, you risk your jam tasting like perfume. You can also swap in your favorite edible flowers here. This is a refrigerator jam with a bit less sugar than some of my other recipes.

—— Makes about 1½ pints

4 cups blueberries

1 cup sugar

1 tablespoon fresh lavender or ½ tablespoon dried (adjust to taste)

Pinch of sea salt

2 cups water

1 Combine the blueberries, sugar, lavender, salt, and water in a saucepan.

2 Cook over medium heat, stirring occasionally, until the mixture comes to a boil. Then reduce the heat to a simmer and cook, stirring occasionally, until the jam coats the back of a spoon, about 20 minutes.

3 Allow the jam to cool and spoon it into airtight containers. Store it in the refrigerator, where it will last for 2 to 3 weeks.

Raspberry-Beet Jam

A crisp, cheery, colorful treat that makes the prettiest gift! This jam is very red, and the color really pops on your plate. The beets add a crunchy texture, perfect for topping yogurt and ice cream. It's great year-round: rich enough for winter, but bright enough to top your summer bakes, too. The addition of beets means that this jam takes longer to cook, but fear not, the flavor and texture are still delightful.

— Makes about 3 pints

- **4–6 medium beets, grated (4 packed cups)**
- **2 cups raspberries**
- **2 cups sugar**
- **½ teaspoon salt**
- **⅔ cup water**
- **⅛ cup red wine vinegar**
- **1½ teaspoons citric acid or 6 tablespoons bottled lemon juice (if canning)**

Raspberry-Beet Jam

1. In a large saucepan, combine the beets, raspberries, sugar, salt, water, and vinegar.
2. Cover and simmer, stirring occasionally, until the beets begin to soften, about 20 minutes.
3. Remove the lid and continue simmering, stirring frequently, until the liquid is reduced by half, about 20 minutes. You should have a very loose jam consistency that coats the back of a spoon (the beets won't break down like the berries: That's okay!).
4. If refrigerating, cool the jam and pack it into an airtight container. It will last in the fridge for 2 weeks or more.
5. If canning, add the citric acid to the mixture and stir to combine. Place six half-pint jars or three pint jars in your hot water bath canner, heat it up, remove the hot jars with tongs, and spoon jam into them, leaving ½ inch of headspace.
6. Run a chopstick or other thin, nonmetal utensil along the inner edges of the jars to release any air bubbles. Wipe the rims of the jars with a clean, damp cloth. Add the lids and bands and screw down to hand tightness.
7. Process half-pints for 12 minutes and pints for 15 minutes in a hot water bath canner, adjusting for altitude (see page 39) if needed.
8. Let the jars cool for 24 hours before testing the seals (see page 36), then store out of direct sunlight at room temperature.

Blue Strawberry Jam

This is a fun take on berry jam, with a bit of a sour kick to keep things balanced. I love the flavor with fresh bread or with goat cheese and crackers. I use a potato masher partway through cooking to get a nice, smooth texture, but you can omit that step if you wish. Save your strawberry tops to make Strawberry-Top Shrub (page 265) or Strawberry-Top Lime Syrup (page 269).

—— Makes 4 pints

- **6 cups sliced strawberries, tops removed**
- **3 cups blueberries**
- **5 cups sugar**
- **½ tablespoon salt**
- **½ cup red wine vinegar (5% acidity) or bottled lemon juice**
- **¼ cup water**

1 Combine the strawberries, blueberries, sugar, salt, vinegar, and water in a large pot and bring to a boil, stirring occasionally.

2 Reduce the heat and simmer over medium-low, stirring occasionally. After 10 to 15 minutes, mash the fruit with a potato masher (or an immersion blender) to start breaking it down.

3 Continue cooking until the jam coats the back of a spoon, about 20 minutes.

4 If refrigerating, let the jam cool and pack it into airtight containers, where it will last for 2 weeks or more.

5 If canning, place four pint or eight half-pint jars in your hot water bath canner and heat it up. Then, using tongs, remove the hot jars from the canner and pack the hot jam into the jars, leaving ½ inch of headspace.

6 Run a chopstick or other thin, nonmetal utensil along the inner edges of the jars to release any air bubbles. Wipe the rims of the jars with a clean, damp cloth. Add the lids and bands and screw down to hand tightness.

7 Process half-pints for 12 minutes and pints for 15 minutes in a hot water bath canner, adjusting for altitude (see page 39) if needed.

8 Let the jars cool for 24 hours before testing the seals (see page 36), then store out of direct sunlight at room temperature.

Sunny Blueberry-Corn Jam

Many moons ago, I worked at a vegetarian café where one of my favorite dishes was waffles with blueberries, corn, lemon zest, and sour cream folded into the batter. I still make them at home, but I made this jam to replicate the experience in a snap, when I'm not making batter from scratch. Add a spoonful of sour cream to your waffles and pancakes (or fold into the batter). Tip: Adding the corn toward the end of cooking your jam helps it keep its texture.

—— Makes about 2 pints

- **4 cups blueberries**
- **3 cups sugar**
- **¼ teaspoon salt**
- **Zest of 2 lemons**
- **Juice of 1 lemon**
- **1½ cups fresh corn kernels (or frozen, thawed and drained)**
- **½ teaspoon citric acid or 1 tablespoon bottled lemon juice (if canning)**

1 Add the blueberries, sugar, salt, lemon zest, and lemon juice to a medium saucepan.

2 Heat the mixture over medium-high, stirring frequently and mashing the berries with a potato masher or the back of a spoon until most are crushed. Cook until the mixture coats the back of a spoon, 10 to 15 minutes.

(continued on next page)

Sunny Blueberry-Corn Jam *continued*

3 Add the corn and cook for 5 minutes longer.

4 If refrigerating, let the jam cool and store in an airtight container, where it will last for 2 weeks or more.

5 If canning, add the citric acid. Place two pint or four half-pint jars in your hot water bath canner and heat it up. Then, using tongs, remove the hot jars from the canner and add the hot jam to the jars, leaving ½ inch of headspace.

6 Run a chopstick or other thin, nonmetal utensil along the inner edges of the jars to release any air bubbles. Wipe the rims of the jars with a clean, damp cloth. Add the lids and bands and screw down to hand tightness.

7 Process half-pints for 12 minutes and pints for 15 minutes in a hot water bath canner, adjusting for altitude (see page 39) if needed.

8 Let the jars cool for 24 hours before testing the seals (see page 36), then store out of direct sunlight at room temperature.

Sunny Blueberry-Corn Jam

Solstice Refrigerator Jam

I love to make foods that celebrate the seasons. The return of the sun in winter, which happens to coincide with citrus season, is a welcome sight. I often celebrate the sun with two brightly flavored fruits with floral notes: Meyer lemon and strawberry. When I lived in Florida, I could find both from local growers during the winter solstice, which was how this refrigerator jam recipe came to be.

—— Makes about 2 pints

- **1 cup water**
- **4 cups strawberries, quartered, tops removed**
- **1¼ cups sugar**
- **½ teaspoon salt**
- **Zest and juice of 1 large Meyer lemon**

1 Bring the water to a boil in a large pot. Once boiling, add the strawberries, sugar, salt, and lemon zest and juice, and stir to combine.

2 Simmer over medium-high heat, stirring occasionally, until it reaches the desired thickness, 15 to 20 minutes.

3 Let the jam cool, then spoon into jars. It will last for about 2 weeks in the fridge.

Cherries

An in-season cherry is just about the most sensual and decadent food I can imagine. These recipes were tested with ripe, red cherries, but play with other available varieties that you enjoy, like golden-yellow Rainier. Just be sure to choose firm cherries without bruises or wrinkled skin.

DRYING

Cherries are delicious dried and easy to process. You may want to pretreat sour cherries by soaking them in syrup for a more palatable snack (see page 79).

Otherwise, wash and drain your ripe cherries, then stem and pit them. You can leave them whole, halve them, or chop them. For whole cherries, dip in boiling water for 30 seconds, then immediately transfer to an ice bath to crack the skins and make your cherries easier to dry. For cut cherries, no blanching is necessary.

Dry cherries at 135 to 140°F/57 to 60°C for 24 to 36 hours (whole) or 10 to 16 hours (pieces), or until dry but slightly pliable. Store them in an airtight container out of direct sunlight and away from high humidity, where they will last for at least 4 months.

FRUIT LEATHER

Cherries are excellent in fruit leather, holding their taste and texture well; follow the general guidance on page 94. If you use sour cherries rather than sweet ones, you may want to blend them with other fruit.

FREEZING

Pit your cherries before freezing.

For syrup packing, use 40 to 50 percent sugar syrup and cool completely before pouring over your cherries to completely cover, then sealing and freezing (see more on page 19). The University of Georgia Cooperative Extension's publication *So Easy to Preserve* recommends adding ½ teaspoon of ascorbic acid per quart when freezing sweet cherries for the best quality.

To sugar pack sour cherries, add ¾ cup sugar per quart of pitted cherries, mix to dissolve the sugar, then pack into containers, leaving sufficient headspace (see page 19).

You can also simply freeze your pitted cherries in a single layer on a rimmed sheet pan for 4 to 6 hours or until frozen through. Once frozen, pack into a freezer-safe, airtight container with no headspace and store. Cherries will last for at least 2 months if properly stored.

Ways to Preserve Cherries	Shelf-stable	Fast	Low waste	Ready meals and ingredients	Big flavor
Smoked Cherry Pit Old-Fashioned Bitters (page 276)	X			X	X
Bourbon-Honey Cherries (page 277)				X	X
Smoked Old-Fashioned Jam (page 278)			X	X	X

INFUSING

Cherry-infused vinegar is really lovely in a dressing for fruit salads and spinach salads (especially ones with goat cheese). It's also nice added to sauces for red meat and pork.

Cherry shrubs and liqueurs make for great drinking. They are fantastic when also infused with orange zest, star anise, and other warming spices like cinnamon. For a summertime take, try infusing cherry with lime zest.

See the general guidance for vinegars, shrubs, and liqueurs on page 66.

Smoked Cherry Pit Old-Fashioned Bitters

These bitters are perfect for smoky cocktails and mocktails. You can also try stirring the Smoked Old-Fashioned Jam (page 278) into drinks for a similar effect. Choose between infusing the smoked cherry pits in bourbon for a traditional old-fashioned flavor profile or in apple cider vinegar for an alcohol-free version.

NOTE: Cherry pits contain cyanide (as do many foods), but not in a harmful dose here, and it isn't released unless the pit is cracked or crushed. That said, only use a few drops of cherry-pit bitters at a time, and enjoy occasionally.

— Makes 1 half-pint

- **¼ cup cherry pits, from smoked cherries if possible**
- **4 (3-inch) strips orange zest**
- **Bourbon (I use Maker's Mark) or apple cider vinegar, to cover**

1. After pitting your smoked cherries for Smoked Old-Fashioned Jam (page 278), return the pan to the smoker and smoke the pits at 150°F/66°C for 15 to 20 minutes. If you are using pits from cherries that were not smoked, smoke your pits for 20 to 25 minutes. They should smell nice and smoky but still have a hint of cherry, too.

2. Combine the smoked cherry pits and orange zest in a half-pint jar. Pour bourbon over them to cover. Close with a lid and let the bitters sit for at least 3 weeks. Bitters will last for at least 2 months if stored properly.

PICKLING

Cherries hold up well to pickling and, while they can be pickled in a hot brine and canned, I prefer to keep a bit more of their snap and texture by quick-pickling them in the refrigerator, using a brine with the ratio of 1 cup water and ½ cup vinegar to 1 tablespoon salt. Add 1 tablespoon sugar, if you wish, and adjust the salt to your taste. Try adding your favorite fresh herbs, baking spices, and citrus zest. I also like pickled cherries with ginger and turmeric.

For more general pickling guidance, see page 53.

MAKING SYRUP AND JAM

Cherry syrups are *excellent* in beverages: A splash in a glass of soda water makes me feel like a kid again. You can add a strip or two of fresh lime zest to your cherry syrup for an extra-delicious treat. Or, if you love the flavor of cherry pie, add some baking spices, like allspice and cinnamon (I usually do about 1 cinnamon stick and 1 teaspoon whole allspice per quart of syrup).

See the general guidance for syrup making (page 79). Cherries are also one of my favorite fruits for making cheong (see page 80).

Bourbon-Honey Cherries

These are one of my most-requested holiday gifts. They're one of my dad's favorites, and maybe they will become one of yours as well. You can use these, and the resulting cherry-bourbon-honey syrup, as a stand-in for Luxardo cherries in drinks and desserts. I leave the pits in these for the aesthetics, but if you have a cherry pitter and can pull them out while leaving the fruit intact, by all means, remove them.

I prefer to can these, which will cook them through and give them a softer texture, but I've also made a refrigerated variation. In this case, let them sit for about a week before serving.

— Makes 4 half pints

- **2 pints cherries, washed, stemmed, and pitted (optional)**
- **½–1 cup good-quality honey**
- **4 cups bourbon**

1 Place jars in your hot water bath canner and heat it up. Then, using tongs, remove the hot jars from the canner.

2 Pack the cherries into the hot jars, leaving 1 inch of headspace. Avoid smashing them in, but if a few get a little squished, that's okay.

3 Add 2 tablespoons to ¼ cup of honey per half-pint, depending on how sweet you want your cherries. Add bourbon to fill the remainder of the jar, leaving ½ inch of headspace.

4 For canning, run a chopstick or other thin, nonmetal utensil along the inner edges of the jars to release any air bubbles. Wipe the rims of the jars with a clean, damp cloth. Add the lids and bands and screw down to hand tightness.

5 Process half-pints in a hot water bath canner for 25 minutes, adjusting for altitude (see page 39) if needed.

6 Let the jars cool for 24 hours before testing the seals (see page 36), then store out of direct sunlight at room temperature.

VARIATION: REFRIGERATOR BOURBON CHERRIES

These are firmer and fresher than their canned counterparts. Heat the honey and bourbon together, whisking constantly, just until the honey is dissolved (but before boiling). Pour over the cherries while warm, allow to cool, and store in an airtight container in the refrigerator for at least 72 hours before serving.

VARIATION: HONEY CHERRIES

You can also make these without bourbon: Fill your hot jars with cherries and make a syrup that's ¼ cup water to each 1 cup of honey. Heat enough to combine and pour over the cherries. Allow to cool, then refrigerate.

Bourbon-Honey Cherries

Smoked Old-Fashioned Jam

The old-fashioned is my favorite cocktail, and this recipe uses the smoker to build in an extra layer of flavor to emulate the smokiness of the whiskey. If you already have the smoker going, this is a great way to get a little extra use out of it. (You can use this same recipe with nonsmoked cherries, too.) Few pleasures in life are as great as eating a warm cherry fresh off the smoker to test its flavor. I recommend engaging in this action regularly and with gusto.

It's nice to serve the jam with cheese and bread, accompanied with cocktails/mocktails using the bitters to tie everything together.

— Makes about 4 half-pint jars

- 2 pounds red cherries
- 2½ cups granulated sugar
- ½ cup turbinado sugar
- 1 teaspoon salt
- 4 (3- to 4-inch) strips orange zest
- Juice of 1 orange
- ¼ cup water
- 1 teaspoon citric acid (if canning)

1 Spread the cherries out on a sheet pan or in a large cast-iron skillet or Dutch oven. Smoke your cherries at 200 to 220°F/93 to 105°C for 20 to 30 minutes until they've softened and have a smoky aroma (but not overwhelmingly so—you still want them to taste like cherries).

2 Add the smoked cherries to a large pot along with the sugars, salt, orange zest, orange juice, and water. Cook over medium heat until cherries are soft and the mixture is a loose jam consistency, 20 to 30 minutes.

3 If you're separating out the pits after cooking, do so now. Fish out the pieces of orange rind, too.

4 If refrigerating, allow the jam to cool and store it in an airtight container in the fridge, where it will last for at least 2 weeks.

5 If canning, whisk the citric acid in 1 tablespoon of boiling water to dissolve, then add to the jam. Place four half-pint jars in your hot water bath canner and heat it up. Then, using tongs, remove the hot jars from the canner.

6 Fill the hot jars with hot jam, leaving ½ inch of headspace.

7 Run a chopstick or other thin, nonmetal utensil along the inner edges of the jars to release any air bubbles. Wipe the rims of the jars with a clean, damp cloth. Add the lids and bands and screw down to hand tightness.

8 Process half-pints for 12 minutes in a hot water bath canner, adjusting for altitude (see page 39) if needed.

9 Let the jars cool for 24 hours before testing the seals (see page 36), then store out of direct sunlight at room temperature.

Save the Pits to Make Bitters!

If you want to make Smoked Cherry Pit Old-Fashioned Bitters (page 276), you have two options regarding the pits: Remove and smoke the pits separately for bitters, or smoke and cook your jam down, then strain, pressing cooked cherries with the back of a spoon to release the pits (my preference, as your bitters have the potential to capture more smoky cherry flavor). Both can be time consuming, but such is the nature of pitting cherries. I promise it's worth it!

Citrus

When I visited my grandma as a child, we would wake up with the sun, paddle our kayaks in the canal behind her house, then pull fresh grapefruit from the tree by the laundry room for breakfast.

Citrus fruit refers to a range of thick-fleshed fruits with pulp and aromatic skin including oranges, lemons, limes, grapefruits, and others. Citrus fruits in the Northern Hemisphere come into season, by and large, in fall and winter. Fresh, in-season citrus is absolutely divine, and preserving means you can enjoy those bright, sunny flavors any time of year. Choose firm fruits that are heavy for their size.

DRYING

Large citrus pieces aren't ideal for drying because the pulp lacks a firm texture and the water content is high. This means they take a long time to dry, and when they do, they're not terribly exciting to eat. However, you can dry citrus peels in thin slices to use in everything from desserts to potpourri sachets.

PEELS

Citrus peels dry beautifully. I highly recommend using dried peels and dried rounds of citrus as garnishes and decorations (I love making garlands from dried rounds of fruit). Ground dried peels also make a flavorful seasoning powder to sprinkle on drinks and desserts.

Ways to Preserve Citrus	Shelf-stable	Fast	Low waste	Ready meals and ingredients	Big flavor
Frozen Citrus Juice Cubes (page 280)				X	
Meyer Limoncello (page 280)				X	X
Citrus Cleaning Vinegar (page 281)			X	X	X
Holiday Citrus Spice Vinegar (page 282)				X	X
Pickled Limes (page 282)				X	X
Salt-Preserved Citrus (page 283)	X			X	X
Yuzu Kosho (page 285)				X	X
Tangerine, Rose, and Turmeric Syrup (page 285)				X	X
Sugar-Packed Citrus Syrup (page 286)				X	X
Simple Kumquat Marmalade (page 286)				X	X

To dry citrus peels: Wash your citrus to remove any waxy coatings. Using a vegetable peeler, cut strips of peel from the fruit, avoiding the white pith underneath. No need to pretreat your peels before drying: Just arrange the peels in a single layer on a dehydrator tray and dry at 125 to 135°F/52 to 57°C for 8 to 12 hours, until dry enough to snap when bent.

You can save your citrus juice from these to add to other preserving projects or meals, or just freeze it (see below) to have on hand later.

THIN SLICES

To dry citrus slices: Wash your citrus to remove any waxy coatings. Cut your unpeeled citrus into thin rounds, ⅛ inch thick. Lay in a single layer on your dehydrator trays and dry at 135 to 140°F/57 to 60°C.

You can also play with color for your dried citrus if using as a garnish or garland. I place thin rounds of citrus in my winter mulled wine, for example, then dry out the wine-stained fruit and turn it into a fragrant, beautiful garland to decorate my home. You could paint your rounds with edible paints or dye them with other colorful kitchen ingredients (like blue butterfly pea flower tea).

FREEZING

Fruit sections, with seeds and membranes removed, can be packed in syrup or citrus juice, leaving sufficient headspace (see page 19), and then frozen. Make sure to use fruit that's heavy for its size, fully ripe, and free of mold or soft spots. It will last for 1 month or more if properly stored.

FROZEN CITRUS JUICE CUBES

Freezing is the perfect way to preserve the juice from citrus peeled for other projects, like infused liqueurs, culinary vinegars, or flavorful syrups (like Tangerine, Rose, and Turmeric Syrup, page 285). Or, if you have peels still attached to your juiced citrus pieces, save them to make Citrus Cleaning Vinegar (page 281).

Squeeze your citrus juice into ice cube trays and freeze, then store your cubes in an airtight container with no headspace. Note that 1 cube equals the juice of 1 lemon, or about 2 tablespoons. To make 1-tablespoon servings instead, just fill your ice cube trays half full. When frozen, transfer cubes to ziplock bags and store in the freezer, where they will last for 1 month or more.

INFUSING

Citrus is a classic in drinks. A strip of citrus zest enhances just about anything, from a bourbon cocktail to a glass of bubble water. That means it's the perfect flavoring for liqueurs, but it's equally at home in vinegar, making a fragrant, flavorful addition to your meals and drinks.

Citrus-infused vinegars are also *the best* for seasoning and for cleaning. The bitter piths are best left out of ones you plan to eat, as they can make the whole vinegar bitter. But for cleaning vinegar? There's no need to take the time to remove bitter piths or seeds.

You can make citrus-infused vinegars following the basic instructions on page 173; see page 68 for general guidance on shrubs and liqueurs. Here are a few of my favorites.

Meyer Limoncello

You can use Eureka or Lisbon lemon (the varieties most commonly sold in grocery stores) in place of one of the Meyer lemons for a bit more zip. Make rosemary lemonade (see facing page) at the same time to make sure none of the juice from the lemons goes to waste!

—— Makes about 1½ pints

- **6 large Meyer lemons**
- **2 cups vodka**
- **1 cup sugar**

1. Peel the zest from the lemons using a vegetable peeler and place it in a container with a sealing lid, leaving 1 inch of headspace.

2. Add vodka to the container to completely cover the zest, leaving ½ inch of headspace.

3. Seal the lid and label the container with the date—it will be ready to drink after 2 weeks, but it will get better the longer it sits. I leave mine in the pantry; you could also put yours in the fridge.

4. Once it's ready, strain out the peels. Then whisk in 1 cup of the sugar until dissolved. Store the limoncello in airtight containers, like narrow-necked, flip-top bottles, in the fridge or in a cool, dark place. Serve chilled. It will last for 2 months or more if properly stored.

Citrus Cleaning Vinegar

This simple infusion packs a powerful cleaning punch and smells great to boot. Use as a spray cleaner for most surfaces (check that metal surfaces are nonreactive prior to using). Do not use on granite or marble, as vinegar can etch the surface.

— Makes ½ gallon

- **1–2 cups of citrus peels or leftover citrus from juicing (any variety)**
- **¾ cup distilled white vinegar**
- **¼ cup water**

1. Put the citrus peels in a half-gallon nonreactive container, such as a large glass jar, and pour the vinegar over the top. Allow the citrus to steep in vinegar for 1 month out of direct sunlight, then strain. Undiluted vinegar will last for months if properly stored.

2. To use: Combine the strained citrus vinegar and water in a 1:4 ratio of vinegar to water in a spray bottle.

Bonus Rosemary Lemonade

A great use for the Meyer lemon juice left over from the limoncello is lemonade. Squeeze the juice from the six lemons into a pitcher. Zest another lemon and add that juice, too.

Using the back of a knife, tap one or two rosemary sprigs along the stem to gently bruise and release the oils. Add the rosemary, a pinch of salt, 2 cups of filtered water, and 1 cup of sugar to a pan and slowly bring to a simmer over medium-low heat. Cook, stirring occasionally, for 5 to 10 minutes. Pour the mixture over the lemon zest and juice and let sit at room temperature for 1 to 2 hours. To serve, fill a glass halfway with the lemonade mixture, and add sparkling or still water to taste.

Holiday Citrus Spice Vinegar

You can use this fragrant, delicious vinegar to jazz up fruit salads or cranberry sauce, mix into drinks and desserts, or even make marinades. The spicing on this vinegar is flexible based on your preferences, but the goal is to get a classic orange spice profile that, at least for me, signals holiday meals and wassail and cozy winter days.

Use any vinegar you want: For more of a wassail flavor profile, try a red wine vinegar. For a vinegar that highlights the citrus and spice itself without adding any flavor, try distilled white vinegar. Or for something that leans heavily into fall and winter produce, try apple cider vinegar. As always, using the best-quality vinegar will yield the best results.

— Makes 1 quart

- **1 large orange, peel on, sliced in ¼-inch-thick rounds**
- **1 cinnamon stick**
- **1 star anise**
- **1 teaspoon whole allspice berries**
- **1 teaspoon whole cloves**
- **Vinegar, to cover**

1 Add the orange, cinnamon, star anise, allspice, and cloves to a quart jar. Pour vinegar over the ingredients to cover, seal the lid tightly, and store the jar out of direct sunlight.

2 Start tasting after 2 to 3 weeks, and strain once it has a flavor you enjoy. (I find this vinegar takes about 1 month to finish.)

3 Store the finished vinegar in an airtight container at room temperature. It will last for at least 1 month.

SALTING AND PICKLING

Sour, salty citrus preserves are some of my favorites: the perfect enhancement to food during cooking, or as a zingy topping. Make sure to reserve the liquid from these recipes for making salad dressings, marinades, or Pickle Brine Martinis (page 69), or for pickling other fruits and vegetables.

Pickled Limes

Thinly sliced pickled limes are a flavor-packed garnish for your meals. Play with different vinegars here. I like apple cider vinegar and distilled white vinegar best, though white wine and rice wine can be good, too.

— Makes about 1 quart

- **3 limes, peels on, thinly sliced**
- **1 bunch cilantro, chopped**
- **1 medium yellow onion, thinly sliced**
- **2 tablespoons to ¼ cup salt**
- **½ cup apple cider vinegar or distilled white vinegar, plus more to cover**

1 Add the limes, cilantro, and onion to a quart jar, leaving ½ to 1 inch of headspace.

2 In a small bowl, whisk the salt into the vinegar to dissolve. Pour the mixture over the limes. Add more vinegar to cover as needed.

3 Screw on the lid and give your jar a gentle shake to distribute the salt solution evenly. Store the limes in the fridge and let them pickle for at least 2 to 3 days before using. These will last for 2 weeks or more in the fridge.

Salt-Preserved Citrus

Salt-preserved lemons, common in Moroccan cuisine, are the most famous type of preserved citrus, but the method can be used for other types of citrus, too. Note that less juicy citrus might need some extra juice to completely cover it in its brine, whereas a very juicy citrus won't.

While not traditional, you can also get creative and add in some dried herbs and spices. Some of my favorite flavor pairings include grapefruit and lavender, orange and tarragon, orange and cinnamon, lemon and bay leaf, tangerine and garam masala (this salt preserve is great blended up as a paste and added, in a very small amount, to a chocolate cake batter), tangerine and oregano, and any citrus with rosemary, nutmeg, and lavender, or with peppercorn, bay leaf, and cayenne.

Lemons

Salt

1 Cut a deep X through the middle of each whole lemon (basically, cut them into quarters but not quite all the way through), then rub the lemons all over with salt. Make sure to fill the X with salt as well. Pack the lemons into a clean jar, really squishing them in to make sure their juice is released. They should be completely covered with juice (you can add more juice, if you need to).

Alternatively, cut the lemons into quarters or thick slices, and layer these with salt in a jar. Begin with ½ tablespoon salt in the bottom, then layer three or four quarters or two slices, followed by more salt, pressing down as you go until the jar is full and the slices are covered in brine.

2 In both cases, sprinkle 1 to 2 teaspoons more salt on the surface of the brine. Allow the lemons to cure out of direct sunlight for 4 weeks or so, until they are soft. Preserved lemons can be stored on the counter or in the fridge, ensuring the fruit stays entirely submerged under the brine, for at least 1 month.

VARIATION: SALT-PRESERVED CITRUS PASTE

Salt-preserved citrus is a delicious ready-to-go ingredient that I use in many meals, but I find it gets even more use in my kitchen after I give the softened, preserved lemons a quick blitz in a food processor or blender. The resulting sour and salty paste is flavor-packed and super easy to stir into anything from an aioli to dressing to a rub for roasted vegetables to sauce for ice cream. I even use it as a pickling bed for hard-boiled eggs! Store in the refrigerator between uses.

STEP 1

STEP 2

Salt-Preserved Citrus (page 283)

Yuzu Kosho

Yuzu kosho is a spicy, citrusy, salty condiment that's perfect for stirring into soups and sauces. I love the way it cuts the richness of dairy, meat, and fatty seafood. While you can buy it, it's incredibly simple to make. If you don't have yuzu, this works with grapefruit, lemon, or any citrus you prefer. Red togarashi chiles are traditional, but you can swap these for other chiles if needed (bird's-eye chiles work well).

To make it, use equal parts by weight of citrus zest (bust out that Microplane!) and chiles, plus one-quarter of their total weight of salt.

— Makes about 1 cup

- **4 yuzu fruit or other citrus (enough to equal 0.8 ounces/20 grams when zested)**
- **1–2 fresh chiles (enough to equal 0.8 ounces/20 grams when diced)**
- **2 teaspoons salt**

1 Grate the zest from the citrus using a Microplane, then save the leftover citrus. You'll need a bit of it later on in the recipe; the rest can be juiced for drinks or to freeze (see Frozen Citrus Juice Cubes, page 280).

2 Next, cut your chiles in half, remove the seeds (for less heat, remove the ribs, too), and finely dice them. It can be helpful to wear gloves for this step.

3 Use a kitchen scale to check that you have roughly equal amounts of citrus zest and diced chiles. (It's okay if the proportions are a little off, but try to get as close as you can for the best flavor.) Blend with a food processor, mortar and pestle, or blender until a paste forms.

4 Add the salt, blending until the crystals have dissolved. Add a bit of citrus juice from your reserved citrus to make a smooth paste.

5 Pack your paste into an airtight jar with no headspace. Some people use it fresh; others let it age in the fridge for anywhere from 1 week to 3 months or more. If you want to freeze it, pack into an airtight container with no headspace, or into ice cube trays (transfer the cubes to a container once frozen), and use within 1 year.

MAKING SYRUPS AND PRESERVES

Marmalade is a classic citrus preserve, but it's just the tip of the iceberg when it comes to sweet citrus possibilities. Syrups, made just from zest or with the addition of other flavors, are another favorite.

Tangerine, Rose, and Turmeric Syrup

This syrup is full of possibilities. I sometimes add 1 to 2 teaspoons more turmeric or an extra ¼ cup rose petals to highlight different flavors. I save and freeze the tangerine juice in cubes to add to my beverages. Substitute lemons or oranges as you prefer.

— Makes about 2 pints

- **4 large tangerines**
- **4 cups sugar**
- **¼ cup dried rose petals**
- **½ tablespoon turmeric powder**
- **¼ teaspoon salt**
- **2 cups water**
- **½ teaspoon citric acid (if canning)**

1 Use a vegetable peeler to remove the peels from the tangerines in strips, taking care to exclude the bitter pith. Set aside the fruit for another use.

2 Add the peels, sugar, rose petals, turmeric, salt, and water to a saucepan set over medium heat.

3 Bring to almost a boil, stirring frequently until the sugar is dissolved. Reduce to a simmer, stirring occasionally, until colorful and fragrant, 15 to 18 minutes.

(continued on next page)

Tangerine, Rose, and Turmeric Syrup *continued*

4 Strain with a fine-mesh strainer, pressing with the back of a spoon to remove as much liquid as possible.

5 If refrigerating, let the syrup cool and store in an airtight container. It will last for at least 2 weeks in the fridge.

6 If canning, whisk in the citric acid until dissolved. Place two pint or four half-pint jars in your hot water bath canner and heat it up. Then, using tongs, remove the hot jars.

7 Fill the hot jars with hot syrup, leaving ½ inch of headspace.

8 Run a chopstick or other thin, nonmetal utensil along the inner edges of the jars to release any air bubbles. Wipe the rims of the jars with a clean, damp cloth. Add the lids and bands and screw down to hand tightness.

9 Process half-pints for 10 minutes and pints for 12 minutes in a hot water bath canner, adjusting for altitude (see page 39) if needed.

10 Let the jars cool for 24 hours before testing the seals (see page 36), then store out of direct sunlight at room temperature.

SUGAR-PACKED CITRUS SYRUP

You can experiment with steeped citrus in sugar to make syrup (for more on this technique, see Cheong, page 80). Simply pack equal parts citrus slices or wedges and sugar in a jar, with whatever other flavorings you want (pine, peppercorns, chiles, rose petals, cinnamon, etc.): You want equal parts sugar and citrus, plus other flavors (such as spices) to taste. Seal the jar and set it out of direct sunlight. Give it a stir once in a while when it gets syrupy, adding a little more sugar if it starts to ferment and you don't want it to (fermentation stops at about 65 percent sugar). It will be ready in 1 to 2 months, at which point you can strain it and store the syrup in the fridge or, if you prefer, at room temperature out of direct sunlight.

Simple Kumquat Marmalade

Kumquats taste like little bursts of sunshine, and they also make an absolutely beautiful marmalade. Rather than using shreds of citrus zest, this marmalade uses the sliced whole fruit. It's perfect for breakfast or alongside snacks and desserts, and it makes a stunning gift.

— Makes about 2 pints

2–3 pounds fresh kumquats
1 cup sugar
2 fresh (preferred) or dried bay leaves
½ teaspoon sea salt
1 cup water

1 Thinly slice the kumquats into little rounds, removing the seeds as you go.

2 Place the sliced fruit in a nonreactive bowl and add ½ cup of the sugar. Toss to coat the kumquats evenly.

3 Let the kumquats sit for 8 to 12 hours, covered with a tea towel or lid, in the refrigerator. This will remove some of the bitterness from the fruit and start the preserving process.

4 Add the kumquats, the remaining ½ cup sugar, bay, salt, and water to a pot. Bring the mixture to a simmer and cook until the water is reduced to a thick syrup.

5 Let the marmalade cool and store it in an airtight container in the fridge, where it will last for at least 2 weeks.

Cranberries

Cranberries are native to North America, and in the precolonial United States, Indigenous communities preserved and ate cranberries in a variety of ways, including sweetened in a sauce with maple sugar and in pemmican, which is meat or fish plus berries, pounded into a pulp, shaped into cakes, and dried in the sun. These practices have been carried forward today in some communities.

European colonists began cultivating cranberries in the early 1800s, and this took off as an industry in Massachusetts. Cultivation spread later to Wisconsin and as far west as Oregon. Indigenous wisdom already existed for drying and curing cranberries in syrup, but many European colonizers ate cranberries primarily during the 2-month period they were in season.

Canned cranberry sauce and cranberry juice cocktail didn't become available in stores until a century later. And the can-shaped log of jellied cranberry that some of us eat by the slice on holidays wasn't available nationwide until 1941.

When shopping for cranberries, look for firm fruits with tight (not wrinkled) skin. Fresh ones will float in water or bounce slightly when dropped on the ground, thanks to the four air-filled chambers inside them.

FREEZING

There are many ways home cooks can enjoy the tart, tangy magic of cranberries year-round.

The easiest, if you buy bags of cranberries at the store, is to just toss the bag(s) in the freezer as is, then rinse the fruit with cold water before using them to make cranberry sauce and other dishes (no need to thaw).

However, bags of cranberries often contain a few soft or bruised berries, so you might prefer to go through them first. If you do remove them from the bag (or if you get berries unbagged), pack them into containers with ½ inch of headspace, or freeze for 8 to 12 hours in a single layer on a rimmed sheet pan or tray and then package when frozen through. They will last for several months or more if properly stored.

INFUSING

To make an infused vinegar, I like to halve my cranberries so they impart their flavor to the vinegar more quickly (start tasting and testing after 2 weeks). You can also leave them whole and start tasting after 3 to 4 weeks. Pull the vinegar when it has a flavor you like, then sweeten if desired for shrubs, or use as is in cooking.

Ways to Preserve Cranberries

	Shelf-stable	Fast	Low waste	Ready meals and ingredients	Big flavor
Cranberry-Orange Vodka (page 288)	X			X	X
Zesty Cranberry Sauce (page 288)				X	X

Cranberry-Orange Vodka

This is the easiest way to use up that extra bag of cranberries you bought on sale, and it tastes like cranberry sauce in a glass. I mix the finished product with unsweetened soda water, but you can add simple syrup if it's too tart for you. It also makes a great holiday gift!

— Makes 2–3 cups

- **8 whole allspice berries**
- **6 whole cloves**
- **2 cinnamon sticks**
- **1 (12-ounce) bag fresh cranberries**
- **2 navel oranges or tangerines**
- **Vodka, to cover**

1. Lightly toast the allspice, cloves, and cinnamon in a small pan over medium heat until fragrant, then add them to a quart jar.

2. Cut the cranberries in half and add them to the jar with the spices. Peel the zest from the oranges using a vegetable peeler and add it to the jar. Pour vodka over the ingredients to cover.

3. Cover the jar and set it aside for at least 1 week, shaking occasionally. The flavor will get stronger the longer it sits.

4. Strain the liquid into a jar or other container with an airtight lid. Store at room temperature or in the refrigerator.

MAKING SYRUPS AND PRESERVES

Tart cranberries also make delicious, sweet preserves, the most well-known being cranberry sauce. There are as many cranberry sauce recipes as there are berries in a bog, but I tend toward ones that balance sweet and tart. If you want a new way to play with cranberries, try cranberry syrup; use it as a dessert sauce or in drinks.

To make cranberry syrup, follow the general guidance on page 79. For best results, cook your syrup until the berries split and the syrup is a nice red color. Leave it pulpy or strain it through a fine-mesh sieve, or, if you want to remove all of the pulp, strain it through butter muslin or cheesecloth.

Zesty Cranberry Sauce

This is the cranberry sauce I made for family holidays in my undergraduate years. This recipe makes just enough for a small holiday gathering (four to six people), but it can easily be increased to feed more.

— Makes about 2 half-pints

- **1 cup sugar**
- **Zest and juice of 1 orange**
- **½ cup water**
- **3 cups fresh cranberries**
- **5 whole cloves**
- **1 cinnamon stick**

1. Combine the sugar, orange zest and juice, and water in a medium saucepan and bring to a boil.

2. Add the cranberries, cloves, and cinnamon, and simmer until the cranberries burst and become soft. Remove the cloves and cinnamon stick.

3. Serve warm, at room temperature, or cold. Or let it cool and store in an airtight container in the fridge, where it will last for at least 2 weeks.

Figs and Dates

Figs, a contender for the original fruit in the Garden of Eden, and dates, whose tree is the home of the mythical Phoenix in Pliny the Elder's *Natural History*, are ancient holy foods and deserve a place in every kitchen today—not just because they're sacred but also because they're delicious. Both are among the oldest cultivated fruits, and our history of stewarding them dates back to the Neolithic.

DRYING

Drying is an easy way to preserve figs and dates for later use. They work perfectly rehydrated or used as is, or they can be enjoyed as a snack. Dates in particular are a top choice for fruit-based snacks because they are sweet and sticky enough to just roll with other ingredients (think date balls). I use dried dates for the recipes in this section.

FIGS

I have the greatest success drying figs whole or halved (for larger figs). If I slice them, the sugary, sticky pieces can stick to my dehydrator trays.

To dry whole figs, dip them in boiling water for 30 to 60 seconds, then immediately plunge them in ice water to crack and loosen the skins so they can dry more evenly. For halved figs, skip this step.

Then, dip your figs in a pretreatment solution (see page 90) to prevent discoloring during drying. Arrange your figs in a single layer on dehydrator trays, then dry at 125 to 135°F/52 to 57°C for 6 to 12 hours (for halved figs, this may be slightly less) until dried but pliable. Allow the dried figs to cool completely, then pack and store. Dried figs will last for months if properly stored.

DATES

Most of us encounter dates as dried fruit. If you have fresh dates to dry, give them a gentle wash, dip in a pretreatment solution (see page 90), then line your dehydrator trays with nonstick material like waxed paper and dry at 125°F/52°C for 24 hours. Dates should be dry on the outside, with a skin that almost snaps, and with a tacky, sugary interior that is sticky but not wet. You can also go the traditional route and dry dates in the sun in a well-ventilated place. Dried dates will last for months if properly stored.

FRUIT LEATHER

Mashed-up ripe figs and dates both work well in fruit leather; follow the directions on page 94.

Ways to Preserve Figs and Dates	Shelf-stable	Fast	Low waste	Ready meals and ingredients	Big flavor
Silan (page 290)				X	X
Vanilla-Fig Syrup (page 290)				X	X
Fig Jam (page 291)				X	X

FREEZING

Figs can be frozen in a 40 percent syrup (see page 19), adding ¾ teaspoon ascorbic acid or ½ cup bottled lemon juice per quart of syrup. Pack, leaving appropriate headspace (see page 19), and freeze.

Figs can also be frozen dry (not in syrup). To prevent darkening, dissolve ¾ teaspoon ascorbic acid in 3 tablespoons water per quart of fruit, and sprinkle or brush the solution evenly over them before freezing. Freeze on a rimmed sheet pan lined with parchment paper or a silicone mat for 8 to 12 hours, then pack into containers with no headspace. Or pack into containers, leaving headspace (see page 19), then freeze. Frozen figs will last for 2 months or more if properly stored.

INFUSING

Fig liqueurs are delicious and lovely to enjoy alongside a dessert dusted with fig-leaf sugar (see page 403). For fig shrubs, I particularly like using white wine vinegar or apple cider vinegar.

Dates can be infused in vinegar, too. Their sweetness and depth of flavor can lend some interesting notes to savory, meaty dishes and stews. I like dates infused in apple cider vinegar. You can also make date liqueurs, which are especially good with citrus as another flavor note. I like to fill a jar with dates, add a few strips of orange peel, cover it with vodka or whiskey, and let it sit for a month. When I'm ready to serve it, I sweeten it to taste (though I rarely need to) and mix it with a little bit of pomegranate juice or pomegranate molasses.

For steps to make shrubs, vinegars, and liqueurs, see the general guidance for shrubs and liqueurs (page 68).

MAKING SYRUPS AND JAMS

Dates and figs are both naturally sweet, so it's no surprise that they're perfect for sweet preserves. I love both as syrups, which are wonderful in drinks and desserts (or eaten from the jar with a spoon).

Silan

Silan is a date syrup, sometimes used as a honey substitute, which appears in various sweet and savory dishes across Middle Eastern and Maghrebi cuisines. It's delicious and easy to make, though it does take about 2 hours on the stove. Use it in place of honey or other favorite syrups like cane syrup or maple syrup.

— Makes about 2 pints

2 pounds dates

9 cups water

1 Combine the dates and water in a large saucepan, bring the mixture to a boil, then reduce it to a simmer.

2 Simmer for about 2 hours, stirring occasionally at first and frequently toward the end. Add more water if needed. The dates should be covered during the cooking process until they break down and dissolve into the water, forming a thick, dark syrup.

3 Remove the silan from the heat, strain it through cheesecloth or a fine-mesh strainer, then allow it to cool.

4 Bottle and store in the refrigerator, where it will last for several weeks.

Vanilla-Fig Syrup

This decadent syrup uses the seeds from half a vanilla bean for flavoring. To get to the seeds, just split the bean lengthwise, then scrape with the back of a knife to remove the seeds. You can reserve the pod and other half of the bean to make Vanilla Extract or Vanilla Sugar (page 68).

— Makes about 2 pints

1 pound figs, quartered
2 cups granulated sugar
¾ cup turbinado sugar or ½ cup packed light brown sugar
¼ cup honey
2 (2-inch) strips lemon peel
Seeds from ½ vanilla bean
¼ teaspoon salt
2½ cups water
½ teaspoon citric acid or 2 tablespoons bottled lemon juice (if canning)

1 Add the figs, sugars, honey, lemon peel, vanilla bean seeds, salt, and water to a saucepan. Bring the mixture to a boil, then reduce to a simmer and cook over medium-low heat, stirring occasionally, until thickened and flavorful, about 20 minutes.

2 Strain the syrup through a fine-mesh strainer or, for a smoother texture, use cheesecloth or butter muslin, gently pressing to remove liquid.

3 If refrigerating, store your syrup in an airtight container in the fridge, where it will last for at least 2 weeks.

4 If canning, add the citric acid to the syrup. Place two pint or four half-pint jars in your hot water bath canner and heat it up. Then, using tongs, remove the hot jars from the canner.

5 Fill the hot jars with hot syrup, leaving ½ inch of headspace.

6 Run a chopstick or other thin, nonmetal utensil along the inner edges of the jars to release any air bubbles. Wipe the rims of the jars with a clean, damp cloth. Add the lids and bands and screw down to hand tightness.

7 Process half-pints or pints for 10 minutes in a hot water bath canner, adjusting for altitude (see page 39) as needed.

8 Let the jars cool for 24 hours before testing the seals (see page 36), then store out of direct sunlight at room temperature.

Fig Jam

Figs make delicious jam, which is perfect on a cheese board or in your grilled cheese sandwich.

—— Makes about 3 pints

4–4½ pounds fresh figs
6 cups sugar
½ teaspoon salt
¾ cup water
Flavorings such as 1–2 teaspoons fresh thyme leaves or 2–3 teaspoons ground baking spices (optional)
¼ cup bottled lemon juice or apple cider vinegar (5% acidity)

1 Add the figs to a heatproof bowl, cover with boiling water, and let them sit for 10 minutes. Drain, remove the stems, and roughly chop.

2 If canning, sterilize the jars (see page 31) by boiling for 10 minutes.

3 Add the figs, sugar, salt, water, and any flavorings (if using) to a large, high-sided pot and bring to a boil, stirring frequently. Continue cooking the jam and stirring it frequently until thick, 15 to 20 minutes.

4 If refrigerating, pack the jam into an airtight container and store in the fridge, where it will last for at least 2 weeks.

5 If canning, add the lemon juice, cook for 1 minute longer, then immediately ladle into hot, sterilized jars, leaving ¼ inch of headspace.

6 Run a chopstick or other thin, nonmetal utensil along the inner edges of the jars to release any air bubbles. Wipe the rims of the jars with a clean, damp cloth. Add the lids and bands and screw down to hand tightness.

7 Process half-pints or pints in a hot water bath canner for 5 minutes, adjusting for altitude (see page 39) if needed.

8 Let the jars cool for 24 hours before testing the seals (see page 36), then store out of direct sunlight at room temperature.

Grapes

Grapes are a perfect snack as is, but if you grow your own, you know that when they're in season the bounty can surpass your appetite, which is where preserving comes in handy. Grapes make great preserves, from jams to drinks to pickles and more. While I offer my suggestions for what grape varieties to use, these methods work with any grape, so experiment to your heart's content.

Choose firm, fresh grapes without wrinkles, soft spots, or bruises.

DRYING

Raisins are just dried grapes. They are a long-loved snack and easy to make at home when you have a bumper grape crop. Wash and drain your grapes after removing from the stems. Leave seedless grapes whole; cut seeded grapes (like muscadines and scuppernongs) in half and seed.

Whole grapes need to have the skins checked (cracked and loosened) so the air can evenly penetrate them. To do this, submerge them in boiling water for 30 to 60 seconds, then immediately shock in ice water and drain thoroughly. Arrange in a single layer on dehydrator trays, then dry at 125 to 135°F/52 to 57°C for 12 to 20 hours or until dried but pliable. Condition your raisins (see page 92), then store in an airtight container out of direct sunlight and away from high humidity, where they will last for at least 4 months.

FREEZING

Grapes, when thawed, have a softer texture than never-frozen grapes. I have the most luck freezing them in 40 percent syrup (see page 19) then using them in desserts. You can, however, freeze grapes in a single layer on a rimmed sheet pan, then pack and store with no headspace; this is what I do when I want to add them to smoothies or chilled, blended soups.

Ways to Preserve Grapes	Shelf-stable	Fast	Low waste	Ready meals and ingredients	Big flavor
Muscadine Gin (page 293)				X	X
Pickled Grapes (page 293)				X	X
Pickled Muscadines (page 294)				X	X
Muscadine Soda Syrup (page 294)				X	X
Grape Preserves Without Pectin (page 295)				X	X
Grape Juice for Jelly (page 295)				X	X
Muscadine or Black Grape Catsup (page 296)				X	X

INFUSING

Grapes of any variety can be infused in distilled spirits like vodka or in vinegar for delicious drinks. Darker, more robust-flavored grapes make for the most flavorful infusions. Follow the infused spirits and infused vinegar directions on page 66.

PICKLING

Pickled grapes are delicious on their own or as a nice balance in fruit or chicken salads. I find that this process works best with flavorful, firm grapes, which hold their taste and texture during pickling.

Muscadine Gin

I love how the flavors of muscadines (wild grapes with a strong, complex taste) and juniper go together in this fruit-infused gin. It makes for an easy, ready-to-go cocktail—just add your favorite bubbles!

—— Makes 1 pint

1 cup quartered muscadine grapes

Gin, to cover

1. Add the grapes to a pint jar. Pour gin over the grapes to completely cover, leaving ½ inch of headspace.

2. Let the gin steep in the fridge or on the counter, making sure the grapes stay submerged (or shake at least once a day) for 1 to 2 weeks. Strain when it has a flavor you like, squeezing the grapes to release excess liquor. Store the gin in an airtight container. It will last for several weeks or more stored on the counter, or it will last for 1 month or more stored in the fridge.

Pickled Grapes

These refrigerator pickles are perfect on charcuterie boards, alongside grilled and roasted meats, or as a garnish for squash bisques. You can add seasonings and spices if you want, but they're perfect as is.

—— Makes about 1 quart

About 1 pound (3 cups) grapes, any variety

1½ tablespoons sugar

1 tablespoon salt

1½ cups water

1 cup vinegar (see note)

NOTE: I use red wine or sherry vinegar with red grapes, and white wine or apple cider vinegar with white grapes. But there's room for experimentation: I've used homemade ginger vinegar to great effect here, too.

1. Put the grapes in a quart jar.

2. Make the brine: In a medium bowl, combine the sugar, salt, water, and vinegar, and stir until the sugar and salt are dissolved.

3. Pour the brine over the grapes and seal the jar tightly. Let the grapes pickle in the fridge for 3 to 7 days. They will keep in the fridge for several weeks, getting softer and more sour the longer they sit.

Pickled Muscadines

I started making this recipe when I was working on my PhD, when I first discovered the magic of muscadines. The warm spices complement the intense flavor of the grapes and add some nice depth that is perfect for cool-weather snacking.

—— Makes about 1 quart

- **1 pound muscadine grapes (2–3 cups)**
- **1½ teaspoons coriander seeds**
- **1 teaspoon black peppercorns**
- **1 (2½-inch) cinnamon stick**
- **1 cup granulated sugar**
- **1 bay leaf**
- **½ teaspoon sea salt**
- **1 cup red wine vinegar**

1. Rinse and dry the grapes, halve them, and remove the seeds. Place the grapes in a bowl.
2. Add the coriander, peppercorns, and cinnamon to a saucepan and toast over medium-high until fragrant, about 5 minutes.
3. Add the sugar, bay leaf, salt, and vinegar to the spice mixture and bring to a boil.
4. Remove the mixture from the heat and immediately pour it over the grapes. Set the bowl aside to cool.
5. Once the mixture is cool, cover the bowl and refrigerate for at least 8 hours (you can also pour the grapes and brine into jars before popping them in the fridge). The pickles will last for at least 3 weeks in the fridge.

MAKING SYRUP, JELLY, AND PRESERVES

Sweet grape preserves remind me of childhood: They're a classic for peanut butter and jelly sandwiches, and grape syrup with soda water makes a grape soda that leaves the canned stuff in the dust.

Muscadine Soda Syrup

I find muscadines to be way more grapey than many commercial varieties, and this muscadine soda syrup is full of flavor. However, if you don't have access to muscadines, this syrup is still delicious when made with other grape varieties. If you prefer white grapes, try scuppernongs if you can get them.

—— Makes about 1 pint

- **About 2 pounds (4 cups) muscadine grapes**
- **1 cup packed light brown sugar**
- **1 cup granulated sugar**
- **1–2 tablespoons good-quality honey (or your favorite vegan equivalent)**
- **¼ teaspoon salt**
- **1 cup water**

1. Blend the grapes in a blender with water or crush with a mortar and pestle until you have a chunky purée. (Note that muscadine skins are thicker than those of many grape varieties, so the grapes may not purée down so much as break open. That's okay!)
2. Combine the grapes with the sugars, honey, salt, and water in a medium saucepan. Bring the mixture to a boil, then reduce the heat and simmer over medium-low until flavorful and slightly thickened, stirring occasionally, 12 to 15 minutes.
3. Strain in a fine-mesh strainer, pressing to extract all the liquid. If there are still chunks in the liquid, pass them through cheesecloth or finer mesh, if desired.
4. Cool the syrup completely and store it in the fridge in an airtight container, where it will last for 2 to 3 weeks.

Grape Preserves Without Pectin

Grape preserves are synonymous with peanut butter and jelly, and grape jelly made at home is extra delicious. Use homemade grape juice here (see right) rather than store-bought, which can yield hit-or-miss results as it's made for drinking, not jelly making. (I know I go on a lot about scuppernongs and muscadines, but seriously, they make a great jelly.)

—— Makes about 4 half-pints

4 cups grape juice (see right)

3 cups sugar

1 Sterilize your jars by processing them in a hot water bath for 10 minutes.

2 Combine the grape juice and sugar in a saucepan and bring to a boil over high heat, stirring frequently. Continue cooking, stirring frequently, until the mixture reaches 220°F/105°C or it sheets from a spoon (rather than dripping).

3 Remove from the heat and immediately skim off any foam.

4 Pour the hot jelly into hot, sterilized jars, leaving ¼ inch of headspace.

5 Run a chopstick or other thin, nonmetal utensil along the inner edges of the jars to release any air bubbles. Wipe the rims of the jars with a clean, damp cloth. Add the lids and bands and screw down to hand tightness.

6 Process half-pints for 5 minutes in a hot water bath canner, adjusting for altitude (see page 39) if needed.

7 Let the jars cool for 24 hours before testing the seals (see page 36), then store out of direct sunlight at room temperature.

Grape Preserves Without Pectin

Grape Juice for Jelly

When making juice for jelly versus juice for drinking, use mostly very ripe fruit, mixed with a smaller ratio of firm fruit: about 3 parts ripe fruit to 1 part very firm fruit. This helps you get the texture you need in your jelly.

—— Makes about 6 cups

3½ pounds grapes

½ cup water

1 Wash and stem your grapes: Roughly three-quarters of the grapes should be fully ripe, and the remaining quarter should be firm, if possible.

2 Put the grapes in a pot and crush them with a potato masher until uniformly mashed, or blend them in a blender, then add to a pot. Add the water and bring to a boil. Reduce the heat to low and simmer for about 10 minutes, stirring occasionally, then remove from heat. For best results, let stand in a cool place overnight.

(continued on next page)

Grape Juice for Jelly *continued*

3 Strain the mixture through several layers of cheesecloth or a damp jelly bag until all the juice strains out. Do not press, which can result in a cloudier final product.

4 Use the juice to make Grape Preserves Without Pectin, page 295.

Muscadine or Black Grape Catsup

As we venture once again into the world of creative ketchup-y condiments (see also Mushroom Ketchup on page 188), we're playing with grapes. I originally saw grape catsup in my 1903 copy of *New Era Home Economics and Cookery* and adapted it to my kitchen. You can use this recipe with muscadines, though you'll have to strain the seeds from your pulp (the flavor payoff is worth it), or you can adapt it to any red or black grape you want (dark, plump grapes will give you the most flavor).

This sweet-and-sour condiment is great alongside roasted vegetables, dolloped next to fatty dishes to cut the heaviness, or just enjoyed with cheese and charcuterie. Truth be told, I ran out of tomato ketchup recently and never replenished, being quite happy to use this instead.

— Makes about 1 quart

- **About 3 pounds (5 cups) muscadine grapes**
- **2 cups sugar**
- **1 teaspoon salt**
- **Freshly ground black pepper**
- **½ teaspoon ground allspice**
- **½ teaspoon ground cinnamon**
- **¼ teaspoon ground cloves**
- **½ cup apple cider vinegar or red wine vinegar**

Black Grape Catsup

1 To make grape pulp: Combine the grapes with just enough water to blend them in a blender, and do so until chunky-smooth (slightly pulpy, but with the seeds still intact).

2 Combine the grape pulp, sugar, salt, pepper to taste, allspice, cinnamon, cloves, and vinegar in a large, high-sided saucepan over medium-high heat. Bring the mixture to a boil, then reduce to a simmer.

3 Simmer, stirring frequently, until thickened, about 15 minutes. Skim the scum off the surface about halfway through.

4 Allow the catsup to cool completely, then store it in an airtight container in the refrigerator, where it will last for at least 2 weeks.

Melons

Cantaloupe, Honeydew, Watermelon

Melons are thick-rinded, watery fruits with large seeds either clustered in the center (as with honeydew and cantaloupe) or distributed throughout the flesh of the fruit (as with watermelon). Melons are the epitome of good late-summer eating. When I'm in Georgia, I keep a hungry eye out for folks with watermelon trucks who, if I'm very lucky, will also be selling bags of boiled peanuts.

But watermelons aren't summer's only delight: Cantaloupes and honeydew melons, which include a wide range of modern hybrids as well as heirloom varieties (like muskmelons or Delice de la Table), are equally succulent and wonderful with an unbeatable texture that feels almost like velvet on my palate. While honeydew can be divisive melons (I love them, but I know many honeydew detractors out there), I bet you boots to buttons if you try one ripe and in season, you'll come to love them, too.

FREEZING

Remove melon rinds and cut your melons into cubes, slices, or balls, depending on how you plan to use them.

Pack your melons into containers leaving ½ inch of headspace and freeze, or pack in syrup. Make a syrup by heating 1¾ cups sugar in 4 cups water; stir to dissolve the sugar completely. Let cool, then pour over the fruit to cover, package leaving headspace (page 19), and freeze. It will last for 1 month or more in the freezer if properly stored.

Tip: Watermelon, seeded (or skip that step if you buy seedless), then cut into ½-inch cubes and packed away in the freezer, makes the perfect milkshake when blended with vanilla ice cream. If you've ever been to a Cook Out restaurant in July or August, you know what I'm talking about.

WATERMELON JUICE

You can also blend your watermelon into juice for drinking fresh (it lasts for a few days) or freezing in ice cube trays to add to drinks later (or use it in Watermelon Syrup, page 300, or Watermelon Caramel Sauce, page 300). The basic guideline

Ways to Preserve Melons

	Shelf-stable	Fast	Low waste	Ready meals and ingredients	Big flavor
Watermelon Juice (page 297)				X	X
Mimi's Pickled Watermelon Rinds (page 298)			X	X	X
Watermelon Rind Slaw (page 299)			X	X	X
Watermelon Syrup (page 300)				X	X
Watermelon Caramel Sauce (page 300)				X	X

is that 8 cups cubed melon equals about ½ cup pulp and 3 cups juice. Add cubed watermelon (rind removed) to a blender and blend it until smooth. Then strain it through a nut milk bag or three layers of cheesecloth in a colander for 15 to 20 minutes, or until the liquid is almost entirely drained. Reserve the pulp, if desired, for other projects.

Other less watery melons can also be juiced in this way. Just note that you'll get less juice, of course.

PICKLING

Pickled watermelon relies on the rind, not the fruit itself, which is too soft to pickle. Pickled watermelon rinds are an example of our ancestors' ingenuity in putting every bit and scrap of food to delicious effect. And my watermelon rind recipe comes down from my own family line to you.

Mimi's Pickled Watermelon Rinds

Mimi's Pickled Watermelon Rinds

Each year Mimi (my great-grandmother Helen) would make these pickles, and my father and aunt have fond memories of enjoying them when they went to Mimi's house. Now the recipe has come to me, and I make them each year to share. This recipe, Mimi's original, is part ferment and part quick pickle: a simple overnight soak in brine that *just* starts to ferment the rinds, followed by boiling in brine until translucent. You can easily adapt this recipe to other spices, as you prefer.

NOTE: In Mimi's original recipe, the rinds are boiled in water until translucent and then packed in the pickling brine, but I opt to save a step and boil the rinds directly in the pickling brine.

— Makes about 6 pints

1 medium watermelon (about 10 pounds), flesh removed and rind cut into ½- to 1-inch cubes

FOR OVERNIGHT BRINE

2 tablespoons salt

1 quart water

FOR PICKLING BRINE

3 pounds granulated or brown sugar

2–3 (2- to 3-inch) pieces ginger

2 cinnamon sticks

1 tablespoon whole cloves

4 cups distilled white vinegar or apple cider vinegar

1 cup water

1 Make the overnight brine: Add the salt to the water and whisk until dissolved. Place the watermelon rinds in a bowl and pour the brine over them. The brine should completely cover the rinds (if not, make more brine using the same ratio of salt to water); weight the rinds with a plate or bowl if needed. Cover with a tea towel or cheesecloth and allow to sit at room temperature for 8 to 12 hours.

2 After soaking, drain and rinse the rinds with cold water. Transfer them to a pot, cover with cold water, and boil until just tender. Drain and set aside.

3 If canning, place 12 half-pint jars or 6 pint jars in your hot water bath canner and heat it up.

4 Make the pickling brine: Combine the sugar, ginger, cinnamon, cloves, vinegar, and water in a large pot and bring to a boil. Boil for 5 minutes.

5 Drop the rinds into the boiling syrup and boil until they are translucent and can be pierced easily with a knife. Remove from the heat.

6 If refrigerating, let the pickles cool and store them in an airtight container in the fridge, where they will last for 1 month or more.

7 If canning, using tongs, remove the hot jars from the canner. Pack the rinds into hot jars, leaving 1 inch of headspace. Pour the hot syrup over them, leaving ½ inch of headspace.

8 Run a chopstick or other thin, nonmetal utensil along the inner edges of the jars to release any air bubbles. Wipe the rims of the jars with a clean, damp cloth. Add the lids and bands and screw down to hand tightness.

9 Process half-pints for 12 minutes and pints for 15 minutes in a hot water bath canner, adjusting for altitude (see page 39) if needed.

10 Let the jars cool for 24 hours before testing the seals (see page 36), then store out of direct sunlight at room temperature.

Watermelon Rind Slaw

This is another favorite way to use up watermelon rinds and to have a sour side or sandwich topping at the ready. I like this slaw because it gives me a taste of summer all year long. Before you grate the watermelon rind (with a food processor or box grater), peel off the green outer skin with a vegetable peeler.

— Makes 4 pints

- **1 clove garlic, minced**
- **¼ cup sugar**
- **2 tablespoons salt**
- **1 tablespoon sesame seeds**
- **1–2 teaspoons red pepper flakes**
- **3 cups rice wine vinegar**
- **½ cup water**
- **½ tablespoon shoyu**
- **½ large watermelon's rind, grated (about 8 cups)**

1 Make the brine: Combine the garlic, sugar, salt, sesame seeds, pepper flakes, vinegar, water, and shoyu in a pot. Heat until boiling.

2 Meanwhile, if canning, place four pint jars in your hot water bath canner and heat it up. Then, using tongs, remove the hot jars from the canner.

3 Place the grated watermelon rind in a bowl, then pour the hot brine over the top to cover.

4 If refrigerating, allow the slaw to cool and store it in an airtight container. Let it sit in the fridge for 2 days before eating. It will last for 3 weeks or more.

5 If canning, loosely pack the watermelon into hot jars, leaving 1 inch of headspace. Pour the brine over, leaving ½ inch of headspace.

6 Run a chopstick or other thin, nonmetal utensil along the inner edges of the jars to release any air bubbles. Wipe the rims of the jars with a clean, damp cloth. Add the lids and bands and screw down to hand tightness.

7 Process pints in a hot water bath canner for 18 minutes, adjusting for altitude (see page 39) if needed.

8 Let the jars cool for 24 hours before testing the seals (see page 36), then store out of direct sunlight at room temperature.

MAKING SYRUP AND PRESERVES

Sweet melon preserves help that summertime flavor linger through the year. Melon's delicate flavor requires some gentle handling, which helps to preserve its floral, sweet taste.

Watermelon Syrup

Unlike many other fruits, melons tend to lose their succulent, delicate flavor when exposed to heat, which can make syrups a challenge. The best option? Make cold syrups by combining melon juice with sugar and whatever other flavors you want, then store them in the fridge. Choose ripe, juicy melons in your favorite variety.

These syrups don't last as long as cooked or canned versions, but if you add vodka or vinegar, cold syrups will last for at least a couple of weeks. And the flavor payoff is worth it: I've never had these syrups around long enough to go bad.

— Makes about 1 quart

- **3 cups Watermelon Juice (page 297)**
- **1–1¼ cups sugar**
- **1–2 tablespoons vinegar (any kind) or vodka (optional)**
- **Flavorings such as lime zest, tajin, cracked black pepper, salt, or fresh mint (optional)**

1. Whisk together the watermelon juice and sugar to dissolve the sugar. Add the vinegar, and stir in any flavorings to taste (if using). Allow to sit for 8 to 12 hours in the refrigerator.

2. If needed, whisk again to dissolve the sugar the rest of the way. The syrup will last in the fridge for 2 to 3 weeks.

Watermelon Caramel Sauce

Watermelon caramel is an unexpected way to use up an excess of fresh fruit. The cooking process alters the flavor of the watermelon a bit, giving it a somewhat earthy taste that evokes watermelon's botanical relationship to squash, which then evolves into that familiar watermelon flavor as it lingers.

Watermelon caramel is a thin, pourable sauce that I eat over ice cream or whisk into drinks. It only makes sense to can it if the canner's already running, as this recipe makes a small amount. Otherwise just store it in the fridge.

— Makes ½ pint

- **4 cups Watermelon Juice (page 297)**
- **1 cup plus 1 tablespoon sugar**
- **1 teaspoon salt**
- **1 (2-inch) strip citrus zest (optional)**

1. Bring the watermelon juice to a boil, then reduce to a simmer and cook over medium heat until it is reduced by a little more than half (to about 1¾ cups) and is thickened, about 30 minutes. Stir occasionally at first and then frequently.

2. Add the sugar, salt, and citrus zest (if using) and continue to cook the syrup until it is thickened and coats the back of a spoon, 10 to 12 minutes. Remove from the heat and remove the zest strip (if using).

3. Cool the sauce completely and store in an airtight container in the fridge, where it will last for at least 2 weeks.

Preserving Around the World

Anatolia, with Chef Ebru Baybara Demir

Turkish cuisine is rooted in history and in geography: "In these lands, food carries a story," says chef Ebru Baybara Demir. In Anatolia, every type of food is preserved: from cheese tucked in boiled, salted whey to keep it fresh through winter to pounded and drained meat mixed with salt and spices to make sausages, or meat buried in jars underground. And, of course, there are vinegars and pickled fruits and vegetables. To keep bread from going stale, cooks pound it into a kind of hardtack, called peksimet. Tomatoes and peppers are turned into paste, vegetables are dried, and yogurt, flour, and vegetables are cooked then dried for future soups.

"In Anatolia, nothing goes to waste," says Demir. "Grapes grown in the Aegean region are made into wines, must, fruit leather, and molasses. Residue from fruit-juice production, which would normally be considered waste, is transformed into a traditional sweet called cevizli sucuk [a walnut-stuffed, molasses-based sweet] in Turkish cuisine. These not only extend the lifespan of the food but also serve as natural sweeteners, offering an alternative to artificial ones."

Preserves are central to Turkish food: "In Anatolian cuisine, preserved products are just as essential as fresh ones. In Türkiye, a smell that reminds everyone of their childhood is onions sautéed in tomato paste, as this base is the foundation of many dishes." Pomegranate molasses, olives and jams for breakfast, and bulgar wheat, dried then cooked, are staples. Harvest celebrations take place between September and October, she says, adding, "In the past, without refrigerators and given that we live in a hot region of Mesopotamia, preservation methods became a fundamental part of our culture. In rural areas, people didn't follow a calendar; many of our elders know they were born during harvest and celebration times but can't give exact dates. During this period, the harvest is not done for each product individually but celebrated collectively as part of a preservation ritual," with each person chipping in to assist in preserving and to share in the bounty.

Anatolian cuisine is rooted in historic practices, the land's abundance, and the diversity of cultures and religious communities that make up this area, which means traditions can vary between communities or even families. "Today, this diversity is crucial; the natural preservation techniques we once relied on during times of plenty are now critical for maximizing the use of scarce resources." She, like me, sees that a connection to the past gives us a more resilient future:

> As discussions around sustainability in food production become more prevalent, we often turn to technology for solutions. However, if we look back to our heritage, we can find environmentally friendly methods to enhance food durability. Our culinary culture promises much more than just seasonal consumption of vegetables; it offers the potential for year-round food availability without harming the environment. Ultimately, I believe our efforts in ensuring food durability are essential, and we are fortunate to inherit such a rich cultural legacy to guide us.

Pomegranates

You've probably had grenadine, a syrup made from pomegranate juice, and fresh pomegranate seeds, but I've been experimenting with pomegranate seed preservation and have discovered that they make wonderful refrigerator pickles and can be canned when preserved in honey. Choose a pomegranate with firm skin that's heavy for its size and free of soft spots, knicks, and blemishes.

PICKLING

Pomegranate seeds (also called arils) are naturally tart, but pickling adds a bit of extra punch. When combined with spices, these pickled seeds make the perfect topping for rich dairy or creamy hummus, as well as vegetables, meat, and fish.

Ways to Preserve Pomegranates

	Shelf-stable	Fast	Low waste	Ready meals and ingredients	Big flavor
Harissa-Pickled Pomegranate Seeds (page 303)		X		X	X
Pomegranate Seeds in Honey (page 303)				X	X
Grenadine (Pomegranate Syrup) (page 304)				X	X

Harissa-Pickled Pomegranate Seeds

Harissa-Pickled Pomegranate Seeds

Delicate pomegranate seeds make a truly delicious refrigerator pickle, balancing pomegranate's flavor with a sweet-and-sour brine and a burst of harissa. Serve alongside rice, roasted vegetables (give it a try with Brussels sprouts!), seafood, or meat. The brine is also delicious whisked with olive oil for a simple vinaigrette.

—— Makes 1 pint

- **Seeds of 1 pomegranate**
- **1½–2 teaspoons harissa paste or 1–1½ teaspoons harissa powder**
- **¼ cup pomegranate juice**
- **1 tablespoon sugar**
- **½ tablespoon salt**
- **½ cup apple cider vinegar**
- **½ cup water**

1 Combine the pomegranate seeds and harissa in a pint jar.

2 Make the brine: In a small bowl, whisk together the pomegranate juice, sugar, salt, vinegar, and water until the sugar and salt are dissolved.

3 Pour the brine into the jar, leaving ½ inch of headspace. Screw on the lid and allow to pickle for 8 to 12 hours in the fridge before using. The pomegranate seeds will last for at least 3 weeks in the refrigerator.

CANNING

Canning pomegranate seeds is tricky because they tend to lose their crisp texture. The best method I've found is to use half-pint jars. This results in a shorter processing time, which helps keep their texture intact.

Pomegranate Seeds in Honey

This is the perfect way to keep pomegranate on hand for drinks and for topping meals. The pomegranate seeds in this recipe stay the most firm when the honey steeps in the fridge, but if you want a shelf-stable version, a short canning time in small jars helps minimize potential mushiness. You may have extra syrup left over, too, which would be wonderful for other kitchen experiments or just to stir into beverages.

—— Makes about 5 half-pints

- **1½ cups honey**
- **½ cup water**
- **Seeds of 1 large pomegranate**
- **Flavorings such as fresh mint, strips of citrus zest, or ½ to 1 teaspoon harissa powder (optional)**
- **1 tablespoon bottled lemon or lime juice**

1 Place five half-pint jars in your hot water bath canner and heat it up. Then, using tongs, remove the hot jars from the canner.

2 Combine the honey and water in a small pot and heat until the honey is just dissolved and pourable.

3 Divide the pomegranate seeds and flavorings into hot jars, leaving 1 inch of headspace. Pour the hot syrup over the pomegranate to cover, leaving ½ inch of headspace.

4 Run a chopstick or other thin, nonmetal utensil along the inner edges of the jars to release any air bubbles. Wipe the rims of the jars with a clean, damp cloth. Add the lids and bands and screw down to hand tightness.

5 Process half-pints in a hot water bath canner for 12 minutes, adjusting for altitude (see page 39) if needed.

6 Let the jars cool for 24 hours before testing the seals (see page 36), then store out of direct sunlight at room temperature.

MAKING SYRUP

You've probably had grenadine in your cocktails or your Shirley Temple, but did you know you can make your own? Plus, making pomegranate syrup at home means you can customize it with other flavors you enjoy.

Fruit syrups can have fruit pieces or be made from juice. They make a colorful and delicious addition to your pantry.

Grenadine (Pomegranate Syrup)

Grenadine reminds me of hot summer days and cold drinks (try it with chilled soda water or in a gin and tonic), but its tart flavor works in cooler weather, too. Think drizzled on roasted or fresh pears or added to wintertime drinks.

Grenadine, or pomegranate syrup, can be made with the seeds and juice of a whole pomegranate or with bottled juice. The molasses adds a depth of flavor, but if you don't have it, this grenadine is delicious without it.

— Makes about 1½ cups

Seeds of 1 pomegranate (about 1½ cups)
¼ teaspoon salt
1 cup water
1 tablespoon pomegranate molasses or Apple Cider Molasses (page 256)

1 Add the pomegranate seeds, salt, water, and molasses to a medium saucepan and bring to a boil.

2 Reduce the heat and simmer over medium-low until the pomegranate seeds just start to break down, 15 to 20 minutes.

3 Remove from the heat and let rest about 5 minutes; the syrup will thicken a bit as it cools.

4 Strain the grenadine through a fine-mesh strainer, cool, then store in an airtight container in the fridge, where it will last for at least 3 weeks.

VARIATION: SMOKY LIME GRENADINE

This is a great way to add an unexpected smoky twist in grenadine for whiskey, cocktails, or mocktails. Make syrup as above, but add 2 (2-inch) strips of lime zest and ½ teaspoon smoked paprika. Note: A light touch is critical here, as smoked paprika can easily overwhelm the flavors of fruit.

Stone Fruits

Apricots, Nectarines, Peaches, Plums

Biting into a fresh peach, the juice running down my chin and maybe even my arm, is the pinnacle of summer fruit luxury. Stone fruits really are better when in season, juicy and bursting with flavor, while their shipped-in wintertime counterparts can be grainy and bland. Use these recipes to create your own luxurious stone fruit flavors that you can enjoy year-round, and swap out added flavors as you see fit. (Have you tried peaches with basil? Divine!)

Stone fruits are natural partners to many preservation processes, giving you a taste of summer whenever you wish. They break apart into luscious cooked sweet preserves like jam, dry into snacks with a burst of flavor, or can be mixed with sugar and allowed to sit for cheong (see page 80), one of the simplest fruit preserves out there.

Choose firm stone fruits with smooth, unwrinkled flesh that are free of bruises and blemishes.

DRYING

Most stone fruits lend themselves well to drying for later use as a snack or an ingredient for other dishes. Store dried stone fruits in an airtight container in a cool, dark place, where they will last for 2 months or more.

Ways to Preserve Stone Fruits	Shelf-stable	Fast	Low waste	Ready meals and ingredients	Big flavor
Apricot-Plum Fruit Leather (page 306)				X	X
Smoked Dried Peaches (page 307)	X			X	X
Peach Shrub (page 308)				X	X
Peach Country Wine (page 309)				X	X
Floral Pickled Peaches (page 309)				X	X
Peach-and-Coriander Syrup (page 311)				X	X
Stone Fruit Jam (page 312)				X	X
Tomato-Peach Refrigerator Jam (page 312)				X	X

APRICOTS

Pit and halve your apricots, or cut them into slices if you prefer. Steam blanch for 3 to 4 minutes or in syrup for 10 minutes, dip in an ascorbic acid or fruit juice dip (page 90), and dehydrate for 24 to 36 hours at 125 to 135°F/52 to 57°C.

NECTARINES AND PEACHES

If you're sulfuring (see page 91), pit and halve your fruit first (and peel, if you wish). If you're steam or syrup blanching (see page 90), leave the fruit whole during the blanching process, then halve. You can also make an ascorbic acid solution (page 90) to dip your fruit in before drying.

These can also be dried in slices or quarters; I usually opt for slices because it reduces the drying time. Once they're pretreated, pop them in the dehydrator at 125 to 135°F/52 to 57°C, then dry for 36 to 48 hours for whole fruit, about 20 hours for quarters, and 8 to 10 hours for slices.

PLUMS

To make prunes from your plums, leave whole (cut out pits) and sulfur (see page 91). If you're air-drying your whole plums (see page 88), cut out pits and dip in boiling water for 30 seconds, followed by submerging in ice water, to check the skins. For a dehydrator, rinse with hot tap water first (no need to check skins), then lay on trays. Whole prunes take about 24 to 36 hours to dry at 125 to 135°F/52 to 57°C.

FRUIT LEATHER

Stone fruits are a common choice for fruit leathers, as they can be ground to a paste easily, dry well, and taste delicious on their own or in combination. Amardeen, a Syrian dried apricot paste, is dried in sheets and is just one of many stone fruit leathers in the world.

Apricot-Plum Fruit Leather

Throughout history, apricots have been preserved whole and dried, packed in syrup, and turned into paste. A 1653 recipe for apricot paste, from *The French Cook*, shared with me by food historian David Shields, shows equal parts sugar to fruit. And we see heavily sugared stone fruit pastes in cookbooks through the next century, including Elizabeth Raffald's 1769 apricot paste recipe, which begins with boiling apricots separately, then mashing them and cooking them with sugar.

This recipe, my adaptation of Martha Washington's apricot and plum paste, uses rose water for extra flavor. The original is boiled with sugar and dried over a fire, whereas I make mine as fruit leather in a dehydrator and prefer little to no added sugar.

— Makes 1 sheet of fruit leather (8×10 inches or 10×12 inches, depending on juiciness of fruit)

- **3–4 apricots, pitted and cubed (about 1 cup)**
- **3–4 plums, pitted and cubed (about 1 cup)**
- **½ cup sugar (optional)**
- **1–2 tablespoons rose water**
- **2 teaspoons lemon juice**

1. Add the apricots, plums, sugar (if using), rose water, and lemon juice to a blender and blend to a pulp.

2. Pour the pulp onto a drying tray or baking sheet lined with parchment paper or a silicone mat, spreading evenly and avoiding the edges, to about ⅛ inch thick.

3. Dry in the dehydrator at 140°F/60°C for 6 to 10 hours, or until the center feels tacky, not wet, and your finger does not leave an indent behind.

4. Peel the fruit leather up from the tray while still warm, then roll it up, allow to cool, cut into serving sizes if desired, and wrap it in plastic or waxed paper. Store at room temperature for 1 month in an airtight container, or freeze for up to 1 year.

Smoked Dried Peaches

In her book *Summer Kitchens*, Olia Hercules shares a recipe for dried smoked pears, which are preserved at the height of the season and added to soups and other savory dishes throughout the year. I decided to work up a Georgia peach version.

Just as in Hercules's recipe, the peaches are dried beforehand to remove moisture, then smoked. This means you get a good smoky flavor, but you don't have to leave your peaches in the smoker for an extended period to preserve them. This is a good recipe to make when you've got your hot smoker already going and have a bit more fuel to use.

6 peaches, halved, pits removed

1. Arrange the peaches cut side up on a baking sheet. Set your dehydrator to 135°F/57°C, or preheat the oven to warm or its lowest setting. To save energy, using a dehydrator is best.

2. Dry the peaches until dried to the touch and shriveled, turning once halfway through. (Note: This process can take 1 to 2 days in either a dehydrator or oven, so I highly recommend putting all the fruit you want to dry and smoke in the oven at the same time to save energy.)

3. Light your smoker and bring it to 150°F/66°C.

4. Smoke your dried peaches for 20 to 30 minutes, until shriveled and distinctly smoky. Allow them to cool on a wire cooling rack and store in an airtight container. They will last for at least 2 months.

Drying Olives

We eat olives as a savory food, but they are, botanically speaking, fruit. Fresh, uncured olives are not good eating when dried (or, really, in general), as they are bitter and tough.

However, you can dry your olives after curing, after removing the pits. This can also be a nice way to use up extra canned olives once the tin is open, or just to experiment with different olive textures.

You can dehydrate olives just until they start to wrinkle to concentrate their flavor. Dry in a dehydrator at 125 to 135°F/52 to 57°C for just a few hours, or in the sun for part of the day, depending on the olive size and type.

If you dry sliced olives until crisp, you can also grind them up into olive powder, which makes a divine umami sprinkle to go on all your savory dishes.

INFUSING

Stone fruits make delicious shrubs and liqueurs (see page 68). Plums are especially nice in shrubs, and as an added bonus, the phrase "plum shrub" is incredibly fun to say. Or try my peach shrub (see facing page).

Peach Shrub

I love this shrub because it is a great way to use up soft peaches that are about to go bad. No need to peel the peaches. I find white wine vinegar or apple cider vinegar best complements the flavor of peaches.

You can take the strained fruit from this recipe, which will be sour from the vinegar, and mash it into a pulp or leave as is and use as a sauce or relish (think a sour fruit chutney, or a dipping sauce for meat or roasted vegetables).

Very ripe peaches, sliced or cut into ½- to 1-inch dice

Flavorings such as a cinnamon stick, rosemary sprig, rose petals, lavender flowers, or your favorite herbs and spices (optional)

White wine vinegar or apple cider vinegar, to cover

Sugar

1. Add the peaches to fill your jar half to three-quarters full. Add additional flavors (if using). Then fill the jar the rest of the way with vinegar, making sure to completely cover the fruit, leaving ½ inch of headspace.

2. Seal the jar and let it sit in the fridge or at room temperature for 2 to 3 weeks, checking occasionally to make sure fruit stays under the vinegar.

3. Once it has a flavor you enjoy, strain and whisk in sugar to taste until dissolved.

4. Store the shrub in the fridge or at room temperature. It will last longer in the fridge, where it will keep for a couple of months (or more).

Process, Not Just Product

The Foxfire Book is devoted to the traditional skills of Appalachian folks, and my 1972 copy, which always sat on my grandpaw's nightstand, includes a recipe for muscadine (wild grape) wine. In it, grapes are mashed by hand, blended with sugar, where you then "let it work [ferment] for about a week, until it quits." You'll notice this kind of process-based indicator, rather than a time-based indicator, in many fermentation recipes (including mine), because fermentation does not always happen at the same speed.

In practical terms, this means that you let it ferment until it gets active and then the activity dies down, which is a sign that the mixture has completed its initial bout of fermentation. The mixture is strained, put back in the churn with more sugar, and fermented "until it quits" again.

Fermentation is influenced by time and temperature. Slower fermentation happens at lower temperatures, and fermentation happens more quickly at higher temperatures (and this also influences the microbial communities present). Time matters, too: The microbial makeup of your ferment changes the longer it goes, as do the flavors (and acidity, or percentage of alcohol, up to a point at least) and you can pull it at different times based on the flavor and final product you want. But to get that final product, you have to stay connected to the process and watch it unfold in its own time.

PICKLING AND FERMENTING

Pickled and fermented fruit is a forever favorite. Stone fruits lend themselves to these processes especially well, offering a range of flavors: sweet, sour, spicy, and beyond.

Peach Country Wine

Country wine is sometimes made with pitched yeast (that is, a yeast starter added to the juice before fermenting). But I like to keep things wild and rely on the yeasts already on my peaches. This is a very accessible way to dip your toes into the world of homemade country wines because it requires no special equipment. The possible results range more widely than using pitched yeast (you might get more sour or funky flavors, for example), but the fun of experimentation, plus the simplicity of this practice, makes it worth a try even if you're skeptical of creating something especially funky.

—— Makes about ½ gallon

- **6 pounds ripe peaches, pitted and chopped**
- **5 cups sugar, plus more for carbonation (optional)**

1. Place the peaches in a blender or food processor and blend them to a chunky pulp, or mash them with a potato masher.

2. Pour the pulp into a large jar or crock. Cover it with a cloth and secure with a rubber band or twine. Let it sit at room temperature, stirring several times a day, until the mixture stops bubbling, 7 to 10 days.

3. Strain the mixture through a mesh bag or cheesecloth, squeezing out as much of the liquid as you can. Transfer the juice back into your fermentation jar or crock. You can experiment with pulp in marinades and sauces, or just toss it in the compost.

4. Add the sugar and stir until it is dissolved. Cover the jar or crock with a cloth and let the liquid ferment again, stirring daily. The mixture will bubble eagerly for the first few days, then start to slow down. Once the bubbling has mostly subsided and the brew tastes alcoholic, it's ready to serve. (I tend to let my taste buds guide me, but you can also test the ABV with a hydrometer, if you prefer, and there are many instructions online for doing so.)

5. Pour the wine into swing-top bottles. At this point, you can carbonate your wine or enjoy it as is. To carbonate, add 2 tablespoons of sugar per gallon of wine (caster sugar is easiest to work with here), and whisk to dissolve. Tightly cap your bottles and allow to ferment at room temperature for several days until good and bubbly. The wine will be quite sweet at this point, as many country wines are. You can age it in the bottles in a cool place for 1 to 2 months to mellow out the sweetness a bit; just make sure your bottles are completely full and tightly capped to minimize the amount of oxygen coming into contact with the wine.

Floral Pickled Peaches

Pickling is a really nice use for firm peaches. My early-season peaches tend to go into pickles, relishes, chutneys—things where that dense texture will hold up; later in the season, I make jams, fruit wines, and other preserves that rely on a heady, intense peach flavor and can work with soft, ripe, succulent fruit. For a less intense pickle, make refrigerator pickles.

I include a few variations for floral peaches here, but I encourage you to make this recipe your own, based on what's in your garden. The brine can be enjoyed as a shrub after the peaches have been eaten.

(continued on next page)

Floral Pickled Peaches *continued*

— Makes 2 pints

¼ cup salt

¼ cup sugar

2 cups apple cider vinegar, white wine vinegar, or distilled white vinegar (for refrigerator pickles; 4 cups for canned pickles)

2 cups water (for refrigerator pickles only)

2 tablespoons agastache flowers

2 tablespoons rose petals

2 teaspoons fresh mugwort flowers

Herbs and spices (try the suggestions above, or make your own blend)

6 firm peaches, pitted and cut into ¼- to ½-inch slices

Floral Pickled Peaches

1 If canning, place two pint or four half-pint jars in your hot water bath canner and heat it up. Then, using tongs, remove the hot jars from the canner.

2 Make the brine: Combine the salt, sugar, vinegar, and water (if making refrigerator pickles) in a large pot and bring to a boil, stirring. Boil until the salt and sugar are completely dissolved.

3 Divide the flowers and other flavorings between the jars or other nonreactive containers with an airtight lid. Add the sliced peaches. Pour the hot brine over the herbs and peaches, leaving ½ inch of headspace.

4 If refrigerating, let cool and store your pickles in the fridge, where they will last for at least 2 weeks.

5 If canning, run a chopstick or other thin, nonmetal utensil along the inner edges of the jars to release any air bubbles. Wipe the rims of the jars with a clean, damp cloth. Add the lids and bands and screw down to hand tightness.

6 Process pint jars in a hot water bath canner for 20 minutes, adjusting for altitude (see page 39) if needed.

7 Let the jars cool for 24 hours before testing the seals (see page 36), then store out of direct sunlight at room temperature.

VARIATION: PICKLED PEACHES WITH SPICES

If you prefer spices over flowers, for two pints, add 1 bay leaf (cut in half, divided between your jars), ½ teaspoon fresh rosemary leaves, and ½ teaspoon black peppercorns. Or ½ teaspoon peppercorns and 1 sprig of tarragon, divided between jars.

VARIATION: BLUE BOUQUET PICKLED PEACHES

Blue butterfly pea flower peaches have a bright, colorful brine (and the peaches do change hue somewhat; they change color more with more flowers). Add ½ to 1 tablespoon dried blue butterfly pea flowers per jar.

MAKING SYRUPS AND JAMS

Stone fruit syrups and jams distill summer's hot days and bright flavors so much that I pause to linger in the moment, feeling warm and comforted, each time I eat them in winter. These are a few of my favorites.

Peach-and-Coriander Syrup

Syrups are absolutely wonderful for when you have peaches that are very soft and starting to get wrinkly—not moldy or unsafe to eat, just past their prime. If you need a quick, simple way to use your very soft peaches, a syrup is one of your top options; others include freezing them as purée (see page 20), making peach wine (see page 308), or making peach shrubs (see page 308). This recipe yields too small an amount to practically can on its own, but it's nice to can if you have the canner already going. Or you can increase the recipe to make a larger amount for canning.

Swap out other stone fruit and flavorings (like stems from fresh basil you've used for other projects) to make syrups all your own.

— Makes about 1 pint

- **1 pound peaches, pitted and sliced (about 3 cups)**
- **3 cups sugar**
- **2 teaspoons coriander seeds**
- **½ teaspoon black peppercorns**
- **½ teaspoon salt**
- **2 cups water**
- **¼ teaspoon citric acid (if canning)**

1. If canning, place a pint jar in your hot water bath canner and heat it up.
2. Add the peaches, sugar, coriander, peppercorns, salt, and water to a large saucepan and bring to a boil over medium-high heat. Reduce to a simmer and cook, stirring often, until thickened and reduced, 15 to 20 minutes.
3. Strain the mixture through a fine-mesh strainer, pressing with the back of a spoon to remove as much liquid as possible. (You can save the solids to use in a crumble, crisp, or other dessert, or just compost them.)
4. If refrigerating, allow the syrup to cool completely, then pour into an airtight container. It will last for several weeks in the fridge.
5. If canning, using tongs, remove the hot jar from the canner. Pour the hot syrup into the hot jar, leaving ½ inch of headspace (see note).
6. Run a chopstick or other thin, nonmetal utensil along the inner edge of the jar to release any air bubbles. Wipe the rim of the jar with a clean, damp cloth. Add the lid and band and screw down to hand tightness.
7. Process the pint in a hot water bath canner for 15 minutes, adjusting for altitude (see page 39) if needed.
8. Let the jar cool for 24 hours before testing the seal (see page 36), then store out of direct sunlight at room temperature.

NOTE: If you're canning syrup and find you don't have quite enough syrup to completely fill your jar, you can add a splash of vinegar (this won't quite make it a shrub, but it will add a nice sour flavor).

Stone Fruit Jam

I use this recipe with whatever surplus of stone fruits I have. In Georgia, that means lots of peaches, but where you are it might mean plums, apricots, or a blend of fruits.

— Makes about 4 pints or 8 half-pints

- **5½–6 cups pitted, crushed peaches**
- **6–7 cups sugar**
- **½ teaspoon salt**
- **2 tablespoons lemon juice (bottled if canning)**
- **Dried or fresh flavorings (see note; optional)**

1 Combine the peaches, sugar, salt, lemon juice, and any dried flavorings in a large pot over medium-high heat. Bring to a boil, stirring frequently.

2 Turn down to simmer over medium heat, stirring often, until the fruit has softened and broken down and it coats the back of a spoon, about 15 minutes. For slightly underripe fruits that are not breaking down easily, mash with a potato masher.

3 Meanwhile, if canning, place four pint or eight half-pint jars in your hot water bath canner and heat it up. Then, using tongs, remove the hot jars from the canner.

4 If refrigerating, remove the jam from the heat, allow it to cool, and store it in an airtight container in the fridge, where it will last for at least 2 weeks.

5 If canning, spoon the hot jam into hot jars, leaving ½ inch of headspace.

6 Run a chopstick or other thin, nonmetal utensil along the inner edges of the jars to release any air bubbles. Wipe the rims of the jars with a clean, damp cloth. Add the lids and bands and screw down to hand tightness.

7 Process half-pints for 12 minutes and pints for 15 minutes in a hot water bath canner, adjusting for altitude (see page 39) if needed.

8 Let the jars cool for 24 hours before testing the seals (see page 36), then store out of direct sunlight at room temperature.

NOTE: Add flavorings like dried herbs and spices (such as ½ to 1 teaspoon lavender, 1 tablespoon ground baking spices, or dried citrus peel) at the beginning; add fresh herbs (like finely chopped leaves of 2 or 3 mint sprigs) at the end.

Tomato-Peach Refrigerator Jam

Summertime in a jar! I make this one jar at a time as I have a few tomatoes come in and a few extra peaches on the counter, and I always have a jar in the fridge as a summery treat when I need a last-minute, unexpected condiment. I find the flavors stay their brightest when the jam is kept in the fridge, rather than canned, where it will last for weeks.

— Makes about 1 pint

- **2 large tomatoes, cut into 1-inch dice, juices reserved**
- **1 peach, pitted, skin on or peeled, cut into ½-inch dice, juices reserved**
- **¾ cup sugar**
- **Pinch of salt**
- **½ cup water**
- **Handful of fresh herbs such as basil, agastache, or tarragon, cut into chiffonade (optional)**

1 Add the tomatoes and peach, with their juices, and the sugar, salt, and water to a saucepan.

2 Bring to a boil over medium-high heat, then reduce to a simmer, stirring frequently, until the mixture has a loose, jammy consistency, 15 to 20 minutes. I like some chunks in the jam, but if you don't, use your food processor, immersion blender, blender, or potato masher to smooth it out.

3 Remove the jam from the heat, stir in the herbs (if using) and allow to cool. Store it in the fridge, where it will last for at least 2 weeks.

Tropical Fruits

Coconuts, Guava, Mango, Papaya, and Pineapple

Tropical fruits can refer to many things, but I like to classify these warm-weather crops together, as, at least in my house, I tend to eat them in combination. Some (like guava and mango) overlap in some of their preserving methods, while others (like coconut) can be a bit different. In all cases, choose the freshest fruit possible with firm flesh and skin and without bruises and blemishes. For coconuts, choose a coconut with damp-feeling fibers and no cracks in the shell, and one that sounds like it's full of milk when shaken.

DRYING

Some people dry coconut in a well-ventilated area in the sun: Cut into thin slices, then rotate every day or so to dry evenly over the course of a couple of weeks. Be sure the coconut is in a sunny and dry area, as this will help it dry more quickly and prevent pathogen growth.

Many cooks dry their hulled coconut in a dehydrator in very thin (less than ¼ inch) slices or grated. Dry coconut on a low temperature (105 to 110°F/41 to 43°C) for 8 to 12 hours, checking every couple of hours. Grated coconut only takes about 4 to 6 hours in most cases, depending on the freshness of your coconut; you can also dry grated coconut in the oven. Allow it to cool completely, and store it in an airtight container in the

Ways to Preserve Tropical Fruits	Shelf-stable	Fast	Low waste	Ready meals and ingredients	Big flavor
Mango-Peel Shrub (page 314)				X	X
Mango-Peel Bitters (page 315)				X	X
Mango Pickles (page 315)		X		X	X
Canned Pickled Mango (page 316)				X	X
Pickled Papaya (page 316)				X	X
Tepache (page 317)			X	X	X
Mango-Pit Mead (page 318)			X		X
Guava Paste (page 318)				X	X
Mango-Pit Syrup (page 319)			X	X	X
Mango Black Pepper Refrigerator Jam (page 319)				X	X

refrigerator. Dried shredded coconut can be used in recipes or added to fruit leathers for some extra texture and flavor.

Guava does not dry well, as its flesh tends toward a grainy, seedy final product. You can, however, make Guava Paste (page 318) for pastries, which you can also use like quince paste on fruit and cheese trays or other grazing board–type meals.

Mango can be puréed and used in fruit leathers; I like to add a bit of coconut, too. Follow the general guidance for fruit leather (see page 94). Or cut mango in slices that are ¼ inch thick or less, arrange on a dehydrator tray, and dry at 135°F/57°C for 6 to 12 hours or until dry.

Pineapple dries well: Use ripe, fresh pineapple, remove the peels and core (save for tepache!), and cut into ½-inch slices. There's no need to pretreat pineapple before drying. Dry in a dehydrator at 135°F/57°C for 24 to 36 hours until dry but pliable. If you plan to eat dried pineapple as a snack, you can also add flavorings to it before drying—try dusting with a little bit of cocoa powder and/or red chili powder, or rub your sliced fruit with a bit of lime zest. Store dried tropical fruits in an airtight container out of direct sunlight, where they will last for at least 1 month.

FREEZING

You can freeze fresh, dehulled coconut. Shred or chop for faster freezing and ease of use later, then pack into containers, leaving ½ inch of headspace, and freeze.

Mango purée can be packed into containers with headspace (see page 19), then frozen. Or cut peeled mangos into slices, arrange on a tray, and freeze. Then pack into a container with no headspace.

Pack sliced, diced, or crushed pineapple tightly into containers with headspace (see page 19) and freeze. Or arrange cubes or slices onto a tray, then freeze. Then pack into a container with no headspace. They will last for at least 2 months in the freezer if properly stored.

INFUSING

Infusing is a great way to use up those last bits and bobs of tropical fruit. I offer mango versions here, but you can also make infused vinegar or spirits with bits of pineapple or other fruit (just follow the directions on page 66). Pineapple shrubs, in particular, are a favorite of mine. They're perfect to have around in case you have a hankering for Tepache (page 317) but don't have any available.

Mango-Peel Shrub

Sweet and tart, this shrub is perfect for your summer drinks—alcoholic (soda, whiskey, sprig of rosemary) or not (soda water).

— Makes 1 quart or 2 pints

Peels of 6 mangoes
¼–½ cup sugar
Pinch of salt
2–3 cups apple cider vinegar

1. Pack the mango peels, sugar, and salt into one quart jar or two pint jars, leaving 1 inch of headspace.

2. Pour the vinegar over to completely cover, then close the lid and shake to dissolve the sugar.

3. Let the shrub steep, gently shaking or stirring every few days. Start taste testing after 2 weeks. When it has a flavor you enjoy, strain and store your shrub in an airtight container with no headspace. It can be kept at room temperature for about 2 weeks or refrigerated for at least 3 weeks.

Mango-Peel Bitters

Unlike most bitters that risk overpowering other subtle, light flavors, these are at home in anything from a glass of Meyer lemonade to a delicate cocktail. They have a little kick from the peppercorns and are perfect for lighter rum and whiskey drinks in summer. Double the recipe, if desired, to make it in a pint jar.

—— Makes about 1 cup

- **1 teaspoon black peppercorns**
- **Peels of 2 mangoes**
- **2 (3- to 4-inch) strips orange peel**
- **Vodka or bourbon, to cover**

1 Add the peppercorns to the bottom of a half-pint jar or other food-safe airtight container. Pack the strips of mango and orange peel lengthwise, starting on the outside and layering to the inside, leaving 1¾ inches of headspace.

2 Add vodka to cover.

3 Let the bitters steep for 1 month, then strain and store in an airtight container with no headspace. They can be kept at room temperature or refrigerated and will last for 2 months or more.

PICKLING AND FERMENTING

Pickled mangoes are wonderful on fish and are equally at home on fresh green salads and fruit salads. And tepache? That might be my favorite beverage on Earth.

Mango Pickles

Mango lends itself beautifully to preservation: It is wonderful in fruit butters and curds, achar (Indian pickled condiments), chutneys, and all kinds of pickles. You can preserve luscious, fresh, fragrant mangoes as well as tarter green mangoes. Experiment with using this technique with other firm tropical fruits like fresh pineapple, too.

—— Makes about 1 quart

- **3 firm, fresh mangoes, peeled, pitted, and cut into ½-inch-thick slices or cubes**
- **1 small bunch cilantro**
- **1 fresh red bird's-eye chile, thinly sliced**
- **1 clove garlic, peeled and halved**
- **2 cups rice wine vinegar, brown rice vinegar, or apple cider vinegar**
- **2 cups water**
- **1–2 tablespoons salt**

1 Add mangoes, cilantro, chile, and garlic to a quart jar.

2 Make the brine: Combine the vinegar, water, and salt in a pot over medium heat, whisking just until the salt is dissolved.

3 Pour the brine over the mango until it is completely covered.

4 Let the mango pickle for 8 to 12 hours in the fridge before using. Store it in the fridge in an airtight container, where it will last for at least 1 week.

Canned Pickled Mango

This is a nice way to save your mango for later, when you'll want a spiced and spicy pickle in a pinch. A medium-size mango, peeled and pitted, is just about enough sliced fruit to fill a pint jar. For pickles, you can leave it sliced or cut the slices into strips or small cubes.

— Makes 2 pints

- **1½ tablespoons salt**
- **1½ cups apple cider vinegar**
- **½ cup water**
- **1–2 fresh red bird's-eye chiles, halved**
- **1–1½ teaspoons ground garam masala**
- **2 firm mangos, peeled, pitted, and cut into ¼-inch slices**

1. Make the brine: Combine the salt, vinegar, and water in a pot over medium heat, whisking just until the salt is dissolved.
2. Meanwhile, place two pint jars in your hot water bath canner and heat it up. Then, using tongs, remove the hot jars from the canner.
3. Divide the chiles and garam masala between the hot jars. Pack the jars with the sliced mango, leaving ½ inch of headspace. Pour the brine over them to completely cover, leaving ½ inch of headspace.
4. Run a chopstick or other thin, nonmetal utensil along the inner edges of the jars to release any air bubbles. Wipe the rims of the jars with a clean, damp cloth. Add the lids and bands and screw down to hand tightness.
5. Process pints in a hot water bath canner for 12 minutes, adjusting for altitude (see page 39) if needed.
6. Let the jars cool for 24 hours before testing the seals (see page 36), then store out of direct sunlight at room temperature.

Pickled Papaya

Pickled Papaya

Made with semi-ripe papaya, this recipe is loosely inspired by the pickled papaya from the website Malaysian Chinese Kitchen. I love making this spicy, tangy pickle to serve alongside rice and fish. Choose a papaya that's still firm, with the flesh just beginning to turn yellow. If it's too ripe, it can turn to mush when canning. Too green and it may be too tannic for your tastes (but give it a try; I love green papaya pickle). It's fun to play with different varieties of chiles for different flavors: more heat from bird's-eye, less heat and a bit of smoke from habanero, for example.

Alternatively, you can thinly slice papaya on a mandoline, pour the cooled brine over it, and pickle in the fridge for at least 3 hours. A firm, just-ripe papaya can work as a refrigerator pickle, but be aware that ripe papayas tend to lose their texture quickly in this recipe.

— Makes 2 pints

- **1 semi-ripe papaya, peeled and seeded**
- **2 cups sugar**
- **1½ tablespoons salt**
- **1 teaspoon turmeric powder**
- **2 cups apple cider vinegar or brown rice vinegar (5% acidity)**
- **1 cup water**
- **1–2 tablespoons red pepper flakes or 1–2 dried bird's-eye chiles**

1 If canning, place two pint jars in your hot water bath canner and heat it up. Using tongs, remove the hot jars from the canner.

2 Meanwhile, thinly slice the papaya ¼ inch thick. Cut wider pieces from the base of the fruit in half before slicing.

3 Make the brine: Combine the sugar, salt, turmeric, vinegar, and water in a large saucepan and bring to a boil.

4 Divide the pepper flakes evenly between the two jars (or if using whole chiles, place 1 chile in the bottom of each jar). Fill the jars with the papaya, leaving 1 inch of headspace.

5 Pour hot brine over to cover completely, leaving ½ inch of headspace.

6 If refrigerating, cool and let pickle in the fridge for 12 to 24 hours before eating. The pickles will last for at least 2 weeks in the fridge.

7 If canning, run a chopstick or other thin, nonmetal utensil along the inner edges of the jars to release any air bubbles. Wipe the rims of the jars with a clean, damp cloth. Add the lids and bands and screw down to hand tightness.

8 Process pints in a hot water bath canner for 12 minutes, adjusting for altitude (see page 39) if needed.

9 Let the jars cool for 24 hours before testing the seals (see page 36), then store out of direct sunlight at room temperature.

Tepache

Tepache, a fermented pineapple drink originally from Mexico, is one of my absolute favorite beverages. Popular in many Caribbean and Latin American countries, tepache can have a lot of regional variation (for instance, I have a Dominican friend who doesn't drink it with spices, but my friend from Acapulco, Mexico, does).

Though pineapple is the traditional base, you can apply the tepache method to whatever fresh fruit you desire. For this recipe, you'll need a 1- to 2-gallon food-safe, nonreactive crock or container. I call for the whole pineapple, but you can use just the core and rind if that's what you have.

(continued on next page)

Tepache

Tepache *continued*

— Makes about 1 gallon

- **1 pineapple, skin on, crown discarded, cut into wedges**
- **2 cups sugar (turbinado, granulated, or brown)**
- **1 tablespoon whole allspice berries**
- **3 whole cloves**
- **1 cinnamon stick**
- **About 1 gallon water**

1 Combine the pineapple, sugar, allspice, cloves, and cinnamon in a 1- to 2-gallon crock or other food-safe container. Add enough water to cover the pineapple, then stir to dissolve the sugar.

2 Cover the mixture with a lid or a tea towel to keep bugs out. For nonalcoholic or very lightly alcoholic tepache, let it sit for 2 to 3 days. For alcoholic tepache, let it sit for 5 to 7 days. Stir the ferment several times a day.

3 Strain your tepache and store in the fridge, using within several weeks.

Mango-Pit Mead

This is an easy, delicious way to use mango pits without a lot of prep time (but, yes, some wait time). Adjust the water and honey to suit your taste, and play with adding seasonings if you'd like: A little bit of fresh rosemary, a couple of strips of citrus zest, or some black peppercorns would be good here. Of course, you can use mango flesh, too; just swap out the pits for the flesh.

— Makes about 1½ quarts

- **6 mango pits**
- **6 cups room-temperature water**
- **2 cups honey**

1 Combine the mango pits, water, and honey in a ½-gallon jar or crock. Stir to dissolve the honey (don't worry if all of the honey doesn't dissolve right now; it will later!).

2 Cover and let sit at room temperature out of direct sunlight, stirring two or three times per day.

3 The mixture will start bubbling, then the bubbling will become less intense after 7 to 10 days. At this point, you have a fresh mead! If you like to carbonate or age your meads, now's the time to do that (see page 60).

4 Store the mead in the refrigerator in an airtight container; it will last for at least 1 month, though the flavor may shift over time.

MAKING SYRUPS AND PRESERVES

Syrups and sweet preserves are a beautiful way to use tropical fruits, giving you a ready ingredient for desserts, or just a topping for toast.

Guava Paste

If you find yourself with fresh guavas, I highly recommend making guava paste. It's a staple in sweet and savory dishes including pastelitos de guayaba, one of my favorite pastries.

- **Fresh guavas, peeled, seeded, and cubed**
- **Sugar**
- **Lemon juice**

1 Weigh the guava and add it to a large pot along with the appropriate amount of water: 1 cup of water per pound of guava. Simmer until very tender, about 30 minutes. Strain, reserving the cooking water.

2 Purée the guava (in a blender, with an immersion blender, or by mashing until smooth) to a thick smoothie consistency; add some of the cooking water, if needed, to help it blend.

3 Measure the pulp and return it to the pot along with the appropriate amount of sugar and lemon juice: 1 cup of sugar per 1 cup of pulp, and the juice of 1 lemon per 2 cups of pulp).

4 Simmer on low, stirring occasionally, until the guava is darkened and thickened. It should be reduced by about half, just starting to form into a paste.

5 Transfer the paste to a parchment-lined mold (like a loaf pan). Let it cool, chill for 8 to 12 hours in the fridge, then cut it into cubes. Store in an airtight container in the refrigerator, where it will last for 2 weeks or more.

Mango-Pit Syrup

This syrup offers instant gratification for enjoying the magic of mango pits. Yes, it's great in drinks, but it's also a really nice all-purpose syrup for desserts and snacks (try it drizzled on fruit salad or yogurt). Adding the spices later means you can extract as much mango flavor as possible, making for a final product where the fruit shines through.

— Makes about 1½ pints

- **2 mango pits**
- **2 cups sugar**
- **Pinch of salt**
- **2 cups water**
- **1–2 tablespoons total of coriander seeds and black pepper, or 1 teaspoon garam masala**
- **1 (2- to 3-inch) strip lemon zest, diced (optional)**

1 Add mango pits, sugar, salt, and water to a saucepan and bring to a boil. Reduce the heat to a simmer and cook until flavorful, stirring occasionally, 20 to 30 minutes.

2 Add the coriander and black pepper and lemon zest, and simmer until it's as spicy as you like, 10 to 15 minutes.

3 Remove from the heat, strain, and store your cooled syrup in an airtight container in the fridge, where it will last for at least 2 weeks.

Mango Black Pepper Refrigerator Jam

I am a big lover of jams that ride the line between sweet and savory applications, and this one fits the bill perfectly. It's at home on a cheese or charcuterie plate or as a glaze for chicken, but it shines equally well on toast, filling pastries, or in any other traditional jam uses.

— Makes about 2 pints

- **6 mangoes, peeled, pitted, and cut into 1-inch dice**
- **2 cups sugar**
- **1½–2 teaspoons freshly ground black pepper**
- **1 teaspoon salt**
- **Juice of 1 orange**

1 Add the mangoes, sugar, pepper, salt, and orange juice to a high-sided skillet and bring to a boil. Reduce to a simmer and cook, stirring frequently, until the mixture coats the back of a spoon, about 25 minutes.

2 If the mixture is still chunky and you prefer a smoother jam, mash it with a potato masher or use an immersion blender.

3 Let it cool and store in the fridge in an airtight container, where it will last for at least 2 weeks.

Mango Black Pepper Refrigerator Jam

Bread Miso (page 326)

CHAPTER 8

Grains and Legumes

Grains	322
Legumes	330

Tempeh (page 336)

Grains and legumes are all seeds. Grains are small, dry seeds (sometimes with a hull/fruit layer, and sometimes not), and the term typically refers to cereals or the seeds of grasses (e.g., wheat, corn, rice). However, *grains* can also refer to the seeds of other plants, like amaranth and buckwheat. Legumes are the edible seeds of legume plants (Fabaceae family), and they include peas, lentils, shell beans, and peanuts.

We have been harvesting, drying, and eating grains and legumes since before the dawn of agriculture (when humans started growing them intentionally and at scale). And while they are shelf-stable when dried—provided they are stored away from moisture and pests—they offer other preserving possibilities, too.

Grains

Grains are seeds from cereal crops: grasses that have been selectively bred for millennia for the purpose of cultivating said seeds. They are packed with nutrition and easy to store. And grains have adapted to growing in many different climates. They are also more affordable and less resource-intense than some other agricultural products (certainly less than animal products). It's not surprising, then, that grains make up so much of so many people's diets around the world. The word *cereal* comes from the name Ceres (Roman goddess of the harvest, whose Greek counterpart is Demeter): Cereal is a word with abundance, security, and food for the future woven into its very fabric.

There are also what some folks call pseudo grains, which are prepared and eaten like grains but are from different botanical families than cereal crops. These include quinoa, wild rice, buckwheat, and amaranth (among others). In this book, if it walks like a grain and talks like a grain, we'll be preserving it like a grain, but knowing the distinction between cereals and other grains is, if nothing else, a neat fact to pull out at parties (depending on the kinds of parties you go to).

The germ on whole grains contains fats, which can go rancid at room temperature. Some people store their whole grains in the freezer, but I usually store mine out of direct sunlight at room temperature in an airtight container (like a mason jar). Try to use them within 6 months. If you do decide to freeze them, just like with any frozen food, freeze them right when you get them: Don't wait until they're about to go rancid. And make sure to label them before they go in the freezer!

Ways to Preserve Grains

	Shelf-stable	Fast	Low waste	Ready meals and ingredients	Big flavor
Tarhana (page 325)	X			X	X
Bread Miso (page 326)			X	X	X
Beet Kvass (page 328)				X	X
Basic Mirin/Not-Mirin Method (page 330)				X	X

DRYING

Drying and storing grains for eating or growing is the same process. If you decide to plant your dried grains, don't let the seeds sit for years before you do. They'll be more vital the sooner they go in the ground (within a year of drying is my benchmark).

Fresh grains can be dried at home in the sun, in a dehydrator, or in an oven set to the lowest setting (though this last one is the hardest, in my opinion). In all cases, spread your grains out in a single layer on a rimmed sheet pan or a dehydrator tray without overcrowding.

For sun-drying: Cover with cheesecloth or a screen to prevent insect activity, then set in direct sunlight to dry. For best results, check your grains after 6 to 8 hours, at which point you may wish to gently roll or shake them around to make sure they dry evenly on all sides before continuing to dry the rest of the way (about 12 to 18 hours total). I like to set them out in the early morning, then bring them in at dusk before the nightly dew settles.

For a dehydrator, dry grains you'll plant as seeds between 100 to 110°F/38 to 43°C (keep the temperature below 113°F/45°C to preserve enzymatic activity so your seeds can grow later). Dry for 6 to 8 hours; I usually check after 3 to 4. If your seeds are smaller than the slots in your dehydrator trays, line the trays with waxed paper before drying.

In the oven, dry your seeds on the lowest setting. Note that most ovens don't go below about 150°F/66°C, which means the enzymatic activity of the seeds will be killed off (so you can't plant them), but you can still cook with them.

In addition to drying your harvested fresh grains, you can dry sprouted grains as well as spent grains from brewing. You can even dehydrate cooked grains.

Dried grains can be ground into flour and used in baking (like breads, some desserts, and pancakes) or kept whole and added to soups, stews, and other dishes. Cooked grains, like rice, can be dried then rehydrated (a popular method for making quicker-cooking rice easier to carry when camping). Dehydrate cooked grains at least at 150°F/66°C, which prevents pathogenic microbes from growing on wet grains as they dry.

The Anatomy of a Grain

As seeds, grains contain plenty of nutrition for a baby grass plant to grow (that's also why they're such nourishing food for us). Grains are made of the following:

HULL. This is a tough outer coating that protects the grain as it grows. Hulls are too tough for us to eat, so even whole grains you buy at the market have these removed (historically, creative uses of hulls have included livestock feed and sowans, a Scottish oat porridge that I talk about in *Our Fermented Lives*). The process of threshing cracks the hulls so they can be removed, and winnowing separates the hulls (called chaff, once they're off the grains) from the edible grains themselves.

BRAN. Below the hull lies the bran, a layer that completely envelops the grain, providing additional protection. It also contains lots of fiber and B vitamins, which we get when we enjoy whole-grain foods.

ENDOSPERM. This is the largest part of the grain, and the part we eat when we eat refined grains (whereas other parts are removed). The endosperm gives energy to the grain, storing carbohydrates and some other nutrients to support the baby plant's growth.

GERM. The word *germinate* gives you a good idea of what this part of the plant does: It contains the plant embryo or, in other words, the part that would grow into another plant. This part of the grain has proteins, vitamins, and minerals. This is also where the fats in the grain live (the ones that can make it go rancid), which is why it's important to store your grains correctly and use them within 6 months or so.

Refined grains (like white flour and white rice) have the germ and/or bran removed, giving them their light color, while whole grains have the germ, endosperm, and bran intact.

Tarhana

Tarhana is a soup mixture that hails from Turkey, made from a combination of grains, vegetables, pulses (edible seeds of legume plants), and yogurt that is fermented and then dried and powdered. It is then rehydrated into a nourishing soup. This recipe can be a jumping-off point for your own experimentation, and the flavor can be shifted to meet your needs and what you have on hand. The ingredients I list are commonly found in tarhana, but you may find that your version has more herbs, omits tomato, or something else.

I finely grind my tarhana powder after drying. This gives the soup a smoother texture and shorter cooking time.

—— Makes about 1 quart

- **6 cups plain Greek yogurt (without added thickeners) or strained homemade yogurt**
- **3–4 pounds fresh Roma tomatoes, diced**
- **3 large red bell peppers, diced**
- **3 cups roughly chopped fresh aromatic greens (my usual mixture is parsley, basil, scallions, oregano, and mint)**
- **2 cloves garlic, minced**
- **2 cups uncooked bulgur wheat**
- **2 cups dried chickpeas**
- **1 cup dried split peas**
- **¾ cup unrefined salt**
- **¾ cup all-purpose flour, plus more as needed**

1 Combine the yogurt, tomatoes, bell peppers, greens, garlic, bulgur, chickpeas, split peas, and salt in a large nonreactive bowl. Mash together with your hands to create a uniform mixture.

2 Sprinkle the flour over the mixture and mash again, thoroughly combining until you have a loose but cohesive mixture. (If your yogurt and veggies have a lot of liquid in them, the mixture may be watery. If so, just add a bit more flour.)

3 Cover the dough with a tea towel to keep out bugs and set it aside at room temperature to ferment, stirring daily, for 7 to 10 days. The finished dough should have a slightly sour but still pleasant smell. When it smells good to you, it's ready to go.

4 Roll the fermented dough into small balls about the size of a quarter, and place them on a parchment-lined baking sheet. Allow them to sit out in the hot sun until they begin to dry, about 12 hours. Turn the balls over and allow to continue drying until they feel dry to the touch, 12 to 24 hours longer. Bring inside overnight to avoid dampness from the night air, and place in a dry part of the house with good air circulation (it can help to point a fan on them). (Alternatively, you can dry them in a dehydrator set to 135°F/57°C, turning after 8 hours and checking them again after another 8 to 10 hours.)

5 Break the balls apart by hand. If you notice that the mixture still feels a bit wet, place it on a parchment-lined sheet and gently dry it in an oven on the lowest setting, or in a dehydrator set to 135°F/57°C. Note that most ovens do not go down to 135°F/57°C, which means that your oven-dried tarhana will not have active cultures. If you put it in the oven, be sure to check it regularly so it doesn't burn!

6 Grind the pieces using a food processor, a coffee grinder reserved for spices, or a mortar and pestle. You'll end up with a fragrant, nutritious dry soup powder. Store your powder in an airtight container at room temperature and use it within a month.

TO MAKE A BOWL OF SOUP:

1 Place the desired amount of tarhana in a bowl and sprinkle it with water (I usually use about 1 tablespoon tarhana per 1 cup of finished soup). Let it sit for about 1 hour.

2 Melt a little butter in a pan over medium heat. If desired, sauté veggies, like onion and bell pepper, and minced or finely diced beef in the butter. Then add the tarhana powder and cook for just 15 to 30 seconds.

(continued on next page)

Tarhana *continued*

3 Add about 1 cup stock or water and gently bring the resulting soup to a boil over medium heat (use more stock for thin soup and less for a thick and flavorful stew). For a thicker-bodied soup, whisk in a bit of tomato paste.

4 Garnish with chopped herbs, if desired, and serve hot.

FREEZING

You can freeze cooked grains in ziplock bags or airtight containers in the freezer. For best results, pack grains in a thin, flat layer in ziplock bags, press out all the air possible, and freeze flat for easier storage. Use within 3 months. Consider freezing grains in premeasured portions so you can easily add them to recipes.

For best texture, use frozen grains straight from the freezer. Thaw in the microwave in 30-second to 1-minute intervals until warmed through, or heat over low to medium-low on the stovetop until warmed through.

FERMENTING

Fermentation is my first port of call for just about any food, and grains are no different. Sometimes I make sour and funky wild-fermented beers, or bread, or Tarhana (page 325), or amazake or mirin (see page 330), but I also use fermentation to preserve food and cut down on food waste. And it's the perfect way to breathe new life into day-old bread.

PRESERVING BREAD

Fermenting grains into bread was (and is) one of our primary ways of turning these shelf-stable grains into nourishing food. Most breads are eaten fresh or relatively fresh, but bread will sometimes be kept as a ready-to-eat food, especially thin flatbreads or cracker/biscuit-type foods that have less moisture and thus can be stored longer without molding than a puffy, yeasted bread can (hardtack is an infamous example). Fermented breads and quickbreads are a cornerstone of many global diets, and there are many wonderful resources out there for exploring the magical world of bread (see a few in Resources, page 410).

The age-old question of what to do with stale bread challenges us to reduce food waste and stretch resources. Bread is often worked into other dishes as a way to solve this problem. Stews thickened with bread, like ribollita, as well as breadcrumbs or homemade croutons made from stale bread, are two well-known examples. Or you could try one of these recipes.

Bread Miso by Kirsten K. Shockey

The idea for this miso is to ferment stale bread, ends, crusts, and even slightly burnt toast (seriously!) into varieties a tasty paste. Use sourdough, rye bread, or your favorite bread. You can also mix different. Since you may not have enough bread at one time, you can also save your ends in an airtight container in the freezer until you are ready to make it.

It takes a bit of time for the bread to soak up the liquid, but don't be tempted to take a shortcut and use breadcrumbs; you'll have a better final texture using bread chunks. When I wait for the water to soak in and slowly hydrate the koji and bread, the whole thing is much tastier, with a smooth, pastelike consistency.

— Makes about 2½ cups

340 grams bread bits
170 grams rice koji (see Resources, page 410)
61 grams sea salt, plus more for packing in jar
2 cups water (boiled and cooled to around 100°F/38°C)

1 Prepare the bread by cutting it into crouton-size pieces and toasting it to a near char. When the bread has cooled, place it in a bowl and add the koji, salt, and water.

2 Massage it together and let it sit. It will take some time for the hard-toasted bread to hydrate. After an hour or so, massage again. When the mixture feels moist and the ingredients are well combined, it is ready to pack into a jar.

3 Using a bit of boiled water, cooled to handle, rinse the inside of your fermentation jar, making sure to coat all of the surface. Then sprinkle about 1 tablespoon of salt into the jar, coating the vessel's sides and bottom.

4 Spoon the mixture into your jar, removing as many air bubbles as possible.

5 Set a small piece of unbleached cotton cloth or parchment paper cut to fit the diameter of your vessel on top. Sprinkle about ½ tablespoon of salt along the edges of this cover to seal any gaps. Weight the miso as best you can with weights or a salt-filled plastic bag.

6 Cover the jar with cloth, securing it in place with a string. Set in a cool spot and allow it to ferment. Ferment for 6 months or more, but feel free to taste it much earlier.

7 When you are ready to harvest your miso, open it up. You may need to scrape off the top surface of the miso until you get to something that looks nice and rich in color. You can either strain off the tamari (the liquid pooling on the top of the miso) or you can mix it back into the miso and eat it as is. Your miso may be chunky; if you prefer a smoother paste, process it in a grinder or food processor. Store in an airtight container. The miso will keep indefinitely in the refrigerator.

Room to Experiment

This recipe gives measurements, but these are rooted in some general guidelines: I use 2 parts bread to 1 part koji and 12 percent salt, because I know it works and I am happy with the results. Feel free to play around with this a bit to suit your tastes, though I'd caution you to not go too low (much lower than 10 percent) on the salt—low salt levels can cause pathogen growth. Some folks even add a bit of their sourdough starter to the mix, though I haven't experimented with that yet. These pastes can be smooth and umami-rich or a little funky and yeasty, or lactic. It's all in controlling the ferment with salt, temperature, and time. (Hint: The lower the salt and the higher the moisture content, the more lactic and funky your miso will taste.)

Bread Miso

Beet Kvass

This Russian and eastern European beverage is a delicious, versatile health tonic. Kvass, or kvas, is typically made with beets (but you can also try adding in other root vegetables, like carrots or a bit of horseradish), and it traditionally includes bread, which makes it a really nice way to use up those last bits of bread you've got lying about. Kvass yields two products: the refreshing drink itself, plus lightly pickled vegetables that can be eaten fresh or added to dishes.

Beet Kvass

Kvass, which is slightly salty and sour, is also a great medium for pickling eggs (and beet kvass turns them a lovely pink color). Just pop peeled, hard-boiled eggs in kvass and let them sit in the fridge for a couple of days before enjoying. I've even used kvass in my pasta or potato boiling water to add some color (pink potatoes!) and flavor.

— Makes about 1½ quarts

- **3 beets, cut into large cubes**
- **½ cup cubed yeasted bread, or the equivalent size heel of bread (see note)**
- **2 teaspoons sea salt**
- **6 cups water**

NOTE: Toss in large chunks or slices of bread (rye bread tastes particularly delicious) to keep it from dissolving entirely as it ferments. If you don't eat gluten, you can omit the bread (I would not substitute gluten-free bread); without the bread, the kvass will ferment a bit more slowly, so add an extra day or two to the ferment time.

1. Combine the beets and bread in your fermentation vessel.
2. Make the brine: Add the salt and water to a small bowl and whisk to dissolve the salt. Pour the brine over the beets. Cover the jar with a towel or cheesecloth, secured with twine if needed.
3. Allow the kvass to ferment, gently stirring twice daily, until it is slightly tangy and sour and a deep purple-red hue, 1 to 2 days.
4. Strain and store in the fridge. Use within 2 weeks.

FERMENTED PORRIDGES

In the past, and in some places today, soaking and fermenting dried grains before cooking them into porridge was and is a common practice (sour porridges in various West African cultures are a good example).

If you're planning to cook porridge in bulk (say, to prep meals for the week), pre-fermenting the grains offers several benefits: It reduces cooking time and provides extra flavor and nutrients, and the grains will last a few days longer in the fridge.

I enjoy fermented porridge regularly. While I think it has the best texture when eaten soon after cooking, it will keep in the fridge, cooked, for a week or so. For most modern cooks with modern kitchens, fermenting porridge isn't a necessity for our daily lives, but in the past, it offered people a way to have a cook-and-go meal at the ready, with a shorter cooking time than unfermented grains. Porridges can be made of just about anything you want. Global porridge traditions are reflective of the grains eaten and grown more widely in a culture, including oatmeal in Scotland and millet in Senegal.

Fermenting Grains and Beans Before Cooking

For much of human history, preservation as a concept extended beyond just preserving food to resource preservation in general, including preserving cooking fuel. Pre-fermenting grains and beans allows the microbes to do a lot of the work for you in breaking down starches and softening the seeds, meaning the cook had to haul and use less precious water and fuel (and time) to prepare a meal. Today, we often take energy use for granted, but we'd do well to return to a holistic mindset of preservation and intentional consumption. Perhaps fermented grains could be a small part of this shift.

MIRIN (AND NOT-MIRIN) COOKING ALCOHOLS

Dried grains are shelf-stable for long periods, but once those grains are cooked, that's no longer true. So what do we do with the leftovers? In my ongoing search for ways to use up cooked grains, I've turned back to an old favorite: fermentation and infusing—in particular, making koji-based cooking alcohols.

Mirin is a seasoning made with white rice, koji, and a distilled alcohol called shochu. It is sometimes called rice cooking wine in Western supermarkets (though that's not technically accurate). Mirin is incredibly versatile, and there are several different kinds on the market today. But store-bought mirin has nothing on the homemade stuff. I definitely recommend making it yourself!

To make what I call "not-mirin," I use the same method as making mirin in small batches at home, but I apply it to a whole range of other grains. I often have lots of grain, and many different types of grains, in my house. Sometimes I get a bit overenthusiastic at the store and find that I have more amaranth, purple barley, or spelt than I can reasonably expect to use. Turning those grains into not-mirin is an unexpected way to use them, and each one offers its own unique flavor profile. Some are more pronounced, some more subtle, and some, like that purple barley, also impart a nice color. It won't taste like (and isn't) traditional mirin, but it's fun to experiment with this process.

A note about grain tenderness: Cook grains for not-mirin to an al dente sort of tenderness. They should each have a bit of bite left so they won't turn to total mush. It's not a huge deal if they do; you'll just be left with a cloudier final product.

You can also depart from traditional mirin by using different alcohols. Vodka is a good choice, since it's a neutral spirit, if shochu isn't available. I've tried bourbon before, too, and the results were tasty, but it was basically a flavor-packed bourbon for drinking rather than something I would use to season savory foods (it would be nice on desserts, though). If you have a spirit that you especially enjoy, this can be an interesting way to play around with it.

Basic Mirin/Not-Mirin Method

The mirin-making process is simple, and the product itself is leaps and bounds better than what you can find at a supermarket. Mirin uses white rice, and not-mirin uses other grains; both use the same process.

1 part prepared koji

1 part cooked grain

2 parts distilled alcohol such as shochu (the traditional choice) or vodka

1. Add the koji, grain, and alcohol to a screw-top bottle or jar, close the lid, and shake to combine.

2. Steep for 3 to 6 months at room temperature out of direct sunlight (I check and shake the jar about once a week).

3. Once it's ready, strain out the grains and store in an airtight container at room temperature, where it will last for at least several months.

VARIATION: MORNING OATS NOT-MIRIN

Usually, I make just enough morning oatmeal for one small bowl, but once in a while I get overzealous. If you find you have extra morning oatmeal (even loaded with cinnamon and sugar), you can cool it, then toss it in a jar with koji and vodka, using the ratios in the recipe above. Once it's ready, I find it to be an interesting seasoning to add to desserts or to dessert sauces like caramel. The spices mellow and shift, and it's more sweet-and-savory than purely sweet.

Legumes

While grains are often dried before use, this is not true for all legumes, which can be eaten fresh or dried. This chapter deals with *dried* (or prepared from dried) beans and legumes, or in other words, beans you rehydrate and cook. If you're working with fresh legumes like green beans, they're included in the Vegetables chapter (starting on page 103) since the techniques we use to prepare fresh beans and peas are closer to how we prepare fresh vegetables than their dried counterparts.

DRYING

Drying fresh legumes is a shelf-stable way to preserve them for cooking or, in the case of shell beans or peas, for future planting.

SHELL BEANS

When growing shell beans for drying, let them grow until the pods are brown and dried out. This ensures the beans inside are fully mature. Harvest before or between rainstorms, when the pods are dry, to prevent mold.

You can blanch and dehydrate shell beans for cooking (see page 332), though drying them as seeds is easier and results in both edible beans and viable seeds. To dry, spread out the pods in a single layer in a well-ventilated area and let dry for 2 to 4 weeks until beans are completely dried through. Doing this, rather than drying at higher heat in a dehydrator, helps preserve the enzymes that make for viable seeds.

Once dried, you can shell the beans by hand for small amounts, or thresh them if you're harvesting at scale. Label and store beans for planting as you would beans for eating. And if you're eating them, remember to save enough beans to plant next year. Store dried beans in an airtight container, like a mason jar, out of direct sunlight. Some people also freeze their beans to prevent rancidity (see page 13). Dried beans will last for about a year if kept away from heat, light, and moisture.

To dry green peas for eating later, shell the peas, then steam blanch for 3 minutes or water blanch for 2 minutes. Dry the peas for 8 to 10 hours

Ways to Preserve Legumes

	Shelf-stable	Fast	Low waste	Ready meals and ingredients	Big flavor
Tempeh (page 336)				X	X
Amino Sauces (page 337)				X	X
Tofu "Feta" with Mushroom Shio Koji (page 338)				X	X
White Miso (page 339)	X			X	X

in a dehydrator at 140°F/60°C until dried hard and wrinkled. Store in an airtight container out of direct sunlight, where they'll last for several months.

PEANUTS

If you grow fresh peanuts and don't plan to boil them right after harvesting, you can dry them for storage until you're ready to roast and serve them. Because peanuts are legumes, not tree nuts, they are preserved similarly to other legumes.

Peanuts can be dried shelled or unshelled, by spreading them out in a single layer on dehydrator trays and drying at 130°F/55°C until the shells have hardened enough to be brittle. The nuts themselves should be tender but not shriveled. Store dried peanuts at room temperature out of direct sunlight in an airtight container, where they will last for 2 months or more.

Historically and today, people cured, and still cure, peanuts by hanging the plants in a warm, dry place with low humidity (like a garden shed or a window). If the humidity is too high, the peanuts will rot rather than air-dry. And if exposed to sunlight, the peanuts might dry unevenly, so be sure to check and turn your drying plant as needed.

FREEZING

Freezing is one of the easiest ways to preserve your legumes, and you're probably already well versed in the magic of having frozen peas at the ready to toss into quick dinners for some extra bulk and nutrition. That same magic extends to legumes of all kinds; I typically freeze fresh beans as well as peas, so I have a variety of tastes and textures to choose from. Frozen legumes will keep for 2 months or more if properly stored.

PEAS

The way you process peas depends on their maturity.

For peas with flat pods, in which the inner pea has not yet developed, and for pods with small but not fully developed peas, trim the ends and cut the pods into pieces 2 to 4 inches long. Blanch them for 3 minutes (or 2 minutes, if the pods are very small and flat), then shock in an ice bath to cool (see page 17). Drain thoroughly. Pack them into ziplock bags or containers, leaving ½ inch of headspace. Or freeze in a single layer on a rimmed sheet pan until frozen through, then transfer to ziplock bags or containers, leaving no headspace.

For green peas that are mature (but not so old that they're starchy), shell the peas, blanch them for 1½ to 2 minutes (2½ minutes for larger peas), then shock and drain thoroughly. Pack and freeze them as instructed above.

For field peas or black-eyed peas, select tender, well-filled pods and shell them. Blanch the peas for 2 minutes, then shock and drain thoroughly. Pack and freeze them as instructed above.

SHELL BEANS

For fresh butter, pinto, lima, and other shell beans, harvest them while the seed is still in the green stage (not fully mature), and wash, shell, and sort the beans according to size. Blanch small beans for 2 minutes, medium beans for 3 minutes, and large beans for 4 minutes. Cool promptly and package, leaving ½ inch of headspace, and freeze. Or freeze in a single layer on a rimmed sheet pan until frozen through, then package leaving no headspace.

How to Boil Peanuts

1. Harvest or buy raw, fresh (green) peanuts. Scrub if needed to remove dirt.
2. Fill a pot with enough water to cover the peanuts by several inches. Add enough salt to make it as salty as the sea.
3. Bring the water to a boil. Add the raw green peanuts, shell on, with whatever spices you want.
4. Simmer the peanuts over low heat, covered, until tender, 5 to 8 hours.
5. Drain and enjoy while still hot.

COOKED BEANS AND PEAS

Once you've cooked your beans or peas into a soup (or just into a pot of beans), freezing them is one of the easiest ways to have ready meals for later.

If you want to freeze cooked beans to use as an ingredient later (say, cooked kidney beans for chili), let your beans cool to room temperature, then gently pat them dry. Then measure them out in 1- to 2-cup portions, place them in freezer-safe containers with 1 inch of headspace, and freeze. When using frozen cooked beans in other dishes, add them to liquid that is simmering (not boiling) to prevent splitting.

When freezing beans in broth or sauce, bean soups, and stocks, it's easiest to use ziplock bags (I rely on reusable silicone ones to minimize waste). Fill your bag, pressing out any air from the top before sealing completely. Label with ingredients and date, then lay flat on a rimmed sheet pan in the freezer. Once frozen, these flat bags stack easily.

BOILED PEANUTS

If you have leftover boiled peanuts from your last get-together (see sidebar), you can freeze them! Boiled peanuts are already cooked, so they don't need to be blanched. Just drain them very thoroughly. Freeze them in a single layer on a rimmed sheet pan before packing into airtight freezer-safe containers with no headspace, or pack into a container with ½ inch of headspace, then freeze.

FREEZING TOFU

I learned to properly freeze and thaw tofu from food writer Su-Jit Lin, who notes that you can freeze any firmness of tofu except silken. Freezing can open expansive new possibilities, as it removes some water from the tofu, making it denser and chewier than its nonfrozen counterparts. It's perfect for adding meaty texture to stir-fries, soups, and scrambles, or in place of meat in a sandwich.

Drain your water-packed tofu, then wrap in a clean kitchen towel or paper towels and gently squeeze out any excess liquid. You can freeze the tofu block as is, but for best results, cut tofu into cubes or strips, which makes it thaw faster. Place tofu in an airtight container with a bit of space between each piece. Or (my preference) freeze in a single layer on a sheet pan lined with a silicone mat for 4 to 6 hours or until frozen through, then transfer to an airtight container with no headspace. Tofu will last for several months in the freezer.

To thaw, simply place on a rimmed plate or in a bowl in the refrigerator for several hours, or place in warm water to thaw more quickly. Then gently press out any excess water before using.

CANNING

Canned beans are a great ready-to-go ingredient, saving the steps of soaking and cooking beans each time you're making a meal. If you grow and use lots of beans, it can make sense to consolidate your efforts by canning, saving you time and energy later on.

Pressure Canning Fresh Shell Beans and Field Peas

Fresh peas, including black-eyed peas and field peas, can be pressure canned as a ready-to-go ingredient later. So can fresh lima beans, which are perfect for wintertime soups.

1 Place jars in your pressure canner and heat it up. Then, using tongs, remove the hot jars from the canner.

2 Hot pack or raw pack your jars:

TO HOT PACK: Add shelled peas or fresh beans to a pot, add boiling water to cover, and boil for 3 minutes. Loosely pack peas into hot jars (reserve your hot cooking liquid), leaving 1 inch of headspace. Add salt if you wish: ½ teaspoon to pints and 1 teaspoon to quarts. Fill the jars with hot cooking liquid, leaving 1 inch of headspace.

TO RAW PACK: Pack the shelled raw peas or beans into jars loosely, without pressing, leaving 1 inch of headspace for pints and 1½ inches of headspace for quarts. For large lima beans or other large beans like butterbeans, leave 1¼ inch of headspace for quarts.

Add salt if you wish: ½ teaspoon to pints and 1 teaspoon to quarts. Fill the jars with boiling water, leaving 1 inch of headspace.

3 Run a chopstick or other thin, nonmetal utensil along the inner edges of the jars to release any air bubbles. Wipe the rims of the jars with a clean, damp cloth. Add the lids and bands and screw down to hand tightness.

4 Set your pressure canner at 10 pounds pressure (weighted gauge) or 11 pounds pressure (dial gauge) and process pints for 40 minutes and quarts for 50 minutes, adjusting for altitude (see page 39) if needed.

5 Allow the canner to depressurize completely. Let the jars cool for 24 hours before testing the seals (see page 40), then store out of direct sunlight at room temperature.

Pressure Canning Fresh Green or English Peas

1 Place jars in your pressure canner and heat it up. Then, using tongs, remove the hot jars from the canner.

2 Hot pack or raw pack your jars:

TO HOT PACK: Add the peas to a pot with water to cover, bring to a rolling boil, and boil for 2 minutes. Spoon the peas into hot jars without pressing down, leaving 1 inch of headspace. Add salt if desired: ½ teaspoon to pints and 1 teaspoon to quarts. Add the hot cooking liquid to cover, leaving 1 inch of headspace.

(continued on next page)

Pressure Canning Fresh Green or English Peas *continued*

TO RAW PACK: Pack your shelled raw peas into jars loosely, without pressing down, and add salt (the same ratios as above), if desired. Add boiling water to cover, leaving 1 inch of headspace.

3 Run a chopstick or other thin, nonmetal utensil along the inner edges of the jars to release any air bubbles. Wipe the rims of the jars with a clean, damp cloth. Add the lids and bands and screw down to hand tightness.

4 Set your pressure canner at 10 pounds pressure (weighted gauge) or 11 pounds pressure (dial gauge) and process pints or quarts for 40 minutes, adjusting for altitude (see page 39) if needed.

5 Allow the canner to depressurize completely. Let the jars cool for 24 hours before testing the seals (see page 40), then store out of direct sunlight at room temperature.

Pressure Canning Bean Soups

1 Select, wash, and prepare vegetables, meat, and seafoods as described for the specific foods. Cover the meat with water and cook until tender, then cool and remove bones. Cook the vegetables. For each cup of dried beans or peas, add 3 cups of water, boil for 2 minutes, remove from the heat, soak for 1 hour, and heat to a boil. Drain and combine with the meat broth, tomatoes, or water to cover. Boil for 5 minutes. Caution: Do not thicken. Salt to taste, if desired.

2 Meanwhile, as you cook the soup, place jars in your pressure canner and heat it up. Then, using tongs, remove the hot jars from the canner.

3 Once you're ready to can, fill hot jars halfway with the solid mixture. Add the remaining liquid, leaving 1 inch of headspace. Run a chopstick or other thin, nonmetal utensil along the inner edges of the jars to release any air bubbles. Wipe the rims of the jars with a clean, damp cloth. Add the lids and bands and screw down to hand tightness.

4 Set your pressure canner at 10 pounds pressure (weighted gauge) or 11 pounds pressure (dial gauge) and process pints for 60 minutes and quarts for 75 minutes, adjusting for altitude (see page 39) if needed.

5 Allow the canner to depressurize completely. Let the jars cool for 24 hours before testing the seals (see page 40), then store out of direct sunlight at room temperature.

A few notes:

- If your soup contains seafood, *it must be canned for 100 minutes rather than the times listed above*—yes, even if it's mostly vegetables with just a few pieces of shrimp thrown in.
- Canning thick, dense soups is unwise for the same reason it's not safe to can squash butters (page 33): The mixture is simply too thick for the heat from canning to penetrate effectively. Make sure to *not* thicken your soup before canning. If you happen to step away for a bit and it thickens, simply cool and freeze it instead.
- This is the tip of the iceberg for prepared bean meals made in a pressure canner. The USDA and University of Georgia Cooperative Extension also offer recipes for canning beans in tomatoes and molasses for classic baked beans, for example.

Preserving Around the World

England and Denmark, with Chef Matthew Parker

Matthew Francis Parker is a chef and rescued food preserver based in rural Denmark, where he operates Kiosken på Odden, a natural wine, cheese, and deli shop that features products from culinary artisans from across Europe, including his own in-house preserves made largely from food that otherwise might be thrown out by local farmers and producers. As an Englishman living abroad, his food-preserving practice is informed by all the places he's called home.

"I will always have an intrinsic love and respect for British traditions of cooking, preserving, and fermenting," he says, and he's expanded on that experience through training in Chinese, South Korean, and Japanese culinary traditions, as well as a move abroad. Today he blends his culinary training and his cultural background "as a way to be creative in my own explorations and processes."

How does this inspire his own preserving life? His most common preserving technique is lactofermentation: "I love to use the resources within my local ecology and live close to the sea, so I collect beautiful, clean seawater (à la Pascal Baudar) and use it as my brine for my lacto-based ferments," he says. He also plays with vinegars and with koji, using locally sourced grains and pulses as well as excess bread and other rescued food.

Like many preservers through the centuries, Parker uses what's around him. "I have found that when I feel my most creative and inspired is when I limit my larder to what I can source directly from my surroundings. . . . Taking this local produce and experimenting with it in interesting ways, using my broad culinary interests and background to preserve them, translates so much into the products that I create." And while he shapes the place he lives with the products he creates, place shapes him, too: Since moving to Denmark in 2019, his preserved food intake has increased dramatically, including pickles as a side to meals and sweet preserves with breakfast. Plus he has made a variety of preserved herring and whole grain, dark, and sour rye bread.

"Before I moved here, I had no real food-preserving traditions. My time, money, and resources were limited to a small apartment in London," he says. Life was about survival, plus long hours in the service industry. But all that has changed: Now his local community engages in existing preserving traditions and develops new ones all their own. Autumn apples are preserved into cider, and mackerel breeding season is a chance to catch and preserve fish.

"I perpetually wonder, how can I positively engage with and secure this indispensable, intangible cultural heritage preservation within my own community and share this knowledge with a wider audience of interested parties?"

For Parker, food preserving is a way of life, one he hopes to continue sharing through everything from artist residencies to public education. And it's all about a shift in lifestyle and perspective that offers rich rewards. "It takes us all a consistent dedication, year on year, maintaining the energy and enthusiasm to continue the craft of preserving," he notes. There are practical considerations, like what to harvest and preserve when, plus the creative side: recipe development, research, and documenting processes, and ensuring processes like foraging are sustainable over the long term.

The value of this work is more than monetary: "The modern world is mainly capitalist, largely monocultured, and trend driven. The globalized societies that most of us live in, where convenience is king, have not been created by us; rather, they have been imposed on us. Anarchism through the free transit of knowledge and community building through intangible cultural preservation is an integral part of empowering ourselves within our own societies."

FERMENTING

Fermentation, my favorite way to play with preserving beans and grains, produces delicious, versatile results.

Tempeh

I originally developed this tempeh recipe for Joe Yonan's *Mastering the Art of Plant-Based Cooking*, a book that has quickly become a treasure in my kitchen. Tempeh is from Indonesia and is traditionally made with soybeans. However, you can experiment with versions made with whatever beans you like (my hands-down favorite is black-eyed peas). Tempeh is also a great way to use up cooked beans; however, ones that are overly salted or made with fats may not work as well.

Tempeh requires a thermophilic (heat-loving) starter, *Rhizopus oryzae*, which grows between 85 and 91°F/29 and 32°C. I make this with the oven off and pilot light on (or the oven light, if using an electric oven). Some people use bread-proofing boxes or improvised insulated chambers (like a cooler filled with water and a sous vide set to 85 to 90°F/29 to 32°C, in which you float a pan of water with your tempeh). If you make yours in the oven like I do, make sure no one else in the house is using the oven: I leave a little sticky note on the oven controls so I remember not to turn it on while my tempeh ferments.

— Makes four 8-ounce blocks

- **1 pound dried soybeans or your bean of choice (about 2½ cups), soaked 8 to 12 hours and drained**
- **2½ tablespoons distilled white vinegar or apple cider vinegar**
- **1 teaspoon powdered tempeh starter (see Resources, page 410)**
- **6 large banana leaves, or 2 or 3 quart-size ziplock bags or parchment paper (see note)**

NOTE: Tempeh is traditionally fermented wrapped in banana leaves, which help regulate moisture and temperature, but you can also use ziplock bags with a few holes punched in them (I love reusable silicone bags as a lower-waste option), or parchment paper.

1. In a Dutch oven or large saucepan, combine the soybeans with enough water to cover by 2 inches, or use a pressure cooker and cover them with 4 inches of water.

2. On the stovetop, bring the soybeans to a boil, reduce the heat to medium-low, and cook until very tender (they should squish easily when gently pressed between your fingers), up to 3 hours. If using a pressure cooker, cook them on high pressure for 45 minutes, then let the pressure naturally release. (The cook time will vary depending on the age and variety of the beans, so if necessary, return them to pressure and continue cooking in 5- to 10-minute increments, using manual release, until they are tender.)

3. Drain the beans, reserving the cooking water, and let cool to just above room temperature.

4. **Optional:** For a smoother-textured final product, gently rub the beans between your hands to remove their skins. Don't worry about getting all of them; just pick out the skins that come off easily.

5. Transfer your beans to a large bowl and toss them with the vinegar and tempeh starter until evenly coated.

6. **If using banana leaves:** Cut four of the leaves in half on either side of the thick vein running down the middle, and compost the vein. (Reserve the other two banana leaves in case any tear.) Divide the beans between the banana-leaf halves, spreading them into the center and folding the leaf edges over to make packets. Secure these with twine.

   If using ziplock bags: Divide your beans among the bags. Press out the air as best you can, seal the zipper, and fold the top half of the bag down so all of your beans are in the bottom. Using a skewer or the tip of a paring knife, poke four to six holes in each bag.

   If using parchment: Divide beans among squares of parchment, folding the edges over and pressing out the air. Using a skewer or the tip of a paring knife, poke four to six holes in each packet.

7 Place your leaves, bags, or packets on a perforated sheet pan, a small cooling rack, or the rack of a roasting pan. This helps air circulate around your tempeh more evenly and keeps it from getting soggy.

8 Make sure your oven is off and cooled. Place the pan of tempeh on the top rack closest to the oven light. (If you have a gas oven with no oven light, place the pan on the bottom rack closest to the pilot light.)

9 After 24 hours, check on the tempeh: You want to see a bit of light, fuzzy growth, which means the spores are multiplying. You should also check moisture and adjust the temperature. Make sure the bottom of the tempeh isn't soggy; if it is, set it on a wire rack or another perforated pan to allow for more air circulation. And now's the time to move it away from the heat source a bit, to the center rack, so it doesn't overheat as the spores continue to multiply.

10 Let the tempeh sit undisturbed for another 24 hours, or until it has a clear white mat of mold around it and it holds its shape firmly. Refrigerate in an airtight container for up to 2 weeks or freeze for up to 4 months.

Tempeh

Amino Sauces

Amino sauces are simply a flavorful mixture of legumes, koji, flavorings, and salt. The method is similar to making shoyu (soy sauce); however, while traditional shoyu uses only soybeans and wheat, amino sauces can use other beans and grains. Also unlike shoyu, in which the legumes are inoculated with koji before being made into sauce, this amino sauce recipe uses koji grains directly in the sauce itself and is fermented for a shorter period.

The best thing about amino sauces is that you can make a whole range of interesting flavor combinations. I make one with green peanuts and all the seasonings I normally put in boiled peanuts. You can even add fruit—persimmon and red bean is a particular recent favorite—but keep in mind that fruit (and any other flavorings with natural sugars) can invite other microbes and additional water to the party, so keep an eye on how the flavors develop as the sauce ages. Use amino sauces anywhere you'd like a savory kick—marinades, dressings, sauces, soups, even baked goods.

— Makes ½–1 pint

1½–2 cups nuts or cooked, cooled beans
3–3½ tablespoons unrefined salt (see note)
1½ tablespoons dried koji
Flavorings (optional)

NOTE: Amino sauces require more salt than lactoferments because they're fermenting for a longer period. The salt should comprise around 10 percent of the solution.

1 Combine the nuts, salt, koji, and flavorings (if using) in a pint jar. Add enough water to fill the jar. Tighten the lid and shake to dissolve the salt.

2 Allow the mixture to ferment at room temperature, shaking daily. Check it regularly for kahm yeast (a white film that won't hurt you or your ferment) and scrape off any that you see. How long you let it ferment is up to you.

(continued on next page)

Amino Sauces *continued*

3 When the ferment achieves a taste and smell that you like, use it! I'll sometimes let an amino sauce age on the counter for 1 month and then age it in the fridge for many more months. Other times, I let it ferment entirely at room temperature for many months, provided that it continues to taste and smell good.

4 I tend to store these experimental amino sauces in the fridge once they reach the desired flavor. At room temperature, their flavor shifts can be more variable than traditional shoyu, which is historically stored at room temperature and keeps a more stable flavor. But this version should keep in the fridge for years.

Tofu "Feta" with Mushroom Shio Koji

If you get in the habit of making Shio Koji (page 74) regularly, this particular dish is easy to make when you have some tofu to use up. If you're vegan or lactose intolerant and miss feta cheese, this salty, slightly crumbly, savory option may be the answer for you. The saltiness soaks all the way through the tofu, so it really mimics feta cheese. And it shifts the texture a bit, too, pulling just enough moisture from the tofu that it crumbles nicely.

I add mushrooms because their savoriness combined with the shio koji packs a one-two punch for mimicking cheesy and meaty flavors in vegan feta. I use winecap mushrooms when I have them, but crimini, sliced portabello, or other full-flavored mushrooms will work well, too. If you don't have or don't like mushrooms, you can leave them out and still end up with a delicious vegan cheese.

— Makes 1 pound

- **2 cups koji**
- **2 cups water**
- **4 tablespoons unrefined salt**
- **½ pound full-flavored mushrooms, sliced ½ inch thick (optional)**
- **16 ounces firm or extra-firm tofu, cubed**

1 Begin by fermenting the shio koji: Combine the koji, water, salt, and mushrooms (if using) in a quart jar. Put on the lid and let the mixture ferment at room temperature for 1 to 2 weeks, stirring or shaking daily and burping the jar as needed.

2 Once the shio koji is ready, put the tofu in another quart jar, add shio koji to cover, place the jar the fridge, and allow it to sit for 8 to 12 hours.

3 Give the tofu a taste and see if you like the flavor. If it doesn't seem salty/savory enough, let it keep going up to 24 hours (or longer, if needed).

Using Your Shio Koji

Don't throw away the shio koji after you use it to make feta! You can use it to marinate other things, too, after straining out the tofu. Shio koji adds some nice depth to soups and stocks and marinades for just about anything (just adjust for salt accordingly).
If you eat meat and dairy, it's nice for marinating chicken or halloumi cheese (be careful how long you leave it on your halloumi, which already is a bit salty) or for veggies. The strained liquid is also nice in sauces and baked goods.

4 Carefully scoop your tofu feta out of the shio koji and store it in an airtight container in the fridge; use within 1 week. The marinated mushrooms can also be diced up and used as a salty, savory addition to dishes.

White Miso

I wrote this recipe for Joe Yonan's *Mastering the Art of Plant-Based Cooking*, and it's an easy, accessible entry point to miso making.

For this recipe, I use prepared rice koji, since it's often easiest to source in local markets and works well for beginners. Traditionally, miso is made by growing koji directly on the substrate (the soybeans) then grinding this into a paste and fermenting, which you can also do if you prefer.

— Makes about 1 quart

1 cup dried soybeans (to yield roughly 2 cups cooked beans), soaked 8 to 12 hours and drained

2 cups rice or barley koji (see Resources, page 410)

5 tablespoons fine sea salt, plus extra for sprinkling and more as needed

1 In a Dutch oven or large saucepan, combine the soybeans with enough water to cover by 2 inches, or use an Instant Pot or other pressure cooker and cover them with 4 inches of water. On the stovetop, bring the soybeans to a boil, reduce the heat to medium-low, and cook until very tender (they should squish easily when gently pressed between your fingers), up to 3 hours. If using an Instant Pot or other pressure cooker, cook them on high pressure for 45 minutes, then let the pressure naturally release. (The cook time will vary depending on the age and variety of the beans, so if necessary, return them to pressure and continue to cook in 5- to 10-minute increments, using manual release, until very tender.)

2 Drain the beans, reserving the cooking water, and let them cool to room temperature.

3 Transfer the beans to a food processor and add the koji and salt. Process until they form a thick paste. If it's too dry to form a dense ball without cracking, add a bit more cooking water.

4 Pack the soybean mixture into a clean glass jar or jars using the back of a clean spoon or ladle, pressing down after each addition to remove any air bubbles. Leave about 2 inches of headspace at the top of the jars so the miso and liquid don't leak out.

5 Cut a piece of cheesecloth slightly larger than the mouth of the jar, fold over the edges, and place it directly on top of the soybean mixture. Next, sprinkle a thin layer of salt on top of the cheesecloth, paying special attention to spread it all the way to the edges of the soybean mixture. This helps keep unwanted molds from growing on top. Place a fermentation weight on top of the salt and seal the jar with a lid.

6 Check the miso every few days, looking for signs of unwanted mold growth or large air pockets. If you find a fuzzy white mold, scrape it off and sprinkle on a bit more salt. If you find colorful or black mold, it's safest to toss the miso and try again. If you find that the miso is bubbling away and forming large air pockets, it can be helpful to press it down again with a clean utensil, then reapply the cheesecloth, salt, and weight. Don't worry if a small amount of caramel-colored liquid floats to the top: This is tamari, a wonderful seasoning that you can use like light soy sauce. Don't throw it away!

7 After 2 to 3 weeks, taste the miso. If you're happy with the flavor, it's done fermenting and is ready to use. If it still tastes like beans and not quite like miso paste yet, it needs more time. Continue to taste it once a week until it is ready.

8 To store: Refrigerate miso for up to 6 months. Refrigerate the tamari separately for up to 4 months.

Pickled Shrimp
(page 381)

CHAPTER 9

Dairy, Meat, Seafood, and Eggs

Dairy	342	Seafood	375
Meat and Poultry	360	Eggs	387

Shoyuzuke Eggs
(page 390)

Animal proteins require a bit of a different approach than fruits and vegetables. Because of their protein and fat content, they react differently to various preservation techniques, and not every technique (like hot water bath canning) is safe. Preserving proteins can feel intimidating to many new home preservers because of the risk of spoilage or illness. Don't be afraid! Start with something simple that is easy to tell if you've done it right (like making jerky, freezing stock, or making fresh cheese), then move on to other projects as you gain confidence.

Dairy

We don't know who the first cheesemaker was, but they were probably an accidental one. The same is true for yogurt. As legend has it, a Neolithic traveler in the Fertile Crescent carried milk in an animal skin to drink as they traveled. The hot sun, plus the microbes on the animal skin, made for a pleasantly sour result: in other words, the first yogurt.

Fermented dairy encompasses many different tastes, textures, and even colors, from yogurt to butter to cheese, and many more besides. We see dairy fermentation in various yogurt-making traditions in eastern Europe and the Middle East, in the dizzying numbers of cheeses and cultured butters at our disposal, and in more historic forms like bog butter—butter that was put in a peat bog, sometimes thousands of years ago, to be preserved and then forgotten about. (I say this in every book I write, but I'll say it here, too: It's one of my life's missions to sample bog butter. If you give me even a small taste of bog butter, you will have a friend for life.)

While the animal-skin yogurt story is romantic, the truth is that dairy preservation was probably born of experiments in multiple places where livestock were kept, out of a need to preserve this very quick-to-spoil food. But maybe the animal skin full of yogurt was a happy accident among those experiments—the two aren't mutually exclusive.

We now have many simple ways to preserve milk for longer than our ancestors could, including just sticking it in the fridge (or freezing it). But if you want it to last for longer than the expiration date on the carton, or you really relish experimentation like I do, dairy fermentation can be a fruitful, joyful playground. In this section, I outline a few of my favorite techniques and recipes.

FREEZING

Dairy may not be the first thing that springs to mind when you think of freezer-friendly foods, but in many cases you can freeze it, depending on what kind of dairy product you have and how you plan to use it later.

CHEESE

Can you freeze cheese? The answer is, perhaps frustratingly, "It depends." Soft, unaged cheeses like goat cheese and cream cheese tend to do alright with freezing, maintaining their flavor and texture, but keeping air away from them is important to preserving their quality. Pack soft, unaged cheeses in freezer-safe containers with no headspace, pressing down to release as many pockets of air as possible. This works best in smaller containers, like 4-ounce Tupperware, rather than in larger containers like pint jars. Top with the lid and freeze.

Some other more firm unaged cheeses, like paneer, often freeze well, too: Follow the instructions for hard cheeses here.

Aged soft cheeses, like Brie, and washed rind cheeses, like Taleggio, should never be frozen. However, aged hard cheeses can be frozen; they do best when wrapped very tightly to prevent freezer burn. You can vacuum seal your cheese, then freeze it, or wrap it tightly in plastic wrap or beeswax wrap and store it in zippered freezer bags, pressing out as much air as possible before sealing.

Cheese can be stored in the freezer for up to 6 months.

CHEESE RINDS

Freezing rinds from your hard cheeses, like parmesan, once you've grated out their delicious innards, is an absolute must-do for homemade soup and stock aficionados. Simply pop your rinds in a freezer-safe container as you go through them.

Ways to Preserve Dairy

	Shelf-stable	Fast	Low waste	Ready meals and ingredients	Big flavor
Basic Fresh Cheese (page 349)		X		X	
Halloumi (page 349)				X	X
Paneer (page 350)				X	X
Ricotta (page 351)			X	X	X
Cream Cheese (page 351)				X	X
Basic Yogurt (page 356)				X	X
Basic Cultured Butter and Buttermilk (page 358)				X	X
Lavender Caramels (page 360)				X	X

Pull one out as needed to plunge into your stock or soup as it cooks, which imparts a rich, cheesy depth to whatever you're making.

BUTTER

The length of time you can freeze butter depends on its salt content: Salted butter can be frozen for 6 months, but unsalted butter only lasts in the freezer for 3 months. You can cut butter directly from frozen to use in cooking, if desired.

MILK AND CREAM

It is possible to freeze milk and cream, but freezing does change the texture somewhat. Freeze heavy cream in an airtight container for up to 2 months; once thawed, it will no longer whip well, but it can still be used in small amounts in sauces or in frozen desserts.

Milk can be frozen for 3 months and added to recipes when thawed, though it's not as pleasant for drinking as fresh, unfrozen

Natural Cheesemaking

David Asher has devoted his life to natural cheesemaking, authoring books and teaching classes to connect people to the powerful transformative process of turning milk into cheese. Milk becomes its best and fullest self through fermentation, a process it naturally wants to engage in. "Keeping milk as milk is actually a really challenging thing to do," Asher says, "and it goes against nature to do so—milk is meant for greater things; it's meant to transform to cheese." Depending on how you handle this one simple ingredient, you can transform it in a thousand different ways:

> Anything is possible: We don't typically understand that about milk, cheese, and fermentation. We think you have to be in this part of the world to make this style of cheese, or that part of the world to make that type of cheese. You know you can't make a Camembert if you're in Normandy, but milk is capable of making these extraordinary transformations anywhere, as long as origins are respected. And if the cheese is made right, the cheese tastes right. It evolves the right way.

In cheesemaking, it's all about creating the right environment: When you create the right circumstances, you get extraordinary results, and you don't need to be in a specific location or in a hyper-sterile modern facility (remember, people have been making cheeses for thousands of years). Cheesemaking also teaches us that mistakes aren't always a bad thing:

> Every cheese that exists out there, every cheese that has been invented, has probably been a mistake. Somebody did something "wrong," they forgot about the cheese overnight and it fermented, it developed acidity and then the next day the cheesemaker came back to the curd, and it was forgotten about and over-fermented, but they tasted it and it was yogurt that had transformed through this inherent microbiological transformation into something more amazing than it was before. Cheese is capable of miraculous transformation, as is any fermentation, as are ourselves.

milk. Freezing milk can sometimes result in separation: If this happens, just give it a stir before adding to a recipe.

Milk and cream should both be thawed in the refrigerator.

CHEESEMAKING

Cheesemaking, and dairy fermentation in general, have a long history. Milk is harder to keep fresh for any period than it is to ferment, and so we started fermenting milk pretty early on (2000 BCE, according to Sumerian clay tablets, but dairy fermentation almost certainly started earlier). The first batches were probably happy accidents, and the type of milk used depended on what animals were around (camels, goats, etc.). Milk naturally wants to become cheese, and while the particulars of cheesemaking can go in many directions, at its most basic the process is quite easy.

Cheese, made from curdling and then straining milk, sometimes pressing the curds (and sometimes aging them or treating them in various ways—more on that later!) is one example of fermented milk. But yogurt and cultured butter are, too. Both offer ways to make milk last longer. Butter was often stored in cool places, from root cellars to peat bogs, which kept it cool and helped keep it from going rancid for a longer period.

Using up whey from cheesemaking is an important part of the preserving process, too, as whey accounts for 85 to 90 percent of the original volume of milk. It's filled with nutrients and is a versatile ingredient in its own right. Learn how to use whey on page 355.

MAKING YOUR OWN CHEESE

There are as many ways to make cheese as there are grains of sand on a beach: Local tradition and terroir, access to ingredients, personal preferences, and more all factor into making each cheese unique.

Fresh cheese, at its most basic (see page 349) is very simple, as are many of the things you can do with it after. You start with a milk (cow, goat, sheep, etc.) and rennet or an acid (lemon juice, vinegar, etc.), and from there the world is your cheesemaking oyster. Certain types of cheeses require certain starters or preparations, but you get to know their particularities and preferences the more you make them. The big thing is to try it and have fun, and to enjoy the process as well as the product.

Dairy That Doesn't Freeze Well

Yogurt, sour cream, and buttermilk, all of which are acidic, do not preserve their texture well with freezing.

So how does frozen yogurt work, then? The answer is that it has added sugar and other ingredients to give it a palatable texture and flavor, and frozen yogurt is typically churned to keep ice crystals small. Plus it's served frozen, eliminating the problem of thawing it to find a less-than-delicious mess.

RENNET AND BEYOND: MANY WAYS TO CURDLE CHEESE

At the core of cheesemaking is the need to curdle the milk and to separate the curds (solids) from whey (liquid). There are many methods of curdling. Rennet, made from enzymes typically found in a ruminant animal's stomach, is commonly used in cheesemaking, as it contains enzymes as well as acidity to support proper curdling and texture, but you can also make some cheeses (like my Basic Fresh Cheese, page 349) using another acid like vinegar. If you're a vegetarian, curdling fresh cheeses with vinegar/acid only or making Yogurt Cheese (page 352) or milk kefir cheese (page 352) are good options for enjoying the magic of cheesemaking without rennet.

Other acids will curdle milk but won't coagulate or thicken the curds as effectively as rennet. But cheesemaking is all about making cheese your own, so experiment with the ingredients you want to use and tinker with them as you need. You can also look to the wide world of fermentation history and to your own stores of ferments: Thistle and nettle were used in Scotland and Ireland prior to Roman occupation, for example, to coagulate and thicken milk, and some cheesemakers still use them today.

The brine from recent lactoferments can be used to flavor and culture butter (see page 358) or to add flavor and a microbial community to your cheese. Homemade vinegar can be used in place of store-bought, and you can also make yogurt cheeses by straining yogurt until very thick. Claudia Lucero, Cheesy Experience Officer at Urban Cheesecraft in Portland, Oregon, says, "Each acid will add a flavor. I like to match the acid to the final use of the cheese. My favorite pairings are yogurt whey for paneer, apple cider vinegar for queso blanco, and lemon juice for ricotta. You can also use citric acid, which doesn't give much flavor."

Many of my fermenting friends also make a more passive cheese using milk kefir grains. Milk kefir (a fermented milk drink similar to

Seasonal Protein

You may not think of them as seasonal like fruits and vegetables, but animal products are seasonal, too. Historically, and in some communities today, seasons are a critical factor in the availability of animal proteins, and how you preserve your food is impacted by how long you'll need to be eating it.

Animals give birth in spring, giving us dairy and springtime foods like lamb, and any larger adult animals (like cattle) are often slaughtered in fall to reduce competition for limited wintertime supplies of feed. Their meat is then preserved to last through winter.

Chickens, ducks, and other birds also reproduce with seasonal cycles. Hens are most likely to go broody and hatch their eggs in spring or summer. Eggs themselves are seasonal: Hens begin laying with the sunlight of longer days in early spring, then stop laying in fall when the days grow shorter, reserving their energy in winter to stay warm in colder months.

Eggs found in grocery stores during winter are from hens who have been exposed to artificial sunlight, which tricks their bodies into continuing to lay eggs after their internal compass has said it's time to stop, and which reduces their quality of life considerably. But since most modern people don't think of eggs as seasonal food, they probably don't realize that year-round laying isn't a part of the hen's natural physiology.

Protein preservation is another example of our ingenuity in storing food supplies for later. And learning how to preserve proteins when you have them helps you live more seasonally, and to source from seasonal producers (like your local farmers' market). It also results in delicious products from cheese to pickled eggs to charcuterie and beyond.

thin yogurt) naturally separates if left out long enough, and you can strain off the solids (just fish out the grains to use in your next kefir batch) to make a tangy fresh cheese without having to heat and separate milk.

Most styles of renneted cheese are made by warming then culturing the milk with either a mesophilic or thermophilic starter (see page 354), then adding rennet and allowing it to curdle, cutting and stirring the curds before they form, straining, and salting the cheese. Some include additional steps like washing the rinds, cooking the curds longer, pressing, or aging. Again, it's beautiful to explore all cheese has to offer; see page 413 to dive into cheesemaking resources.

CHEESEMAKING BEST PRACTICES

The specifics differ depending on the type of cheese you're making, but there are a few universal basics to consider: Milk quality (use the best and most local you can), heat, and acidity. Lucero encourages her cheesemaking students to remember, "Although it may not look like the cheese you aimed to make, it is likely still a valid cheese somewhere in the world!" Embracing the process is part of the fun, and she adds,

> Cheesemaking is a craft, and it is not always predictable even for experienced professionals. So the biggest mistake is to expect to be a skilled artisan on your first try. If you successfully separated curds from whey, you made cheese! Drain the curds, add salt and herbs to taste, and celebrate your rustic cheese. Beyond that, practice lots to get familiar with all the factors that have to line up just right for the end goal. Then you can skillfully adjust the factors for more predictable results.

There are a few best practices, too: The first is cleanliness. Sterilize equipment to prevent cross contamination and use clean, new cheesecloth. Though, in cheesemaking as in life, there are exceptions to every rule, and around the world you'll find cheesemakers working with established microbial colonies in containers and in wrappings (like leaves) to give their cheese certain effects and protect against pathogen growth. This is a very deep rabbit hole to explore, but whether you wrap your cheese in leaves or eat it fresh, keep your utensils and cooking pots clean so you're only introducing the microbes you want.

Fermenter Annie Simpkins also recommends good recordkeeping with cooking times, aging times, temperatures, and pH so that if your cheese turns out very well, you can repeat what you did.

An Ancient Art for Modern Times

Cheesemaking can offer you a lifetime of experimentation in different styles, preparations, and aging processes. It gives us the opportunity to explore traditions from around the world and adapt those traditions to the places we live and the ingredients we have available.

You might try wrapping your fresh cheese in foraged edible leaves, like grape leaves, or you might experiment with pressing and aging it in different conditions. You might find you love making fresh yogurt cheeses simply by straining your fresh Greek yogurt until very thick. Or you might love to age your cheese for months or even years. To dive down that rabbit hole yourself, check out the cheesemaking books in Resources on page 413.

Learn what environment your style of cheese thrives in. (If you're using a cheesemaking kit, follow the instructions; if you're making it up as you go, take a peek at recipes for similar kinds of cheeses for inspiration.) Lucero says, "Each style of cheese will have its own requirements regarding temperature, acidity, humidity levels."

Fresh ingredients are critical, and local is best. Cheesemaking offers a chance to play with what's already around you (like fresh or dried herbs from your garden, and, of course, dairy) and use it to create a practice all your own.

FRESH CHEESES

Fresh cheeses, made with either rennet and/or an acid like vinegar or lemon juice, encompass a wide variety of possibilities, from paneer to cottage cheese to halloumi and beyond. Here are a few basic versions of fresh cheeses, all of which will last in the fridge for about 5 days, though in some cases, like halloumi packed in brine (see page 349), it can last longer.

This basic process of curdling milk and straining the curds from the whey is at the core of all cheesemaking: Make sure to check out the cheesemaking resources on page 413 for more. To order rennet and other cheesemaking supplies, see the supplier list on page 410.

Why Cheesemakers Love Cheese

To inspire you on your journey, I asked some of my cheesemaking friends why cheesemaking has captured their hearts and shaped how they cook and eat.

Cheesemaking feels less intimidating when we remember what a natural process it is. Claudia Lucero says, "Milk wants to become cheese! When you provide the right conditions, like warmth, for example, milk just starts the process. Our job is to guide this process along in a way that rewards us with delicious results." Kat Kocsis, a UK-based chef focused on foraging and fermenting, loves the thrill of the process: "Making your own cheese is like harvesting your first vegetable from your garden and cooking with it."

London-based fermenter Annie Simpkins revels in the possibilities of cheese: "I love the infinite ways that liquid perishable milk can be transformed into a longer-lasting solid, which tastes so delicious. It's fascinating how cheesemakers have taken advantage of the leaves, drinks, minerals, and plants in their environment to enhance their cheeses and make them unique."

London-based fermenter and educator Anna Drozdova grew up with Russian and Latvian culinary traditions, and fermentation, including homemade cheese, has always been a big part of her life. She notes that even simple cheesemaking methods can be used to produce a variety of results: "I have only made the simplest of cheeses that need no specific equipment and are fairly fast to prepare, like cream cheese, cottage cheese, paneer, mascarpone, and labneh." But she notes that by making her own cheese, she's in control of what goes into it and of the final flavor: It can be more or less sour or salty, and she can add the seasonings she's craving at a given time.

STEP 2

STEP 3

Basic Fresh Cheese

This is perfect for when you have just a little bit of milk to use up, or you only want a little bit of cheese. This cheese is light and lemony, with a fluffy texture that spreads nicely.

—— Makes about 1 cup

4 cups whole milk

Juice of 1 lemon or 2 tablespoons of another acid like apple cider vinegar

Salt

1 Pour the milk into a nonreactive pan and heat until boiling.

2 Remove from the heat and immediately add the lemon juice and salt to taste. Gently stir to break apart curds and whey.

3 Allow the curds and whey to cool. Strain, using a cheesecloth placed inside a colander, until it is the consistency you want (the longer you strain it, the firmer and drier the cheese will get).

4 Store your cheese in the fridge in an airtight container for 1 to 2 weeks.

Halloumi

Many fresh cheeses are made by heating milk, adding rennet, letting it sit and separate, cutting the curds, then straining and shaping. The particulars of each determine exactly what cheese you'll end up with—and with halloumi, cooking the curds in whey gives it its distinct texture. You can press black cumin seeds (or your favorite dried herbs or spices) into the cheese while hot, if desired. Halloumi is traditionally made with sheep's milk, but you can use whatever milk you have on hand.

(continued on next page)

Halloumi *continued*

—— Makes 3–4 cups

- **1 gallon milk**
- **⅓ cup water**
- **2 teaspoons liquid rennet**
- **½–1 teaspoon salt**
- **1 tablespoon black cumin seeds (optional)**

1. Heat the milk to 95°F/35°C in a large pot, stirring frequently to prevent scorching.

2. Meanwhile, whisk the water and rennet together in a small bowl.

3. Add the rennet solution to the milk and stir gently. Cover the pot with a lid set ajar, or a tea towel, and set it aside for 30 minutes.

4. Line a colander with cheesecloth and place it over a nonreactive pot.

5. Gently whisk the milk to break apart the curds and strain through the cheesecloth, reserving the whey. Let it strain until the whey is drained out, about 1 hour.

6. Sprinkle the salt to taste evenly over the curds in the cheesecloth.

7. Remove to a cutting board, and fold the curds over, if needed, to make a 2-inch-thick block.

8. Bring the leftover whey to a boil.

9. Meanwhile, place cheesecloth or reusable muslin over and under the cheese, and press with your hands until no more whey can be pressed out.

10. When the whey is at a low boil, gently drop in pieces of cheese (anywhere from bite-size to several inches wide, depending on your preference) and boil them until they float, about 5 minutes.

11. Remove the cooked cheese to a cutting board, saving the whey if making a brine for storage (see note). Sprinkle the cumin (if using) over the cheese while still hot, and gently press it into the surface.

12. Allow the cheese to cool completely before storing. Store it in an airtight container in the fridge for up to 1 week.

NOTE: For longer storage, make a brine using a ratio of ½ tablespoon salt to 2 cups whey. Pack the cooled, cooked cheese into a sterilized jar, then pour the cooled brine over to cover completely. Store in the fridge for up to 1 month.

Paneer

This recipe is from Claudia Lucero of Urban Cheesecraft, who says, "I love paneer as a gateway cheese for complete first-timers!" She says it's also a great way to quickly use up milk before it goes bad. "Paneer is practically fail-proof, and did I mention . . . you can fry it!" Paneer also freezes beautifully.

—— Makes about 2 cups

- **1 gallon milk**
- **About ¼ cup apple cider vinegar**

1. Boil the milk.

2. While stirring gently, add the vinegar until you see curds.

3. Drain the curds through a cheesecloth while still warm. Save the whey for other projects, if desired.

4. Press the bundle of curds by setting a plate with some kind of weight (like cans of beans) on top of it for at least 1 hour.

5. Once the cheese is drained and firm, cut into cubes.

6 You can fry firm cubes of your cheese in avocado oil or ghee—paneer does not melt. To finish, simply toss the crispy golden cubes in garlic powder and sea salt, or use them in any dish where you would use chicken or tofu. Store in an airtight container in the fridge and use in 1 to 2 weeks.

Ricotta

Ricotta is cooked whey—an ideal way to get all those last precious bits out of your cheesemaking efforts. You can make ricotta with just whey or whey combined with milk (as below), which produces more curds. Note: Use whey for ricotta within a few hours of making cheese.

— Makes 1–2 cups

4 cups whey from cheesemaking

4 cups whole milk

2 tablespoons lemon juice or vinegar

Salt (optional)

1 Combine the whey, milk, and lemon juice in a large pot (you can also use a double boiler) and bring to a boil over medium heat.

2 Reduce to a simmer and cook until curds form, 10 to 15 minutes, stirring constantly to prevent scorching.

3 Remove the pot from the heat and let it cool for 10 minutes.

4 Strain the ricotta through cheesecloth over a bowl or sink for 1 to 2 hours, until it has a consistency you like.

5 Salt it lightly, or don't salt to use for sweet applications.

6 Store your ricotta in an airtight container with no headspace in the fridge, where it will last for 1 week or more.

Cream Cheese

Store-bought cream cheese, which often contains lots of stabilizers and other ingredients, rarely tastes as good as homemade. This recipe relies on a mesophilic starter to get cream cheese's signature tang. This can be purchased from a cheesemaking supplier (see Resources, page 410). Mesophilic starters prefer cooler temperatures, as opposed to thermophilic yogurt, which prefers warmer incubation temperatures. I make this with whole milk, but you can substitute half-and-half for a richer and denser final product. Play around with mixing in extra flavors, too, after straining. My favorite is sliced green olives or finely diced root vegetables.

— Makes about 3 cups

1 gallon whole milk (not ultra-pasteurized), brought to room temperature

1 packet mesophilic starter

Salt

1 Pour the milk into a large container, then whisk in the starter to dissolve. Let it sit, covered, for 16 to 24 hours at room temperature until thickened and slightly sour.

2 Stir in salt to taste, then strain the cheese through a cheesecloth-lined colander until it's as thick as you'd like. A thicker but still spreadable block-style cream cheese is best strained for 8 to 12 hours: Just tie the opposite corners of your cheesecloth together to make a bundle, then thread a long-handled wooden spoon through the opening and hang over a bowl to capture the whey.

3 Store the cheese in an airtight container in the fridge, where it will last for 1 week or more. If desired, fold in flavorings like chopped herbs, finely diced vegetables, or ground spices before storing.

VARIATION: WHIPPED CREAM CHEESE

For whipped cream cheese, strain until you've reached the consistency of a very thick yogurt (4 to 6 hours), then beat the cheese with a hand mixer or in a blender until it has a lighter, fluffier texture.

BRINING AND OIL PRESERVING

I picked up a used copy of Aida Karaoglan's *Food for the Vegetarian: Traditional Lebanese Recipes* during my first year of college, and it remains one of my most treasured books. It's how I first learned to make labneh (strained yogurt cream cheese), which I still make and use at least monthly. (You can learn more about yogurt cheese at right.) It's also where I learned to make oil-packed cheese, which remains a favorite in my household, and which inspired me to think about cheese as a foodstuff to be preserved in liquid rather than just eating my yogurt cheese fresh.

The most popular way to preserve cheese is in a brine, typically made of salted whey, that the cheese is packed in to reduce its contact with air. Some brines include extra ingredients (like vinegar) to flavor the cheese. You can also pack your cheese in olive oil. Of course, cheese can be aged, wrapped in leaves, washed in spirits, and any number of possibilities. But if you've got fresh cheese you want to play with today, brining and oil packing are your two easiest options.

TO STORE FRESH CHEESE IN BRINE, the easiest option is to whisk salt into room-temperature whey until dissolved (I do ¼ cup salt per quart of whey), add your cheese balls/cubes/etc. to a sterilized container, and pour the brine over to cover. Use within 1 week. For longer storage, make a saturated brine, like what is used for feta cheese, by combining 1 teaspoon of distilled white or apple cider vinegar, 1 tablespoon of calcium chloride, 2¼ pounds of salt, and 1 gallon of water.

Aged cheeses are also salted before aging in brine made from whey or from vinegar, calcium chloride, water, and salt (or just vinegar, water, and salt). You can learn more about brining aged cheeses in the cheesemaking books in Resources (page 410).

Brine presents a wonderful opportunity to add extra flavor to cheese and to experiment, if you wish. While the flavor typically comes from salt, I know many home cheesemakers who add herbs and spices to the brine, and some who even experiment with plopping their fresh cheese in brines from other projects (like kimchi or sauerkraut brine, full sour pickle brine, etc.).

TO STORE FRESH CHEESE IN OIL, gently roll cheese into marble-size or slightly larger balls. Chill for 1 to 2 hours until firm. Drop into sterilized jars. Add olive oil to cover, plus spices and seasonings (like dried herbs or red pepper flakes), and screw on the lid. Oil-packed cheese is traditionally stored at room temperature, but modern food-safety guidelines encourage storing dairy in the fridge. Note that oil can solidify in the refrigerator: If this happens, remove the cheese from the fridge an hour or so before you plan to eat it to let it come to room temperature. It will last for about 1 month in the fridge. Serving with some of the olive oil will soften the cheese and make it nice and spreadable.

YOGURT CHEESE

Yogurt-based cheeses are essentially very thick strained yogurt. This differs from cheesemaking in which one heats milk, adds acid to curdle it, and separates curds from whey. Labneh is a yogurt-based cheese more well known to Western eaters, but there are many yogurt cheeses across the Middle East and elsewhere.

To make your own yogurt cheese, you have a couple of options. One is to make fresh yogurt and strain it the way you would Greek yogurt (see page 356). Once it has a Greek yogurt consistency, tie the opposite corners of your cheesecloth together in two separate knots to make a pouch. Thread a wooden spoon or other long, sturdy utensil through the hole at the top of your pouch and let it hang over a bowl in the fridge overnight. In the morning, you'll have a scoopable, spreadable cheese. For a fun addition, try rolling your cheese in dried herbs and spices.

I also make cheese with yogurt starter or milk kefir by letting it sit and culture for long enough that it separates naturally. This results in a rather tangy cheese, particularly with yogurt, but I love the flavor. Once it separates, strain off the whey by pouring the cheese through cheesecloth, then pack in an airtight container and store in the fridge, where it will last for 2 weeks or more.

Oil-packed cheese

Microbial Starters for Cheesemaking

Some cheesemakers use an acid (like lemon juice) in cheesemaking, while others rely on microbial starters. This is a deep and magical rabbit hole to explore: You can use kefir grains (which can be purchased online and can only be grown from other kefir grains), unpasteurized buttermilk or yogurt, clabber (curdled milk), or whey (which is not as consistent in its results but still works much of the time).

Mesophilic and thermophilic starters refer to the different temperatures that the microbial communities in your starter prefer to work at: Mesophilic cultures, like milk kefir, prefer cooler temperatures, just cooler than body temperature (68 to 95°F/20 to 35°C), while thermophilic (heat-loving) cultures, like yogurt, prefer 99 to 113°F/ 37 to 45°C.

There are places for both in cheesemaking. Thermophilic cultures tend to have a lower pH and thus taste more acidic than their mesophilic counterparts. And there is a world of cheesemaking resources to help you decide which you want to use.

The microbial communities in your cheese can also shift over time, between the make (primary fermentation) and the aging process (which David Asher describes as a secondary fermentation).

VEGAN CHEESE

Plant-based cheeses are made with all kinds of fun ingredients, from cooked vegetables blended together to nuts, nutritional yeast, and beyond. One of my favorites is vegan kimcheese: Nutmeats are soaked in kimchi brine (any fermented brine can be substituted) for 8 hours or longer, blended in a food processor or blender until smooth, then strained with cheesecloth or pressed in a cheese mold.

Like dairy cheeses, you can wrap vegan cheeses in edible leaves, add spices, and so on. Chef Kat Kocsis encourages budding vegan cheesemakers to read up on specific ingredients and vegan cheese styles to learn best practices, such as what humidity and temperature are best for vegan chickpea cheddar (for example) versus a cheese made of nuts, what salt percentages work best, etc.

To learn more about vegan cheesemaking, check out Resources (page 410).

KOJI-PRESERVED CHEESE

I've used shio koji to make vegan tofu feta for years (see my recipe on page 338), but I was inspired after Chef Kat Kocsis shared her favorite ways to use koji in cheese preserving. Yes, cheese lasts longer than fresh dairy, but, especially with fresh cheeses like mozzarella, it can still go bad. When her fresh mozzarella is almost out of date, Kocsis pops it in a jar of Shio Koji (page 74) to cover completely. It keeps the cheese safe for a couple of months, but the shio koji alters the flavor dramatically, offering another avenue for exploration. "In a week's time, your mozzarella will taste like mild cheddar. In 3 weeks it will taste like a strong parmesan, and after 5 weeks you will have to play with the strongest blue cheese you ever experienced."

She also likes to make "cheeso" (cheese miso) that has a long shelf life and an "out-of-this-world flavor profile" using soft, creamy cheese and/ or the hard edges of old, cracked cheese. Blend with fresh rice koji and some salt (and a bit of liquid, if you need to), then let it sit and age. This process is experimental and very fun, so if koji making and koji experiments are in your practice, I encourage you to take your miso recipes and map them in a new direction.

MAKING YOGURT

Yogurt making is an ancient art that you can easily carry on in your own home. Yogurt relies on the inoculation of specific beneficial microbes, so it requires a starter culture to make the magic happen. Families have passed on heritage yogurt starters for generations, even carrying them to new continents. But if your family, like many, has no such starter, fear not: You can purchase starters online (see Resources, page 410), get some from a friend (my favorite way), or even get a small container of plain, organic yogurt with live cultures from the grocery store and use that.

What to Do with All That Whey?

Cheesemaking results in two products: curds (what we use for our cheese) and whey (the liquid left behind). You'll notice that even a small batch of cheese produces a lot of whey. There's no reason to toss it, though! Whey is an incredibly versatile and tasty food. Here are some of my favorite ways to use it.

- **STARTER FOR FUTURE BATCHES OF CHEESE:** You can read more about this in David Asher's books (see Resources, page 410).
- **STARTER FOR FERMENTATION PROCESSES:** Whey is sometimes used as a starter culture in lactofermentation and other fermentation processes.
- **SMOOTHIES:** Adds a protein boost plus nutrients (like whey powder does).
- **SOUPS AND SAUCES:** Adds some salt and tang.
- **SYRUPS:** You can experiment with reducing whey down into syrups and adding it to dressings. This is a fun way to play with sweet/sour/salty flavors in fruit syrups.
- **MARINADES AND BRINES:** Use as a base when working with meat.
- **SOFT CHEESES:** Cook down to get the remaining solids for ricotta or other foods like gjetost (a toasted, caramel-colored cheese).
- **BATHS:** This isn't everyone's cup of tea, but whey is great for your skin. I don't ever measure how much whey I put in my bathtub ("a lot" would be a good estimate), but make sure to strain out all the solid bits first. Your drainpipes will thank you.
- **FOR CRITTERS AND GARDEN:** Plants and pets (including chickens) love whey as a treat. For plants, I mix unsalted whey half and half, or less, with water and use as fertilizer for acid-loving plants.
- **BAKING:** Replace water or other liquids in batters and doughs with whey.
- **OTHER RECIPES:** Whey is the perfect springboard for experimentation. Urban Cheesecraft's Claudia Lucero uses it in Brazilian limeade, cream-of-broccoli soup, corn and squash chowder, and risotto.

For more ways to use whey, see the cheesemaking books in Resources, page 413.

Unlike sourdough starters, which are fed separately before baking, your yogurt starter isn't fed separately from making a batch of yogurt. Since the whole batch is also your starter, make sure to save a bit (rather than eating every last drop) so you can make yogurt again. (Most people save 2 tablespoons; I'm paranoid and make a new batch of yogurt when I'm down to about 2 cups to ensure I never run out.)

KEEPING YOGURT WARM DURING INCUBATION

There are a number of ways to keep yogurt warm during incubation. A yogurt maker is one option, but by all means, it's not the only one. Here's how to keep your yogurt warm using materials you have on hand.

OVEN. An oven keeps heat in, so it's the perfect choice for making yogurt. Wrap your pot of inoculated milk in a tea towel, place in the middle of the oven, and either keep the oven light on but the oven off (for electric ovens), or keep the pilot light on but the oven off (for gas ovens).

COOLER. A cooler can keep things warm as well as cool. Place your starter in the cooler, then add hot water bottles. You can also place a covered container of inoculated milk in a cooler filled with warm water, making sure the water stays at least 1 inch below the edge of the container so it doesn't get in your milk. If you're worried about the water cooling off too much in the night, you can even use a sous vide machine, stuck on the edge of your cooler, to keep the water a consistent temperature.

HEATING PADS AND HOT WATER BOTTLES. You can wrap your container in hot water bottles or heating pads (just be sure these aren't so hot that they scald the milk or create too-hot spots on your container).

INSTANT POTS, SLOW COOKERS, AND RICE COOKERS. Like yogurt makers, the "keep warm" function on these machines holds their contents at a steady temperature. Follow the manufacturer's instructions if you go this route (there is a yogurt-making setting on Instant Pot cookers, but note that it sterilizes the milk first, so wait to add your starter until the milk cools).

Basic Yogurt

When you get to the end of your batch of yogurt, save at least a couple of tablespoons to start your next batch, and then do this for your future batches. This will be your starter culture, which will eventually develop its own unique tangy flavor.

—— Makes 1 quart

4 cups milk

1 tablespoon yogurt starter

1. In a medium saucepan, heat your milk to 162°F/72°C and keep it at that temperature for at least 15 seconds (this pasteurizes your milk, killing any existing microbes).

2. Allow the milk to cool to room temperature, then pour it into a nonreactive pan or bowl, and whisk in the starter culture. Cover with a tea towel.

3. Place the milk and culture mixture in an incubator, where it will be warmer than room temperature, ideally 110 to 115°F/43 to 46°C. Allow it to sit in the incubator for 8 to 12 hours, then refrigerate.

4. You can leave your yogurt at this consistency or strain it by pouring it into a colander lined with cheesecloth. Straining it for a few hours will produce thick Greek-style yogurt, while straining longer (8 to 12 hours, or more, in the fridge) will give you a thick cheeselike consistency. Save the whey: It's full of active cultures and is great to add into lactofermentation projects (for whey ideas, see page 355). Store yogurt in an airtight container in the fridge, where it will last for 2 weeks or more.

VARIATION: GREEK YOGURT

Greek yogurt is just yogurt that's been strained, removing some of the liquid to give it a thicker texture. After making your yogurt, line a colander with cheesecloth, pour the yogurt in, and let it sit until it's as thick as you like. The longer it strains, the thicker it gets. Once it's strained, scoop your Greek yogurt into jars and store in the fridge. Make sure to save the liquid you strain off: it's great to use in smoothies or as you would use whey.

VARIATION: VEGAN YOGURT

Making nondairy yogurt is, in most cases, the same process as dairy yogurt, except you use nondairy milk, like soy or oat, and a vegan yogurt starter. Some people stir in some store-bought probiotic capsules, or you can purchase a vegan yogurt starter online. The latter is perhaps the easiest for new vegan yogurt makers—just follow the package directions.

Different plant-based milks will offer different flavors and textures, and different starters can yield slightly different results, too. So the best thing to do is experiment and see what you like best.

Basic Yogurt

Sourcing and Caring for Heirloom Yogurt Cultures

My yogurt culture is one of my most precious heirlooms—so precious that it's written into my will to be passed on to my fermentation friends after I'm gone. You can start your own yogurt from any live culture yogurt; however, I encourage you to source a starter from a friend or neighbor, or find an heirloom starter online (see Resources, page 410) if you can. You might have luck posting in neighborhood groups or in fermentation forums online, too.

Heirloom starters offer a complexity of flavor that I love: Each one has its own personality. My starter is a combination of volunteer spoonfuls from at least 20 people's heirloom starters, some of which are over a century old, blended together over the course of about 2 decades. Some people prefer to use only one heirloom starter. However, as starters are not microbially constant, I prefer to embrace the waves of change and create a starter that combines the microbial memories of favorite people and places.

No matter how you source your starter, use the directions for yogurt making (page 355) to incubate it (and remember to save a couple of spoonfuls, or preferably more, to start your next batch when you run low).

Yogurt Makers

I tend to shy away from extra appliances when a simpler technique will do, but many people love yogurt makers and find that having the appliance as a set-and-forget option makes them more likely to prepare yogurt regularly.

If you want to try a yogurt maker, here are a few things to consider.

CAPACITY: Consider how much yogurt you typically go through, and make sure to get a machine that's large enough to meet your needs. Think about the space you have to store it, too.

FUNCTIONALITY AND FEATURES: Do you want a stand-alone yogurt maker or a device (like the Instant Pot) that can make yogurt along with other functions? What about other features, like an automatic shutoff or a "keep warm" setting?

ELECTRIC VERSUS NONELECTRIC: All yogurt makers are, in essence, insulated chambers that keep milk consistently warm as it cultures. Electric yogurt makers do this with a built-in heating element, while nonelectric yogurt makers simply create an insulated environment that reduces a loss of heat, but they do not heat the milk itself.

CULTURING BUTTER AND BUTTERMILK

Unlike regular butter, cultured butter has live cultures, and the flavor is a bit tangier and more nuanced than regular butter. I love making these highly customizable recipes—they're a favorite way to use up scraps from other fermentation projects. The most basic version is simply a tablespoon of homemade yogurt whisked into cream and allowed to sit overnight before beating into butter the next day. This (or using other cultures, like a previous batch of buttermilk) is cultured butter the traditional way. You can also experiment with other starter cultures to play with a range of flavors, like blue cheese, fire cider, and banana (see page 359).

Basic Cultured Butter and Buttermilk

This recipe produces the tangy, rich, flavorful butter (and buttermilk) of your dreams.

— Makes about 2 cups

4 cups heavy whipping cream (not ultra-pasteurized)

1 tablespoon plain yogurt

1. Combine the cream and yogurt in a non-reactive mixing bowl and whisk together. Cover with a clean cloth or towel, and allow to rest at room temperature for 6 to 12 hours (the longer the culture time, the tangier the butter).

2. Using an electric mixer, beat the cream until it forms butter, 5 to 10 minutes. Initially you'll get a thick whipped cream and might think you're done. Keep going! You'll know you have butter when the buttermilk and butter separate.

3. Pour off the buttermilk into a separate container and store in the fridge. Use it within 2 to 3 days for the freshest flavor, though it will keep for up to 1 week.

Butter and buttermilk separate after beating.

Massaging butter under cold water removes buttermilk and helps the butter stay fresh longer.

4 Gently massage the butter under cold water until the water runs clear to remove the excess buttermilk. This will prolong the life of your butter.

5 Transfer the butter to a jar or other lidded vessel and store in the fridge. Like your buttermilk, cultured butter tastes best when used relatively soon after it's made, though it can keep in the fridge for 2 to 3 weeks.

CULTURING BUTTER WITH OTHER CULTURES

You can make cultured butter using all kinds of ferments beyond yogurt or buttermilk. I was inspired to jump down this rabbit hole by Maine-based chef and fermenter Sean Doherty, whose experiments culturing butter with blue cheese (which is *so good*) inspired me to start my own. Each ferment imparts its unique qualities to butter, giving you another layer of flavor when you use that butter in dishes or as a spread.

The process is the same as for making cultured butter; just substitute another ferment for the yogurt. For most, I use 2 to 4 tablespoons of ferment per 4 cups of cream. This is a great space to play around and see what tastes best to you. In all cases, make sure you're using live cultures.

My favorites include:

- Crumbled blue cheese
- Fire Cider (page 399) made with unpasteurized vinegar
- Live-culture pickle brine
- Unpasteurized vinegars

Lavender Caramels

Is your heavy cream inching toward the expiration date, but you don't have plans for using it? Try these caramels, possibly the first recipe I ever tested and wrote, which remain an in-demand treat among friends and family. The caramels are rich and buttery, and the lavender accents the flavors perfectly. The recipe makes quite a few of them, and they're good for gifts!

— Makes 30–40 caramels

- **4 tablespoons butter, plus more for greasing**
- **1 cup sugar**
- **1 tablespoon dried lavender flowers**
- **Pinch of salt**
- **1 cup heavy cream**
- **¼ cup plus 2 tablespoons honey**

1. Grease a loaf pan with butter.
2. Combine the butter, sugar, lavender, salt, cream, and honey in a high-sided skillet over medium heat. Cook, stirring constantly with a wooden spoon, until thickened, 10 to 15 minutes.
3. Test the mixture for doneness by dropping a little bit into very cold water. If it holds its shape until gently pressed (called the soft ball stage in candy making), it is done.
4. Immediately pour the caramel into the pan. Let cool.
5. Cut the caramel into bite-size squares or rectangles. Wrap each one in waxed paper (like saltwater taffy). Store them in a cool, dry location, where they will keep for up to 2 weeks.

Meat and Poultry

Like dairy, meat spoils quickly, which means it needs to be preserved or processed as soon as possible after the animal is killed. Refrigeration temporarily slows decay, and freezing preserves meat even longer, but prior to refrigeration and/or in places without consistent access to it, other forms of meat preservation were and are absolutely essential.

We've come up with countless creative ways to preserve meat and use up every part of an animal, including fermentation, drying, smoking, salting, quick pickling, canning, and more, each important for processing different cuts, preserving using different methods (e.g., canned beef stew versus a piece of jerky), and for different culinary uses. Our ancestors have a long history of preserving meat, including pickled meats going back to at least fifth-century BCE Babylon and Egypt.

I encourage you to find the best quality meat you can, and, if you're able, to source from local providers. It can be a lot of fun to think seasonally about your animal proteins, as local farms and farmers' markets may have different meat products available at different times of year.

FREEZING

Meat, game, and poultry, whether whole, in pieces, or ground, tends to freeze well. As with produce, get fresh, high-quality meat and freeze it as soon as possible (save for small game, like rabbits, which you should skin, dress, and refrigerate for at least 24 hours, or until the meat is no longer rigid, then package and freeze).

FREEZING MEAT

Package unseasoned, raw meat in meal-size portions. If you buy meat from the store, it will need to be repackaged, as the cling film it's wrapped in is not water-vapor resistant (unless it's heavy-duty freezer film, in which case, no other packaging is needed!).

If packaging patties, place two layers of freezer paper or wrap between your patties. This makes them easier to separate, and they will thaw faster.

Ways to Preserve Meat and Poultry

	Shelf-stable	Fast	Low waste	Ready meals and ingredients	Big flavor
Chicken Soup (page 364)	X			X	
Geographically Indeterminate Ham (page 369)				X	X
Amana Pickled Ham (page 371)				X	X
Mole-Inspired Beef Jerky (page 374)				X	X

Wrapping meat helps prevent freezer burn.

There are a few avenues to freezing meat: Vacuum sealing is a straightforward and foolproof method; however, it can also be wasteful and expensive, and it requires specialty equipment. Meat can be wrapped in butcher or freezer paper, which is my preference, then labeled with contents and date. Or it can be placed in a ziplock bag using the air displacement method (page 20). Freezer bags are especially good for ground meat, stew meat, and other meat that's frozen in small quantities.

Provided your freezer is consistently at 0°F/–18°C or lower, frozen meat and game will maintain their taste and texture for months: steaks or roasts for 1 year, pork chops for 4 to 6 months, ground meat for 3 months, and sausages for 2 months.

You can cook meat from frozen, but for best texture and flavor, thaw meat completely in the refrigerator before cooking. Be sure to thaw on a rimmed tray or in a high-sided container to keep meat juices contained.

FREEZING POULTRY

Poultry also freezes well, though some poultry meat may turn dark around the bones when frozen. This darkening is normal and won't impact safety or flavor.

For game birds (quail, duck, pheasant, etc.), freeze following the same directions as for poultry. Use frozen poultry and game birds within 4 months for the best flavor and texture. If you process your own birds, eviscerate and clean them, then chill them below 40°F/4°C for 24 hours prior to freezing.

Whole, skin-on birds freeze well (fryers or broilers freeze best): For short-term storage (under 1 month), simply place in a plastic freezer bag, press out the air, seal, and freeze. For longer-term storage, wrap first in freezer paper or foil and seal airtight, then freeze immediately. Whatever method you choose, make the bird as compact as possible (press the wings and legs into the body and fold wings in) to prevent freezer burn.

Do not stuff poultry before freezing: Freezing and thawing stuffed birds at home can easily introduce pathogens to the stuffing. If you like stuffing, place it inside the thawed bird just before cooking. Or the more food-safe option is to make dressing to go on the side.

Halves, quarters, and pieces should have two layers of freezer wrap or paper between them, as with meat patties, then be packaged in airtight wrap as for whole birds. You can either package pieces of a whole bird together, or put like pieces with like (breasts, thighs, wings, etc.), depending on what you have and how you plan to prepare it.

Thoroughly clean and wash giblets and livers. Freeze in a single layer on a rimmed sheet pan with space between each, then pack tightly in freezer bags or freezer-safe containers with no headspace. Use livers within 1 month and giblets within 3 months.

FREEZING GROUND MEAT KEBABS

There are a few ways to go about freezing kebab-shaped ground meat, but I find I have the best luck when I treat it the way I treat blanched vegetables: that is, to place kebabs in a single layer on a sheet pan, freeze just until frozen, then pack into a freezer-proof container. This helps them freeze evenly, which can help prevent freezer burn later.

To make your own, follow your favorite ground meat–based kebab recipe, but do not cook. Freeze uncovered in a single layer on a rimmed sheet pan lined with waxed paper. (Note: In general, raw meat is frozen unseasoned; however, I make an exception with kebabs.) Place in the freezer until frozen through: 4 to 12 hours, depending on size. Transfer frozen ground meat to a freezer-proof container with 1 inch of headspace: in a single layer, if possible, for kebabs or other irregularly shaped meats, and with slices of butcher paper between each patty if freezing multiple layers. Thaw for 8 to 12 hours in the fridge when ready to cook. Kebabs will last in the freezer for 2 to 3 months.

MAKING AND FREEZING STOCK

Few things rival the flavor boost that a high-quality stock adds to meals. And you can use your food scraps, those leftover bits and bobs from cooking, to get it.

See page 20 for my Scrappy Soup Stock recipe. Store your stems, ends, bones, etc., in a freezer-safe container until you have enough to make a pot of stock (I use a 1-gallon reusable silicone zippered bag, then dump its contents into my Instant Pot or slow cooker, with water to cover, once it's full.) Simmer for 6 to 8 hours until it's fragrant and flavorful. As with any stock, you can add aromatics or other ingredients you like. I always add pieces of kelp (then simmer covered so it retains its iodine in the stock), pieces of dried mushrooms like reishi, and spices like peppercorn. And, of course, salt to taste.

You can make stock with whole ingredients, too—this is a fantastic way to get the most out of the carcass of a rotisserie chicken. Simply pack your chicken (whole or carcass) or other bones (you can buy beef soup bones from butchers, or you may have leftover bones, like ham bones or turkey bones from holiday meals). Add them in as is: Some meat on the bones is totally fine and adds to the flavor. (I love using bones from smoked meats as well.) You can also just use whole, raw chickens, or chicken pieces, if you prefer.

Once your meat and bones are in the pot, add aromatics. The traditional French combination is celery, carrot, and onion (called mirepoix), and I also add lots of whole garlic cloves, peppercorns, salt to taste, and maybe some herbs and spices (like herbes de Provence), depending on how I plan to use it. However, the ingredients in your stock are only limited by your imagination, and it's a good chance to play with the broths and stocks from your favorite cuisines. This is also a great place to throw onion scraps, the tops of carrots, celery leaves, or whatever other scraps you think would be good in stock. One note: A lot of dark leafy greens and brassicas (plants in the cabbage and mustard family) can sometimes result in a bitter stock.

Add a splash of vinegar to taste (I add about ½ cup per Instant Pot or slow cooker batch), which helps release collagen from connective tissue in meat and makes for a better final texture and flavor.

You can make the same thing with shrimp shells and fish bones, too: Gently simmer to make a flavorful fish or shellfish stock (I usually am light-handed with the other aromatics here so that I don't overwhelm the delicate flavor of the seafood).

Simmer the stock on the stove or in your slow cooker for 4 to 8 hours (or longer), until it's fragrant and flavorful.

Cool completely, then add to freezer-safe containers and store in the freezer. For wide-mouthed (freezer-safe) mason jars, or other freezer-safe glass containers, leave 1 to 2 inches of headspace to give the stock room to expand as it freezes. If you're pouring your stock into freezer bags, seal completely and lay flat on a sheet pan so they'll freeze flat and stack easily when frozen. You can also pour cooled stock into a greased muffin tin or an ice cube tray if you want small, ready-to-use portions, or reduce it to make concentrated stock (see below). Seal the cubes in a container or bag with no headspace, or vacuum seal, after completely frozen. Stock will last for several months or more in the freezer if properly stored.

FREEZING CONCENTRATED STOCK CUBES

Homemade stocks are much healthier, and tastier, than anything available commercially, and concentrating them gives you a ready ingredient for meals. Strain a finished stock, then cook it down to about half its volume for a concentrated, gelatinous stock. You can do this by simmering it on the stove or in a slow cooker on low for at least several hours (I usually do overnight in a slow cooker).

Cool completely, then scoop into ice cube trays, tap them gently on the counter to release any air bubbles, and freeze. Once frozen, transfer to a freezer-safe container with no headspace; they will last for several months or more. The result is delicious, homemade bouillon-ish cubes, ready to go when you need a splash of stock flavor in a hurry.

CANNING

Meat, poultry, and game are low-acid foods and thus have to be pressure canned. While it's possible, technically, to can ground or chopped meat in water, these do better frozen, as the taste and texture of the final product are a much higher quality. Strips, cubes, and chunks of meat do well pressure canned, though, and you'll get the best results with a hot pack (rather than raw pack) technique.

Pressure Canning Meat

1. Start with fresh, high-quality meat that's been chilled.
2. To take some of the gamey flavor from strongly flavored wild meats, make a brine that's 1¼ tablespoons of salt per quart of water. Soak the meat in the brine for an hour, then rinse.
3. Meanwhile, place jars in your pressure canner and heat it up. Then, using tongs, remove the hot jars from the canner.
4. Remove excess fat and cut the meat into 1-inch chunks.
5. Precook the meat to rare (roast, stew, or sauté it), using only a small amount of cooking fat (just enough so it doesn't stick).
6. Pack your hot meat loosely into hot jars, leaving 1 inch of headspace.
7. Add salt to the jars: ½ teaspoon per pint, or 1 teaspoon per quart.
8. Fill each jar with boiling broth, water, stock, or tomato juice, leaving 1 inch of headspace.
9. Run a chopstick or other thin, nonmetal utensil along the inner edges of the jars to release any air bubbles. Wipe the rims of the jars with a clean, damp cloth. Add the lids and bands and screw down to hand tightness.
10. Set your pressure canner at 11 pounds pressure (dial gauge) or 10 pounds pressure (weighted gauge) and process pints for 75 minutes and quarts for 90 minutes, adjusting for altitude (see page 39) if needed.
11. Allow the canner to depressurize completely. Let the jars sit for 24 hours before testing the seals (see page 40), then store out of direct sunlight at room temperature.

Chicken Soup

This herbal, garlicky soup is perfect for winter cold and flu season, but its comforting, warming flavor is fantastic any time! I love using Scrappy Soup Stock (page 20) in this recipe.

— Makes about 4 quarts

- 2 pounds boneless chicken, fat trimmed, cut into 1-inch dice (you can also use leftover cooked chicken, if desired)
- Salt
- Freshly ground black pepper
- 1–2 tablespoons butter or neutral vegetable oil
- 10 cups stock
- 10 stalks celery, sliced ½ inch thick
- 6 carrots, sliced ½ inch thick
- 2 yellow onions, cut into ½-inch dice
- 6 cloves garlic, minced, or 4–5 tablespoons Three-Root Paste (page 108)
- 1–2 tablespoons herbes de Provence
- ½ tablespoon dark soy sauce
- Pasta or grains (optional), for serving

1. Salt and pepper the chicken to taste. Heat 1 tablespoon of the butter in a large pot, add the chicken, and cook over medium heat until browned slightly and cooked through, 10 to 15 minutes.
2. Deglaze the pot with a splash of the stock, if needed, before removing the chicken. Set aside.

3 Add 1 tablespoon of the butter to the pot if needed. Sweat the celery, carrots, and onions in the pot for 5 minutes, then add the garlic and sauté until just golden, 2 to 3 minutes.

4 Increase the heat to high. Add the stock to the pot, along with the chicken, 1 teaspoon of pepper, the herbes de Provence, and the soy sauce. Season with salt to taste.

5 Add the jars to the pressure canner to heat. Then, using tongs, remove the hot jars from the canner.

6 Boil the soup for 5 minutes, then transfer to the hot jars. Fill them halfway with solids, then add the boiling stock to cover, leaving 1 inch of headspace.

7 Run a chopstick or other thin, nonmetal utensil along the inner edges of the jars to release any air bubbles. Wipe the rims of the jars with a clean, damp cloth. Add the lids and bands and screw down to hand tightness.

8 Set your pressure canner at 11 pounds pressure (dial gauge) or 10 pounds pressure (weighted gauge) and process quarts for 75 minutes, adjusting for altitude (see page 39) if needed.

9 Allow the canner to depressurize completely. Let the jars sit for 24 hours before testing the seals (see page 40), then store out of direct sunlight at room temperature.

10 To serve: Pour the soup into a saucepan and simmer until heated through. Some grains and pasta can be added when you're ready to open and serve your soup: Bring the soup to a boil, add the desired amount of pasta or grains, and cook until tender. Dense grains with a long cooking time are best cooked separately, then added before serving. To make that more worth your while, cook a bigger batch so you have leftover grains to enjoy for meals to come.

Chicken Soup

Preserving Around the World

South Carolina Lowcountry, with Amethyst Ganaway

Amethyst Ganaway is a chef and food writer from North Charleston, South Carolina, who has dedicated her life to preserving and sharing Lowcountry cuisine and the stories of Black cooks in the South. The Lowcountry, or low-lying coastal areas of South Carolina, consists of salt marshes, beaches, and palmetto trees.

She says, "In the Lowcountry, it's a mix of Gullah Geechee (descendants of enslaved West Africans), Indigenous, French Huguenot, German, and English communities [whose traditions] make up our cuisine."

The food here is special, unlike anything else. Ganaway notes that "our cuisine in the Lowcountry is diverse. It's heavily rooted in land/sea to table, more than I think a lot of other places in the United States are. What I love most is that even if you don't have a lot, you'll always be able to eat well."

And this mix of cuisines has led to rich food-preserving traditions: "Pickling and canning are the most popular here, in my opinion—of course pickled okra, but also pickled eggs, pigs' feet, hot sausages, green tomatoes, etc. I also love our fruit jams like plums, peaches, and strawberries." Pickles are a side dish at every meal, and smoked fish is rehydrated: "Preserved foods really see a moment to shine in cooler months after the summer crops have been preserved, and, outside of that, pickled ingredients are always on the table or in the fridge for a snack!"

And preserving does more than add some zing to meals. "Preserving is a huge part of preserving cultural knowledge," says Ganaway. "It's seen a lot more with people who really have a close tie to the land and who understand the importance of knowing how to preserve ingredients."

CURING AND FERMENTING

The world of sour, salty meats is a magical one indeed. From salami to naem to ham, there are many options. This section offers an overview of some simple, accessible ways to explore curing and fermenting meat.

Let's begin by looking at the terminology, which can be confusing to the newly initiated. The word *cure* is often used interchangeably with *ferment*, especially when talking about meat and dairy products. Sometimes, however, *curing* refers to proteins packed in salt or sugar (like Salt-Cured Egg Yolks, page 391). A peek at the recipe will tell you which technique it is.

Some cured meats, like salami (the name for which comes from *salare*, which means "to salt"), are fermented with nitrates, which is critical to inhibiting the growth of pathogens. Historically, celery (which contains naturally occurring nitrates) was a popular source, as was saltpeter (potassium nitrate), which appears in recipes going back to the Middle Ages. Today, you can purchase industrially produced nitrates from butcher supply companies, and there's a rich world of possibilities to explore for fermented meat lovers. (Check out the resources listed on page 413 when you're ready to deep dive.)

The word *drying* typically refers to letting meat dry slowly as part of the preserving process, whereas the word *dehydrating* means a process that relies on faster drying (think using a dehydrator), resulting in products like dried fish or beef jerky. In places where the climate is not conducive to drying, meat and seafood are often smoked to remove moisture and impart flavor.

To add to the confusion, the terms we use to describe our fermented meats are often time-based. In *Preservation*, Christina Ward says the names change based on fermentation time. For instance, Scandinavian cured salmon is called surlaks, but cure it for longer and it becomes gravlax, which is similar to lox. She adds, "Many revered local culinary delicacies are often related to other items from different areas. Slight variations in spice and technique are often the only difference."

Brining

You've probably heard of "wet brining" (literally submerging your meat in brine, or a liquid mixture of salt and water) and "dry brining" (actually salting; this is a dry rub, thus not a brine at all). Brining imparts a flavor and prevents spoilage (make sure to keep your meat weighted and completely submerged under the brine!). In some cases, this is a chance to ferment the meat; in others, the brine is used to flavor the muscle and alter the texture. Dry rubbing also can impart flavor, and it draws out moisture from the meat, as does sugaring. You may see some brines that have salt as well as sugar: I have encountered preserved meats made with sugar and no salt, but it's much more rare than salted meats.

If you're preserving meat by brining, follow the brine ratios in your recipe. You may be surprised by the amount of salt you're using, but it's necessary for a safe final product, and most of it washes away.

Preserving Meat

Meredith Leigh is an activist and educator and the author of *The Ethical Meat Handbook*. Meredith shared her wisdom about beginning your own journey of meat preserving, a process that she considers easier than making sourdough.

JS: What are your favorite things about preserving meat?

ML: I love that it requires me to pay attention to my environment and the natural processes I am attempting to harness. There is an inherent cultivation of mindfulness and rooting to place that come with preservation practice. When folks are feeling uneasy about meat preservation, I encourage them to start small. In my teaching, I strive to explain all of the potential risks and the knowledge that we have to help us eliminate those risks. If people are willing to learn that, there is very little they can do to make uninformed errors that would harm themselves or others.

JS: What's the best preserving project for someone completely new to meat preservation to tackle?

ML: Familiarize yourself with the process of salt curing first by tackling a whole muscle product that will eventually be cooked. An example of this would be bacon, or a roasted cured ham, or rillettes or confit. If someone is feeling more adventurous and wants to go for a noncooked but fully preserved item, I would recommend trying bresaola. This is a whole-muscle cure using beef, which has low water activity and is generally pretty easy to produce without problems for a beginner.

JS: What are some basic dos and don'ts of safely preserving meat?

ML: Keeping surfaces, tools, hands, etc., clean is important. I'm not advocating bleaching your home before preserving, but I do see a lot of equipment like sausage stuffers and meat grinders that have been haphazardly cleaned and stored, and the fat and meat lurking in the crevices or on neglected gaskets can harbor pathogens. Also, keeping processing cold, and knowing the purpose of some additives, like nitrates, and when you can or cannot use them, is important. Do your homework and you'll be just fine.

JS: What are a few best practices for drying cured meats?

ML: Creating the right environment is important here. If you don't live in a climate that has moderate humidity and cooler temperatures for an extended period of the year, this is probably not the best technique to start out with. You want temperatures cool enough (higher than refrigerator temps but lower than room temp) and moderate humidity so the meat can slowly dry without molding or becoming rancid.

JS: What are a few best practices for smoking meat?

ML: This is the place to start if you live in an extremely humid climate or a very cold climate. Best practices depend on the type of smoking you are trying to do, but for beginners I would say curing meat thoroughly in salt and then hot smoking to cook it is probably the easiest way to get started.

JS: What is a simple charcuterie-making method you'd recommend readers start with if they've never cured meat before?

ML: I would say salt curing is the place to start. This is only the beginning stage of the process, so the next step will be to move on to learning how to smoke or dry meats after salt curing, but if you learn to salt cure and cook meat, you'll get the reward of amplified flavor and texture that curing brings while also learning fundamentals of preservation that apply across most charcuterie practice.

JS: What other simple preservation methods do you recommend for readers new to meat preservation?

ML: Learn to make a basic fresh sausage. Understanding how to create texture, bind, balance flavor, use the equipment and all of that on a cooked, nonpreserved sausage product will go a long way to preparing you for fermented sausage production.

HAMS

People have strong opinions about ham. All hams are cut from the hind leg of a hog, and there are many regional varieties and flavoring possibilities for hams.

Different names sometimes denote different preparations. Hams can be sold bone-in, partially boned, or boneless. All hams are cured unless it specifically says uncured on the package, and hams are sold cooked, uncooked, or partially cooked (hams need to be baked before serving, unless they're cooked; then they just need to be heated through). Some are aged, some are smoked, some are spiced in certain ways. There's a lot to explore! Here are a few common varieties.

BLACK FOREST HAM. This boneless German ham is seasoned with juniper, garlic, and other spices and cold smoked.

CITY HAM. While country hams have been produced for centuries, the method for making city ham came about with the advent of refrigeration. City ham is cured in brine or injected with brine rather than dry-cured. After just a few days of curing, the ham is smoked and refrigerated to stay fresh. Because of its shorter, less-intensive production time, it is more affordable than country ham. It also has a milder flavor.

COUNTRY HAM. This ham is dry-cured in salt, smoked, then dried for at least 6 months. Most are uncooked and need to be cooked before serving.

HONEY OR MAPLE HAM. This wet-cured ham is made with a brine that includes honey or maple to give it its characteristic sweetness.

IRISH HAM. This ham is wet-brined then smoked over peat or juniper for a smoky, piney flavor. Traditionally this needs to be soaked and scrubbed before baking.

JAMÓN IBÉRICO. This Spanish ham is dry-cured for 2 years.

PICNIC HAM. Technically speaking, this isn't a ham: It's made from the upper part of the foreleg and part of the shoulder, and this cut is what makes it a picnic ham. It can be smoked or unsmoked.

PROSCIUTTO. This Italian ham is unsmoked, salt-cured, and air-dried, giving it a concentrated flavor.

JAMÓN SERRANO. A dry-cured Spanish ham, it has a robust flavor.

SPECK. An Italian ham, it is cured similarly to prosciutto and lightly smoked.

VIRGINIA HAM. This ham, produced in the state of Virginia, is salt-cured and smoked low and slow using traditional methods.

Curing your own ham is a relatively easy entry point to working with meat. Meredith Leigh has wonderful ham recipes in *The Ethical Meat Handbook*, should you ever be curious to make your own. Rather than reinventing the wheel, I decided to take ham making in a different direction: Using the process from Leigh's smoked fiochetto ham recipe as inspiration, I swapped out the seasonings in the brine and ended up with a ham that's neither fully Southern nor Italian. Nor clearly of anywhere else. I call it geographically indeterminate ham.

Geographically Indeterminate Ham

Ham doesn't have to be from Virginia. This is a small ham that's a nice project for folks who just want a few pounds of finished product. I used a bone-in, uncured, uncooked ham. Look for a ham that's 4 to 5 pounds so the ratio of curing salt to ham is correct. The final flavor is savory and meaty, but also bright from the seasonings.

(continued on next page)

Geographically Indeterminate Ham *continued*

— Makes one 4–5 pound ham

- 1½ pounds kosher salt (I use Diamond Crystal)
- 2 cups packed light brown sugar
- 5 ounces cure #1 (pink curing salt)
- 2 gallons water
- ¼ cup black peppercorns
- 1–2 tablespoons coriander seeds
- 3 small sprigs rosemary
- Zest of 2 large lemons, cut into strips
- ½ bottle dry, full-bodied red wine
- 16 ounces cane syrup
- 1 (4–5 pound) ham, uncooked and uncured, lightly trimmed of fat
- 2 (180 cu in.) bag hickory wood chips (or your favorite wood chip)

1. Make the brine: Combine the salt, sugar, cure #1, and water in a pot and heat enough to dissolve the salt and sugar. Cool slightly. Then add the peppercorns, coriander, rosemary, lemon zest, wine, and cane syrup, and allow to cool completely to room temperature.

2. Add the ham, weighting it to ensure it is completely submerged below the brine.

3. Let it cure in the brine for 5 to 7 days in the fridge, turning daily, ensuring it is fully under the brine again after being turned.

4. The day before smoking, remove the ham from the brine and discard the brine. Rinse the ham thoroughly to remove the curing salts, pat it dry, and leave it uncovered on a tray in the refrigerator overnight to dry out slightly.

5. The next day, set the ham out on the counter a couple of hours before smoking it to remove the chill, and heat your smoker to 150 to 180°F/66 to 82°C. Smoke the ham over the hickory chips until its internal temperature reaches 160°F/71°C.

6. Remove the ham from the smoker and let it rest for 15 to 30 minutes. Store it in the refrigerator, where it will last for about 2 weeks.

PICKLING

Pickling is a popular way to preserve meat: Essentially, you're making a quick pickle like you would with a veggie, but you're submerging meat in the brine instead. I have fond memories of Amish pickled ham. And in the South, you'll often see pickled pigs' feet (trotters). Wherever you live in the world, there are probably long-standing meat-pickling traditions all around you. Cretan apaki—smoked pork loin steeped in vinegar to prolong its shelf life—is a good example. Some meats that are cooked in a strong, pickle-y brine are considered pickled, even though they aren't soaking in a cold brine for a long period; Indian achari lamb and Korean jangjorim (soy-braised beef) are good examples.

Meats can be pickled for a relatively short time, like sauerbraten, a German dish made from rump roast marinated with wine, vinegar, and seasonings for a couple of days before cooking. Or they can be pickled for longer in a strong, sour brine (like Amana Pickled Ham, page 371) then plucked out of the pickling jar as needed. Historic texts show that pickling meat has, not surprisingly, a long history as a method for lengthening shelf life, like xāmīz, a Middle Persian dish (third through ninth centuries CE) made of vinegar-brined meat prepared from a variety of animals and served cold.

Some fermented meats (like Thai or Lao naem) are classed as pickled meats, depending on who you ask: I treat quick pickling and fermenting as separate processes since, well, they technically are. Some people also refer to salt-cured meats as pickled.

Pickling meat is done with vinegar and salt: The meat can be submerged in a brine to pickle slowly like a refrigerator pickle (see the vegetable version of this on page 54) or cooked in a hot brine so it absorbs the sour liquid more quickly. In many cases, quick pickling doesn't substantially increase the shelf life unless the meat is stored completely submerged.

Amana Pickled Ham

Pickled ham is simply cooked ham in a quick pickling solution. I first had pickled ham while living in Iowa City, where it would grace the table each time I ate in the nearby Amana Colonies (my recipe is loosely based on the one from the Ronneburg restaurant's cookbook from 1981, *The Ronneburg Recipe Album*). This pickled ham is always served with onions but only sometimes with spices added to the brine. However, I fell in love with a version that was studded with a few whole cloves, so I use them every time.

—— Makes 2 quarts

1 teaspoon salt

3 cups apple cider vinegar or distilled white vinegar

1½ cups water

1 pound cooked ham, cut into ½-inch cubes (4 cups)

1 medium white or yellow onion, sliced

Spices such as 1 teaspoon whole cloves, 1 teaspoon whole pickling spice blend, or ½ teaspoon ground black pepper (optional)

1 Make the brine: Combine the salt, vinegar, and water in a large bowl or other food-safe container.

2 Divide the ham, onions, and spices (if using) evenly between two quart jars.

3 Pour the brine over to completely cover, and refrigerate for at least 24 hours. It will last for about 2 weeks in the refrigerator.

SMOKING

Smoking is done over smoldering (rather than flaming) wood chunks or chips. Hot-smoked meats (like southern BBQ) are typically smoked between 190 to 300°F/88 to 150°C. The hot smoke adds flavor while also cooking the meat low and slow. Hours of cooking time results in tender meat and a smoky, flavorful final product. Cold smoking is done at much lower temperatures, usually to add flavor rather than to cook the meat. Before being smoked, meat must be brined or salt cured, which removes some moisture and prevents spoilage during the slow smoking process.

To learn more about smoking meat, see the meat and seafood books in Resources (page 410).

Smoking Meat

1 If you're using a dry-rub cure before smoking, rub it all over the meat, on all sides. If you're using a wet brine, pour it over the meat in a nonreactive container; make sure the meat is weighted down and completely submerged as it brines.

2 Allow the meat to cure for the time specified in your recipe. In some cases, this might be for just a week or so; in other cases, it might be months. Cure dry-rubbed meat in the fridge on a rack over a rimmed pan (like a roasting pan), which will catch any cure that falls off and any liquid that is pulled from the meat. Turn meat and re-rub with cure as needed. If your meat is submerged in brine, check it from time to time to make sure it stays completely submerged.

3 When it's time to smoke, rinse the meat if your recipe calls for it, and heat your smoker following the manufacturer's instructions.

4 Smoke the meat for the time specified in your recipe, making sure that it reaches the recommended internal temperature.

5 Let the smoked meat cool completely before storing it. Many smoked, cured meats that make good beginner projects still contain a good amount of moisture and need to be stored in the fridge.

DRYING

Meat, particularly beef and some game meats, can be dried into jerky to extend their shelf life. Jerky can be made with beef, venison, mutton, elk, chicken, and turkey without pretreating. However, if you're making bear or pork jerky, you need to freeze the meat for a month prior in order to kill any potential trichinae present in the meat. Jerky is made with lean meat, like top or bottom round, as you want very little intermuscular fat or connective tissue, which makes for a tough final product.

Making Meat Jerky

1 Trim away any fat on the meat. Cut the meat in ¼-inch-thick slices, then cut them into 1-inch-wide strips. This can be easier to do if the meat is partially frozen (or have your butcher cut the initial thin slices).

2 Season the meat, if you like, with a dry rub or marinade.

3 Safe jerky making requires a relatively high-temperature smoker, dehydrator, or oven (start at 160°F/71°C) to kill pathogenic microorganisms: You can turn the heat down to 140°F/60°C halfway through drying. Smoke your jerky for 4 to 5 hours or until chewy and firm but still somewhat pliable; or dry in the dehydrator or oven for 16 to 24 hours, turning once, until it has a slightly pliable but dry texture.

4 Allow the jerky to cool completely, then store it in airtight containers in a cool, dry place, where it will last for several weeks, or keep it in the refrigerator (lasts for at least 1 month) or freezer (lasts for 6 months or more).

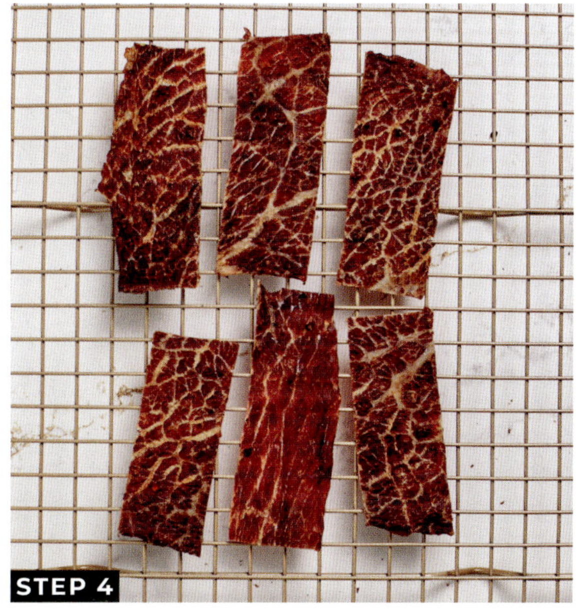

DRY RUBS

You can make dry rubs for jerky with or without curing salts like Morton Tender Quick, which contain nitrates or nitrites (this is different from Prague powder or pink salts, which are more concentrated), but note that curing salts help maintain a better color and texture on the final product.

To make a dry rub with curing salt, for each pound of lean meat, combine the following in a bowl: 1 tablespoon of commercial curing salt, like Morton Tender Quick, 1 teaspoon of sugar, and 1 to 2 teaspoons of any desired seasonings (garlic powder, black pepper, cayenne, lemon pepper, etc.). Rub all surfaces of meat with the cure and allow it to cure in the refrigerator for 1 hour. Rinse the cure thoroughly from the meat, then pat it dry with paper towels before dehydrating.

To make a dry rub without curing salt, liberally season the meat with salt on both sides, along with any desired seasonings. Layer the meat in a covered container in the refrigerator for 6 to 12 hours. Rinse and pat dry before dehydrating.

If I'm dehydrating meat to rehydrate in other dishes later (like in a stew), I'll simply salt and dry it without smoking to give me the greatest versatility.

MARINADES

You can also make wet marinades for jerky. The soy sauce marinade I use for white fish (see page 382) works well here and gives you a product similar to Korean yukpo (especially if you add the optional sugar). I use it on fish for just a few hours, whereas I'll marinate beef overnight.

You can also make my mole-inspired jerky marinade on this page.

If you want to add Morton Tender Quick in either version, use ½ tablespoon per 1 pound of meat. If you want to use pink curing salt, follow the label directions for the weight of meat; a little goes a long way.

Marinate meat for at least 2 hours to overnight, then pat dry and arrange on trays in your oven or dehydrator in a single layer, without overlap.

Mole-Inspired Beef Jerky

Mole refers to a family of Mexican sauces that use a range of ingredients, including chiles, nuts, spices, and sometimes chocolate. I remember eating mole at friends' houses when I was growing up, and I still find it one of the most comforting smells and tastes. Give this a try on your favorite meats, if you don't love beef.

— Makes enough marinade for 1 pound of meat

2 cloves garlic, minced
3 teaspoons unsweetened cocoa powder
½–1 teaspoon red pepper flakes (optional)
½ teaspoon coriander powder
¼ teaspoon cumin seeds
¼ teaspoon hot paprika
¼ teaspoon smoked paprika
¼ cup dark soy sauce
¼ cup water
1 teaspoon tomato paste
Zest of 1 small lime

1. In a bowl, whisk together the garlic, cocoa powder, pepper flakes (if using), coriander, cumin, hot paprika, smoked paprika, soy sauce, water, tomato paste, and lime zest. Pour the marinade over the sliced meat in a resealable bag or in a flat container, making sure all sides are covered.

2. Let sit, covered, in the fridge for 4 to 12 hours.

3. Remove the meat from the marinade and gently pat dry.

4. Dry the marinated meat slices in a dehydrator at 150°F/66°C for 16 to 24 hours or until dried but still pliable (or smoke using the directions on page 372). Store the jerky in an airtight container out of direct sunlight, where it will last for several weeks; for longer-lasting jerky, store it in the refrigerator (lasts for at least 1 month) or freezer (lasts for 6 months or more).

Seafood

Seafood is fun and easy to preserve, from quickly packaging and freezing to smoking low and slow, and to drying, pickling, and beyond. Fish, like all food, needs to be preserved when it's at peak freshness, which means as soon as possible after it's caught. If you're catching the fish yourself, this is easy to do. If you're buying fish from the store, you'll need to check for freshness: It should smell fresh (like the ocean, with a mild smell rather than a strong fishy smell), the flesh should be firm and tight, and the eyes clear rather than cloudy. When selecting shellfish like clams, oysters, and mussels, check that the shells are tightly closed: Open shells mean the shellfish has died and is not safe to eat. Choose shrimp with firm flesh and shells that are solidly in place (rather than loose or slimy), and with clear eyes, if they have their heads on.

Once your seafood is put up, what do you do with it? Preserved fish is a fantastic kitchen staple, lending itself to simple platters with spreads, breads, and maybe some olives and pickles, or as an add-in or topping for pizza, pasta sauce, dressings, or whatever else. Frozen fish thaws easily and relatively quickly, making it a star for weeknight meals. And seafood stock is a wonderful base for soups or even for pasta-cooking water in dishes like shrimp scampi.

FREEZING

Freezing is one of the easiest ways to preserve fish when you're short on time or low on energy. Fish does, however, require a bit of special handling to maintain its quality and texture once it's thawed.

If you have whole, fresh fish, make sure to remove the entrails before freezing. Depending on the size of the fish and how you want to prepare it, you can leave fish whole, break it down into steaks, or cut it into fillets. Fish steaks and fillets that are ½ inch thick or more, or whole small to medium fish, tend to freeze best.

Ways to Preserve Seafood	Shelf-stable	Fast	Low waste	Ready meals and ingredients	Big flavor
Frozen Seafood Stock (page 377)			X	X	X
Lemon-Miso Fish Jerky Marinade (page 378)				X	X
Garlic-Shoyu Fish Jerky Marinade (page 378)				X	X
Pickled Shrimp (page 381)				X	X
Pickled White Fish (page 382)				X	X
Pickled Salmon (page 382)				X	X
Pickled Oysters (page 384)				X	X

STEP 1

PRETREATING FISH

Pretreating fish preserves flavor and texture. Base the exact pretreatment solution on whether your fish is fatty or lean (see below), but in either case, dip your fish in the solution for 20 seconds.

For fatty fish, like mackerel, tuna, mullet, trout, and salmon, dip the fish in an ascorbic acid solution (2 tablespoons ascorbic acid dissolved in 4 cups cold water).

For lean fish, which includes most freshwater fish as well as grouper, cod, flounder, tilapia, and snapper, among others, dip it in a brine made of ¼ cup salt to 4 cups cold water.

You can also make a brine of ¼ cup salt, 2 tablespoons ascorbic acid, and 4 cups cold water, which will pretreat any fish you have on hand.

PREPARING AND PACKAGING

If you'll only be storing your fish for 1 to 2 weeks (or less), wrapping it in plastic freezer wrap usually works just fine. But if you plan to store it longer term in the freezer, properly freezing is critical to prevent freezer burn and an undesirable texture. For longer-term storage, vacuum seal your fillets, package in ziplock bags with the air displacement method (see page 20), or glaze them with ice. Try to use fatty fish within 3 months and lean fish within 6 months, after which the quality of the thawed fish declines.

STEP 2

Ice Glazing

1 Place unwrapped, pretreated fish on a sheet pan in the freezer to freeze (I recommend lining the sheet pan with a silicone mat to prevent sticking).

2 Once the fish is frozen, dip it in an ice bath, then place it back in the freezer for a few minutes to set.

3 Repeat this process of dipping and freezing until the fish is coated with a ¼-inch-thick glaze of ice. Wrap in moisture-resistant paper or place in freezer bags.

STEP 3

FREEZING SHELLFISH

Clams, scallops, and oysters are, according to best practices, frozen live, which keeps their shells tightly shut during freezing. Place them shell-on in a moisture-vapor-resistant bag, press out the air, and freeze.

To save freezer space, shucked scallops can be placed in a freezer-safe container with ½ inch of headspace, then sealed and frozen. The same process is used for clams: Shuck them and drain the liquid before packing. Oysters should be shucked and the oyster liquor reserved, taking care to remove any sand or bits of shell. Place them in a freezer-safe container or freezer bag with the liquor, leaving ½ inch of headspace, then seal and freeze.

Seafood expert Hank Shaw uses ice glazing (page 376) for shucked clams and oysters, and for shrimp, storing the frozen seafood in a freezer bag. As he says, it's basically like doing IQF (individual quick freezing, a typically more industrial process) at home, and it helps your shellfish retain their quality. Note that shellfish's texture can change with freezing, so frozen oysters especially (but also clams) are best saved for soups and stews.

Lobster should be frozen uncooked, either whole and shell-on, or after cleaning, freezing just the tails (with shells). Wrap in moisture-vapor-resistant wrap, then freeze. Crab freezes best when not picked (which means the meat is not pulled out of the shell). Instead, remove back legs, gills, and entrails, either while raw or after boiling for 5 minutes. If you do boil your crab prior to freezing, cool quickly in the refrigerator after cooking. The claws and bodies can be ice-glazed (page 376) and wrapped in freezer wrap.

Shrimp can be frozen cooked or raw, shelled or unshelled, though raw (with shells on but heads removed) will last longest. Chill shrimp in the refrigerator for 1 to 2 hours before freezing, then package in freezer bags or freezer-safe containers, with ¼ inch of headspace, and freeze. To make shrimp easiest to separate while frozen, I freeze it on a rimmed sheet pan in a single layer with a little space between each shrimp, then package. Shellfish will last in the freezer for 2 months or more if properly stored.

FROZEN SEAFOOD STOCK

Fish stock and shellfish stock are excellent staples to have in the freezer, adding some variety to your meals alongside meat-based and vegetable stocks. Follow the directions for making stock earlier in this chapter (page 363), but swap out the chicken carcass with bony fish or shrimp shells. Cook low and slow. You won't need to cook for as many hours: Usually 4 to 6 hours will do it (but as with any stock, follow your senses!). For instructions on freezing stock, see page 363.

SALTING AND DRYING FISH

Salted seafood shapes the flavors of meals eaten by millions and perhaps billions of people a day, from dried fish in West Africa to salted dried shrimp in Mexico and the many, many variations of dried fish and shellfish used across the many diverse cuisines in Asia and Southeast Asia.

There's a huge range of options to explore in the world of salted fish: Some are smoked, some are air-dried, some are fermented, and the treatments of preserved fish can and do take up whole chapters of books (see Resources, page 410). Whole fish and shellfish can be preserved, as can other fishy products (fish roe, like dried bottarga, is preserved, too).

Fish is salted before it is dried, which helps draw out moisture and inhibits pathogen growth.

FISH JERKY

Fish jerky, like other jerkies, is a versatile snack for camping and road trips. It is a bit stinkier than beef jerky, though, so be prepared for a not-unpleasant but definitely present fish smell if you keep it stuffed at the bottom of your backpack during a hike.

Fish jerky is best made with lean fish (like mahi mahi, bass, or pike), as fatty or oily fish (like salmon or trout) can more easily go rancid. You technically *can* make it with fatty fish, but be sure to eat it soon after you do.

Another nice thing about fish jerky is that you can customize the flavor with the level of smoking or the type of marinade. I offer two of my favorites here: a deep, flavorful, soy sauce–based marinade that can stand up to full-flavor fish and a lighter, brighter marinade that's heavier on the lemon zest and lighter on the deep umami flavors so that delicate fish aren't overpowered.

Making Fish Jerky

You can enjoy your jerky as a snack or rehydrate it in other dishes like chowders (just be sure to adjust the salt in the original recipe to account for the salt and seasonings in the jerky).

1 Start by filleting and skinning your fish (unless you're using very small fish, like smelt; then just clean them and remove the heads—no deboning or skinning needed). Then cut into thin strips 1 inch wide.

2 If desired, hot smoke fish at 150°F/66°C or below until the fish takes on as much smoky flavor as you like but is not cooked. Remember that the smoky flavor will concentrate a bit once the fish is fully dried. I typically don't do this unless my smoker is already running, as it really only needs a short amount of time (anywhere from 3 to 30 minutes, depending on your desired flavor).

3 Make a marinade and pour it over your fish strips in a lidded food-safe container or zippered bag. Marinate in the refrigerator for 4 to 8 hours. If the fish strips aren't completely covered by marinade, flip them halfway through.

4 Once they're marinated, gently place your fish strips in a slotted or mesh strainer, letting the juice drip off them for 5 to 10 minutes, then gently pat them dry with paper towels (or a clean, unlinted cloth).

5 Arrange your fish in a single layer without touching on dehydrator trays, or on a rack tray in the oven. A dehydrator is the easiest, most energy-efficient option. I usually do 145°F/63°C for 4 to 6 hours, or until the fish has a chewy, jerkylike texture. For the oven, preheat it to 150°F/66°C and dehydrate the fish for 8 to 12 hours with the door propped open to release moisture.

6 Dry your fish until it has the leathery, chewy texture of jerky.

7 Let it cool completely at room temperature. Once it has completely cooled, you can pack it tightly in an airtight container or in a ziplock bag, or vacuum-seal it. Label, then store at room temperature in a cool, dark place (use within 1 month); in the refrigerator (use within 3 to 6 months); or in the freezer (use within 10 to 12 months).

Lemon-Miso Fish Jerky Marinade

This is my go-to for when I want a bright, flavorful marinade to go with my fish. Lemon and fish is a classic combination, and did you know that it came about because of humoral medicine? It's true! The cold, wet fish was thought to be balanced by the hot, dry (in humoral speak) nature of the lemon. So you're eating a bit of history every time you eat lemon and fish!

— Makes enough for 1 pound of fish

- 1 cup dry white wine
- 3 tablespoons white miso paste
- 1 teaspoon honey
- Zest of 1 lemon

Combine the wine, miso, honey, and lemon zest and mix well.

Garlic-Shoyu Fish Jerky Marinade

This deep, savory marinade is perfect for full-flavor fish or just for when you want a snack that packs a lot of flavor into each bite.

—— Makes enough for 1 pound of fish

- **2 cloves garlic, minced**
- **1 tablespoon light brown sugar**
- **½ tablespoon granulated sugar (optional)**
- **½–1 teaspoon red pepper flakes**
- **¼ cup dark soy sauce**
- **1 teaspoon sesame oil**

Combine the garlic, brown sugar, granulated sugar (if using), pepper flakes, soy sauce, and oil and mix well.

SMOKING

Hot smoking, the most common way people smoke fish in North America, means that you're smoking above 150°F/66°C and below 225°F/107°C—in other words, cooking over low heat, which adds a distinct smoky flavor. Hot smoking does not dramatically increase the shelf life of your fish unless it's hot smoked *and* dried further (think fish jerky), but it does increase the fish's shelf life in the fridge by a few days or so.

With cold smoking, seafood is typically cured first to remove some moisture, then cold smoked to preserve it further. Cold smoking typically happens around 90°F/32°C, for anywhere from half a day to several days, and the curing process beforehand is critical to preventing bacterial growth during smoking.

Smoked fish is first dry-salted (some people say dry-brined, which, if we want to get picky, is incorrect, because brines have water), or brined. Dry-salting is easiest; I follow Hank Shaw's advice in *Hook, Line, and Supper* and thickly coat the fish in salt, then let it sit for 1 hour per pound of fish. This draws out some moisture, which helps preserve the fish as well as season the flesh itself.

See page 96 for more information about smoking.

CANNING

Yes, it's possible to can fish: But you need to follow some exacting specifications to do it safely. For that reason, I usually freeze or pickle it instead.

Seafood is low acid and thus needs to be pressure canned. The texture of canned seafood is best for things like spreads, dips, and maybe stews. (Think of when you buy tinned fish at the store—you'd use your canned fish in a similar way.) In tested recipes from the USDA and in the University of Georgia Cooperative Extension's publication *So Easy to Preserve*, fish is pressure canned in just salt and water. There are some recipes that also increase the acidity of the canned fish by including vinegar or tomato sauce. If you go that route, make sure to use a trusted recipe from a trusted source (see canning books in Resources, page 411).

With canning, always follow the manufacturer's guidance and safe practices for your canner and the food you're canning. My canner, for example, includes a big warning that it isn't safe for smoked seafood.

PICKLING

Pickling is a simple way to preserve fish. Pickling helps extend the shelf life of this very perishable food, but it will only add maybe a week or two (or maybe a bit more, depending on the method) to your fish's edibility—it won't add months like jerky (see page 377) or years like fish sauce (see page 385).

There are rich fish-pickling traditions all over the world, from escabeche (one of my favorites; see page 381) to ceviche (raw fish lightly pickled in citrus juice) to pickled herring (my least favorite childhood food, despite my grandpaw's efforts, but now one I crave). Pickled fish retains its form, so it is a good choice if you like eating chunks of fish on or in dishes.

Quick pickling involves placing fish in an acidic brine, which adds flavor and enhances shelf life. You can quick pickle any seafood, but I especially enjoy this method for salmon, white fish, and shrimp. Pickled fish can be served cooked or served as is on bread or crackers, or with other accompaniments.

Preserving Around the World

Japan, with Nancy Singleton Hachisu

Nancy Singleton Hachisu is a cookbook author and food journalist whose book, *Preserving the Japanese Way*, was my introduction to Japanese food preservation techniques years ago and reflects a deep knowledge of and appreciation for Japanese cuisine.

"Salt is *the* vehicle for preserving foods in Japan," Hachisu says, "and given that Japan is an island nation, a large amount of preservation practices involve fish." Some popular preserves include half-dried fish (ichiyaboshi), dried overnight then grilled before being eaten. In Niigata, shiobiki shake (salt-dried salmon) is dried in salt for 7 to 10 days before being eaten.

Fish nukazuke (distinct from vegetable nukazuke) is a strongly flavored fish preserve from Ishikawa, made of very well salted fish packed in rice bran and fermented. Kusaya (literally "stinky") is a pungent fish from the Izu Peninsula, made by gutting and butterflying small fish, heads on, and soaking them in a perpetual brine that is reused for each batch, with more salt added each time. Kusaya are air-dried, then grilled before serving.

But salt preservation is not limited to seafood: Miso is made by mixing soybeans with rice koji, barley koji, or soybean koji and salt. For shoyu, koji spores are propagated on steamed soybeans and roasted cracked wheat, then salt and pristine well or mountain water are mixed in to create a mash (moromi). The mash is fermented for a year and then pressed into shoyu (and is leaps and bounds better than the "soy sauce" available at many American grocery chains).

Hachisu says that "quick salt-, miso-, or shoyu-pickling is the most common," for daily pickle consumption, though many people buy prepackaged. "The rural community in Japan is disappearing," she notes, as the landscape of work and life changes, which means much preserving and pickling is done by larger companies. However, miso making does still happen, as does some home vegetable pickling.

"Actual long-term preservation methods involving fruit or vegetables are few," she says, including "umeboshi (salt-brined, sun-dried sour plums), takuan (half-dried daikon, packed in salt, aromatics, and rice bran), hakusai (lactofermented napa cabbage with salt as the balancing agent), and narazuke (sun-dried cucumber and uri, packed in sweetened sake lees for several months)."

Preserved proteins and vegetables are regular features on Japanese tables, such as dried fish or fish eggs to go with sake or shochu, grilled dried or semi-dried fish, and pickled or preserved vegetables alongside miso soup and rice for breakfast or to end a meal.

Climate and the rhythm of the seasons play a role in what is preserved, and how. In cold areas like Niigata, longer salted fish preparations take place in snowy months. In southern coastal areas, half-day dried fish is made during cool months from early winter to early spring. Miso and shoyu are started in cool weather, and their fermentation ramps up during the hot, humid summer. Produce preservation matches what is seasonally available and appropriate to the seasonal temperature and humidity. For example, umeboshi and narazuke are started in summer.

At its core, Japanese cuisine is about quality ingredients presented with care. Hachisu also notes that engaging in Japanese preservation practices means participating in traditions with deep roots that need to be carried forward into the future: Using the terms *miso* or *shoyu* to describe amino sauces and amino pastes without any resemblance to the Japanese products is a case in point. "This kind of cultural appropriation is more like cultural annihilation. Miso has a 1,000-year-old tradition, and shoyu has been made using this current method for hundreds of years. These are critical traditions worth protecting for the future of Japan."

Pickled Shrimp

Unlike escabeche (below), this pickled shrimp is first boiled in liberally salted water until *just* cooked through. You can add seasonings (like lemon peel or Old Bay) to the water for an extra layer of flavor if you like.

— Makes about 1 quart

- **12½ cups water**
- **3–4 cups whole shrimp, deveined and heads removed**
- **2 teaspoons Old Bay seasoning**
- **1 teaspoon salt**
- **1½ cups distilled white vinegar**
- **2 (3-inch) strips lemon zest**
- **½ small white or yellow onion, cut into ¼-inch slices**
- **1 jalapeño, cut into ¼-inch slices**
- **Juice of 1 lemon**

1. Bring 12 cups (3 quarts) of the water to boil and season, if desired. Add the shrimp and cook until it just turns pink and cooks through but is not overcooked, 3 to 5 minutes.

2. Drain the shrimp and shock it in cold water to stop cooking.

3. Make the brine by combining the Old Bay, salt, vinegar, and remaining ½ cup water in a small pot and heating it just enough to dissolve the salt.

4. Add 1 strip of lemon zest to the bottom of a quart jar, then layer the onion, jalapeño, and shrimp, topping with the remaining lemon strip and leaving 1 inch of headspace.

5. Whisk the lemon juice into the brine. Pour the brine over the shrimp mixture to cover completely, add the lid, and let the shrimp pickle for 24 hours in the fridge before eating. It will last for 2 weeks or more in the fridge.

Escabeche and Trusting Your Instincts

In the book *Grand Dishes* by Anastasia Miari and Iska Lupton, which highlights grandmothers' culinary practices in various countries, one of the women profiled is Clara Maria in Madrid, Spain. Clara Maria, who founded the Alambique culinary school and shop, is an escabeche enthusiast: "You can escabeche anything, from partridge and game to chicken. It's a popular classic with all Spaniards. The verb *escabechar* in Spanish simply means 'to cook and preserve in vinegar,' which I like to do a lot, but using only very good-quality Spanish vinegar."

I love how she considers her relationship between cooking and the rest of her life:

> It's so important to have faith in whatever you go into. You must believe in what you do, very much. You have to believe it is going to happen. That's why I made a success of Alambique, because I truly believed in it. It's a question of character. Sometimes you do something and you think, "Oh, I am crazy, this is ridiculous, I'm going to lose everything." But if you are sure of what you're doing, it's magic. It opens all the doors. All you must do is believe.

This mixture of instinct and belief in what you're doing is important in preserving, too. When we learn how to preserve, and believe in ourselves and the success of whatever we're making, we can follow best practice along with our instincts with flavors and ingredients to make something more magical than we ever could have imagined.

Pickled White Fish

Pickled white fish, like pike and herring, hails from Scandinavia and eastern Europe, also finding its home in communities in North America that immigrated from these areas (like parts of the Upper Midwest). I love using lean white ocean fish, like mahi mahi, for this, too.

Some white fish (like mahi mahi) you can eat and pickle raw. All other fish need to be frozen first to kill potential pathogens (including tapeworms, carried by some freshwater fish, which is one reason why we cook them before eating). In this recipe, we brine the fish first in just salt and water, then layer it with spices and a traditional vinegar-based pickling brine.

You can change up the spicing in this brine to your heart's content!

— Makes about 1 quart

SALT BRINE

- ¼ cup salt
- 2 cups water

FISH

- 1 pound of filleted white fish
- 1 small red onion, thinly sliced
- 6 (3-inch) strips lemon zest, thinly sliced
- 1 bay leaf

PICKLING BRINE

- ¼–⅓ cup sugar
- 1½ teaspoons whole allspice berries
- ½ teaspoon coriander seeds
- ¼ teaspoon juniper berries (optional)
- 2 cups apple cider vinegar or white wine vinegar
- 2 cups water

1 Make the salt brine: Combine the salt and water in a small pot. Heat just enough to dissolve the salt. Let it cool to room temperature. If you are using fish that cannot be eaten raw, freeze the fish for 8 to 12 hours. See local fishing guidelines for information about the safety of your catch.

2 Pour the cooled brine over the fish and let it soak in the fridge for 6 to 8 hours.

3 Make the pickling brine: Combine the sugar, allspice, coriander, juniper (if using), vinegar, and water in a pot and heat just until the sugar is dissolved. Let it cool to room temperature.

4 Cut the fish into 1-inch cubes and layer it in a quart jar with the onion, lemon zest, and bay leaf.

5 Pour the cooled pickling brine over the top and let it sit in the refrigerator for at least 1 day before eating. It will last for about 1 month stored in the refrigerator.

Pickled Salmon

I learned this technique from *The Salmon Sisters: Feasting, Fishing, and Living in Alaska* by Emma Teal Laukitis and Claire Neaton. Salmon is layered in salt to remove some moisture, rinsed and soaked to keep it from getting *too* salty, then popped into an aromatic brine and kept in the fridge to be snacked on as you wish. This is the perfect option for folks who want a bit of salmon for breakfast and snacks, but who don't want to go to the trouble of pressure canning or smoking.

You can cut your salmon into chunks or squares or slices: It's perfect layered on crackers and breads. Just note that thicker pieces will take longer to pickle all the way through. This salmon is at home on a bagel, with a smattering of capers, Cream Cheese (page 351), and fresh scallions.

— Makes 1 quart

FISH

- 2–3 cups kosher salt
- 2–3 pounds raw salmon fillets, skin removed
- Strips of zest from 1 lemon
- ½ small white or yellow onion, cut into ¼-inch-thick slices

PICKLING BRINE

- ¼–⅓ cup sugar
- 3 (3-inch) strips lemon zest, thinly sliced
- 1 bay leaf
- 2 teaspoons black peppercorns
- 2 cups apple cider vinegar or white wine vinegar
- 1 cup water

1 In a flat, lidded container, layer a ¼-inch-deep layer of kosher salt, then arrange a single layer of salmon over it. Cover that with another ¼-inch layer of salt. Add strips of lemon zest between each layer, about 3 per fillet, for a little bit more flavor and aroma.

2 Place the container in the fridge and let it sit for 24 hours.

3 Rinse the salt from the fillets. Layer the fillets in a container and fill it with tap water. Place the container in the fridge and let the fillets soak for about 8 hours.

4 Drain the fillets, pat them dry, and cut them into about 1-inch cubes.

5 Pop a couple of strips of lemon zest into the bottom of a quart jar or other nonreactive container, then layer the onion and salmon, leaving 1 inch of headspace.

6 Make the pickling brine: Combine the sugar, lemon zest, bay leaf, peppercorns, vinegar, and water, and heat just until the sugar is dissolved. Let cool to room temperature.

7 Pour the cooled pickling brine over the salmon until completely submerged, and let it sit in the fridge for at least 1 day before eating. It will last for 2 to 3 weeks in the refrigerator.

VARIATION: SMOKED SALMON

If you want a bit of a smoky bite, you can indeed put your fish in the smoker after soaking but before brining, until fragrant. It's important to use a low temperature (120 to 150°F/49 to 66°C) and shorter smoke time (think half an hour or so rather than hours), as the texture of the final pickled salmon is best when using salmon that hasn't been cooked with heat. Or use smoked salt in place of regular salt, or add a dash of smoked paprika to taste.

Pickled Salmon

Pickled Oysters

Pickled oysters were once synonymous with New York City cuisine, according to Mark Kurlansky's *The Big Oyster*. This recipe is inspired by the flavors of an eighteenth-century recipe for pickled oysters, which was probably the most common preparation for New York City's famous oysters at the time.

— Makes about 1 pint

- 1 pint shucked, raw oysters with their liquor reserved (20–24 oysters)
- 1 teaspoon salt
- ½ teaspoon black peppercorns
- ¼ teaspoon ground allspice
- ⅛ teaspoon grated nutmeg
- 1 cup apple cider vinegar, white wine vinegar, or Artichoke Vinegar (page 115)

1. Combine the oysters and their liquor, salt, peppercorns, allspice, nutmeg, and vinegar in a pot over medium-high heat. Bring to a boil, then reduce the heat and simmer until the oysters are cooked through, occasionally stirring (gently), 6 to 8 minutes.

2. Remove from the heat, skim any scum off the surface, and cool the oysters to room temperature.

3. Store the pickled oysters in an airtight container in the fridge, where they will keep for 1 week or more.

Fermenting Fish: A Global Tradition

Some forms of pickled fish are traditionally fermented rather than quick pickled. Dutch maatjes herring, for example, is cured in 8 to 10 percent brine for a relatively short amount of time. Swedish surströmming (literally "sour herring") is lightly brined in 3 to 4 percent salt, then fermented in barrels for 1 or 2 months; it's then transferred to a saltier environment and sealed, where the fermentation continues.

In Filipino burong isda (fish fermented with rice) and balao-balao (shrimp fermented with rice), the fish (or shrimp) and their juices, plus cooked and cooled rice, are packed in a jar with garlic and ginger and sometimes also red yeast rice (angkak), then fermented and later served with sautéed garlic and onion.

Many fish ferments are strong-smelling, some like ammonia, but the flavor is nuanced if pungent. I passed a wonderful, memorable evening with my friends from Súrkál fermentation company in Iceland as we shared various fermented meats, fishes, cheeses, bread made in a geothermal spring, and mead and beer from friends. We also had skata, fermented skate typically served at Christmas, and while it was strongly flavored, I was pleasantly surprised by the taste.

FISH SAUCE AND SALTED FISH

One aspect of our ancestors' meat and fish preserving practices was not just to make meat and fish last longer but also to extend one's salt stores as far as they could go. According to legend, surströmming, or fermented herring, was discovered accidentally by Swedes trying to save salt. This is similar to the origin stories we often hear about the development of fish sauce, whether we're talking about Roman garum or the fish sauces of East and Southeast Asia. All were created to add a big dose of umami flavor plus salt, requiring less salt than if it used salt alone.

Fish sauce appears to have originated in China, and the preservation method then spread outward around the world, according to Mark Kurlansky in *Salt: A World History*. Sprinkling salt directly on food was far less common in ancient times than salting food by adding condiments, and fish fermented in salt was a popular choice.

According to the *Geoponica*, a Greek agricultural manual written around 900 CE, liquamen or garum (the fish sauce used in ancient Greece and Rome) is made by salting fish intestines in a vessel alongside small whole fish, also salted. The salty mixture is then set in the sun and frequently shaken or moved. The heat from the sun (as well as the enzymes in the intestines) break down the fish, and once a good bit of liquid has seeped out, the whole thing is strained through a basket. The liquid (or liquamen/garum) strains through the basket into the vessel below, while the solids (or allec) remain in the basket.

On page 386 is my basic fish sauce, a modern version of those ancient techniques. You can find more recipes in the books listed beginning on page 411. *Koji Alchemy* by Rich Shih and Jeremy Umansky, for example, has a method for making fish sauce with koji.

Fish sauce is a flavor-packed condiment with ancient roots.

Making Fish Sauce

Fish sauce can be made from many different sea creatures and is a great way to preserve fish while also adding an umami burst to your meals. The guts (which provide enzymes needed for breaking down the fish) are left intact, and the fish are layered in salt until a transparent, rich, salty liquid (the fish sauce) separates out. I make mine in a jar and *carefully* pour the sauce out when it's done.

Recipes vary in the amount of salt they use. Some use a 1:10 or 1:8 ratio of salt to fish (1 pound salt to 8 pounds fish, for example), and some use much more salt (e.g., 1:4 ratio). Use small fish (such as mackerel, sardines, and smelt) and cut them into pieces if they run large. Herbs and spices can sometimes be packed in with the fish, too, but are optional. This can be a fun place to play around with flavors!

1 Place a layer of salt in the bottom of a glass jar or other food-safe vessel with a lid.

2 Place a layer of fish and herbs (if using), and another layer of salt (like making a lasagna, but with fish) on top. Press down each layer as you go to remove any air bubbles. Continue layering. Make sure the last layer you put on is a thick layer of salt to protect your fish from the elements.

3 Place a nonreactive, food-safe weight on top of the layers to keep everything in place, and top the vessel with a lid.

4 Let the fish ferment for at least 6 months (1 year or more is best) on the counter. Setting it in the sun will result in accelerated enzymatic action; however, it will do just fine out of direct sunlight. Your fish sauce is ready when it has a layer of transparent liquid on top (typically the color and clarity, though certainly not the flavor, of maple syrup).

5 Slowly pour off the fish sauce into a bowl, taking care not to upset the remaining solids in your jar. Once you have poured off as much liquid as you can, transfer your fish sauce to a jar. Historically, this liquid was kept at room temperature out of direct sunlight, where it would last for at least a couple of months, but if you prefer you can store it in the fridge, where it will last for years.

6 If you're up for it and would like to capture every bit of fish sauce, transfer the fish concoction left in your fermentation vessel into a cheesecloth-lined mesh sieve set over a bowl. Press the remaining liquid into the bowl to get a cloudy, but still very delicious, fish sauce. This will also store in the fridge indefinitely.

Meat Amino Sauces and Beyond

You can apply this same method of heavily salting and letting sit to other proteins, too. Some people call them garum as a nod to the ancient Greek and Roman term, but I prefer "amino sauce," as it acknowledges that the process cultivates umami but also keeps these sauces conceptually distinct from global fish sauce traditions. You can find examples made with freshly ground beef and one with bee pollen in *The Noma Guide to Fermentation*, and you can find many other examples of creative koji-based sauces in *Koji Alchemy*.

Eggs

Eggs are pretty magical; they have powerful symbolism in creation myths and springtime rituals across many global cultures. I could get metaphysical here about the power and magic of eggs, but they are also just plain good eating. When I used to keep chickens and quail, I had eggs in abundance and thus needed to preserve many eggs quite often. I froze them, pickled them, and ate eggs with pretty much every meal from March to September (I didn't can them, though, as there is no safe method for canning eggs).

My story is part of a long, rich, worldwide tradition: millions of hands over thousands of years working to preserve eggs, through burying in ashes or in the ground, pickling, freezing, curing in salt, or drying. By preserving our eggs, which hens don't naturally lay in cooler, darker months, we offer ourselves ongoing nutrition, making them both delicious and a part of our individual and collective food security.

For preserving, eggs should be as fresh as possible. You can test their freshness by gently placing the eggs in a bowl of water. Those that lie flat are fresh. Those that stand on their ends have gas starting to build up inside, which means they're older. And those that float are either rotting or well on their way there.

If you purchase your eggs refrigerated, continue to refrigerate them. Once eggs have been refrigerated, they cannot be stored on the counter. Refrigerated eggs should be used within 3 to 5 weeks.

Working with Non-Chicken Eggs

Many of these recipes can be easily adapted to your quail, duck, ostrich, or whatever other eggs. Just adjust times for pickling and curing up or down, depending on size (larger size = longer cure). For freezing, follow the same methods as for chicken eggs.

Ways to Preserve Eggs

	Shelf-stable	Fast	Low waste	Ready meals and ingredients	Big flavor
Shoyuzuke Eggs (page 390)		X		X	X
Pickled Eggs in Vinegar (page 391)		X		X	X
Salt-Cured Egg Yolks (page 391)		X		X	X
Misozuke (Miso-Pickled) Eggs (page 392)		X		X	X
Preserved Lemon Eggs (page 393)		X		X	X

The Best Way to Boil an Egg

I boiled a lot of eggs testing recipes for this book. Prior to that, my hard-boiled egg technique had been hit or miss. But hundreds of eggs later, I can safely say my technique has improved considerably. There are many ways to hard-boil an egg—bringing to a boil then turning off the water, using a pressure cooker, or even baking them. But for preserving hard-boiled eggs, where you want an egg that's got a firm yolk or, in the case of Shoyuzuke Eggs (page 390), a jammy yolk (not runny), I prefer this method.

The ice bath is a critical step here: It cools the shells quickly, helping them separate more cleanly from the egg so peeling is a *lot* easier than hard-boiling and letting them cool naturally.

Here's how I hard-boil eggs:

1. Add 6 eggs to a large saucepan or pot and add water to cover by 2 inches. Replace any egg that floats with a fresh egg.
2. Bring the water just to a boil, then reduce the heat, gently stir to cover the eggs, and simmer for 11 minutes.
3. Carefully scoop the eggs into an ice bath and let them sit for 5 minutes.
4. Gently tap and roll the eggs on a counter or cutting board, then carefully peel off the shells.
5. Store hard-boiled eggs in the fridge, where they will last for 2 to 3 days.

FREEZING

Freezing is one of the faster ways to preserve eggs; however, note that cooked egg whites shouldn't be frozen. You *can* freeze them, but the texture is like eating a sponge made of weirdly dense but also kind of runny rubber. I do not recommend it.

To freeze whole eggs, start with fresh, raw eggs and crack them into a bowl (I crack them into a separate bowl first, just in case one is rotten, then add them to the larger bowl). Whisk the eggs to combine yolks and whites, but be careful not to beat in air. Optional, but recommended to prevent graininess later: Add 1½ tablespoons of sugar or corn syrup, or ½ teaspoon of salt per cup of egg, and stir to combine. Strain the eggs through a sieve or colander, then package them with ½ inch of headspace, seal, and freeze. Three tablespoons of egg mixture equals one whole egg.

Or you can freeze whole eggs my favorite way—in ice cube trays. Simply pour your egg mixture into an ice cube tray that holds about 3 tablespoons of liquid per cube. Place your trays in the freezer and freeze until solid, then remove the cubes and package them in a vapor- and moisture-resistant container. Seal it and pop it back in the freezer, where the eggs will last for at least 1 or 2 months.

To freeze egg yolks, separate your eggs, then gently stir or whisk your yolks to break them up, being careful not to beat in air. Optional, but recommended to prevent graininess later: Add 1½ tablespoons sugar or corn syrup, or ½ teaspoon salt per cup of egg, and stir to combine. Strain the yolks through a sieve, then package leaving ½ inch of headspace. Seal and freeze (or freeze in ice cube trays as directed above). One tablespoon of yolk mixture equals one egg yolk.

To freeze egg whites, separate your eggs, then gently stir or whisk your whites to break them up, being careful not to beat in air. (You don't need to add sugar or salt to the whites, as the fatty yolks are the only part of the egg that gets pasty and hard to work with after freezing.) Strain the whites through a sieve, then package leaving ½ inch of headspace. Seal and freeze (or freeze in ice cube trays as directed previously). Two tablespoons of egg white mixture equals one fresh egg white.

Another great way to freeze egg whites (from the new *Joy of Cooking*) is in amounts that suit your favorite baked-goods recipes, like angel food cake. You can still whip thawed egg whites, so this is a great answer to the eternal conundrum of what to do with all the egg whites after making a yolk-heavy recipe.

Kimchi Eggs, Kvass Eggs, and Other Fermented Brine Pickles

Finished ferments like kimchi, beet kvass, and full sour-pickle brine (three of my favorites) can be reimagined as pickling mediums for your delicious hard-boiled eggs, each offering its own flavor profile to the finished product. Get creative with your favorite pickling brines and see where that takes you!

To make these eggs, just add hard-boiled and peeled eggs to a jar, leaving 1 inch of headspace, then pour brine over to completely cover and allow to pickle in the fridge. They should be ready in a day or two. They will last for at least 1 week if kept under the brine.

Eggs pickled in beet kvass can range from pink to red to sometimes purple!

PICKLING AND CURING

Pickling and salt curing are two of my favorite ways to preserve eggs, as they offer a simple, accessible, and delicious way to preserve your eggs that results in some decadent ready ingredients to use in later meals.

Whole eggs are, in most cases, hard-boiled then peeled prior to being plopped in a jar of brine or rolled in miso. But for every rule there's an exception, and you can cure raw eggs, too. Cured raw egg yolks (see page 391) remain one of my favorite ways to instantly add richness to a dish.

Shoyuzuke Eggs

Shoyuzuke Eggs

I first learned this process from Kirsten Shockey, and it has become a staple for salty, tangy eggs to top my salads, soups, and noodles. If you've ever had a jammy egg on ramen with a salty taste and slightly brown outside, this is what you were eating. The shoyu (soy sauce) really shines in this recipe, so be sure to use a good-quality, naturally fermented one.

This versatile brine can vary based on your taste: Add a splash more mirin to sweeten it a bit more, bright strips of lemon zest, or some seasonal herbs and aromatics you love (think springtime garlic scapes or green shoots from your onions).

— Makes 6 eggs

- **6 eggs**
- **1½ cups water**
- **1 cup good-quality soy sauce (shoyu or tamari)**
- **2–3 tablespoons mirin**
- **1½–2 tablespoons rice wine vinegar**
- **¼ cup herbs or aromatics (for example, fresh chiles, fresh loosely packed herbs, scallions, slices of ginger, garlic cloves)**
- **1 strip kombu (seaweed)**

1. Hard-boil and peel your eggs using the instructions on page 388. For ramen eggs with a more jammy yolk, reduce cook time by 1 to 2 minutes.

2. Make the brine: Mix the water, soy sauce, mirin, vinegar, herbs, and kombu in a quart jar.

3. Gently drop the eggs into the brine, making sure they are all completely covered. Add the lid and refrigerate for 7 to 12 hours.

4. These eggs will keep in the fridge for up to 10 days. The brine can be reused one more time for a second batch.

Pickled Eggs in Vinegar

When you think "pickled eggs," you probably think of the ones pickled in distilled white vinegar, maybe with some beet added and a couple of spices, like those you might get at a bar or gas station. As you'll see throughout this section, there are many other ways to pickle eggs, but this version remains a delicious classic.

Like with all pickle recipes, you can adjust the spices up and down, or swap things out, to match your own preferences. I love pickled eggs with five-spice powder, for example, or with thyme, rosemary, and a burst of red pepper flakes.

— Makes 6 eggs

- **6 eggs**
- **1 tablespoon black peppercorns**
- **1 tablespoon sugar**
- **½–1 tablespoon ground ginger**
- **½ tablespoon whole allspice berries**
- **1 teaspoon red pepper flakes**
- **1 teaspoon salt**
- **2 cups distilled white vinegar or apple cider vinegar (5% acidity)**

1. Hard-boil and peel your eggs using the instructions on page 388.
2. Gently pack the cooled eggs into sterilized jars (two pints or one quart).
3. Make the brine: In a medium saucepan, combine the peppercorns, sugar, ginger, allspice, pepper flakes, salt, and vinegar and simmer over medium heat for 5 to 6 minutes.
4. Pour the hot brine over the eggs, seal, and place in the refrigerator.
5. Keep the eggs refrigerated and use within 1 month.

Salt-Cured Egg Yolks

A cured egg yolk is a thing of magic. The salt removes much of the water from the yolk, rendering it dense and grateable, with a salty savoriness that I adore (it's a wonderful stand-in for grated parmesan). Removing some water from the yolks lengthens their shelf life, too, though they should still be stored in the fridge.

— Makes 4 egg yolks

- **3 cups salt**
- **4 eggs**

1. In a flat-bottomed 1-quart container, spread half of the salt in an even layer.
2. Create small divots, evenly spaced, in the salt with the back of a spoon or the bottom of an uncracked egg: These are where your yolks will live.
3. One at a time, separate the whites from the eggs, reserving the whites for another use. Gently place each yolk in its little divot on the salt bed, then add the remaining salt in an even layer to cover.
4. Pop the (airtight) lid on your container, place it in the fridge, and wait for 5 to 7 days. Remove the yolks from the salt and store in an airtight container in the fridge, where they will last for about 1 month. The salt can be reused for subsequent batches.

VARIATION: SALTY AND SWEET

You can also make these with half salt and half sugar (about 2 cups of each, depending on the size of your container). Just whisk the salt and sugar together to evenly combine before using. You can also make it with just sugar using the same method.

PICKLING BEDS

Burying food in a pickling bed is a time-honored way to preserve it for future eating, and we can turn our attention toward Japan for prolific examples of the pickling bed in action.

Miso is a classic pickling-bed base. Eggs can be buried in whatever kind of miso you wish. If you make or buy unconventional misos (those made from something besides soybeans), they can be fun to experiment with here, too.

The sky's the limit with pickling-bed possibilities. You might pickle in deep, dark, rich tianmanjiang, a Chinese condiment made from fermented bread and sometimes beans (hence its other name, sweet bean sauce). Sake kasu (the lees, or sediment, left from brewing sake) is also a popular pickling-bed choice. I've used ground or mashed-up lactofermented vegetables (especially those that went unexpectedly mushy but have a good flavor) as a pickling bed for eggs and veggies. Each imparts a different flavor—from mouth-puckeringly sour to bracingly salty, from mild and mellow to rich and spiced—and part of the joy is in the discovery.

If you are a fermenter or lover of ferments, pickling beds open up a new realm of experimentation and discovery. And if you're not, I still encourage you to at least try enrobing your eggs in miso, just for the incredible flavor. Who knows, you might become a pickling-bed lover, too!

Misozuke Eggs

Misozuke (Miso-Pickled) Eggs

The magic of these eggs is in their salty, deep flavor and their deceptively easy production, but they also showcase practical preservation at its finest: Yes, you easily extend the life of hard-boiled eggs, but you can also reuse the pickling bed for many subsequent batches—meaning that nothing is wasted, and delicious, umami-rich preserves are always within reach. I learned this process from Nancy Singleton Hachisu's excellent book *Preserving the Japanese Way*.

Miso-cured eggs are phenomenal with rice, hearty soups, or sliced on a salad. You will undoubtedly find many other great uses for them, too. I recommend starting with a small batch of six eggs, especially if you're using a miso you haven't tried before. You can always make a larger batch later. While white miso is the standard option, so many other possibilities exist, and I encourage you to explore with your favorite misos and see what you like best.

— Makes 6 eggs

6 eggs

1 pound miso

1. Hard-boil and peel your eggs using the instructions on page 388.

2. Divide the miso evenly among the eggs: Gently press about 3 tablespoons of miso into a flat disc or pancake shape in the palm of your hand, place an egg in the middle, and then gently fold the miso around the egg. Gently (always gently!), completely enclose the egg in the miso.

3. Repeat with all 6 eggs, then store in an airtight container in the fridge for about 4 hours. After 4 hours have passed, remove the miso (yes, even if you aren't using the eggs immediately), then pack your used miso in a resealable container in the fridge for subsequent batches (you can reuse it multiple times, particularly with very salty misos).

4 For larger batches, you can spread a layer of miso in the bottom of a container, then evenly lay your hard-boiled eggs across it and pack a layer of miso over the top of them to completely cover each one. Hachisu recommends doing no more than two layers of eggs in your container, to prevent crushing the bottom layer, and waiting 6 hours to accommodate the larger number of eggs. These last for 1 week or more in the fridge.

Preserved Lemon Eggs

A bright, flavorful way to mix up your hard-boiled egg routine, these eggs are inspired by misozuke (miso-cured eggs) and use a similar process. Preserved lemons, or another citrus of your choice preserved using that same method, make some of the best-tasting and lovely eggs I've ever had, with a nice, firm texture and a bright, enticing lemony flavor that's really nice on a Niçoise salad or just about anything else.

— Makes 4 eggs

4 eggs

1 pint preserved lemons (see page 283)

1 Hard-boil and peel your eggs using the instructions on page 388.

2 Meanwhile, put the preserved lemons in a blender or food processor, liquid and all, and blend into a paste.

3 Add a ½-inch layer of lemon paste in the bottom of a flat-bottomed container with an airtight lid. (I reuse plastic takeout containers about the size of a soup bowl for this, but use what you have on hand.)

4 Layer the eggs on top, leaving a little space between them.

5 Spread the remaining paste over to cover, ensuring it gets between the eggs.

6 Seal the lid and let the eggs sit in the fridge for 1 to 3 days. They will get saltier, more flavorful, and denser (the salt draws water from the egg as it cures) the longer they sit. I find my sweet spot for these eggs is at 1 to 2 days, after which they're too salty for me.

7 Once they're done curing, remove the eggs and gently wipe off any remaining paste (you can reuse the paste once more for another batch of eggs).

8 Store in an airtight container in the fridge and use within 1 month.

What to Do with Eggshells?

These are my favorite ways to use up all those eggshells:

INFUSED VINEGAR. This is literally just eggshells in a jar, covered with vinegar. It can be added sparingly to your garden to increase calcium.

SCOURING SOLUTION FOR CLEANING. Dry your eggshells in a dehydrator or low oven for a few hours to dry out the inner membrane completely. Allow to cool, then finely grind and store in an airtight container. Mix with soap to make a cleaning scrub, but avoid using it on surfaces that can scratch easily.

MINERALS FOR THE GARDEN. Finely crush your eggshells (this helps them break down more easily) and add them to your compost or turn into garden beds.

FOOD FOR CHICKENS. If you keep your own birds, crushing the eggshells and feeding them back to your flock helps your hens replenish the resources their bodies spend in making eggs to nourish you.

CHAPTER 10

Other Preserving Experiments

Preserving for Medicine and Self-Care	396
Crafting as Preserving	401
Regrowth	402
Playing with Flowers	402
Playing with Leaves	403

Fish-Skin Parchment
(page 401)

I want this book to be the beginning of your own abundant preserving journey, not the end. One thing that has been fulfilling in my own journey is combining my other nonpreserving interests, like crafts, art, and time in nature, with my preserving practice. So, to set you on your path, here are a few other directions your journey could take you. You might be surprised where it leads.

Preserving for Medicine and Self-Care

Preserving the abundance around you becomes a part of your lifestyle the more you do it, and the practice of preserving seeps into your life beyond the kitchen. My food-preserving practice has grown to encompass many of the crafts, herbal medicines, and body-care products I make for myself and my loved ones. To me, it's a reminder that for most of history our culinary and medicinal practices have been deeply interwoven, which is part of the reason I started to pursue herbalism.

The information in this section offers a glimpse into the possibilities of using herbs and other ingredients from your garden for home and body. I hope it gives you a sense of the magic that a life rooted in preserving and the seasons can provide.

SALVES

You can preserve the healing power of plants with skin salves, both to moisturize the skin and to soothe acute conditions like bug bites, eczema, or burns. Two of my go-tos are rose salve and a salve called (charmingly) wound charm.

Melt 1 cup of oil (olive, almond, or whatever is your favorite) and 1 ounce of beeswax with ½ to 1 cup of botanicals. You can play with the ratios to impact texture and strength, but this ratio is a good starting point. Heat over a double boiler to slowly infuse your botanicals in your oil, strain it through cheesecloth, pour into jars, and let cool. Here are a few of my favorites.

Healing Rose Skin Salve

Tip: To make a thinner salve, use less beeswax. For an extra-thick, dense salve, use more.

— Makes about 1½ pints

- **1 ounce grated beeswax**
- **1 cup oil (olive, almond, or your favorite)**
- **1 cup packed fresh rose petals or ½ cup dried rose petals**

1. Combine the beeswax, oil, and rose petals in a double boiler. Heat over medium or medium-high heat for 20 to 30 minutes to warm the oil, melt the wax, and infuse the rose.

2. Line a strainer with cheesecloth, place it over a bowl, and strain the oil through it. Or, if you like, leave the rose petals in the oil for visual effect, bearing in mind they will stick to you when you use the salve.

3. Pour the warm salve into heatproof half-pint or smaller jars, let it cool, then put on the lids. Store the salve in a cool, dry location out of direct sunlight, where it will keep for at least 6 months.

Icelandic Wound Charm

I feel closer to the earth in Iceland than in many places, and this closeness to nature seems to be part of the culture there, manifesting even in the herbal salves available for sale in the airport—one of which, labeled "wound charm," became an instant favorite of mine.

This recipe mimics the Icelandic unguent in form and function. It's absolute magic on small cuts, scrapes, and bug bites, making it a summertime staple in my household. If you enjoy making your own salves, I hope you'll give this one a try.

—— Makes 2–2½ pints

- **1 cup packed fresh yarrow flowers**
- **½ cup packed fresh chickweed**
- **⅓ cup dried or ½ cup packed fresh flowers**
- **¼ cup packed fresh mugwort flowers and/or leaves**
- **¼ cup packed fresh violet leaves**
- **1 (4-inch) piece fresh curly dock root**
- **2 cups extra-virgin olive oil**
- **2 ounces grated beeswax**

1. Combine the herbs and oil in a double boiler and heat slowly for about 1 hour, gently stirring and pressing occasionally (a wooden spoon works best here) for maximum extraction.

2. Line a strainer with cheesecloth, place it over a bowl, and strain the oil into it. Allow everything to cool slightly so it's safe to handle.

3. Wrap up the cheesecloth and squeeze out as much oil as you can from the plant matter.

4. Place the oil in a saucepan and add the beeswax. Heat slowly, stirring constantly, until the beeswax is just melted. Remove from the heat.

5. Pour into half-pint or smaller heatproof jars, let them cool, then put on the lids. Store the salve in a cool, dry location, out of direct sunlight, where it will keep for at least 6 months.

Icelandic Wound Charm

INFUSED OILS

You can preserve dried herbs and other skin-safe aromatics, like citrus zest, in oil for use as body oils using the same process you'd use to make flavored culinary oils.

To warm-infuse oils, gently heat the oil and aromatics over a double boiler until fragrant and (in the case of edible aromatics) flavorful.

To cold infuse, add dried botanicals to a jar (it's important not to use fresh, which could lead to pathogen growth) and leave at least 1 inch of headspace. Make sure the plant matter stays completely under the oil to prevent spoilage. Let steep for 2 to 4 weeks, until the oil has a fragrance and/or flavor you enjoy. Strain and store at room temperature.

HERBAL TEAS

Herbal teas are simply dried herbs steeped in water, strained, and enjoyed hot or iced. Your garden's abundance can be dried in bundles or in a dehydrator (see page 92), then turned into delicious, healing teas. I choose herbs based on their medicinal qualities as well as their flavor, and I usually blend herbal teas: I love adding a sweet note, a floral note, and either a bitter or citrus note. You can, of course, also make tea using just one herb (like peppermint, for digestion).

Calming Winter Herbal Tea

The herbs in this tasty tea help soothe digestion and calm your nervous system. Rose also is a healer for the heart and for grief, helping you enter the new year with an open heart and with a balm for what ails you. It's a perfect, soothing hot tea as is, or it can be sweetened with honey, flavored with a slice of lemon, or served with your other favorite tea add-ins.

— Makes 1 pint

1 cup dried lemon verbena leaves
⅔ cup dried peppermint leaves
¼ cup dried rose petals

1. In a bowl, mix together the lemon verbena, peppermint, and rose petals until evenly combined. Pour into a pint jar or divide between smaller jars with airtight lids. Store out of direct sunlight, where the tea will last for months.

2. To make tea, use 1 to 2 tablespoons per 8-ounce cup of hot water. Infuse for 5 to 10 minutes or until it's as strong as you'd like.

HERBAL TINCTURES

If you, like me, enjoy herbal medicine making from your foraged and cultivated finds, alcohol tinctures are a shelf-stable and simple way to do so, particularly for extracting resins. They're also simple to take and can travel with you. You can make tinctures with fresh or dried edible flowers, herbs, and spices. A few that I always have on hand are passionflower (which I take every night), wild lettuce, tulsi, medicinal mushroom blends, rose, mimosa flower, goldenrod, chamomile, vervain, elderberry, and violet leaf. As with any remedy, use your best judgment when deciding what herbs to take, and check with a healthcare professional to discuss their relationship with your own medical history and medications. If using watery fresh herbs, take care to not pack the jars too tightly, which can dilute the tincture considerably.

Passionflower Tincture

Here's the most basic approach to making tinctures, using passionflower as an example. Essentially, you steep your botanicals for a couple of weeks to 1 month, then strain and bottle.

— Makes 1 cup

¾ cup fresh passionflower
1 cup distilled spirits (40 proof or higher) such as vodka, Everclear, or whiskey

1. Fill a half-pint jar loosely with the flowers, leaving 1 inch of headspace, then fill to completely cover with the distilled spirits.

2. Add the lid and allow to steep for about 1 month, checking occasionally to make sure the flowers remain submerged (if they keep floating to the top, just give it a gentle shake once a day).

3. Strain the tincture with a fine-mesh strainer, then decant it into dropper bottles. I recommend labeling with the proof of the alcohol and the measurements for each ingredient so you can replicate particularly effective batches again.

FIRE CIDER

Fire cider is a health tonic that was popularized by herbalist Rosemary Gladstar, and it is part of a long, worldwide tradition of using infused vinegars as health tonics, like four thieves vinegar, which is said to have originated during the Black Plague.

Fire cider is typically made with unpasteurized apple cider vinegar. It also commonly uses hot peppers and alliums (onions and garlic). Aside from that, the ingredients are extremely flexible and vary from person to person and even batch to batch. I classify my ingredients into three main groups—roots, shoots and fruits, and spices—and mix and match between them. You might add a blend of fresh chiles, your favorite whole spices, fresh herbs, little bits of vegetable matter (like the tops of onions, beets, or strawberry), or herb stems from other cooking projects! The goal is to get as much goodness packed into the jar as possible.

Fire Cider

Fire cider can be enjoyed as a health tonic by the shot glass or spoonful, or it can be incorporated into recipes, dressings, and marinades as a flavorful stand-in for apple cider vinegar. I love using it in vinaigrette since it already has all the flavor I need—just whisk with olive oil and serve.

I purposefully did not give measurements for the ingredients, as this recipe is meant to be adapted to what you like and have on hand.

— Makes 1 pint

Roots, such as onion, garlic, turmeric, ginger, horseradish, and carrot

Shoots and fruits, such as strips of citrus zest, thyme, rosemary, parsley, wild greens, dried cherries, and elderberries

Spices, such as chiles (any variety), cinnamon sticks, star anise, and cloves

Unpasteurized apple cider vinegar

Honey (optional)

1. Slice, cube, or coarsely chop the roots, and cut the hot peppers in halves or quarters.

2. Pack all of the roots, shoots and fruits, and spices tightly into a pint jar, and fill it all the way to the neck with the vinegar, making sure everything is submerged. Cover with a tightly fitting lid.

3. Let it steep at room temperature for at least 1 month. If bits of herbs and spices float to the top, gently shake the jar each day to redistribute them.

4. Once it's ready, strain the aromatics. If you want to add honey, stir it in now or whisk it in when serving. Bottle the finished fire cider and store at room temperature; it will keep for months.

VARIATION: SPRING BERRY CIDER

I make a lot of my fire cider in late summer to have it ready to go for winter cold and flu season, but I also like to make a berry-rich version in spring. It's a great tonic, and its deep, vibrant color makes it fun. Follow the recipe above, but pack in lots of fresh-as-can-be berries, too. Blueberries, strawberries, raspberries, blackberries, and mulberries are my go-tos, but use whatever is fresh and available to you.

VARIATION: FALL-SPICED CIDER

I like to pull in cozy mulled-cider vibes to this version. Though fire cider is not itself sweet, some people do add honey after steeping or when serving, and this particular version is a great one to sweeten up, if desired. Think of your favorite mulling spices—cinnamon, cloves, allspice, etc.—and other seasonal flavors you enjoy (like orange or even rosemary). I think turmeric tastes great in this one, too. I typically leave out the garlic and onions here, instead opting for lots of ginger and citrus. And, of course, it still has plenty of hot peppers; I prefer the flavor of red to green peppers in this version.

VARIATION: FIVE-SPICE CIDER

For this one, I use lots of fresh ginger, plus shredded licorice or star anise, Sichuan peppercorns, and a little each of cinnamon, cloves, and fennel.

Community Care with Fire Cider

Cultivating a preserving practice often means we have food to share, and it gives us the opportunity to be of service to the people around us. Fire cider is an important component of my own mutual aid work, and fire cider is a great, simple way to support your community's health and tickle their palates, particularly if you're short on time and want to make one simple thing that can be distributed widely.

As I talk about in the Introduction to this book, preserving, to me, is a holistic practice: one that has the potential to feed and nourish us and our loved ones, to play and experiment, to engage in reciprocity with community and the natural world, and perhaps to walk a bit more lightly on the earth.

Fire cider is so easy to make in quantity that you will almost certainly find yourself with more of it than you can use. Check with local mutual aid groups, food rescue or distribution organizations, community gardens, community-focused herbalists, and other resources in your area. Sometimes there will be a request and need for fire cider, or the fire cider might fit into a larger program of distribution that someone is already doing. I also have luck posting its availability on social media. It seems to always end up going where it's needed the most.

BITTERS

Bitters, potent infusions of botanicals in alcohol, are used medicinally to stimulate salivation and digestion. If you don't imbibe at all, you can also make them with vinegar; just be mindful that it can change the final flavor versus using alcohol.

As far as what alcohol to use to infuse your bitters, the sky's the limit, though it makes the most sense to use either a neutral spirit (like vodka or whiskey) rather than a spirit that's already infused or distilled with flavorful botanicals (like gin). This gives you more control over the taste of the final product.

The key to bitters is, well, bitter things, like the following:

- Artichoke/cardoon
- Cacao nibs
- Chamomile
- Chicory
- Bitter citrus like trifoliate orange
- Coffee
- Dandelion
- Gentian
- Goldenrod
- Mango peel
- Muscadine grape skins
- Sage
- Tobacco
- Yarrow

1. Pack your botanicals into a half-pint jar. I usually do a ratio of 2 parts bittering ingredients to 1 part other more pleasantly flavored botanicals.
2. Add alcohol or vinegar to cover. Put on the lid.
3. Let steep out of direct sunlight for at least 1 month, making sure the botanicals stay completely submerged.
4. Once your bitters are ready, strain them (and squeeze your botanicals to get all of the liquid out that you can).
5. Store bitters in a glass container (I prefer to use dropper bottles for ease of use).

Bitters are commonly used on their own, as a predinner digestif, or mixed into drinks, but they also feel at home in dishes that could use some bitter depth, like stews. Or like desserts (think a few drops of citrus bitters to balance a saccharine-sweet strawberry pie filling, or coffee bitters to add some complexity to a chocolate sauce). There's also the famous hangover cure of bitters in soda water. I've field-tested this one a number of times and, to my delight, it works quite well.

Crafting as Preserving

When we use what's available to its best and fullest extent, that sometimes that means imagining how we might use parts of our food in nonedible ways. Think dyes for textiles made from beets or onion skins, dye bundles made from flowers rolled up in fabric then steamed, or textiles dyed by hammering colorful plant matter into them to make prints. There are inks to be made from spices or, if you want to make a very historically accurate ink, from the old wasp galls on a nearby oak tree. Or you can boil down plant matter to make homemade watercolor paints, which is an easy and accessible way to play with your food and to see what colors emerge from what foods (hint: It isn't always the color they are when fresh).

In the garden, vines can be woven into baskets, corn husks can be shaped into dolls or various other figures, and flowers can be pressed and dried or added to pulp in a papermaking mold and turned into paper. Of course, you can also just spend time in your garden or in nature, observing, drawing, painting, writing, and appreciating.

You can even use some animal-based leftovers for crafts, if that's of interest. I've seen many examples of people honoring chickens and other animals after eating them by repurposing their bones in crafts and jewelry. Or, if you make fish and remove the skins, try your hand at fish-skin parchment. I especially recommend this if you enjoy calligraphy or bookbinding, but it's a fun and easy craft for everyone.

FISH-SKIN PARCHMENT

Fish skin has been used for parchment, clothing, and more in Alaska Native communities and in various other communities around the world (there are, for example, some records of its creation in Germany, as described by Peter Verheyan). Artist Joel Isaak is a fantastic creator of fish-skin goods rooted in Native Alaskan traditions.

Fish-skin parchment making is a relatively quick process, as curing and drying skins goes, and because fish skins from store-bought fish tend to be small, you don't need a ton of space to do it. You can use the skins from scaled but skin-on fillets purchased from the store. Or use skins from fish you caught. Bear in mind that the skin from fillets works best here, as the fins result in holes in the final product.

Start by gently skinning the fillet, reserving the meat to cook later. Soak the skin in undyed detergent. (I use Dr. Bronner's dish soap, which I buy by the gallon jug, but any undyed detergent will do.) Let it soak for an hour or so, then rinse and repeat until the skin is no longer oily and any remaining flesh on it has softened.

Using a metal spatula or (my preference) the back of a knife, *gently* scrape the inside of the skin at a 45-degree angle to remove any remaining flesh. Spread your parchment out on a box and hold it in place with push pins: To do this, start by gently patting your fish skin dry with lintless cloths or paper towels. Then stretch the skin out flat across a cardboard box (one without printing or dyes that could transfer to the skin), securing it with push pins.

Place the skin in direct sunlight until dried. This can take a few hours or longer depending on heat, humidity, etc. Fish parchment can be used like other animal parchments for writing and/or book binding.

Fish skin parchment is an unexpected and fun craft to make with your kitchen leftovers.

Regrowth

Part of the fun of preserving and gardening is getting to watch the life cycle of your plants from seed to plate to compost and back again. But even if you just have a windowsill with a few pots, you can garden.

Try regrowing veggie scraps as a way to use your leftovers to grow entirely new food: The root ends of scallions, for example, can be popped into the soil to make new scallions, and you can plant potatoes that sprouted to grow more potatoes, or do the same with sprouted onion ends and garlic bulbs. And, of course, you can also save and regrow seeds. There are plenty of wonderful resources to guide you; just look online or ask at your local library.

Playing with Flowers

When you find yourself with a bounty of blooms, it's nice to have some recipes for how to use them. And they bring such joy to the kitchen, it can be worth seeking them out. Don't use flowers from a florist unless you know they use strictly organic blooms. I cover flowers elsewhere (see, for example, flowerkraut, page 136), but here are more ideas to expand your floral culinary practice.

FLOWER YEASTS. If you love fermenting, collecting yeasts from your favorite edible flowers is a fun way to work with plants in your practice (and delicious, too). Make a starter with your flowers, water, and sugar, then use it like you would use Ginger Bug (page 37).

HYDROSOLS AND ESSENTIAL OILS. If you have a still to distill beverages or essential oils, you can make hydrosols, which are made from water distilled with plant matter (like fresh flowers and herbs). Essential oils can be separated from the hydrosol and used separately or kept in the hydrosol. But note that it takes *a lot* of plant matter to make even an ounce of essential oil (think 60,000 roses for 1 ounce of essential oil!). Two famous examples of hydrosols are rose water and orange-blossom water (though there are also versions made through other methods, like infusing).

FLOWER ESSENCES. Flower essences offer a way to work with the gentle, energetic medicine of plants. Like many healing traditions, there are many ways to go about making them. Some people insist you float a flower in water for a certain number of hours or days, some people only use rainwater or wild-collected water, some only let it sit out in sunlight or moonlight. I make mine with what's available, which sometimes is just tap water.

Playing with Leaves

Few things are as satisfying as stepping on a crunchy leaf in autumn, *except* possibly infusing fragrant, edible leaves in sugar. Teresa Finney from At Heart Panaderia in Atlanta taught me how to make fig-leaf sugar. Just wash the leaves, dry them out in the oven on its lowest setting (or in a dehydrator at 135 to 145°F/57 to 63°C) until crisp, then grind them down and add to sugar. I usually do half leaves and half sugar; adjust up or down to suit your taste. You can also substitute your favorite leaves here: I love grinding tea leaves, mixing them with sugar, and using it to coat shortbread, or making lemon balm sugar to add to my tea or coffee.

Baking with Botanicals and Preserves

Teresa Finney, owner of At Heart Panaderia, has devoted her career to the craft of pan dulce: Spanish for "sweet bread." "In Mexican baking, pan dulce consists of breads like conchas, but also cookies and even cake," she says. "I make all the aforementioned pan dulce, including some savory stuff like empanadas and flour tortillas. I am mainly inspired by the southeastern seasons and the food and ingredients I grew up eating." Finney's Mexican-American heritage is foundational to her work: "I pull all the time from childhood memories of family using masa harina, for example. Masa harina, the ancestral ingredient of nixtamalized corn flour, is found in many of my bakery menu items. I use it a lot in cakes, cookies, and sometimes the conchas. I'm drawn to masa harina especially because the scent, the flavor evoke such a sense of home to me."

She also folds preserves into her baked goods: filling cakes with jam, stirring fruit vinegars in jam as a way to bring in more acid beyond lemon. Flowers, like hibiscus, stud curds and buttercreams and are mixed with sugar to dust on conchas fresh from the oven. It's important for the jam to be well set, not runny, for cake fillings, she cautions, otherwise your cake might not cook all the way through.

For Finney, baking is a source of confidence and a reminder of her capability, flexibility, and ingenuity. But it's also a source of beauty: Her signature cake style is studded with edible flowers. She encourages bakers to research flowers before baking with them or even using them as decorative toppings to be sure they're edible: "I'd suggest people visit any farmers' markets closest to them, talk to any flower farmers to be sure the florals aren't being sprayed with harmful pesticides, etc." If you haven't baked with preserves before, start with jam—it's an easy filling and adds a nice tart component to rich cakes.

Conclusion: Preserving in Community

While I preserve *a lot* of food, I still have access to multiple supermarkets and farmers' markets. So if I don't can enough of one thing, or bugs get in my grain, or whatever, I am still able to eat and conveniently get whatever I need to fill my pantry. In other words, the stakes are different than if I lived far out of town, off-grid, away from services and stores, or regularly struggled to afford food.

The preserving landscape is different today than it was for our ancestors, too. People preserved food because they had to, but they weren't doing it alone. Pooling resources and labor was common; foods were purchased at markets or from neighbors, or bartered or traded. What exactly our ancestors' preservation practices looked like depended on the full context of their lives: where they lived, the relationships they had with others, access to resources, etc. And the same is true of us.

Today, we have a false sense of individualism because our current social landscape has taught us that we can buy anything we need to fix any problem. We've forgotten a deep, human truth—we need each other to survive, and pooling our energy and resources together is the way to do it. That's part of the beauty of a preserving practice. It asks us to tap into ways of knowing and living that defy capitalistic individualism, and it asks us to return to reciprocity, slowness, an appreciation of process as well as product, and care for community. There's a lot of magic in a jar. And the perspective we cultivate in filling it makes up a lot of that magic.

Our food preservation practices happen within the context of our lives: both the people we share our lives with and the activities with which we fill our days. The foods we preserve, and how we share them, reflect those contexts. So I like to think of my preservation practice in terms of preserving in community.

Community means our human communities as well as the natural world, and the ways we fit within, nourish, and are nourished by each. Here's how that might look for you in your own abundant preserving life.

Sharing the Bounty: Feeding Communities

Sharing the food you preserve is a tangible act of care and nourishment, one humans have been practicing for a very, very long time and even before we were *Homo sapiens* (sharing activities are well documented among primates, for example). So when you share that jar of jam or pickles, you're participating in a tangible act of love that stretches forward and backward through the generations.

How does this look practically? You might donate to a local food pantry. However, not all pantries take homemade goods; or they only take certain foods (like dehydrated and vacuum-sealed produce). The guidelines vary from group to group, so please check before donating (and before embarking on a big preserving project to donate).

However, food pantries are not your only option for sharing the bounty: Organizations that redistribute food (like Umi Feeds in Atlanta), free fridges, mutual-aid groups, neighborhood/university food pantries, and other community organizations may also be able to take your preserves (but again, ask first).

You can donate directly to friends and local mutual-aid groups by posting notices about preserved goods that you have available. And, of course, give your pickles, ferments, jams, or whatever else to friends and family as gifts.

Community Food Preservation

Community food preservation has a long history around the world. From kimjang (kimchi-making parties) in Korea to pickling and jam-making in church basements in the American Midwest, we've been coming together to preserve our food for many generations.

This is partly practical—as the saying goes, many hands make light work—so if you all combine forces to make labor-intensive foods, you're all getting what you need and helping others do the same. But it also supports community in a couple of ways: First, by spending time together creating something by hand, you have the chance to talk with others and learn from them while actively engaged in a task. Second, you're putting aside food to nourish your community later on in the season.

There are probably food-preserving gatherings happening near you. These may include food-preserving meetups, which you might find through your local Cooperative Extension office, community/virtual notice boards, social media, or organizations like 4-H. Some community and religious groups also host canning and preserving gatherings, or you might find a secular version at a cooking school, a community/shared kitchen, or a community garden. You might also attend a swap, where rather than gathering to preserve food, you gather to share what you've made. Those are nice because you can share your goodies and get some new things to try in return.

Hosting your own preserving gathering can be a lot of fun, too. First of all, consider how much space you have versus how much space you need: If I want to have 20 people over to can tomatoes but have a galley kitchen, that's going to be uncomfortable for everyone. If your space doesn't match your needs, you can either find a larger kitchen space to host you or modify the get-together to match the space you have.

Then, think of what supplies and ingredients you might need: What do you need to buy? What can people bring? Next, think of the format of the actual day: Where will you set everyone up? Will everyone be doing the same thing, or will one person be blanching and peeling tomatoes while another purées, another fills jars, and another fills the canner? Make sure to have things around to make the day enjoyable, like snacks to graze on and drinks (I love to share homemade sodas at these events).

Finally, remember that this gathering is meant to be fun as well as practical. Invite people who you enjoy being around, who you're eager to learn from, or who otherwise enrich the space with their presence. Go at a relaxed pace (plan to spend hours doing this; food-preserving gatherings are not 30- to 60-minute affairs), encourage folks to take breaks when they need to, and just enjoy each other's company. And, of course, celebrate the wonderful food you've put together when you're finished.

MAKING COMMUNITY FOOD AND MEDICINE

Fire cider is both ancient and modern. The term (and exact concept of) *fire cider* can be traced to herbalist Rosemary Gladstar in the 1970s or 1980s. But it is rooted in a much more ancient tradition of medicinal vinegars, including four thieves vinegar, which is connected to one of my favorite pieces of fermentation-related lore: Four thieves were going around during the Plague stealing from everyone, and when they were arrested, they were asked why they weren't getting sick. It was because they were taking a protective medicine (called four thieves vinegar as a result).

Making Fire Cider (page 399) is a great excuse to gather your favorite people together, everyone bringing ingredients to contribute and together making jars for each person to take home. I recommend making an evening (or afternoon) of it with snacks, some laughs, maybe some wine.

Fire cider takes little time to assemble, so this would also be a great time to make some other nourishing foods for self and loved ones—maybe a big batch of sauerkraut or kimchi, or some tinctures, or maybe you could prep food to dehydrate. And there's always canning. Many hands are welcome when canning big batches of late-summer and autumn produce.

Or you can enjoy your fire cider–making ritual solo: My favorite way to do this is to craft a jar for myself and another to give away to someone who needs it.

Feeding Communities Through Teaching and Sharing

Part of the beauty of food preserving, and something that I've witnessed in my own life and the lives of friends in fermenting and food preserving communities, is the centrality of knowledge sharing. Passing down techniques and traditions is an important part of this work, because we're not only keeping important traditions alive but also connecting future generations to the thread of the past.

In a moment where many people feel disconnected from their food, rebuilding those connections is critical: Many of us have experienced natural disasters or have been in situations where food and water access were limited. So what do we do if we don't have electricity to cook with or access to fully stocked grocery shelves? Knowing how to continue to care for ourselves, even with limited resources, is an important gift to give to the future.

Educating and learning can happen in so many different forms: learning side by side with a friend or family member in person; taking or teaching classes, online (like many of mine) or in person; or going to talks hosted by local community groups like your public library or community garden; reading books; or even connecting with other enthusiasts on social media (for a fermentation example, check out #KojiBuildsCommunity).

Sourcing Locally

Preserving food in community also means supporting community with our food-purchasing habits: Sourcing intentionally not only helps support local farmers and businesses but also helps us maintain a more robust and healthy food system.

As we saw during the COVID-19 pandemic in 2020, many people didn't have grocery options besides big chain stores. And when those stores' shelves were bare, people had to get creative to find other options. With so many big supermarket chains (and other chains that sell food) outpricing and overwhelming smaller local sellers and small local farmers, we lose more than local businesses and the income they kept in our community (though both are already a big loss)—we lose a literal source of nourishment. We also lose the ability to choose who we support. The more big chain stores take over, the less power we have over our food supply and the less agency we have in choosing what food we have access to.

But we can reimagine our food supplies in part through what and how we buy, for those with the means to do so. In 2020, while the large grocery store a couple of miles away was nearly devolving into fistfights over gallons of milk, I could walk to one of the two small corner markets near me and find at least some food I wanted, no fistfights involved. Why? Because the owners worked very hard alongside their suppliers to keep shelves stocked, getting creative about swapping out products when they needed. Yes, everyone was short on toilet paper for a while there, but by and large, those smaller markets had less volatility in their supply, and certainly were more pleasant to deal with, than the larger grocery chains. And they focused their attention on buying from local producers (and asked for feedback from the local community), which meant strengthened community connections and a stronger local economy at a moment when everything felt particularly isolated and sideways.

You may or may not have a locally owned grocery near you, but it's worth checking. Here are some other options.

- Visit farmers' markets, farm stands, U-pick days at farms, and pop-up markets.
- Some community gardens will let members sell their produce on a given day (or have a way for you to reach out to buy from members).
- Local free/barter/buy nothing groups sometimes include listings for excess produce.
- For wild game meat, local hunters or a local meat locker might be able to point you in the right direction.
- Agriculture-focused organizations, like 4-H or your county Extension service, may keep a list of local producers you can buy from. Your chamber of commerce or other local government resources might, too.
- Some farmers sell sides of beef or other meat in quantity: Essentially, you buy a share in an animal, and then you receive the meat when it's slaughtered. It's often a lot of meat, but if you've got the space and time to put it up, it's usually a good deal.
- Check your community for local foods-focused nonprofits and other organizations dealing with food systems or with slow eating/living or sustainability. They might have some good leads (and possibly also events where you can mingle with, and sample from, suppliers).
- While the produce is not always 100 percent local, state farmers' markets can also be a good choice for produce.
- You can reach out directly to farmers; you may be able to place a bulk order if you're buying in quantity.
- And finally, if you want to order from a farmer you love but can't make it to the farmers' market (and don't want to buy in bulk), CSAs are a great option for getting some variety in your own diet and sending some support their way.
- Also check out the Resources section (page 410) for information on smaller-scale grain mills and other suppliers.

The Natural World Is Our Community, Too

Reciprocity means living all aspects of our lives in relationship, and it often asks us to unweave and reweave the stories we currently hold about giving and taking. Balancing give-and-take with our loved ones? Sure, that's easy! Balancing give-and-take with the natural world or, more shockingly still, asking permission and listening? Maybe that takes a bit more learning.

Many of us have been taught to have an extractive relationship with anything and everything nonhuman in this world (and sometimes also with other humans). We see each plant, or mineral deposit, or water source as a resource to use until it is depleted; then we'll find another. But what if we saw each of them as parts of our community, just as we are?

Robin Wall Kimmerer says in *Braiding Sweetgrass*, "Give thanks for what you have been given. Give a gift, in reciprocity for what you have taken. Sustain the ones who sustain you and the earth will last forever. In the teachings of my Potawatomi ancestors, responsibilities and gifts are understood as two sides of the same coin."

The gift you give is sometimes your gratitude, sometimes your stewardship and careful tending of the health of the land, sometimes your time. But however it looks, I promise if you begin from a place of wonder and appreciation, your relationship with the land will transform. And when you cultivate reciprocity with the natural world, you'll find you always have exactly what you need.

ACKNOWLEDGMENTS

Countless hands have shaped this work, and like any great project, it is the culmination of the many wells of knowledge and the hard work of many people. The book's journey began with a conversation with my agents, Lisa and Sally Ekus of the Ekus Group, about my interest in writing it (of course, I jumped at the chance). Everyone at the Ekus Group and the Jean V. Naggar Literary Agency have been, and continue to be, incredible advocates for my work and facilitators of my growth as a writer.

My editor, Carleen Madigan, continues to be kind, thorough, and creative, inspiring and urging me to create more beautiful and useful work than I could ever imagine. Emma Sector brings her magic to each Storey book I write, too, helping my writing to reach my ideal readers, to clarify my ideas, and to shape the story of my work as we share it around the world.

I'm so blessed to work with everyone at Storey, including Emma and Carleen but also everyone in design, photography, shipping, printing, and beyond who worked to bring this book to life. That includes (but isn't limited to!) Carolyn Eckert, Sarah Slattery, Ian O'Neill, Nancy Ringer, and Kim Dergarabedian.

Thank you to Steven Satterfield for letting us use your beautiful space for photos, Iain Bagwell for your skilled photography, and Jessamine Starr for stepping in to help me prep food (and keep me sane!) throughout our photoshoot.

Others who have supported my work include:

The natural world: To the land without which none of this work or life itself is possible, I want to offer my deepest gratitude. To each place I've been, and each place I have yet to go: May our relationship continue to cultivate a sense of wonder, stewardship, and reciprocity. In particular, I want to thank the land and people of every place where I worked on this book: in Atlanta and Cork, as well as western Alabama, North Carolina, West Cork, Edinburgh, London, South Carolina, Alaska, Copenhagen, and across Georgia (and a few other places, too).

And to all of those ancestors who preserved food and kept their families alive using the skills shared in this book, which can be here only because of each person who chose to continue these traditions. It's some of the most unseen, underappreciated, and most important work anyone has ever done. May my work do honor to the continued legacy of passing these skills down to future generations.

To my husband, Cian, whose love has healed and expanded my life in ways that imagine new possibilities and new futures.

To Victoria Peri Detherage, who has been an absolute lifesaver, a sanity-inducing problem solver, and a massive support during the process of bringing this book to life (while also getting married, launching two businesses, and moving part-time to another country).

Watching the writers I coach reconnect with the joy of their writing also helped me deepen into the joy of writing my own work, and I hope that joy is evident in every page of this book.

I'm grateful for all opportunities to have quiet, reflective space to write, financial support, and all the other ways a book can be nurtured as it comes into the world, including at artist residencies at Wildacres in North Carolina, and Hambidge in north Georgia.

To my mentors: Many seen and unseen stories pass through a life of preserving traditions. But those mentors who have had the greatest impact include Kirsten Shockey, Christopher Shockey, Sandor Katz, K. Anne Amienne, Mara Jane King, Meredith Leigh, Wade Fox, Rich Shih, Jeremy Umansky, Sean Doherty, Ken Fornataro, Melissa Gross, Gary Burnett, Kathy Burnett, and many, many others.

To my family, including Dave Skinner: I wish everyone could experience the joy of having a father who offers them both unconditional love and weekly conversations on everything from kitchen equipment to the nature of the universe. To Jan Horton, Jeremy Horton, Jonathan Horton, and Jameson Horton, Tonish Horton, and Kristen

Schreiber. And to Sinéad O'Sullivan, Bernard O'Sullivan, Maria O'Donovan, Kay O'Sullivan, Tim Murphy, and Chloe O'Sullivan. And to Joyce Lenoir, Gwen Cradle, and Connie Boyd. And to family no longer with us, particularly Jean Sibbald, Margaret Skinner Meints, Margaret Arrington, David Huntley, Julian Huntley, Margery Skinner, Bill Skinner, and Gene Sibbald. And to my pets, my cats and birds, who provided comic relief and stress-relieving snuggles.

This book was made possible by the labor of the many farmers and food producers whose hard work provided the abundance of food used to test each recipe. My thanks especially goes to Crack in the Sidewalk Farmlet, Southern Cap Mushrooms, Rodgers Greens and Roots, Jon Jackson and Comfort Farms, Dave "Smoke" McClusky, Burlap and Barrel, Caribe United Farm, Cosmos Farm, Four Bellies Farm, Georgia Proud and Pearsons Provisions, Middle Georgia Growers Coop, Rag & Frass Farm, Snapfinger Farm, Quay Co-op, Sevananda, Grant Wallace, My Goodness, Cork Urban Soil Project, and the many great folks at The English Market.

An incomplete list of friends who have cheered me on, supported my work in some way, or inspired my work include John Becker, Megan Scott, Ellen Ireland, Lauren Harris, Patrick Hendershot, Robbie Astrove and Jess Pfeffer, Rose McAdoo, KC Hysmith, Erica Clahar, Amy Halloran, Taffy Elrod, Leni Sorensen, Cassandra Loftin, John Gibson and John Bluhm, Elliot McNally, Kimberly Coburn, Pru Hardi, Brandon Sheats, Joey Hernandez, Sarah Higgins, Bettina Makalintal, Abi Balinget, Amethyst Ganaway, Michael Twitty, Joe Yonan, Lisa Hecht, Paola Briseño González, Adrian Miller, Wade Fox, Justin Haines, Haley Murphy, Heather Luttrell, Alana Fuselier, Karl Gorline, Sarah and Jeremy Fisher, Paul Harper, Mick O'Dwyer, Phoebe O'Regan, Virginia O'Gara, Naoise Ní Gealbháin, George Long, Chris Wiersema, Anne Marsh, Janisse Ray, Jessamine Starr, Emma Janzen, Bart Sasso, Nialle Sylvan, Melanie Styles, Hannah Crum, Risa Dickens, Regina Sexton, Jim Meehan, Jade Nguyen, Kara Strauss, and Alana Fuselier for helping me look and feel my best, and many, many others.

I interviewed some incredible people for this book to learn more about preserving in different global cultures and about how we find and use food-preserving information. My eternal gratitude to Nguyễn Thiên Ân, David Asher, J. P. McMahon, April McGregor, Ashley English, Claudia Lucero, Kat Kocsis, Anna Drozdova, Annie Simpkins, Melanie McIntosh, Amethyst Ganaway, Katsu Lash, Matthew Parker, Su-Jit Lin, Mark Vail, Jonathan Hollister, Ryan Cohen, Nancy Singleton Hachisu, Leela Punyaratabandhu, Teresa Finney, Jeanette Hurt, Ebru Baybara Demir and Ebru Tuncay, and Christina Ward for being so generous with their time and knowledge.

And finally, to everyone who plunged their hands into a crock of sauerkraut with me, or stood over a boiling canning bath together in the heat of summer, who taught me about everything from root cellars to rutabagas, or who I've shared some of my preserved foods with. There are literally hundreds of you. Thank you all, I love you.

Resources

SOME FAVORITE SUPPLIERS

You can also look for supplies at your local farm supply store, hardware store, grocer, or specialty food store. Your local Extension service, community garden, or library may have ideas for where to purchase preserving supplies as well.

Fermentation Tools (Jars, Crocks, etc.)

All American
https://allamerican1930.com
Pressure canners

Ball
https://ballmasonjars.com
Jars

Excalibur
https://excaliburdehydrator.com
Dehydrators

Kerr
https://kerrcanningjars.com
Jars

Kilner
https://kilnerjar.com
Jars

Le Parfait
https://leparfait.us
Jars

Ohio Stoneware
https://stonewareoutlet.com
Fermentation crocks

Roots & Harvest
https://rootsandharvest.com
General preserving supplies and tools

Seasonings

Beautiful Briny Sea
https://beautifulbrinysea.com

Burlap & Barrel
https://burlapandbarrel.com

Penzeys
https://penzeys.com

Starter Cultures and Kits

Craft Butchers' Pantry
https://butcherspantry.com
Meat preservation supplies

Cultures for Health
https://culturesforhealth.com
Fermentation and cheesemaking supplies

Fermentaholics
https://fermentaholics.com
Fermentation supplies

GEM Cultures
http://gemcultures.com
Starter cultures

Kawashimaya (Japan)
https://thejapanstore.jp
Wide selection of starter cultures, seasonings, and other foods

The Koji Kitchen (UK)
https://thekojikitchen.com
Starter cultures and workshops

New England Cheese Making Supply Company
https://cheesemaking.com
Cheesemaking kits and supplies

OV Dairy Supplies (UK)
https://ovdairysupplies.co.uk
Cheesemaking kits and supplies

South River Miso Company
https://southrivermiso.com
Starter cultures

Quercus Cooperage
https://qcooperage.com/products/

Urban Cheesecraft
https://urbancheesecraft.com
Cheesemaking kits and supplies

TRUSTWORTHY PRESERVING RESOURCES

Living in a world where all the information you want is at your fingertips is both a blessing and a curse. I can, in about 5 seconds, get thousands of recipes for canned strawberry jam (for example) without even having to get up from the couch. But the fact that anyone can publish anything on the internet, or as a self-published book, or as an AI-generated book, means we need to approach food preserving sources with cautious optimism, making sure that they're trustworthy.

Now, more than ever, it's important to know how to evaluate sources so you can choose ones that meet your needs and help you expand your culinary horizons. Finding good information created by knowledgeable folks is especially critical when we're talking about food preserving, because some types of preserving carry real risks if done incorrectly. A recipe that gives you incorrect processing times for canning or the wrong salt ratios for meat preserving is a recipe that might make you sick.

How do you know a good preserving recipe when you see one? What is a "trusted" source when it comes to preserving? There are some guidelines that work for any kind of source, and they apply to cookbooks, too.

You can see complete guidance on how to identify resources, plus resources from information literacy experts Dr. Jonathan Hollister and Ryan Cohen, whom I interviewed for this book, at https://root-kitchens.com/essential-resources.

One of my favorite quick ways to evaluate information is the CRAAP test, which is a good first step for quickly assessing whether a resource is trustworthy and appropriate to your needs:

CURRENCY: Is the information current?

RELEVANCE: Does this information meet your needs?

AUTHORITY: What expertise does the creator of this information have? Where/how was it published? Large social media followings or celebrity status do not correlate with someone's ability to find, evaluate, create, or share trustworthy information. In other words, rather than believing that a guy in a lab coat on YouTube is a scientist, check to see if he is.

ACCURACY: Is this information correct? Is it corroborated by other sources?

PURPOSE: Why was this information created and shared? Who funded it?

The following books and articles all pass the CRAAP test and are trusted sources for more information about preserving. You can also make use of your local Cooperative Extension Service's website or the National Center for Home Food Preservation website. For more on evaluating trustworthy resources, visit https://root-kitchens.com/essential-resources.

General Preserving

For a complete list of preserving-related resources, please visit https://root-kitchens.com/essential-resources.

Acheson, Hugh. *Pick a Pickle.* Potter Style, 2014.

Ball Newell Brands. *Ball Blue Book Guide to Preserving*. Ball, 2020.

English, Ashley. *Homemade Living: Canning & Preserving with Ashley English.* Lark Books, 2010.

Goldstein, Darra, Cortney Burns, and Richard Martin. *Preserved: Condiments*. Hardie Grant, 2023.

———. *Preserved: Drinks.* Hardie Grant, 2024.

———. *Preserved: Fruit*. Hardie Grant, 2023.

———. *Preserved: Vegetables.* Hardie Grant, 2024.

Hisamatsu, Ikuko. *Quick & Easy Tsukemono*. JOIE, Inc, 2005.

Hobson, Phyllis. *Making & Using Dried Foods*. Storey, 1994.

Hui, Y. H., Sue Ghazala, Dee M. Graham, K. D. Murrell, and Wai-Kit Nip, eds. *Handbook of Vegetable Preservation and Processing*. CRC Press, 2005.

Hurt, Jeanette. *Dehydrating*. Penguin Random House, 2022.

Marrone, Teresa. *The Beginner's Guide to Dehydrating Food.* Storey, 2018.

Rombauer, Irma S., Marion Rombauer Becker, Ethan Becker, John Becker, and Megan Scott. *Joy of Cooking*. Rev. ed. Scribner, 2019.

Solomon, Karen. *Asian Pickles*. Ten Speed Press, 2014.

University of Georgia Cooperative Extension Service. *So Easy to Preserve*. 6th ed. Cooperative Extension Service, University of Georgia, 2014.

USDA Complete Guide to Home Canning, 2015 Revision. USDA Extension Service. https://nchfp.uga.edu/resources/entry/about-the-usda-guide-to-home-canning-2015-revision.

Ward, Christina. *Preservation*. Process Media, 2017.

Fermentation

Battcock, Mike, and Sue Azam-Ali. "Fermented Fruits and Vegetables: A Global Perspective." *FAO Agricultural Services Bulletin* 134. Food and Agriculture Organization of the United Nations, 1998. http://www.fao.org/docrep/x0560e/x0560e05.htm#Fer.

Buhner, Stephen Harrod. *Sacred and Herbal Healing Beers*. Brewers Publications, 1998.

Caruso, Giuseppe. *The Botany of Beer*. Columbia University Press, 2022.

Christensen, Emma. *Brew Better Beer*. Ten Speed Press, 2015.

———. *Modern Cider*. Ten Speed Press, 2017.

———. *True Brews*. Ten Speed Press, 2013.

Crum, Hannah, and Alex LaGory. *The Big Book of Kombucha*. Storey, 2016.

Davis, Holly. *Ferment*. Chronicle Books, 2017.

Dirar, Hamid A. *The Indigenous Fermented Foods of the Sudan*. CAB International, 1993.

Kang, Mingoo, Joshua David Stein, and Nadia Cho. *Jang: The Soul of Korean Cooking*. Artisan, 2024.

Katz, Sandor Ellix. *The Art of Fermentation*. Chelsea Green, 2012.

———. "Dosas and Idlis: Turn Beans to Bread." *Fermentation Magazine* (winter 2019). https://www.myfermentation.com/grains/dosas-and-idlis-zerz1905zbut/.

———. *Fermentation as Metaphor*. Chelsea Green, 2020.

———. *Wild Fermentation*. Chelsea Green, 2016.

Lukas, Kathryn, and Shane Peterson. *The Farmhouse Culture Guide to Fermenting*. Ten Speed Press, 2019.

Malle, Bettina, and Helge Schmikl. *The Artisanal Vinegar Maker's Handbook*, trans. Paul Lehmann. Spikehorn Press, 2015.

Marsden, Emma, and Aggie MacKenzie. *The Miracle of Vinegar*. HarperCollins UK, 2019.

McGovern, Patrick E. *Ancient Brews*. W. W. Norton, 2017.

Redzepi, René, and David Zilber. *The Noma Guide to Fermentation*. Artisan, 2018.

Rosenblum, Harry. *Vinegar Revival*. Clarkson Potter, 2017.

Shepard, Sue. *Pickled, Potted, and Canned*. Simon & Schuster, 2000.

Shih, Rich, and Jeremy Umansky. *Koji Alchemy*. Chelsea Green, 2020.

Shockey, Christopher, and Kirsten K. Shockey. *The Big Book of Cidermaking*. Storey, 2020.

Shockey, Kirsten K., and Christopher Shockey. *Fermented Vegetables, 10th Anniversary Edition*. Storey, 2024.

———. *Fiery Ferments*. Storey, 2017.

———. *Miso, Tempeh, Natto & Other Tasty Ferments*. Storey, 2019.

Singleton Hachisu, Nancy. *Preserving the Japanese Way*. Andrews McMeel, 2015.

Skinner, Julia. *Our Fermented Lives*. Storey, 2022.

Watson, Ben. *Cider: Hard and Sweet*. 3rd ed. Countryman, 2013.

Zimmerman, Jereme. *Make Mead Like a Viking*. Chelsea Green, 2015.

Making Cheese and Yogurt

Asher, David. *The Art of Natural Cheesemaking*. Chelsea Green, 2015.

———. *Milk Into Cheese*. Chelsea Green, 2024.

Caldwell, Gianaclis. *Homemade Yogurt & Kefir*. Storey, 2020.

———. *Mastering Artisan Cheesemaking*. Chelsea Green, 2012.

———. *Mastering Basic Cheesemaking*. New Society Publishers, 2016.

Carr, Morgan McGlynn. *The Modern Cheesemaker*. White Lion, 2019.

Carroll, Ricki. *Home Cheese Making*, 4th Ed. Storey, 2018.

———. *Making Cheese, Butter & Yogurt*. Storey, 1983.

Facaros, Dana, and Michael Pauls. "Formadi Frant," Italian Food Decoder, accessed November 1, 2020, https://www.facarospauls.com/apps/italian-food-decoder/10757/formadi-frant.

Lucero, Claudia. *Cooking with Whey*. Storey, 2022.

———. *Instant Pot Cheese*. Storey, 2020.

———. *One-Hour Cheese*. Workman, 2014.

———. *One-Hour Dairy-Free Cheese*. Workman, 2019.

McAthy, Karen. *The Art of Plant-Based Cheesemaking*, 2nd Ed. New Society Publishers, 2021.

Saxelby, Anne. *The New Rules of Cheese*. Ten Speed Press, 2020.

Freezing

Christensen, Ashley, and Kaitlyn Goalen. *It's Always Freezer Season*. Ten Speed Press, 2021.

Conner, Polly, and Rachel Tiemeyer. *From Freezer to Cooker*. Rodale, 2020.

———. *From Freezer to Table*. Rodale, 2017.

Schmidt, Crystal. *Freeze Fresh*. Storey, 2022.

Meat, Eggs, and Seafood

Grigson, Jane. *Charcuterie and French Pork Cookery*. Grub Street Publishing, 2008.

Haase, Hendrik, Robert Klanten, and Sven Ehmann. *Crafted Meat*. Gestalten Verlag, 2015.

Leigh, Meredith. *Pure Charcuterie*. New Society Publishers, 2018.

———. "How to Make Charcuterie: The Art of Meat Preservation." https://www.fermentationschool.com/courses/how-to-make-charcuterie.

Marianski, Stanley, and Adam Marianski. *German Sausages*. Bookmagic, 2019.

———. *Home Production of Quality Meats and Sausages*. Bookmagic, 2010.

———. *Spanish Sausages*. Bookmagic, 2018.

Marianski, Stanley, Adam Marianski, and Robert Marianski. *Meat Smoking and Smokehouse Design*. Bookmagic, 2012.

McDade, Chris. *The Magic of Tinned Fish*. Artisan, 2021.

Raichlen, Steven. *Project Smoke*. Workman, 2016.

Ruhlman, Michael, and Brian Polcyn. *Charcuterie*. W. W. Norton, 2005.

INDEX

A

acidity
- canning methods for acidic food, 27
- jams and jellies and, 81

air displacement method, 20
air-drying, 88
Aji Dulce Pepper Relish, 205
alcohol, 57
alcohol fermentation, 45
altitude adjustments, 39
Amana Pickled Ham, 371
amino sauces, 337–338, 386
apples, 246–258
- Apple Cider Molasses, 255–256
- Apple Pie Filling, 256–257
- Apple Relish, 251
- Basic Applesauce, 258
- drying/dried, 246–247, 248
- Fermented Squash-and-Apple Relish, 238–239
- Five-Spice Apple Rings, 250
- freezing, 248
- Green Tomato Refrigerator Jam, 235
- Mapple (Maple and Apple) Butter, 253–254
- Old Apple Vinegar, 252–253
- Persimmon, Apple, and Cranberry Refrigerator Pickles, 249
- Pickled Apples with Sage, 251–252
- Quick-Cooked Squash-and-Apple Relish, 239
- repurposing mushy and bruised, 254
- Sweet-and-Sour Five-Spice Apples, 249–250
- vinegar and, 252–253

apricots, 305–312
- Apricot-Plum Fruit Leather, 306

Aromatic Herbal Salt, 96
aromatic roots, 104–114
artichokes, 115–116
- Artichoke Vinegar or Liquor, 115
- Feta and Herb Salad with Artichoke Vinaigrette, 116
- Pickled Artichoke or Cardoon Stems, 116

ascorbic acid dips, 90
asparagus, 117–120
- Asparagus-End Relish, 120
- Asparagus Refrigerator Pickles, 119
- Herbes-de-Provence-Pickled Asparagus, 118

Avocado Cubes, Frozen, 23

B

baking with botanicals and preserves, 403
bananas, 259–262
- Banana Chips, 260
- Banana "Ice Cream," 261
- Banana Jam, 262
- Banana Vinegar, 261
- flavors to pair with, 260

Basil Burst Syrup, 175
beans, cooked, 332. *See also* legumes
Beef Jerky, Mole-Inspired, 374
beet greens, 169–170
beets, 121–128
- Beet Kvass, 328
- Beet–Pasta Sauce Cubes, 122–123
- Easy Yogurt Sauce, 123
- Fermented Beet-and-Carrot Sauce, 127
- Fermented Pastrami Beets, 124–125
- Fermented Rainbow Roots and Spinach Salad, 170
- Kimchi Beets, 127–128
- Pickled Pastrami Beets, 125–126
- Quick Beet Soup, 123
- Rainbow Roots Soup Starter, 107
- Raspberry-Beet Jam, 272
- Raspberry-Beet Syrup, 268
- Root Vegetable Jam, 146
- Smoked Pastrami-Fermented Beets, 125

berries, 262–274
- Blueberry-Lavender Refrigerator Jam, 271
- Blue Strawberry Jam, 273
- Chilled Blueberry Soup, 265
- dry packed, 263

freezing, 18
Ginger-Berry Syrup, 269–270
Raspberry-Beet Jam, 272
Raspberry-Beet Syrup, 268
Refrigerator Pickled Blackberries, 266
Refrigerator Pickled Strawberries, 266–267
soda from, 269
Solstice Refrigerator Jam, 274
Spring Berry Cider, 399
Strawberry-Jalapeño Shrub, 266
Strawberry Jam, 270
Strawberry-Top Lime Syrup, 269
Strawberry-Top Shrub, 265
Strawberry-Wine Refrigerator Jam, 271
sugar packed, 263
Sunny Blueberry-Corn Jam, 273–274
Sweet-and-Savory Macerated Strawberry Sauce, 268
syrup packed, 263
See also individual berries

best practices
for canning, 32, 41
for cheesemaking, 347–348
for freezing, 15–16
for freezing shellfish, 377
importance of, 4, 5
for lactofermentation, 46–47
for preserving meats, 368
for root cellars, 14
for vegan cheesemaking, 354

Bird's-Eye and Serrano Sauce, 207

bitters
about, 400–401
Butternut Squash Peel Bitters, 239–240
Mango-Peel Bitters, 315
Smoked Cherry Pit Old-Fashioned Bitters, 276, 278

blackberries
with pickled peppers, 204
Refrigerator Pickled Blackberries, 266

Black Forest ham, 369

blanching
fruits and vegetables, 16–17, 90
stinging nettle, 243

blueberries
Blueberry-Lavender Refrigerator Jam, 271
Blueberry Lavender Syrup, 270
Blue Strawberry Jam, 273
Chilled Blueberry Soup, 265
Sunny Blueberry-Corn Jam, 273–274

Blue Strawberry Jam, 273
boiled peanuts, 332
bok choy, 130

bourbon
Bourbon-Honey Cherries, 277
Smoked Cherry Pit Old-Fashioned Bitters, 276

bran, 324
brassicas, 128–141
Bread-and-Butter Carrots, 145
Bread-and-Butter Green Tomatoes, 233

breads
Beet Kvass, 328
Bread Miso, 326–327
preserving, 326–327

brine
flavored, 134
Kimchi-Inspired Pickle Brine, 113
perpetual brine ferments, 52
ratios for, 49
Refrigerator Pickle Brine, 113
using after fermentation, 50, 97

broccoli
Broccoli-Stem Refrigerator Relish, 141
drying, 128
freezing, 130

Brussels sprouts, 129, 130
bulgur wheat, Tarhana, 325–326
"burping" ferments, 46

butter
culturing, 97, 358–359
freezing, 344

buttermilk, 97, 358–359
Butternut Squash Peel Bitters, 239–240

C

cabbage
Coriander-and-Mustard Canned Sauerkraut, 138
Curtido, 138–139
drying, 129
freezing, 130
Quick-Pickled Chowchow, 140
Sauerkraut, 135

Candied Jalapeños, Easy, 210–211
canners, choosing, 28–29

canning
basics of, 27
best practices for, 41
development of, 26
equipment for, 28–29
finding and customizing recipes for, 32–33
hot pack, 32
hot water bath, 27, 34–36
jars for, 30–31
pH and, 27
pressure, 27, 37–40
raw pack, 32
safety and, 41
sterilization and, 31, 39
See also individual foods

canning racks, 28
cantaloupe, 297–300
Caponata, 162
Caramels, Lavender, 360
carbonated soda, naturally, 58–59
Cardoon Stems, Pickled Artichoke or, 116

carrots, 142–146
Bread-and-Butter Carrots, 145
Carrot "Lox," 143
Curtido, 138–139
Fermented Beet-and-Carrot Sauce, 127
Fermented Carrot Sticks, 144
Fermented Rainbow Roots and Spinach Salad, 170
Frozen Mirepoix, 196–197

carrots, *continued*
  Frozen Trinity, 196–197
  Kimchi, 132
  pesto from tops of, 145
  Quick-Pickled Carrots, 144
  Rainbow Roots Soup Starter, 107
  Ready-to-Go Okra Soup Cubes, 192
  Root Vegetable Jam, 146
  Sour Corn, 152
cauliflower
  Canned Cauliflower Pickles, 134
  drying, 130
  freezing, 130
  Quick-Pickled Cauliflower, 131
Celeriac, Pickled, 150
celery, 148–150
  Caponata, 162
  Celery Vinegar, 149
  Celery Vodka, 149
  Frozen Mirepoix, 196–197
  Rainbow Roots Soup Starter, 107
chard, 169–170
cheese
  Basic Fresh Cheese, 349
  brining, 352–355
  Cream Cheese, 351
  freezing, 343
  fresh, 348–349
  Halloumi, 349–350
  koji-preserved, 354–355
  oil preserving, 352–355
  Paneer, 350–351
  Ricotta, 351
  vegan, 354
cheesemaking, 344, 345–351
cheese rids, 343–344
cheong, making, 80
cherries, 275–278
  Bourbon-Honey Cherries, 277
  Smoked Cherry Pit Old-Fashioned Bitters, 276, 278
  Smoked Old-Fashioned Jam, 278
Chicken Soup, 364–365
chickpeas, Tarhana, 325–326
chickweed, Icelandic Wound Charm, 397
Chocolate Hot Sauce, Red Chile, 207
Choose-Your-Own-Adventure Herbal Soda, 176–177
Chowchow
  Fermented, 139–140
  Quick-Pickled, 140
cider
  Apple Cider Molasses, 255–256
  Fall-Spiced Cider, 399
  Fire Cider, 399–400
  Five-Spice Cider, 399
  pasteurized, 66–69
  Spring Berry Cider, 399
cilantro
  Mango Pickles, 315
  Pickled Limes, 282
  with pickled peppers, 204
  Sofrito Cubes, 202
citrus, 279–286
  Citrus Cleaning Vinegar, 281
  Citrus-Pickled Turmeric, 113
  Citrus Syrup, 270
  drying peels from, 279–280
  drying slices of, 280
  Frozen Citrus Juice Cubes, 280
  Holiday Citrus Spice Vinegar, 282
  Meyer Limoncello, 280–281
  Pickled Limes, 282
  Salt-Preserved Citrus, 283
  Salt-Preserved Citrus Paste, 283
  Simple Kumquat Marmalade, 286
  Sugar-Packed Citrus Syrup, 286
  Tangerine, Rose, and Turmeric Syrup, 285–286
  Yuzu Kosho, 285
city ham, 369
cleaning sprays, 98
cocktails, 68–69, 99
cocoa powder, Red Chile Chocolate Hot Sauce, 207
coconuts, 313–319
cold smoke, 96
collards, 169–170
community, 4, 404–407
compost, 98
containers
  for canning, 30–31
  freezer-safe, 18
coriander
  Coriander-and-Mustard Canned Sauerkraut, 138
  Peach-and-Coriander Syrup, 311
  with pickled peppers, 204
corn (fresh), 150–152
  Corncob Stock, 151
  Quick-Pickled Corn, 151
  Sour Corn, 152
  Sunny Blueberry-Corn Jam, 273–274
Cornichons, 157–158
country ham, 369
country wine
  basic, 62–63
  Peach Country Wine, 309
crabapples, 246–258
  drying, 248
crackers, 99
crafting as preserving, 401
cranberries, 287–288
  Apple Relish, 251
  Cranberry-Orange Vodka, 288
  Persimmon, Apple, and Cranberry Refrigerator Pickles, 249
  Zesty Cranberry Sauce, 288
cream, 344–345
Cream Cheese, 351
crocks, for fermentation, 47–49
cucumbers, 154–160
  Canned Dill Pickle Chips, 159
  Cornichons, 157–158
  Dill Refrigerator Pickles, 156–157
  Garlic Refrigerator Pickles, 157
  Half Sours and Full Sours, 156
  Mountain Cabin Cucumber Salad, 160
  preventing mushy pickles from, 154
  Summery Cucumber Salad, 158
  Sweet-and-Sour Cucumber Salad, 158

Cultured Butter and Buttermilk, Basic, 358–359
curing meats, 367, 369–370
curly dock root, Icelandic Wound Charm, 397
currants, 262–274
Curtido, 138–139

D

daikon radish
- fermented, 217
- Kimchi, 132

dairy
- about, 342
- brining, 352–355
- butter, 344
- cheese, 343
- cheesemaking, 344, 345–351
- cheese rids, 343–344
- cream, 344–345
- freezing, 343
- milk, 344–345
- oil preserving, 352–355
- yogurt, 345

dates, 289–291
- Silan, 290

dehydrating
- about, 89–90
- checking whole fruits and vegetables, 93
- drying temperatures and times for, 91
- pretreating fruits and vegetables before, 90
- reducing food waste and, 99
- seasoning blends for, 95–96
- tips for, 93
- using a dehydrator, 92
- *See also* drying; fruit leather; *individual foods*

Demir, Ebru Baybara, 301
dill weed
- Dill Refrigerator Pickles, 156–157
- Dill Squash Refrigerator Pickles, 223
- Green Tomato Dill Chips, 228
- Quick-Pickled Dilly Beans, 167–168
- Summery Cucumber Salad, 158

Doc's Hot Sauce, 209
dog treats, 99
Dressing, Leek-Top, 179
drying
- air-drying, 88
- dehydrating, 89–90, 92–94
- oven drying, 88–89
- pretreating fruits and vegetables before, 90
- reconstituting foods after, 97
- reducing food waste and, 97–99
- seasonings for, 95–96
- storing foods after, 96–97
- temperatures and times for, 91
- *See also* dehydrating; *individual foods*

dry packing, 18, 19, 263
dry rubs, 374

E

eggplant, 161–164
- Caponata, 162
- Pickled Mini Eggplant, 164

eggs, 387–393
- boiling, 388
- curing, 390
- freezing, 388–389
- Misozuke (Miso-Pickled) Eggs, 392–393
- non-chicken, 387
- pickled, 389–393
- Pickled Eggs in Vinegar, 391
- Preserved Lemon Eggs, 393
- Salt-Cured Egg Yolks, 391
- Shoyuzuke Eggs, 390

eggshells, 393
egg storage, 15
elderberries
- Elderberry Syrup, 267–268
- working with, 267

endosperm, 324
equipment
- for canning, 28–29
- for fermentation, 47–49

escabeche, 381
essences, flower, 403
essential oils, 402–403
ethylene gas, 14

F

fennel, 164–166
- Fennel-Strawberry Vinegar, 165
- Quick-Pickled Fennel, 166

fermentation
- alcohol, 57
- best practices for, 46–47
- brine ratios for, 49
- canned pickles, 55–56
- cheesemaking, 344, 345–351
- country wine, 62–63
- differing time for, 308
- equipment for, 47–49
- guidance for, 75
- introduction to, 44–46
- koji, 70–74
- lactofermentation, 45, 46
- making kraut, 50–51
- mead/melomel, 60–61
- naturally carbonated soda, 58–59
- perpetual brine ferments, 52
- quick pickles, 53–56
- refrigerator pickles, 54
- soda, 57–59
- using ferments, 45
- using scraps from, 97
- vinegar, 64–69
- *See also individual foods*

Feta and Herb Salad with Artichoke Vinaigrette, 116
figs, 289–291
- Fig Jam, 291
- Vanilla-Fig Syrup, 290–291

Fire Cider, 399–400
fish
- canning, 379
- drying temperatures for, 91
- fermenting, 384
- fish-skin parchment, 401
- freezing, 16

fish, *continued*
Garlic-Shoyu Fish Jerky Marinade, 379
Lemon-Miso Fish Jerky Marinade, 378
making jerky, 377–378
pickling, 379, 382–383
salted, 385
salting and drying, 377–379
seasoning blends from, 95
smoking, 379, 383
See also seafood
fish sauce
about, 385
Fish Sauce–Inspired Pickled Brine, 113
making, 386
five-spice
Five-Spice Apple Rings, 250
Five-Spice Cider, 399
Five-Spice Syrup, 270
Sweet-and-Sour Five-Spice Apples, 249–250
flowers
Icelandic Wound Charm, 397
playing with, 402–403
freeze-drying, 23
freezer burn, 16, 23
freezer jam, 83
Freezer-Safe Lion's Mane Mushroom Cutlets, 185–186
freezing
best practices for, 15–16
containers for, 18
in cubes, 20–23
preparing foods for, 16–20
See also individual foods
French Fries, 213
Fruit Honey, Vegan, 81
fruit juice dips, 90
fruit leather
Apricot-Plum Fruit Leather, 306
from berries and currants, 263
from cherries, 275
from figs and dates, 289
making, 94
reducing food waste and, 99
from stone fruits, 306
fruits
blanching, 16–17
checking whole, 93
drying temperatures for, 91
freezing, 15–16, 18
pretreating before drying, 90
in root cellars, 14
Smoothie Cubes, 22
sugar and syrup packed, 18–19
using overripe, 99
See also individual fruits

G

Ganaway, Amethyst, 366
garlic, 104–114
Dill Refrigerator Pickles, 156–157
Garlic in Honey, 109
Garlic Refrigerator Pickles, 157
Garlic-Shoyu Fish Jerky Marinade, 379
Kimchi-Inspired Pickle Brine, 113
Mushroom Broth, 186–187
pickled, 111
Rainbow Roots Soup Starter, 107
Tarhana, 325–326
Three-Root Paste, 108
Geographically Indeterminate Ham, 369–370
germ (of grain), 324
gin, Muscadine Gin, 293
ginger, 104–114
Fermented Ginger Beer, 110
Ginger-Berry Syrup, 269–270
Masala Syrup, 114
pickled, 111
Three-Root Paste, 108
ginger bug, 57
grains, 322–330
anatomy of, 324
Basic Mirin/Not-Mirin Method, 330
drying, 323
fermented porridges, 329
fermenting, 326
fermenting before cooking, 329
freezing, 326
mirin, 329–330
Morning Oats Not-Mirin, 330
Tarhana, 325–326
grapes, 292–296
Grape Juice for Jelly, 295–296
Grape Preserves Without Pectin, 295
Muscadine Gin, 293
Muscadine or Black Grape Catsup, 296
Muscadine Soda Syrup, 294
Pickled Grapes, 293
Pickled Muscadines, 294
green beans, 167–168
Fermented Dilly Beans, 168
Fermented Green Beans, 168
Quick-Pickled Dilly Beans, 167–168
Green Pine Cone Syrup, 242
greens
dark and leafy, 169–171
Fermented Rainbow Roots and Spinach Salad, 170
Green Smoothie Cubes, 169–170
tender, 172–178
using, 107
Green Tomato Dill Chips, 228
Green Tomato Refrigerator Jam, 235
Grenadine (Pomegranate Syrup), 304
Grenadine, Smoky Lime, 304
guava, 313–319
Guava Paste, 318–319

H

Habanero Sauces, 207
Hachisu, Nancy Singleton, 380
Halloumi, 349–350
hams, 369–370, 371
Harissa-Pickled Pomegranate Seeds, 303
headspace
for canning, 31
for freezing, 19
Healing Rose Skin Salve, 396

herbal teas, 398
herbal tinctures, 398
Herbes-de-Provence-Pickled Asparagus, 118
herbs, 172–178
- Aromatic Herbal Salt, 96
- Choose-Your-Own-Adventure Herbal Soda, 176–177
- drying temperatures for, 91
- Feta and Herb Salad with Artichoke Vinaigrette, 116
- Herbal Sauce, 177
- Herb Bud Salt, 175–176
- Herb-Infused Vinegar, 173–174
- Pickled Herb Buds, 176
- Savory Sage Refrigerator Paste, 178
- Tarhana, 325–326
- *See also individual herbs*

honey
- Bourbon-Honey Cherries, 277
- Garlic in Honey, 109
- honey ham, 369
- honey syrup dips, 90
- Hot Honey, 203
- Pomegranate Seeds in Honey, 303

honeydew, 297–300
horseradish, 104–114
- Fermented Horseradish Paste, 107
- Horseradish and Orange "Kosho," 113
- Horseradish Vinegar, 114
- Prepared Horseradish, 111
- Quick-Pickled Horseradish and Scallion Paste, 111

Hot-and-Sour Bird's-Eye Sauce, 209
hot pack, 32
hot smoke, 96
hot water bath canning
- altitude adjustments for, 39
- equipment for, 28
- method for, 34–36
- pH and, 27

hull, 324
humidity, for root cellars, 14
hydrosols, 402

ice glazing, 376
Icelandic Wound Charm, 397
infused vinegars and liquors, 66–69
infusing
- Herb-Infused Vinegar, 173–174
- Kimchi-Lemongrass Infused Vinegar, 134
- Leek-Infused Vinegar, 178
- liquors, 66–69, 115
- oils, 397
- reducing food waste and, 98
- *See also individual foods*

Irish ham, 369

jalapeños
- Easy Candied Jalapeños, 210
- Fermented Salsa, 234
- Jalapeño Relish, 205
- pickled peppers and, 204
- Ready-to-Go Okra Soup Cubes, 192
- Sofrito Cubes, 202
- Spicier Yogurt Leek Sauce, 179
- Strawberry-Jalapeño Shrub, 266
- Tomatillo Salad, 233

Jamón Ibérico, 369
Jamón Serrano, 369
jams
- about, 78
- Banana Jam, 262
- Blueberry-Lavender Refrigerator Jam, 271
- Blue Strawberry Jam, 273
- Fig Jam, 291
- freezer, 83
- Green Tomato Refrigerator Jam, 235
- making, 82–83
- Mango Black Pepper Refrigerator Jam, 319
- Raspberry-Beet Jam, 272
- Red Quince Marmalade, 255
- Root Vegetable Jam, 146
- science of, 81
- Simple Kumquat Marmalade, 286
- Smoked Old-Fashioned Jam, 278
- Solstice Refrigerator Jam, 274
- Stone Fruit Jam, 312
- Strawberry Jam, 270
- Strawberry-Wine Refrigerator Jam, 271
- Tomato-Peach Refrigerator Jam, 312
- White Quince Marmalade, 254–255

jar lifters, 29
jars for canning, 30–31, 39
jellies
- about, 78
- Grape Juice for Jelly, 295–296
- making, 84–85
- science of, 81

kale, 169–170
kimchi
- Kimchi, 132
- Kimchi Beets, 127–128
- kimchi eggs, 389
- Kimchi-Inspired Pickle Brine, 113
- Kimchi-Lemongrass Infused Vinegar, 134

kohlrabi, 130
koji
- Bread Miso, 326–327
- cheese preserved with, 354–355
- cultivating, 70–71
- fermentation with, 45, 70
- growing, 72–73
- reusing, 338
- Tofu "Feta" with Mushroom Shio Koji, 338–339

koji, *continued*
using for preservation, 74
White Miso, 339
kojiban, 70
kraut
making, 50–51
playing with, 136–137
Kumquat Marmalade, Simple, 286
kvass
Beet Kvass, 328
kvass eggs, 389
Lettuce Kvass, 181

L

labeling, 6
lactofermentation, 45, 46
Lask, Katsu, 112
lavender
Blueberry-Lavender Refrigerator Jam, 271
Blueberry Lavender Syrup, 270
Lavender Caramels, 360
leaves, playing with, 403
leeks, 178–179
Leek-Infused Vinegar, 178
Leek-Top Dressing, 179
Yogurt Leek Sauce, 179
legumes
Amino Sauces, 337–338
canning, 333–334
drying, 330–331
fermenting, 336–339
fermenting before cooking, 329
freezing, 331–333
pressure canning bean soups, 334
Tarhana, 325–326
Tempeh, 336–337
Tofu "Feta" with Mushroom Shio Koji, 338–339
White Miso, 339
Lemongrass Infused Vinegar, Kimchi-, 134
lemons
Citrus-Pickled Turmeric, 113
Lemon-Miso Fish Jerky Marinade, 378
Meyer Limoncello, 280–281
Preserved Lemon Eggs, 393
Rosemary Lemonade, 281
Salt-Preserved Citrus, 283
lemon verbena leaves, Calming Winter Herbal Tea, 398
lettuce, 180–181
Lettuce Kvass, 181
Soy Sauce–Pickled Romaine Lettuce, 181
lids and bands for canning, 30–31
limes
Pickled Limes, 282
Smoky Lime Grenadine, 304
liquids, freezing, 18
liquors, infused, 66–69, 115
local sourcing, 406–407

M

mango, 313–319
Canned Pickled Mango, 316
Mango Black Pepper Refrigerator Jam, 319
Mango-Peel Bitters, 315
Mango-Peel Shrub, 314
Mango Pickles, 315
Mango-Pit Mead, 318
Mango-Pit Syrup, 319
maple ham, 369
Mapple (Maple and Apple) Butter, 253–254
marinades, 374
Garlic-Shoyu Fish Jerky Marinade, 379
Lemon-Miso Fish Jerky Marinade, 378
marmalades
Red Quince Marmalade, 255
Simple Kumquat Marmalade, 286
White Quince Marmalade, 254–255
See also jams
Martini, Pickle Brine, 69
Masala Syrup, 114
McMahon J. P., 224
mead/melomel, 60–61
meats
about, 360
amino sauces and, 386
brining, 367
curing and fermenting, 367, 369–370
drying, 372–374
drying temperatures for, 91
dry rubs for, 374
freezing, 16, 18, 360–362
freezing ground, 362
making jerky, 373, 374
marinades for, 374
Mole-Inspired Beef Jerky, 374
pickling, 370–371
preserving, 368
pressure canning, 364
smoking, 372
See also individual meats
meat stock, 20
medicine, preserving for, 396–401, 405–406
melons, 297–300
Meyer lemons
Meyer Limoncello, 280–281
Rosemary Lemonade, 281
microbial starters for cheese-making, 354
milk, 344–345
Mirepoix, Frozen, 196–197
mirin, 329–330
miso
Bread Miso, 326–327
Lemon-Miso Fish Jerky Marinade, 378
Misozuke (Miso-Pickled) Eggs, 392–393
pickling beds and, 392
White Miso, 339
mocktails, 68–69
molasses
Apple Cider Molasses, 256–257
varieties of, 257
Mugolio, 242
mugwort, Icelandic Wound Charm, 397

muscadines
- Muscadine Gin, 293
- Muscadine or Black Grape Catsup, 296
- Muscadine Soda Syrup, 294
- Pickled Muscadines, 294

mushrooms, 182–190
- Dried Mushroom Tea, 184
- Freezer-Safe Lion's Mane Mushroom Cutlets, 185–186
- Frozen Mushroom "Scallops," 186
- Marinated Mushrooms, 189–190
- Mushroom Broth, 186–187
- Mushroom Jerky, 184–185
- Mushroom Ketchup, 188–189
- Quick-Pickled Mushrooms, 188
- Tea-Pickled Mushrooms, 187
- Tofu "Feta" with Mushroom Shio Koji, 338–339

mustard greens, 169–170

N

napa cabbage, Kimchi, 132
natural cheesemaking, 344
nectarines, 305–312
nettle, working with, 243
Nguyễn Thiên Ân, 216
"not-mirin," 329–330
nuts
- drying temperatures for, 91
- storing, 12

O

oils
- essential, 402–403
- infused, 397

okra, 191–195
- Lauren's Pickled Okra, 194–195
- Okra and Tomatoes: Small Batches, 193
- Ready-to-Go Okra Soup Cubes, 192

olives
- Caponata, 162
- drying, 307

onions, 195–200
- Bread-and-Butter Green Tomatoes, 233
- Canned Dill Pickle Chips, 159
- Caponata, 162
- Fermented Salsa, 234
- Frozen Mirepoix, 196–197
- Frozen Trinity, 196–197
- Marinated Mushrooms, 189–190
- Mushroom Broth, 186–187
- Mushroom Ketchup, 188–189
- Okra and Tomatoes: Small Batches, 193
- Pickled Limes, 282
- with pickled peppers, 204
- Pickled Red Onions with Mustard, 199
- Pickled Sweet Onions, 198
- Rainbow Roots Soup Starter, 107
- Ready-to-Go Okra Soup Cubes, 192
- Rosemary Cocktail Onions, 199–200
- Sofrito Cubes, 202
- Soup à l'Oignon Cubes, 197–198
- Summer Harvest Tomato Sauce, 230, 232
- Summery Cucumber Salad, 158
- Tomatillo Salad, 233

oranges
- Citrus-Pickled Turmeric, 113
- Cranberry-Orange Vodka, 288
- Holiday Citrus Spice Vinegar, 282
- Horseradish and Orange "Kosho," 113

oven drying, 88–89
Oysters, Pickled, 384

P

pan dulce, 403
Paneer, 350–351
pantry storage, 12–13
paocai, 52
papaya, 313–319
- Pickled Papaya, 316–317

parchment, fish-skin, 401
Parker, Matthew, 335
parsnips, 130
Passionflower Tincture, 398
Pasta Sauce Cubes, Beet–, 122–123
pastrami-spiced beets, 124–125
peaches, 305–312
- Blue Bouquet Pickled Peaches, 311
- Floral Pickled Peaches, 309–310
- Peach-and-Coriander Syrup, 311
- Peach Country Wine, 309
- Peach Shrub, 308
- Pickled Peaches with Spices, 310
- Smoked Dried Peaches, 307
- Stone Fruit Jam, 312
- Tomato-Peach Refrigerator Jam, 312

peanuts, 331, 332
pears, 246–258
- drying, 247

peas, 331–332
- English, 333–334
- field, 333
- fresh, 333–334
- split, 325–326
- Tarhana, 325–326

pectin, 81, 82
peppermint leaves, Calming Winter Herbal Tea, 398
peppers, bell, 200–207, 209–211
- Caponata, 162
- Frozen Trinity, 196–197
- pressure canning, 210
- quick-pickling, 203–204
- roasted, 204
- Roasted Pepper Cubes, 202
- Sofrito Cubes, 202
- Sour Corn, 152
- Sweet-and-Sour Cucumber Salad, 211
- Tarhana, 325–326

peppers, hot, 200–207, 209–211
- Aji Dulce Pepper Relish, 205
- Bird's-Eye and Serrano Sauce, 207
- Canned Pickled Mango, 316

peppers, hot, *continued*
- Doc's Hot Sauce, 209
- Easy Candied Jalapeños, 210–211
- Fermented Hot Sauce, 207
- Fermented Salsa, 234
- Habanero Sauces, 207
- Hot-and-Sour Bird's-Eye Sauce, 209
- Hot Honey, 203
- Hot Pepper Vinegar, 203
- Jalapeño Relish, 205
- Mango Pickles, 315
- pressure canning, 210
- quick-pickling, 203–204
- Ready-to-Go Okra Soup Cubes, 192
- Red Chile Chocolate Hot Sauce, 207
- Roasted Pepper Cubes, 202
- Sofrito Cubes, 202
- Strawberry-Jalapeño Shrub, 266
- Tomatillo Salad, 233

perpetual brine ferments, 52
Persimmon, Apple, and Cranberry Refrigerator Pickles, 249
pH for canning, 27
Pickle Brine Martini, 69
pickle powders, 95–96
pickles/pickling
- Amana Pickled Ham, 371
- Asparagus Refrigerator Pickles, 119
- Basic Pickled Rhubarb, 218
- Blue Bouquet Pickled Peaches, 311
- Canned Cauliflower Pickles, 134
- Canned Dill Pickle Chips, 159
- Canned Pickled Mango, 316
- canned pickles, 55–56
- carrots and, 143
- Citrus-Pickled Turmeric, 113
- Cornichons, 157–158
- Dill Refrigerator Pickles, 156–157
- Dill Squash Refrigerator Pickles, 223
- Fish Sauce–Inspired Pickled Brine, 113
- Floral Pickled Peaches, 309–310
- Garlic Refrigerator Pickles, 157
- Half Sours and Full Sours, 156
- Harissa-Pickled Pomegranate Seeds, 303
- Herbes-de-Provence-Pickled Asparagus, 118
- Lauren's Pickled Okra, 194–195
- Mimi's Pickled Watermelon Rinds, 298–299
- Misozuke (Miso-Pickled) Eggs, 392–393
- Mountain Cabin Cucumber Salad, 160
- Pickled Apples with Sage, 251–252
- Pickled Artichoke or Cardoon Stems, 116
- Pickled Celeriac, 150
- Pickled Eggs in Vinegar, 391
- Pickled Grapes, 293
- Pickled Herb Buds, 176
- Pickled Limes, 282
- Pickled Mini Eggplant, 164
- Pickled Muscadines, 294
- Pickled Oysters, 384
- Pickled Papaya, 316–317
- Pickled Pastrami Beets, 125–126
- Pickled Peaches with Spices, 310
- Pickled Red Onions with Mustard, 199
- Pickled Red Radishes, 215
- Pickled Salmon, 382–383
- Pickled Scapes and Scallions, 221
- Pickled Shrimp, 381
- Pickled Sweet Onions, 198
- Pickled White Fish, 382
- preventing mushy, 154
- Quick-Pickled Carrots, 144
- Quick-Pickled Cauliflower, 131
- Quick-Pickled Chowchow, 140
- Quick-Pickled Corn, 151
- Quick-Pickled Dilly Beans, 167–168
- Quick-Pickled Fennel, 166
- Quick-Pickled Horseradish and Scallion Paste, 111
- Quick-Pickled Mushrooms, 188
- quick pickles, 53
- Refrigerator Pickled Blackberries, 266
- Refrigerator Pickled Strawberries, 266–267
- refrigerator pickles, 54
- Slightly Sweet-and-Sour Pickled Radishes, 217
- Soy Sauce–Pickled Romaine Lettuce, 181
- Sweet-and-Sour Cucumber Salad, 158
- Tea-Pickled Mushrooms, 187
- Tomato Refrigerator Pickles, 232–233

pickling beds, 392
picnic ham, 369
pineapple, 313–319
- Tepache, 317–318

Pine Cone Syrup, Green, 242
plums, 305–312
- Apricot-Plum Fruit Leather, 306

pomegranates, 302–304
- Grenadine (Pomegranate Syrup), 304
- Harissa-Pickled Pomegranate Seeds, 303
- Pomegranate Seeds in Honey, 303

porridges, fermented, 329
potatoes, 212–214
- French Fries, 213
- pressure canning, 213

poultry
- about, 360
- Chicken Soup, 364–365
- freezing, 362
- *See also* meats

power outages, 21
pressure canners, 28–29
pressure canning
- altitude adjustments for, 39
- equipment for, 28–29
- method for, 37–40
- pH and, 27

- prosciutto, 369
- protein, seasonal, 346
- pulp, using, 99
- pumpkin, canning safety and, 33
- Pumpkincello, 240
- Punyaratabandhu, Leela, 208

Q

- Quick-Cooked Squash-and-Apple Relish, 239
- Quick-Pickled Cauliflower, 131
- Quick-Pickled Chowchow, 140
- Quick-Pickled Horseradish and Scallion Paste, 111
- Quick-Pickled Mushrooms, 188
- quinces, 246–258
  - drying, 248
  - Red Quince Marmalade, 255
  - White Quince Marmalade, 254–255
  - working with, 252

- radishes, 214–215, 217
  - Fermented Daikon, 217
  - Pickled Red Radishes, 215
  - Slightly Sweet-and-Sour Pickled Radishes, 217
- Rainbow Roots Soup Starter, 107
- raisins
  - Apple Relish, 251
  - Root Vegetable Jam, 146
- raspberries
  - Raspberry-Beet Jam, 272
  - Raspberry-Beet Syrup, 268
- raw foods, drying temperatures for, 91
- raw pack, 32
- Red Chile Chocolate Hot Sauce, 207
- Red Quince Marmalade, 255
- refrigerator storage, 15
- regrowth, 402
- relishes
  - Aji Dulce Pepper Relish, 205
  - Apple Relish, 251
  - Asparagus-End Relish, 120
  - Broccoli-Stem Refrigerator Relish, 141
  - Fermented Squash-and-Apple Relish, 238–239
  - Jalapeño Relish, 205
  - Quick-Cooked Squash-and-Apple Relish, 239
- rennet, 345–346
- rhubarb, 218–219
  - Basic Pickled Rhubarb, 218
  - Rhubarb and Black Pepper Relish, 219
  - syrups using, 219
- Ricotta, 351
- root cellaring, 13–14
- roots, aromatic, 104–114
- Root Vegetable Jam, 146
- rosemary
  - Rosemary and Thyme Syrup, 174–175
  - Rosemary Cocktail Onions, 199–200
  - Rosemary Lemonade, 281
- rose petals
  - Calming Winter Herbal Tea, 398
  - Five-Spice Apple Rings, 250
  - Floral Pickled Peaches, 309–310
  - Healing Rose Skin Salve, 396
  - Strawberry Rose Syrup, 270
  - Tangerine, Rose, and Turmeric Syrup, 285–286
- rutabaga, 130

- sachets, 98
- safety
  - for canning, 41
  - canning recipes and, 32–33
  - spoilage and, 6
- sage
  - Pickled Apples with Sage, 251–252
  - Savory Sage Refrigerator Paste, 178
- salmon
  - Pickled Salmon, 382–383
  - Smoked Salmon, 383
- salt
  - Aromatic Herbal Salt, 96
  - celery salt, 149
  - Herb Bud Salt, 175–176
  - Salt-Cured Egg Yolks, 391
  - Salt-Preserved Citrus, 283
  - Salt-Preserved Citrus Paste, 283
- salves, 396–397
- sauces
  - Amino Sauces, 337–338
  - Beet–Pasta Sauce Cubes, 122–123
  - Bird's-Eye and Serrano Sauce, 207
  - Doc's Hot Sauce, 209
  - Easy Yogurt Sauce, 123
  - Fermented Beet-and-Carrot Sauce, 127
  - Fermented Hot Sauce, 207
  - freezing, 18
  - Habanero Sauces, 207
  - Herbal Sauce, 177
  - Hot-and-Sour Bird's-Eye Sauce, 209
  - Red Chile Chocolate Hot Sauce, 207
  - Spicier Yogurt Leek Sauce, 179
  - Summer Harvest Tomato Sauce, 230, 232
  - Sweet-and-Savory Macerated Strawberry Sauce, 268
  - Yogurt Leek Sauce, 179
  - Zesty Cranberry Sauce, 288
- Sauerkraut, 135
  - Coriander-and-Mustard Canned, 138
- Savory Sage Refrigerator Paste, 178
- scallions, 220–221
  - Pickled Scapes and Scallions, 221
  - Quick-Pickled Horseradish and Scallion Paste, 111

scapes, 220–221
  Pickled Scapes and Scallions, 221
seafood
  about, 375
  canning, 379
  fermenting, 384
  freezing, 375–377
  ice glazing, 376
  Lemon-Miso Fish Jerky Marinade, 378
  Pickled Shrimp, 381
  pickling, 379, 381, 381–383
  pretreating before freezing, 376
  salting and drying, 377–379
  smoking, 379, 383
seafood stock, 20
seasoning blends
  celery-leaf seasoning, 149
  for drying, 95–96
  reducing food waste and, 97, 99
seaweed, preserving, 171
self-care, preserving for, 396–401
Serrano Sauce, Bird's-Eye and, 207
shallots, 195–200
  Fermented Rainbow Roots and Spinach Salad, 170
shell beans, 330–331, 332, 333
shellfish, freezing, 377. *See also* seafood
Shio Koji, 74
Shoyuzuke Eggs, 390
Shrimp, Pickled, 381
shrubs, 68
Silan, 290
Skin Salve, Healing Rose, 396
small-space storage, 14
Smoked Cherry Pit Old-Fashioned Bitters, 278
Smoked Dried Peaches, 307
Smoked Old-Fashioned Jam, 278
smoking
  about, 96
  meats, 372
  seafood, 379
Smoky Lime Grenadine, 304
Smoothie Cubes, 22
soda
  about, 57
  Choose-Your-Own-Adventure Herbal Soda, 176–177
  Herbal Soda, 176
  naturally carbonated soda, 58–59
solar dehydrators, 90
Solstice Refrigerator Jam, 274
soups
  Chicken Soup, 364–365
  Chilled Blueberry Soup, 265
  freezing, 18
  frozen seafood stock, 377
  making and freezing stocks, 363
  Mushroom Broth, 186–187
  pressure canning bean, 334
  Quick Beet Soup, 123
  Rainbow Roots Soup Starter, 107
  Ready-to-Go Okra Soup Cubes, 192
  Soup à l'Oignon Cubes, 197–198
  stock for, 20
soybeans
  Tempeh, 336–337
  White Miso, 339
Soy Sauce–Pickled Romaine Lettuce, 181
speck, 369
Spiced Root Syrup, 114
spices, drying temperatures for, 91
spinach, 169–170
  Fermented Rainbow Roots and Spinach Salad, 170
spores, dispersing koji, 71
squash, summer, 222–223
  Dill Squash Refrigerator Pickles, 223
squash, winter, 236–240
  Butternut Squash Peel Bitters, 239–240
  Fermented Squash-and-Apple Relish, 238–239
  pressure canning, 238
  Quick-Cooked Squash-and-Apple Relish, 239
steamer baskets, 18
sterilization of jars, 31, 39
stinging nettle, working with, 243
stock
  freezing concentrated stock cubes, 363
  frozen seafood, 377
  making and freezing, 363
  scrappy, 20
  See also soups
stone fruits, 305–312
  Apricot-Plum Fruit Leather, 306
  Blue Bouquet Pickled Peaches, 311
  Floral Pickled Peaches, 309–310
  Peach-and-Coriander Syrup, 311
  Peach Country Wine, 309
  Peach Shrub, 308
  Pickled Peaches with Spices, 310
  Smoked Dried Peaches, 307
  Stone Fruit Jam, 312
  Tomato-Peach Refrigerator Jam, 312
storage
  of canned food, 41
  of dried foods, 96–97
  labeling and, 6
strawberries
  Blue Strawberry Jam, 273
  Fennel-Strawberry Vinegar, 165
  with pickled peppers, 204
  Refrigerator Pickled Strawberries, 266–267
  Solstice Refrigerator Jam, 274
  Strawberry-Jalapeño Shrub, 266
  Strawberry Jam, 270
  Strawberry-Top Lime Syrup, 269
  Strawberry-Top Shrub, 265
  Strawberry-Wine Refrigerator Jam, 271
  Sweet-and-Savory Macerated Strawberry Sauce, 268

sugar, in jellies and jams, 81, 82
Sugar-Packed Citrus Syrup, 286
sugar packing, 18–19, 263
sugar syrup dips, 90
Su-Jit Lin, 153
sulfuring/sulfite dips, 91
Summer Harvest Tomato Sauce, 230, 232
Sunny Blueberry-Corn Jam, 273–274
Sweet-and-Sour Five-Spice Apples, 249–250
Sweet-and-Sour Roasted Red Pepper Jam, 211
sweet potatoes, 225–226
  Sweet Potato Fly, 226
syrup packing, 18–19, 263
syrups
  about, 78
  aromatic roots and, 114
  Blueberry Lavender Syrup, 270
  from cherries, 276–277
  citrus, 285–286
  Citrus Syrup, 270
  Five-Spice Syrup, 270
  Ginger-Berry Syrup, 269–270
  Grenadine (Pomegranate Syrup), 304
  herbs in, 174–175
  making, 79
  Mango-Pit Syrup, 319
  Muscadine Soda Syrup, 294
  Peach-and-Coriander Syrup, 311
  Silan, 290
  Strawberry Rose Syrup, 270
  Sugar-Packed Citrus Syrup, 286
  Vanilla-Fig Syrup, 290–291
  variations for berry, 270
  Watermelon Syrup, 300
  Zesty Cranberry Sauce, 288

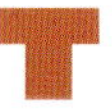

tangerines
  Cranberry-Orange Vodka, 288
  Tangerine, Rose, and Turmeric Syrup, 285–286
Tarhana, 325–326
teas
  Calming Winter Herbal Tea, 398
  Dried Mushroom Tea, 184
  herbal, 398
  Tea-Pickled Mushrooms, 187
Tempeh, 336–337
temperature
  for drying foods, 91
  for hot water bath canning, 27
  for pantries, 12
  for pressure canning, 27
  for refrigerators, 15
  for root cellars, 14
Three-Root Paste, 108
Thyme Syrup, Rosemary and, 174–175
tinctures, herbal, 396
tofu
  freezing, 332–333
  Tofu "Feta" with Mushroom Shio Koji, 338–339
tomatillos, 227–235
  canning, 230
  Tomatillo Salad, 233
tomatoes, 227–235
  Bread-and-Butter Green Tomatoes, 233
  canning, 229
  Caponata, 162
  Fermented Salsa, 234
  Green Tomato Dill Chips, 228
  Green Tomato Refrigerator Jam, 235
  Okra and Tomatoes: Small Batches, 193
  Quick-Pickled Chowchow, 140
  Ready-to-Go Okra Soup Cubes, 192
  Sofrito Cubes, 202
  Summer Harvest Tomato Sauce, 230, 232
  Tarhana, 325–326
  Tomato Cocktail Syrup, 234
  Tomato-Peach Refrigerator Jam, 312
  Tomato Refrigerator Pickles, 232–233
Trinity, Frozen, 196–197
tropical fruits, 313–319
  Canned Pickled Mango, 316
  Guava Paste, 318–319
  Mango Black Pepper Refrigerator Jam, 319
  Mango-Peel Bitters, 315
  Mango-Peel Shrub, 314
  Mango Pickles, 315
  Mango-Pit Mead, 318
  Mango-Pit Syrup, 319
  Pickled Papaya, 316–317
  Tepache, 317–318
tsukemono, 53
tsukudani, 171
turmeric, 104–114
  Citrus-Pickled Turmeric, 113
  Tangerine, Rose, and Turmeric Syrup, 285–286
  Three-Root Paste, 108
turnips, 130

Vanilla Extract, 68
Vanilla-Fig Syrup, 290–291
Vanilla Sugar, 68
vegan cheese, 354
Vegan Fruit Honey, 81
Vegan Yogurt, 357
vegetables
  blanching, 16–17
  checking whole, 93
  drying temperatures for, 91
  freezing, 15–16, 18
  jellies and jams from, 85
  pretreating before drying, 90
  in root cellars, 14
  scraps from for soup, 20
  Smoothie Cubes, 22
  using wilted, 99
  See also individual vegetables
vinegar
  about, 64
  apples and, 252–253
  artichokes and, 115
  Banana Vinegar, 261
  Celery Vinegar, 149

vinegar, *continued*
- Citrus Cleaning Vinegar, 281
- fermentation with, 45
- Horseradish Vinegar, 114
- Hot Pepper Vinegar, 203
- infused, 66–69
- infusing with stinging nettle, 243
- Leek-Infused Vinegar, 178
- making, 64–65
- Pickled Eggs in Vinegar, 391
- seasoning blends after infusing, 95
- Spring Greens Vinegar, 242

violet leaves, Icelandic Wound Charm, 397
Virginia ham, 369
vodka
- Celery Vodka, 149
- Cranberry-Orange Vodka, 288
- Pumpkincello, 240

waste, reducing, 97–98
water damage, 14
watermelon, 297–300
- Mimi's Pickled Watermelon Rinds, 298–299
- Watermelon Caramel Sauce, 300
- Watermelon Juice, 297–298
- Watermelon Rind Slaw, 299
- Watermelon Syrup, 300

weights, for fermentation, 47–49
whey, uses for, 355
White Fish, Pickled, 382
White Quince Marmalade, 254–255
wild plants, 241–243
- Mugolio, 242
- Spring Greens Vinegar, 242

wine
- basic country, 62–63
- Beet–Pasta Sauce Cubes, 122
- Caponata, 162
- fermentation and, 57
- Geographically Indeterminate Ham, 369–370
- Lemon-Miso Fish Jerky Marinade, 378
- Mushroom Jerky, 184
- Peach Country Wine, 309
- Peach Shrub, 308
- Quick-Pickled Mushrooms, 188
- solids from, 95
- Soup à l'Oignon Cubes, 197–198
- Strawberry-Wine Refrigerator Jam, 271
- vinegar and, 64, 65

Wound Charm, Icelandic, 397

yarrow flowers, Icelandic Wound Charm, 397
yeasts, flower, 402
yogurt
- Basic Yogurt, 356
- cheese from, 352
- Easy Yogurt Sauce, 123
- frozen, 345
- Greek Yogurt, 356–357
- heirloom cultures for, 357
- making, 355–358
- Spicier Yogurt Leek Sauce, 179
- Tarhana, 325–326
- Vegan Yogurt, 357
- Yogurt Leek Sauce, 179

yogurt makers, 358
Yuzu Kosho, 285

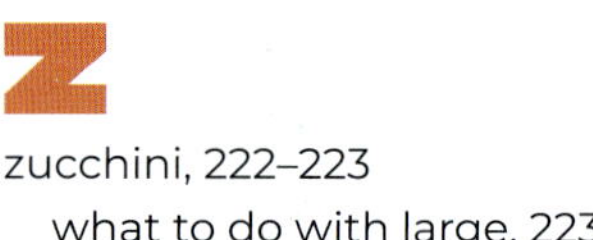

zucchini, 222–223
- what to do with large, 223